The William James Reader Vol I

The William James Reader Vol I

By Dr. William James

Essays in Radical Empiricism
The Meaning of Truth
What is an Emotion?
The Varieties of Religious Experience

Essays in Radical Empiricism

Table of Contents

EDITOR'S PREFACE

The present volume is an attempt to carry out a plan which William James is known to have formed several years before his death. In 1907 he collected reprints in an envelope which he inscribed with the title 'Essays in Radical Empiricism'; and he also had duplicate sets of these reprints bound, under the same title, and deposited for the use of students in the general Harvard Library, and in the Philosophical Library in Emerson Hall.

Two years later Professor James published The Meaning of Truth and A Pluralistic Universe, and inserted in these volumes several of the articles which he had intended to use in the ' Essays in Radical Empiricism.' Whether he would nevertheless have carried out his original plan, had he lived, cannot be certainly known. Several facts, however, stand out very clearly. In the first place, the articles included in the original plan but omitted from his later volumes are indispensable to the understanding of his other writings. To these articles he repeatedly alludes. Thus, in The Meaning of Truth, he says: "This statement is probably excessively obscure to any one who has not read my two articles 'Does Consciousness Exist?' and 'A World of Pure Experience. ' " Other allusions have been indicated in the present text. In the second place, the articles originally brought together as 'Essays in Radical Empiricism' form a connected whole. Not only were most of them written consecutively within a period of two years, but they contain numerous cross-references. In the third place, Professor James regarded 'radical empiricism' as an independent doctrine. This he asserted expressly: "Let me say that there is no logical connexion between pragmatism, as I understand it, and a doctrine which I have recently set forth as 'radical empiricism.' The latter stands on its own feet. One may entirely reject it and still be a pragmatist." Finally, Professor James came toward the end of his life to regard 'radical empiricism' as more fundamental and more important than 'pragmatism.' In the Preface to The Meaning of Truth (1909), the author gives the following explanation of his desire to continue, and if possible conclude, the controversy over pragmatism: " I am interested in another doctrine in philosophy to which I give the name of radical empiricism, and it seems to me that the establishment of the pragmatist theory of truth is a step of first-rate importance in making radical empiricism prevail."

In preparing the present volume, the editor has therefore been governed by two motives. On the one hand, he has sought to preserve and make accessible certain important articles not to be found in Professor James's other books. This is true of Essays 1, II IV, V, VIII, IX, x, Xi, and XII. On the other hand, he has sought to bring together in one volume a set of essays treating systematically of one independent, coherent, and fundamental doctrine. To this end it has seemed best to include three essays (III VI, and VII), which, although included in the original plan, were afterwards reprinted elsewhere;

and one essay, XII, not included in the original plan. Essays III, VI, and VII are indispensable to the consecutiveness of the series, and are so interwoven with the rest that it is necessary that the student should have them at hand for ready consultation. Essay XII throws an important light on the author's general 'empiricism,' and forms an important link between 'radical empiricism' and the author's other doctrines.

In short, the present volume is designed not as a collection but rather as a treatise. It is intended that another volume shall be issued which shall contain papers having biographical or historical importance which have not yet been reprinted in book form. The present volume is intended not only for students of Professor James's philosophy, but for students of metaphysics and the theory of knowledge. It sets forth systematically and within brief compass the doctrine of 'radical empiricism.'

A word more may be in order concerning the general meaning of this doctrine. In the Preface to the Will to Believe (1898), Professor James gives the name "radical empiricism" to his " philosophic attitude," and adds the following explanation: "I say 'empiricism,' because it is contented to regard its most assured conclusions concerning matters of fact as hypotheses liable to modification in the course of future experience; and I say 'radical,' because it treats the doctrine of monism itself as an hypothesis, and, unlike so much of the halfway empiricism that is current under the name of positivism or agnosticism or scientific naturalism, it does not dogmatically affirm monism as something with which all experience has got to square." An 'empiricism' of this description is a "philosophic attitude" or temper of mind rather than a doctrine, and characterizes all of Professor James's writings. It is set forth in Essay XII of the present volume.

In a narrower sense, 'empiricism' is the method of resorting to particular experiences for the solution of philosophical problems. Rationalists are the men of principles, empiricists the men of facts. Or, "since principles are universals, and facts are particulars, perhaps the best way of characterizing the two tendencies is to say that rationalist thinking proceeds most willingly by going from wholes to parts, while empiricist thinking proceeds by going from parts to wholes." Again, empiricism "remands us to sensation." The "empiricist view" insists that, "as reality is created temporally day by day, concepts . . . can never fitly supersede perception.... The deeper features of reality are found only in perceptual experience. Empiricism in this sense is as yet characteristic of Professor James's philosophy as a whole. It is not the distinctive and independent doctrine set forth in the present book.

The only summary of 'radical empiricism I in this last and narrowest sense appears in the Preface to The Meaning of Truth; and it must be reprinted here as the key to the text that follows.[1]

" Radical empiricism consists (1) first of a postulate, (2) next of a statement of fact, (3) and finally of a generalized conclusion." (1) "The postulate is that the only things that shall be debatable among philosophers shall be things definable in terms drawn from experience. (Things of an unexperienceable nature may exist ad libitum, but they form no part of the material for philosophic debate.) "This is "the principle of pure experience" as "a methodical postulate." This postulate corresponds to the notion which the author repeatedly attributes to Shadworth Hodgson, the notion "that realities are only what they are 'known as.'" In this sense 'radical empiricism' and pragmatism are closely allied. Indeed, if pragmatism be defined as the assertion that "the meaning of any proposition can always be brought down to some particular consequence in our future practical experience, . . . the point lying in the fact that the experience must be particular rather than in the fact that it must be active"; then pragmatism and the above postulate come to the same thing. The present book, however, consists not so much in the assertion of this postulate as in the use of it. And the method is successful in special applications by virtue of a certain "statement of fact" concerning relations. "The statement of fact is that the relations between things, conjunctive as well as disjunctive, are just as much matters of direct particular experience, neither more so nor less so, than the things themselves." This is the central doctrine of the present book. It distinguishes 'radical empiricism' from the "ordinary empiricism" of Hume, J. S. Mill, etc., with which it is otherwise allied. It provides an empirical and relational version of 'activity,' and so distinguishes the author's voluntarism from a view with which it is easily confused — the view which upholds a pure or transcendent activity. It makes it possible to escape the vicious disjunctions that have thus far baffled philosophy: such disjunctions as those between consciousness and physical nature, between thought and its object, between one mind and another, and between one 'thing' and another. These disjunctions need not be 'overcome' by calling in any "extraneous trans-empirical connective support"; they may now be avoided by regarding the dualities in question as only differences of empirical relationship among common empirical terms. The pragmatistic account of 'meaning' and 'truth,' shows only how a vicious disjunction between 'idea' and 'object' may thus be avoided. The present volume not only presents pragmatism in this light; but adds similar accounts of the other dualities mentioned above.

Thus while pragmatism and radical empiricism. do not differ essentially when regarded as methods, they are independent when regarded as doctrines. For it would be possible to hold the pragmatistic theory of 'meaning' and 'truth,' without basing it on any fundamental theory of relations, and without extending such a theory of relations to residual philosophical problems; without, in short, holding either to the above 'statement of fact,' or to the following 'generalized conclusion.' "The generalized conclusion is that therefore the parts of experience hold together from next to next by relations that are themselves parts of experience. The directly apprehended universe needs., in short, no extraneous transempirical connective support, but possesses in its own right a concatenated or continuous structure." When thus generalized, 'radical empiricism' is not only a theory of knowledge comprising pragmatism as a special chapter, but a metaphysic as well. It excludes " the hypothesis of trans-empirical reality." It is the author's most rigorous statement of his theory that reality is an "experience-continuum." It is that positive and constructive 'empiricism' of which Professor James said: "Let empiricism once become associated with religion, as hitherto, through some strange misunderstanding, it has been associated with irreligion, and I believe that a new era of religion as well as of philosophy will be ready to begin."

The editor desires to acknowledge his obligations to the periodicals from which these essays have been reprinted, and to the many friends of Professor James who have rendered valuable advice and assistance in the preparation of the present volume.

Ralph Barton Perry.

Cambridge, Massachusetts.

January 8, 1912.

DOES 'CONSCIOUSNESS' EXIST?[1]

'Thoughts' and 'things' are names for two sorts of object, which common sense will always find contrasted and will always practically oppose to each other. Philosophy, reflecting on the contrast, has varied in the past in her explanations of it, and may be expected to vary in the future. At first, "spirit and matter,' 'soul and body,' stood for a pair of equipollent substances quite on a par in weight and interest. But one day Kant undermined the soul and brought in the transcendental ego, and ever since then the bipolar relation has been very much off its balance. The transcendental ego seems nowadays in rationalist quarters to stand for everything, in empiricist quarters for almost nothing. In the hands of such writers as Schuppe, Rehmke, Natorp, Munsterberg — at any rate in his earlier writings, Schubert-Soldern and others, the spiritual principle attenuates itself to a thoroughly ghostly condition, being only a name for the fact that the 'content' of experience is known. It loses personal form and activity — these passing over to the content — becomes a bare Bewusstheit or Bewusstsein überhaupt, of which in its own right absolutely nothing can be said.

I believe that 'consciousness,' when once it has evaporated to this estate of pure diaphaneity, is on the point of disappearing altogether. It is the name of a nonentity, and has no right to a place among first principles. Those who still cling to it are clinging to a mere echo, the faint rumor left behind by the disappearing 'soul' upon the air of philosophy. During the past year, I have read a number of articles whose authors seemed just on the point of abandoning the notion of consciousness,[2] and substituting for it that of an absolute experience not due to two factors. But they were not quite radical enough, not quite daring enough in their negations. For twenty years past I have mistrusted 'consciousness' as an entity; for seven or eight years past I have suggested its non-existence to my students, and tried to give them its pragmatic equivalent in realities of experience. It seems to me that the hour is ripe for it to be openly and universally discarded.

To deny plumply that 'consciousness' exists seems so absurd on the face of it — for undeniably 'thoughts' do exist — that I fear some readers will follow me no farther. Let me then immediately explain that I mean only to deny that the word stands for an entity, but to insist most emphatically that it does stand for a function. There is, I mean, no aboriginal stuff or quality of being,[3] contrasted with that of which material objects are made, out of which our thoughts of them are made; but there is a function in experience which thoughts perform, and for the performance of which this quality of being is invoked. That function is knowing. 'Consciousness' is supposed necessary to explain the fact that things not only are, but get reported, are known. Whoever blots out the notion of consciousness from his list of first principles must still provide in some way for that function's being carried on.

My thesis is that if we start with the supposition that there is only one primal stuff or material in the world, a stuff of which everything is composed, and if we call that stuff 'pure experience,' then knowing can easily be explained as a particular sort of relation towards one another into which portions of pure experience may enter. The relation itself is a part of pure experience; one of its 'terms' becomes the subject or bearer of the knowledge, the knower,[4] the other becomes the object known. This will need much explanation before it can be understood. The best way to get it understood is to contrast it with the alternative view; and for that we may take the recentest alternative, that in which the evaporation of the definite soul-substance has proceeded as far as it can go without being yet complete. If neo-Kantism has expelled earlier forms of dualism, we shall have expelled all forms if we are able to expel neo-Kantism in its turn.

For the thinkers I call neo-Kantian, the word consciousness today does no more than signalize the fact that experience is indefeasibly dualistic in structure. It means that not subject, not object, but object-plus-subject is the minimum that can actually be. The subject-object distinction meanwhile is entirely different from that between mind and matter, from that between body and soul. Souls were detachable, had separate destinies; things could happen to them. To consciousness as such nothing can happen, for, timeless itself, it is only a witness of happenings in time, in which it plays no part. It is, in a word, but the logical correlative of 'content' in an Experience of which the peculiarity is that fact comes to light in it, that awareness of content takes place. Consciousness as such is entirely impersonal — 'self' and its activities belong to the content. To say that I am self-conscious, or conscious of putting forth volition, means only that certain contents, for which 'self' and 'effort of will' are the names, are not without witness as they occur.

Thus, for these belated drinkers at the Kantian spring, we should have to admit consciousness as an 'epistemological' necessity, even if we had no direct evidence of its being there.

But in addition to this, we are supposed by almost every one to have an immediate consciousness of consciousness itself. When the world of outer fact ceases to be materially present, and we merely recall it in memory, or fancy it, the consciousness is believed to stand out and to be felt as a kind of impalpable inner flowing, which, once known in this sort of experience, may equally be detected in presentations of the outer world. "The moment we try to fix our attention upon consciousness and to see what, distinctly, it is," says a recent writer, "it seems to vanish. It seems as if we had before us a mere emptiness. When we try to introspect the sensation of blue, all we can see is the blue; the other element is as if it were diaphanous. Yet it can be distinguished, if we look attentively enough, and know that there is something to look for."[6] "Consciousness" (Bewusstheit), says another philosopher, "is inexplicable and hardly describable, yet all conscious experiences have this in common that what we call their content has this peculiar reference to a centre for which 'self ' is the name, in virtue of which reference alone the content is subjectively given, or appears. . . . While in this way consciousness, or reference to a self, is the only thing which distinguishes a conscious content from any sort of being that might be there with no one conscious of it, yet this only ground of the distinction defies all closer explanations. The existence of consciousness, although it is the fundamental fact of psychology, can indeed be laid down as certain, can be brought out by analysis, but can neither be defined nor deduced from anything but itself."[6]

'Can be brought out by analysis,' this author says. This supposes that the consciousness is one element, moment, factor — call it what you like — of an experience of essentially dualistic inner constitution, from which, if you abstract the content, the consciousness will remain revealed to its own eye. Experience, at this rate, would be much like a paint of which the world pictures were made. Paint has a dual constitution, involving, as it does, a menstruum[7] (oil, size or what not) and a mass of content in the form of pigment suspended therein. We can get the pure menstruum by letting the pigment settle, and the pure pigment by pouring off the size or oil. We operate here by physical subtraction; and the usual view is, that by mental subtraction we can separate the two factors of experience in an analogous way — not isolating them entirely, but distinguishing them enough to know that they are two.

II

Now my contention is exactly the reverse of this. Experience, I believe, has no such inner duplicity; and the separation of it into consciousness and content comes, not by way of subtraction, but by way of addition — the addition, to a given concrete piece of it, of other sets of experiences, in connection with which severally its use or function may be of two different kinds. The paint will also serve here as an illustration. In a pot in a paint-shop, along with other paints, it serves in its entirety as so much saleable matter. Spread on a canvas, with other paints around it, it represents, on the contrary, a feature in a picture and performs a spiritual function. Just SO, I maintain, does a given undivided portion of experience, taken in one context of associates, play the part of a knower, of a state of mind, of 'consciousness'; while in a different context the same undivided bit of experience plays the part of a thing known, of an objective 'content.' In a word, in one group it figures as a thought, in another group as a thing. And, since it can figure in both groups simultaneously we have every right to speak of it as subjective and objective both at once. The dualism connoted by such double-barrelled terms as 'experience,' ' phenomenon," 'datum," Vorfindung' — terms which, in philosophy at any rate, tend more and more to replace the single-barrelled terms of 'thought' and 'thing' — that dualism, I say, is still preserved in this account, but reinterpreted, so that, instead of being mysterious and elusive, it becomes verifiable and concrete. It is an affair of relations, it falls outside, not inside, the single experience considered, and can always be particularized and defined.

The entering wedge for this more concrete way of understanding the dualism was fashioned by Locke when he made the word 'idea' stand indifferently for thing and thought, and by Berkeley when he said that what common sense means by realities is exactly what the philosopher means by ideas. Neither Locke nor Berkeley thought his truth out into perfect clearness, but it seems to me that the conception I am defending does little more than consistently carry out the 'pragmatic' method which they were the first to use.

If the reader will take his own experiences, he will see what I mean. Let him begin with a perceptual experience, the 'presentation,' so called, of a physical object, his actual field of vision, the room he sits in, with the book he is reading as its centre; and let him for the present treat this complex object in the commonsense way as being 'really' what it seems to be, namely, a collection of physical things cut out from an environing world of other physical things with which these physical things have actual or potential relations. Now at the same time it is just those self-same things which his mind, as we say, perceives; and the whole philosophy of perception from Democritus's time downwards has been just one long wrangle over the paradox that what is evidently one reality should be in two places at once, both in outer space and in a person's mind. 'Representative' theories of perception avoid the logical paradox, but on the other hand they violate the reader's sense of life, which knows no intervening mental image but seems to see the room and the book immediately just as they physically exist.

The puzzle of how the one identical room can be in two places is at bottom just the puzzle of how one identical point can be on two lines. It can, if it be situated at their intersection; and similarly, if the 'pure experience' of the room were a place of intersection of two processes, which connected it with different groups of associates respectively, it could be counted twice over, as belonging to either group, and spoken of loosely as existing in two places, although it would remain all the time a numerically single thing.

Well, the experience is a member of diverse processes that can be followed away from it along entirely different lines. The one self-identical thing has so many relations to the rest of experience that you can take it in disparate systems of association, and treat it as belonging with opposite contexts.[8] In one of these contexts it is your 'field of consciousness'; in another it is 'the room in which you sit,' and it enters both contexts in its wholeness, giving no pretext for being said to attach itself to consciousness by one of its parts or aspects, and to outer reality by another. What are the two processes, now, into which the room-experience simultaneously enters in this way?

One of them is the reader's personal biography, the other is the history of the house of which the room is part. The presentation, the experience, the that in short (for until we have decided what it is it must be a mere that) is the last term of a train of sensations, emotions, decisions, movements, classifications, expectations, etc., ending in the present, and the first term of a series of similar 'inner' operations extending into the future, on the reader's part. On the other hand, the very same that is the terminus ad quem of a lot of previous physical operations, carpentering, papering, furnishing, warming, etc., and the terminus a quo of a lot of future ones. in. which it will be concerned when undergoing the destiny of a physical room. The physical and the mental operations form curiously incompatible groups. As a room, the experience has occupied that spot and had that environment for thirty years. As your field of consciousness it may never have existed until now. As a room, attention will go on to discover endless new details in it. As your mental state merely, few new ones will emerge under attention's eye. As a room, it will take an earthquake, or a gang of men, and in any case a certain amount of time, to destroy it. As your subjective state, the closing of your eyes, or any instantaneous play of your fancy will suffice. In the real world, fire will consume it. In your mind, you can let fire play over it without effect. As an outer object, you must pay so much a month to inhabit it. As an inner content, you may occupy it for any length of time rent-free. If, in short, you follow it in the mental direction, taking it along with events of personal biography solely, all sorts of things are true of it which are false, and false of it which are true if you treat it as a real thing experienced, follow it in the physical direction, and relate it to associates in the outer world.

III

So far, all seems plain sailing, but my thesis will probably grow less plausible to the reader when I pass from percepts to concepts, or from the case of things presented to that of things remote. I believe, nevertheless, that here also the same law holds good. If we take conceptual manifolds, or memories, or fancies, they also are in their first intention mere bits of pure experience, and, as such, are single thats which act in one context as objects, and in another context figure as mental states. By taking them in their first intention., I mean ignoring their relation to possible perceptual experiences with which they may be connected, which they may lead to and terminate in, and which then they may be supposed to 'represent.' Taking them in this way first, we confine the problem to a world merely 'thoughtof' and not directly felt or seen.[9] This world, just like the world of percepts, comes to us at first as a chaos of experiences, but lines of order soon get traced. We find that any bit of it which we may cut out as an example is connected with distinct groups of associates, just as our perceptual experiences are, that these associates link themselves with it by different relations,[10] and that one forms the inner history of a person, while the other acts as an imper. sonal 'objective' world, either spatial and temporal, or else merely logical or mathematical, or otherwise 'ideal.'

The first obstacle on the part of the reader to seeing that these non-perceptual experiences have objectivity as well as subjectivity will probably be due to the intrusion into his mind of percepts, that third group of associates with which the non-perceptual experiences have relations, and which, as a whole, they 'represent,' standing to them as thoughts to things. This important function of the non-perceptual experiences complicates the question and confuses it; for, so used are we to treat percepts as the sole genuine realities that, unless we keep them out of the discussion, we tend altogether to overlook the objectivity that lies in nonperceptual experiences by themselves. We treat them,'knowing' percepts as they do, as through and through subjective, and say that they are wholly constituted of the stuff called consciousness, using this term now for a kind of entity, after the fashion which I am seeking to refute.[11]

Abstracting, then, from percepts altogether, what I maintain is, that any single non-perceptual experience tends to get counted twice over, just as a perceptual experience does, figuring in one context as an object or field of objects, in another as a state of mind: and all this without the least internal self-diremption on its own part into consciousness and content. It is all consciousness in one taking; and, in the other, all content.

I find this objectivity of non-perceptual experiences, this complete parallelism in point of reality between the presently felt and the remotely thought, so well set forth in a page of Munsterberg's Grundzuge, that I will quote it as it stands.

"I may only think of my objects," says Professor Munsterberg; "yet, in my living thought they stand before me exactly as perceived objects would do, no matter how different the two ways of apprehending them may be in their genesis. The book here lying on the table before me, and the book in the next room of which I think and which I mean to get, are both in the same sense given realities for me, realities which I acknowledge and of which I take account. If you agree that the perceptual object is not an idea within me, but that percept and thing, as indistinguishably one, are really experienced there, outside, you ought not to believe that the merely thought-of object is hid away inside of the thinking subject. The object of which I think, and of whose existence I take cognizance without letting it now work upon my senses, occupies its definite place in the outer world as much as does the object which I directly see."

"What is true of the here and the there, is also true of the now and the then. I know of the thing which is present and perceived, but I know also of the thing which yesterday was but is no more, and which I only remember. Both can determine my present conduct, both are parts of the reality of which I keep account. It is true that of much of the past I am uncertain, just as I am uncertain of much of what is present if it be but dimly perceived. But the interval of time does not in principle alter my relation to the object, does not transform it from an object known into a mental state. . . . The things in the room here which I survey, and those in my distant home of which I think, the things of this minute and those of my long-vanished boyhood, influence and decide me alike, with a reality which my experience of them directly feels. They both make up my real world, they make it directly, they do not have first to be introduced to me and mediated by ideas which now and here arise within me. . . . This not-me character of my recollections and expectations does not imply that the external objects of which I am aware in those experiences should necessarily be there also for others. The objects of dreamers and hallucinated persons are wholly without general validity. But even were they centaurs and golden mountains, they still would be 'off there,' in fairy land, and not 'inside' of ourselves."[12]

This certainly is the immediate., primary, naif, or practical way of taking our thought-of-world. Were there no perceptual world to serve as its 'reductive,' in Taine's sense, by being 'stronger' and more genuinely 'outer' (so that the whole merely thought-of world seems weak and inner in comparison), our world of thought would be the only world, and would enjoy complete reality in our belief. This actually happens in our dreams, and in our day-dreams so long as percepts do not interrupt them.

And yet, just as the seen room (to go back to our late example) is also a field of consciousness, so the conceived or recollected room is also a state of mind; and the doubling-up of the experience has in both cases similar grounds.

The room thought-of, namely, has many thought-of couplings with many thought-of-things. Some of these couplings are inconstant, others are stable. In the reader's personal history the room occupies a single date — he saw it only once perhaps, a year ago. Of the house's history, on the other hand, it forms a permanent ingredient. Some couplings have the curious stubbornness, to borrow Royce's term, of fact; others show the fluidity of fancy — we let them come and go as we please. Grouped with the rest of its house, with the name of its town, of its owner, builder, value, decorative plan, the room maintains a definite foothold, to which, if we try to loosen it, it tends to return, and to reassert itself with force.[13] With these associates, in a word, it coheres, while to other houses, other towns, other owners, etc., it shows no tendency to cohere at all. The two collections, first of its cohesive, and, second, of its loose associates, inevitably come to be contrasted. We call the first collection the system of external realities, in the midst of which the room, as 'real,' exists; the other we call the stream of our internal thinking, in which, as a 'mental image,' it for a moment floats.[14] The room thus again gets counted twice over. It plays two different roles, being Gedanke and Gedachtes, the thought-of-an-object, and the object-thought-of, both in one; and all this without paradox or mystery, just as the same material thing may be both low and high, or small and great, or bad and good, because of its relations to opposite parts of an environing world.

As 'subjective' we say that the experience represents; as 'objective' it is represented. What represents and what is represented is here numerically the same; but we must remember that no dualism of being represented and representing resides in the experience per se. In its pure state, or when isolated., there is no selfsplitting of it into consciousness and what the consciousness is 'of.' Its subjectivity and objectivity are functional attributes solely, realized only when the experience is 'taken,' i. e., talked-of, twice, considered along with its two differing contexts respectively, by a new retrospective experience, of which that whole past complication now forms the fresh content.

The instant field of the present is at all times what I call the 'pure' experience. It is only virtually or potentially either object or subject as yet. For the time being, it is plain, unqualified actuality, or existence, a simple that. In this naif immediacy it is of course valid; it is there, we act upon it; and the doubling of it in retrospection into a state of mind and a reality intended thereby, is just one of the acts. The 'state of mind,' first treated explicitly as such in retrospection, will stand corrected or confirmed, and the retrospective experience in its turn will get a similar treatment; but the immediate experience in its passing is always ' truth,'[15] practical truth, something to act on, at its own movement. If the world were then and there to go out like a candle, it would remain truth absolute and objective, for it would be 'the last word,' would have no critic, and no one would ever oppose the thought in it to the reality intended.[16]

I think I may now claim to have made my thesis clear. Consciousness connotes a kind of external relation, and does not denote a special stuff or way of being. The peculiarity of our experiences, that they not only are, but are known, which their 'conscious' quality is invoked to explain, is better

explained by their relations these relations themselves being experiences —
to one another.

IV

Were I now to go on to treat of the knowing of perceptual by conceptual
experiences, it would again prove to be an affair of external relations. One
experience would be the knower, the other the reality known; and I could
perfectly well define, without the notion of `consciousness,' what the knowing
actually and practically amounts to —leading-towards, namely, and
terminating-in percepts, through a series of transitional experiences which
the world supplies. But I will not treat of this, space being insufficient.[17] I will
rather consider a few objections that are sure to be urged against the entire
theory as it stands.

V

First of all, this will be asked: "If experience has not 'conscious' existence,
if it be not partly made of 'consciousness,' of what then is it made? Matter we
know, and thought we know, and conscious content we know, but neutral and
simple 'pure experience' is something we know not at all. Say what it consists
of — for it must consist of something — or be willing to give it up!"

To this challenge the reply is easy. Although for fluency's sake I myself
spoke early in this article of a stuff of pure experience, I have now to say that
there is no general stuff of which experience at large is made. There are as
many stuffs as there are 'natures' in the things experienced. If you ask what
any one bit of pure experience is made of, the answer is always the same: "It
is made of that, of just what appears, of space, of intensity, of flatness,
brownness, heaviness, or what not." Shadworth Hodgson's analysis here
leaves nothing to be desired.[18] Experience is only a collective name for all
these sensible natures, and save for time and space (and, if you like, for
'being') there appears no universal element of which all things are made.

VI

The next objection is more formidable, in fact it sounds quite crushing when
one hears it first.

"If it be the self-same piece of pure experience, taken twice over, that serves
now as thought and now as thing" —so the objection runs — "how comes it
that its attributes should differ so fundamentally in the two takings. As thing,
the experience is extended; as thought, it occupies no space or place. As thing,
it is red, hard, heavy; but who ever heard of a red, hard or heavy thought? Yet
even now you said that an experience is made of just what appears, and what
appears is just such adjectives. How can the one experience in its
thing-function be made of them, consist of them, carry them as its own
attributes, while in its thought-function it disowns them and attributes them
elsewhere. There is a self-contradiction here from which the radical dualism
of thought and thing is the only truth that can save us. Only if the thought is
one kind of being can the adjectives exist in it 'intentionally' (to use the
scholastic term); only if the thing is another kind, can they exist in it

constitutively and energetically. No simple subject can take the same adjectives and at one time be qualified by it, and at another time be merely 'of' it, as of something only meant or known."

The solution insisted on by this objector, like many other common-sense solutions, grows the less satisfactory the more one turns it in one"s mind. To begin with, are thought and thing as heterogeneous as is commonly said?

No one denies that they have some categories in common. Their relations to time are identical. Both, moreover, may have parts (for psychologists in general treat thoughts as having them); and both may be complex or simple. Both are of kinds, can be compared, added and subtracted and arranged in serial orders. All sorts of adjectives qualify our thoughts which appear incompatible with consciousness, being as such a bare diaphaneity. For instance, they are natural and easy, or laborious. They are beautiful, happy, intense, interesting, wise, idiotic, focal, marginal, insipid, confused, vague, precise, rational, casual, general, particular, and many things besides. Moreover, the chapters on 'Perception' in the psychology-books are full of facts that make for the essential homogeneity of thought with thing. How, if 'subject' and 'object' were separated 'by the whole diameter of being,' and had no attributes in common, could it be so hard to tell, in a presented and recognized material object, what part comes in through the senseorgans and what part comes 'out of one's own head'? Sensations and apperceptive ideas fuse here so intimately that you can no more tell where one begins and the other ends, than you can tell, in those cunning circular panoramas that have lately been exhibited, where the real foreground and the painted canvas join together.[19]

Descartes for the first time defined thought as the absolutely unextended, and later philosophers have accepted the description as correct. But what possible meaning has it to say that, when we think of a foot-rule or a square yard, extension is not attributable to our thought? Of every extended object the adequate mental picture must have all the extension of the object itself. The difference between objective and subjective extension is one of relation to a context solely. In the mind the various extents maintain no necessarily stubborn order relatively to each other, while in the physical world they bound each other stably, and, added together, make the great enveloping Unit which we believe in and call real Space. As 'outer,' they carry themselves adversely, so to speak, to one another, exclude one another and maintain their distances; while, as 'inner,' their order is loose, and they form a durcheinander in which unity is lost.[20] But to argue from this that inner experience is absolutely inextensive seems to me little short of absurd. The two worlds differ, not by the presence or absence of extension, but by the relations of the extensions which in both worlds exist.

Does not this case of extension now put us on the track of truth in the case of other qualities? it does; and I am surprised that the facts should not have been noticed long ago. Why, for example, do we call a fire hot, and water wet, and yet refuse to say that our mental state, when it is 'of' these objects, is either wet or hot? 'Intentionally,' at any rate, and when the mental state is a vivid image, hotness and wetness are in it just as much as they are in the physical experience. The reason is this, that, as the general chaos of all our experiences gets sifted, we find that there are some fires that will always burn sticks and always warm our bodies, and that there are some waters that will always put out fires; while there are other fires and waters that will not act at all. The general group of experiences that act, that do not only possess their natures intrinsically, but wear them adjectively and energetically, turn. ing them against one another, comes inevitably to be contrasted with the group whose members, having identically the same natures, fail to manifest them in the 'energetic' way.'[21] make for myself now an experience of blazing fire; I place it near my body; but it does not warm me in the least. I lay a stick upon it, and the stick either burns or remains green, as I please. I call up water, and pour it on the fire, and absolutely no difference ensues. I account for all such facts by calling this whole train of experiences unreal, a mental train. Mental fire is what won't burn real sticks; mental water is what won't necessarily (though of course it may) put out even a mental fire. Mental knives may be sharp, but they won't cut real wood. Mental triangles are pointed, but their points won't wound. With 'real' objects, on the contrary, consequences always accrue; and thus the real experiences get sifted from the mental ones, the things from our thoughts of them, fanciful or true, and precipitated together as the stable part of the whole experience-chaos, under the name of the physical world. Of this our perceptual experiences are the nucleus, they being the originally strong experiences. We add a lot of conceptual experiences to them, making these strong also in imagination, and building out the remoter parts of the physical world by their means; and around this core of reality the world of laxly connected fancies and mere rhapsodical objects floats like a bank of clouds. In the clouds, all sorts of rules are violated which in the core are kept. Extensions there can be indefinitely located; motion there obeys no Newton's laws.

VII

There is a peculiar class of experiences to which, whether we take them as subjective or as objective, we assign their several natures as attributes, because in both contexts they affect their associates actively, though in neither quite as 'strongly' or as sharply as things affect one another by their physical energies. I refer here to appreciations, which form an ambiguous sphere of being, belonging with emotion on the one hand, and having objective 'value' on the other, yet seeming not quite inner nor quite outer, as if a diremption had begun but had not made itself complete.[22]

Experiences of painful objects, for example, are usually also painful experiences; perceptions of loveliness, of ugliness, tend to pass muster as lovely or as ugly perceptions; intuitions of the morally lofty are lofty intuitions. Sometimes the adjective wanders as if uncertain where to fix itself. Shall we speak of seductive visions or of visions of seductive things? Of wicked desires or of desires for wickedness? Of healthy thoughts or of thoughts of healthy objects? Of good impulses, or of impulses towards the good? Of feelings of anger, or of angry feelings? Both in the mind and in the thing, these natures modify their context, exclude certain associates and determine others, have their mates and incompatibles. Yet not as stubbornly as in the case of physical qualities, for beauty and ugliness, love and hatred, pleasant and painful can, in certain complex experiences, coexist.

If one were to make an evolutionary construction of how a lot of originally chaotic pure experiences became gradually differentiated into an orderly inner and outer world, the whole theory would turn upon one's success in explaining how or why the quality of an experience, once active, could become less so, and, from being an energetic attribute in some cases, elsewhere lapse into the status of an inert or merely internal 'nature.' This would be the 'evolution' of the psychical from the bosom of the physical, in which the esthetic, moral and otherwise emotional experiences would represent a halfway stage.

VIII

But a last cry of non possumus will probably go up from many readers. "All very pretty as a piece of ingenuity," they will say," but our consciousness itself intuitively contradicts You. We, for our part, know that we are conscious. We feel our thought, flowing as a life within us, in absolute contrast with the objects which it so unremittingly escorts. We can not be faithless to this immediate intuition. The dualism is a fundamental datum: Let no man join what God has put asunder."

My reply to this is my last word, and I greatly grieve that to many it will sound materialistic. I can not help that, however, for 1, too, have my intuitions and I must obey them. Let the case be what it may in others, I am as confident as I am of anything that, in myself, the stream of thinking (which I recognize emphatically as a phenomenon) is only a careless name for what, when scrutinized, reveals itself to consist chiefly of the stream of my breathing. The 'I think' which Kant said must be able to accompany all my objects, is the 'I breathe' which actually does accompany them. There are other internal facts besides breathing (intracephalic muscular adjustments, etc., of which I have said a word in my larger Psychology), and these increase the assets of 'consciousness,' so far as the latter is subject to immediate perception;[23] but breath, which was ever the original of 'spirit,' breath moving outwards, between the glottis and the nostrils, is, I am persuaded, the essence out of which philosophers have constructed the entity known to them as consciousness. That entity is fictitious, while thoughts in the concrete are fully real. But thoughts in the concrete are made of the same stuff as things are.

I wish I might believe myself to have made that plausible in this article. In another article I shall try to make the general notion of a world composed of pure experiences still more clear.

Endnotes

1. [Reprinted from the Journal of Philosophy, Psychology and Scientific Methods, vol. I No. 18, September 1, 1904. For the relation between this essay and those which follow, cf. below.]

2. Articles by Baldwin, Ward, Bawden, King, Alexander and others. Dr. Perry is frankly over the border.

3. [Similarly, there is no "activity of 'consciousness' as such."]

4. In my Psychology I have tried to show that we need no knower other than the 'passing thought.' [Principles of Psychology, vol. I, pp. 338 ff.]

5. G. E. Moore: Mind, Vol. XII, N. S., [1903], p. 450.

6. Paul Natorp: Einleitung in die Psychologie, 1888, pp. 14, 112.

7. "Figuratively speaking, consciousness may be said to be the one universal solvent, or menstruum, in which the different concrete kinds of psychic acts and facts are contained, whether in concealed or in obvious form." G. T. Ladd: Psychology, Descriptive and Explanatory, 1894, p. 30.

8. [For a parallel statement of this view, cf. the author's Meaning of Truth.]

9. [For the author's recognition of "concepts as a co-ordinate realm " of reality, cf. his Meaning of Truth, note; A Pluralistic Universe; Some Problems of Philosophy; and below. Note. Giving this view the name 'logical realism,' he remarks elsewhere that his philosophy "may be regarded as: somewhat eccentric in its attempt to combine logical realism with an otherwise empiricist mode of thought"

10. Here as elsewhere the relations are of course experienced rela. tions, members of the same originally chaotic manifold of non. perceptual experience of which the related terms themselves are parts.

11. Of the representative function of non-perceptual experience am a whole, I will say a word in a subsequent article: it leads too far into the general theory of knowledge for much to be said about it in a short paper like this. Munsterberg; Grundzuge der Psychologie, vol. I, p. 48.

13. Cf. A. L. Hodder: The Adversaries of the Sceptic, pp. 94-99.

14. For simplicity's sake I confine my exposition to 'external' reality. But there is also the system of ideal reality in which the room plays its part. Relations of comparison, of classification, serial order, value, also are stubborn, assign a definite place to the room, unlike the incoherence of its places in the mere rhapsody of our successive thoughts.

15. Note the ambiguity of this term, which is taken sometimes objectively and sometimes subjectively.

16. In the Psychological Review for July [19041, Dr. R. B. Perry has published a view of Consciousness which comes nearer to mine than any other with which I am acquainted. At present, Dr. Perry thinks every field of experience is so much 'fact.' It becomes 'opinion' or 'thought' only in retrospection, when a fresh experience, thinking the same object. alters and corrects it. But the corrective experience becomes itself in turn corrected, sad thus experience as a whole is a process in which what is objective originally forever turns subjective. turns into our apprehension of the object. I strongly recommend Dr. Perry's admirable article to my readers.

17. I have given it partial account of the matter in Mind, vol. x p. V. 1885 [reprinted in The Meaning of Truth], and in the Psychological Review, vol. II, p. 105, 1895 [partly reprinted in The Meaning of Trut. See also C. A. Strong's article in the Journal of Philosophy, Psychology and Scientific Methods. vol. I, p. 253, May 19, 1904. I hope myself very soon to recur to the matter.

18. [Cf. Shadworth Hodgson: The Metaphysic of Experience, vol. I, passim; The Philosophy of Reflection, bk. II ch. IV, §3. ED.]

19. Spencer's proof of his 'Transfigured Realism' (his doctrine that there is an absolutely non-mental reality) comes to mind as a splendid instance of the impossibility of establishing radical heterogeneity between thought and thing.

All his painfully accumulated points of difference run gradually into their opposites, and are full of exceptions.

20. I speak here of the complete inner life in which the mind plays freely with its materials. Of course the mind's free play is restricted when it seeks to copy real things in real space.

21. [But there are also "mental activity trains," in which thoughts do "work on each other."]

22. [This topic in resumed below.)

23. [Principles of Psychology, vol. I, pp. 299-305.]

A WORLD OF PURE EXPERIENCE[1]

It is difficult not to notice a curious unrest in the philosophic atmosphere of the time, a loosening of old landmarks, a softening of oppositions, a mutual borrowing from one an other on the part of systems anciently closed, and an interest in new suggestions, however vague, as if the one thing sure were the inadequacy of the extant school-solutions. The dissatisfaction with these seems due for the most part to a feeling that they are too abstract and academic. Life is confused and superabundant, and what the younger generation appears to crave is more of the temperament of life in its philosophy, even though it were at some cost of logical rigor and of formal purity. Transcendental idealism is inclining to let the world wag incomprehensibly, in spite of its Absolute Subject and his unity of purpose. Berkeleyan idealism is abandoning the principle of parsimony and dabbling in panpsychic speculations. Empiricism flirts with teleology; and, strangest of all, natural realism, so long decently buried, raises its head above the turf, and finds glad hands outstretched from the most unlikely quarters to help it to its feet again. We are all biased by our personal feelings, I know, and I am personally discontented with extant solutions; so I seem to read the signs of a great unsettlement, as if the upheaval of more real conceptions and more fruitful methods were imminent, as if a true landscape might result, less clipped, straight-edged and artificial.

If philosophy be really on the eve of any considerable rearrangement, the time should be propitious for any one who has suggestions of his own to bring forward. For many years past my mind has been growing into a certain type of Weltanshauung. Rightly or wrongly, I have got to the point where I can hardly see things in any other pattern. I propose, therefore, to describe the pattern as clearly as I can consistently with great brevity, and to throw my description into the bubbling vat of publicity where, jostled by rivals and tom by critics, it will eventually either disappear from notice, or else, if better luck befall it, quietly subside to the profundities, and serve as a possible ferment of new growths or a nucleus of new crystallization.

RADICAL EMPIRICISM

I give the name of 'radical empiricism' to my Weltanschauung. Empiricism is known as the opposite of rationalism. Rationalism tends to emphasize universals and to make wholes prior to parts in the order of logic as well as in that of being. Empiricism, on the contrary, lays the explanatory stress upon the part, the element, the individual, and treats the whole as a collection and the universal as an abstraction. My description of things, accordingly, starts with the parts and makes of the whole being of the second order. It is essentially a mosaic philosophy, a philosophy of plural facts, like that of Hume and his descendants, who refer these facts neither to Substances in which

they inhere nor to an Absolute Mind that creates them as its objects. But it
differs from the Humian type of empiricism in one particular which makes me
add the epithet radical.

To be radical, an empiricism must neither admit into its constructions any
element that is not directly experienced, nor exclude from them any element
that is directly experienced. For such a philosophy, the relations that connect
experiences must themselves be experienced relations, and any kind of
relation experienced must be accounted as 'real' as anything else in the
system. Elements may indeed be redistributed, the original placing of things
getting corrected, but a real place must be found for every kind of thing
experienced, whether term or relation, in the final philosophic arrangement.

Now, ordinary empiricism, in spite of the fact that conjunctive and
disjunctive relations present themselves as being fully co-ordinate parts of
experience, has always shown a tendency to do away with the connections of
things, and to insist most on the disjunctions. Berkeley's nominalism, Hume's
statement that whatever things we distinguish are as 'loose and separate' as
if they had 'no manner of connection,' James Mill's denial that similars have
anything 'really' in common, the resolution of the causal tie into habitual
sequence, John Mill's account of both physical things and selves as composed
of discontinuous possibilities, and the general pulverization of all Experience
by association and the mind-dust theory, are examples of what I mean.[2]

The natural result of such a world-picture has been the efforts of
rationalism to correct its incoherencies by the addition of transexperiential
agents of unification, substances, intellectual categories and powers, or Selves;
whereas, if empiricism had only been radical and taken everything that
comes without disfavor, conjunction as well as separation, each at its face
value, the results would have called for no such artificial correction. Radical
empiricism, as I understand it, does full justice to conjunctive relations,
without, however, treating them as rationalism always tends to treat them,
as being true in some supernal way, as if the unity of things and their variety
belonged to different orders of truth and vitality altogether.

CONJUNCTIVE RELATIONS

Relations are of different degrees of intimacy. Merely to be 'with' one
another in a universe of discourse is the most external relation that terms can
have, and seems to involve nothing whatever as to farther consequences.
Simultaneity and time-interval come next, and then space-adjacency and
distance. After them, similarity and difference, carrying the possibility of
many inferences. Then relations of activity, tying terms into series involving
change, tendency, resistance, and the causal order generally. Finally, the
relation experienced between terms that form states of mind, and are
immediately conscious of continuing each other. The organization of the Self
as a system of memories, purposes, strivings, fulfilments or disappointments,
is incidental to this most intimate of all relations, the terms of which seem in
many cases actually to compenetrate and suffuse each other's being.[3]

Philosophy has always turned on grammatical particles. With, near, next,
like, from, towards, against, because, for, through, my —these words

designate types of conjunctive relation arranged in a roughly ascending order of intimacy and inclusiveness. A priori, we can imagine a universe of withness but no nextness; or one of nextness but no likeness, or of likeness with no activity, or of activity with no purpose, or of purpose with no ego. These would be universes, each with its own grade, of unity. The universe of human experience is, by one or another of its parts, of each and all these grades.

Whether or not it possibly enjoys some still more absolute grade of union does not appear upon the surface.

Taken as it does appear, our universe is to a large extent chaotic. No one single type of connection runs through all the experiences that compose it. If we take space-relations, they fail to connect minds into any regular system. Causes and purposes obtain only among special series of facts. The self-relation seems extremely limited and does not link two different selves together. Prima facie, if you should liken the universe of absolute idealism to an aquarium, a crystal globe in which goldfish are swimming, you would have to compare the empiricist universe to something more like one of those dried human heads with which the Dyaks of Borneo deck their lodges. The skull forms a solid nucleus; but innumerable feathers, leaves, strings, beads, and loose appendices of every description float and dangle from it, and, save that they terminate in it, seem to have nothing to do with one another. Even so my experiences and yours float and dangle, terminating, it is true, in a nucleus of common perception, but for the most part out of sight and irrelevant and unimaginable to one another. This imperfect intimacy, this bare relation of withness between some parts of the sum total of experience and other parts, is the fact that ordinary empiricism over-emphasizes against rationalism, the latter always tending to ignore it unduly. Radical empiricism, on the contrary, is fair to both the unity and the disconnection. It finds no reason for treating either as illusory. It allots to each its definite sphere of description, and agrees that there appear to be actual forces at work which tend, as time goes on, to make the unity greater.

The conjunctive relation that has given most trouble to philosophy is the co-conscious transition, so to call it, by which one experience passes into another when both belong to the same self. About the facts there is no question. My experiences and your experiences are 'with' each other in various external ways, but mine pass into mine, and yours pass into yours in a way in which yours and mine never pass into one another. Within each of our personal histories, subject, object, interest and purpose are continuous or maybe continuous.[4] Personal histories are processes of change in time, and the change itself is one of the things immediately experienced. 'Change' in this case means continuous as opposed to discontinuous transition. But continuous transition is one sort of a conjunctive relation; and to be a radical empiricist means to hold fast to this conjunctive relation of all others, for this is the strategic point, the position through which, if a hole be made, all the corruptions of dialectics and all the metaphysical fictions pour into our philosophy. The holding fast to this relation means taking it at its face value, neither less nor more; and to take it at its face value means first of all to take it just as we feel it, and not to confuse ourselves with abstract talk about it, involving words that drive us to invent secondary conceptions in order to neutralize their suggestions and to make our actual experience again seem rationally possible.

What I do feel simply when a later moment of my experience succeeds an earlier one is that though they are two moments, the transition from the one to the other is continuous. Continuity here is a definite sort of experience; just as definite as is the discontinuity-experience which I find it impossible to avoid when I seek to make the transition from an experience of my own to one of yours. In this latter case I have to get on and off again, to pass from a thing lived to another thing only conceived, and the break is positively experienced and noted. Though the functions exerted by my experience and by yours may be the same (e. g., the same objects known and the same purposes followed), yet the sameness has in this case to be ascertained expressly (and often with difficulty and uncertainty) after the break has been felt; whereas in passing from one of my own moments to another the sameness of object and interest is unbroken, and both the earlier and the later experience are of things directly lived.

There is no other nature, no other whatness than this absence of break and this sense of continuity in that most intimate of all conjunctive relations, the passing of one experience into another when they belong to the same self. And this whatness is real empirical 'content,' just as the whatness of separation and discontinuity is real content in the contrasted case. Practically to experience one's personal continuum in this living way is to know the originals of the ideas of continuity and of sameness, to know what the words stand for concretely, to own all that they can ever mean. But all experiences have their conditions; and over-subtle intellects, thinking about the facts here, and asking how they are possible, have ended by substituting a lot of static objects of conception for the direct perceptual experiences. "Sameness," they have said, "must be a stark numerical identity; it can't run on from next to next. Continuity can't mean mere absence of gap; for if you say two things are in immediate contact, at the contact how can they be two? If, on the other hand, you put a relation of transition between them, that itself is a third thing, and needs to be related or hitched to its terms. An infinite series is involved," and so on. The result is that from difficulty to difficulty, the plain conjunctive experience has been discredited by both schools, the empiricists leaving things permanently disjoined, and the rationalist remedying the looseness by their Absolutes or Substances, or whatever other fictitious agencies of union they may have employed.[5] From all which artificiality we can be saved by a couple of simple reflections: first, that conjunctions and separations are, at all events, co-ordinate phenomena which, if we take experiences at their face value, must be accounted equally real; and second, that if we insist on treating things as really separate when they are given as continuously joined, invoking, when union is required, transcendental principles to overcome the separateness we have assumed, then we ought to stand ready to perform the converse act. We ought to invoke higher principles of disunion, also, to make our merely experienced disjunctions more truly real. Failing thus, we ought to let the originally given continuities stand on their own bottom. We have no right to be lopsided or to blow capriciously hot and cold.

The first great pitfall from which such a radical standing by experience will save us is an artificial conception of the relations between knower and known. Throughout the history of philosophy the subject and its object have been treated as absolutely discontinuous entities; and thereupon the presence of the latter to the former, or the 'apprehension' by the former of the latter, has assumed a paradoxical character which all sorts of theories had to be invented to overcome. Representative theories put a mental 'representation,' 'image,' or 'content' into the gap, as a sort of intermediary. Common-sense theories left the gap untouched, declaring our mind able to clear it by a self-transcending leap. Transcendentalist theories left it impossible to traverse by finite knowers, and brought an Absolute in to perform the saltatory act. All the while, in the very bosom of the finite experience, every conjunction required to make the relation intelligible is given in full. Either the knower and the known are: (1) the self-same piece of experience taken twice over in different contexts; or they are (2) two pieces of actual experience belonging to the same subject, with definite tracts of conjunctive transitional experience between them; or (3) the known is a possible experience either of that subject or another, to which the said conjunctive transitions would lead, if sufficiently prolonged.

To discuss all the ways in which one experience may function as the knower of another, would be incompatible with the limits of this essay.[6] I have just treated of type 1, the kind of knowledge called perception.[7] This is the type of case in which the mind enjoys direct 'acquaintance' with a present object. In the other types the mind has 'knowledge-about' an object not immediately there. Of type 2, the simplest sort of conceptual knowledge, I have given some account in two [earlier] articles.[8] Type 3 can always formally and hypothetically be reduced to type 2, so that a brief description of that type will put the present reader sufficiently at my point of view, and make him see what the actual meanings of the mysterious cognitive relation may be.

Suppose me to be sitting here in my library at Cambridge, at ten minutes' walk from 'Memorial Hall,' and to be thinking truly of the latter object. My mind may have before it only the name, or it may have a clear image, or it may have a very dim image of the hall, but such intrinsic differences in the image make no difference in its cognitive function. Certain extrinsic phenomena, special experiences of conjunction, are what impart to the image, be it what it may, its knowing office.

For instance, if you ask me what hall I mean by my image, and I can tell you nothing; or if I fail to point or lead you towards the Harvard Delta; or if, being led by you, I am uncertain whether the Hall I see be what I had in mind or not; you would rightly deny that I had ` meant' that particular hall at all, even though my mental image might to some degree have resembled it. The resemblance would count in that case as coincidental merely, for all sorts of things of a kind resemble one another in this world without being held for that reason to take cognizance of one another.

On the other hand, if I can lead you to the hall, and tell you of its history and present uses; if in its presence I feel my idea, however imperfect it may have been, to have led hither and to be now terminated; if the associates of the image and of the felt hall run parallel, so that each term of the one context corresponds serially, as I walk, with an answering term of the others; why then my soul was prophetic, and my idea must be, and by common consent would be, called cognizant of reality. That percept was what I meant, for into it my idea has passed by conjunctive experiences of sameness and fulfilled intention. Nowhere is there jar, but every later moment continues and corroborates an earlier one.

In this continuing and corroborating, taken in no transcendental sense, but denoting definitely felt transitions, lies all that the knowing of a percept by an idea can possibly contain or signify. Wherever such transitions are felt, the first experience knows the last one. Where they do not, or where even as possibles they can not, intervene, there can be no pretence of knowing. In this latter case the extremes will be connected, if connected at all, by inferior relations — bare likeness or succession, or by 'withness' alone. Knowledge of sensible realities thus comes to life inside the tissue of experience. It is made; and made by relations that unroll themselves in time. Whenever certain intermediaries are given, such that, as they develop towards their terminus, there is experience from point to point of one direction followed, and finally of one process fulfilled, the result is that their starting-point thereby becomes a knower and their terminus an object meant or known. That is all that knowing (in the simple case considered) can be known—as, that is the whole of its nature, put into experiential terms. Whenever such is the sequence of our experiences we may freely say that we had the terminal object 'in mind' from the outset, even although at the outset nothing was there in us but a flat piece of substantive experience like any other, with no self-transcendency about it, and no mystery save the mystery of coming into existence and of being gradually followed by other pieces of substantive experience, with conjunctively transitional experiences between. That is what we mean here by the object's being 'in mind.' Of any deeper more real way of being in mind we have no positive conception, and we have no right to discredit our actual experience by talking of such a way at all.

I know that many a reader will rebel at this. "'Mere intermediaries,'" he will say, "even though they be feelings of continuously growing fulfilment, only separate the knower from the known, whereas what we have in knowledge is a kind of immediate touch of the one by the other, an 'apprehension' in the etymological sense of the word, a leaping of the chasm as by lightning, an act by which two terms are smitten into one, over the head of their distinctness. All these dead intermediaries of yours are out of each other, and outside of their termini still."

But do not such dialectic difficulties remind us of the dog dropping his bone and snapping at its image in the water? If we knew any more real kind of union aliunde, we might be entitled to brand all our empirical unions as a sham. But unions by continuous transition are the only ones we know of, whether in this matter of a knowledge—about that terminates in an acquaintance, whether in personal identity, in logical predication through the copula 'is,' or elsewhere. If anywhere there were more absolute unions realized, they could only reveal themselves to us by just such conjunctive results. These are what the unions are worth, these are all that we can ever practically mean by union, by continuity. Is it not time to repeat what Lotze said of substances, that to act like one is to be one?[9] Should we not say here that to be experienced as continuous is to be really continuous, in a world where experience and reality come to the same thing? In a picture gallery a painted hook will serve to hang a painted chain by, a painted cable will hold a painted ship. In a world where both the terms and their distinctions are affairs of experience, conjunctions that are experienced must be at least as real as anything else. They will be 'absolutely' real conjunctions, if we have no transphenomenal Absolute ready, to derealize the whole experienced world by, at a stroke. If, on the other hand, we had such an Absolute, not one of our opponents' theories of knowledge could remain standing any better than ours could; for the distinctions as well as the conjunctions of experience would impartially fall its prey. The whole question of how 'one' thing can know 'another' would cease to be a real one at all in a world where otherness itself was an illusion.[10]

So much for the essentials of the cognitive relation, where the knowledge is conceptual in type, or forms knowledge 'about' an object. It consists in intermediary experiences (possible, if not actual) of continuously developing progress, and, finally, of fulfilment, when the sensible percept, which is the object, is reached. The percept here not only verifies the concept, proves its function of knowing that percept to be true, but the percept's existence as the terminus of the chain of intermediaries creates the function. Whatever terminates that chain was, because it now proves itself to be, what the concept 'had in mind.'

The towering importance for human life of this kind of knowing lies in the fact that an experience that knows another can figure as its representative, not in any quasi-miraculous 'epistemological' sense, but in the definite practical sense of being its substitute in various operations, sometimes physical and sometimes mental, which lead us to its associates and results. By experimenting on our ideas of reality, we may save ourselves the trouble of experimenting on the real experiences which they severally mean. The ideas form related systems, corresponding point for point to the systems which the realities form; and by letting an ideal term call up its associates systematically, we may be led to a terminus which the corresponding real term would have led to in case we had operated on the real world. And this brings us to the general question of substitution.

SUBSTITUTION

In Taine's brilliant book on 'Intelligence,' substitution was for the first time named as a cardinal logical function, though of course the facts had always been familiar enough. What, exactly, in a system of experiences, does the 'substitution' of one of them for another mean?

According to my view, experience as a whole is a process in time, whereby innumerable particular terms lapse and are superseded by others that follow upon them by transitions which, whether disjunctive or conjunctive in content, are themselves experiences, and must in general be accounted at least as real as the terms which they relate. What the nature of the event called 'superseding' signifies, depends altogether on the kind of transition that obtains. Some experiences simply abolish their predecessors without

continuing them in any way. Others are felt to increase or to enlarge their
meaning, to carry out their purpose, or to bring us nearer to their goal. They
represent' them, and may fulfil their function better than they fulfilled it
themselves. But to 'fulfil a function' in a world of pure experience can be
conceived and defined in only one possible way. In such a world transitions
and arrivals (or terminations) are the only events that happen, though they
happen by so many sorts of path. The only function that one experience can
perform is to lead into another experience; and the only fulfilment we can
speak of is the reaching of a certain experienced end. When one experience
leads to (or can lead to) the same end as another, they agree in function. But
the whole system of experiences as they are immediately given presents itself
as a quasi-chaos through which one can pass out of an initial term in many
directions and yet end in the same terminus, moving from next to next by a
great many possible paths.

Either one of these paths might be a functional substitute for another, and
to follow one rather than another might on occasion be an advantageous thing
to do. As a matter of fact, and in a general way, the paths that run through
conceptual experiences, that is, through 'thoughts' or 'ideas' that 'know' the
things in which they terminate, are highly advantageous paths to follow. Not
only do they yield inconceivably rapid transitions; but, owing to the 'universal'
character[11] which they frequently possess, and to their capacity for
association with one another in great systems, they outstrip the tardy
consecutions of the things themselves, and sweep us on towards our ultimate
termini in a far more labor-saving way than the following of trains of sensible
perception ever could. Wonderful are the new cuts and the short-circuits
which the thought-paths make. Most thought-paths, it is true, are substitutes
for nothing actual; they end outside the real world altogether, in wayward
fancies, utopias, fictions or mistakes. But where they do re-enter reality and
terminate therein, we substitute them always; and with these substitutes we
pass the greater number of our hours.

This is why I called our experiences, taken all together, a quasi-chaos.
There is vastly more discontinuity in the sum total of experiences than we
commonly suppose. The objective nucleus of every man's experience, his own
body, is, it is true, a continuous percept; and equally continuous as a percept
(though we may be inattentive to it) is the material environment of that body,
changing by gradual transition when the body moves. But the distant parts
of the physical world are at all times absent from us, and form conceptual
objects merely, into the perceptual reality of which our life inserts itself at
points discrete and relatively rare. Round their several objective nuclei, partly
shared and common and partly discrete, of the real physical world,
innumerable thinkers, pursuing their several lines of physically true
cogitation, trace paths that. intersect one another only at discontinuous
perceptual points, and the rest of the time are quite incongruent; and around
all the nuclei of shared 'reality,' as around the Dyak's head of my late
metaphor, floats the vast cloud of experiences that are wholly subjective, that
are non-substitutional, that find not even an eventual ending for themselves
in the perceptual world — the mere day-dreams and joys and sufferings and
wishes of the individual minds. These exist with one another, indeed, and

with the objective nuclei, but out of them it is probable that to all eternity no interrelated system of any kind will ever be made.

This notion of the purely substitutional or conceptual physical world brings us to the most critical of all the steps in the development of a philosophy of pure experience. The paradox of self-transcendency in knowledge comes back upon us here, but I think that our notions of pure experience and of substitution, and our radically empirical view of conjunctive transitions, are Denkmittel that will carry us safely through the pass.

WHAT OBJECTIVE REFERENCE IS.

Whosoever feels his experience to be something substitutional even while he has it, may be said to have an experience that reaches beyond itself. From inside of its own entity it says 'more,' and postulates reality existing elsewhere. For the transcendentalist, who holds knowing to consist in a salto mortale across an 'epistemological chasm,' such an idea presents no difficulty; but it seems at first sight as if it might be inconsistent with an empiricism like our own. Have we not explained that conceptual knowledge is made such wholly by the existence of things that fall outside of the knowing experience itself — by intermediary experiences and by a terminus that fulfils? Can the knowledge be there before these elements that constitute its being have come? And, if knowledge be not there, how can objective reference occur?

The key to this difficulty lies in the distinction between knowing as verified and completed, and the same knowing as in transit and on its way. To recur to the Memorial Hall example lately used, it is only when our idea of the Hall has actually terminated in the percept that we know 'for certain' that from the beginning it was truly cognitive of that. Until established by the end of the process, its quality of knowing that, or indeed of knowing anything, could still be doubted; and yet the knowing really was there, as the result now shows. We were virtual knowers of the Hall long before we were certified to have been its actual knowers, by the percept's retroactive validating power. Just so we are 'mortal' all the time, by reason of the virtuality of the inevitable event which will make us so when it shall have come.

Now the immensely greater part of all our knowing never gets beyond this virtual stage. It never is completed or nailed down. I speak not merely of our ideas of imperceptibles like ether-waves or dissociated 'ions,' or of 'ejects' like the contents of our neighbors' minds; I speak also of ideas which we might verify if we would take the trouble, but which we hold for true although unterminated perceptually, because nothing says 'no' to us, and there is no contradicting truth in sight. To continue thinking unchallenged is, ninety-nine times out of a hundred, our practical substitute for knowing in the completed sense. As each experience runs by cognitive transition into the next one, and we nowhere feel a collision with what we elsewhere count as truth or fact, we commit ourselves to the current as if the port were sure. We live, as it were, upon the front edge of an advancing wave-crest, and our sense of a determinate direction in falling forward is all we cover of the future of our path. It is as if a differential quotient should be conscious and treat itself as an adequate substitute for a traced-out curve. Our experience, inter alia, is of variations of rate and of direction, and lives in these transitions more than in the journey's end. The experiences of tendency are sufficient to act upon —what more could we have done at those moments even if the later verification comes complete?

This is what, as a radical empiricist, I say to the charge that the objective reference which is so flagrant a character of our experiences involves a chasm and a mortal leap. A positively conjunctive transition involves neither chasm nor leap. Being the very original of what we mean by continuity, it makes a continuum wherever it appears. I know full well that such brief words as these will leave the hardened transcendentalist unshaken. Conjunctive experiences separate their terms, he will still say: they are third things interposed, that have themselves to be conjoined by new links, and to invoke them makes our trouble infinitely worse. To 'feel' our motion forward is impossible. Motion implies terminus; and how can terminus be felt before we have arrived? The barest start and sally forwards, the barest tendency to leave the instant, involves the chasm and the leap. Conjunctive transitions are the most superficial of appearances, illusions of our sensibility which philosophical reflection pulverizes at a touch. Conception is our only trustworthy instrument, conception and the Absolute working hand in hand. Conception disintegrates experience utterly, but its disjunctions are easily overcome again when the Absolute takes up the task.

Such transcendentalists I must leave, provisionally at least, in full possession of their creed.'[12] have no space for polemics in this article, so I shall simply formulate the empiricist doctrine as my hypothesis, leaving it to work or not work as it may.

Objective reference, I say then, is an incident of the fact that so much of our experience comes as an insufficient and consists of process and transition. Our fields of experience have no more definite boundaries than have our fields of view. Both are fringed forever by a more that continuously develops, and that continuously supersedes them as life proceeds. The relations, generally speaking, are as real here as the terms are, and the only complaint of the transcendentalist's with which I could at all sympathize would be his charge that, by first making knowledge to consist in external relations as I have done, and by then confessing that nine-tenths of the time these are not actually but only virtually there, I have knocked the solid bottom out of the whole business, and palmed off a substitute of knowledge for the genuine thing. Only the admission, such a critic might say, that our ideas are self-transcendent and 'true' already, in advance of the experiences that are to terminate them, can bring solidity back to knowledge in a world like this, in which transitions and terminations are only by exception fulfilled.

This seems to me an excellent place for applying the pragmatic method. When a dispute arises, that method consists in auguring what practical consequences would be different if one side rather than the other were true. If no difference can be thought of, the dispute is a quarrel over words. What then would the self-transcendency affirmed to exist in advance of all experiential mediation or termination, be known as? What would it practically result in for us, were it true?

It could only result in our orientation, in the turning of our expectations and practical tendencies into the right path; and the right path here, so long as we and the object are not yet face to face (or can never get face to face, as in the case of ejects), would be the path that led us into the object's nearest neighborhood. Where direct acquaintance is lacking, 'knowledge about' is the next best thing, and an acquaintance with what actually lies about the object, and is most closely related to it, puts such knowledge within our grasp. Ether-waves and your anger, for example, are things in which my thoughts will never perceptually terminate, but my concepts of them lead me to their very brink, to the chromatic fringes and to the hurtful words and deeds which are their really next effects.

Even if our ideas did in themselves carry the postulated self-transcendency, it would still remain true that their putting us into possession of such effects would be the sole cash-value of the self-transcendency for us. And this cash-value, it is needless to say, is verbatim et literatim what our empiricist account pays in. On pragmatist principles therefore, a dispute over self-transcendency is a pure logomachy. Call our concepts of ejective things selftranscendent or the reverse, it makes no difference, so long as we don't differ about the nature of that exalted virtue's fruits — fruits for us, of course, humanistic fruits. If an Absolute were proved to exist for other reasons, it might well appear that his knowledge is terminated in innumerable cases where ours is still incomplete. That, however, would be a fact indifferent to our knowledge. The latter would grow neither worse nor better, whether we acknowledged such an Absolute or left him out.

So the notion of a knowledge still in transitu and on its way joins hands here with that notion of a 'pure experience' which I tried to explain in my [essay] entitled 'Does Consciousness Exist?' The instant field of the present is always experience in its 'pure' state, plain unqualified actuality, a simple that, as yet undifferentiated into thing and thought, and only virtually classifiable as objective fact or as some one's opinion about fact. This is as true when the field is conceptual as when it is perceptual. 'Memorial Hall' is 'there' in my idea as much as when I stand before it. I proceed to act on its account in either case. Only in the later experience that supersedes the present one is this naif immediacy retrospectively split into two parts, a 'consciousness' and its 'content,' and the content corrected or confirmed.

While still pure, or present, any experience — mine, for example, of what I write about in these very lines — passes for 'truth.' The morrow may reduce it to 'opinion.' The transcendentalist in all his particular knowledges is as liable to this reduction as I am: his Absolute does not save him. Why, then, need he quarrel with an account of knowing that merely leaves it liable to this inevitable condition? Why insist that knowing is a static relation out of time when it practically seems so much a function of our active life? For a thing to be valid, says Lotze, is the same as to make itself valid. When the whole universe seems only to be making itself valid and to be still incomplete (else why its ceaseless changing?) why, of all things, should knowing be exempt? Why should it not be making itself valid like everything else? That some parts of it may be already valid or verified beyond dispute, the empirical philosopher, of course, like any one else, may always hope.

THE CONTERMINOUSNESS OF DIFFERENT MINDS[13]

With transition and prospect thus enthroned in pure experience, it is impossible to subscribe to the idealism of the English school. Radical empiricism has, in fact, more affinities with natural realism than with the views of Berkeley or of Mill, and this can be easily shown.

For the Berkeleyan school, ideas (the verbal equivalent of what I term experiences) are discontinuous. The content of each is wholly immanent, and there are no transitions with which they are consubstantial and through which their beings may unite. Your Memorial Hall and mine, even when both are percepts, are wholly out of connection with each other. Our lives are a congeries of solipsisms, out of which in strict logic only a God could compose a universe even of discourse. No dynamic currents run between my objects and your objects. Never can our minds meet in the same.

The incredibility of such a philosophy is flagrant. It is 'cold, strained, and unnatural' in a supreme degree; and it may be doubted whether even Berkeley himself, who took it so religiously, really believed, when walking through the streets of London, that his spirit and the spirits of his fellow wayfarers had absolutely different towns in view.

To me the decisive reason in favor of our minds meeting in some common objects at least is that, unless I make that supposition, I have no motive for assuming that your mind exists at all. Why do I postulate your mind? Because I see your body acting in a certain way. Its gestures, facial movements, words and conduct generally, are 'expressive,' so I deem it actuated as my own is, by an inner life like mine. This argument from analogy is my reason, whether an instinctive belief runs before it or not. But what is 'your body' here but a percept in my field? It is only as animating that object, my object, that I have any occasion to think of you at all. If the body that you actuate be not the very body that I see there, but some duplicate body of your own with which that has nothing to do, we belong to different universes, you and 1, and for me to speak of you is folly. Myriads of such universes even now may coexist, irrelevant to one another; my concern is solely with the universe with which my own life is connected.

In that perceptual part of my universe which I call your body, your mind and my mind meet and may be called conterminous. Your mind actuates that body and mine sees it ; my thoughts pass into it as into their harmonious cognitive fulfilment; your emotions and volitions pass into it as causes into their effects.

But that percept hangs together with all our other physical percepts. They are of one stuff with it; and if it be our common possession, they must be so likewise. For instance, your hand lays hold of one end of a rope and my hand lays hold of the other end. We pull against each other. Can our two hands be mutual objects in this experience, and the rope not be mutual also? What is true of the rope is true of any other percept. Your objects are over and over again the same as mine. If I ask you where some object of yours is, our old Memorial Hall, for example, you point to my Memorial Hall with your hand which I see. If you alter an object in your world, put out a candle, for example, when I am present, my candle ipso facto goes out. It is only as altering my objects that I guess you to exist. if your objects do not coalesce with my objects, if they be not identically where mine are, they must be proved to be positively somewhere else. But no other location can be assigned for them, so their place must be what it seems to be, the same.[14]

Practically, then, our minds meet in a world of objects which they share in common, which would still be there, if one or several of the minds were destroyed. I can see no formal objection to this supposition's being literally true. On the principles which I am defending, a 'mind' or 'personal consciousness' is the name for a series of experiences run together by certain definite transitions, and an objective reality is a series of similar experiences knit by different transitions. If one and the same experience can figure twice, once in a mental and once in a physical context (as I have tried, in my article on 'Consciousness,' to show that it can), one does not see why it might not figure thrice, or four times, or any number of times, by running into as many different mental contexts, just as the same point, lying at their intersection, can be continued into many different lines. Abolishing any number of contexts would not destroy the experience itself or its other contexts, any more than abolishing some of the point's linear continuations would destroy the others, or destroy the point itself.

I well know the subtle dialectic which insists so that a term taken in another relation must needs be an intrinsically different term. The crux is always the old Greek one, that the same man can't be tall in relation to one neighbor, and short in relation to another, for that would make him tall and short at once. In this essay I can not stop to refute this dialectic, so I pass on, leaving my flank for the time exposed.[15] But if my reader will only allow that the same 'now' both ends his past and begins his future; or that, when he buys an acre of land from his neighbor, it is the same acre that successively figures in the two estates; or that when I pay him a dollar, the same dollar goes into his pocket that came out of mine; he will also in consistency have to allow that the same object may conceivably play a part in, as being related to the rest of, any number of otherwise entirely different minds. This is enough for my present point: the common-sense notion of minds sharing the same object offers no special logical or epistemological difficulties of its own; it stands or falls with the general possibility of things being in conjunctive relation with other things at all.

In principle, then, let natural realism Pass for possible. Your mind and mine may terminate in the same percept, not merely against it, as if it were a third external thing, but by inserting themselves into it and coalescing with it, for such is the sort of conjunctive union that appears to be experienced when a perceptual terminus 'fulfils.' Even so, two hawsers may embrace the same pile, and yet neither one of them touch any other part except that pile, of what the other hawser is attached to.

It is therefore not a formal question, but a question of empirical fact solely, whether, when you and I are said to know the 'same' Memorial Hall, our minds do terminate at or in a numerically identical percept. Obviously, as a plain matter of fact, they do not. Apart from color-blindness and such possibilities, we see the Hall in different perspectives. You may be on one side of it and I on another. The percept of each of us, as he sees the surface of the Hall, is moreover only his provisional terminus. The next thing beyond my percept is not your mind, but more percepts of my own into which my first percept develops, the interior of the Hall, for instance, or the inner structure of its bricks and mortar. If our minds were in a literal sense conterminous, neither could get beyond the percept which they had in common, it would be an ultimate barrier between them — unless indeed they flowed over it and became 'co-conscious' over a still larger part of their content, which (thought-transference apart) is not supposed to be the case. In point of fact the ultimate common barrier can always be pushed, by both minds, farther than any actual percept of either, until at last it resolves itself into the mere notion of imperceptibles like atoms or ether, so that, where we do terminate in percepts, our knowledge is only speciously completed, being, in theoretic strictness, only a virtual knowledge of those remoter objects which conception carries out.

Is natural realism, permissible in logic, refuted then by empirical fact? Do our minds have no object in common after all?

Yes, they certainly have Space in common.

On pragmatic principles we are obliged to predicate sameness wherever we can predicate no assignable point of difference. If two named things have every quality and function indiscernible, and are a t the same time in the same place, they must be written down as numerically one thing under two different names. But there is no test discoverable, so far as I know, by which it can be shown that the place occupied by your percept of Memorial Hall differs from the place occupied by mine. The percepts themselves may be shown to differ; but if each of us be asked to Point out where his percept is, we point to an identical spot. All the relations, whether geometrical or causal, of the Hall originate or terminate in that spot wherein our hands meet, and where each of us begins to work if he wishes to make the Hall change before the other's eyes. Just so it is with our bodies. That body of yours which you actuate and feel from within must be in the same spot as the body of yours which I see or touch from without. 'There' for me means where I place my finger. If you do not feel my finger's contact to be 'there' in my sense, when I place it on your body, where then do you feel it? Your inner actuations of your body meet my finger there: it is there that you resist its push, or shrink back, or sweep the finger aside with your hand. Whatever farther knowledge either of us may acquire of the real constitution of the body which we thus feel, you from within and I from without, it is in that same place that the newly conceived or perceived constituents have to be located, and it is through that space that your and my mental intercourse with each other has always to be carried on, by the mediation of impressions which I convey thither, and of the reactions thence which those impressions may provoke from you.

In general terms, then, whatever differing contents our minds may eventually fill a place with, the place itself is a numerically identical content of the two minds, a piece of common property in which, through which, and over which they join. The receptacle of certain of our experiences being thus common, the experiences themselves might some day become common also. If that day ever did come, our thoughts would terminate in a complete empirical identity, there would be an end, so far as those experiences went, to our discussions about truth. No points of difference appearing, they would have to count as the same.

CONCLUSION

With this we have the outlines of a philosophy of pure experience before us. At the outset of my essay, I called it a mosaic philosophy. In actual mosaics the pieces are held together by their bedding, for which bedding the Substances, transcendental Egos, or Absolutes of other philosophies may be taken to stand. In radical empiricism there is no bedding; it is as if the pieces clung together by their edges, the transitions experienced between them forming their cement. Of course such a metaphor is misleading, for in actual experience the more substantive and the more transitive parts run into each other continuously, there is in general no separateness needing to be overcome by an external cement; and whatever separateness is actually experienced is not overcome, it stays and counts as separateness to the end. But the metaphor serves to symbolize the fact that Experience itself, taken at large, can grow by its edges. That one moment of it proliferates into the next by transitions which, whether conjunctive or disjunctive, continue the experiential tissue, can not, I contend, be denied. Life is in the transitions as much as in the terms connected; often, indeed, it seems to be there more emphatically, as if our spurts and sallies forward were the real firing-line of the battle, were like the thin line of flame advancing across the dry autumnal field which the farmer proceeds to burn. In this line we live prospectively as well as retrospectively. It is 'of' the past, inasmuch as it comes expressly as the past's continuation; it is 'of' the future in so far as the future, when it comes, will have continued it.

These relations of continuous transition experienced are what make our experiences cognitive. In the simplest and completest cases the experiences are cognitive of one another. When one of them terminates a previous series of them with a sense of fulfilment, it, we say, is what those other experiences 'had in view.' The knowledge, in such a case, is verified; the truth is 'salted down.' Mainly, however, we live on speculative investments, or on our prospects only. But living on things in posse is as good as living in the actual, so long as our credit remains good. It is evident that for the most part it is good, and that the universe seldom protests our drafts.

In this sense we at every moment can continue to believe in an existing beyond. It is only in special cases that our confident rush forward gets rebuked. The beyond must, of course, always in our philosophy be itself of an experiential nature. If not a future experience of our own or a present one of our neighbor, it must be a thing in itself in Dr. Prince's and Professor Strong's sense of the term —that is, it must be an experience for itself whose relation to other things we translate into the action of molecules, ether-waves, or whatever else the physical symbols may be.[16] This opens the chapter of the relations of radical empiricism to panpsychism, into which I can not enter now.[17]

The beyond can in any case exist simultaneously — for it can be experienced to have existed simultaneously — with the experience that practically postulates it by looking in its direction, or by turning or changing in the direction of which it is the goal. Pending that actuality of union, in the virtuality of which the 'truth,' even now, of the postulation consists, the beyond and its knower are entities split off from each other. The world is in so far forth a pluralism of which the unity is not fully experienced as yet. But, as fast as verifications come, trains of experience, once separate, run into one another; and that is why I said, earlier in my article, that the unity of the world is on the whole undergoing increase. The universe continually grows in quantity by new experiences that graft themselves upon the older mass; but these very new experiences often help the mass to a more consolidated form.

These are the main features of a philosophy of pure experience. It has innumerable other aspects and arouses innumerable questions, but the points I have touched on seem enough to make an entering wedge. In my own mind such a philosophy harmonizes best with a radical pluralism, with novelty and indeterminism, moralism and theism, and with the 'humanism' lately sprung upon us by the Oxford and the Chicago schools.[18] I can not, however, be sure that all these doctrines are its necessary and indispensable allies. It presents so many points of difference, both from the common sense and from the idealism that have made our philosophic language, that it is almost as difficult to state it as it is to think it out clearly, and if it is ever to grow into a respectable system, it will have to be built up by the contributions of many co-operating minds. It seems to me, as I said at the outset of this essay, that many minds are, in point of fact, now turning in a direction that points towards radical empiricism. If they are carried farther by my words, and if then they add their stronger voices to my feebler one, the publication of this essay will have been worth while.

Endnotes

1. [Reprinted from the Journal of Philosophy, Psychology and Scientific Methods, vol. 1, 1904. No. 90, September 29, and No. 21, October 13. Pp. 52-46 have also been reprinted, with some. omissions, alterations and additions, in The Meaning of Truth. The alterations have been adopted in the present text. This essay is referred to in A Pluralistic Universe.]

2. [Cf. Berkeley: Principles of Human Knowledge, Introduction; Hume: An Enquiry Concerning Human Understanding, sect. vil, part n; James mill: Analysis of the Phenomena of the Human Mind. ch. VIII; J. S. Mill: An Examination of Sir William Hamilton's Philosophy, ch. XI, XII; W. K. Clifford: Lectures and Essays, pp. 274 ff.]

3. [See "The Experience of Activity."]

4. The psychology books have of late described the facts here with approximate adequacy. I may refer to the chapters on 'The Stream of Thought' and on the Self in my own Principles of Psychology, as well as to S. H. Hodgson's Metaphysic of Experience, vol. I, ch. VII and VIII.

5. [See "The Thing and its Relations."]

6. For brevity's sake I altogether omit mention of the type constituted by knowledge of the truth of general propositions. This type has been thoroughly and, so far as I can see, satisfactorily, elucidated in Dewey's Studies in Logical Theory. Such propositions are reducible to the S-is-P form; and the 'terminus' that verifies and fulfils is the SP in combination. Of course percepts may be

involved in the mediating experiences, or in the 'satisfactoriness' of the P in its new position.

7. [See above.]

8. [On the Function of Cognition," Mind, vol. X, 1885, and "The Knowing of Things Together," Psychological Review, vol. II, 1895. These articles are reprinted, the former in full, the latter in part, in The Meaning of Truth.) These articles and their doctrine, unnoticed apparently by any one else, have lately gained favorable comment. from Professor Strong. ['A Naturalistic Theory of the Reference of Thought to Reality,' Journal of Philosophy, Psychology and Scientific Methods, vol. I. 1904.] Dr. Dickinson S. Miller has independenly thought out the same results ["The Meaning of Truth and Error," Philosophical Review, vol. II, 1893; "The Confusion of Function and Content in Mental Analysis," Psychological Review, vol. n, 1895], which Strong accordingly dubs the James-Miller theory of cognition.

9. [Cf. H. Lotze: Metaphysik, §§ 37-39, 97, 98, 243.]

10. Mr. Bradley, not professing to know his absolute aliunde, nevertheless derealizes Experience by alleging it to be everywhere infected with self-contradiction. His arguments seem almost purely verbal, but this is no place for arguing that point out. [Cf. F. H. Bradley; Appearance and Reality, passim.]

11. Of which all that need be said in this essay is that it also can be conceived as functional, and defined in terms of transitions, or of the possibility of such. [Cf. Principles of Psychology, vol. I, pp. 473-480. vol. II, pp. 337-340; Pragmatism, p. 966; Some Problems of Philosophy, pp. 63-74; Meaning of Truth.]

12. [Cf. below.]

13. [Cf." How Two Minds Can Know One Thing."]

14. The notion that our objects are inside of our respective heads is not seriously defensible, so I pass it by.

15. [The argument is resumed below.]

16. Our minds and these ejective realities would still have space (or pseudo-space, as I believe Professor Strong calls the medium of interaction between 'things-in-themselves') in common. These would exist where, and begin to act whore, we locate the molecules, etc., and where we perceive the sensible phenomena explained thereby. [Cf. Morton Prince: The Nature of Mind, and Human Automatism, part I, ch. III, IV; C. A. Strong: Why the Mind Has a Body, ch. XII.]

17. [Cf. below, A Pluralistic Universe. Lect. IV-VII.]

18. I have said something of this latter alliance in an article entitled 'Humanism and Truth,' in Mind, October, 1904. [Reprinted in The Meaning of Truth. Cf. also "Humanism and Truth Once More."]

THE THING AND ITS RELATIONS[1]

Experience in its immediacy seems perfectly fluent. The active sense of living which we all enjoy, before reflection shatters our instinctive world for us, is self-luminous and suggests no paradoxes. Its difficulties are disappointments and uncertainties. They are not intellectual contradictions.

When the reflective intellect gets at work, however, it discovers incomprehensibilities in the flowing process. Distinguishing its elements and parts, it gives them separate names, and what it thus disjoins it can not easily put together. Pyrrhonism, accepts the irrationality and revels in its dialectic elaboration. Other philosophies try, some by ignoring, some by resisting, and some by turning the dialectic procedure against itself, negating its first negations, to restore the fluent sense of life again, and let redemption take the place of innocence. The perfection with which any philosophy may do this is the measure of its human success and of its importance in philosophic history. In [the last essay], 'A World of Pure Experience,' I tried my own hand sketchily at the problem, resisting certain first steps of dialectics by insisting in a general way that the immediately experienced conjunctive relations are as real as anything else. If my sketch is not to appear too naif, I must come closer to details, and in the present essay I propose to do so.

'Pure experience' is the name which I gave to the immediate flux of life which furnishes the material to our later reflection with its conceptual categories. Only new-born babes, or men in semi-coma from sleep, drugs, illnesses, or blows, may be assumed to have an experience pure in the literal sense of a that which is not yet any definite what, tho' ready to be all sorts of whats; full both of oneness and of manyness, but in respects that don't appear; changing throughout, yet so confusedly that its phases interpenetrate and no points, either of distinction or of identity, can be caught. Pure experience in this state is but another name for feeling or sensation. But the flux of it no sooner comes than it tends to fill itself with emphases, and these salient parts become identified and fixed and abstracted; so that experience now flows as if shot through with adjectives and nouns and prepositions and conjunctions. Its purity is only a relative term, meaning the proportional amount of unverbalized sensation which it still embodies.

Far back as we go, the flux, both as a whole and in its parts, is that of things conjunct and separated. The great continua of time, space, and the self envelope everything, betwixt them, and flow together without interfering. The things that they envelope come as separate in some ways and as continuous in others. Some sensations coalesce with some ideas, and others are irreconcilable. Qualities compenetrate one space, or exclude each other from it. They cling together persistently in groups that move as units, or else they separate. Their changes are abrupt or discontinuous; and their kinds resemble or differ; and, as they do so, they fall into either even or irregular series.

In all this the continuities and the discontinuities are absolutely co-ordinate matters of immediate feeling. The conjunctions are as primordial elements of 'fact' as are the distinctions and disjunctions. In the same act by which I feel that this passing minute is a new pulse of my life, I feel that the old life continues into it, and the feeling of continuance in no wise jars upon the simultaneous feeling of a novelty. They, too, compenetrate harmoniously. Prepositions, copulas, and conjunctions, 6 is," ' is n't," then," before," in," on," beside,' 'between,' "next,' 'like,' 'unlike,' 'as,' 'but,' flower out of the stream of pure experience, the stream of concretes or the sensational stream, as naturally as nouns and adjectives do, and they melt into it again as fluidly when we apply them to a new portion of the stream.

II

If now we ask why we must thus translate experience from a more concrete or pure into a more intellectualized form, filling it with ever more abounding conceptual distinctions, rationalism and naturalism give different replies.

The rationalistic answer is that the theoretic life is absolute and its interests imperative; that to understand is simply the duty of man; and that who questions this need not be argued with, for by the fact of arguing he gives away his case.

The naturalist answer is that the environment kills as well as sustains us, and that the tendency of raw experience to extinguish the experient. himself is lessened just in the degree in which the elements in it that have a practical bearing upon life are analyzed out of the continuum and verbally fixed and coupled together, so that we may know what is in the wind for us and get ready to react in time. Had pure experience, the naturalist says, been always perfectly healthy, there would never have arisen the necessity of isolating or verbalizing any of its terms. We should just have experienced inarticulately and unintellectually enjoyed. This leaning on 'reaction' in the naturalist account implies that, — whenever we intellectualize a relatively pure experience, we ought to do so for the sake of redescending to the purer or more concrete level again; and that if an intellect stays aloft among its abstract terms and generalized relations, and does not reinsert itself with its conclusions into some particular point of the immediate stream of life, it fails to finish out its function and leaves its normal race unrun.

Most rationalists nowadays will agree that naturalism gives a true enough account of the way in which our intellect arose at first, but they will deny these latter implications. The case, they will say, resembles that of sexual love. Originating in the animal need of getting another generation born, this passion has developed secondarily such imperious spiritual needs that, if you ask why another generation ought to be born at all, the answer is: 'Chiefly that love may go on.' Just so with our intellect: it originated as a practical means of serving life; but it has developed incidentally the function of understanding absolute truth; and life itself now seems to be given chiefly as a means by which that function may be prosecuted. But truth and the understanding of it lie among the abstracts and universals, so the intellect now carries on its higher business wholly in this region, without any need of redescending into pure experience again.

If the contrasted tendencies which I thus designate as naturalistic and rationalistic are not recognized by the reader, perhaps an example will make them more concrete. Mr. Bradley, for instance, is an ultra-rationalist. He admits that our intellect is primarily practical, but says that, for philosophers, the practical need is simply Truth. Truth, moreover, must be assumed 'consistent.' Immediate experience has to be broken into subjects and qualities, terms and relations, to be understood as truth at all. Yet when so broken it is less consistent then ever. Taken raw, it is all undistinguished. Intellectualized, it is all distinction without oneness. 'Such an arrangement may work, but the theoretic Problem is not solved.' The question is 'how the diversity can exist in harmony with the oneness.' To go back to pure experience is unavailing. 'Mere feeling gives no answer to our riddle.' Even if your intuition is a fact, it is not an understanding. 'It is a mere experience, and furnishes no consistent view.' The experience offered as facts or truths 'I find that my intellect rejects because. they contradict themselves. They offer a complex of diversities conjoined in a way which it feels is not its way and which it can not repeat as its own. . . . For to be satisfied, my intellect must understand, and it can not understand by taking a congeries in the lump.'[2] So Mr. Bradley, in the sole interests of 'understanding' (as he conceives that function), turns his back on finite experience forever. Truth must lie in the opposite direction, the direction of the Absolute; and this kind of rationalism and naturalism, or (as I will now call it) pragmatism, walk thenceforward upon opposite paths. For the one, those intellectual products are most true which, turning their face towards the Absolute, come nearest to symbolizing its ways of uniting the many and the one. For the other, those are most true which most successfully dip back into the finite stream of feeling and grow most easily confluent, with some particular wave or wavelet. Such confluence not only proves the intellectual operation to have been true (as an addition may 'prove' that a subtraction is already rightly performed), but it constitutes, according to pragmatism, all that we mean by calling it true. Only in so far as they lead us, successfully or unsuccessfully, back into sensible experience again, are our abstracts and universals true or false at all.[3]

III

In Section VI of [the last essay], I adopted in a general way the common-sense belief that one and the same world is cognized by our different minds; but I left undiscussed the dialectical arguments which maintain that this is logically absurd. The usual reason given for its being absurd is that it assumes one object (to wit, the world) to stand in two relations at once; to my mind, namely, and again to yours; whereas a term taken in a second relation can not logically be the same term which it was at first.

I have heard this reason urged so often in discussing with absolutists, and it would destroy my radical empiricism so utterly, if it were valid, that I am bound to give it an attentive ear, and seriously to search its strength.

For instance, let the matter in dispute be term M, asserted to be on the one hand related to L, and on the other to N; and let the two cases of relation be symbolized by L — M and M — N respectively. When, now, I assume that the experience may immediately come and be given in the shape L —M — N, with no trace of doubling or internal fission in the M, I am told that this is all a popular delusion, that L — M — N logically means two different experiences, L — M and M — N, namely; and that although the Absolute may, and indeed must, from its superior point of view, read its own kind of unity into M's two editions, yet as elements in finite experience the two M's lie irretrievably asunder, and the world between them is broken and unbridged.

In arguing this dialectic thesis, one must avoid slipping from the logical into the physical point of view. It would be easy, in taking a concrete example to fix one's ideas by, to choose one in which the letter M should stand for a collective noun of some sort, which noun, being related to L by one of its parts and to N by another, would inwardly be two things when it stood outwardly in both relations. Thus, one might say: 'David Hume, who weighed so many stone by his body, influences posterity by his doctrine.' The body and the doctrine are two things, between which our finite minds can discover no real sameness, though the same name covers both of them. And then, one might continue: 'Only an Absolute is capable of uniting such a non-identity.' We must, I say, avoid this sort of example, for the dialectic insight, if true at all, must apply to terms and relations universally. It must be true of abstract units as well as of nouns collective; and if we prove it by concrete examples we must take the simplest, so as to avoid irrelevant material suggestions.

Taken thus in all its generality, the absolutist contention seems to use as its major premise Hume's notion 'that all our distinct perceptions are distinct existences, and that the mind never perceives any real connexion among distinct existences.'[4] Undoubtedly, since we use two phrases in talking first about 'M's relation to L' and then about 'M's relation to N,' we must be having, or must have had, two distinct perceptions; — and the rest would then seem to follow duly. But the starting-point of the reasoning here seems to be the fact of the two phrases; and this suggests that the argument may be merely verbal. Can it be that the whole dialectic consists in attributing to the experience talked about a constitution similar to that of the language in which we describe it? Must we assert the objective doubleness of the M merely because we have to name it twice over when we name its two relations?

Candidly, I can think of no other reason than this for the dialectic conclusion;[5] for, if we think, not of our words, but of any simple concrete matter which they may be held to signify, the experience itself belies the paradox asserted. We use indeed two separate concepts in analyzing our object, but we know them all the while to be but substitutional, and that the M in L — M and the M in M — N mean (i.e., are capable of leading to and terminating in) one self-same piece, M, of sensible experience. This persistent identity of certain units (or emphases, or points, or objects, or members — call them what you will) of the experiencecontinuum, is just one of those conjunctive features of it, on which I am obliged to insist so emphatically.[6] For samenesses are parts of experience's indefeasible structure. When I hear a bell-stroke and, as life flows on, its after image dies away, I still hark back to it as 'that same bell-stroke.' When I see a thing M, with L to the left of it and N to the right of it, I see it as one M; and if you tell me I have had to "take' it

twice, I reply that if I 'took' it a thousand times I should Still see it as a unit.[7]
Its unity is aboriginal, just as the multiplicity of my successive takings is
aboriginal. It comes unbroken as that M, as a singular which I encounter;
they come broken, as those takings, as my plurality of operations. The unity
and the separateness are strictly co-ordinate. I do not easily fathom why my
opponents should find the separateness so much more easily understandable
that they must needs infect the whole of finite experience with it, and relegate
the unity (now taken as a bare postulate and no longer as a thing positively
perceivable) to the region of the Absolute's mysteries. I do not easily fathom
this, I say, for the said opponents are above mere verbal quibbling; yet all that
I can catch in their talk is the substitution of what is true of certain words for
what is true of what they signify. They stay with the words, — not returning
to the stream of life whence all the meaning of them came, and which is
always ready to reabsorb them.

IV

For aught this argument proves, then, we may continue to believe that one
thing can be known by many knowers. But the denial of one thing in many
relations is but one application of a still profounder dialectic difficulty. Man
can't be good, said the sophists, for man is man and good is good; and Hegel[8]
and Herbart in their day, more recently A. Spir,[9] and most recently and
elaborately of all, Mr. Bradley, informs us that a term can logically only be a
punctiform unit, and that not one of the conjunctive relations between things,
which experience seems to yield, is rationally possible.

Of course, if true, this cuts off radical empiricism without even a shilling.
Radical empiricism takes conjunctive relations at their face value, holding
them to be as real as the terms united by them.[10] The world it represents as
a collection, some parts of which are conjunctively and others disjunctively
related. Two parts, themselves disjoined, may nevertheless hang together by
intermediaries with which they are severally connected, and the whole world
eventually may hang together similarly, inasmuch as some path of
conjunctive transition by which to pass from one of its parts to another may
always be discernible. Such determinately various hanging-together may be
called concatenated union, to distinguish it from the 'through-and-through'
type of union, 'each in all and all in each' (union of total conflux, as one might
call it), which monistic systems hold to obtain when things are taken in their
absolute reality. In a concatenated world a partial conflux often is
experienced. Our concepts and our sensations are confluent; successive states
of the same ego, and feelings of the same body are confluent. Where the
experience is not of conflux, it may be of conterminousness (things with but
one thing between); or of contiguousness (nothing between); or of likeness; or
of nearness; or of simultaneousness; or of in-ness; or of on-ness; or of for-ness;
or of simple with-ness; or even of mere and-ness, which last relation would
make of however disjointed a world otherwise, at any rate for that occasion a
universe 'of discourse.' Now Mr. Bradley tells us that none of these relations,
as we actually experience them, can possibly be real.[11] My next duty,
accordingly, must be to rescue radical empiricism from Mr. Bradley.

Fortunately, as it seems to me, his general contention, that the very notion of relation is unthinkable clearly, has been successfully met by many critics.[12]

It is a burden to the flesh, and an injustice both to readers and to the previous writers, to repeat good arguments already printed. So, in noticing Mr. Bradley, I will confine myself to the interests of radical empiricism solely.

V

The first duty of radical empiricism, taking given conjunctions at their face-value, is to class some of them as more intimate and some as more external. When two terms are similar, their very natures enter into the relation. Being what they are, no matter where or when, the likeness never can be denied, if asserted. It continues predicable as long as the terms continue. Other relations, the where and the when, for example, seem adventitious. The sheet of paper may be "off" or 'on' the table, for example; and in either case the relation involves only the outside of its terms. Having an outside, both of them, they contribute by it to the relation. It is external: the term's inner nature is irrelevant to it. Any book, any table, may fall into the relation, which is created pro hac vice, not by their existence, but by their casual situation. It is just because so many of the conjunctions of experience seem so external that a philosophy of pure experience must tend to pluralism in its ontology. So far as things have space-relations, for example, we are free to imagine them with different origins even. If they could get to be, and get into space at all, then they may have done so separately. Once there, however, they are additives to one another, and, with no prejudice to their natures, all sorts of space-relations may supervene between them. The question of how things could come to be anyhow, is wholly different from the question what their relations, once the being accomplished, may consist in.

Mr. Bradley now affirms that such external relations as the space-relations which we here talk of must hold of entirely different subjects from those of which the absence of such relations might a moment previously have been plausibly asserted. Not only is the situation different when the book is on the table, but the book itself is different as a book, from what it was when it was off the table.[13] He admits that "such external relations seem possible and even existing. . . . That you do not alter what you compare or rearrange in space seems to common sense quite obvious, and that on the other side there are as obvious difficulties does not occur to common sense at all. And I will begin by pointing out these difficulties. . . . There is a relation in the result, and this relation, we hear, is to make no difference in its terms. But, if so, to what does it make a difference? [Does n't it make a difference to us onlookers, at least?] and what is the meaning and sense of qualifying the terms by it? [Surely the meaning is to tell the truth about their relative position.[14] If, in short, it is external to the terms, how can it possibly be true of them? [Is it the 'intimacy' suggested by the little word 'of,' here, which I have underscored, that is the root of Mr. Bradley's trouble?] ... If the terms from their inner nature do not enter into the relation, then, so far as they are concerned, they seem related for no reason at all. . . . Things are spatially related, first in one way, and then become related in another way, and yet in no way themselves are altered; for the relations, it is said, are but external. But I reply that, if so, I can not understand the leaving by the terms of one set of relations and their adoption of another fresh set. The process and its result to the terms, if they contribute nothing to it [Surely they contribute to it all there is 'of' it !] seem irrational throughout. [If 'irrational' here means simply 'non-rational,' or nondeducible from the essence of either term singly, it is no reproach; if it means 'contradicting' such essence, Mr. Bradley should show wherein and how.] But, if they contribute anything, —they must surely be affected internally. [Why so, if they contribute only their surface? In such relations as 'on," a foot away," between,' ' next,' etc., only surfaces are in question.] . . . If the terms contribute anything whatever, then the terms are affected [inwardly altered?] by the arrangement. . . . That for working purposes we treat, and do well to treat, some relations as external merely I do not deny, and that of course is not the question at issue here. That question is . . . whether in the end and in principle a mere external relation [i. e., a relation which can change without forcing its terms to change their nature simultaneously] is possible and forced on us by the facts."[15]

Mr. Bradley next reverts to the antinomies of space, which, according to him, prove it to be unreal, although it appears as so prolific a medium of external relations; and he then concludes that "Irrationality and externality can not be the last truth about things, Somewhere there must be a reason why this and that appear together. And this reason and reality must reside in the whole from which terms and relations are abstractions, a whole in which their internal connection must lie, and out of which from the background appear those fresh results which never could have come from the premises." And he adds that "Where the whole is different, the terms that qualify and contribute to it must so far be different. . . . They are altered so far only [How far? farther than externally, yet not through and through?] but still they are altered. . . . I must insist that in each case the terms are qualified by their whole [Qualified how? —Do their external relations, situations, dates, etc., changed as these are in the new whole, fail to qualify them 'far' enough?], and that in the second case there is a whole which differs both logically and psychologically from the first whole; and I urge that in contributing to the change the terms so far are altered."

Not merely the relations, then, but the terms are altered: und zwar 'so far.' But just how far is the whole problem; and 'through-and-through' would seem (in spite of Mr. Bradley's somewhat undecided utterances[16]) to be the full Bradleyan answer. The 'whole' which he here treats as primary and determinative of each part's manner of 'contributing,' simply must, when it alters, alter in its entirety. There must be total conflux of its parts, each into and through each other. The 'must' appears here as a Machtspruch, as an ipse dixit of Mr. Bradley's absolutistically tempered 'understanding,' for he candidly confesses that how the parts do differ as they contribute to different wholes, is unknown to him.[17]

Although I have every wish to comprehend the authority by which Mr. Bradley's understanding speaks, his words leave me wholly unconverted. 'External relations' stand with their withers all unwrung, and remain, for aught he proves to the contrary, not only practically workable, but also perfectly intelligible factors of reality.

VI

Mr. Bradley's understanding shows the most extraordinary power of perceiving separations and the most extraordinary impotence in comprehending conjunctions. One would naturally say 'neither or both,' but not so Mr. Bradley. When a common man analyzes certain whats from out the stream of experience, he understands their distinctness as thus isolated. But this does not prevent him from equally well understanding their combination with each other as originally experienced in the concrete, or their confluence with new sensible experiences in which they recur as 'the same.' Returning into the stream of sensible presentation, nouns and adjectives, and thats and abstract whats, grow confluent again, and the word 'is' names all these experiences of conjunction. Mr. Bradley understands the isolation of the abstracts, but to understand the combination is to him impossible.[18] "To understand a complex AB," he says, "I must begin with A or B. And beginning, say with A, if I then merely find B, I have either lost A, or I have got beside A, [the word 'beside' seems here vital, as meaning a conjunction 'external' and therefore unintelligible] something else, and in neither case have I understood.[19] For my intellect can not simply unite a diversity, nor has it in itself any form or way of togetherness, and you gain nothing if, beside A and B, you offer me their conjunction in fact. For to my intellect that is no more than another external element. And 'facts,' once for all, are for my intellect not true unless they satisfy it. . . . The intellect has in its nature no principle of mere togetherness."[20]

Of course Mr. Bradley has a right to define 'intellect' as the power by which we perceive separations but not unions —provided he give due notice to the reader. But why then claim that such a maimed and amputated power must reign supreme in philosophy, and accuse on its behoof the whole empirical world of irrationality? It is true that he else. where attributes to the intellect a proprius motus of transition, but says that when he looks for these transitions in the detail of living experience, he 'is unable to verify such a solution.'[21]

Yet he never explains what the intellectual transitions would be like in case we had them. He only defines them negatively — they are not spatial, temporal, predicative, or causal; or qualitatively or otherwise serial; or in any way relational as we naively trace relations, for relations separate terms, and need themselves to be hooked on ad infinitum. The nearest approach he makes to describing a truly intellectual transition is where he speaks of A and B as being 'united, each from its own nature, in a whole which is the nature of both alike.'[22] But this (which, pace Mr. Bradley, seems exquisitely analogous to 'taking' a congeries in a 'lump,' if not to 'swamping') suggests nothing but that conflux which pure experience so abundantly offers, as when 'space,' 'white' and 'sweet—' are confluent in a 'lump of sugar,' or kinesthetic, dermal, and optical sensations confluent in 'my hand.'[23] All that I can verify in the transitions which Mr. Bradley's intellect desiderates as its proprius motus is a reminiscence of these and other sensible conjunctions (especially spaceconjunctions), but a reminiscence so vague that its originals are not recognized. Bradley in short repeats the fable of the dog, the bone, and its image in the water. With a world of particulars, given in loveliest union, in conjunction definitely various, and variously definite, the 'how' of which you 'understand' as soon as you see the fact of them,[24] for there is no 'how' except the constitution of the fact as given; with all this given him, I say, in pure experience, he asks for some ineffable union in the abstract instead, which, if he gained it, would only be a duplicate of what he has already in his full possession. Surely he abuses the privilege which society grants to all us philosophers, of being puzzle-headed.

Polemic writing like this is odious; but with absolutism in possession in so many quarters, omission to defend my radical empiricism against its best known champion would count as either superficiality or inability. I have to conclude that its dialectic has not invalidated in the least degree the usual conjunctions by which the world, as experienced, hangs so variously together. In particular it leaves an empirical theory of knowledge[25] intact, and lets us continue to believe with common sense that one object may be known, if we have any ground for thinking that it is known, to many knowers.

In [the next essay] I shall return to this last supposition, which seems to me to offer other difficulties much harder for a philosophy of pure experience to deal with than any of absolutism's dialectic objections.

Endnotes

1. [Reprinted from The Journal of Philosophy, Psychology and Scientific Methods, vol. II, No. 2, January 19, 1905. Reprinted also as Appendix A in A Pluralistic Universe, pp. 347-369. The author's corrections have been adopted in the present text. ED.]

2. [F. H. Bradley: Appearance and Reality, second edition, pp. 152-153. 23, 118, 104, 108-109, 570.]

3. Compare Professor MacLennan's admirable Auseinandersetzung with Mr. Bradley, in The Journal of Philosophy, Psychology and Scientific Methods, vol. I, 119041, pp. 403 ff.. especially pp. 406-407.

4. [Hume: Treatise of Human Nature, Appendix, Selby-Bigge's edition, p. 636.]

5. Technically, it seems classable as a 'fallacy of composition.' A duality, predicable of the two wholes, L — M and M — N, is forthwith predicated of one of their puts. M.

6. See above.

7. I may perhaps refer here to my Principles of Psychology, vol. 1, pp. 459 ff. It really seems 'weird' to have to argue (as I am forced now to do) for the notion that 'it is one sheet of paper (With it& two surfaces and all that ties between) which is both under my pen and on the table while I write — the 'claim' that it is two sheets seems so brazen. Yet I sometimes suspect the absolutists of sincerity !

8. [For the authors criticism of Hegel's view of relations, cf. Will to Believe, pp. 278-279. ED.]

9. [Cf. A. Spir: Denken und Wirklichkeit, part I, bk. III, ch. IV (containing also account of Herbart). ED.)

10. [See above.]

11. Here again the reader must beware of slipping from logical into phenomenal considerations. It may well be that we attribute a certain

relation falsely, because the circumstances of the case, being complex, have deceived us. At a railway station we may take our own train, and not the one that fills our window, to be moving. We here put motion in the wrong place in the world, but in its original place the motion is a part of reality. What Mr. Bradley means is nothing like this, but rather that such things as motion are nowhere real, and that, even in their aboriginal and empirically incorrigible seats, relations are impossible of comprehension.

12. Particularly so by Andrew Seth Pringle-Pattison, in his Man and the Cosmos; by L. T. Hobhouse, in chapter XII ("The Validity of Judgment ") of his Theory of Knowledge; and by F. C. S. Schiller, in his Humanism, essay xi. Other fatal reviews (in my opinion) are Hodder's, in the Psychological Review, vol. I, [1894], p. 307; Stout's in the Proceedings of the Aristotelian Society, 1901—2, p. 1; and MacLennan's in [The Journal of Philosophy, Psychology and Scientific Methods, vol. 1, 1904, p. 403].

13. Once more, don't slip from logical into physical situations. Of course, if the table be wet, it will moisten the book, or if it be slight enough and the book heavy enough, the book will break it down. But such collateral phenomena are not the point at issue. The point is whether the successive relations 'on' and 'not-on' can rationally (not physically) hold of the same constant terms, abstractly taken. Professor A. E. Taylor drops from logical into material considerations when he instances color-contrast as a proof that A, 'as contradistinguished from B, is not the same thing as mere A not 6 any way affected'. Note the substitution, for 'related' of the word 'affected.' which begs the whole question.

14. But "is there any sense," asks Mr. Bradley, peevishly, on p. 579, "and if so, what sense in truth that is only outside and 'about' things? " Surely such a question may be left unanswered.

15. Appearance and Reality, second edition, pp. 575-576.

16. I say ' undecided,' because, apart from the 'so far,' which sounds terribly half-hearted, there are passages in these very Pam in which Mr. Bradley admits the pluralistic thesis. Read, for example, what he says, on p. 578, of a billiard ball keeping its 'character' unchanged, though, in its change of place, its 'existence' gets altered; or what he says, on p. 579, of the possibility that an abstract quality A, B, or C. in a thing, 'may throughout remain unchanged' although the thing be altered; or his admission that in red-hairedness, both as analyzed out of a man and when given with the rest of him, there may be 'no change.' Why does he immediately add that for the pluralist to plead the non-mutation of such abstractions would be an ignoratio elenchi? It is impossible to admit it to be such. The entire elenchus and inquest is just as to whether parts which you can abstract from existing wholes can also contribute to other wholes without changing their inner nature. If they can thus mould various wholes into new gestaltqualitaten, then it follows that the same elements are logically able to exist in different wholes [whether physically able would depend on additional hypotheses]; that partial changes are thinkable, and through-and-through change not a dialectic necessity; that monism is only an hypothesis; and that an additively constituted universe is a rationally respectable hypothesis also. All the them of radical empiricism, in short, follow.

17. Op. cit.

18. So far as I catch his state of mind, it is somewhat like this: 'Book.' table,'' on' — how does the existence of these three abstract elements result in this book being livingly on this table. Why is n't the table on the book? Or why does n't the 'on' connect itself with another book, or something that is not a table? Must n't something in each of the three elements already determine the two others to it, so that they do not settle elsewhere or float vaguely? Must n't the whole fact be prefigured in each part. and exist de jure before it can exist defacto? But if so, in what can the jural existence consist, if not in a spiritual miniature of the whole fact's constitution actuating every partial factor as its purpose? But is this anything but the old metaphysical fallacy of looking behind a fact in esse for the ground of the fact. and finding it in the shape of the very same fact in posse? Somewhere we; must leave off with a constitution behind which there is nothing.

19. Apply this to the can of 'book-on-table'! W. J.

20. Op. cit.

21. Op. cit.

22. Op. cit.

23. How meaningless is the contention that in such wholes (or in 'book-on-table,' 'watch-in-pocket,' etc.) the relation is an additional entity between the terms, needing itself to be related again to each! Both Bradley and Royce lovingly repeat this piece of profundity.

24. The 'why' and the 'whence' am entirely other questions, not under discussion, as I understand Mr. Bradley. Not how experience gets itself born, but how it can be what it is after it is born. is the puzzle.

25. Above.

HOW TWO MINDS CAN KNOW ONE THING[1]

In [the essay] entitled 'Does Consciousness Exist?' I have tried to show that when we call an experience 'conscious,' that does not mean that it is suffused throughout with a peculiar modality of being ('psychic' being) as stained glass may be suffused with light, but rather that it stands in certain determinate relations to other portions of experience extraneous to itself. These form one peculiar 'context' for it; while, taken in another context of experiences, we class it as a fact in the physical world. This 'pen, ' for example, is, in the first instance, a bald that, a datum, fact, phenomenon, content, or whatever other neutral or ambiguous name you may prefer to apply. I called it in that article a 'pure experience.' To get classed either as a physical pen or as some one's percept of a pen, it must assume a function, and that can only happen in a more complicated world. So far as in that world it is a stable feature, holds ink, marks paper and obeys the guidance of a hand, it is a physical pen. That is what we mean by being 'physical,' in a pen. So far as it is instable, on the contrary, coming and going with the movements of my eyes, altering with what I call my fancy, continuous with subsequent experiences of its 'having been' (in the past tense), it is the percept of a pen in my mind. Those peculiarities are what we mean by being 'conscious,' in a pen.

In Section VI of another [essay] I I tried to show that the same that, the same numerically identical pen of pure experience, can enter simultaneously into many conscious contexts, or, in other words, be an object for many differ. ent minds. I admitted that I had not space to treat of certain possible objections in that article; but in [the last essay] I took some of the objections up. At the end of that [essay] I said that still more formidable-sounding objections remained; so, to leave my pure experience theory in as strong a state as possible, I propose to consider those objections now.

I

The objections I previously tried to dispose of were purely logical or dialectical. No one identical term, whether physical or psychical, it had been said, could be the subject of two relations at once. This thesis I sought to prove unfounded. The objections that now confront us arise from the nature supposed to inhere in psychic facts specifically. Whatever may be the case with physical objects, a fact of con. sciousness, it is alleged (and indeed very plausibly), can not, without self-contradiction, be treated as a portion of two different minds, and for the following reasons.

In the physical world we make with impunity the assumption that one and the same material object can figure in an indefinitely large number of different processes at once. When, for instance, a sheet of rubber is pulled at its four corners, a unit of rubber in the middle of the sheet is affected by all four of the pulls. It transmits them each, as if it pulled in four different ways at once itself. So, an air-particle or an ether-particle 'compounds' the different directions of movement imprinted on it without obliterating their several individualities. It delivers them distinct, on the contrary, at as many several 'receivers' (ear, eye or what not) as may be 'tuned' to that effect. The apparent paradox of a distinctness like this surviving in the midst of compounding is a thing which, I fancy, the analyses made by physicists have by this time sufficiently cleared up.

But if, on the strength of these analogies, one should ask: "Why, if two or more lines can run through one and the same geometrical point, or if two or more distinct processes of activity can run through one and the same physical thing so that it simultaneously plays a role in each and every process, might not two or more streams of personal consciousness include one and the same unit of experience so that it would simultaneously be a part of the experience of all the different minds?" one would be checked by thinking of a certain peculiarity by which phenomena of consciousness differ from physical things.

While physical things, namely, are supposed to be permanent and to have their 'states,' a fact of consciousness exists but once and is a state. Its esse is sentiri; it is only so far as it is felt; and it is unambiguously and unequivocally exactly what is felt. The hypothesis under consideration would, however, oblige it to be felt equivocally, felt now as part of my mind and again at the same time not as a part of my mind, but of yours (for my mind is not yours), and this would seem impossible without doubling it into two distinct things, or, in other words, without reverting to the ordinary dualistic philosophy of insulated minds each knowing its object representatively as a third thing, — and that would be to give up the pureexperience scheme altogether.

Can we see, then, any way in which a unit of pure experience might enter into and figure in two diverse streams of consciousness without turning itself into the two units which, on our hypothesis, it must not be?

II

There is a way; and the first step towards it is to see more precisely how the unit enters into either one of the streams of consciousness alone. Just what, from being ' pure,' does its becoming 'conscious' once mean?

It means, first, that new experiences have supervened; and, second, that they have borne a certain assignable relation to the unit supposed. Continue, if you please, to speak of the pure unit as 'the pen.' So far as the pen's successors do but repeat the pen or, being different from it, are 'energetically'[3] related to it, it and they will form a group of stably existing physical things. SO far, however, as its successors differ from it in another well-determined way, the pen will figure in their context, not as a physical, but as a mental fact. It will become a passing 'percept,' my percept of that pen. What now is that decisive well-determined way?

In the chapter on 'The Self,' in my Principles, of Psychology, I explained the continuous identity of each personal consciousness as a name for the practical fact that new experiences[4] come which look back on the old ones, find them 'warm,' and greet and appropriate them as 'mine.' These operations mean, when analyzed empirically, several tolerably definite things, viz.:

1. That the new experience has past time for its 'content,' and in that time a pen that 'was';

2. That 'warmth' was also about the pen: in the sense of a group of feelings ('interest' aroused, 'attention' turned, 'eyes' employed, etc.) that were closely connected with it and that now recur and evermore recur with unbroken vividness, though from the pen of now, which may be only an image, all such vividness may have gone;

3. That these feelings are the nucleus of 'me';

4. That whatever once was associated with them was, at least for that one moment, 'mine' — my implement if associated with hand-feelings, my 'percept' only, if only eye-feelings and attention-feelings were involved.

The pen, realized in this retrospective way as my percept, thus figures as a fact of 'conscious' life. But it does so only so far as 'appropriation' has occurred; and appropriation is part of the content of a later experience wholly additional to the originally 'pure' pen. That pen, virtually both objective and subjective, is at its own moment actually and intrinsically neither. It has to be looked back upon and wed, in order to be classed in either distinctive way. But its use, so called, is in the hands of the other experience, while it stands, throughout the operation, passive and unchanged.

If this pass muster as an intelligible account of how an experience originally pure can enter into one consciousness, the next question is as to how it might conceivably enter into two.

III

Obviously no new kind of condition would have to be supplied. All that we should have to postulate would be a second subsequent experience, collateral and contemporary with the first subsequent one, in which a similar act of appropriation should occur. The two acts would interfere neither with one another nor with the originally pure pen. It would sleep undisturbed in its own past, no matter how many such successors went through their several appropriative acts. Each would know it as 'my' percept, each would class it as a 'conscious' fact.

Nor need their so classing it interfere in the least with their classing it at the same time as a physical pen. Since the classing in both cases depends upon the taking of it in one group or another of associates, if the superseding experience were of wide enough 'span' it could think the pen in both groups simultaneously, and yet distinguish the two groups. It would then see the whole situation conformably to what we call 'the representative theory of cognition,' and that is what we all spontaneously do. As a man philosophizing 'popularly,' I believe that what I see myself writing with is double — I think it in its relations to physical nature, and also in its relations to my personal life; I see that it is in my mind, but that it also is a physical pen.

The paradox of the same experience figuring in two consciousnesses seems thus no paradox at all. To be 'conscious' means not simply to be, but to be reported, known, to have awareness of one's being added to that being; and this is just what happens when the appropriative experience supervenes. The pen-experience in its original immediacy is not aware of itself, it simply is, and the second experience is required for what we call awareness of it to occur.[5]

The difficulty of understanding what happens here is, therefore, not a logical difficulty: there is no contradiction involved. It is an ontological difficulty rather. Experiences come on an enormous scale, and if we take them all together, they come in a chaos of incommensurable relations that we can not straighten out. We have to abstract different groups of them, and handle these separately if we are to talk of them at all. But how the experiences ever get themselves made, or why their characters and relations are just such as appear, we can not begin to understand. Granting, however, that, by hook or crook, they can get themselves made, and can appear in the successions that I have so schematically described, then we have to confess that even although (as I began by quoting from the adversary) 'a feeling only is as it is felt,' there is still nothing absurd in the notion of its being felt in two different ways at once, as yours, namely, and as mine. It is, indeed, 'mine' only as it is felt as mine, and 'yours' only as it is felt as yours. But it is felt as neither by itself, but only when 'owned' by our two several remembering experiences, just as one undivided estate is owned by several heirs.

IV

One word, now, before I close, about the corollaries of the views set forth. Since the acquisition of conscious quality on the part of an experience depends upon a context coming to it, it follows that the sum total of all experiences, having no context, can not strictly be called conscious at all. It is a that, an Absolute, a 'pure' experience on an enormous scale, undifferentiated and undifferentiable into thought and thing. This the post-Kantian idealists have always practically acknowledged by calling their doctrine an Identitatsphilosophie. The question of the Beseelung of the All of things ought not, then, even to be asked. No more ought the question of its truth to be asked, for truth is a relation inside of the sum total, obtaining between thoughts and something else, and thoughts, as we have seen, can only be contextual things. In these respects the pure experiences of our philosophy are, in themselves considered. so many little absolutes, the philosophy of pure experience being only a more comminuted Identitas-philosophie.[6]

Meanwhile, a pure experience can be postulated with any amount whatever of span or field. If it exert the retrospective and appropriative function on any other piece of experience, the latter thereby enters into its own conscious stream. And in this operation time intervals make no essential difference. After sleeping, my retrospection is as perfect as it is between two successive waking moments of my time. Accordingly if, millions of years later, a similarly retrospective experience should anyhow come to birth, my present thought would form a genuine portion of its long-span conscious life. 'Form a portion,' I say, but not in the sense that the two things could be entitatively or substantively one —they cannot, for they are numerically discrete facts —but only in the sense that the functions of my present thought, its knowledge, its purpose, its content and 'consciousness.' in short, being inherited, would be continued practically unchanged. Speculations like Fechner's, of an Earth-soul, of wider spans of consciousness enveloping narrower ones throughout the cosmos, are, therefore, philosophically quite in order, provided they distinguish the functional from the entitative point of view, and do not treat the minor consciousness under discussion as a kind of standing material of which the wider ones consist.[7]

Endnotes

1. [Reprinted from The Journal of Philosophy, Psychology and Scientific Methods, vol. 14 No. 7, March 30, 1905.]

2. " A World of Pure Experience."

3. [For an explanation of this expression, see above.]

4. I call them 'passing thoughts' in the book .

5. Shadworth Hodgson has laid great stress on the fact that the minimum of consciousness demands two subfeelings, of which the second retrospects the first. (Cf. the section 'Analysis of Minima' in his Philosophy of Reflection, vol. I, p. 248; also the chapter entitled 'The Moment of Experience' in his Metaphysic of Experience, vol. I, p. 84.) 'We live forward, but we understand backward' is a phrase of Kierkegaard's which Hoffding quotes. [H. Hoffding: " A Philosophical Confession," Journal of Philosophy, Psychology and Scientific Methods, vol. II, 1905, p. 86.]

6. [Cf. below.]

7. [Cf. A Pluralistic Universe. Lect. IV,'Concerning Fechner,' and Lect. V. 'The Compounding of Consciousness.']

THE PLACE OF AFFECTIONAL FACTS
IN A WORLD OF PURE EXPERIENCE[1]

Common sense and popular philosophy are as dualistic as it is possible to be. Thoughts, we all naturally think, are made of one kind of substance, and things of another. Consciousness, flowing inside of us in the forms of con

ception or judgment, or concentrating itself in the shape of passion or emotion, can be directly felt as the spiritual activity which it is, and known in contrast with the space-filling objective 'content' which it envelopes and accompanies. In opposition to this dualistic philosophy, I tried, in [the first essay] to show that thoughts and things are absolutely homogeneous as to their material, and that their opposition is only one of relation and of function. There is no thought-stuff different from thing-stuff, I said; but the same identical piece of 'pure experience' (which was the name I gave to the materia prima of everything) can stand alternately for a 'fact of consciousness' or for a physical reality, according as it is taken in one context or in another. For the right understanding of what follows, I shall have to presuppose that the reader will have read that [essay].[2]

The commonest objection which the doctrine there laid down runs up against is drawn from the existence of our 'affections.' In our pleasures and pains, our loves and fears and angers, in the beauty, comicality, importance or preciousness of certain objects and situations., we have, I am told by many critics, a great realm of experience intuitively recognized as spiritual, made, and felt to be made, of consciousness exclusively, and different in nature from the space-filling kind of being which is enjoyed by physical objects. In Section VII. of [the first essay], I treated of this class of experiences very inadequately, because I had to be so brief. I now return to the subject, because I believe that, so far from invalidating my general thesis, these phenomena, when properly analyzed, afford it powerful support.

The central point of the pure-experience theory is that 'outer' and 'inner' are names for two groups into which we sort experiences according to the way in which they act upon their neighbors. Any one 'content,' such as hard, let us say, can be assigned to either group. In the outer group it is 'strong,' it acts ' energetically' and aggressively. Here whatever is hard interferes with the space its neighbors occupy. It dents them; is impenetrable by them; and we call the hardness then a physical hardness. In the mind, on the contrary, the hard thing is nowhere in particular, it dents nothing, it suffuses through its mental neighbors, as it were, and interpenetrates them. Taken in this group we call both it and them 'ideas' or 'sensations'; and the basis of the two groups respectively is the different type of interrelation, the mutual impenetrability, on the one hand, and the lack of physical interference and interaction, on the other.

That what in itself is one and the same entity should be able to function thus differently in different contexts is a natural consequence of the extremely complex reticulations in which our experiences come. To her offspring a tigress is tender, but cruel to every other living thing — both cruel and tender, therefore, at once. A mass in movement resists every force that operates contrariwise to its own direction, but to forces that pursue the same direction, or come in at right angles, it is absolutely inert. It is thus both energetic and inert; and the same is true (if you vary the associates properly) of every other piece of experience. It is only towards certain specific groups of associates that the physical energies, as we call them, of a content are put forth. In another group it may be quite inert.

It is possible to imagine a universe of experiences in which the only alternative between neighbors would be either physical interaction or complete inertness. In such a world the mental or the physical status of any piece of experience would be unequivocal. When active, it would figure in the physical, and when inactive, in the mental group.

But the universe we live in is more chaotic than this, and there is room in it for the hybrid or ambiguous group of our affectional experiences, of our emotions and appreciative perceptions. In the paragraphs that follow I shall try to show: (1) That the popular notion that these experiences are intuitively given as purely inner facts is hasty and erroneous; and (2) That their ambiguity illustrates beautifully my central thesis that subjectivity and objectivity are affairs not of what an experience is aboriginally made of, but of its classification. Classifications depend on our temporary purposes. For certain purposes it is convenient to take things in one set of relations, for other purposes in another set. In the two cases their contexts are apt to be different In the case of our affectional experiences we have no permanent and steadfast purpose that obliges us to be consistent, so we find it easy to let them float ambiguously, sometimes classing them with our feelings, sometimes with more physical realities, according to caprice or to the convenience of the moment. Thus would these experiences, so far from being an obstacle to the pure experience philosophy, serve as an excellent corroboration of its truth.

First of all, then, it is a mistake to say, with the objectors whom I began by citing, that anger, love and fear are affections purely of the mind. That, to a great extent at any rate, they are simultaneously affections of the body is proved by the whole literature of the JamesLange theory of emotion.[3] All our pains, moreover, are local, and we are always free to speak of them in objective as well as in subjective terms. We can say that we are aware of a painful place, filling a certain bigness in our organism, or we can say that we are inwardly in a 'state' of pain. All our adjectives of worth are similarly ambiguous — I instanced some of the ambiguities [in the first essay].[4] Is the preciousness of a diamond a quality of the gem? or is it a feeling in our mind? Practically we treat it as both or as either, according to the temporary direction of our thought. 'Beauty,' says Professor Santayana, 'is pleasure objectified'; and in Sections 10 and 11 of his work, The Sense of Beauty, he treats in a masterly way of this equivocal realm. The various pleasures we receive from an object may count as 'feelings' when we take them singly, but when they combine in a total richness, we call the result the 'beauty' of the object, and treat it as an outer attribute which our mind perceives. We discover beauty just as we discover the physical properties of things. Training is needed to make us expert in either line. Single sensations also maybe ambiguous. Shall we say an 'agreeable degree of heat,' or an 'agreeable feeling' occasioned by the degree of heat? Either will do; and language would lose most of its esthetic and rhetorical value were we forbidden to project words primarily connoting our affections upon the objects by which the affections are aroused. The man is really hateful; the action really mean; the situation really tragic — all in themselves and quite apart from our opinion. We even go so far as to talk of a weary road, a giddy height, a jocund morning or a sullen sky; and the term 'indefinite' while usually applied only to our apprehensions, functions as a fundamental physical qualification of things in Spencer's 'law of evolution,' and doubtless passes with most readers for all right.

Psychologists, studying our perceptions of movement, have unearthed experiences in which movement is felt in general but not ascribed correctly to the body that really moves. Thus in optical vertigo, caused by unconscious movements of our eyes, both we and the external universe appear to be in a whirl. When clouds float by the moon, it is as if both clouds and moon and we ourselves shared in the motion. In the extraordinary case of amnesia of the Rev. Mr. Hanna, published by Sidis and Goodhart in their important work on Multiple Personality, we read that when the patient first recovered consciousness and "noticed an attendant walk across the room, he identified the movement with that of his own. He did not yet discriminate between his own movements and those outside himself."[5] Such experiences point to a primitive stage of perception in which discriminations afterwards needful have not yet been made. A piece of experience of a determinate sort is there, but there at first as a 'pure' fact. Motion originally simply is; only later is it confined to this thing or to that. Something like this is true of every experience, however complex, at the moment of its actual presence. Let the reader arrest himself in the act of reading this article now. Now this is a pure experience, a phenomenon, or datum, a mere that or content of fact. 'Reading' simply is, is there; and whether there for some one's consciousness, or there for physical nature, is a question not yet put. At the moment, it is there for neither; later we shall probably judge it to have been there for both.

With the affectional experiences which we are considering, the relatively 'pure' condition lasts. In practical life no urgent need has yet arisen for deciding whether to treat them as rigorously mental or as rigorously physical facts. So they remain equivocal; and, as the world goes, their equivocality is one of their great conveniences.

The shifting place of 'secondary qualities' in the history of philosophy[6] is another excellent proof of the fact that 'inner' and 'outer' are not coefficients with which experiences come to us aboriginally stamped, but are rather results of a later classification performed by us for particular needs. The common-sense stage of thought is a perfectly definite practical halting-place, the place where we ourselves can proceed to act unhesitatingIy. On this stage of thought things act on each other as well as on us by means of their secondary qualities. Sound, as such, goes through the air and can be intercepted. The heat of the fire passes over, as such, into the water which it sets a-boiling. It is the very light of the arc-lamp which displaces the darkness of the midnight street, etc. By engendering and trans-locating just these qualities, actively efficacious as they seem to be, we ourselves succeed in altering nature so as to suit us; and until more purely intellectual, as distinguished from practical, needs had arisen, no one ever thought of calling these qualities subjective. When, however, Galileo, Descartes, and others found it best for philosophic purposes to class sound, heat, and light along with pain and pleasure as purely mental phenomena, they could do so with impunity.[7]

Even the primary qualities are undergoing the same fate. Hardness and softness are effects on us of atomic interactions, and the atoms themselves are neither hard nor soft, nor solid nor liquid. Size and shape are deemed subjective by Kantians; time itself is subjective according to many philosophers ;[8] and even the activity and causal efficacy which lingered in physics long after secondary qualities were banished are now treated as illusory projections outwards of phenomena of our own consciousness. There are no activities or effects in nature, for the most intellectual contemporary school of physical speculation. Nature exhibits only changes, which habitually coincide with one another so that their habits are describable in simple 'laws.'[9]

There is no original spirituality or materiality of being, intuitively discerned, then; but only a translocation of experiences from one world to another; a grouping of them with one set or another of associates for definitely practical or intellectual ends.

I will say nothing here of the persistent ambiguity of relations. They are undeniable parts of pure experience; yet, while common sense and what I call radical empiricism stand for their being objective, both rationalism and the usual empiricism claim that they are exclusively the 'work of the mind' — the finite mind or the absolute mind, as the case may be.

Turn now to those affective phenomena which more directly concern us.

We soon learn to separate the ways in which things appeal to our interests and emotions from the ways in which they act upon one another. It does not work to assume that physical objects are going to act outwardly by their sympathetic or antipathetic qualities. The beauty of a thing or its value is no force that can be plotted in a polygon of compositions, nor does its 'use' or 'significance' affect in the minutest degree its vicissitudes or destiny at the hands of physical nature. Chemical 'affinities' are a purely verbal metaphor; and, as I just said, even such things as forces, tensions, and activities can at a pinch be regarded as anthropomorphic projections. So far, then, as the physical world means the collection of contents that determine in each other certain regular changes, the whole collection of our appreciative attributes has to be treated as falling outside of it. If we mean by physical nature whatever lies beyond the surface of our bodies, these attributes are inert throughout the whole extent of physical nature.

Why then do men leave them as ambiguous as they do, and not class them decisively as purely spiritual?

The reason would seem to be that, although they are inert as regards the rest of physical nature, they are not inert as regards that part of physical nature which our own skin covers. It is those very appreciative attributes of things, their dangerousness, beauty, rarity, utility, etc., that primarily appeal to our attention. In our commerce with nature these attributes are what give emphasis to objects; and for an object to be emphatic, whatever spiritual fact it may mean, means also that it produces immediate bodily effects upon us, alterations of tone and tension, of heart-beat and breathing, of vascular and visceral action. The 'interesting' aspects of things are thus not wholly inert physically, though they be active only in these small corners of physical nature which our bodies occupy. That, however, is enough to save them from being classed as absolutely non-objective.

The attempt, if any one should make it, to sort experiences into two absolutely discrete groups, with nothing but inertness in one of them and nothing but activities in the other, would thus receive one check. It would receive another as soon as we examined the more distinctively mental group; for though in that group it be true that things do not act on one another by their physical properties, do not dent each other or set fire to each other, they yet act on each other in the most energetic way by those very characters which are so inert extracorporeally. It is by the interest and importance that experiences have for us, by the emotions they excite, and the purposes they subserve, by their affective values, in short, that their consecution in our several conscious streams, as 'thoughts' of ours, is mainly ruled. Desire introduces them; interest holds them; fitness fixes their order and con. nection. I need only refer for this aspect of our mental life, to Wundt's article 'Ueber psychische Causalitat,' which begins Volume X of his Philosophische Studien.[10]

It thus appears that the ambiguous or amphibious status which we find our epithets of value occupying is the most natural thing in the world. It would, however, be an unnatural status if the popular opinion which I cited at the outset were correct. If 'physical' and 'mental' meant two different kinds of intrinsic nature, immediately, intuitively, and infallibly discernible, and each fixed forever in whatever bit of experience it qualified, one does not see how there could ever have arisen any room for doubt or ambiguity. But if, on the contrary, these words are words of sorting, ambiguity is natural. For then, as soon as the relations of a thing are sufficiently various it can be sorted variously. Take a mass of carrion, for example, and the 'disgustingness' which for us is part of the experience. The sun caresses it, and the zephyr wooes it as if it were a bed of roses. So the disgustingness fails to operate within the realm of suns and breezes, — it does not function as a physical quality. But the carrion 'turns our stomach' by what seems a direct operation — it does function physically, therefore, in that limited part of physics. We can treat it as physical or as non-physical according as we take it in the narrower or in the wider context, and conversely, of course, we must treat it as non-mental or as mental.

Our body itself is the palmary instance of the ambiguous. Sometimes I treat my body purely as a part of outer nature. Sometimes, again, I think of it as 'mine,' I sort it with the 'me,' and then certain local changes and determinations in it pass for spiritual happenings. Its breathing is my 'thinking,' its sensorial adjustments are my 'attention,' its kinesthetic alterations are my Works,' its visceral perturbations are my 'emotions.' The obstinate controversies that have arisen over such statements as these (which sound so paradoxical, and which can yet be made so seriously) prove how hard it is to decide by bare introspection what it is in experiences that shall make them either spiritual or material. It surely can be nothing intrinsic in the individual experience. It is their way of behaving towards each other, their system of relations, their function; and all these things vary with the context in which we find it opportune to consider them.

I think I may conclude, then (and I hope that my readers are now ready to conclude with me), that the pretended spirituality of our emotions and of our attributes of value, so far from proving an objection to the philosophy of pure experience, does, when rightly discussed and accounted for, serve as one of its best corroborations.

Endnotes

1. [Reprinted from The Journal Of Philosophy, Psychology and Scientific Methods, vol. ii. No. 11, May 25, 1905]

2. It will be still better if he shall have also read the [essay] entitled 'A World of Pure Experience.' which follows [the first] and develops its ideas still farther.

3. [Cf. The Principles Of Psychology, VOL II, ch. XXV; read "The Physical Basis of Emotion." The Psychological Review, Vol. 16 1894, P. 516].

4. [See above.]

5. [See above.].

6. [Cf. Janet and Séailles: History of the Problem of Philosophy, trans, by Monahan, part I, ch. III.]

7. [Cf. Descartes: Meditation II; Principles of Philosophy, part I, XLVIII.]

8. [Cf. A. E. Taylor: Elements of Metaphysics, bk. III, ch. IV.]

9. [Cf. K. Pearson: Grammar of Science, ch. III.]

10. It is enough for my present purpose if the appreciative characters but seem to act thus. Believers in an activity an sich, other than our mental experiences of activity. will find some farther reflections on the subject in my address on 'The Experience of Activity.' [The next essay.]

THE EXPERIENCE OF ACTIVITY[1]

Brethren of the Psychological Association:

In casting about me for a subject for your President this year to talk about it has seemed to me that our experiences of activity would form a good one; not only because the topic is so naturally interesting, and because it has lately led to a good deal of rather inconclusive discussion, but because I myself am growing more and more Interested in a certain systematic way of handling questions, and want to get others interested also, and this question strikes me as one in which, although I am painfully aware of my inability to communicate new discoveries or to reach definitive conclusions, I yet can show, in a rather definite manner, how the method works.

The way of handling things I speak of, is, as you already will have suspected, that known sometimes as the pragmatic method, sometimes as humanism, sometimes as Deweyism, and in France, by some of the disciples of Bergson, as the Philosophie nouvelle. Professor Woodbridge's Journal of Philosophy[2] seems unintentionally to have become a sort of meeting place for those who follow these tendencies in America. There is only a dim identity among them; and the most that can be said at present is that some sort of gestation seems to be in the atmosphere, and that almost any day a man with a genius for finding the right word for things may hit upon some unifying and conciliating formula that will make so much vaguely similar— aspiration crystallize into more definite form.

I myself have given the name of 'radical empiricism' to that version of the tendency in question which I prefer; and I propose, if you will now let me, to illustrate what I mean by radical empiricism, by applying it to activity as an example, hoping at the same time incidentally to leave the general problem of activity in a slightly — I fear very slightly — more manageable shape than before.

Mr. Bradley calls the question of activity a scandal to philosophy, and if one turns to the current literature of the subject — his own writings included — one easily gathers what he means. The opponents cannot even understand one another. Mr. Bradley says to Mr. Ward: " I do not care What your oracle is, and your preposterous psychology may here be gospel if you please; . . . but if the revelation does contain a meaning, I will commit myself to this: either the oracle is so confused that its signification is not discoverable, or, upon the other hand, if it can be pinned down to any definite statement, then that statement will be false."[3] Mr. Ward in turn says of Mr. Bradley: "I cannot even imagine the state of mind to which his description applies. ... [It] reads like an unintentional travesty of Herbartian psychology by one who has tried to improve upon it without being at the pains to master it."[4] Munsterberg excludes a view opposed to his own by saying that with any one who holds it a Verstandigung with him is "grundsatzlick ausgeschlossen"; and Royce, in a review of Stout,[5] hauls him over the coals at great length for defending 'efficacy ' in a way which I, for one, never gathered from reading him, and which I have heard Stout himself say was quite foreign to the intention of his text.

In these discussions distinct questions are habitually jumbled and different points of view are talked of durcheinander. (1) There is a psychological question: " Have we perceptions of activity? and if so, what are they like, and when and where do we have them? (2) There is a metaphysical question: "Is there a fact of activity? and if so, what idea must we frame of it? What is it like? and what does it do, if it does anything?" And finally there is a logical question: (3) "Whence do we know activity? By our own feelings of it solely? or by some other source of information?" Throughout page after page of the literature one knows not which of these questions is before one; and mere description of the surface—show of experience is proferred as if it implicitly answered every one of them. No one of the disputants, moreover, tries to show what pragmatic consequences his own view would carry, or what assignable particular differences in any one's experience it would make if his adversary's were triumphant.

It seems to me that if radical empiricism be good for anything, it ought, with its pragmatic method and its principle of pure experience, to be able to avoid such tangles, or at least to simplify them somewhat. The pragmatic method starts from the postulate that there is no difference of truth that does n't make a difference of fact somewhere; and it seeks to determine the meaning of all differences of opinion by making the discussion hinge as soon as Possible upon some practical or particular issue. The principle of pure experience is also a methodical postulate. Nothing shall be admitted as fact, it says, except what can be experienced at some definite time by some experient; and for every feature of fact ever so experienced, a definite place must be found somewhere in the final system of reality. In other words: Everything real must be experienceable somewhere, and every kind of thing experienced must somewhere be real.

Armed with these rules of method let us see what face the problems of activity present to us.

By the principle of pure experience, either the word 'activity' must have no meaning at all, or else the original type and model of what it means must lie in some concrete kind of experience that can be definitely pointed out. Whatever ulterior judgments we may eventually come to make regarding activity, that sort of thing will be what the judgments are about. The first step to take, then, is to ask where in the stream of experience we seem to find what we speak of as activity. What we are to think of the activity thus found will be a later question.

Now it is obvious that we are tempted to affirm activity wherever we find anything going on. Taken in the broadest sense, any apprehension of something doing, is an experience of activity. Were our world describable only by the words 'nothing happening,' 'nothing changing,' 'nothing doing,' we should unquestionably call it an 'inactive' world. Bare activity then, as we may call it, means the bare fact of event or change. 'Change taking place' is a unique content of experience, one of those 'conjunctive' objects which radical empiricism seeks so earnestly to rehabilitate and preserve. The sense of activity is thus in the broadest and vaguest way synonymous with the sense of 'life.' We should feel our own subjective life at least, even in noticing and proclaiming an otherwise inactive world. Our own reaction on its monotony would be the one thing experienced there in the form of something coming to pass.

This seems to be what certain writers have in mind when they insist that for an experient, to be at all is to be active. It seems to justify, or at any rate to explain, Mr. Ward's expression that we are only as we are active,[6] for we are only as experients; and it rules out Mr. Bradley's contention that "there is no original experience of anything like activity."[7] What we ought to say about activities thus elementary, whose they are, what they effect, or whether indeed they effect anything at all — these are later questions, to be answered only when the field of experience is enlarged.

Bare activity would thus be predicable, though there were no definite direction, no actor, and no aim. Mere restless zigzag movement, or a wild Ideenflucht, or Rhapsodie der Wahrnehmungen, as Kant would say,[8] would constitute an active as distinguished from an inactive world.

But in this actual world of ours, as it is given, a part at least of the activity comes with definite direction; it comes with desire and sense of goal; it comes complicated with resistances which it overcomes or succumbs to, and with the efforts which the feeling of resistance so often provokes; and it is in complex experiences like these that the notions of distinct agents, and of passivity as opposed to activity arise. Here also the notion of causal efficacy comes to birth. Perhaps the most elaborate work ever done in descriptive psychology has been the analysis by various recent writers of the more complex activity situations.[9] In their descriptions, exquisitely subtle some of them,[10] the activity appears as the gestaltqualitat or the fundirte inhalt (or as whatever else you may please to call the conjunctive form) which the content falls into when we experience it in the ways which the describers set forth. Those factors in those relations are what we mean by activity-situations; and to the possible enumeration and accumulation of their circumstances and ingredients there would seem to be no natural bound. Every hour of human life could contribute to the picture gallery; and this is the only fault that one can find with such descriptive industry —where is it going to stop? Ought we to listen forever to verbal pictures of what we have already in concrete form in our own breasts?[11] They never take us off the superficial plane. We knew the facts already — les spread out and separated, to be sure — but we knew them still. We always felt our own activity, for example, as 'the expansion of an idea with which our Self is identified, against an obstacle';[12] and the following out of such a definition through a multitude of cases elaborates the obvious so as to be little more than an exercise in synonymic speech.

All the descriptions have to trace familiar outlines, and to use familiar terms. The activity is, for example, attributed either to a physical or to a mental agent, and is either aimless or directed. If directed it shows tendency. The tendency may or may not be resisted. If not, we call the activity immanent, as when a body moves in empty space by its momentum, or our thoughts wander at their own sweet will. If resistance is met, its agent complicates the situation. If now, in spite of resistance, the original tendency continues, effort makes its appearance, and along with effort, strain or squeeze. Will, in the narrower sense of the word, then comes upon the scene, whenever, along with the tendency, the strain and squeeze are sustained. But the resistance may be great enough to check the tendency, or even to reverse its path. In that case, we (if 'we' were the original agents or subjects of the tendency) are overpowered. The phenomenon turns into one of tension simply, or of necessity succumbed to, according as the opposing power is only equal, or is superior to ourselves.

Whosoever describes an experience in such terms as these describes an experience of activity. If the word have any meaning, it must denote what there is found. There is complete activity in its original and first intention. What it is 'known-as' is what there appears. The experiencer of such a situation possesses all that the idea contains. He feels the tendency, the obstacle, the will, the strain, the triumph, or the passive giving up, just as he feels the time, the space, the swiftness or intensity, the movement, the weight and color, the pain and pleasure, the complexity, or whatever remaining characters the situation may involve. He goes through all that ever can be imagined where activity is supposed. If we suppose activities to go on outside of our experience, it is in forms like these that we must suppose them, or else give them some other name; for the word ' activity' has no imaginable content whatever save these experiences of process, obstruction, striving, strain, or release, ultimate qualia as they are of the life given us to be known.

Were this the end of the matter, one might think that whenever we had successfully lived through an activity-situation we should have to be permitted, without provoking contradiction, to say that we had been really active, that we had met real resistance and had really prevailed. Lotze somewhere says that to be an entity all that is necessary is to gelten as an entity, to operate, or be felt, experienced, recognized, or in any way realized, as such.[13] In our activity-experiences the activity assuredly fulfils Lotze's demand. It makes itself gelten. It is witnessed at its work. No matter what activities there may really be in this extraordinary universe of ours, it is impossible for us to conceive of any one of them being either lived through or authentically known otherwise than in this dramatic shape of something sustaining a felt purpose against felt obstacles and overcoming or being overcome. What 'sustaining' means here is clear to anyone who has lived through the experience, but to no one else; just as 'loud,' 'red,'' sweet,' mean something only to beings with ears, eyes, and tongues. The percipi in these originals of experience is the esse; the curtain is the picture. If there is anything hiding in the background, it ought not to be called activity, but should get itself another name.

This seems so obviously true that one might well experience astonishment at finding so many of the ablest writers on the subject flatly denying that the activity we live through in these situations is real. Merely to feel active is not to be active, in their sight. The agents that appear in the experience are not real agents, the resistances do not really resist, the effects that appear are not really effects at all.[14] It is evident from this that mere descriptive analysis of any one of our activity-experiences is not the whole story, that there is something still to tell about them that has led such able writers to conceive of a Simon—pure activity, of an activity an sich, that does, and does n't merely appear to us to do, and compared with whose real doing all this phenomenal activity is but a specious sham.

The metaphysical question opens here; and I think that the state of mind of one possessed by it is often something like this: " It is all very well," we may imagine him saying, "to talk about certain experience-series taking on the form of feelings of activity, just as they might take on musical or geometric forms. Suppose that they do so; suppose we feel a will to stand a strain. Does our feeling do more than record the fact that the strain is sustained? The real activity, meanwhile, is the doing of the fact; and what is the doing made of before the record is made. What in the will enables it to act thus? And these trains of experience themselves, in which activities appear, what makes them go at all? Does the activity in one bit of experience bring the next bit into being? As an empiricist you cannot say so, for you have just declared activity to be only a kind of synthetic object, or conjunctive relation experienced between bits of experience already made. But what made them at all? What propels experience uberhaupt into being? There is the activity that operates; the activity felt is only its superficial sign."

To the metaphysical question, popped upon us in this way, I must pay serious attention ere I end my remarks; but, before doing so, let me show that without leaving the immediate reticulations of experience, or asking what makes activity itself act, we still find the distinction between less real and more real activities forced upon us, and are driven to much soul-searching on the purely phenomenal plane.

We must not forget, namely, in talking of the ultimate character of our activity—experiences, that each of them is but a portion of a wider world, one link in the vast chain of processes of experience out of which history is made. Each partial process, to him who lives through it, defines itself by its origin and its goal; but to an observer with a wider mindspan who should live outside of it, that goal would appear but as a provisional halting-place, and the subjectively felt activity would be seen to continue into objective activities that led far beyond. We thus acquire a habit, in discussing activity-experiences, of defining them by their relation to something more. If an experience be one of narrow span, it will be mistaken as to what activity it is and whose. You think that you are acting while you are only obeying someone's push. You think you are doing this, but you are doing something of which you do not dream. For instance, you think you are but drinking this glass; but you are really creating the liver-cirrhosis that will end your days. You think you are just driving this bargain, but, as Stevenson says somewhere, you are laying down a link in the policy of mankind.

Generally speaking, the onlooker, with his wider field of vision, regards the ultimate outcome of an activity as what it is more really doing; and the most previous agent ascertainable, being the first source of action, he regards as the most real agent in the field. The others but transmit that agent's impulse; on him we put responsibility; we name him when one asks us 'Who's to blame?'

But the most previous agents ascertainable, instead of being of longer span, are often of much shorter span than the activity in view. Brain-cells are our best example. My brain-cells are believed to excite each other from next to next (by contiguous transmission of katabolic alteration, let us say) and to have been doing so long before this present stretch of lecturing-activity on my part began. If any one cell-group stops its activity, the lecturing will cease or show disorder of form. Cessante causa, cessat et effectus — does not this look as if the short-span brain activities were the more real activities, and the lecturing activities on my part only their effects? Moreover, as Hume so clearly pointed out,[15] in my mental activity-situation the words physically to be uttered are represented as the activity's im. mediate goal. These words, however, cannot be uttered without intermediate physical processes in the bulb and vagi nerves, which processes nevertheless fail to figure in the mental activity-series at all. That series, therefore, since it leaves out vitally real steps of action, cannot represent the real activities. It is something purely subjective; the facts of activity are elsewhere. They are something far more interstitial, so to speak, than what my feelings record.

The real facts of activity that have in point of fact been systematically pleaded for by philosophers have, so far as my information goes, been of three principal types.

The first type takes a consciousness of wider time-span than ours to be the vehicle of the more real activity. Its will is the agent, and its purpose is the action done.

The second type assumes that 'ideas' struggling with one another are the agents, and that the prevalence of one set of them is the action.

The third type believes that nerve-cells are the agents, and that resultant motor discharges are the acts achieved.

Now if we must de-realize our immediately felt activity-situations for the benefit of either of these types of substitute, we ought to know what the substitution practically involves. What practical difference ought it to make if, instead of saying naively that 'I' am active now in delivering this address., I say that a wider thinker is active, or that certain ideas are active, or that certain nerve-cells are active, in producing the result?

This would be the pragmatic meaning of the three hypotheses. Let us take them in succession in seeking a reply.

If we assume a wider thinker, it is evident that his purposes envelope mine. I am really lecturing for him; and although I cannot surely know to what end, yet if I take him religiously, I can trust it to be a good end, and willingly connive. I can be happy in thinking that my activity transmits his impulse, and that his ends prolong my own. So long as I take him religiously, in short, he does not de-realize my activities. He tends rather to corroborate the reality of them, so long as I believe both them and him to be good.

When now we turn to ideas, the case is different, inasmuch as ideas are supposed by the association psychology to influence each other only from next to next. The 'span' of an idea or pair of ideas, is assumed to be much smaller instead of being larger than that of my total conscious field. The same results may get worked out in both cases, for this address is being given anyhow. But the ideas supposed to 'really' work it out had no prevision of the whole of it;

and if I was lecturing for an absolute thinker in the former case, so, by similar reasoning, are my ideas now lecturing for me, that is, accomplishing unwittingly a result which I approve and adopt. But, when this passing lecture is over, there is nothing in the bare notion that ideas have been its agents that would seem to guarantee that my present purposes in lecturing will be prolonged. I may have ulterior developments in view; but there is no certainty that my ideas as such will wish to, or be able to, work them out.

The like is true if nerve-cells be the agents. The activity of a nerve-cell must be conceived of as a tendency of exceedingly short reach., an 'impulse' barely spanning the way to the next cell — for surely that amount of actual 'process' must be 'experienced' by the cells if what happens between them is to deserve the name of activity at all. But here again the gross resultant, as I perceive it, is indifferent to the agents, and neither wished or willed or foreseen. Their being agents now congruous with my will gives me no guarantee that like results will recur again from their activity. In point of fact, all sorts of other results do occur. My mistakes, impotencies, perversions, mental obstructions, and frustrations generally, are also results of the activity of cells. Although these are letting me lecture now, on other occasions they make me do things that I would willingly not do.

The question Whose is the real activity? is thus tantamount to the question What will be the actual results? Its interest is dramatic; how will things work out? If the agents are of one sort, one way; if of another sort, they may work out very differently. The pragmatic meaning of the various alternatives, in short, is great. It makes no merely verbal difference which opinion we take up.

You see it is the old dispute come back! Materialism and teleology; elementary short-span actions summing themselves 'blindly,' or fax foreseen ideals coming with effort into act.

Naively we believe, and humanly and dramatically we like to believe, that activities both of wider and of narrower span are at work in life together, that both are real, and that the long-span tendencies yoke the others in their service, encouraging them in the right direction, and damping them when they tend in other ways. But how to represent clearly the modus operandi of such steering of small tendencies by large ones is a problem which metaphysical thinkers will have to ruminate upon for many years to come. Even it such control should eventually grow clearly picturable, the question how far it is successfully exerted in this actual world can be answered only by investigating the details of fact. No philosophic knowledge of the general nature and constitution of tendencies, or of the relation of larger to smaller ones, can help us to predict which of all the various competing tendencies that interest us in this universe are likeliest to prevail. We know as an empirical fact that far-seeing tendencies often carry out their purpose, but we know also that they are often defeated by the failure of some comtemptibly small process on which success depends. A little thrombus in a statesman's meningeal artery will throw an empire out of gear. I can therefore not even hint at any solution of the pragmatic issue. I have only wished to show you that that issue is what gives the real interest to all inquiries into what kinds of activity may be real. Are the forces that really act in the world more foreseeing or more blind? As between 'our' activities as 'we' experience them, and those of our ideas, or of our braincells, the issue is well-defined.

I said a while back[16] that I should return to the 'metaphysical' question before ending; so, with a few words about that, I will now close my remarks.

In whatever form we hear this question propounded, I think that it always arises from two things, a belief that causality must be exerted in activity, and a wonder as to how causality is made. If we take an activity-situation at its face-value, it seems as if we caught in flagrante delicto the very power that makes facts come and be. I now am eagerly striving, for example, to get this truth which I seem half to perceive, into words which shall make it show more clearly. If the words come, it will seem as if the striving itself had drawn or pulled them into actuality out from the state of merely possible being in which they were. How is this feat performed? How does the pulling pull? How do I get my hold on words not yet existent, and when they come by what means have I made them come? Really it is the problem of creation; for in the end the question is: How do I make them be? Real activities are those that really make things be, without which the things are not, and with which they are there. Activity, so far as we merely feel it, on the other hand, is only an impression of ours, it may be maintained; and an impression is, for all this way of thinking, only a shadow of another fact.

Arrived at this point, I can do little more than indicate the principles on which, as it seems to me, a radically empirical philosophy is obliged to rely in handling such a dispute.

If there be real creative activities in being, radical empiricism must say, somewhere they must be immediately lived. Somewhere the that of efficacious causing and the what of it must be experienced in one, just as the what and the that of 'cold' are experienced in one whenever a man has the sensation of cold here and now. It boots not to say that our sensations are fallible. They are indeed; but to see the thermometer contradict us when we say 'it is cold' does not abolish cold as a specific nature from the universe. Cold is in the arctic circle if not here. Even so, to feel that our train is moving when the train beside our window moves, to see the moon through a telescope come twice as near, or to see two pictures as one solid when we look through a stereoscope at them, leaves motion, nearness, and solidity still in being — if not here, yet each in its proper seat elsewhere. And wherever the seat of real causality is, as ultimately known 'for true' (in nerve-processes, if you will, that cause our feelings of activity as well as the movements which these seem to prompt), a philosophy of pure experience can consider the real causation as no other nature of thing than that which even in our most erroneous experiences appears to be at work. Exactly what appears there is what we mean by working, though we may later come to learn that working was not exactly there. Sustaining, persevering, striving, paying with effort as we go, hanging on, and finally achieving our intention — this is action, this is effectuation in the only shape in which, by a pure experience-philosophy, the whereabouts of it anywhere can be discussed. Here is creation in its first intention, here is causality at work.[17] To treat this offhand as the bare illusory surface of a world whose real causality is an unimaginable ontological principle hidden in the cubic deeps, is, for the more empirical way of thinking, only animism in another shape. You explain your given fact by your 'principle,' but the principle itself, when you look clearly at it, turns out to be nothing but a previous little spiritual copy of the fact. Away from that one and only kind of fact your mind, considering causality, can never get.[18] I conclude, then, that real effectual causation as an ultimate nature, as a 'category,' if you like, of reality, is just what we feel it to be, just that kind of conjunction which our own activity-series reveal. We have the whole butt and being of it in our hands; and the healthy thing for philosophy is to leave off grubbing underground for what effects effectuation, or what makes action act, and to try to solve the concrete questions of where effectuation in this world is located, of which things are the true causal agents there, and of what the more remote effects consist.

From this point of view the greater sublimity traditionally attributed to the metaphysical inquiry, the grubbing inquiry, entirely disappears. If we could know what causation really and transcendentally is in itself, the only use of the knowledge would be to help us to recognize an actual cause when we had one, and so to track the future course of operations more intelligently out. The mere abstract inquiry into causation's hidden nature is not more sublime than any other inquiry equally abstract. Causation inhabits no more sublime level than anything else. It lives, apparently, in the dirt of the world as well as in the absolute, or in man's unconquerable mind. The worth and interest of the world consists not in its elements, be these elements things, or be they the conjunctions of things; it exists rather in the dramatic outcome in the whole process, and in the meaning of the succession stages which the elements work out.

My colleague and master, Josiah Royce, in a page of his review of Stout's Analytic Psychology[19] has some fine words on this point with which I cordially agree. I cannot agree with his separating the notion of efficacy from that of activity altogether (this I understand to be one contention of his) for activities are efficacious whenever they are real activities at all. But the inner nature both of efficacy and of activity are superficial problems, I understand Royce to say; and the only point for us in solving them would be their possible use in helping us to solve the far deeper problem of the course and meaning of the world of life. Life, says our colleague, is full of significance, of meaning, of success and of defeat, of hoping and of striving, of longing, of desire, and of inner value. It is a total presence that embodies worth. To live our own lives better in this presence is the true reason why we wish to know the elements of things; so even we psychologists must end on this pragmatic note.

The urgent problems of activity are thus more concrete. They are all problems of the true relation of longer-span to shorter-span activities. When, for example, a number of 'ideas' (to use the name traditional in psychology) grow confluent in a larger field of consciousness, do the smaller activities still co-exist with the wider activities then experienced by the conscious subject? And, if so, do the wide activities accompany the narrow ones inertly, or do they exert control? Or do they perhaps utterly supplant and replace them and short-circuit their effects? Again, when a mental activity-process and a braincell series of activities both terminate in the same muscular movement, does the mental process steer the neural processes or not? Or, on the other hand, does it independently shortcircuit their effects? Such are the questions that we must begin with. But so far am I from suggesting any definitive answer to such questions, that I hardly yet can put them clearly. They lead, however, into that region of panpsychic and ontologic speculation of which Professors Bergson and Strong have lately enlarged the literature in so able and interesting a way.[20] The results of these authors seem in many respects dissimilar, and I understand them as yet but imperfectly; but I cannot help suspecting that the direction of their work is very promising, and that they have the hunter's instinct for the fruitful trails.

Endnotes

1. President's Address before the American Psychological Association, Philadelphia Meeting, December, 1904. [Reprinted from The Psychological Review, vol. XII, No. 1, Jan., 1905. Also reprinted, with some omissions, as Appendix B. A Pluralistic Universe, pp. $70-894. Pp. 166-167 have also been reprinted in Some Problem of Philosophy, p. 212. The present essay is referred to in ibid., p. 219, note. The author's corrections have been adopted for the present text. ED.]

2. [The Journal of Philosophy, Psychology and Scientific Methods.]

3. Appearance and Reality, second edition, pp. 116-117. — Obviously written at Ward, though Ward's name is not mentioned.

4. [Mind, vol. XII, 1887, pp. 573-574.]

5. Mind, N. S., vol. VI, [1897] p. 379.

6. Naturalism and Agnosticism, vol. II, p. 245. One thinks naturally of the peripatetic actus primus and actus secundus here. [" Actus autem est duplex: primus et secundus. Actus quidem primus eat forma, et integritas sei. Actus autem secundus est operatio." Thomas Aquinas : Summa Theologica, edition of Leo XIII. (1894), vol. I. p. 891. Cf. also Blanc: Dictionnaire do Philosophie, under 'acte.' ED.]

7. [Appearance and Reality, second edition, p. 116.]

8. [Kritik der reinen Vernunft, Werke, (1905), vol. IV, p. 110 (trans. by Max Mullur, second edition, p. 128) .]

9. I refer to such descriptive work as Ladd's (Psychology, Descriptive and Explanatory, part 1. chap. V, part 11, chap. XI, part III, chaps. XXV and XXVI); as Sully's (The Human Mind, part V); as Stout's (Analytic Psychology, book I, chap. VI, and book II, chaps. I, II, and III); as Bradley's (in his long series of analytic articles on Psychology in Mind); as Titchener's (Outline of Psychology, part I, chap. VI); as Shand's (Mind, N. S., III, 449; IV, 450; VI, 289); as Ward's (Mind, XII, 67; 564); an Loveday's (Mind, N. S.. X, 455); as Lipps's (Vom Fuhlen, Wollen und Denken, 1902, chaps. II,IV, VI); and as Bergson's (Revue Philosophique, LIII, 1) — to mention only a few writings which I immediately recall.

10. Their existence forms a curious commentary on Prof. Munsterberg's dogma that will-attitudes are not describable. He himself has contributed in a superior way to their description, both in his Willenshandlung. and in his Grundzuge [der Psychologie], part II, chap. IX, 17.

11. I ought myself to cry peccavi, having been a voluminous sinner in my own chapter on the will. [Principles of Psychology, vol. II, chap. XXVI.]

12. [Cf. F. H. Bradley, Appearance and Reality, second edition, pp. 96-97.]

13. [Cf. above.]

14. Verborum gratia: "The feeling of activity is not able, qua feeling,to tell us anything about activity" (Loveday: Mind, N. S., vol. X, 119011, p. 463); "A sensation or feeling or sense of activity ... is not, looked at in another way, an experience of activity at all. It is a mere sensation shut up within which you could by no reflection get the idea of activity. . . . Whether this experience is or is not later on a character essential to our perception and our idea of activity, it, as it comes first, is not in itself an experience of activity at all. It, as it comes first, is only so for extraneous reasons and only so for an outside observer" (Bradley, Appearance and Reality, second edition, p. 605); "In dem Tatigkeitsgefuhle liegt an sich nicht der geringste Beweis für das Vorhandensein einer psychischen Tätigkeit" (Münsterberg: Grundzage der Psychologie). I could multiply similar quotations and would have introduced some of them into my text to make it more concrete, save that the mingling of different points of view in most of these author's discussions (not in Munsterberg's) make it impossible to disentangle exactly what they mean. I am sure in any case, to be accused of misrepresenting them totally, even in this note, by omission of the context, so the less I name names and the more I stick to abstract characterization of a merely possible style of opinion, the safer it will be. And apropos of misunderstandings, I may add to this note a complaint on my own account. Professor Stout, in the excellent chapter on 'Mental Activity,' in vol. I of his Analytic Psychology, takes me to task for identifying spiritual activity with certain muscular feelings and gives quotations to bear him out. They are from certain paragraphs on 'the Self,' in which my attempt was to show what the central nucleus of the activities that we call 'ours' is. [Principles of Psychology, vol. I, pp. 299-305.] I found it in certain intracephalic movements which we habitually oppose, as 'subjective,' to the activities of the transcorporeal world. I sought to show that there is no direct evidence that we feel the activity of an inner spiritual agent as such (I should now say the activity of I consciousness' as such, see [the first essay], 'Does Consciousness Exist?'). There are. in fact, three distinguishable 'activities, in the field of discussion: the elementary activity involved in the mere that of experience, in the fact that something is going on, and the farther specification of this something into two whats, an activity felt as 'ours,' and an activity ascribed to objects. Stout, as I apprehend him, identifies 'our' activity with that of the total experience-process, and when I circumscribe it as a part thereof, accuses me of treating it as a sort of external appendage to itself, as if I 'separated the activity from the process which is active.' But all the processes in question are active, and their activity is inseparable from their being. My book raised only the question of which activity deserved the name of 'ours.' So far as we are 'persons,' and contrasted and opposed to an 'environment,' movements in our body figure as our activities; and I am unable to find any other activities that are ours in this strictly personal sense. There is a wider sense in which the whole 'choir of heaven and furniture of the earth,' and their activities, are ours, for they are our 'objects.' But 'we' are here only another name for the total process of experience, another name for all

that is, in fact; and I was dealing with the personal and individualized self exclusively in the passages with which Professor Stout finds fault.

The individualized self, which I believe to be the only thing properly called self, is a part of the content of the world experienced. Ile world experienced (otherwise called the 'field of consciousness') comes at all times with our body as its centre, centre of vision, centre of action, centre of interest. Where the body is is 'here'; when the body acts is 'now'; what the body touches is 'this'; all other things are 'there' and 'then' and 'that.' These words of emphasized position imply a systematization of things with reference to a focus of action and interest which lies in the body; and the systematization is now so instinctive (was it ever not so?) that no developed or active experience exists for us at all except in that ordered form. So far as 'thoughts' and 'feelings' can be active, their activity terminates in the activity of the body, and only through first arousing its activities can they begin to change those of the rest of the world. [Cf. also A Pluralistic Universe, p. 344, note 8. ED.] The body is the storm centre, the origin of co-ordinates, the constant place of stress in all that experience-train. Everything circles round it. and is felt from its point of view. The word 'I' then, is primarily a noun of position, just like 'this' and 'here.' Activities attached to I this ' position have prerogative emphasis, and, if activities have feelings, must be felt in a peculiar way. The word 'my' designates the kind of emphasis. I see no inconsistency whatever in defending, on the one hand, 'my' activities as unique and opposed to those of outer nature, and, on the other hand, in affirming, after introspection, that they consist in movements in the head. The 'my' of them is the emphasis, the feeling of perspective-interest in which they are dyed.

15. [Enquiry Concerning Human Understanding, sect. VII, part 1, Selby-Bigge's edition, pp. 65 ff.)

16. Below.

17. Let me not be told that this contradicts [the first essay], 'Does Consciousness Exist?' in which it was said that while 'thoughts' and 'things' have the same natures, the natures work 'energetically' on each other in the things (fire bums, water wets, etc.) but not in the thoughts. Mental activity-trains are composed of thoughts, yet their members do work on each other, they check, sustain, and introduce. They do so when the activity is merely associational as well as when effort is there. But, and this is my reply, they do so by other parts of their nature than those that energize physically. One thought in every developed activity-series is a desire or thought of purpose, and all the other thoughts acquire a feeling tone from their relation of harmony or oppugnancy to this. The interplay of these secondary tones (among which 'interest,' 'difficulty,' and 'effort' figure) runs the drama in the mental series. In what we term the physical drama these qualities play absolutely no part. The subject needs careful working out; but I can see no inconsistency.

18. I have found myself more than once accused in print of being the assertor of a metaphysical principle of activity. Since literary misunderstandings retard the settlement of problems, I should like to say that such an interpretation of the pages I have published on Effort and on Will is absolutely foreign to what I meant to express. [Principles of Psychology, vol.

II ch. XXVI.] I owe all my doctrines on this subject to Renouvier; and Renouvier, as I understand him, is (or at any rate then was) an out and out phenomenist, a denier of 'forces' in the most strenuous sense. [Cf. Ch. Renouvier: Esquisse d'une Classication cation Systématique des Doctrines Philosophiques (1885), vol. II, pp. 390-392; Essais de Critique Générale (1859), vol. II, It IX, xiii. For an acknowledgment of the author's general indebtedness to Renouvier, cf. Some Problems of Philosophy, p. 165, note. ED.] Single clauses in my writing, or sentences read out of their connection, may possibly have been compatible with a transphenomenal principle of energy; but I defy anyone to show a single sentence which, taken with its context, should be naturally held to advocate that view. The misinterpretation probably arose at first from my defending (after Renouvier) the indeterminism of our efforts. 'Free will' was supposed by my critics to involve a supernatural agent. As a matter of plain history the only 'free will' I have ever thought of defending is the character of novelty in fresh activity-situations. If an activity-process is the form of a whole 'field of consciousness,' and if each field of consciousness is not only in its totality unique (as is now commonly admitted) but has its elements unique (since in that situation they are all dyed in the total) then novelty is perpetually entering the world and what happens there is not pure repetition, as the dogma of the literal uniformity of nature requires. Activity-situations come, in short, each with an original touch. A 'principle' of free will if there were one, would doubtless manifest itself in such phenomena, but I never saw, nor do I now see, what the principle could do except rehearse the phenomenon beforehand, or why it ever should be invoked.

19. Mind, N. S., vol. VI, 1897; cf. pp. 392-393.

20. [Cf. A Pluralistic Universe, Lect. VI (on Bergson) ; H. Bergson: Creative Evolution, trans. by A. Mitchell; C. A. Strong: Why the Mind has a Body, ch. XII. ED.]

THE ESSENCE OF HUMANISM[1]

Humanism is a ferment that has 'come to stay.'[2] It is not a single hypothesis or theorem, and it dwells on no new facts. It is rather a slow shifting in the philosophic perspective, making things appear as from a new centre of interest or point of sight. Some writers are strongly conscious of the shifting, others half unconscious, even though their own vision may have undergone much change. The result is no small confusion in debate, the half-conscious humanists often taking part against the radical ones, as if they wished to count upon the other side.[3]

If humanism really be the name for such a shifting of perspective, it is obvious that the whole scene of the philosophic stage will change in some degree if humanism prevails. The emphasis of things, their foreground and background distribution, their sizes and values, will not keep just the same.[4] If such pervasive consequences be involved in humanism, it is clear that no pains which philosophers may take, first in defining it, and then in furthering, checking, or steering its progress, will be thrown away.

It suffers badly at present from incomplete definition. Its most systematic advocates, Schiller and Dewey, have published fragmentary programs only; and its bearing on many vital philosophic problems has not been traced except by adversaries who, scenting heresies in advance, have showered blows on doctrines — subjectivism and scepticism, for example that no good humanist finds it necessary to entertain. By their still greater reticences, the anti-humanists have, in turn, perplexed the humanists. Much of the controversy has involved the word 'truth.' It is always good in debate to know your adversary's point of view authentically. But the critics of humanism never define exactly what the word 'truth' signifies when they use it themselves. The humanists have to guess at their view; and the result has doubtless been much beating of the air. Add to all this, great individual differences in both camps, and it becomes clear that nothing is so urgently needed, at the stage which things have reached at present, as a sharper definition by each side of its central point of view.

Whoever will contribute any touch of sharpness will help us to make sure of what's what and who is who. Anyone can contribute such a definition, and, without it, no one knows exactly where he stands. If I offer my own provisional definition of humanism[5] now and here, others may improve it, some adversary may be led to define his own creed more sharply by the contrast, and a certain quickening of the crystallization of general opinion may result.

I

The essential service of humanism, as I conceive the situation, is to have seen that though one part of our experience may lean upon another part to make it what it is in any one of several aspects in which it may be considered, experience as a whole is self-containing and leans. on nothing.

Since this formula also expresses the main contention of transcendental idealism, it needs abundant explication to make it unambiguous. It seems, at first sight, to confine itself to denying theism and pantheism. But, in fact, it need not deny either ; everything would depend on the exegesis; and if the formula ever became canonical, it would certainly develop both right-wing and left-wing interpreters. I myself read humanism theistically and pluralistically. If there be a God, he is no absolute all-experiencer, but simply the experiencer of widest actual conscious span. Read thus, humanism is for me a religion susceptible of reasoned defence, though I am well aware how many minds there are to whom it can appeal religiously only when it has been monistically translated. Ethically the pluralistic form of it takes for me a stronger hold on reality than any other philosophy I know of — it being essentially a social philosophy, a philosophy of 'co,' in which conjunctions do the work. But my primary reason for advocating it is its matchless intellectual economy. It gets rid, not only of the standing 'problems' that monism engenders (problem of evil,' 'problem of freedom,' and the like), but of other metaphysical mysteries and paradoxes as well.

It gets rid, for example, of the whole agnostic controversy, by refusing to entertain the hypothesis of trans-empirical reality at all. It gets rid of any need for an absolute of the Bradleyan type (avowedly sterile for intellectual purposes) by insisting that the conjunctive relations found within experience are faultlessly real. It gets rid of the need of an absolute of the Roycean type (similarly sterile) by its pragmatic treatment of the problem of knowledge [a treatment of which I have already given a version in two very inadequate articles].[6] As the views of knowledge, reality and truth imputed to humanism have been those so far most fiercely attacked, it is in regard to these ideas that a sharpening of focus seems most urgently required. I proceed therefore to bring the views which I impute to humanism in these respects into focus as briefly as I can.

II

If the central humanistic thesis be accepted, it will follow that, if there be any such thing at all as knowing, the knower and the object known must both be portions of experience. One part of experience must, therefore, either (1) Know another part of experience — in other words, parts must, as Professor Woodbridge says,[7] represent one another instead of representing realities outside of 'consciousness' — this case is that of conceptual knowledge; or else (2) They must simply exist as so many ultimate thats or facts of being, in the first instance; and then, as a secondary complication, and without doubling up its entitative singleness, any one and the same that must figure alternately as a thing known and as a knowledge of the thing, by reason of two divergent kinds of context into which, in the general course of experience, it gets woven.[8]

This second case is that of sense-perception. There is a stage of thought that goes beyond common sense, and of it I shall say more presently; but the common-sense stage is a perfectly definite halting-place of thought, primarily for purposes of action; and, so long as we remain on the common-sense stage

of thought, object and subject fuse in the fact of ' presentation' or
sense-perception —the pen and hand which I now see writing, for example,
are the physical realities which those words designate. In this case there is no
self-transcendency implied in the knowing. Humanism, here, is only a more
comminuted Identititsphilosophie.[9]

In case (1), on the contrary, the representative experience does transcend
itself in knowing the other experience that is its object. No one can talk of the
knowledge of the one by the other without seeing them as numerically distinct
entities, of which the one lies beyond the other and away from it, along some
direction and with some interval, that can be definitely named. But, if the
talker be a humanist, he must also see this distance-interval concretely and
pragmatically, and confess it to consist of other intervening experiences —of
possible ones, at all events, if not of actual. To call my present idea of my dog,
for example, cognitive of the real dog means that, as the actual tissue of
experience is constituted, the idea is capable of leading into a chain of other
experiences on my part that go from next to next and terminate at last in
vivid sense-perceptions of a jumping, barking, hairy body. Those are the real
dog, the dog's full presence, for my common sense. If the supposed talker is a
profound philosopher, although they may not be the real dog for him, they
mean the real dog, are practical substitutes for the real dog, as the
representation was a practical substitute for them, that real dog being a lot of
atoms, say, or of mind-stuff, that lie where the sense-perceptions lie in his
experience as well as in my own.

III

The philosopher here stands for the stage of thought that goes beyond the
stage of common sense; and the difference is simply that he 'interpolates" and
'extrapolates,' where common sense does not. For common sense, two men see
the same identical real dog. Philosophy, noting actual differences in their
perceptions, points out the duality of these latter, and interpolates something
between them as a more real terminus —first, organs, viscera, etc.; next, cells;
then, ultimate atoms; lastly, mind-stuff perhaps. The original sense-termini
of the two men, instead of coalescing with each other and with the real
dog-object, as at first supposed, are thus held by philosophers to be separated
by invisible realities with which, at most, they are conterminous.

Abolish, now, one of the percipients, and the interpolation changes into
'extrapolation.' The sense-terminus of the remaining percipient is regarded by
the philosopher as not quite reaching reality. He has only carried the
procession of experiences, the philosopher thinks, to a definite, because
practical, halting-place somewhere on the way towards an absolute truth that
lies beyond.

The humanist sees all the time, however, that there is no absolute
transcendency even about the more absolute realities thus conjectured or
believed in. The viscera and cells are only possible percepts following upon
that of the outer body. The atoms again, though we may never attain to
human means of perceiving them, are still defined perceptually. The
mind-stuff itself is conceived as a kind of experience; and it is possible to
frame the hypothesis (such hypotheses can by no logic be excluded from

philosophy) of two knowers of a piece of mind-stuff and the mind-stuff itself becoming 'confluent' at the moment at which our imperfect knowing might pass into knowing of a completed type. Even so do you and I habitually represent our two perceptions and the real dog as confluent, though only provisionally, and for the common-sense stage of thought. If my pen be inwardly made of mind-stuff, there is no confluence now between that mind-stuff and my visual perception of the pen. But conceivably there might come to be such confluence; for, in the case of my hand, the visual sensations and the inward feelings of the hand, its mind-stuff, so to speak, are even now as confluent, as any two things can be.

There is, thus, no breach in humanistic epistemology. Whether knowledge be taken as ideally perfected, or only as true enough to pass muster for practice, it is hung on one continuous scheme. Reality, howsoever remote, is always defined as a terminus within the general possibilities of experience; and what knows it is defined as an experience that 'represents' it, in the sense of being substitutable for it in our thinking because it leads to the same associates, or in the sense of 'pointing to it' through a chain of other experiences that either intervene or may intervene.

Absolute reality here bears the same relation to sensation as sensation bears to conception or imagination. Both are provisional or final termini, sensation being only the terminus at which the practical man habitually stops, while the philosopher projects a 'beyond' in the shape of more absolute reality. These termini, for the practical and the philosophical stages of thought respectively, are self-supporting. They are not 'true' of anything else, they simply are, are real. They 'lean on nothing,' as my formula said. Rather does the whole fabric of experience lean on them, just as the whole fabric of the solar system, including many relative positions, leans, for its absolute position in space, on any one of its constituent stars. Here, again, one gets a new Identitatsphilosophie in pluralistic form.[10]

IV

If I have succeeded in making this at all clear (though I fear that brevity and abstractness between them may have made me fail), the reader will see that the 'truth' of our mental operations must always be an intra-experiential affair. A conception is reckoned true. by common sense when it can be made to lead to a sensation. The sensation, which for common sense is not so much 'true 3' as 4; real.,' is held to be provisionally true by the philosopher just in so far as it covers (abuts at, or occupies the place of) a still more absolutely real experience, in the possibility of which to some remoter experient the philosopher finds reason to believe.

Meanwhile what actually does count for true to any individual trower, whether he be philosopher or common man, is always a result of his apperceptions. If a novel experience, conceptual or sensible, contradict too emphatically our pre-existent system of beliefs, in ninety-nine cases out of a hundred it is treated as false. Only when the older and the newer experiences are congruous enough to mutually apperceive and modify each other, does what we treat as an advance in truth result. [Having written of this point in an article in reply to Mr. Joseph's criticism of my humanism, I will say no more about truth here, but refer the reader to that review.[11]] In no case, however, need truth consist in a relation between our experiences and something archetypal or trans-experiential. Should we ever reach absolutely terminal experiences, experiences in which we all agreed, which were superseded by no revised continuations, these would not be true, they would be real, they would simply be, and be indeed the angles, corners, and linchpins of all reality, on which the truth of everything else would be stayed. Only such other things as led to these by satisfactory conjunctions would be 'true.' Satisfactory connection of some sort with such termini is all that the word 'truth' means. On the common-sense stage of thought sense-presentations serve as such termini. Our ideas and concepts and scientific theories pass for true only so far as they harmoniously lead back to the world of sense.

I hope that many humanists will endorse this attempt of mine to trace the more essential features of that way of viewing things. I feel almost certain that Messrs. Dewey and Schiller will do so. If the attackers will also take some slight account of it, it may be that discussion will be a little less wide of the mark than it has hitherto been.

Endnotes

1. [Reprinted from The Journal of Philosophy, Psychology and Scientific Methods, vol. II. No. 5, March 2, 1905. Also reprinted, with slight changes in The Meaning of Truth. The author's corrections have been adopted for the present text. ED.]

2. [Written apropos of the appearance of three articles in Mind, N. S., vol. XIV, No. 53, January, 1905: " ' Absolute' and 'Relative' Truth," H. 131. Joachim; "Professor James on 'Humanism and Truth,'" H. W. B. Joseph; " Applied Axioms," A. Sidgwick. Of these articles the second and third "continue the humanistic (or pragmatistic) controversy," the first "deeply connects with it," Bpi)

3. Professor Baldwin, for example. His address 'On Selective Thinking' (Psychological Review, [vol. v], 1808, reprinted in his volume, Development and Evolution) seems to we an unusually well-written pragmatic manifesto. Nevertheless in 'The Limits of Pragmatism' (ibid., [vol. XI], 1904), he (much less clearly) joins in the attack.

4. The ethical changes, it seems to me, are beautifully made evident in Professor Dewey's series of articles, which will never get the attention they deserve till they are printed in a book. I mean: 'The Significance of Emotions,' Psychological Review, vol. 11, [1895], p. is; 'The Reflex Arc Concept in Psychology,' ibid., vol. III, [1896], p. 357; 'Psychology and Social Practice,' ibid., vol. VII, [1900], p. 105; ' Interpretation of Savage Mind, 'ibid., vol. IX, [1902], p. 217; 'Green's Theory of the Moral Motive,' Philosophical Review, vol. I, [1892], p. 593; 'Self-realization as the Moral Ideal,' ibid., vol. II, [1893], p. 652; 'The Psychology of Effort.' ibid., vol. VI, [1897], p. 48; 'The Evolutionary Method as Applied to Mortality,' ibid., Vol. XI, [1902]. pp. 107, 358; 'Evolution and Ethics,' Monist, vol. VIII, [1898], p. 321; to mention only a few.

5. [The author employs the term 'humanism' either as a synonym for 'radical empiricism'; or as that general philosophy of life of which 'radical

empiricism' the theoretical ground. For other discussions of 'humanism.' cf. below, essay xi, and The Meaning of Truth, essay III. ED.]

6. [Omitted from reprint in Meaning of Truth. The articles referred to are 'Does Consciousness Exist?' and 'A World of Pure Experience,']

7. In Science, November 4, 1904, p. 599.

8. This statement is probably excessively obscure to any one who has not read my two articles. 'Does Consciousness Exist?' and 'A World of Pure Experience.'

9. [Cf. above and below.]

10. [Cf. above.]

11. [Omitted from reprint in Meaning of Truth. The review referred to is reprinted under the title" Humanism and Truth Once More." ED.]

Is Radical Empiricism Solopsistic? [1]

If all the criticisms which the humanistic Weltanschauung is receiving were as sachgemass as Mr. Bode's,[2] the truth of the matter would more rapidly clear up. Not only is it excellently well written, but it brings its own point of view out clearly, and admits of a perfectly straight reply.

The argument (unless I fail to catch it) can be expressed as follows:

If a series of experiences be supposed, no one of which is endowed immediately with the selftranscendent function of reference to a reality beyond itself, no motive will occur within the series for supposing anything beyond it to exist. It will remain subjective, and contentedly subjective, both as a whole and in its several parts.

Radical empiricism, trying, as it does, to account for objective knowledge by means of such a series, egregiously fails. It can not explain how the notion of a physical order, as distinguished from a subjectively biographical order, of experiences, ever arose.

It pretends to explain the notion of a physical order, but does so by playing fast and loose with the concept of objective reference. On the one hand, it denies that such reference implies self-transcendency on the part of any one experience; on the other hand, it claims that experiences point. But, critically considered, there can be no pointing unless self-transcendency be also allowed. The conjunctive function of pointing, as I have assumed it, is, according to my critic, vitiated by the fallacy of attaching a bilateral relation to a term ad quo, as if it could stick out substantively and, maintain itself in existence in advance of the term ad quem which is equally required for it to be a concretely experienced fact. If the relation be made concrete, the term ad quem is involved, which would mean (if I succeed in apprehending Mr. Bode rightly) that this latter term, although not empirically there, is yet noetically there, in advance—in other words it would mean that any experience that ' points' must already have transcended itself, in the ordinary 'epistemological' sense of the word transcend.

Something like this, if I understand Mr. Bode's text, is the upshot of his state of mind. It is a reasonable sounding state of mind, but it is exactly the state of mind which radical empiricism, by its doctrine of the reality of conjunctive relations, seeks to dispel. I very much fear — so difficult does mutual understanding seem in these exalted regions — that my able critic has failed to understand that doctrine as it is meant to be understood. I suspect that he performs on all these conjunctive relations (of which the aforesaid 'pointing' is only one) the usual rationalistic act of substitution — he takes them not as they are given in their first intention, as parts constitutive of experience's living flow, but only as they appear in retrospect, each fixed as a determinate object of conception, static, therefore, and contained within itself.

Against this rationalistic tendency to treat experience as chopped up into discontinuous static objects, radical empiricism protests. It insists on taking conjunctions at their 'face-value,' just as they come. Consider, for example, such conjunctions as 'and,' 'with,' ' near,' ' plus,' ' towards.' While we live in such conjunctions our state is one of transition in the most literal sense. We are expectant of a 0; more' to come, and before the more has come, the transition, nevertheless, is directed towards it. I fail otherwise to see how, if one kind of more comes, there should be satisfaction and feeling of fulfilment; but disappointment if the more comes in another shape. One more will continue, another more will arrest or deflect the direction, in which our experience is moving even now. We can not, it is true, name our different living 'ands' or 'withs' except by naming the different terms towards which they are moving us, but we live their specifications and differences before those terms explicitly arrive. Thus, though the various 'ands" are all bilateral relations, each requiring a term ad quem to define it when viewed in retrospect and articulately conceived, yet in its living moment any one of them may be treated as if it 'stuck out' from its term a quo and pointed in a special direction, much as a compass-needle (to use Mr. Bode's excellent simile) points at the pole, even though it stirs not from its box.

In Professor Hoffding's massive little article in The Journal of Philosophy, Psychology and Scientific Methods,[3] he quotes a saying of Kierkegaard's to the effect that we live forwards, but we understand backwards. Understanding backwards is, it must be confessed, a very frequent weakness of philosophers, both of the rationalistic and of the ordinary empiricist type. Radical empiricism alone insists on understanding forwards also, and refuses to substitute static concepts of the understanding for transitions in our moving life. A logic similar to that which my critic seems to employ here should, it seems to me, forbid him to say that our present is, while present, directed towards our future, or that any physical movement can have direction until its goal is actually reached.

At this point does it not seem as if the quarrel about self-transcendency in knowledge might drop? Is it not a purely verbal dispute? Call it self-transcendency or call it pointing, whichever you like — it makes no difference so long as real transitions towards real goals are admitted as things given in experience, and among experience's most indefeasible parts. Radical empiricism, unable to close its eyes to the transitions caught in actu, accounts for the self-transcendency or the pointing (whichever you may call it) as a process that occurs within experience, as an empirically mediated thing of which a perfectly definite description can be given. 'Epistemology,' on the other hand, denies this; and pretends that the self-transcendency is unmediated or, if mediated, then mediated in a super-empirical world. To justify this pretension, epistemology has first to transform all our conjunctions into static objects, and this, I submit, is an absolutely arbitrary act. But in spite of Mr. Bode's maltreatment of conjunctions, as I understand them — and as I understand him — I believe that at bottom we are fighting for nothing different, but are both defending the same continuities of experience in different forms of words.

There are other criticisms in the article in question, but, as this seems the most vital one, I will for the present, at any rate, leave them untouched.

Endnotes

1. [Reprinted from The Journal of Philosophy, Psychology and Scientific Methods, vol. II, No. 9, April 27, 1905.]

2. [B. H. Bode: "'Pure Experience' and the External World," Journal of Philosophy, Psychology and Scientific Methods, vol. II, 1905, P. 128.]

3. Vol. 11, [1905], pp. 85-92.

MR. PITKIN'S REFUTATION
OF 'RADICAL EMPIRICISM'[1]

Although Mr. Pitkin does not name me in his acute article on radical empiricism,[2] [...] I fear that some readers, knowing me to have applied that name to my own doctrine, may possibly consider themselves to have been in at my death.

In point of fact my withers are entirely unwrung. I have, indeed, said[3] that 'to be radical, an empiricism must not admit into its constructions any element that is not directly experienced! But in my own radical empiricism this is only a methodological postulate, not a conclusion supposed to flow from the intrinsic absurdity of transempirical objects. I have never felt the slightest respect for the idealistic arguments which Mr. Pitkin attacks and of which Ferrier made such striking use; and I am perfectly willing to admit any number of noumenal beings or events into philosophy if only their pragmatic value can be shown.

Radical empiricism and pragmatism have so many misunderstandings to suffer from, that it seems my duty not to let this one go any farther, uncorrected.

Mr. Pitkin's 'reply' to me,[4] perplexes me by the obscurity of style which I find in almost all our younger philosophers. He asks me, however, two direct questions which I understand, so I take the liberty of answering.

First he asks: Do not experience and science show 'that countless things are[5] experienced as that which they are not or are only partially?' I reply: Yes, assuredly, as, for example, 'things' distorted by refractive media, 'molecules,' or whatever else is taken to be more ultimately real than the immediate content of the perceptive moment.

Secondly: "If experience is self-supporting[6] (in any intelligible sense) does this fact preclude the possibility of (a) something not experienced and (b) action of experience upon a noumenon?"

My reply is: Assuredly not the possibility of either — how could it? Yet in my opinion we should be wise not to consider any thing or action of that nature, and to restrict our universe of philosophic discourse to what is experienced or, at least, experienceable.[7]

Endnotes

1. [Reprinted from the Journal of Philosophy, Psychology and Scientific Methods, vol. III, No. 96, December 20, 1906; and ibid., vol. IV, No. 4, February 14, 1907, where the original is entitled "A Reply to Mr. Pitkin." Ed.]

2. [W. B. Pitkin: "A Problem of Evidence in Radical Empiricism," ibid., vol. III, No. 24. November 22, 1906. ED.]

3. [Above. ED.]

4. [" In Reply to Professor James." Journal of Philosophy, Psychology and Scientific Methods, vol. IV, No. 2, January 17,1907, ED.]

5. Mr. Pitkin inserts the clause: 'by reason of the very nature of experience itself.' Not understanding just what reason is meant, I do not include this clause in my answer.

6. [See above. ED.]

7. [Elsewhere, in speaking of 'reality' as "conceptual or perceptual experiences," the author says. "This is meant merely to exclude reality of an 'unknowable' sort, of which no account in either perceptual or conceptual terms can be given. It includes, of course, any amount of empirical reality independent of the knower." Meaning of Truth, P. 100, note. ED.]

HUMANISM AND TRUTH ONCE MORE.[1]

Mr. Joseph's criticism of my article 'Humanism and Truth "[2] is a useful contribution to the general clearing up. He has seriously tried to comprehend what the pragmatic movement may intelligibly mean; and if he has failed, it is the fault neither of his patience nor of his sincerity, but rather of stubborn tricks of thought which he could not easily get rid of. Minute polemics, in which the parties try to rebut every detail of each of the other's charges, are a useful exercise only to the disputants. They can but breed confusion in a reader. I will therefore ignore as much as possible the text of both our articles (mine was inadequate enough) and treat once more the general objective situation. As I apprehend the movement towards humanism, it is based on no particular discovery or principle that can be driven into one precise formula which thereupon can be impaled upon a logical skewer. It is much more like one of those secular changes that come upon public opinion over-night, as it were, borne upon tides 'too full for sound or foam,' that survive all the crudities and extravagances of their advocates, that you can pin to no one absolutely essential statement, nor kill by any one decisive stab.

Such have been the changes from aristocracy to democracy, from classic to romantic taste, from theistic to pantheistic feeling, from static to evolutionary ways of understanding life —changes of which we all have been spectators. Scholasticism still opposes to such changes the method of confutation by single decisive reasons, showing that the new view involves self-contradiction, or traverses some fundamental principle. This is like stopping a river by planting a stick in the middle of its bed. Round your obstacle flows the water and 'gets there all the same.' In reading Mr. Joseph, I am not a little reminded of those Catholic writers who refute Darwinism by telling us that higher species can not come from lower because minus nequit gignere plus, or that the notion of transformation is absurd, for it implies that species tend to their own destruction, and that would violate the principle that every reality tends to persevere in its own shape. The point of view is too myopic, too tight and close to take in the inductive argument. You can not settle questions of fact by formal logic. I feel as if Mr. Joseph almost pounced on my words singly, without giving the sentences time to get out of my mouth.

The one condition of understanding humanism is to become inductive-minded one. self, to drop rigorous definitions, and follow lines of least resistance 'on the whole.' "In other words," Mr. Joseph may probably say, "resolve your intellect into a kind of slush." "'Even so," I make reply, —"if you will consent to use no politer word." For humanism, conceiving the more 'true' as the more 'satisfactory' (Dewey's term) has to renounce sincerely rectilinear arguments and ancient ideals of rigor and finality. It is in just this temper of renunciation, so different from that of pyrrhonistic scepticism, that the spirit of humanism essentially consists. Satisfactoriness has to be measured by a multitude of standards, of which some, for aught we know, may fail in any given case; and what is 'more' satisfactory than any alternative in sight, may to the end be a sum of pluses and minuses, concerning which we can only trust that by ulterior corrections and improvements a maximum of the one and a minimum of the other may some day be approached. It means a real change of heart, a break with absolutistic hopes, when one takes up this view of the conditions of belief.

That humanism's critics have never imagined this attitude inwardly, is shown by their invariable tactics. They do not get into it far enough to see objectively and from with out what their own opposite notion of truth is. Mr. Joseph is possessed by some such notion; he thinks his readers to be full of it, he obeys it, works from it, but never even essays to tell us what it is. The nearest he comes to doing so is where[3] he says it is the way "we ought to think," whether we be psychologically compelled to or not.

Of course humanism agrees to this: it is only a manner of calling truth an ideal. But humanism explicates the summarizing word "ought' into a mass of pragmatic motives from the midst of which our critics think that truth itself takes flight. Truth is a name of double meaning. It stands now for an abstract something defined only as that to which our thought ought to conform; and again it stands for the concrete propositions within which we believe that conformity already reigns — they being so many 'truths.' Humanism sees that the only conformity we ever have to deal with concretely is that between our subjects and our predicates, using these words in a very broad sense. It sees moreover. that 'this conformity is 'validated' (to use Mr. Schiller's term) by an indefinite number of pragmatic tests that vary as the predicates and subjects vary. If an S gets superseded by an SP that gives our mind a completer sum of satisfactions, we always say, humanism points out, that we have advanced to a better position in regard to truth.

Now many of our judgments thus attained are retrospective. The S'es, so the judgment runs, were SP's already ere the fact was humanly recorded. Common sense, struck by this state of things, now rearranges the whole field; and traditional philosophy follows her example. The general requirement that predicates must conform to their subject, they translate into an ontological theory. A most previous Subject of all is substituted for the lesser subjects and conceived of as an archetypal Reality; and the conformity required of predicates in detail is reinterpreted as a relation which our whole mind, with all its subjects and predicates together, must get into with respect to this Reality. It, meanwhile, is conceived as eternal, static, and unaffected by our thinking. Conformity to a non-human Archetype like this is probably the notion of truth which my opponent shares with common sense and philosophic rationalism.

When now Humanism, fully admitting both the naturalness and the grandeur of this hypothesis, nevertheless points to its sterility, and declines to chime in with the substitution, keeping to the concrete and still lodging truth between the subjects and the predicates in detail, it provokes the outcry which we hear and which my critic echoes.

One of the commonest parts of the outcry is that humanism is subjectivistic altogether — it is supposed to labor under a necessity of 'denying trans-perceptual reality.'[4] It is not hard to see how this misconception of humanism may have arisen; and humanistic writers, partly from not having sufficiently guarded their expressions, and partly from not having yet "got round" (in the poverty of their literature) to a full discussion of the subject, are doubtless in some degree to blame. But I fail to understand how any one with a working grasp of their principles can charge them wholesale with subjectivism. I myself have never thought of humanism as being subjectivistic farther than to this extent, that, inasmuch as it treats the thinker as being himself one portion of reality, it must also allow that some of the realities that he declares for true are created by his being there. Such realities of course are either acts Of his, or relations between other things and him, or relations between things, which, but for him, would never have been traced. Humanists are subjectivistic, also in this, that, unlike rationalists (who think they carry a warrant for the absolute truth of what they now believe in in their present pocket), they hold all present beliefs as subject to revision in the light of future experience. The future experience, however, may be of things outside the thinker; and that this is so the humanist may believe as freely as any other kind of empiricist philosopher.

The critics of humanism (though here I follow them but darkly) appear to object to any infusion whatever of subjectivism into truth. All must be archetypal; every truth must pre-exist to its perception. Humanism sees that an enormous quantity of truth must be written down as having pre-existed to its perception by us humans. In countless instances we find it most satisfactory to believe that, though we were always ignorant of the fact, it always was a fact that S was SP. But humanism separates this class of cases from those in which it is more satisfactory to believe the opposite, e.g., that S is ephemeral, or P a passing event, or SP created by the perceiving act. Our critics seem on the other hand, to wish to universalize the retrospective type of instance. Reality must pre-exist to every assertion for which truth is claimed. And, not content with this overuse of one particular type of judgment, our critics claim its monopoly. They appear to wish to cut off Humanism from its rights to any retrospection at all.

Humanism says that satisfactoriness is what distinguishes the true from the false. But satisfactoriness is both a subjective quality, and a present one. Ergo (the critics appear to reason) an object, qua true, must always for humanism be both present and subjective, and a humanist's belief can never be in anything that lives outside of the belief itself or antedates it. Why so preposterous a charge should be so current, I find it hard to say. Nothing is more obvious than the fact that both the objective and the past existence of the object may be the very things about it that most seem satisfactory, and that most invite us to believe them. The past tense can figure in the humanist's world, as well of belief as of representation, quite as harmoniously as in the world of any one else.

Mr. Joseph gives a special turn to this accusation. He charges me[5] with being self-contradictory when I say that the main categories of thought were evolved in the course of experience itself. For I use these very categories to define the course of experience by. Experience, as I talk about it, is a product of their use; and yet I take it as true anteriorly to them. This seems to Mr.

Joseph to be an absurdity. I hope it does not seem such to his readers; for if experiences can suggest hypotheses at all (and they notoriously do so) I can see no absurdity whatever in the notion of a retrospective hypothesis having for its object the very train of experiences by which its own being, along with that of other things, has been brought about. If the hypothesis is 'satisfactory' we must, of course, believe it to have been true anteriorly to its formulation by ourselves. Every explanation of a present by a past seems to involve this kind of circle, which is not a vicious circle. The past is causa existendi of the present, which in turn is causa cognoscendi of the past. If the present were treated as causa existendi of the past, the circle might indeed be vicious.

Closely connected with this pseudo-difficulty is another one of wider scope and greater complication — more excusable therefore.[6] Humanism, namely, asking how truth in point of fact is reached, and seeing that it is by ever substituting more satisfactory for less satisfactory opinions, is thereby led into a vague historic sketch of truth's development. The earliest 'opinions,' it thinks, must have been dim, unconnected 'feelings,' and only little by little did more and more orderly views of things replace them. Our own retrospective view of this whole evolution is now, let us say, the latest candidate for 'truth' as yet reached in the process. To be a satisfactory candidate, it must give some definite sort of a picture of what forces keep the process going. On the subjective side we have a fairly definite picture — sensation, association, interest, hypothesis, these account in a general way for the growth into a cosmos of the relative chaos with which the mind began.

But on the side of the object, so to call it roughly, our view is much less satisfactory. Of which of our many objects are we to believe that it truly was there and at work before the human mind began? Time, space, kind, number, serial order, cause, consciousness, are hard things not to objectify — even transcendental idealism leaves them standing as 'empirically real.' Substance, matter, force, fall down more easily before criticism, and secondary qualities make almost no resistance at all. Nevertheless, when we survey the field of speculation, from Scholasticism through Kantism to Spencerism, we find an ever-recurring tendency to convert the pre-human into a merely logical object, an unknowable ding-an-sich, that but starts the process, or a vague materia prima that but receives our forms.[7]

The reasons for this are not so much logical as they are material. We can postulate an extra-mental that freely enough (though some idealists have denied us the privilege), but when we have done so, the what of it is hard to determine satisfactorily, because of the oppositions and entanglements of the variously proposed whats with one another and with the history of the human mind. The literature of speculative cosmology bears witness to this difficulty. Humanism suffers from it no more than any other philosophy suffers, but it makes all our cosmogonic theories so unsatisfactory that some thinkers seek relief in the denial of any primal dualism. Absolute Thought or 'pure experience' is postulated, and endowed with attributes calculated to justify the belief that it may 'run itself.' Both these truth-claiming hypotheses are nondualistic in the old mind-and-matter sense; but the one is monistic and the other pluralistic as to the world process itself. Some humanists are non-dualists of this sort — I myself am one und zwar of the pluralistic brand.

But doubtless dualistic humanists also exist, as well as non-dualistic ones of the monistic wing.

Mr. Joseph pins these general philosophic difficulties on humanism alone, or possibly on me alone. My article spoke vaguely of a 'most chaotic pure experience' coming first, and building up the mind.[8] But how can two structureless things interact so as to produce a structure? my critic triumphantly asks. Of course they can't, as purely so-named entities. We must make additional hypotheses. We must beg a minimum of structure for them. The kind of minimum that might have tended to increase towards what we now find actually developed is the philosophical desideratum here. The question is that of the most materially satisfactory hypothesis. Mr. Joseph handles it by formal logic purely, as if he had no acquaintance with the logic of hypothesis at all.

Mr. Joseph again is much bewildered as to what a humanist can mean when he uses the word knowledge. He tries to convict me[9] of vaguely identifying it with any kind of good. Knowledge is a difficult thing to define briefly, and Mr. Joseph shows his own constructive hand here even less than in the rest of his article. I have myself put forth on several occasions a radically pragmatist account of knowledge,[10] the existence of which account my critic probably does not know of — so perhaps I had better not say anything about knowledge until he reads and attacks that. I will say, however, that whatever the relation called knowing may itself prove to consist in, I can think of no conceivable kind of object which may not become an object of knowledge on humanistic principles as well as on the principles of any other philosophy.[11]

I confess that I am pretty steadily hampered by the habit, on the part of humanism's critics, of assuming that they have truer ideas than mine of truth and knowledge, the nature of which I must know of and can not need to have re-defined. I have consequently to reconstruct these ideas in order to carry on the discussion (I have e.g. had to do so in some parts of this article) and I thereby expose myself to charges of caricature. In one part of Mr. Joseph's attack, however, I rejoice that we are free from this embarrassment. It is an important point and covers probably a genuine difficulty, so I take it up last.

When, following Schiller and Dewey, I define the true as that which gives the maximal combination of satisfactions, and say that satisfaction is a many-dimensional term that can be realized in various ways, Mr. Joseph replies, rightly enough, that the chief satisfaction of a rational creature must always be his thought that what he believes is true, whether the truth brings him the satisfaction of collateral profits or not. This would seem, however, to make of truth the prior concept, and to relegate satisfaction to a secondary place.

Again, if to be satisfactory is what is meant by being true, whose satisfactions, and which of his satisfactions, are to count? Discriminations notoriously have to be made; and the upshot is that only rational candidates and intellectual satisfactions stand the test. We are then driven to a purely theoretic notion of truth, and get out of the pragmatic atmosphere altogether. And with this Mr. Joseph leaves us — truth is truth, and there is an end of the matter. But he makes a very pretty show of convicting me of self-stultification in according to our purely theoretic satisfactions any place in the humanistic scheme. They crowd the collateral satisfactions out of house and home, he thinks, and pragmatism has to go into bankruptcy if she recognizes them at all.

There is no room for disagreement about the facts here; but the destructive force of the reasoning disappears as soon as we talk concretely instead of abstractly, and ask, in our quality of good pragmatists, just what the famous theoretic needs are known as and in what the intellectual satisfactions consist. Mr. Joseph, faithful to the habits of his party, makes no attempt at characterizing them, but assumes that their nature is self-evident to all.

Are they not all mere matters of consistency — and emphatically not of consistency between an Absolute Reality and the mind's copies of it, but of actually felt consistency among judgments, objects, and manners of reacting, in the mind? And are not both our need of such consistency and our pleasure in it conceivable as outcomes of the natural fact that we are beings that develop mental habits — habit itself proving adaptively beneficial in an environment where the same objects, or the same kinds of objects, recur and follow 'law'? If this were so, what would have come first would have been the collateral profits of habit, and the theoretic life would have grown up in aid of these. In point of fact this seems to have been the probable case. At life's origin, any present perception may have been 'true' —if such a word could then be applicable. Later, when reactions became organized, the reactions became 'true' whenever expectation was fulfilled by them. Otherwise they were 'false' or 'mistaken' reactions. But the same class of objects needs the same kind of reaction, so the impulse to react consistently must gradually have been established, with a disappointment felt whenever the results frustrated expectation. Here is a perfectly plausible germ for all our higher consistencies. Nowadays, if an object claims from us a reaction of the kind habitually accorded only to the opposite class of objects, our mental machinery refuses to run smoothly. The situation is intellectually unsatisfactory. To gain relief we seek either to preserve the reaction by re-interpreting the object, or, leaving the object as it is, we react in a way contrary to the way claimed of us. Neither solution is easy. Such a situation might be that of Mr. Joseph, with me claiming assent to humanism from him. He can not apperceive it so as to permit him to gratify my claim; but there is enough appeal in the claim to induce him to write a whole article in justification of his refusal. If he should assent to humanism, on the other hand, that would drag after it an unwelcome, yea incredible, alteration of his previous mental beliefs. Whichever alternative he might adopt, however, a new equilibrium of intellectual consistency would in the end be reached. He would feel, which-ever way he decided, that he was now thinking truly. But if, with his old habits unaltered, he should simply add to them the new one of advocating humanism quietly or noisily, his mind would be rent into two systems, each of which would accuse the other of falsehood. The resultant situation, being profoundly unsatisfactory, would also be instable.

Theoretic truth is thus no relation between our mind and archetypal reality. It falls within the mind, being the accord of some of its processes and objects with other processes and objects —'accord' consisting here in well-definable relations. So long as the satisfaction of feeling such an accord is denied us, whatever collateral profits may seem to inure from what we believe in are but as dust in the balance — provided always that we are highly organized intellectually, which the majority of us are not. The amount of accord which satisfies most men and women is merely the absence of violent clash between their usual thoughts and statements and the limited sphere of sense-perceptions in which their lives are cast. The theoretic truth that most of us think we 'ought' to attain to is thus the possession of a set of predicates that do not contradict their subjects. We preserve it as often as not by leaving other predicates and subjects out.

In some men theory is a passion, just as music is in others. The form of inner consistency is pursued far beyond the line at which collateral profits stop. Such men systematize and classify and schematize and make synoptical tables and invent ideal objects for the pure love of unifying. Too often the results, glowing with 'truth' for the inventors, seem pathetically personal and artificial to bystanders. Which is as much as to say that the purely theoretic criterion of truth can leave us in the lurch as easily as any other criterion.

I think that if Mr. Joseph will but consider all these things a little more concretely, he may find that the humanistic scheme and the notion of theoretic truth fall into line consistently enough to yield him also intellectual satisfaction.

Endnotes

1. [Reprinted without change from Mind, N. S., vol. XIV, No. 54, April, 1905, pp. 190-198. Pages 245-247, and pp. 261-265, have also been reprinted in The Meaning of Truth, pp. 64-57, and pp. 97-100. The present essay is referred to above.]

2. ' Humanism and Truth' first appeared in Mind, N. S., vol. XIII, No. 52. October, 1904. It is reprinted in The Meaning of Truth, pp. 51-101. Cf. this article passim. Mr. H. W. B. Joseph's criticism, entitled " Professor James on ' Humanism and Truth, appeared in Mind, N. S., vol. XIV, No. 53, January. 1905. ED.]

3. Op. cit.

4. [Cf. above]

5. Op. cit.

6. [This] Mr. Joseph deals with (though in much too pettifogging and logic-chopping a way) on pp. 33-34 of his article.

7. Compare some elaborate articles by M. Le Roy and M. Wilbois in the Revue de Métaphysique et de Morale, vols. VIII, IX, and X, [1900, 1901, and 1902.]

8. [Cf. The Meaning of Truth.]

9. [Joseph: op. cit.]

10. [Most recently in two articles, "Does 'Consciousness' Exist?" and "A World of Pure Experience." [See above.]

11. For a recent attempt, effective on the whole, at squaring humanism. with knowing, I may refer to Prof. Woodbridge's very able address at the Saint Louis Congress, "The Field of Logic," printed in Science, N. Y., November 4, 1904.

ABSOLUTISM AND EMPIRICISM[1]

No seeker of truth can fail to rejoice at the terre-à-terre sort of discussion of the issues between Empiricism and Transcendentalism (or, as the champions of the latter would probably prefer to say, between Irrationalism and Rationalism) that seems to have begun in Mind .[2] It would seem as if , over concrete examples like Mr. J. S. Haldane's, both parties ought inevitably to come to a better understanding. As a reader with a strong bias towards Irrationalism, I have studied his article[3] with the liveliest admiration of its temper and its painstaking effort to be clear. But the cases discussed failed to satisfy me, and I was at first tempted to write a Note animadverting upon them in detail. The growth of the limb, the sea's contour, the vicarious functioning of the nerve-centre, the digitalis curing the heart, are unfortunately not cases where we can see any through-and-through conditioning of the parts by the whole. They are all cases of reciprocity where subjects, supposed independently to exist, acquire certain attributes through their relations to other subjects. That they also exist through similar relations is only an ideal supposition, not verified to our understanding in these or any other concrete cases whatsoever.

If, however, one were to urge this solemnly, Mr. Haldane's friends could easily reply that he only gave us such examples on account of the hardness of our hearts. He knew full well their imperfection, but he hoped that to those who would not spontaneously ascend to the Notion of the Totality, these cases might prove a spur and suggest and symbolize something better than themselves. No particular case that can be brought forward is a real concrete. They are all abstractions from the Whole, and of course the "through-and-through " character can not be found in them. Each of them still contains among its elements what we call things, grammatical subjects, forming a sort of residual caput mortuum of Existence after all the relations that figure in the examples have been told off. On this "existence," thinks popular philosophy, things may live on, like-the winter bears on their own fat, never entering relations at all, or, if entering them, entering an entirely different set of them from those treated of in Mr. Haldane's examples. Thus if the digitalis were to weaken instead of strengthening the heart, and to produce death (as sometimes happens), it would determine itself, through determining the organism, to the function of "kill" instead of that of "cure." The function and relation seem adventitious, depending on what kind of a heart the digitalis gets hold of, the digitalis and the heart being facts external and, so to speak, accidental to each other. But this popular view, Mr. Haldane's friends will continue, is an illusion. What seems to us the "existence " of digitalis and heart outside of the relations of killing or curing, is but a function in a wider system of relations, of which, pro hac vice, we take no account. The larger system determines the existence just as absolutely as the system "kill," or the system "cure," determined the function of the digitalis. Ascend to the absolute system, instead of biding with these relative and partial ones, and you shall see that the law of through-and-throughness must and does obtain.

Of course, this argument is entirely reasonable, and debars us completely from chopping logic about the concrete examples Mr. Haldane has chosen. It is not his fault if his categories are so fine an instrument that nothing but the sum total of things can be taken to show us the manner of their use. It is simply our misfortune that he has not the sum total of things to show it by. Let us fall back from all concrete attempts and see what we can do with his notion of through-and-throughness, avowedly taken in abstracto. In abstract systems the " through-and-through " Ideal is realized on every hand. In any system, as such, the members are only members in the system. Abolish the system and you abolish its members, for you have conceived them through no other property than the abstract one of membership. Neither rightness nor leftness, except through bi-laterality. Neither mortgager nor mortgagee, except through mortgage. The logic of these cases is this: — If A, then B; but if B, then A: wherefore if either, Both; and if not Both, Nothing.

It costs nothing, not even a mental effort, to admit that the absolute totality of things may be organized exactly after the pattern of one of these " through-and-through " abstractions. In fact, it is the pleasantest and freest of mental movements. Husband makes, and is made by, wife, through marriage; one makes other, by being itself other; everything self-created through its opposite — you go round like a squirrel in a cage. But if you stop and reflect upon what you are about, you lay bare the exact point at issue between common sense and the " through-and-through " school.

What, in fact, is the logic of these abstract systems? It is, as we said above: If any Member, then the Whole System; if not the Whole System, then Nothing. But how can Logic possibly do anything more with these two hypotheses than combine them into the single disjunctive proposition — "Either this Whole System, just as it stands, or Nothing at all." Is not that disjunction the ultimate word of Logic in the matter, and can any disjunction, as such, resolve itself? It may be that Mr. Haldane sees how one horn, the concept of the Whole System, carries real existence with it. But if he has been as unsuccessful as I in assimilating the Hegelian re-editings of the Anselmian proof,[4] he will have to say that though Logic may determine what the system must be, if it is, something else than Logic must tell us that it is. Mr. Haldane in this case would probably consciously, or unconsciously, make an appeal to Fact: the disjunction is decided, since nobody can dispute that now, as a matter of fact, something, and not nothing, is. We must therefore, he would probably say, go on to admit the Whole System in the desiderated sense. Is not then the validity of the Anselmian proof the nucleus of the whole question between Logic and Fact? Ought not the efforts of Mr. Haldane and his friends to be principally devoted to its elucidation? Is it not the real door of separation between Empiricism and Rationalism? And if the Rationalists leave that door for a moment off its hinges, can any power keep that abstract, opaque, unmediated, external, irrational, and irresponsible monster, known to the vulgar as bare Fact, from getting in and contaminating the whole sanctuary with his presence? Can anything prevent Faust from changing "Am Anfang war das Wort " into "Am Anfang war die That? "

Nothing in earth or heaven. Only the Anselmian proof can keep Fact out of philosophy. The question, "Shall Fact be recognized as an ultimate principle? " is the whole issue between the Rationalists and the Empiricism of vulgar thought.

Of course, if so recognized, Fact sets a limit to the " through-and-through " character of the world's rationality. That rationality might then mediate between all the members of our conception of the world, but not between the conception itself and reality. Reality would have to be given, not by Reason, but by Fact. Fact holds out blankly, brutally and blindly, against that universal deliquescence of everything into logical relations which the Absolutist Logic demands, and it is the only thing that does hold out. Hence the ire of the Absolutist Logic —hence its non-recognition, its 'cutting' of Fact.

The reasons it gives for the 'cutting' are that Fact is speechless, a mere word for the negation of thought, a vacuous unknowability, a dog-in-the-manger, in truth, which having no rights of its own, can find nothing else to do than to keep its betters out of theirs.

There are two points involved here: first the claim that certain things have rights that are absolute, ubiquitous and all pervasive, and in regard to which nothing else can possibly exist in its own right; and second that anything that denies this assertion is pure negativity with no positive context whatsoever.

Take the latter point first. Is it true that what is negative in one way is thereby convicted of incapacity to be positive in any other way? The word " Fact " is like the word " Accident," like the word "Absolute" itself. They all have their negative connotation. In truth, their whole connotation is negative and relative. All it says is that, whatever the thing may be that is denoted by the words, other things do not control it. Where fact, where accident is, they must be silent, it alone can speak. But that does not prevent its speaking as loudly as you please, in its own tongue. It may have an inward life, self-transparent and active in the maximum degree. An indeterminate future volition on my part, for example, would be a strict accident as far as my present self is concerned. But that could not prevent it, in the moment in which it occurred, from being possibly the most intensely living and luminous experience I ever had. Its quality of being a brute fact ab extra says nothing whatever as to its inwardness. It simply says to outsiders: 'Hands off!'

And this brings us back to the first point of the Absolutist indictment of Fact. Is that point really anything more than a fantastic dislike to letting anything say 'Hands off '? What else explains the contempt the Absolutist authors exhibit for a freedom defined simply on its " negative " side, as freedom "from," etc.? What else prompts them to deride such freedom? But, dislike for dislike, who shall decide? Why is not their dislike at having me "from" them, entirely on a par with mine at having them "through" me?

I know very well that in talking of dislikes to those who never mention them, I am doing a very coarse thing, and making a sort of intellectual Orson of myself. But, for the life of me, I can not help it, because I feel sure that likes and dislikes must be among the ultimate factors of their philosophy as well as of mine. Would they but admit it! How sweetly we then could hold converse together! There is something finite about us both, as we now stand. We do not know the Absolute Whole yet. Part of it is still negative to us. Among the whats of it Still stalks a mob of opaque thats, without which we cannot think. But just as I admit that this is all possibly provisional that even the Anselmian proof may come out all right, and creation may be a rational system through-and-through, why might they not also admit that it may all be otherwise, and that the shadow, the opacity, the negativity, the "from "—ness, the plurality that is ultimate, may never be wholly driven from the scene. We should both then be avowedly making hypotheses, playing with Ideals. Ah! Why is the notion of hypothesis so abhorrent to the Hegelian mind?

And once down on our common level of hypothesis, we might then admit scepticism, since the Whole is not yet revealed, to be the soundest logical position. But since we are in the main not sceptics, we might go on and frankly confess to each other the motives for our several faiths. I frankly confess mine — I can not but think that at bottom they are. of an aesthetic and not of a logical sort. The "through-and-through" universe seems to suffocate me with its infallible impeccable allpervasiveness. Its necessity, with no possibilities; its relations, with no subjects, make me feel as if I had entered into a contract with no reserved rights, or rather as if I had to live in a large seaside boarding-house with no private bed-room in which I might take refuge from the society of the place. I am distinctly aware, moreover, that the old quarrel of sinner and pharisee has something to do with the matter. Certainly, to my personal knowledge, all Hegelians are not prigs, but I somehow feel as if all prigs ought to end, if developed, by becoming Hegelians. There is a story of two clergymen asked by mistake to conduct the same funeral. One came first and had got no farther than "I am the Resurrection and the Life," when the other entered. "I am the Resurrection and the Life," cried the latter. The "through-and-through" philosophy, as it actually exists, reminds many of us of that clergyman. It seems too buttoned-up and white-chokered and clean-shaven a thing to speak for the vast slow-breathing unconscious Kosmos with its dread abysses and its unknown tides. The "freedom" we want to see there is not the freedom, with a string tied to its leg and warranted not to fly away, of that philosophy. "Let it fly away," we say, "from us I What then?"

Again, I know I am exhibiting my mental grossness. But again, Ich kann nicht anders. I show my feelings; why will they not show theirs? I know they have a personal feeling about the through-and-through universe, which is entirely different from mine, and which I should very likely be much the better for gaining if they would only show me how. Their persistence in telling me that feeling has nothing to do with the question, that it is a pure matter of absolute reason, keeps me for ever out of the pale. Still seeing a that in things which Logic does not expel, the most I can do is to aspire to the expulsion. At present I do not even aspire. Aspiration is a feeling. What can kindle feeling but the example of feeling? And if the Hegelians will refuse to set an example, what can they expect the rest of us to do? To speak more seriously, the one fundamental quarrel Empiricism has with Absolutism is over this repudiation by Absolutism of the personal and aesthetic factor in the construction of philosophy. That we all of us have feelings, Empiricism feels quite sure. That they may be as prophetic and anticipatory of truth as anything else we have, and some of them more so than others, can not possibly be denied. But what hope is there of squaring and settling opinions unless Absolutism will hold parley on this common ground; and will admit that all philosophies are hypotheses, to which all our faculties, emotional as well as logical, help us, and the truest of which will at the final integration of things be found in possession of the men whose faculties on the whole had the best divining power?

Endnotes
1. [Reprinted from Mind, vol. IX, No. 34, April, 1884.]
2. [In 1884.]
3. ["Life and Mechanism," Mind, vol. IX, 1884.]
4. [Cf. P. Janet and G. Raffles: History of the Problem of Philosophy, trans. by Monahan, vol. II, pp. 275-278; 305-307. ED.]

The Meaning of Truth

TABLE OF CONTENTS

PREFACE

The pivotal part of my book named Pragmatism is its account of the relation called 'truth' which may obtain between an idea (opinion, belief, statement, or what not) and its object. 'Truth,' I there say, 'is a property of certain Of our ideas. It means their agreement, as falsity means their disagreement, with reality. Pragmatists and intellectualists both accept this definition as a matter of course.

'Where our ideas [do] not copy definitely their object, what does agreement with that object mean? . . . Pragmatism asks its usual question. " Grant an idea or belief to be true," it says, "what concrete difference will its being true make in any one's actual life? What experiences [may] be different from those which would obtain if the belief were false? How will the truth be realized? What, in short, is the truth's cash-value in experiential terms?" The moment pragmatism asks this question, it sees the answer: True ideas are those that we can assimilate, validate, corroborate, and verify. False ideas are those that we cannot.— That is the practical difference it makes to us to have true ideas; that therefore is the meaning of truth, for it is all that truth is known as.

'The truth of an idea is not a stagnant property inherent in it. Truth happens to an idea. It becomes true, is made true by events. Its verity is in fact an event,, a process, the process namely of its verifying itself, its verification. Its validity is the process of its validation.[1]

'To agree in the widest sense with a reality can only mean to be guided either straight up to it or into its surroundings, or to be put into such working touch with it as to handle either it or something connected with it better than if we disagreed. Better either intellectually or practically. . . . Any idea that helps us to deal, whether practically or intellectually, with either the reality or its belongings, that does net entangle our progress in frustrations, that fits, in fact, and adapts our life to the realitys whole setting, will agree sufficiently to meet the requirement. It will be true of that reality.

'The true, to put it very briefly, is only the expedient in the way of our thinking, just as the right is only the expedient in the way of our behaving. Expedient in almost any fashion, and expedient in the long run and on the whole, of course; for what meets expediently all the experience in sight won't necessarily meet all farther experiences equally satisfactorily. Experience, as we know, has ways of boiling over, and making us correct our present formulas.'

This account of truth, following upon the similar ones given by Messrs. Dewey and Schiller, has occasioned the liveliest discussion. Few critics have defended it, most of them have scouted it. It seems evident that the subject is a hard one to understand, under its apparent simplicity; and evident also, I think, that the definitive settlement of it will mark a turning point in the history of epistemology, and consequently in that of general philosophy. In order to make my own thought more accessible to those who hereafter may have to study the question, I have collected in the volume that follows all the work of my pen that bears directly on the truth-question. My first statement was in 1884, in the article that begins the present volume. The other papers follow in the order of their publication. Two or three appear now for the first time.

One of the accusations which I oftenest have had to meet is that of making the truth of our religious beliefs consist in their 'feeling good' to us, and in nothing else. I regret to have given some excuse for this charge, by the unguarded language in which, in the book Pragmatism, I spoke of the truth of the belief of certain philosophers in the absolute. Explaining why I do not believe in the absolute myself, yet finding that it may secure 'moral holidays' to those who need them, and is true in so far forth (if to gain moral holidays be a good),[2] I offered this as a conciliatory olive-branch to my enemies. But they, as is only too common with such offerings, trampled the gift under foot and turned and rent the giver. I had counted too much on their good will — oh for the rarity of christian charity under the sun! Oh for the rarity of ordinary secular intelligence also! I had supposed it to be matter of common observation that, of two competing views of the universe which in all other respects are equal, but of which the first denies some vital human need while the second satisfies it, the second will be favored by sane men for the simple reason that it makes the world seem more rational. To choose the first view under such circumstances would be an ascetic act, an act of philosophic self-denial of which no normal human being would be guilty. Using the pragmatic test of the meaning of concepts, I bad shown the concept of the absolute to mean nothing but the holiday giver, the banisher of cosmic fear. One's objective deliverance, when one says 'the absolute exists,' amounted, on my showing, just to this, that 'some justification of a feeling of security in presence of the universe,' exists, and that systematically to refuse to cultivate a feeling of security would be to do violence to a tendency in one's emotional life which might well be respected as prophetic.

Apparently my absolutist critics fail to see the workings of their own minds in any such picture, so all that I can do is to apologize, and take my offering back. The absolute is true in no way then, and least of all, by the verdict of the critics, in the way which I assigned!

My treatment of 'God," freedom,' and 'design' was similar. Reducing, by the pragmatic test, the meaning of each of these concepts to its positive experienceable operation, I showed them all to mean the same thing, viz., the presence of 'Promise' in the world. 'God or no God?' means 'promise or no promise? It seems to me that the alternative is objective enough, being a question as to whether the cosmos has one character or another, even though our own provisional answer be made on subjective grounds. Nevertheless christian and non-christian critics alike accuse me of summoning people to say 'God exists,' even when he does n't exist, because forsooth in my philosophy the 'truth' of the saying does n't really mean that he exists in any shape whatever, but only that to say so feels good.

Most of the pragmatist and anti-pragmatist warfare is over what the word 'truth' shall be held to signify, and not over any of the facts embodied in truth-situations; for both pragmatists and anti-pragmatists believe in existent objects, just as they believe in our ideas of them. The difference is that when the pragmatists speak of truth, they mean exclusively something about the ideas, namely their workableness; whereas when anti-pragmatists speak of truth they seem most often to mean something about the objects. Since the pragmatist, if he agrees that an idea is 'really' true, also agrees to whatever it says about its object; and since most anti-pragmatists have already come round to agreeing that, if the object exists, the 'idea that it does so 'is workable; there would seem so little left to fight about that I might well be asked why instead of reprinting my share in so much verbal wrangling, I do not show my sense of 'values' by burning it all up.

I understand the question and I will give my answer. I am interested in another doctrine in philosophy to which I give the name of radical empiricism, and it seems to me that the establishment of the pragmatist theory of truth is a step of first-rate importance in making radical empiricism prevail. Radical empiricism consists first of a postulate, next of a statement of fact, and finally of a generalized conclusion.

The postulate is that the only things that shall be debatable among philosophers shall be things definable in terms drawn from experience. [Things of an unexperienceable nature may exist ad libitum, but they form no part of the material for philosophic debate.]

The statement of fact is that the relations between things, conjunctive as well as disjunctive, are just as much matters of direct particular experience, neither more so nor less so, than the things themselves.

The generalized conclusion is that therefore the parts of experience hold together from next to next by relations that are themselves parts of experience. The directly apprehended universe needs, in short, no extraneous trans-empirical connective support, but possesses in its own right a concatenated or continuous structure.

The great obstacle to radical empiricism in the contemporary mind is the rooted rationalist belief that experience as immediately given is all disjunction and no conjunction, and that to make one world out of this separateness, a higher unifying agency must be there. In the prevalent idealism this agency is represented as the absolute all—witness which 'relates' things together by throwing categories' over them like a net. The most peculiar and unique, perhaps, of all these categories is supposed to be the truth-relation, which connects parts of reality in pairs, making of one of them a knower, and of the other a thing known, yet which is itself contentless experientially, neither describable, explicable, nor reduceable to lower terms, and denotable only by uttering the name 'truth.'

The pragmatist view, on the contrary, of the truth-relation is that it has a definite content, and that everything in it is experienceable. Its whole nature can be told in positive terms. The 'workableness' which ideas must have, in order. to be true, means particular workings, physical or intellectual, actual or possible, which they may set up from next to next inside of concrete experience. Were this pragmatic contention admitted, one great point in the victory of radical empiricism would also be scored, for the relation between an object and the idea that truly knows it, is held by rationalists to be nothing of this describable sort., but to stand outside of all possible temporal experience; and on the relation., so interpreted, rationalism is wonted to make its last most obdurate rally.

Now the anti-pragmatist contentions which I try to meet in this volume can be so easily used by rationalists as weapons of resistance, not only to pragmatism but to radical empiricism also (for if the truth-relation were transcendent, others might be so too), that I feel strongly the strategical importance of having them definitely met and got out of the way. What our critics most persistently keep saying is that though workings go with truth, yet they do not constitute it. It is numerically additional to them, prior to them, explanatory of them, and in no wise to be explained by them, we are incessantly told. The first point for our enemies to establish, therefore, is that something numerically additional and prior to the workings is involved in the truth of an idea. Since the object is additional, and usually prior, most rationalists plead it, and boldly accuse us of denying it. This leaves on the bystanders the impression — since we cannot reasonably deny the existence of the object — that our account of truth breaks down, and that our critics have driven us from the field. Altho in various places in this volume I try to refute the slanderous charge that we deny real existence, I will say here again, for the sake of emphasis, that the existence of the object, whenever the idea asserts it ' truly,' is the only reason, in innumerable cases, why the idea does work successfully, if it work at all; and that it seems an abuse of language, to say the least, to transfer the word 'truth—' from the idea to the object's existence, when the falsehood of ideas that won't work is explained by that existence as well as the truth of those that will.

I find this abuse prevailing among my most accomplished adversaries. But once establish the proper verbal custom, let the word ' truth' represent a property of the idea, cease to make it something mysteriously connected with the object known, and the path opens fair and wide, as I believe, to the discussion of radical empiricism on its merits. The truth of an idea will then mean only its workings, or that in it which by ordinary psychological laws sets up those workings; it will mean neither the idea's object, nor anything 'saltatory' inside the idea, that terms drawn from experience cannot describe.

One word more, ere I end this preface. A distinction is sometimes made between Dewey, Schiller and myself, as if I, in supposing the object's existence, made a concession to popular prejudice which they, as more radical pragmatists, refuse-to make. As I myself under. stand these authors, we all three absolutely agree in admitting the transcendency of the object (provided it be an experienceable object) to the subject, in the truth-relation. Dewey in particular has insisted almost ad nauseam that the whole meaning of our cognitive states and processes lies in the way they intervene in the control and revaluation of independent existences or facts. His account of knowledge is not only absurd, but meaningless, unless independent existences be there of which our ideas take account, and for the transformation of which they work. But because he and Schiller refuse to discuss objects and relations 'transcendent' in the sense of being altogether trans-experiential, their critics pounce on sentences in their writings to that effect to show that they deny the existence within the realm of experience of objects external to the ideas that declare their presence there.[3] It seems incredible that educated and apparently sincere critics should so fail to catch their adversary's point of view.

What misleads so many of them is possibly also the fact that the universes of discourse of Schiller, Dewey, and myself are panoramas of different extent, and that what the one postulates explicitly the other provisionally leaves only in a state of implication, while the reader thereupon considers it to be denied. Schiller's universe is the smallest, being essentially a psychological one. He starts with but one sort of thing, truth-claims, but is led ultimately to the independent objective facts which they assert, inasmuch as the most successfully validated of all claims is that such facts are there. MY universe is more essentially epistemological. I start with two things, the objective facts and the claims, and indicate which claims, the facts being there, will work successfully as the latter's substitutes and which will not. I call the former claims true. Dewey's panorama, if I understand this colleague, is the widest of the three, but I refrain from giving my own account of its complexity. Suffice it that he holds as firmly as I do to objects independent of our judgments. If I am wrong in saying this, he must correct me. I decline in this matter to be corrected at second hand.

I have not pretended in the following pages to consider all the critics of my account of truth, such as Messrs. Taylor, Lovejoy, Gardiner, Bakewell, Creighton, Hibben, Parodi, Salter, Carus, Lalande, Mentré, McTaggart, G. E. Moore, Ladd and others, especially not Professor Schinz, who has published under the title of Anti-pragmatisme an amusing sociological romance. Some of these critics seem to me to labor under an inability almost pathetic, to understand the thesis which they seek to refute. I imagine that most of their difficulties have been answered by anticipation elsewhere in this volume, and I am sure that my readers will thank me for not adding more repetition to the fearful amount that is already there.

95 Irving ST.
Cambridge (Mass.),
August, 1909.

Endnotes

1. But 'verifability,' I add, ' is as good as verification. For one truth-process completed, there are a million in our lives that function in [the] state of nascency. They lead us towards direct verification; lead us into the surroundings of the object they envisage; and then, if everything runs on harmoniously, we are so sure that verification is possible that we omit it, and are usually justified by all that happens.'

2. Op. cit.

3. It gives me pleasure to welcome Professor Carveth Read into the pragmatistic church, so far as his epistemology goes. See his vigorous book, The Metaphysics of Nature, 2d Edition, Appendix A. (London, Black, 1908.) The work What is Reality? by Francis Howe Johnson (Boston, 1891), of which I make the acquaintance only while correcting these proofs, contains some striking anticipations of the later pragmatist view. The Psychology of Thinking, by Irving E. Miller (New York, Macmillan Co., 1909), which has just

appeared, is one of the most convincing pragmatist documents yet published, tho it does not use the word 'pragmatism' at all. While I am making references, I cannot refrain from inserting one to the extraordinarily acute article by H. V. Knox, in the Quarterly Review for April, 1909.

THE FUNCTION OF COGNITION[1]

The following inquiry is (to use a distinction familiar to readers of Mr. Shadworth Hodgson) not an inquiry into the 'how it comes,' but into the 'what it is' of cognition. What we call acts of cognition are evidently realized through what we call brains and their events, whether there be 'souls' dynamically connected with the brains or not. But with neither brains nor souls has this essay any business to transact. In it we shall simply assume that cognition is produced, somehow, and limit ourselves to asking what elements it contains, what factors it implies.

Cognition is a function of consciousness. The first factor it implies is therefore a state of consciousness wherein the cognition shall take place. Having elsewhere used the word 'feeling' to designate generically all states of consciousness considered subjectively, or without respect to their possible function, I shall then say that, whatever elements an act of cognition may imply besides, it at least implies the existence of a feeling. [If the reader share the current antipathy to the word 'feeling,' he may substitute for it, wherever I use it, the word 'idea,' taken in the old broad Lockian sense, or he may use the clumsy phrase 'state of consciousness,' or finally he may say 'thought' instead.]

Now it is to be observed that the common consent of mankind has agreed that some feelings are cognitive and some are simple facts having a subjective, or, what one might almost call a physical, existence, but no such self-transcendent function as would be implied in their being pieces of knowledge. Our task is again limited here. We are not to ask, 'How is self-transcendence possible?' We are only to ask, 'How comes it that common sense has assigned a number of cases in which 'it is assumed not only to be possible but actual? And what are the marks used by common sense to distinguish those cases from the rest?' In short, our inquiry is a chapter in descriptive psychology, — hardly anything more.

Condillac embarked on a quest similar to this by his famous hypothesis of a statue to which various feelings were successively imparted. Its first feeling was supposed to be one of fragrance. But to avoid all possible complication with the question of genesis, let us not attribute even to a statue the possession of our imaginary feeling. Let us rather suppose it attached to no matter, nor localized at any point in space, but left swinging in vacuo, as it were, by the direct creative fiat of a god. And let us also, to escape entanglement with difficulties about the physical or psychical nature of its 'object,' not call it a feeling of fragrance or of any other determinate sort, but limit ourselves to assuming that it is a feeling of q. What is true of it under this abstract name will be no less true of it in any more particular shape (such as fragrance, pain, hardness) which the reader may suppose.

Now, if this feeling of q be the only creation of the god, it will of course form the entire universe. And if, to escape the cavils of that large class of persons who believe that semper idem sentire ac non sentire are the same,[2] we allow the feeling to be of as short a duration as they like, that universe will only need to last an infinitesimal part of a second. The feeling in question will thus be reduced to its fighting weight, and all that befalls it in the way of a cognitive function must be held to befall in the brief instant of its quickly snuffed-out life, — a life, it will also be noticed, that has no other moment of consciousness either preceding or following it.

Well now, can our little feeling, thus left alone in the universe, — for the god and we psychological critics may be supposed left out of the account, — can the feeling, I say, be said to have any sort of a cognitive function? For it to know, there must be something to be known. What is there, on the present supposition? One may reply, 'the feeling's content q.' But does it not seem more proper to call this the feeling's quality than its content? Does not the word 'content' suggest that the feeling has already diremepted itself as an act from its content as an object? And would it be quite safe to assume so promptly that the quality q of a feeling is one and the same thing with a feeling of the quality q? The quality q, so far, is an entirely subjective fact which the feeling carries so to speak endogenously, or in its pocket. If any one pleases to dignify so simple a fact as this by the name of knowledge, of course nothing can prevent him. But let us keep closer to the path of common usage, and reserve the name knowledge for the cognition of 'realities,' meaning by realities things that exist independently of the feeling through which their cognition occurs. If the content of the feeling occur nowhere in the universe outside of the feeling itself, and perish with the feeling, common usage refuses to call it a reality, and brands it as a subjective feature of the feeling's constitution, or at the most as the feeling's dream.

For the feeling to be cognitive in the specific sense, then, it must be self-transcendent; and we must prevail upon the god to create a reality outside of it to correspond to its intrinsic quality q. Thus only can it be redeemed from the condition of being a solipsism. If now the new-created reality resemble the feeling's quality q, I say that the feeling may be held by us to be cognizant of that reality.

This first instalment of my thesis is sure to be attacked. But one word before defending it. 'Reality' has become our warrant for calling a feeling cognitive; but what becomes our warrant for calling anything reality? The only reply is — the faith of the present critic or inquirer. At every moment of his life he finds himself subject to a belief in some realities, even though his realities of this year should prove to be his illusions of the next. Whenever he finds that the feeling he is studying contemplates what he himself regards as a reality, he must of course admit the feeling itself to be truly cognitive. We are ourselves the critics here; and we shall find our burden much lightened by being allowed to take reality in this relative and provisional way. Every science must make some assumptions. Erkenntnisstheoretiker are but fallible mortals. When they study the function of, cognition, they do it by means of the same function in themselves. And knowing that the fountain cannot go higher than its source, we should promptly confess that our results in this field are affected by our own liability to err. The most we can claim is, that what we say about cognition may be counted as true as what we say about anything else. If our hearers agree with us about what are to be held 'realities,' they will perhaps also agree to the reality of our doctrine of the way in which they are known. We cannot ask for more.

Our terminology shall follow the spirit of these remarks. We will deny the function of knowledge to any feeling whose quality or content we do not ourselves believe to exist outside of that feeling as well as in it. We may call such a feeling a dream if we like; we shall have to see later whether we can call it a fiction or an error.

To revert now to our thesis. Some persons will immediately cry out, 'How can a reality resemble a feeling?' Here we find how wise we were to name the quality of the feeling by an algebraic letter q. We flank the whole difficulty of resemblance between an inner state and an outward reality, by leaving it free to any one to postulate as the reality whatever sort of thing he thinks can resemble a feeling, — if not an outward thing, then another feeling like the first one, — the mere feeling q in the critic's mind for example. Evading thus this objection, we turn to another which is sure to be urged.

It will come from those philosophers to whom 'thought,' in the sense of a knowledge of relations, is the all in all of mental life; and who hold a merely feeling consciousness to be no better — one would sometimes say from their utterances, a good deal worse — than no consciousness at all. Such phrases as these, for example, are common today in the mouths of those who claim to walk in the footprints of Kant and Hegel rather than in the ancestral English paths: 'A perception detached from all others, " left out of the heap we call a mind," being out of all relation, has no qualities — is simply nothing. We can no more consider it than we can see vacancy.' 'It is simply in itself fleeting, momentary, unnameable (because while we name it it has become another), and for the very same reason unknowable, the very negation of knowability.' 'Exclude from what we have considered real all qualities constituted by relation, we find that none are left.'

Altho such citations as these from the writings of Professor Green might be multiplied almost indefinitely, they would hardly repay the pains of collection, so egregiously false is the doctrine they teach. Our little supposed feeling, whatever it may be, from the cognitive point of view, whether a bit of knowledge or a dream, is certainly no psychical zero. It is a most positively and definitely qualified inner fact, with a complexion all its own. Of course there are many mental facts which it is not. It knows q, if q be a reality, with a very minimum of knowledge. It neither dates nor locates it. It neither classes nor names it. And it neither knows itself as a feeling, nor contrasts itself with other feelings, nor estimates its own duration or intensity. It is, in short, if there is no more of it than this, a most dumb and helpless and useless kind of thing.

But if we must describe it by so many negations, and if it can say nothing about itself or about anything else, by what right do we deny that it is a psychical zero? And may not the relationists' be right after all?

In the innocent looking word ' about' lies the solution of this riddle; and a simple enough solution it is when frankly looked at. A quotation from a too seldom quoted book, the Exploratio Philosophica of John Grote (London, 1865), p. 60, will form the best introduction to it.

'Our knowledge,' writes Grote, 'may be contemplated in either of two ways, or, to use other words, we may speak in a double manner of the " object" of knowledge. That is, we may either use language thus: we know a thing, a man, etc.; or we may use it thus: we know such and such things about the thing, the man, etc. Language in general, following its true logical instinct, distinguishes between these two applications of the notion of knowledge, the one being gnwnai, noscere, kennen, connaître, the other being eidenai, scrie, wissen, savoir. In the origin, the former may be considered more what I have called phenomenal — it is the notion of knowledge as acquaintance or familiarity with what is known; which notion is perhaps more akin to the phenomenal bodily communication, and is less purely intellectual than the other; it is the kind of knowledge which we have of a thing by the presentation to the senses or the representation of it in picture or type, a Vorstellung. The other, which is what we express in judgments or propositions, what is embodied in Begriffe or concepts without any necessary imaginative representation, is in its origin the more intellectual notion of knowledge. There is no reason, however, why we should not express our knowledge, whatever its kind, in either manner, provided only we do not confusedly express it, in the same proposition or piece of reasoning, in both.'

Now obviously if our supposed feeling of q is (if knowledge at all) only knowledge of the mere acquaintance-type, it is milking a he-goat, as the ancients would have said, to try to extract from it any deliverance about anything under the sun, even about itself. And it is as unjust, after our failure, to turn upon it and call it a psychical nothing, as it would be, after our fruitless attack upon the billy-goat, to proclaim the non-lactiferous character of the whole goat-tribe. But the entire industry of the Hegelian school in trying to shove simple sensation out of the pale of philosophic recognition is founded on this false issue. It is always the 'speechlessness' of sensation, its inability to make any 'statement,'[3] that is held to make the very notion of it meaningless, and to justify the student of knowledge in scouting it out of existence. 'Significance,' in the sense of standing as the sign of other mental states, is taken to be the sole function of what mental states we have; and from the perception that our little primitive sensation has as yet no significance in this literal sense, it is an easy step to call it first meaningless, next senseless, then vacuous, and finally to brand it as absurd and inadmissible. But in this universal liquidation, this everlasting slip, slip, slip, of direct acquaintance into knowledge-about, until at last nothing is left about which the knowledge can be supposed to obtain, does not all 'significance' depart from the situation? And when our knowledge about things has reached its never so complicated perfection, must there not needs abide alongside of it and inextricably mixed in with it some acquaintance with what things all this knowledge is about?

Now, our supposed little feeling gives a what; and if other feelings should succeed which remember the first, its what may stand as subject or predicate of some piece of knowledge-about, of some judgment, perceiving relations between it and other whats which the other feelings may know. The hitherto dumb q will then receive a name and be no longer speechless. But every name, as students of logic know, has its 'denotation'; and the denotation always means some reality or content, relationless ab extra or with its internal relations unanalyzed, like the q which our primitive sensation is supposed to know. No relation-expressing proposition is possible except on the basis of a preliminary acquaintance with such 'facts,' with such contents, as this. Let the q be fragrance, let it be toothache, or let it be a more complex kind of feeling, like that of the full-moon swimming in her blue abyss, it must first come in that simple shape, and be held fast in that first intention, before any knowledge about it can be attained. The knowledge about it is it with a context added. Undo it, and what is added cannot be context.[4]

Let us say no more then about this objection, but enlarge our thesis, thus: If there be in the universe a q other than the q in the feeling, the latter may have acquaintance with an entity ejective to itself; an acquaintance moreover, which, as mere acquaintance, it would be hard to imagine susceptible either of improvement or increase, being in its way complete; and which would oblige us (so long as we refuse not to call acquaintance knowledge) to say not only that the feeling is cognitive, but that all qualities of feeling, so long as there is anything outside of them which they resemble, are feelings of qualities of existence, and perceptions of outward fact.

The point of this vindication of the cognitive function of the first feeling lies, it will be noticed, in the discovery that q does exist elsewhere than in it. In case this discovery were not made, we could not be sure the feeling was cognitive; and in case there were nothing outside to be discovered, we should have to call the feeling a dream. But the feeling itself cannot make the discovery. Its own q is the only q it grasps; and its own nature is not a particle altered by having the self-transcendent function of cognition either added to it or taken away. The function is accidental; synthetic, not analytic; and falls outside and not inside its being.[5]

A feeling feels as a gun shoots. If there be nothing to be felt or hit, they discharge themselves ins blaue hinein. If, however, something starts up opposite them, they no longer simply shoot or feel, they hit and know.

But with this arises a worse objection than any yet made. We the critics look on and see a real q and a feeling of q; and because the two resemble each other, we say the one knows the other. But what right have we to say this until we know that the feeling of q means to stand for or represent just that same other q? Suppose, instead of one q, a number of real q's in the field. If the gun shoots and hits, we can easily see which one of them it hits. But how can we distinguish which one the feeling knows? It knows the one it stands for. But which one does it stand for? It declares no intention in this respect. It merely resembles; it resembles all indifferently; and resembling, per se, is not necessarily representing or standing for at all. Eggs resemble each other, but do not on that account represent, stand for, or know each other. And if you say this is because neither of them is a feeling, then imagine the world to consist of nothing but toothaches, which are feelings, feelings resembling each other exactly, — would they know each other the better for all that?

The case of q being a bare quality like that of toothache-pain is quite different from that of its being a concrete individual thing. There is practically no test for deciding whether the feeling of a bare quality means to represent it or not. It can do nothing to the quality beyond resembling it, simply because an abstract quality is a thing to which nothing can be done. Being without context or environment or principium individuationis, a quiddity with no haecceity, a platonic idea, even duplicate editions of such a quality (were they possible), would be indiscernible, and no sign could be given, no result altered, whether the feeling meant to stand for this edition or for that, or whether it simply resembled the quality without meaning to stand for it at all.

If now we grant a genuine pluralism of editions to the quality q, by assigning to each a context which shall distinguish it from its mates, we may proceed to explain which edition of it the feeling knows, by extending our principle of resemblance to the context too, and saying the feeling knows the particular q whose context it most exactly duplicates. But here again the theoretic doubt recurs: duplication and coincidence, are they knowledge? The gun shows which q it points to and hits, by breaking it. Until the feeling can show us which q it points to and knows, by some equally flagrant token, why are we not free to deny that it either points to or knows any one of the real q 's at all, and to affirm that the word 'resemblance' exhaustively describes its relation to the reality?

Well. as a matter of fact, every actual feeling does show us, quite as flagrantly as the gun, which q it points to; and practically in concrete cases the matter is decided by an element we have hitherto left out. Let us pass from abstractions to possible instances, and ask our obliging deus ex machina to frame for us a richer world. Let him send me, for example, a dream of the death of a certain man, and let him simultaneously cause the man to die. How would our practical instinct spontaneously decide whether this were a case of cognition of the reality, or only a sort of marvellous coincidence of a resembling reality with my dream? Just such puzzling cases as this are what the 'society for psychical research' is busily collecting and trying to interpret in the most reasonable way.

If my dream were the only one of the kind I ever had in my life, if the context of the death in the dream differed in many particulars from the real death's context, and if my dream led me to no action about the death, unquestionably we should all call it a strange coincidence, and naught besides. But if the death in the dream had a long context, agreeing point for point with every feature that attended the real death; if I were constantly having such dreams, all equally perfect, and if on awaking I had a habit of acting immediately as if they were true and so getting 'the start' of my more tardily instructed neighbors,— we should in all probability have to admit that I had some mysterious kind of clairvoyant power, that my dreams in an inscrutable way meant just those realities they figured, and that the word ' coincidence' failed to touch the root of the matter. And whatever doubts any one preserved would completely vanish, if it should appear that from the midst of my dream I had the power of interfering with the course of the reality, and making the events in it turn this way or that, according as I dreamed they should. Then at least it would be certain that my waking critics and my dreaming self were dealing with the same.

And thus do men invariably decide such a question. The falling of the dream's practical consequences into the real world, and the extent of the resemblance between the two worlds are the criteria they instinctively use.[6] All feeling is for the sake of action, all feeling results in action, — today no argument is needed to prove these truths. But by a most singular disposition of nature which we may conceive to have been different, my feelings act upon the realities within my critic's world. Unless, then, my critic can prove that my feeling does not 'point to' those realities which it acts upon, how can he continue to doubt that he and I are alike cognizant of one and the same real world? If the action is performed in one world, that must be the world the feeling intends; if in another world, that is the world the feeling has in mind. If your feeling bear no fruits in my world, I call it utterly detached from my world; I call it a solipsism, and call its world a dream-world. If your toothache do not prompt you to act as if I had a toothache, nor even as if I had a separate existence; if you neither say to me, 'I know now how you must suffer!' nor tell me of a remedy, I deny that your feeling, however it may resemble mine, is really cognizant of mine. It gives no sign of being cognizant, and such a sign is absolutely necessary to my admission that it is.

Before I can think you to mean my world, you must affect my world; before I can think you to mean much of it, you must affect much of it; and before I can be sure you mean it as I do, you must affect it just as l should if I were in your place. Then I, your critic, will gladly believe that we are thinking, not only of the same reality, but that we are thinking it alike, and thinking of much of its extent.

Without the practical effects of our neighbor's feelings on our own world, we should never suspect the existence of our neighbor's feelings at all, and of course should never find ourselves playing the critic as we do in this article. The constitution of nature is very peculiar. In the world of each of us are certain objects called human bodies, which move about and act on all the other objects there, and the occasions of their action are in the main what the occasions of our action would be, were they our bodies. They use words and gestures, which, if we used them, would have thoughts behind them, — no mere thoughts überhaupt, however, but strictly determinate thoughts. I think you have the notion of fire in general, because I see you act towards this fire in my room just as I act towards it, poke it and present your person towards it, and so forth. But that binds me to believe that if you feel 'fire' at all, this is the fire you feel. As a matter of fact, whenever we constitute ourselves into psychological critics, it is not by dint of discovering which reality a feeling 'resembles' that we find out which reality it means. We become first aware of which one it means, and then we suppose that to be the one it resembles. We see each other looking at the same objects, pointing to them and turning them over in various ways, and thereupon we hope and trust that all of our several feelings resemble the reality and each other. But this is a thing of which we are never theoretically sure. Still, it would practically be a case of grübelsucht, if a ruffian were assaulting and drubbing my body, to spend much time in subtle speculation either as to whether his vision of my body resembled mine, or as to whether the body he really meant to insult were not some body in his mind's eye, altogether other from my own. The practical point of view brushes such metaphysical cobwebs away. If what he have in mind be not my body, why call we it a body at all? His mind is inferred by me as a term, to whose existence we trace the things that happen. The inference is quite void if the term, once inferred, be separated from its connection with the body that made me infer it, and connected with another that is not mine at all. No matter for the metaphysical puzzle of how our two minds, the ruffian's and mine, can mean the same body. Men who see each other's bodies sharing the same space, treading the same earth, splashing the same water, making the same air resonant, and pursuing the same game and eating out of the same dish, will never practically believe in a pluralism of solipsistic worlds.

Where, however, the actions of one mind seem to take no effect in the world of the other, the case is different. This is what happens in poetry and fiction. Every one knows Ivanhoe, for example; but so long as we stick to the story pure and simple without regard to the facts of its production, few would hesitate to admit that there are as many different Ivanhoes as there are different minds cognizant of the story.[7] The fact that all these Ivanhoes resemble each other does not prove the contrary. But if an alteration invented by one man in his version were to reverberate immediately through all the other versions, and produce changes therein, we should then easily agree that all these thinkers were thinking the same Ivanhoe, and that, fiction or no fiction, it formed a little world common to them all.

Having reached this point, we may take up our thesis and improve it again. Still calling the reality by the name of q and letting the critic's feeling vouch for it, we can say that any other feeling will be held cognizant of q, provided it both resemble q, and refer to q, as shown by its either modifying q directly, or modifying some other reality, p or r, which the critic knows to be continuous with q. Or more shortly, thus: The feeling of q knows whatever reality it resembles, and either directly or indirectly operates on. If it resemble without operating, it is a dream; if it operate without resembling, it is an error.[8]

It is to be feared that the reader may consider this formula rather insignificant and obvious, and hardly worth the labor of so many pages, especially when he considers that the only cases to which it applies are percepts, and that the whole field of symbolic or conceptual thinking seems to elude its grasp. Where the reality is either a material thing or act, or a state of the critic's consciousness, I may both mirror it in my mind and operate upon it — in the latter case indirectly, of course — as soon as I perceive it. But there are many cognitions, universally allowed to be such, which neither mirror nor operate on their realities.

In the whole field of symbolic thought we are universally held both to intend, to speak of, and to reach conclusions about — to know in short —particular realities, without having in our subjective consciousness any mind-stuff that resembles them even in a remote degree. We are instructed about them by language which awakens no consciousness beyond its sound; and we know which realities they are by the faintest and most fragmentary glimpse of some remote context they may have and by no direct imagination of themselves. As minds may differ here, let me speak in the first person. I am sure that my own current thinking has words for its almost exclusive subjective material, words which are made intelligible by being referred to some reality that lies beyond the horizon of direct consciousness, and of which I am only aware as of a terminal more existing in a certain direction, to which the words might lead but do not lead yet. The subject, or topic, of the words is usually something towards which I mentally seem to pitch them in a backward way, almost as I might jerk my thumb over my shoulder to point at something, without looking round, if I were only entirely sure that it was there. The upshot, or conclusion of the words is something towards which I seem to incline my head forwards, as if giving assent to its existence, tho all my mind's eye catches sight of may be some tatter of an image connected with it, which tatter, however, if only endued with the feeling of familiarity and reality, makes me feel that the whole to which it belongs is rational and real, and fit to be let pass.

Here then is cognitive consciousness on a large scale, and yet what it knows, it hardly resembles in the least degree. The formula last laid down for our thesis must therefore be made more complete. We may now express it thus: A percept knows whatever reality it directly or indirectly operates on and resembles; conceptual feeling, or thought knows[9] a reality, whenever it actually or potentially terminates in a percept that operates on, or resembles that reality, or is otherwise connected with it or with its context. The latter percept may be either sensation or sensorial idea; and when I say the thought must terminate in such a percept, I mean that it must ultimately be capable of leading up thereto, — by the way of practical experience, if the terminal feeling be a sensation; by the way of logical or habitual suggestion, if it be only an image in the mind.

Let an illustration make this plainer. I open the first book I take up, and read the first sentence that meets my eye: 'Newton saw the handiwork of God in the heavens as plainly as Paley in the animal kingdom.' I immediately look back and try to analyze the subjective state in which I rapidly apprehended this sentence as I read it. In the first place there was an obvious feeling that the sentence was intelligible and rational and related to the world of realities. There was also a sense of agreement or harmony between 'Newton,' 'Paley,' and 'God.' There was no apparent image connected with the words 'heavens,' or 'handiwork,' or 'God'; they were words merely. With 'animal kingdom' I think there was the faintest consciousness (it may possibly have been an image of the steps) of the Museum of Zoology in the town of Cambridge where I write. With 'Paley' there was an equally faint consciousness of a small dark leather book; and with 'Newton' a pretty distinct vision of the right-hand lower corner of a curling periwig. This is all the mind-stuff I can discover in my first consciousness of the meaning of this sentence, and I am afraid that even not all of this would have been present had I come upon the sentence in a genuine reading of the book, and not picked it out for an experiment. And yet my consciousness was truly cognitive. The sentence is 'about realities' which my psychological critic —for we must not forget him — acknowledges to be such even as he acknowledges my distinct feeling that they are realities, and my acquiescence in the general rightness of what I read of them, to be true knowledge on my part.

Now what justifies my critic in being as lenient as this? This singularly inadequate consciousness of mine, made up of symbols that neither resemble nor affect the realities they stand for, —how can he be sure it is cognizant of the very realities he, has himself in mind?

He is sure because in countless like cases he has seen such inadequate and symbolic thoughts, by developing themselves, terminate in percepts that practically modified and presumably resembled his own. By 'developing' themselves is meant obeying their tendencies, following up the suggestions nascently present in them, working in the direction in which they seem to point, clearing up the penumbra, making distinct the halo, unravelling the fringe, which is part of their composition, and in the midst of which their more substantive kernel of subjective content seems consciously to lie. Thus I may develop my thought in the Paley direction by procuring the brown leather volume and bringing the passages about the animal kingdom before the critic's eyes. I may satisfy him that the words mean for me just what they mean for him, by showing him in concreto the very animals and their arrangements, of which the pages treat. I may get Newton's works and portraits; or if I follow the line of suggestion of the wig, I may smother my critic in seventeenth-century matters pertaining to Newton's environment, to show that the word ' Newton' has the same locus and relations in both our minds. Finally I may, by act and word, persuade him that what I mean by God and the heavens and the analogy of the handiworks, is just what he means also.

My demonstration in the last resort is to his senses. My thought makes me act on his senses much as he might himself act on them, were he pursuing the consequences of a perception of his own. Practically then my thought terminates in his realities. He willingly supposes it, therefore, to be of them, and inwardly to resemble what his own thought would be, were it of the same symbolic sort as mine. And the pivot and fulcrum and support of his mental persuasion, is the sensible operation which my thought leads me, or may lead, to effect — the bringing of Paley's book, of Newton's portrait, etc., before his very eyes —

In the last analysis, then, we believe that we all know and think about and talk about the same world, because we believe our PERCEPTS are possessed by us in common. And we believe this because the percepts of each one of us seem to be changed in consequence of changes in the percepts of some one else. What I am for you is in the first instance a percept of your own. Unexpectedly, however, I open and show you a book, uttering certain sounds the while. These acts are also your percepts, but they so resemble acts of yours with feelings prompting them, that you cannot doubt I have the feelings too, or that the book is one book felt in both our worlds. That it is felt in the same way, that my feelings of it resemble yours, is something of which we never can be sure, but which we assume as the simplest hypothesis that meets the case. As a matter of fact, we never are sure of it, and, as erkenntnisstheoretiker, we can only say that of feelings that should not resemble each other, both could not know the same thing at the same time in the same way.[10] If each holds to its own percept as the reality, it is bound to say of the other percept, that, though it may intend that reality, and prove this by working change upon it, yet, if it do not resemble it, it is all false and wrong.[11]

If this be so of percepts, how much more so of higher modes of thought! Even in the sphere of sensation individuals are probably different enough. Comparative study of the simplest conceptual elements seems to show a wider divergence still. And when it comes to general theories and emotional attitudes towards life, it is indeed time to say with Thackeray, 'My friend, two different universes walk about under your hat and under mine.'

What can save us at all and prevent us from flying asunder into a chaos of mutually repellent solipsisms? Through what can our several minds commune? Through nothing but the mutual resemblance of those of our perceptual feelings which have this power of modifying one another, which are mere dumb knowledges-of-acquaintance, and which must also resemble their realities or not know them aright at all. In such pieces of knowledge-of-acquaintance all our knowledge-about must end, and carry a sense of this possible termination as part of its content. These percepts, these termini, these sensible things, these mere matters-of-acquaintance, are the only realities we ever directly know, and the whole history of our thought is the history of our substitution of one of them for another, and the reduction of the substitute to the status of a conceptual sign. Contemned though they be by some thinkers, these sensations are the motherearth, the anchorage, the stable rock, the first and last limits, the terminus a quo and the terminus ad quem of the mind. To find such sensational termini should be our aim with all our higher thought. They end discussion; they destroy the false conceit of knowledge; and without them we are all at sea with each other's meaning. If two men act alike on a percept, they believe themselves to feel alike about it; if not, they may suspect they know it in differing ways. We can never be sure we understand each other till we are able to bring the matter to this test.' This is why metaphysical discussions are so much like fighting with the air; they have no practical issue of a sensational kind. 'Scientific' theories, on the other hand, always terminate in definite percepts. You can deduce a possible sensation from your theory and, taking me into your laboratory, prove that your theory is true of my world by giving me the sensation then and there. Beautiful is the flight of conceptual reason through the upper air of truth. No wonder philosophers are dazzled by it still, and no wonder they look with some disdain at the low earth of feeling from which the goddess launched herself aloft. But woe to her if she return not home to its acquaintance; Nirgends haften dann die unsicheren Sohlen — every crazy wind will take her, and, like a fire-balloon at night, she will go out among the stars.

Note. The reader will easily see how much of the account of the truth-function developed later in Pragmatism was already explicit in this earlier article, and how much came to be defined later. In this earlier article we find distinctly asserted:

1. The reality, external to the true idea;

2. The critic, reader, or epistemologist, with his own belief, as warrant for this reality's existence;

3. The experienceable environment, as the vehicle or medium connecting knower with known, and yielding the cognitive relation;

4. The notion of pointing, through this medium, to the reality, as one condition of our being said to know it;

5. That of resembling it, and eventually affecting it, as determining the pointing to it and not to something else.

6. The elimination of the 'epistemological gulf,' so that the whole truth-relation falls inside of the continuities of concrete experience, and is constituted of particular processes, varying with every object and subject, and susceptible of being described in detail.

The defects in this earlier account are:

1. The possibly undue prominence given to resembling, which altho a fundamental function in knowing truly, is so often dispensed with;

2. The undue emphasis laid upon operating on the object itself, which in many cases is indeed decisive of that being what we refer to, but which is often lacking, or replaced by operations on other things related to the object.

3. The imperfect development of the generalized notion of the workability of the feeling or idea as equivalent to that satisfactory adaptation to the particular reality, which constitutes the truth of the idea. It is this more generalized notion, as covering all such specifications as pointing, fitting, operating or resembling, that distinguishes the developed view of Dewey, Schiller, and myself.

4. The treatment of percepts as the only realm of reality. I now treat concepts as a co-ordinate realm.

The next paper represents a somewhat broader grasp of the topic on the writer's part.

Endnotes

1. Read before the Aristotelian Society, December 1, and first published in Mind, vol. x (1885). — This, and the following articles have received a very slight verbal revision, consisting mostly in the omission of redundancy.

2. 'The Relativity of Knowledge,' held in this sense, is, it may be observed in passing, one of the oddest of philosophic superstitions. Whatever facts may be cited in its favor are due to the properties of nerve-tissue, which may be exhausted by too prolonged an excitement. Patients with neuralgias that last unremittingly for days can, however, assure us that the limits of this nerve-law are pretty widely drawn. But if we. physically could get a feeling that should last eternally unchanged, what atom of logical or psychological argument is there to prove that it would not be felt as long as it lasted, and felt for just what it is, all that time? The reason for the opposite prejudice seems to be our reluctance to think that so stupid a thing as such a feeling would necessarily be, should be allowed to fill eternity with its presence. An interminable acquaintance, leading to no knowledge- about, — such would be its condition.

3. See, for example, Gwen's Introduction to Hume Treatise of Human Nature, p. 36.

4. If A enters and B exclaims, 'Did n't you see my brother on the stairs?' we all hold that A may answer, 'I saw him, but did n't know he was your brother; ignorance of brotherhood not abolishing power to see. But those who, on

account of the unrelatedness of the first facts with which we become acquainted, deny them to be 'known' to us, ought in consistency to maintain that if A did not perceive the relationship of the man on the stairs to B, it was impossible he should have noticed him at all.

5. It seems odd to call so important a function accidental. but I do not see how we can mend the matter. Just as, if we start with the reality and ask how it may come to be known, we can only reply by invoking a feeling which shall reconstruct it in its own more private fashion; so, if we start with the feeling and ask how it may come to know, we can only reply by invoking a reality which shall reconstruct it in its own more public fashion. In either case, however, the datum we start with remains just what it was. One may easily get lost in verbal mysteries about the difference between quality of feeling and feeling of quality, between receiving and reconstructing the knowledge of a reality. But at the end we must confess that the notion of real cognition involves an unmediated dualing of the knower and the known. See Bowne's Metaphysics New York, 1882, pp. 403-412, and various passages in Lotze, e. g., Logic, § 308. ['Unmediated' is a bad word to have used. — 1909.]

6. The thoroughgoing objector might, it is true, still return to the charge, and, granting a dream which should completely mirror the real universe, and all the actions dreamed in which should be instantly matched by duplicate actions in this universe, still insist that this is nothing more than harmony, and that it is as far as ever from being made clear whether the dream-world refers to that other world, all of whose details it so closely copies. This objection leads deep into metaphysics. I do not impugn its importance, and justice obliges me to say that but for the teachings of my colleague, Dr. Josiah Royce, I should neither have grasped its full force nor made my own practical and psychological point of view as clear to myself as it is. On this occasion I prefer to stick steadfastly to that point of view; but I hope that Dr. Royce's more fundamental criticism of the function of cognition may ere long see the light. [I referred in this note to Royce's Religious aspect of philosophy, then about to be published. This powerful book maintained that the notion of referring involved that of an inclusive mind that shall own both the real q and the mental q, and use the latter expressly as a representative symbol of the former. At the time I could not refute this transcendentalist opinion. Later, largely through the influence of Professor D. S. Miller I came to see that any definitely experienceable workings would serve as intermediaries quite as well as the absolute mind's intentions would.]

7. That is, there is no real 'Ivanhoe,' not even the one in Sir Walter Scott's mind as he was writing the story. That one is only the first one of the Ivanhoe-solipsisms. It is quite true we can make it the real Ivanhoe if we like, and then say that the other Ivanhoes know it or do not know it, according as they refer to and resemble it or no. This is done by bringing in Sir Walter Scott himself as the author of the real Ivanhoe, and so making a complex object of both. This object, however, is not a story pure and simple. It has dynamic relations with the world common to the experience of all the readers. Sir Walter Scott's Ivanhoe got itself printed in volumes which we all can handle, and to any one of which we can refer to see which of our versions be the true one, i.e., the original one of Scott himself. We can see the manuscript; in short

William James

we can get back to the Ivanhoe in Scott's mind by many an avenue and channel of this real world of our experience, — a thing we can by no means do with either the Ivanhoe or the Rebecca, either the Templar or the Isaac of York, of the story taken simply as such, and detached from the conditions of its production. Everywhere, then, we have the same test: can we pass continuously from two objects in two minds to a third object which seems to be in both minds, because each mind feels every modification imprinted on it by the other? If so, the first two objects named are derivatives, to say the least, from the same third object, and may be held, if they resemble each other, to refer to one and the same reality.

8. Among such errors are those cases in which our feeling operates on a reality which it does partially resemble, and yet does not intend: as for instance, when I take up your umbrella, meaning to take my own. I cannot be said here either to know your umbrella, or my own, which latter my feeling more completely resembles. I am mistaking them both, misrepresenting their context, etc.

We have spoken in the text as if the critic were necessarily one mind, and the feeling criticised another. But the criticised feeling and its critic may be earlier and later feelings of the same mind, and here it might seem that we could dispense with the notion of operating, to prove that critic and criticised are referring to and meaning to represent the same. We think we see our past feelings directly, and know what they refer to without appeal. At the worst, we can always fix the intention of our present feeling and make it refer to the same reality to which any one of our past feelings may have referred. So we need no 'operating' here, to make sure that the feeling and its critic mean the same real q. Well, all the better if this is so! We have covered the more complex and difficult case in our text, and we may let this easier one go. The main thing at present is to stick to practical psychology, and ignore metaphysical difficulties.

One more remark. Our formula contains, it will be observed, nothing to correspond to the great principle of cognition laid down by Professor Ferrier in his Institutes of Metaphysic and apparently adopted by all the followers of Fichte, the principle, namely, that for knowledge to be constituted there must be knowledge of the knowing mind along with whatever else is known: not q, as we have supposed, but q plus myself, must be the least I can know. It is certain that the common sense of mankind never dreams of using any such principle when it tries to discriminate between conscious states that are knowledge and conscious states that are not. So that Ferrier's principle, if it have any relevancy at all, must have relevancy to the metaphysical possibility of consciousness at large, and not to the practically recognized constitution of cognitive consciousness. We may therefore pass it by without further notice here.

9. Is an incomplete 'thought about, that reality, that reality is its 'topic,' etc.

10. Though both might terminate in the same thing and be incomplete thoughts 'about' it.

11. The difference between Idealism and Realism is immaterial here. What is said in the text is consistent with either theory. A law by which my percept shall change yours directly is no more mysterious than a law by which it shall

first change a physical reality, and then the reality change yours. In either case you and I seem knit into a continuous world, and not to form a pair of solipsisms.

12. 'There is no distinction of meaning so fine as to consist in anything but a possible difference of practice. . . . It appears, then, that the rule for attaining the [highest] grade of clearness of apprehension is as follows: Consider what effects, which might conceivably have practical bearings, we conceive the object of our conception to have. Then, our conception of these effects is the whole of our conception of the object.' Charles S. Peirce: 'How to make our Ideas clear,' in Popular Science Monthly, New York, January, 1878, p. 293.

THE TIGERS IN INDIA[1]

There are two ways of knowing things, knowing them immediately or intuitively, and knowing them conceptually or representatively. Altho such things as the white paper before our eyes can be known intuitively, most of the things we know, the tigers now in India, for example, or the scholastic system of philosophy, are known only representatively or symbolically.

Suppose, to fix our ideas, that we take first a case of conceptual knowledge; and let it be our knowledge of the tigers in India, as we sit here. Exactly what do we mean by saying that we here know the tigers? What is the precise fact that the cognition so confidently claimed is known-as, to use Shadworth Hodgson's inelegant but valuable form of words?

Most men would answer that what we mean by knowing the tigers is having them, however absent in body, become in some way present to our thought; or that our knowledge of them is known as presence of our thought to them. A great mystery is usually made of this peculiar presence in absence; and the scholastic philosophy, which is only common sense grown pedantic, would explain it as a peculiar kind of existence, called intentional inexistence, of the tigers in our mind. At the very least, people would say that what we mean by knowing the tigers is mentally pointing towards them as we sit here.

But now what do we mean by pointing, in such a case as this? What is the pointing known-as, here?

To this question I shall have to give a very prosaic answer — one that traverses the prepossessions not only of common sense and scholasticism, but also those of nearly all the epistemological writers whom I have ever read. The answer, made brief, is this : The pointing of our thought to the tigers is known simply and solely as a procession of mental associates and motor consequences that follow on the thought, and that would lead harmoniously, if followed out, into some ideal or real context, or even into the immediate presence, of the tigers. It is known as our rejection of a jaguar, if that beast were shown us as a tiger; as our assent to a genuine tiger if so shown. It is known as our ability to utter all sorts of propositions which don't contradict other propositions that are true of the real tigers. It is even known, if we take the tigers very seriously, as actions of ours which may terminate in directly intuited tigers, as they would if we took a voyage to India for the purpose of tiger-hunting and brought back a lot of skins of the striped rascals which we had laid low. In all this there is no self-transcendency in our mental images taken by themselves. They are one phenomenal fact; the tigers are another; and their pointing to the tigers is a perfectly commonplace intra-experiential relation, if you once grant a connecting world to be there. In short, the ideas and the tigers are in themselves as loose and separate, to use Hume's language, as any two things can be; and pointing means here an operation as external and adventitious as any that nature yields.[2]

I hope you may agree with me now that in representative knowledge there is no special inner mystery, but only an outer chain of physical or mental intermediaries connecting thought and thing. To know an object is here to lead to it through a context which the world supplies. All this was most instructively set forth by our colleague D. S. Miller at our meeting in New York last Christmas, and for re-confirming my sometime wavering opinion, I owe him this acknowledgment.[3]

Let us next pass on to the case of immediate or intuitive acquaintance with an object, and let the object be the white paper before our eyes. The thought-stuff and the thing-stuff are here indistinguishably the same in nature, as we saw a moment since, and there is no context of intermediaries or associates to stand between and separate the thought and thing. There is no 'presence in absence' here, and no 'pointing,' but rather an allround embracing Of the paper by the thought; and it is clear that the knowing cannot now be explained exactly as it was when the tigers were its object. Dotted all through our experience are states of immediate acquaintance just like this. Somewhere our belief always does rest on ultimate data like the whiteness, smoothness, or squareness of this paper. Whether such qualities be truly ultimate aspects of being, or only provisional suppositions of ours,—held-to till we get better informed, is quite immaterial for our present inquiry. So long as it is believed in, We see our object face to face. What now do we mean by 'knowing' such a sort of object as this? For this is also the way in which we should know the tiger if our conceptual idea of him were to terminate by having led us to his lair?

This address must not become too long, so I must give my answer in the fewest words. And let me first say this: So far as the white paper or other ultimate datum of our experience is considered to enter also into some one else's experience, and we, in knowing it, axe held to know it there as well as here; so far, again, as it is considered to be a mere mask for hidden molecules that other now impossible experiences of our own might some day lay bare to view; so far it is a case of tigers in India again — the things known being absent experiences, the knowing can only consist in passing smoothly towards them through the intermediary context that the world supplies. But if our own private vision of the paper be considered in abstraction from every other event, as if it constituted by itself the universe (and it might perfectly well do so, for aught we can understand to the contrary), then the paper seen and the seeing of it are only two names for one indivisible fact which, properly named, is the datum, the phenomenon, or the experience. The paper is in the mind and the mind is around the paper, because paper and mind are only two names that are given later to the one experience, when, taken in a larger world of which it forms a part, its connections are traced in different directions.[4] To know

immediately, then, or intuitively, is for mental content and object to be identical. This is a very different definition from that which we gave of representative knowledge; but neither definition involves those mysterious notions of self-transcendency and presence in absence which are such essential parts of the ideas of knowledge, both of philosophers and of common men.[5]

Endnotes

1. Extracts from a presidential address before the American Psychological Association, published in the Psychological Review, vol. ii, p. 105 (1895).

2. A stone in one field may 'fit,' we say, a hole in another field. But the relation of 'fitting,' so long as no one carries the stone to the hole and drops it in, is only one name for the fact that such an act may happen. Similarly with the knowing of the tigers here and now. It is only an anticipatory name for a 'further associative and terminative process that may occur.

3. See Dr. Miller's articles on Truth and Error, and on Content and Function, in the Philosophical Review, July, 1893, and Nov., 1895.

4. What is meant by this is that 'the experience' can be referred to either of two great associative systems, that of the experiencer's mental history, or that of the experienced facts of the world. Of both of these systems it forms part, and may be regarded, indeed, as one of their points of intersection. One might let a vertical line stand for the mental history; but the same object, O, appears also in the mental history of different persons, represented by the other vertical lines. It thus ceases to be the private property of one experience, and becomes, so to speak, a shared or public thing. We can track its outer history in this way, and represent it by the horizon line. [It is also known representatively at other points of the vertical lines, or intuitively there again, so that the line of its outer history would have to be looped and wandering, but I make it straight for simplicity's sake.] In any case, however, it is the same stuff that figures in all the sets of lines.

5. [The reader will observe that the text is written from the point of view of naif realism or common sense, and avoids raising the idealistic controversy.]

HUMANISM AND TRUTH[1]

Receiving from the Editor of Mind an advance proof of Mr. Bradley's article on 'Truth and Practice,' I understand this as a hint to me to join in the controversy over 'Pragmatism' which seems to have seriously begun. As my name has been coupled with the movement, I deem it wise to take the hint, the more so as in some quarters greater credit has been given me than I deserve, and probably undeserved discredit in other quarters falls also to my lot.

First, as to the word 'pragmatism.' I myself have only used the term to indicate a method of carrying on abstract discussion. The serious meaning of a concept, says Mr. Peirce, lies in the concrete difference to some one which its being true will make. Strive to bring all debated conceptions to that 'pragmatic' test, and you will escape vain wrangling: if it can make no practical difference which of two statements be true, then they are really one statement in two verbal forms; if it can make no practical difference whether a given statement be true or false, then the statement has no real meaning. In neither case is there anything fit to quarrel about: we may save our breath, and pass to more important things.

All that the pragmatic method implies, then, is that truths should have practical[2] consequences. In England the word has been used more broadly still, to cover the notion that the truth of any statement consists in the consequences, and particularly in their being good consequences. Here we get beyond affairs of method altogether; and since my pragmatism and this wider pragmatism are so different, and both an important enough to have different names, I think that Mr. Schiller's proposal to call the wider pragmatism by the name of 'humanism' is excellent and ought to be adopted. The narrower pragmatism may still be spoken of as the 'pragmatic method.'

I have read in the past six months many hostile reviews of Schiller's and Dewey's publications; but with the exception of Mr. Bradley's elaborate indictment, they are out of reach where I write, and I have largely forgotten them. I think that a free discussion of the subject on my part would in any case be more useful than a polemic attempt at rebutting these criticisms in detail. Mr. Bradley in particular can be taken care of by Mr. Schiller. He repeatedly confesses himself unable to comprehend Schiller's views, he evidently has not sought to do so sympathetically, and I deeply regret to say that his laborious article throws, for my mind, absolutely no useful light upon the subject. It seems to me on the whole an ignoratio elenchi, and I feel free to disregard it altogether.

The subject is unquestionably difficult. Messrs. Dewey's and Schiller's thought is eminently an induction, a generalization working itself free from all sorts of entangling particulars. If true, it involves much restatement of traditional notions. This is a kind of intellectual product that never attains a classic form of expression when first promulgated. The critic ought therefore not to be too sharp and logic-chopping in his dealings with it, but should weigh it as a whole, and especially weigh it against its possible alternatives. One should also try to apply it first to one instance, and then to another to see how it will work. It seems to me that it is emphatically not a case for instant execution, by conviction of intrinsic absurdity or of self-contradiction, or by caricature of what it would look like if reduced to skeleton shape. Humanism is in fact much more like one of those secular changes that come upon public opinion overnight, as it were, borne upon tides 'too deep for sound or foam,' that survive all the crudities and extravagances of their advocates, that you can pin to no one absolutely essential statement, nor kill by any one decisive stab.

Such have been the changes from aristocracy to democracy, from classic to romantic taste, from theistic to pantheistic feeling, from static to evolutionary ways of understanding life — changes of which we all have been spectators. Scholasticism still opposes to such changes the method of confutation by single decisive reasons, showing that the new view involves self-contradiction, or traverses some fundamental principle. This is like stopping a river by planting a stick in the middle of its bed. Round your obstacle flows the water and 'gets there all the same.' In reading some of our opponents, I am not a little reminded of those catholic writers who refute darwinism by telling us that higher species cannot come from lower because minus nequit gignere plus, or that the notion of transformation is absurd, for it implies that species tend to their own destruction, and that would violate the principle that every reality tends to persevere in its own shape. The point of view is too myopic, too tight and close to take in the inductive argument. Wide generalizations in science always meet with these summary refutations in their early days; but they outlive them, and the refutations then sound oddly antiquated and scholastic. I cannot help suspecting that the humanistic theory is going through this kind of would be refutation at present.

The one condition of understanding humanism is to become inductive-minded oneself, to drop rigorous definitions, and follow lines of least resistance 'on the whole.' In other words,' an opponent might say, 'resolve your intellect into a kind of slush.' 'Even so,' I make reply, —'if you will consent to use no politer word.' For humanism, conceiving the more 'true' as the more 'satisfactory' (Dewey's term), has sincerely to renounce rectilinear arguments and ancient ideals of rigor and final ity. It is in just this temper of renunciation, so different from that of pyrrhonistic scepticism, that the spirit of humanism essentially consists. Satisfactoriness has to be measured by a multitude of standards, of which some, for aught

we know, may fail in any given case; and what is more satisfactory than any alternative in sight, may to the end be a sum of pluses and minuses, concerning which we can only trust that by ulterior corrections and improvements a maximum of the one and a minimum of the other may some day be approached. It means a real change of heart, a break with absolutistic hopes, when one takes up this inductive view of the conditions of belief.

As I understand the pragmatist way of seeing things, it owes its being to the break-down which the last fifty years have brought about in the older notions of scientific truth. 'God geometrizes,' it used to be said; and it was believed that Euclid's elements literally reproduced his geometrizing. There is an eternal and unchangeable 'reason'; and its voice was supposed to reverberate in Barbara and Celarent. So also of the 'laws of nature,' physical and chemical, so of natural history classifications — all were supposed to be exact and exclusive duplicates of pre-human archetypes buried in the structure of things, to which the spark of divinity hidden in our intellect enables us to penetrate. The anatomy of the world is logical, and its logic is that of a university professor, it was thought. Up to about 1850 almost every one believed that sciences expressed truths that were exact copies of a definite code of non-human realities. But the enormously rapid multiplication of theories in these latter days has well-nigh upset the notion of any one of them being a more literally objective kind of thing than another. There are so many geometries, so many logics, so many physical and chemical hypotheses, so many classifications, each one of them good for so much and yet not good for everything, that the notion that even the truest formula may be a human device and not a literal transcript has dawned upon us. We hear scientific laws now treated as so much 'conceptual shorthand,' true so far as they are useful but no farther. Our mind has become tolerant of symbol instead of reproduction, of approximation instead of exactness, of plasticity instead of rigor. 'Energetics,' measuring the bare face of sensible phenomena so as to describe in a single formula all their changes of 'level,' is the last word of this scientific humanism, which indeed leaves queries enough outstanding as to the reason for so curious a congruence between the world and the mind, but which at any rate makes our whole notion of scientific truth more flexible and genial than it used to be.

It is to be doubted whether any theorizer today, either in mathematics, logic, physics or biology, conceives himself to be literally re-editing processes of nature or thoughts of God. The main forms of our thinking, the separation of subjects from predicates, the negative, hypothetic and disjunctive judgments, are purely human habits. The ether, as Lord Salisbury said, is only a noun for the verb to undulate; and many of our theological ideas are admitted, even by those who call them 'true,' to be humanistic in like degree.

I fancy that these changes in the current notions of truth are what originally gave the impulse to Messrs. Dewey's and Schiller's views. The suspicion is in the air nowadays that the superiority of one of our formulas to another may not consist so much in its literal 'objectivity,' as in subjective qualities like its usefulness, its 'elegance' or its congruity with our residual beliefs. Yielding to these suspicions, and generalizing, we fall into something like the humanistic state of mind. Truth we conceive to mean everywhere, not duplication, but addition; not the constructing of inner copies of already complete realities, but rather the collaborating with realities so as to bring about a clearer result. Obviously this state of mind is at first full of vagueness and ambiguity. 'Collaborating' is a vague term; it must at any rate cover conceptions and logical arrangements. 'Clearer' is vaguer still. Truth must bring clear thoughts, as well as clear the way to action. 'Reality' is the vaguest term of all. The only way to test such a programme at all is to apply it to the various types of truth, in the hope of reaching an account that shall be more precise. Any hypothesis that forces such a review upon one has one great merit, even if in the end it prove invalid: it gets us better acquainted with the total subject. To give the theory plenty of 'rope' and see if it hangs itself eventually is better tactics than to choke it off at the outset by abstract accusations of self-contradiction. I think therefore that a decided effort at sympathetic mental play with humanism is the provisional attitude to be recommended to the reader.

When I find myself playing sympathetically with humanism, something like what follows is what I end by conceiving it to mean.

Experience is a process that continually gives us new material to digest. We handle this intellectually by the mass of beliefs of which we find ourselves already possessed, assimilating, rejecting, or rearranging in different degrees. Some of the apperceiving ideas are recent acquisitions Of our own, but most of them are common-sense traditions of the race. There is probably not a common-sense tradition, of all those which we now live by, that was not in the first instance a genuine discovery, an inductive generalization like those more recent ones of the atom, of inertia, of energy, of reflex action, or of fitness to survive. The notions of one Time and of one Space as single continuous receptacles; the distinction between thoughts and things, matter and mind; between permanent subjects and changing attributes; the conception of classes with subclasses within them; the separation of fortuitous from regularly caused connections; surely all these were once definite conquests made at historic dates by our ancestors in their attempts to get the chaos of their crude individual experiences into a more shareable and manageable shape. They proved of such sovereign use as denkmittel that they are now a part of the very structure of our mind. We cannot play fast and loose with them. No experience can upset them. On the contrary, they apperceive every experience and assign it to its place.

To what effect? That we may the better foresee the course of our experiences, communicate with one another, and steer our lives by rule. Also that we may have a cleaner, clearer, more inclusive mental view.

The greatest common-sense achievement, after the discovery of one Time and one Space, is probably the concept of permanently existing things. When a rattle first drops out of the hand of a baby, he does not look to see where it has gone. Non-perception he accepts as annihilation until he finds a better belief. That our perceptions mean beings, rattles that are there whether we hold them in our hands or not, becomes an interpretation so luminous of what happens to us that, once employed, it never gets forgotten. It applies with equal felicity to things and persons, to the objective and to the ejective realm. However a Berkeley, a Mill, or a Cornelius may criticise it, it works; and in practical life we never think of ' going back' upon it, or reading our incoming experiences in any other terms. We may, indeed, speculatively imagine a state of 'pure' experience before the hypothesis of permanent objects behind its flux had been framed; and we can play with the idea that some primeval genius might have struck into a different hypothesis. But we cannot positively imagine today what the different hypothesis could have been, for the category of trans-perceptual reality is now one of the foundations of our life. Our thoughts must still employ it if they are to possess reasonableness and truth.

This notion of a first in the shape of a most chaotic pure experience which sets us questions, of a second in the way of fundamental categories, long ago wrought into the structure of our consciousness and practically irreversible, which define the general frame within which answers must fall, and of a third which gives the detail of the answers in the shapes most congruous with all our present needs, is, as I take it, the essence of the humanistic conception. It represents experience in its pristine purity to be now so enveloped in predicates historically worked out that we can think of it as little more than an Other, of a That, which the mind, in Mr. Bradley's phrase, 'encounters, ' and to whose stimulating presence we respond by ways of thinking which we call 'true' in proportion as they facilitate our mental or physical activities and bring us outer power and inner peace. But whether the Other, the universal That, has itself any definite inner structure, or whether, if it have any, the structure resembles any of our predicated whats, this is a question which humanism leaves untouched. For us, at any rate, it insists, reality is an accumulation of our own intellectual inventions, and the struggle for 'truth' in our progressive dealings with it is always a struggle to work in new nouns and adjectives while altering as little as possible the old.

It is hard to see why either Mr. Bradley's own logic or his metaphysics should oblige him to quarrel with this conception. He might consistently adopt it verbatim et literatim, if he would, and simply throw his peculiar absolute round it, following in this the good example of Professor Royce. Bergson in France, and his disciples, Wilbois the physicist and Leroy, are thoroughgoing humanists in the sense defined. Professor Milhaud also appears to be one; and the great Poincaré misses it by only the breadth of a hair. In Germany the name of Simmel offers itself as that of a humanist of the most radical sort. Mach and his school, and Hertz and Ostwald must be classed as humanists. The view is in the atmosphere and must be patiently discussed.

The best way to discuss it would be to see what the alternative might be. What is it indeed? Its critics make no explicit statement, Professor Royce being the only one so far who has formulated anything definite. The first service of humanism to philosophy accordingly seems to be that it will probably oblige those who dislike it to search their own hearts and heads. It will force analysis to the front and make it the order of the day. At present the lazy tradition that truth is adaequatio intelleetûs et rei seems all there is to contradict it with. Mr. Bradley's only suggestion is that true thought 'must correspond to a determinate being which it cannot be said to make,' and obviously that sheds no new light. What is the meaning of the word to 'correspond'? Where is the 'being'? What sort of things are, determinations,' and what is meant in this particular case by ' not to make'?

Humanism proceeds immediately to refine upon the looseness of these epithets. We correspond in some way with anything with which we enter into any relations at all. If it be a thing, we may produce an exact copy of it, or we may simply feel it as an existent in a certain place. If it be a demand, we may obey it without knowing anything more about it than its push. If it be a proposition, we may agree by not contradicting it, by letting it pass. If it be a relation between things, we may act on the first thing so as to bring ourselves out where the second will be. If it be something inaccessible, we may substitute a hypothetical object for it, which, having the same consequences, will cipher out for us real results. In a general way we may simply add our thought to it; and if it suffers the addition, and the whole situation harmoniously prolongs and enriches itself, the thought will pass f or true.

As for the whereabouts of the beings thus corresponded to, although they may be outside of the present thought as well as in it, humanism sees no ground for saying they are outside of finite experience itself. Pragmatically, their reality means that we submit to them, take account of them, whether we like to or not, but this we must perpetually do with experiences other than our own. The whole system of what the present experience must correspond to 'adequately' may be continuous with the present experience itself. Reality, so taken as experience other than the present, might be either the legacy of past experience or the content of experience to come. Its determinations for us are in any case the adjectives which our acts of judging fit to it, and those are essentially humanistic things.

To say that our thought does not 'make' this reality means pragmatically that if our own particular thought were annihilated the reality would still be there in some shape, though possibly it might be a shape that would lack something that our thought supplies.

That reality is 'independent' means that there is something in every experience that escapes our arbitrary control. If it be a sensible experience it coerces our attention; if a sequence, we cannot invert it; if we compare two terms we can come to only one result. There is a push, an urgency, within our very experience, against which we are on the whole powerless, and which drives us in a direction that is the destiny of our belief. That this drift of experience itself is in the last resort due to something independent of all possible experience may or may not be true. There may or may not be an extra-experiential 'ding an sich' that keeps the ball rolling, or an 'absolute' that lies eternally behind all the successive determinations which human thought has made. But within our experience itself, at any rate, humanism says, some determinations show themselves as being independent of others; some questions, if we ever ask them, can only be answered in one, way; some beings, if we ever suppose them, must be supposed to have existed previously to the supposing; some relations, if they exist ever, must exist as long as their terms exist.

Truth thus means, according to humanism, the relation of less fixed parts of experience (predicates) to other relatively more fixed parts (subjects); and we are not required to seek it in a relation of experience as such to anything beyond itself. We can stay at home, for our behavior as experients is hemmed in on every side. The forces both of advance and of resistance are exerted by our own objects, and the notion of truth as something opposed to waywardness or license inevitably grows up solipsistically inside of every human life.

So obvious is all this that a common charge against the humanistic authors 'makes me tired.' 'How can a deweyite discriminate sincerity from bluff?' was a question asked at a philosophic meeting where I reported on Dewey's Studies. 'How can the mere[3] pragmatist feel any duty to think truly?' is the objection urged by Professor Royce. Mr. Bradley in turn says that if a humanist understands his own doctrine, ' he must hold any idea, however mad, to be the truth, if any one will have it so.' And Professor Taylor describes pragmatism as believing anything one pleases and calling it truth.

Such a shallow sense of the conditions under which men's thinking actually goes on seems to me most surprising. These critics appear to suppose that, if left to itself, the rudderless raft of our experience must be ready to drift anywhere or nowhere. Even tho there were compasses on board, they seem to say, there would be no pole for them to point to. There must be absolute sailing-directions, they insist, decreed from outside, and an independent chart of the voyage added to the ' mere ' voyage itself, if we are ever to make a port. But is it not obvious that even tho there be such absolute sailing-directions in the' shape of pre-human standards of truth that we ought to follow, the only guarantee that we shall in fact follow them must lie in our human equipment. The 'ought' would be a brutum fulmen unless there were a felt grain inside of our experience that conspired. As a matter of fact the devoutest believers in absolute standards must admit that men fail to obey them. Waywardness is here, in spite of the eternal prohibitions, and the existence of any amount of reality ante rem is no warrant against unlimited error in rebus being incurred. The only real guarantee we have against licentious thinking is the circumpressure of experience itself, which gets us sick of concrete errors, whether there be a trans-empirical reality or not. How does the partisan of absolute reality know what this orders him to think? He cannot get direct sight of the absolute; and he has no means of guessing what it wants of him except by following the humanistic clues. The only truth that he himself will ever practically accept will be that to which his finite experiences lead him of themselves. The state of mind which shudders at the idea of a lot of experiences left to themselves, and that augurs protection from the sheer name of an absolute, as if, however inoperative, that might still stand for a sort of ghostly security, is like the mood of those good people who, whenever they hear of a social tendency that is damnable, begin to redden and to puff, and say 'Parliament or Congress ought to make a law against it,' as if an impotent decree would give relief.

All the sanctions of a law of truth lie in the very texture of experience. Absolute or no absolute, the concrete truth for us will always be that way of thinking in which our various experiences most profitably combine.

And yet, the opponent obstinately urges, your humanist will always have a greater liberty to play fast and loose with truth than will your believer in an independent realm of reality that makes the standard rigid. If by this latter believer he means a man who pretend s to know the standard and who fulminates it, the humanist will doubtless prove more flexible; but no more flexible than the absolutist himself if the latter follows (as fortunately our present-day absolutists do follow) empirical methods of inquiry in concrete affairs. To consider hypotheses is surely always better than to dogmatize ins blaue hinein.

Nevertheless this probable flexibility of temper in him has been used to convict the humanist of sin. Believing as he does, that truth lies in rebus., and is at every moment our own line of most propitious reaction, he stands forever debarred, as I have heard a learned colleague say, from trying to convert opponents, for does not their view, being their most propitious momentary reaction, already fill the bill? Only the believer in the ante-rent brand Of truth can on this theory seek to make converts without self-stultification. But can there be self-stultification in urging any account whatever of truth? Can the definition ever contradict the deed? 'Truth is what I feel like saying' — suppose that to be the definition. 'Well, I feel like saying that, and I want you to feel like saying it, and shall continue to gay it until I get you to agree.' Where is there any contradiction? Whatever truth may be said to be, that is the kind of truth which the saying can be held to carry. The temper which a saying may comport is an extra-logical matter. It may indeed be hotter in some individual absolutist than in a humanist, but it need not be so in another. And the humanist, for his part, is perfectly consistent in compassing sea and land to make one proselyte, if his nature be enthusiastic enough.

'But how can you be enthusiastic over any view of things which you know to have been partly made by yourself, and which is liable to alter during the next minute? How is any heroic devotion to the ideal of truth possible under such paltry conditions?'

This is just another of those objections by which the anti-humanists show their own comparatively slack hold on the realities of the situation. If they would only follow the pragmatic method and ask: 'What is truth known as? What does its existence stand for in the way of concrete goods?'—they would see that the name of it is the inbegriff of almost everything that is valuable in our lives. The true is the opposite of whatever is instable, of whatever is practically disappointing, of whatever is useless, of whatever is lying and unreliable, of whatever is unverifiable and unsupported, of whatever is inconsistent and contradictory, of whatever is artificial and eccentric, of whatever is unreal in the sense of being of no practical account. Here are pragmatic reasons with a vengeance why we should turn to truth — truth saves us from a world of that complexion. What wonder that its very name awakens loyal feeling! In particular what wonder that all little provisional fool's paradises of belief should appear contemptible in comparison with its bare pursuit! When absolutists reject-humanism because they feel it to be untrue, that means that the whole habit of their mental needs is wedded already to a different view of reality, in comparison with which the humanistic world seems but the whim of a few irresponsible youths. Their own subjective apperceiving mass is what speaks here in the name of the eternal natures and bids them reject our humanism — as they apprehend it. Just so with us humanists, when we condemn all noble, clean-cut, fixed, eternal, rational, temple-like systems of philosophy. These contradict the dramatic temperament of nature, as our dealings with nature and our habits of thinking have so far brought us to conceive it. They seem oddly personal and artificial, even when not bureaucratic and professional in an absurd degree. We turn from them to the great unpent and unstayed wilderness of truth as we feel it to be constituted, with as good a conscience as rationalists are moved by when they turn from our wilderness into their neater and cleaner intellectual abodes.[4]

This is surely enough to show that the humanist does not ignore the character of objectivity and independence in truth. Let me turn next to what his opponents mean when they say that to be true, our thoughts must correspond!

The vulgar notion of correspondence here is that the thoughts must copy the reality cognitio fit per assimiliationem cogniti et cog noscentis; and philosophy, without having ever fairly sat down to the question, seems to have instinctively accepted this idea: propositions are held true if they copy the eternal thought; terms are held true if they copy extra-mental realities. Implicitly, I think that the copytheory has animated most of the criticisms that have been made on humanism.

A priori, however, it is not self-evident that the sole business of our mind with realities should be to copy them. Let my reader suppose himself to constitute for a time all the reality there is in the universe, and then to receive the announcement that another being is to be created who shall know him truly. How will he represent the knowing in advance? "'hat will he hope it to be? I doubt extremely whether it could ever occur to him to fancy it as a mere copying. Of what use to him would an imperfect second edition of himself in the new comer's interior be? It would seem pure waste of a propitious opportunity. The demand would more probably be for something absolutely new. The reader would conceive the knowing humanistically, 'the new comer,' he would say, 'must take account of my presence by reacting on it in such a way that good would accrue to us both. If copying be requisite to that end, let there be copying; otherwise not.' The essence in any case would not be the copying, but the enrichment of the previous world.

I read the other day, in a book of Professor Eucken's, a phrase, 'Die erhöhung des vorgefundenen daseins,' which seems to be pertinent here. Why may not thought's mission be to increase and elevate, rather than simply to imitate and reduplicate, existence? No one who has read Lotze can fail to remember his striking comment on the ordinary view of the secondary qualities of matter, which brands them as 'illusory' because they copy nothing in the thing. The notion of a world complete in itself, to which thought comes as a passive mirror, adding nothing to fact, Lotze says is irrational. Rather is thought itself a most momentous part of fact, and the whole mission of the pre-existing and insufficient world of matter may simply be to provoke thought to produce its far more precious supplement.

'Knowing,' in short, may, for aught we can see beforeh and to the contrary, be only one way of getting into fruitful relations with reality, whether copying be one of the relations or not.

It is easy to see from what special type of knowing the copy-theory arose. In our dealings with natural phenomena the great point is to be able to foretell. Foretelling, according to such a writer as Spencer, is the whole meaning of intelligence. When Spencer's 'law of intelligence' says that inner and outer relations must 'correspond,' it means that the distribution of terms in our inner time-scheme and space-scheme must be an exact copy of the distribution in real time and space of the real terms. In strict theory the mental terms themselves need not answer to the real terms in the sense of severally copying them, symbolic mental terms being enough, if only the real dates and places be copied. But in our ordinary life the mental terms are images and the real ones are sensations, and the images so often copy the sensations, that we easily take copying of terms as well as of relations to be the natural significance of knowing. Meanwhile much, even Of this common descriptive truth, is couched in verbal symbols. If our symbols fit the world, in the sense of determining our expectations rightly, they may even be the better for not copying its terms.

It seems obvious that the pragmatic account of all this routine of phenomenal knowledge is accurate. Truth here is a relation, not of our ideas to non-human realities, but of conceptual parts of our experience to sensational parts. Those thoughts are true which guide us to beneficial interaction with sensible particulars as they occur, whether they copy these in advance or not.

From the frequency of copying in the knowledge of phenomenal fact, copying has been supposed to be the essence of truth in matters rational also. Geometry and logic, it has been supposed, must copy archetypal thoughts in the Creator. But in these abstract spheres there is no need of assuming archetypes. The mind is free to carve so many figures out of space, to make so many numerical collections, to frame so many classes and series, and it can analyze and compare so endlessly, that the very superabundance of the resulting ideas makes us doubt the 'objective' pre-existence of their models. It would be plainly wrong to suppose a God whose thought consecrated rectangular but not polar co-ordinates, or Jevons's notation but not Boole's. Yet if, on the other hand, we assume God to have thought in advance of every possible flight of human fancy in these directions, his mind becomes too much like a Hindoo idol with three heads, eight arms and six breasts, too much made up of superfoetation and redundancy for us to wish to copy it, and the whole notion of copying tends to evaporate from these sciences. Their objects can be better interpreted as being created step by step by men, as fast as they successively conceive them.

If now it be asked how, if triangles, squares, square roots, genera, and the like, are but improvised human 'artefacts,' their properties and relations can be so promptly known to be ' eternal,' the humanistic answer is easy. If triangles and genera are of our own production we can keep them invariant. We can make them 'timeless' by expressly decreeing that on the things we mean time shall exert no altering effect, that they are intentionally and it may be fictitiously abstracted from every corrupting real associate and condition. But relations between invariant objects will themselves be invariant. Such relations cannot be happenings, for by hypothesis nothing shall happen to the objects. I have tried to show in the last chapter of my Principles of Psychology[5] that they can only be relations of comparison. No one so far seems to have noticed my suggestion, and I am too ignorant of the development of mathematics to feel very confident of my own view. But if it were correct it would solve the difficulty perfectly. Relations of comparison are matters of direct inspection. As soon as mental objects are mentally compared, they are perceived to be either like or unlike. But once the same, always the same, once different, always different, under these timeless conditions. Which is as much as to say that truths concerning these man-made objects are necessary and eternal. We can change our conclusions only by changing our data fast.

The whole fabric of the a priori sciences can thus be treated as a man-made product. As Locke long ago pointed out, these sciences have no immediate connection with fact. Only if a fact can be humanized by being identified with any of these ideal objects, is what was true of the objects now true also of the facts. The truth itself meanwhile was originally a copy of nothing; it was only a relation directly perceived to obtain between two artificial mental things.[6]

We may now glance at some special types of knowing, so as to see better whether the humanistic account fits. On the mathematical and logical types we need not enlarge further, nor need we return at much length to the case of our descriptive knowledge of the course of nature. So far as this involves anticipation, tho that may mean copying, it need, as we saw, mean little more than 'getting ready' in advance. But with many distant and future objects, our practical relations are to the last degree potential and remote. In no sense can we now get ready for the arrest of the earth's revolution by the tidal brake, for instance; and with the past, tho we suppose ourselves to know it truly, we have no practical relations at all. It is obvious that, altho interests strictly practical have been the original starting-point of our search for true phenomenal descriptions, yet an intrinsic interest in the bare describing function has grown up. We wish accounts that shall be true, whether they bring collateral profit or not. The primitive function has developed its demand for mere exercise. This theoretic curiosity seems to be the characteristically human differentia, and humanism recognizes its enormous scope. A true idea now means not only one that prepares us for an actual perception. It means also one that might prepare us for a merely possible perception, or one that, if spoken, would suggest possible perceptions to others, or suggest actual perceptions which the speaker cannot share. The ensemble of perceptions thus thought of as either actual or possible form a system which it is obviously advantageous to us to get into a stable and consistent shape; and here it is that the common-sense notion of permanent beings finds triumphant use. Beings acting outside of the thinker explain, not only his actual perceptions, past and future, but his possible perceptions and those of every one else. Accordingly they gratify our theoretic need in a supremely beautiful way. We pass from our immediate actual through them into the foreign and the potential, and back again into the future actual, accounting for innumerable particulars, by a single cause. As in those circular panoramas, where a real f oreground of dirt, grass, bushes, rocks and a broken-down cannon is enveloped by a canvas picture of sky and earth and of a raging battle, continuing the foreground so cunningly that the spectator can detect no joint; so these conceptual objects, added to our present perceptual reality, fuse with it into the whole universe of our belief. In spite of all berkeleyan criticism, we do not doubt that they are really there. Tho our discovery of any one of them may only date from now, we unhesitatingly say that it not only is, but was there, if, by so saying, the past appears connected more consistently with what we feel the present to be. This is historic truth. Moses wrote the Pentateuch, we think, because if he did n't, all our reli gious habits will have to be undone. Julius Caesar was real, or we can never listen to history again. Trilobites were once alive, or all our thought about the strata is at sea. Radium, discovered only yesterday, must always have existed, or its analogy with other natural elements, which are permanent, fails. In all this, it is but one portion of our beliefs reacting on another so as to yield the most satisfactory total state of mind. That state of mind, we say, sees truth, and the content of its deliverances we believe.

Of course, if you take the satisfactoriness concretely, as something felt by you now, and if, by truth, you mean truth taken abstractly and verified in the long run, you cannot make them equate, for it is notorious that the temporarily satisfactory is often false. Yet at each and every concrete moment, truth for each man is what that man 'troweth' at that moment with the maximum of satisfaction to himself ; and similarly, abstract truth, truth verified by the long run, and abstract satisfactoriness, long-run satisfactoriness, coincide. If, in short, we compare concrete with concrete and abstract with abstract, the true and the satisfactory do mean the same thing. I suspect that a certain muddling of matters hereabouts is what makes the general philosophic public so impervious to humanism's claims.

The fundamental fact about our experience is that it is a process of change. For the 'trower' at any moment, truth, like the visible area round a man walking in a fog, or like what George Eliot calls 'the wall of dark seen by small fishes eyes that pierce a span in the wide Ocean,' is an objective field which the next moment enlarges and of which it is the critic, and which then either suffers alteration or is continued unchanged. The critic sees both the first trower's truth and his own truth, compares them with each other, and verifies or confutes. His field of view is the reality independent of that earlier trower's thinking with which that thinking ought to correspond. But the critic is himself only a trower; and if the whole process of experience should terminate at that instant, there would be no otherwise known independent reality with which his thought might be compared.

The immediate in experience is always provisionally in this situation. The humanism, for instance, which I see and try so hard to defend, is the completest truth attained from my point of view up to date. But, owing to the fact that all experience is a process, no point of view can ever be the last one. Every one is insufficient and off its balance, and responsible to later points of view than itself. You, occupying some of these later points in your own person, and believing in the reality of others, will not agree that my point of view sees truth positive, truth timeless, truth that counts, unless they verify and confirm what it sees.

You generalize this by saying that any opinion, however satisfactory, can count positively and absolutely as true only so far as it agrees with a standard beyond itself; and if you then forget that this standard perpetually grows up endogenously inside the web of the experiences, you may carelessly go on to say that what distributively holds of each experience, holds also collectively of all experience, and that experience as such and in its totality owes whatever truth it may be possessed of to its correspondence with absolute realities outside of its own being. This evidently is the popular and traditional position. From the fact that finite experiences must draw support from one another, philosophers pass to the notion that experience uberhaupt must need an absolute support. The denial of such a notion by humanism lies probably at the root of most of the dislike which it incurs.

But is this not the globe, the elephant and the tortoise over again? Must not something end by supporting itself? Humanism is willing to let finite experience be self-supporting. Somewhere being must immediately breast nonentity. Why may not the advancing front of experience, carrying its immanent satisfactions and dissatisfactions, cut against the black inane as the luminous orb of the moon cuts the caerulean abyss? Why should anywhere the world be absolutely fixed and finished? And if reality genuinely grows, why may it not grow in these very determinations which here and now are made?

In point of fact it actually seems to grow by our mental determinations, be these never so true.' Take the 'great bear' or 'dipper' constellation in the heavens. We call it by that name, we count the stars and call them seven, we say they were seven before they were counted, and we say that whether any one had ever noted the fact or not, the dim resemblance to a long-tailed (or long-necked?) animal was always truly there. But what do we mean by this projection into past eternity of recent human ways of thinking? Did an 'absolute' thinker actually do the counting, tell off the stars upon his standing number-tally, and make the bear comparison, silly as the latter is? Were they explicitly seven, explicitly bear-like, before the human witness came? Surely nothing in the truth of the attributions drives us to think this. They were only implicitly or virtually what we call. them, and we human witnesses first explicated them and made them 'real.' A fact virtually pre-exists when every condition of its realization save one is already there. In this case the condition lacking is the act of the counting and comparing mind. But the stars (once the mind considers them) themselves dictate the result. The counting in no wise modifies their previous nature, and, they being what and where they are, the count cannot fall out differently. It could then always be made. Never could the number seven be, questioned, if the question once were raised.

We have here a quasi-paradox. Undeniably something comes by the counting that was not there before. And yet that something was always true. In one sense you create it, and in another sense you find it. You have to treat your count as being true beforehand, the moment you come to treat the matter at all.

Our stellar attributes must always be called true, then; yet none the less are they genuine additions made by our intellect to the world of fact. Not additions of consciousness only, but additions of 'content.' They copy nothing that pre-existed, yet they agree with what preexisted, fit it, amplify it, relate and connect it with a ' wain,' a number-tally, or what not, and build it out. It seems to me that humanism is the only theory that builds this case out in the good direction, and this case stands for innumerable other kinds of case. In all such cases, odd as it may sound, our judgment may actually be said to retroact and to enrich the past.

Our judgments at any rate change the character of future reality by the acts to which they lead. Where these acts are acts expressive of trust, —trust, e. g., that a man is honest, that our health is good enough, or that we can make a successful effort, —which acts may be a needed antecedent of the trusted things becoming true, Professor Taylor says[7] that our trust is at any rate untrue when it is made,, i. e., before the action; and I seem to remember that he disposes of anything like a faith in the general excellence of the universe (making the faithful person's part in it at any rate more excellent) as a 'lie in the soul.' But the pathos of this expression should not blind us to the complication of the facts. I doubt whether Professor Taylor would himself be in favor of practically handling trusters of these kinds as liars. Future and present really mix in such emergencies, and one can always escape lies in them by using hypothetic forms. But Mr. Taylor's attitude suggests such absurd possibilities of practice that it seems to me to illustrate beautifully how self-stultifying the conception of a truth that shall merely register a standing fixture may become. Theoretic truth, truth of passive copying, sought in the sole interests of copying as such, not because copying is good for something, but because copying ought schlechthin to be, seems, if you look at it coldly, to be an almost preposterous ideal. Why should the universe, existing in itself, also exist in copies? How can it be copied in the solidity of its objective fulness? And even if it could, what would the motive be? 'Even the hairs of your head are numbered.' Doubtless they are, virtually; but why, as an absolute proposition, ought the number to become copied and known? Surely knowing is only one way of interacting with reality and adding to its effect.

The opponent here will ask: 'Has not the knowing of truth any substantive value on its own account, apart from the collateral advantages it may bring? And if you allow theoretic satisfactions to exist at all, do they not crowd the collateral satisfactions out of house and home, and must not pragmatism go into bankruptcy, if she admits them at all?' The destructive force of such talk disappears as soon as we use words concretely instead of abstractly, and ask, in our quality of good pragmatists, just what the famous theoretic needs are known as and in what the intellectual satisfactions consist.

Are they not all mere matters of consistency and emphatically not of consistency between an absolute reality and the mind's copies of it, but of actually felt consistency among judgments, objects, and habits of reacting, in the mind's own experienceable world? And are not both our need of such consistency and our pleasure in it conceivable as outcomes of the natural fact that we are beings that do develop mental habits —habit itself proving adaptively beneficial in an environment where the same objects, or the same kinds of objects, recur and follow 'law'? If this were so, what would have come first would have been the collateral profits of habit as such, and the theoretic life would have grown up in aid of these. In point of fact, this seems to have been the probable case. At life's origin, any present perception may have been 'true' — if such a word could then be applicable. Later, when reactions became organized, the reactions became 'true' whenever expectation was fulfilled by them. Otherwise they were 'false' or 'mistaken' reactions. But the same class of objects needs the same kind of reaction, so the impulse to react consistently must gradually have been established, and a disappointment felt whenever the results frustrated expectation. Here is a perfectly plausible germ for all our higher consistencies. Nowadays, if an object claims from us a reaction of the kind habitually accorded only to the opposite class of objects, our mental machinery refuses to run smoothly. The situation is intellectually unsatisfactory.

Theoretic truth thus falls within the mind, being the accord of some of its processes and objects with other processes and objects — accord' consisting here in well-definable relations. So long as the satisfaction of feeling such an accord is denied us, whatever collateral profits may seem to inure from what we believe in are but as dust in the balance provided always that we are highly organized intellectually, which the majority of us are not. The amount of accord which satisfies most men and women is merely the absence of violent clash between their usual thoughts and statements and the limited sphere of sense-perceptions in which their lives are cast. The theoretic truth that most of us think we 'ought' to attain to is thus the possession of a set of predicates that do not explicitly contradict their subjects. We preserve it as often as not by leaving other predicates and subjects out.

In some men theory is a passion, just as music is in others. The form of inner consistency is pursued far beyond the line at which collateral profits stop. Such men systematize and classify and schematize and make synoptical tables and invent ideal objects for the pure love of unifying. Too often the results, glowing with 'truth' for the inventors, seem pawthetically personal and artificial to bystanders. Which is as much as to say that the purely theoretic criterion of truth can leave us in the lurch as easily as any other criterion, and that the absolutists, for all their pretensions, are 'in the same boat' concretely with those whom they attack.

I am well aware that this paper has been rambling in the extreme. But the whole subject is inductive, and sharp logic is hardly yet in order. My great trammel has been the nonexistence of any definitely stated alternative on my opponents' part. It may conduce to clearness if I recapitulate, in closing, what I conceive the main points of humanism to be. They are these:

1. An experience, perceptual or conceptual, must conform to reality in order to be true.

2. By 'reality' humanism means nothing more than the other conceptual or perceptual experiences with which a given present experience may find itself in point of fact mixed up.[8]

3. By 'conforming,' humanism means taking account of in such a way as to gain any intellectually and practically satisfactory result.

4. To "take account of" and to be 'satisfactory' are terms that admit of no definition, so many are the ways in which these requirements can practically be worked out.

5. Vaguely and in general, we take account of a reality by preserving it in as unmodified a form as possible. But, to be then satisfactory, it must not contradict other realities outside of it which claim also to be preserved. That we must preserve all the experience we can and minimize contradiction in what we preserve, is about all that can be said in advance.

6. The truth which the conforming experience embodies may be a positive addition to the previous reality, and later judgments may have to conform to it. Yet, virtually at least, it may have been true previously. Pragmatically, virtual and actual truth mean the same thing: the possibility of only one answer, when once the question is raised.

Endnotes

1. Reprinted, with slight verbal revision, from Mind, vol. xiii, N. S., p. 457 (October, 1904). A couple of interpolations from another article in Mind, 'Humanism and truth once more,' in vol. xiv, have been made.

2. ['Practical' in the sense of particular, of course, not in the sense that the consequences may not be mental as well as physical.]

3. I know of no 'mere' pragmatist, if mereness here means, as it seems, the denial of all concreteness to the pragmatist's thought.

4. [I cannot forbear quoting as an illustration of the contrast between humanist and rationalist tempers of mind, in a sphere remote from philosophy, these remarks on the Dreyfus 'affaire,' written by one who assuredly had never heard of humanism or pragmatism. 'Autant que la Révolution, "l'Affaire" est désormais une de nos "origines." Si elle n'a pas fait ouvrir le gouffre, c'est elle du moins qui a rendu patent et visible le long travail souterrain qui, silencieusement, avait preparé In séparation entre nos deux camps d'aujourd'hui, pour écarter enfin, d'un coup soudain, 14 France des traditionalistes (poseurs do principes, chercheurs d'unité, constructeurs do systèmes a; priori) et la France éprise du fait positif et de libre examen; — la France révolutionnaire et romantique si l'on veut, celle qui met très haut l'individu, qui ne veut pas qu'un juste périsse, fut-ce pour sauver la nation, et qui cherche]a vérité dans toutes ses parties aussi bien que dans une vue d'ensemble. . . . Duclaux ne pouvait pas concevoir qu'on préferat quelque chose it la vérité. Mais il voyait autour de lui de fort honnêtes gens qui, mettant en balance la vie d'un homme et la raison d'Etat, lui avouaient de quel poids léger its jugeaient une simple existence individuelle, pour innocente qu'elle fut. C'etaient des classiques, des gens a qui l'ensemble seul importe.' La Vie de Emile Duclaux, par Mme. Em. D., Laval, 1906, pp. 243, 247-248.

5. Vol. ii, pp. 641 ff .

6. [Mental things which are realities of course within the mental world.]

7. In an article criticising Pragmatism (as he conceives it) in the McGill University Quarterly published at Montreal, for May, 1904.

8. This is meant merely to exclude reality of an 'unknowable' sort, of which no account 'in either perceptual or conceptual terms can be given. It includes of course any amount of empirical reality independent of the knower. Pragmatism is thus 'epistemologically' realistic in its account.

THE RELATION BETWEEN
KNOWER AND KNOWN [1]

Throughout the history of philosophy the subject and its object have been treated as absolutely discontinuous entities; and thereupon the presence of the latter to the former, or the 49 apprehension' by the former of the latter, has assumed a paradoxical character which all sorts of theories had to be invented to overcome. Representative theories put a mental 4; representation,' 'image,' or 'content' into the gap, as a sort of intermediary. Commonsense theories left the gap untouched, declaring our mind able to clear it by a self-transcending leap. Transcendentalist theories left it impossible to traverse by finite knowers, and brought an absolute in to perform the saltatory act. All the while, in the very bosom of the finite experience, every conjunction required to make the relation intelligible is given in full. Either the knower and the known are: (1) the self-same piece of experience taken twice over in different contexts; or they are (2) two pieces of actual experience belonging to the same subject, with definite tracts of conjunctive transitional experience between them; or (3) the known is a possible experience either of that subject or another, to which the said conjunctive transitions would lead, if sufficiently prolonged.

To discuss all the ways in which one experience may function as the knower of another, would be incompatible with the limits of this essay. I have treated of type 1, the kind of knowledge called perception, in an article in the Journal of Philosophy, for September 1, 1904, called 'Does consciousness exist?' This is the type of case in which the mind enjoys direct 'acquaintance' with a present object. in the other types the mind has 'knowledge-about' an object not immediately there. Type 3 can always formally and hypothetically be reduced to type 2, so that a brief description of that type will now put the present reader sufficiently at my point of view, and make him see what the actual meanings of the mysterious cognitive relation may be.

Suppose me to be sitting here in my library at Cambridge, at ten minutes' walk from 'Memorial Hall,' and to be thinking truly of the latter object. My mind may have before it only the name, or it may have a clear image, or it may have a very dim image of the hall, but such an intrinsic difference in the image makes no difference in its cognitive function. Certain extrinsic phenomena, special experiences of conjunction, are what impart to the image, be it what it may, its knowing office.

For instance, if you ask me what hall I mean by my image, and I can tell you nothing; or if I fail to point or lead you towards the Harvard Delta; or if, being led by you, I am uncertain whether the Hall I see be what I had in mind or not—, you would rightly deny that I had 'meant' that particular hall at all, even tho my mental image might to some degree have resembled it. The resemblance would count in that case as coincidental merely, for all sorts of things of a kind resemble one another in this world without being held for that reason to take cognizance of one another.

On the other hand, if I can lead you to the hall, and tell you of its history and present uses; if in its presence I feel my idea, however imperfect it may have been, to have led hither and to be now terminated; if the associates of the image and of the felt hall run parallel, so that each term of the one context corresponds serially, as I walk, with an answering term of the other; why then my soul was prophetic, and my idea must be, and by common consent would be, called cognizant of reality. That percept was what I meant, for into it my idea has passed by conjunctive experiences of sameness and fulfilled intention. Nowhere is there jar, but every later moment continues and corroborates an earlier one.

In this continuing and corroborating, taken in no transcendental sense, but denoting definitely felt transitions, lies all that the knowing of a percept by an idea can possibly contain or signify. Wherever such transitions are felt, the first experience knows the last one. Where they do not, or where even as possibles they can not, intervene, there can be no pretence of knowing. In this latter case the extremes will be connected, if connected at all, by inferior relations — bare likeness or succession, or by 'withness' alone. Knowledge of sensible realities thus comes to life inside the tissue of experience. It is made; and made by relations that unroll themselves in time. Whenever certain intermediaries are given, such that, as they develop towards their terminus, there is experience from point to point of one direction followed, and finally of one process fulfilled, the result is that their starting-point thereby becomes a knower and their terminus an object meant or known. That is all that knowing (in the simple case considered) can be known-as, that is the whole of its nature, put into experiential terms. Whenever such is the sequence of our experiences we may freely say that we had the terminal object 'in mind' from the outset, even altho at the outset nothing was there in us but a flat piece of substantive experience like any other, with no self-transcendency about it, and no mystery save the mystery of coming into existence and of being gradually followed by other pieces of substantive experience, with conjunctively transitional experiences between. That is what we mean here by the object's being 'in mind.' Of any deeper more real way of its being in mind we have no positive conception, and we have no right to discredit our actual experience by talking of such a way at all.

I know that many a reader will rebel at this. 'Mere intermediaries,' he will say, 'even tho they be feelings of continuously growing fulfilment, only separate the knower from the known, whereas what we have in knowledge is a kind of immediate touch of the one by the other, an "apprehension" in the etymological sense of the word, a leaping of the chasm as by lightning, an act by which two terms are smitten into one over the head of their distinctness. All these dead intermediaries of yours are out of each other, and outside of their termini still.'

But do not such dialectic difficulties remind us of the dog dropping his bone and snapping at its image in the water? If we knew any more real kind of union aliunde, we might be entitled to brand all our empirical unions as a sham. But unions by continuous transition are the only ones we know of, whether in this matter of a knowledge-about that terminates in an acquaintance, whether in personal identity, in logical prediction through the copula 'is,' or elsewhere. If anywhere there were more absolute unions, they could only reveal themselves to us by just such conjunctive results. These are what the unions are worth, these are all that we can ever practically mean by union, by continuity. Is it not time to repeat what Lotze said of substances,, that to act like one is to be one? Should we not say here that to be experienced as continuous is to be really continuous, in a world where experience and reality come to the same thing? In a picture gallery a painted hook will serve to hang a painted chain by, a painted cable will hold a painted ship. In a world where both the terms and their distinctions are affairs of experience, conjunctions that are experienced must be at least as real as anything else. They will be 'absolutely' real conjunctions, if we have no transphenomenal absolute ready, to derealize the whole experienced world by, at a stroke.

So much for the essentials of the cognitive relation where the knowledge is conceptual in type, or forms knowledge 'about' an object. It consists in intermediary experiences (possible, if not actual) of continuously developing progress, and, finally, of fulfilment, when the sensible percept which is the object is reached. The percept here not only verifies the concept, proves its function of knowing that percept to be true, but the percept's existence as the terminus of the chain of intermediaries creates the function. Whatever terminates that chain was, because it now proves itself to be, what the concept 'had in mind.'

The towering importance for human life of this kind of knowing lies in the fact that an experience that knows another can figure as its representative, not in any quasi-miraculous 'epistemological' sense, but in the definite practical sense of being its substitute in various operations, sometimes physical and sometimes mental, which lead us to its associates and results. By experimenting on our ideas of reality, we may save ourselves the trouble of experimenting on the real experiences which they severally mean. The ideas form related systems, corresponding point for point to the systems which the realities form; and by letting an ideal term call up its associates systematically, we may be led to a terminus which the corresponding real term would have led to in case we had operated on the real world. And this brings us to the general question of substitution.

What, exactly, in a system of experiences, does the 'substitution' of one of them for another mean?

According to my view, experience as a whole is a process in time, whereby innumerable particular terms lapse and are superseded by others that follow upon them by transitions which, whether disjunctive or conjunctive in content, are themselves experiences, and must in general be accounted at least as real as the terms which they relate. What the nature of the event called 'superseding' signifies, depends altogether on the kind of transition that obtains. Some experiences simply abolish their predecessors without continuing them in any way. Others are felt to increase or to enlarge their meaning, to carry out their purpose, or to bring us nearer to their goal. They 'represent' them, and may fulfil their function better than they fulfilled it themselves. But to 'fulfil a function' in a world of pure experience can be conceived and defined in only one possible way. In such a world transitions and arrivals (or terminations) are the only events that happen, tho they happen by so many sorts of path. The only function that one experience can perform is to lead into another experience; and the only fulfilment we can speak of is the reaching of a certain experienced end. When one experience leads to (or can lead to) the same end as another., they agree in function. But the whole system of experiences as they are immediately given presents itself as a quasi-chaos through which one can pass out of an initial term in many directions and yet end in the same terminus, moving from next to next by a great many possible paths.

Either one of these paths might be a functional substitute for another, and to follow one rather than another might on occasion be an advantageous thing to do. As a matter of fact, and in a general way, the paths that run through conceptual experiences, that is, through 'thoughts' or 'ideas' that 'know' the things in which they terminate, are highly advantageous paths to follow. Not only do they yield inconceivably rapid transitions; but, owing to the 'universal' character[2] which they frequently possess, and to their capacity for association with one another in great systems, they outstrip the tardy consecutions of the things themselves, and sweep us on towards our ultimate termini in a far more labor-saving way than the following of trains of sensible perception ever could. Wonderful are the new cuts and the short-circuits the thought-paths make. Most thought-paths, it is true, are substitutes for nothing actual; they end outside the real world altogether, in wayward fancies, utopias, fictions or mistakes. But where they do re-enter reality and terminate therein, we substitute them always; and with these substitutes we pass the greater number of our hours.[3]

Whosoever feels his experience to be something substitutional even while he has it, may be said to have an experience that reaches beyond itself. From inside of its own entity it says 'more,' and postulates reality existing elsewhere. For the transcendentalist, who holds knowing to consist in a salto mortale across an epistemological chasm,' such an idea presents no difficulty; but it seems at first sight as if it might be inconsistent with an empiricism like our own. Have we not explained that conceptual knowledge is made such wholly by the existence of things that fall outside of the knowing experience itself — by intermediary experiences and by a terminus that fulfils? Can the knowledge be there before these elements that constitute its being have come? And, if knowledge be not there, how can objective reference occur?

The key to this difficulty lies in the distinction between knowing as verified and completed, and the same knowing as in transit and on its way. To recur to the Memorial Hall example lately used, it is only when our idea of the Hall has actually terminated in the percept that we know 'for certain' that from the beginning it was truly cognitive of that. Until established by the end of the process, its quality of knowing that, or indeed of knowing anything, could still be doubted; and yet the knowing really was there, as the result now shows. We were virtual knowers of the Hall long before we were certified to have been its actual knowers, by the percept's retroactive validating power. Just so we are ' mortal' all the time, by reason of the virtuality of the inevitable event which will make us so when it shall have come.

Now the immensely greater part of all our knowing never gets beyond this virtual stage. It never is completed or nailed down. I speak not merely of our ideas of imperceptibles like ether-waves or dissociated 'ions,' or of 'ejects' like the contents of our neighbors' minds; I speak also of ideas which we might verify if we would take the trouble, but which we hold for true altho unterminated perceptually, because nothing says 'no' to us, and there is no contradicting truth in sight. To continue thinking unchallenged is, ninety-nine times out of a hundred, our practical substitute for knowing in the completed sense. As each experience runs by cognitive transition into the next one, and we nowhere feel a collision with what we elsewhere count as truth or fact, we commit ourselves to the current as if the port were sure. We live, as it were, upon the front edge of an advancing wave-crest, and our sense of a determinate direction in falling forward is all we cover of the future of our path. It is as if a differential quotient should be conscious and treat itself as an adequate substitute for a traced-out curve. Our experience, inter alia, is of variations of rate and of direction, and lives in these transitions more than in the journey's end. The experiences of tendency are sufficient to act upon — what more could we have done at those moments even if the later verification comes complete?

This is what, as a radical empiricist, I say to the charge that the objective reference which is so flagrant a character of our experiences involves a chasm and a mortal leap. A positively conjunctive transition involves neither chasm nor leap. Being the very original of what we mean by continuity, it makes a continuum wherever it appears. Objective reference is an incident of the fact that so much of our experience comes as an insufficient and consists of process and transition. Our fields of experience have no more definite boundaries than have our fields of view. Both are fringed forever by a more that continuously develops, and that continuously supersedes them as life proceeds. The relations, generally speaking, are as real here as the terms are, and the only complaint of the transcendentalist's with which I could at all sympathize would be his charge that, by first making knowledge to consist in external relations as I have done, and by then confessing that nine-tenths of the time these are not actually but only virtually there, I have knocked the solid bottom out of the whole business, and palmed off a substitute of knowledge for the genuine thing. Only the admission, such a critic might say, that our ideas are self-transcendent and 'true' already; in advance of the experiences that are to terminate them, can bring solidity back to knowledge in a world like this, in which transitions and terminations are only by exception fulfilled.

This seems to me an excellent place for applying the pragmatic method. What would the self-transcendency affirmed to exist in advance of all experiential mediation or termination, be known as? What would it practically result in for us, were it true?

It could only result in our orientation, in the turning of our expectations and practical tendencies into the right path; and the right path here, so long as we and the object are not yet face to face (or can never get face to face, as in the case of ejects), would be the path that led us into the object's nearest neighborhood. Where direct acquaintance is lacking, 'knowledge about' is the next best thing, and an acquaintance with what actually lies about the object, and is most closely related to it, puts such knowledge within our grasp. Ether-waves and your anger, for example, are things in which my thoughts will never perceptually terminate, but my concepts Of them lead me to their very brink, to the chromatic fringes and to the hurtful words and deeds which are their really next effects.

Even if our ideas did in themselves possess the postulated self-transcendency, it would still remain true that their putting us into possession of such effects would be the sole cash-value of the self-transcendency for us. And this cash-value, it is needless to say, is verbatim et literatim what our empiricist account pays In. On pragmatist principles therefore, a dispute over self-transcendency is a pure logomachy. Call our concepts of ejective things self-transcendent or the reverse, it makes no difference, so long as we don't differ about the nature of that exalted virtue's fruits fruits — for us, of course, humanistic fruits.

The transcendentalist believes his ideas to be self-transcendent only because he finds that in fact they do bear fruits. Why need he quarrel with an account of knowledge that insists on naming this effect? Why not treat the working of the idea from next to next as the essence of its self-transcendency? Why insist that knowing is a static relation out of time when it practically seems so much a function of our active life? For a thing to be valid, says Lotze, is the same as to make itself valid. When the whole universe seems only to be making itself valid and to be still incomplete (else why its ceaseless changing?) why, of all things, should knowing be exempt? Why should it not be making itself valid like everything else? That some parts of it may be already valid or verified beyond dispute, the empirical philosopher, of course, like any one else, may always hope.

Endnotes

1. Extract from an article entitled 'A World of Pure Experience,' in the Journal of Philosophy, etc., September 29, 1904.

2. Of which all that need be said in this essay is that it also can be conceived as functional, and defined in terms of transitions, or of the possibility of such.

3. This is why I called our experiences, taken all together, a quasi-chaos. There is vastly more discontinuity in the sum total of experiences than we commonly suppose. The objective nucleus of every man's experience, his own body, is, it is true, a continuous percept; and equally continuous as a percept (though we may be inattentive to it) is the material environment of that body, changing by gradual transition when the body moves. But the distant parts of the physical world are at all times absent from us, and form conceptual objects merely, into the perceptual reality of which our life inserts itself at points discrete and relatively rare. Round their several objective nuclei, partly shared and common partly discrete, of the real physical world, innumerable

thinkers, pursuing their several lines of physically true cogitation, trace paths that intersect one another only at discontinuous perceptual points, and the rest of the time are quite incongruent; and around all the nuclei of shared 'reality' floats the vast cloud of experiences that are wholly subjective, that are non-substitutional, that find not even an eventual ending for themselves in the perceptual world —the mere day-dreams and joys and sufferings and wishes of the individual minds. These exist with one another, indeed, and with the objective nuclei. but out of them it is probable that to all eternity no interrelated system of any kind will ever be made.

THE ESSENCE OF HUMANISM[1]

Humanism is a ferment that has 'come to stay.' It is not a single hypothesis or theorem, and it dwells on no new facts. It is rather a slow shifting in the philosophic perspective, making thin appear as from a new centre of interest or point of sight. Some writers are strongly conscious of the shifting, others half unconscious, even though their own vision may have undergone much change. The result is no small confusion in debate, the half-conscious humanists often taking part against the radical ones, as if they wished to count upon the other side.[2]

If humanism really be the name for such a shifting of perspective, it is obvious that the whole scene of the philosophic stage will change in some degree if humanism prevails. The emphasis of things, their foreground and background distribution, their sizes and values, will not keep just the same.[3] If such pervasive consequences be involved in humanism, it is clear that no pains which philosophers may take, first in defining it, and then in furthering, checking, or steering its progress, will be thrown away.

It suffers badly at present from incomplete definition. Its most systematic advocates, Schiller and Dewey, have published fragmentary programmes only; and its bearing on many vital philosophic problems has not been traced except by adversaries who, scenting heresies in advance, have showered blows on doctrines — subjectivism and scepticism, for example — that no good humanist finds it necessary to entertain. By their still greater reticences, the anti-humanists have, in turn, perplexed the humanists. Much of the controversy has involved the word 'truth.' It is always good in debate to know your adversary's point of view authentically. But the critics of humanism never define exactly what the word 'truth' signifies when they use it themselves. The humanists have to guess at their view; and the result has doubtless been much beating of the air. Add to all this, great individual differences in both camps, and it becomes clear that nothing is so urgently needed, at the stage which things have reached at present, as a sharper definition by each side of its central point of view.

Whoever will contribute any touch of sharpness will help us to make sure of what's what and who is who. Any one can contribute such a definition, and, without it, no one knows exactly where he stands. If I offer my own provisional definition of humanism now and here, others may improve it, some adversary may be led to define his own creed more sharply by the contrast, and a certain quickening of the crystallization of general opinion may result.

I

The essential service of humanism., as I conceive the situation, is to have seen that tho, one part of our experience may lean upon another part to make it what it is in any one of several aspects in which it may be considered, experience as a whole is self-containing and leans on nothing. Since this formula also expresses the main contention of transcendental idealism, it needs abundant explication to make it unambiguous. It seems, at first sight, to confine itself to denying theism and pantheism. But, in fact, it need not deny either; everything would depend on the exegesis; and if the formula ever became canonical, it would certainly develop both right-wing and left-wing interpreters. I myself read humanism theistically and pluralistically. If there be a God, he is no absolute all-experiencer, but simply the experiencer of widest actual conscious span. Read thus, humanism is for me a religion susceptible of reasoned defence, tho I am well aware how many minds there are to whom it can appeal religiously only when it has been monistically translated. Ethically the pluralistic form of it takes for me a stronger hold on reality than any other philosophy I know of — it being essentially a social philosophy, a philosophy of 'co,' in which conjunctions do the work. But my primary reason for advocating it is its matchless intellectual economy. It gets rid, not only of the standing 'problems' that monism engenders ('problem of evil,' 'problem of freedom,' and the like), but of other metaphysical mysteries and paradoxes as well.

It gets rid, for example, of the whole agnostic controversy, by refusing to entertain the hypothesis of trans-empirical reality at all. It gets rid of any need for an absolute of the bradleyan type (avowedly sterile for intellectual purposes) by insisting that the conjunctive relations found within experience are faultlessly real. It gets rid of the need of an absolute of the roycean type (similarly sterile) by its pragmatic treatment of the problem of knowledge. As the views of knowledge, reality and truth imputed to humanism have been those so far most fiercely attacked, it is in regard to these ideas that a sharpening of focus seems most urgently required. I proceed therefore to bring the views which I impute to humanism in these respects into focus as briefly as I can.

II

If the central humanistic thesis be accepted, it will follow that, if there be any such thing at all as knowing, the knower and the object known must both be portions of experience. One part of experience must, therefore, either (1) Know another part of experience — in other words, parts must, as Professor Woodbridge says,[4] represent one another instead of representing realities outside of 'consciousness' —this case is that of conceptual knowledge; or else (2) They must simply exist as so many ultimate thats or facts of being, in the first instance; and then, as a secondary complication, and without doubling up its entitative singleness, any one and the same that in experience must figure alternately as a thing known and as a knowledge of the thing, by reason of two divergent kinds of context into which, in the general course of experience, it gets woven.[5]

This second case is that of sense-perception. There is a stage of thought that goes beyond common sense, and of it I shall say more presently; but the common-sense stage is a perfectly definite halting-place of thought, primarily for purposes of action; and, so long as we remain on the common-sense stage of thought, object and subject fuse in the fact of 'Presentation' or sense-perception — the pen and hand which I now see writing, for example, are the physical realities which those words designate. In this case there is no self-transcendency implied in the knowing. Humanism, here, is only a more comminuted identitätsphilosophie.

In case (1), on the contrary, the representative experience does transcend itself in knowing the other experience that is its object. No one can talk of the knowledge of the one by the other without seeing them as numerically distinct entities, of which the one lies beyond the other and away from it, along some direction and with some interval, that can be definitely named. But, if the talker be a humanist, he must also see this distance interval concretely and pragmatically, and confess it to consist of other intervening experiences — of possible ones, at all events, if not of actual. To call my present idea of my dog, for example, cognitive of the real dog means that, as the actual tissue of experience is constituted, the idea is capable of leading into a chain of other experiences on my part that go from next to next and terminate at last in vivid sense-perceptions of a jumping, barking, hairy body. Those are the real dog, the dog's full presence, for my common sense. If the supposed talker is a profound philosopher, altho they may not be the real dog for him, they mean the real dog, are practical substitutes for the real dog, as the representation was a practical substitute for them, that real dog being a lot of atoms, say, or of mindstuff, that lie where the sense-perceptions lie in his experience as well as in my own.

III

The philosopher here stands for the stage of thought that goes beyond the stage of common sense; and the difference is simply that he 'interpolates' and 'extrapolates,' where common sense does not. For common sense, two men see the same identical real dog. Philosophy, noting actual differences in their perceptions, points out the duality of these latter, and interpolates something between them as a more real terminus —first, organs, viscera, etc.; next, cells; then, ultimate atoms; lastly, mind-stuff perhaps. The original sense-termini of the two men, instead of coalescing with each other and with the real dog-object, as at first supposed, are thus held by philosophers to be separated by invisible realities with which, at most, they are conterminous.

Abolish, now, one of the percipients, and the interpolation changes into 'extrapolation.' The sense-terminus of the remaining percipient is regarded by the philosopher as not quite reaching reality. He has only carried the procession of experiences, the philosopher thinks, to a definite, because practical, halting-place somewhere on the way towards an absolute truth that lies beyond.

The humanist sees all the time, however, that there is no absolute transcendency even about the more absolute realities thus conjectured or believed in. The viscera and cells are only possible percepts following upon that of the outer body. The atoms again, tho, we may never attain to human means of perceiving them, are still defined perceptually. The mind-stuff itself is conceived as a kind of experience; and it is possible to frame the hypothesis (such hypotheses can by no logic be excluded from philosophy) of two knowers of a piece of mind-stuff and the mind-stuff itself becoming 'confluent' at the moment at which our imperfect knowing might pass into knowing of a completed type. Even so do you and I habitually conceive our two perceptions and the real dog as confluent, tho, only provisionally, and for the common-sense stage of thought. If my pen be inwardly made of mind-stuff, there is no confluence now between that mind-stuff and my visual perception of the pen. But conceivably there might come to be such confluence; for, in the case of my hand, the visual sensations and the inward feelings of the hand, its mind-stuff, so to speak, are even now as confluent as any two things can be.

There is, thus, no breach in humanistic epistemology. Whether knowledge be taken as ideally perfected, or only as true enough to pass muster for practice, it is hung on one continuous scheme. Reality, howsoever remote, is always defined as a terminus within the general possibilities of experience; and what knows it is defined as an experience that 'represents' it, in the sense of being substitutable for it in our thinking because it leads to the same associates, or in the sense of 'pointing to it' through a chain of other experiences that either intervene or may intervene.

Absolute reality here bears the same relation to sensation as sensation bears to conception or imagination. Both are provisional or final termini, sensation being only the terminus at which the practical man habitually stops, while the philosopher projects a 'beyond,' in the shape of more absolute reality. These termini, for the practical and the philosophical stages of thought respectively, are self-supporting. They are not 'true' of anything else, they simply are, are real. They 'lean on nothing,' as my formula said. Rather does the whole fabric of experience lean on them, just as the whole fabric of the solar system, including many relative positions, leans, for its absolute position in space, on any one of its constituent stars. Here, again, one gets a new Identitatsphilosophie in pluralistic form.

IV

If I have succeeded in making this at all clear (tho I fear that brevity and abstractness between them may have made me fail), the reader will see that the 'truth' of our mental operations must always be an intraexperiential affair. A conception is reckoned true by common sense when it can be made to lead to a sensation. The sensation, which for common sense is not so much 'true' as 'real,' is held to be provisionally true by the philosopher just in so far as it covers (abuts at, or occupies the place of) a still more absolutely real experience, in the possibility of which, to some remoter experient, the philosopher finds reason to believe.

Meanwhile what actually does count for true to any individual trower, whether he be philosopher or common man, is always a result of his apperceptions. If a novel experience, conceptual or sensible, contradict too emphatically our pre-existent system of beliefs, in ninety-nine cases out of a hundred it is treated as false. Only when the older and the newer experiences are congruous enough to mutually apperceive and modify each other, does what we treat as an advance in truth result. In no case, however, need truth consist in a relation between our experiences and something archetypal or trans-experiential. Should we ever reach absolutely terminal experiences,

experiences in which we all agreed, which were superseded by no revised continuations, these would not be true, they would be real, they would simply be, and be indeed the angles, comers, and linchpins of all reality, on which the truth of everything else would be stayed. Only such other things as led to these by satisfactory conjunctions would be true.' Satisfactory connection of some sort with such termini is all that the word 'truth' means. On the commonsense stage of thought sense-presentations serve as such termini. Our ideas and concepts and scientific theories pass for true only so far as they harmoniously lead back to the world of sense.

I hope that many humanists will endorse this attempt of mine to trace the more essential features of that way of viewing things. I feel almost certain that Messrs. Dewey and Schiller will do so. If the attackers will also take some slight account of it, it may be that discussion will be a little less wide of the mark than it has hitherto been.

Endnotes

1. Reprinted from the Journal of Philosophy, Psychology and Scientific Methods, vol. ii, No. 5, March 2, 1905.

2. Professor Baldwin, for example. His address 'Selective Thinking' (Psychological Review, January, 1898, reprinted in his volume, 'Development and Evolution') seems to me an unusually well written pragmatic manifesto. Nevertheless in 'The Limits of Pragmatism' (ibid., January, 1904), he (much less clearly) joins in the attack.

3. The ethical changes, it seems to me, are beautifully made evident in Professor Dewey's series of articles, which will never get the attention they deserve till they are printed in a book. I mean: 'The Significance of Emotions,' Psychological Review vol. ii, 13; 'The Reflex Are Concept in Psychology,' ibid., iii, 357; 'Psychology and Social Practice,' ibid., vii, 105; 'Interpretation of Savage Mind,' ibid., ix, 217; 'Green's Theory of the Moral Motive,' Philosophical Review, vol. i, 599; 'Self realization as the Moral Ideal,' ibid., ii, 652; 'The Psychology of Effort,' ibid., vi, 43; 'The Evolutionary Method as Applied to Morality,' ibid., xi, 107,353; 'Evolution and Ethics', Monist, vol. viii, 321; to mention only a few.

4. In Science, November 4, 1904, p. 599.

5. This statement is probably excessively obscure to any one who has not read my two articles 'Does Consciousness Exist? and 'A World of Pure Experience' in the Journal of Philosophy, vol. i, 1904.

A WORD MORE ABOUT TRUTH [1]

My failure in making converts to my conception of truth seems, if I may judge by what I hear in conversation, almost complete. An ordinary philosopher would feel disheartened, and a common choleric sinner would curse God and die, after such a reception. But instead of taking counsel of despair, I make bold to vary my statements, in the faint hope that repeated droppings may wear upon the stone, and that my formulas may seem less obscure if surrounded by something more of a 'mass' whereby to apperceive them.

For fear of compromising other pragmatists, whoe'er they be, I will speak of the conception which I am trying to make intelligible, as my own conception. I first published it in the year 1885, in the first article reprinted in the present book. Essential theses of this article were independently supported in 1893 and 1895 by Professor D. S. Miller,[2] and were repeated by me in a presidential address on 'The knowing of things together'[3] in 1895. Professor Strong, in an article in the Journal of Philosophy, etc.,[4] entitled 'A naturalistic theory of the reference of thought to reality,' called our account 'the James-Miller theory of cognition,' and, as I understood him, gave it his adhesion. Yet, such is the difficulty of writing clearly in these penetralia of philosophy, that each of these revered colleagues informs me privately that the account of truth I now give which to me is but that earlier statement more completely set forth — is to him inadequate, and seems to leave the gist of real cognition out. If such near friends disagree, what can I hope from remoter ones, and what from unfriendly critics?

Yet I feel so sure that the fault must lie in my lame forms of statement and not in my doctrine, that I am fain to try once more to express myself.

I

Are there not some general distinctions which it may help us to agree about in advance? Professor Strong distinguishes between what he calls 'saltatory' and what he calls 'ambulatory' relations. 'Difference,' for example, is saltatory, jumping as it were immediately from one term to another, but 'distance' in time or space is made out of intervening parts of experience through which we ambulate in succession. Years ago, when T. H. Green's ideas were most influential, I was much troubled by his criticisms of english sensationalism. One of his disciples in particular would always say to me, 'Yes! terms may indeed be possibly sensational in origin; but relations, what are they but pure acts of the intellect coming upon the sensations from above, and of a higher nature P I well remember the sudden relief it gave me to perceive one day that space-rela tions at any rate were homogeneous with the terms between which they mediated. The terms were spaces, and the relations were other intervening spaces.[5] For the Greenites space- relations had been saltatory, for me they became thenceforward ambulatory.

Now the most general way of contrasting my view of knowledge with the popular view (which is also the view of most epistemologists) is to call my view ambulatory, and the other view saltatory; and the most general way of characterizing the two views is by saying that my view describes knowing as it exists concretely, while the other view only describes its results abstractly taken.

I fear that most of my recalcitrant readers fail to recognize that what is ambulatory in the concrete may be taken so abstractly as to appear saltatory. Distance, for example, is made abstract by emptying out whatever is particular in the concrete intervals — it is reduced thus to a sole 'difference,' a difference of 'place,' which is a logical or saltatory distinction, a so-called 'pure relation.'

The same is true of the relation called 'knowing,' which may connect an idea with a reality. My own account of this relation is ambulatory through and through. I say that we know an object by means of an idea, whenever we ambulate towards the object under the impulse which the idea communicates. If we believe in so-called 'sensible' realities, the idea may not only send us towards its object, but may put the latter into our very hand, make it our . mediate sensation. But, if, as most reflective people opine, sensible realities are not 'real' realities, but only their appearances, our idea brings us at least so far, puts us in touch with reality 's most authentic a earances and substitutes. In any case our idea brings us into the object's neighborhood, practical or ideal, gets us into commerce with it, helps us towards its closer acquaintance, enables us to foresee it, class it, compare it, deduce it, — in short, to deal with it as we could not were the idea not in our possession.

The idea is thus, when functionally considered, an 'instrument for enabling us the better to have to do with the object and to act about it. But it and the object are both of them bits of the general sheet and tissue of reality at large; and when we say that the idea leads us towards the object, that only means that it carries us forward through intervening tracts of that reality into the object's closer neighborhood, into the midst of its associates at least, be these its physical neighbors, or be they its logical congeners only. Thus carried into closer quarters, we are in an improved situation as regards acquaintance and conduct; and we say that through the idea we now know the object better or more truly.

My thesis is that the knowing here is made by the ambulation through the intervening experiences. If the idea led us nowhere, or from that object instead of towards it, could we talk at all of its having any cognitive quality? Surely not, for it is only when taken in conjunction with the intermediate experiences that it gets related to that particular object rather than to any other part of nature. Those intermediaries determine what particular know ing function it exerts. The terminus they guide us to tells us what object it 'means,' the results they enrich us with 'verify' or I refute I it. Intervening experiences are thus as indispensable foundations for a concrete relation of cognition as intervening space is for a relation of distance. Cognition, whenever we take it concretely, means determinate 'ambulation,' through intermediaries, from a terminus a quo to, or towards, a terntinu8ad quem. As the intermediaries are other than the termini, and connected with them by the usual associative bonds (be these 'external' or be they logical, i. e., classificatory, in character), there would appear to be nothing especially unique about the processes of knowing. They fall wholly within experience; and we need use, in describing them, no other categories than those which we employ in describing other natural processes.

But there exist no processes which we cannot also consider abstractly, eviscerating them down to their essential skeletons or outlines; and when we have treated the processes of knowing thus, we are easily led to regard them as something altogether unparalleled in nature. For we first empty idea, object and intermediaries of all their particularities, in order to retain only a general scheme, and then we consider the latter only in its function of giving a result, and not in its character of being a process. In this treatment the intermediaries shrivel into the form of a mere space of separation, while the idea and object retain only the logical distinctness of being the end terms that are separated. In other words, the intermediaries which in their concrete particularity form a bridge, evaporate ideally into an empty interval to cross, and then, the relation of the end-terms having become saltatory, the whole hocus-pocus of erkenntnisstheorie begins, and goes on unrestrained by further concrete considerations. The idea, in 'meaning' an object separated by an 'epistemological chasm' from itself, now executes what Professor Ladd calls a 'salto mortale'; in knowing the object's nature, it now 'transcends' its own. The object in turn becomes 'present' where it is really absent, etc.; until a scheme remains upon our hands, the sublime paradoxes of which some of us think that nothing short of an 'absolute' can explain.

The relation between idea and object, thus made abstract and saltatory, is thenceforward opposed, as being more essential and previous, to its own ambulatory self, and the more concrete description is branded as either false or insufficient. The bridge of intermediaries, actual or possible, which in every real case is what carries and defines the knowing, gets treated as an episodic complication which need not even potentially be there. I believe that this vulgar fallacy of opposing abstractions to the concretes from which they are abstracted, is the main reason why my account of knowing is deemed so unsatisfactory,, and I will therefore say a word more on that general point.

Any vehicle of conjunction, if all its particularities are abstracted from it, will leave us with nothing on our hands but the i inal disjunction which it bridged over. But to escape treating the resultant self-contradiction as an achievement of dialectical profundity, all we need is to restore some part, no matter how small, of what we have taken away. In the case of the epistemological chasm the first reasonable step is to remember that the chasm was filled with some empirical material, whether ideational or sensational, which performed some bridging function and saved us from the mortal leap. Restoring thus the indispensable modicum of reality to the matter of our discussion, we find our abstract treatment genuinely useful. We escape entanglement with special cases without at the same time falling into gratuitous paradoxes. We can now describe the general features of cognition, tell what on the whole it does for us, in a universal way.

We must remember that this whole inquiry into knowing grows up on a reflective level. In any real moment of knowing, what we are thinking of is our object, not the way in which we ourselves are momentarily knowing it. We at this moment, as it happens, have knowing itself for our object; but I think that the reader will agree that his present knowing of that object is included only abstractly, and by anticipation, in the results he may reach. What be concretely has before his mind, as he reasons, is some supposed objective instance of knowing, as he conceives it to go on in some other person, or recalls it from his own past. As such, he, the critic, sees it to contain both an idea and an object, and processes by which the knower is guided from the one towards the other. He sees that the idea is remote from the object, and that, whether through intermediaries or not, it genuinely has to do with it. He sees that it thus works beyond its immediate being, and lays hold of a remote reality; it jumps across, transcends itself. It does all this by extraneous aid, to be sure, but when the aid has come, it has done it and the result is secure. Why not talk of results by themselves, then, without considering means? Why not treat the idea as simply grasping or intuiting the reality, of its having the faculty anyhow, of shooting over nature behind the scenes and knowing things immediately and directly? Why need we always lug in the bridging? —it only retards our discourse to do so.

Such abstract talk about cognition's results is surely convenient; and it is surely as legitimate as it is convenient, so long as we do not forget or positively deny, what it ignores. We may on occasion say that our idea meant always that particular object, that it led us there because it was of it intrinsically and essentially. We may insist that its verification follows upon that original cognitive virtue in it — and all the rest —and we shall do no harm so long as we know that these are only short cuts in our thinking. They are positively true accounts of fact as far as they go, only they leave vast tracts of fact out of the account, tracts of fact that have to be reinstated to make the accounts literally true of any real case. But if, not merely passively ignoring the intermediaries, you actively deny them[6] to be even potential requisites for the results you are so struck by, your epistemology goes to irremediable smash. You are as far off the track as an historian would be, if, lost in admiration of Napoleon's personal power, he were to ignore his marshals and his armies, and were to accuse you of error in describing his conquests as effected by their means. Of such abstractness and one-sidedness I accuse most of the critics of my own account.

In the second lecture of the book Pragmatism, I used the illustration of a squirrel scrambling round a tree-trunk to keep out of sight of a pursuing man: both go round the tree, but does the man go round the squirrel? It all depends, I said, on what you mean by 'going round.' In one sense of the word the man 'goes round,' in another sense he does not. I settled the dispute by pragmatically distinguishing the senses. But I told how some disputants had called my distinction a shuffling evasion and taken their stand on what they called 'plain honest English going-round.' in such a simple case few people would object to Jetting the term in dispute be translated into its concreter equivalents. But in the case of a complex function like our knowing they act differently. I give full concrete particular value for the ideas of knowing in every case I can think of, yet my critics insist that 'plain honest English knowing' is left out of my account. They write as if the minus were on my side and the plus on theirs.

The essence of the matter for me is that altho knowing can be both abstractly and concretely described, and altho the abstract descriptions are often useful enough, yet they are all sucked up and absorbed without residuum into the concreter ones, and contain nothing of any essentially other or higher nature, which the concrete descriptions can be justly accused of leaving behind. Knowing is just a natural process like any other. There is no ambulatory process whatsoever, the results of which we may not describe, if we prefer to, in saltatory terms, or represent in static formulation. Suppose, e. g., that we say a man is 'prudent.' Concretely, that means that he takes out insurance, hedges in betting, looks before he leaps. Do such acts constitute the prudence? are they the man quâ prudent?

Or is the prudence something by itself and independent of them? As a constant habit in him, a permanent tone Of character, it is convenient to call him prudent in abstraction from any one of his acts., prudent in general and without specification, and to say the acts follow from the pre-existing prudence. There are peculiarities in his psycho-physical system that make him act prudently; and there are tendencies to association in our thoughts that prompt some of them to make for truth and others for error. But would the man be prudent in the absence of each and all of the acts? Or would the thoughts be true if they had no associative or impulsive tendencies? Surely we have no right to oppose static essences in this way to the moving processes in which they live embedded.

My bedroom is above my library. Does the 'aboveness' here mean aught that is different from the concrete spaces which have to be moved-through in getting from the one to the other? It means, you may say, a pure topographic relation, a sort of architect's plan among the eternal essences. But that is not the full aboveness, it is only an abbreviated substitute that on occasion may lead my mind towards truer, i. e., fuller, dealings with the real aboveness. It is not an aboveness ante rem, it is a post rem extract from the aboveness in rebus. We may indeed talk, for certain conveniences, as if the abstract scheme preceded, we may say 'I must go up stairs because of the essential aboveness,' just as we may say that the man does prudent acts because of his ingrained prudence,' or that our ideas 'lead us truly because of their intrinsic truth.' But this should not debar us on other occasions from using completer forms of description. A concrete matter of fact always remains identical under any form of description, as when we say of a line, now that it runs from left to right, and now that it runs from right to left. These are but names of one and the same fact, one more expedient to use at one time, one at another. The full facts of cognition, whatever be the way in which we talk about them, even when we talk most abstractly, stand inalterably given in the actualities and possibilities of the experience-continuum.[7] But my critics treat my own more concrete talk as if it were the kind that sinned by its inadequacy, and as if the full continuum left something out.

A favorite way of opposing the more abstract to the more concrete account is to accuse those who favor the latter of 'confounding psychology with logic.' Our critics say that when we are asked what truth means, we reply by telling only how it is arrived at. But since a meaning is a logical relation, static, independent of time, how can it possibly be identified, they say, with any concrete man's experience perishing as this does at the instant of its production? This, indeed, sounds profound, but I challenge the profundity. I defy any one to show any difference between logic and psychology here. The logical relation stands to the psychological relation between idea and object only as saltatory abstractness stands to ambulatory concreteness. Both relations need a psychological vehicle; and the 'logical' one is simply the 'psychological' one disemboweled of its fulness, and reduced to a bare abstractional scheme.

A while ago a prisoner, on being released, tried to assassinate the judge who had sentenced him. He had apparently succeeded in conceiving the judge timelessly, had reduced him to a bare logical meaning, that of being his 'enemy and persecutor,' by stripping off all the concrete conditions (as jury's verdict, official obligation, absence of personal spite, possibly sympathy) that gave its full psychological character to the sentence as a particular man's act in time. Truly the sentence was inimical to the culprit; but which idea of it is the truer one, that bare logical definition of it, or its full psychological specification? The anti-pragmatists ought in consistency to stand up for the criminal's view of the case, treat the judge as the latter's logical enemy, and bar out the other conditions as so much inessential psychological stuff.

II

A still further obstacle, I suspect, stands in the way of my account's acceptance. Like Dewey and like Schiller, I have had to say that the truth of an idea is determined by its satisfactoriness. But satisfactoriness is a subjective term, just as idea is; and truth is generally regarded as 'objective.' Readers who admit that satisfactoriness is our only mark of truth, the only sign that we possess the precious article, will still say that the objective relation between idea and object which the word 'truth' points to is left out of my account altogether. I fear also that the association of my poor name with the 'will to believe' (which 'will,' it seems to me, ought to play no part in this discussion) works against my credit in some quarters. I fornicate with that unclean thing, my adversaries may think, whereas your genuine truth-lover must discourse in huxleyan heroics, and feel as if truth, to be real truth, ought to bring eventual messages of death to all our satisfactions. Such divergences certainly prove the complexity of the area of our discussion; but to my mind they also are based on misunderstandings, which (tho with but little hope of success) I will try to diminish by a further word of explanation.

First, then, I will ask my objectors to define exactly what sort of thing it is they have in mind when they speak of a truth that shall be absolute, complete and objective; and then I will defy them to show me any conceivable standing-room for such a kind of truth outside the terms of my own description. It will fall., as I contend, entirely within the field of my analysis.

To begin with, it must obtain between an idea and a reality that is the idea's object; and, as a predicate, it must apply to the idea and not to the object, for objective realities are not true, at least not in the universe of discourse to which we are now confining ourselves, for there they are taken as simply being, while the ideas are true of them. But we can suppose a series of ideas to be successively more and more true of the same object, and can ask what is the extreme approach to being absolutely true that the last idea might attain to.

The maximal conceivable truth in an idea would seem to be that it should lead to an actual merging of ourselves with the object, to an utter mutual confluence and identification. On the common-sense level of belief this is what is supposed really to take place in senseperception. My idea of this pen verifies itself through my percept; and my percept is held to be the pen for the time being-percepts and physical realities being treated by common sense as identical. But the physiology of the senses has criticised common sense out of court, and the pen 'in itself' is now believed to lie beyond my momentary percept. Yet the notion once suggested, of what a completely consummated acquaintance with a reality might be like, remains over for our speculative purposes. Total conflux of the mind with the reality would be the absolute limit of truth, there could be no better or more satisfying knowledge than that.

Such total conflux, it is needless to say, is already explicitly provided for, as a possibility, in my account of the matter. If an idea should ever lead us not only towards, or up to, or against, a reality, but so close that we and the reality should melt together, it would be made absolutely true, according to me, by that performance.

In point of fact philosophers doubt that this ever occurs. What happens, they think, is only that we get nearer and nearer to realities, we approximate more and more to the all-satisfying limit; and the definition of actually, as distinguished from imaginably, complete and objective truth, can then only be that it belongs to the idea that will lead us as close up against the object as in the nature of our experience is possible, literally next to it, for instance.

Suppose, now, there were an idea that did this for a certain objective reality. Suppose that no further approach were possible, that nothing lay between, that the next step would carry us right into the reality; then that result, being the next thing to conflux, would make the idea true in the maximal degree that might be supposed practically attainable in the world which we inhabit.

Well, I need hardly explain that that degree of truth is also provided for in my account of the matter. And if satisfactions are the marks of truth's presence, we may add that any less true substitute for such a true idea would prove less satisfactory. Following its lead, we should probably find out that we did not quite touch the terminus. We should desiderate a closer approach, and not rest till we had found it.

I am, of course, postulating here a standing reality independent of the idea that knows it. I am also postulating that satisfactions grow pari passu with our approximation to such reality.[8] If my critics challenge this latter assumption, I retort upon them with the former. Our whole notion of a standing reality grows up in the form of an ideal limit to the series of successive termini to which our thoughts 'have led us and still are leading us. Each terminus proves provisional by leaving us unsatisfied. The truer idea is the one that pushes farther; so we are ever beckoned on by the ideal notion of an ultimate completely satisfactory terminus. 1, for one, obey and accept that notion. I can conceive no other objective content to the notion of ideally perfect truth than that of penetration into such a terminus, nor can I conceive that the notion would ever have grown up, or that true ideas would ever have been sorted out from false or idle ones, save for the greater sum of satisfactions, intellectual or practical, which the truer ones brought with them. Can we imagine a man absolutely satisfied with an idea and with all its relations to his other ideas and to his sensible experiences, who should yet not take its content as a true account of reality? The matter of the true is thus absolutely identical with the matter of the satisfactory. You may put either word first in your ways of talking; but leave out that whole notion of satisfactory working or leading (which is the essence of my pragmatistic account) and call truth a static logical relation, independent even of possible leadings or satisfactions, and it seems to me you cut all ground from under you.

I fear that I am still very obscure. But I respectfully implore those who reject my doctrine because they can make nothing of my stumbling language, to tell us in their own name — und zwar very concretely and articulately! — just how the real, genuine and absolutely 'objective' truth which they believe in so profoundly, is constituted and established. They must n't point to the 'reality' itself, for truth is only our subjective relation to realities. What is the nominal essence of this relation, its logical definition, whether or not it be 'objectively' attainable by mortals?

Whatever they may say it is, I have the firmest faith that my account will prove to have allowed for it and included it by anticipation, as one possible case in the total mixture of cases. There is, in short, no room for any grade or sort of truth outside of the framework of the pragmatic system, outside of that jungle of empirical workings and leadings, and their nearer or ulterior terminations, of which I seem to have written so unskilfully.

Endnotes

1. Reprint from the Journal of Philosophy, July 18,1907.
2. Philosophical Review, vol. ii, P. 409, and Psychological Review, vol. ii, p. 533.
3. The relevant parts of which are printed above.
4. Vol. i, p. 253.
5. See my Principles of Psychology, vol. ii, pp. 148-153.
6. This is the fallacy which I have called 'vicious intellectualism' in my book A Pluralistic Universe, Longmans, Green & Co., 1909.
7. The ultimate object or terminus of a cognitive process may in certain instances lie beyond the direct experience of the particular cognizer, but it, of course, must exist as part of the total universe of experience whose constitution, with cognition in it, the critic is discussing.
8. Say, if you prefer to, that dissatisfactions decrease pari passu with such approximation. The approximation may be of any kind assignable approximation in time or in space, or approximation in kind, which in common speech means 'copying.'

PROFESSOR PRATT ON TRUTH

I[1]

Professor J. B. Pratt's paper in the Journal of Philosophy for June 6, 1907, is so brilliantly written that its misconception of the pragmatist position seems doubly to call for a reply.

He asserts that, for a pragmatist, truth cannot be a relation between an idea and a reality outside and transcendent of the idea, but must lie 'altogether within experience,' where it will need 'no reference to anything else to justify it no reference to the object, apparently. The pragmatist must 'reduce everything to psychology,' aye, and to the psychology of the immediate moment. He is consequently debarred from saying that an idea that eventually gets psychologically verified was already true before the process of verifying was complete; and he is equally debarred from treating an idea as true provisionally so long as he only believes that he can verify it whenever he will.

Whether such a pragmatist as this exists, I know not, never having myself met with the beast. We can define terms as we like; and if that be my friend Pratt's definition of a pragmatist, I can only concur with his anti-pragmatism. But, in setting up the weird type, he quotes words from me; so, in order to escape being classed by some reader along with so asinine a being, I will reassert my own view of truth once more.

Truth is essentially a relation between two things, an idea, on the one hand, and a reality outside of the idea, on the other. This relation, like all relations, has its fundamentum, namely, the matrix of experiential circumstance, psychological as well as physical, in which the correlated terms are found embedded. In the case of the relation between 'heir' and 'legacy' the fundamentum is a world in which there was a testator, and in which there is now a will and an executor; in the case of that between idea and object, it is a world with circumstances of a sort to make a satisfactory verification process, lying around and between the two terms. But just as a man may be called an heir and treated as one before the executor has divided the estate, so an idea may practically be credited with truth before the verification process has been exhaustively carried out —the existence of the mass of verifying circumstance is enough. Where potentiality counts for actuality in so many other cases, one does not see why it may not so count here. We call a man benevolent not only for his kind acts paid in, but for his readiness to perform others; we treat an idea as 'luminous' not only for the light it has shed, but for that we expect it will shed on dark problems. Why should we not equally trust the truth of our ideas? We live on credits everywhere; and we use our ideas far oftener for calling up things connected with their immediate objects, than for calling up those objects themselves. Ninety-nine times out of a hundred the only use we should make of the object itself, if we were led up to it by our idea, would be to pass on to those connected things by its means. So we continually curtail verification-processes, letting our belief that they are possible suffice.

What constitutes the relation known as truth, I now say, is just the existence in the empirical world of this fundamentum of circumstance surrounding object and idea and ready to be either short-circuited or traversed at full length. So long as it exists, and a satisfactory passage through it between the object and the Idea is possible, that idea will both be true, and will have been true of that object, whether fully developed verification has taken place or not. The nature and place and affinities of the object of course play as vital a part in making the particular passage possible as do the nature and associative tendencies of the idea; so that the notion that truth could fall alto
gether inside of the thinker's private experience and be something purely psychological, is absurd. It is between the idea and the object that the truth-relation is to be sought and it involves both terms.

But the 'intellectualistic' position, if I understand Mr. Pratt rightly, is. that, altho we can use this fundamentum, this mass of go-between experience, for testing truth, yet the truth-relation in itself remains as something apart. It means, in Mr. Pratt's words, merely 'this simple thing that the object of which one is thinking is as one thinks it.'

It seems to me that the word 'as,' which qualifies the relation here, and bears the whole ' epistemological' burden, is anything but simple. What it most immediately suggests is that the idea should be like the object; but most of our ideas, being abstract concepts, bear almost no resemblance to their objects. The 'as' must therefore, I should say, be usually interpreted functionally, as meaning that the idea shall lead us into the same quarters of experience as the object would. Experience leads ever on and on, and objects and our ideas of objects may both lead to the same goals. The ideas being in that case shorter cuts, we substitute them more and more for their objects; and we habitually waive direct verification of each one of them, as their train passes through our mind, because if an idea leads as the object would lead, we can say, in Mr. Pratt's words, that in so far forth the object is as we think it, and that the idea, verified thus in so far forth, is true enough.

Mr. Pratt will undoubtedly accept most of these facts, but he will deny that they spell pragmatism. Of course, definitions are free to every one; but I have myself never meant by the pragmatic view of truth anything different from what I now describe; and inasmuch as my use of the term came earlier than my friend's, I think it ought to have the right Of way. But I suspect that Professor Pratt's contention is not solely as to what one must think in order to be called a pragmatist. I am sure that he believes that the truth-relation has something more in it than the fundamentum, which I assign can account for. Useful to test truth by, the matrix Of circumstance, he thinks, cannot found the truth-relation in se, for that is trans-empirical and 'saltatory.'

Well, take an object and an idea, and assume that the latter is true of the former — as eternally and absolutely true as you like. Let the object be as much 'as' the idea thinks it, as it is possible for one thing to be 'as' another. I now formally ask of Professor Pratt to tell what this 'as'-ness in itself consists in—for it seems to me that it ought to consist in something assignable and describable, and not remain a pure mystery, and I promise that if he can assign any determination of it whatever which I cannot successfully refer to some specification of what in this article I have called the empirical fundamentum, I will confess my stupidity cheerfully, and will agree never to publish a line upon this subject of truth again.

II

Professor Pratt has returned to the charge in a whole book,[2] which for its clearness and good temper deserves to supersede all the rest of the anti-pragmatistic literature. I wish it might do so; for its author admits all my essential contentions, simply distinguishing my account of truth as 'modified' pragmatism from Schiller's and Dewey's, which he calls pragmatism of the 'radical' sort. As I myself understand Dewey and Schiller, our views absolutely agree, in spite of our different modes of statement; but I have enough trouble of my own in life without having to defend my friends, so I abandon them provisionally to the tender mercy of Professor Pratt's interpretations, utterly erroneous tho, I deem these to be. My reply as regards myself can be very short, for I prefer to consider only essentials, and Dr. Pratt's whole book hardly takes the matter farther than the article to which I retort in Part I of the present paper.

He repeats the 'as' formula, as if it were something that 1, along with other pragmatists, had denied,[3] whereas I have only asked those who insist so on its importance to do something more than merely utter it — to explicate it, for example, and tell us what its so great importance consists in. I myself agree most cordially that for an idea to be true the object must be 'as' the idea declares it, but I explicate the 'as'-ness as meaning the idea's verifiability.

Now since Dr. Pratt denies none of these verifying 'workings' for which I have pleaded, but only insists on their inability to serve as the fundamentum, of the truth-relation, it seems that there is really nothing in the line of fact about which we differ, and that the issue between us is solely as to how far the notion of workableness or verifiability is an essential part of the notion of 'trueness' 'trueness" — being Dr. Pratt's present name for the character of as-ness in the true idea. I maintain that there is no meaning left in this notion of as-ness or trueness if no reference to the possibility of concrete working on the part of the idea is made.

Take an example where there can be no possible working. Suppose I have an idea to which I give utterance by the vocable 'skrkl,' claiming at the same time that it is true. Who now can say that it is false, for why may there not be somewhere in the unplumbed depths of the cosmos some object with which 'skrkl' can agree and have trueness in Dr. Pratt's sense? On the other hand who can say that it is true, for who can lay his hand on that object and show that it and nothing else is what I mean by my word? But yet again, who can gainsay any one who shall call my word utterly irrelative to other reality, and treat it as a bare fact in my mind, devoid of any cognitive function whatever. One of these three alternatives must surely be predicated of it. For it not to be irrelevant (or not-cognitive in nature), an object of some kind must be provided which it may refer to. Supposing that object provided, whether 'skrkl' is true or false of it, depends, according to Professor Pratt, on no intermediating condition whatever. The trueness or the falsity is even now immediately, absolutely, and positively there.

I, on the other hand, demand a cosmic environment of some kind to establish which of them is there rather than utter irrelevancy.[4] I then say, first, that unless some sort of a natural path exists between the 'skrkl' and that object, distinguishable among the innumerable pathways that run among all the realities of the universe, linking them promiscuously with one another, there is nothing there to constitute even the possibility of its referring to that object rather than to any other.

I say furthermore that unless it have some tendency to follow up that path, there is nothing to constitute its intention to refer to the object in question. Finally, I say that unless the path be strown with possibilities of frustration or encouragement, and offer some sort of terminal satisfaction or contradiction, there is nothing to constitute its agreement or disagreement with that object, or to constitute the as-ness (or 'not-asness') in which the trueness (or falseness) is said to consist.

I think that Dr. Pratt ought to do something more than repeat the name 'trueness,' in answer to my pathetic question whether that there be not some constitution to a relation as important as this. The pathway, the tendency, the corroborating or contradicting progress, need not in every case be experienced in full'. but I don't see, if the universe does n't contain them among its possibilities of furniture, what logical material for defining the trueness of my idea is left. But if it do contain them, they and they only am the logical material required.

I am perplexed by the superior importance which Dr. Pratt attributes to abstract trueness over concrete verifiability in an idea, and I wish that he might be moved to explain. It is prior to verification, to be sure, but so is the verifiability for which I contend prior, just as a man's 'mortality' (which is nothing but the possibility of his death) is prior to his death, but it can hardly be that this abstract priority of all possibility to its correlative fact is what so obstinate a quarrel is about. I think it probable that Dr. Pratt is vaguely thinking of something concreter than this. The trueness of an idea must mean something definite in it that determines its tendency to work, and indeed towards this object rather than towards that. Undoubtedly there is something of this sort in the idea, just as there is something in man that accounts for his tendency towards death, and in bread that accounts for its tendency to nourish. What that something is in the case of truth psychology tells us: the idea has associates peculiar to itself, motor as well as ideational; it tends by its place and nature to call these into being, one after another; and the appearance of them in succession is what we mean by the 'workings' of the idea. According to what they are, does the trueness or falseness which the idea harbored come to light. These tendencies have still earlier conditions which, in a general way, biology, psychology and biography can trace. This whole chain of natural causal conditions produces a resultant state of things in which new relations, not simply causal, can now be found, or into which they can now be introduced, — the relations namely which we epistemologists study, relations of adaptation, of substitutability, of instrumentality, of reference and of truth.

The prior causal conditions, altho there could be no knowing of any kind, true or false, without them, are but preliminary to the question of what makes the ideas true or false when once their tendencies have been obeyed. The tendencies must exist in some shape anyhow, but their fruits are truth, falsity, or irrelevancy, according to what they concretely turn out to be. They are not 'saltatory' at any rate, for they evoke their consequences contiguously, from next to next only; and not until the final result of the whole associative sequence, actual or potential, is in our mental sight, can we feel sure what its epistemological significance, if it have any, may be. True knowing is, in fine, not substantially, in itself, or 'as such,,' inside of the idea from the first,, any more than mortality as such is inside of the man,, or nourishment as such inside of the bread. Something else is there first that practically makes for knowing, dying or nourishing, as the case may be. That something is the 'nature ' namely of the first term, be it idea, man, or bread, that operates to start the causal chain of processes which,, when completed, is the complex fact to which we give whatever functional name best fits the case. Another nature, another chain of cognitive workings; and then either another object known or the same object known differently, will ensue.

Dr. Pratt perplexes me again by seeming to charge Dewey and Schiller[5] (I am not sure that he charges me) with an account of truth which would allow the object believed in not to exist,, even if the belief in it were true. 'Since the truth of an idea,' he writes, 'means merely the fact that the idea works, that fact is all that you mean when you say the idea is true.' 'When you say the idea is true'does that mean true for you, the critic, or true for the believer whom you are describing? The critic's trouble over this seems to come from his taking the word ' true' irrelatively, whereas the pragmatist always means 'true for him who experiences the workings! 'But is the object really true or not?' —the critic then seems to ask, — as if the pragmatist were bound to throw in a whole ontology on top of his epistemology and tell us what realities indubitably exist. 'One world at a time, I would seem to be the right reply here.

One other trouble of Dr. Pratt's must be noticed. It concerns the 'transcendence' of the object. When our ideas have worked so as to bring us flat up against the object, next to it, 'is our relation to it then ambulatory or saltatory?' Dr. Pratt mks. If your headache be my object, 'my experiences break off where yours begin,' Dr. Pratt writes, and 'this fact is of great importance, for it bars out the sense of transition and fulfilment which forms so important an element in the pragmatist description of knowledge — the sense of fulfilment due to a continuous passage from the original idea to the known object. If this comes at all when I know your headache, it comes not with the object, but quite on my side of the " epistemological gulf." The gulf is still there to be transcended."

Some day of course, or even now somewhere in the larger life of the universe, different men's headaches may become confluent or be 'co-conscious.' Here and now, however, headaches do transcend each other and, when not felt, can be known only conceptually. My idea is that you really have a headache; it works well with what I see of your expression, and with what I hear you say; but it does n't put me in possession of the headache itself. I am still at one remove, and the headache 'transcends' me, even tho it be in nowise transcendent of human experience generally. But the 'gulf' here is that which the pragmatist epistemology itself fixes in the very first words it uses, by saying there must be an object and an idea. The idea however does n't immediately leap the gulf, it only works from next to next so as to bridge it, fully or approximately. If it bridges it, in the pragmatist's vision of his hypothetical universe, it can be called a 'true' idea. If it only might bridge it, but doesn't, or if it throws a bridge distinctly at it, it still has, in the onlooking pragmatist's eyes, what Professor Pratt calls 'trueness.' But to ask the pragmatist thereupon whether, when it thus fails to coalesce bodily with the object, it is really true or has real trueness, — other words whether the headache he supposes, and supposes the thinker he supposes, to believe in, be a real headache or not, — to step from his hypothetical universe of discourse into the altogether different world of natural fact.

Endnotes

1. Reprinted from the Journal of Philosophy etc., August 15, 1907 (vol. iv, p. 464).

2. J.B. Pratt: What is Pragmatism. New York, The Macmillan Company, 1909. — The comments I have printed were written in March, 1909, after some of the articles printed later in the present volume.

3. Op. cit..

4. Dr. Pratt, singularly enough, disposes of this primal postulate of all pragmatic epistemology, by saying that the pragmatist 'unconsciously surrenders his whole case by smuggling in the idea of a conditioning environment which determines whether or not the experience can work, and which cannot itself be identified with the experience or any part of it.' The 'experience' means here of course the idea, or belief; and the expression 'smuggling in' is to the last degree diverting. If any epistemologist could dispense with a conditioning environment, it would seem to be the antipragmatist, with his immediate saltatory trueness, independent of work done. The mediating pathway which the environment supplies is the very essence of the pragmatist's explanation.

5. Above.

THE PRAGMATIST ACCOUNT OF TRUTH AND ITS MISUNDERSTANDERS[1]

The account of truth given in my volume entitled Pragmatism, continues to meet with such persistent misunderstanding that I am tempted to make a final brief reply. My ideas may well deserve refutation, but they can get none till they are conceived of in their proper shape. The fantastic character of the current misconceptions shows how unfamiliar is the concrete point of view which pragmatism assumes. Persons who are familiar with a conception move about so easily in it that they understand each other at a hint, and can converse without anxiously attending to their P's and Q's. I have to admit, in view of the results, that we have assumed too ready an intelligence, and consequently in many places used a language too slipshod. We should never have spoken elliptically. The critics have boggled at every word they could boggle at, and refused to take the spirit rather than the letter of our discourse. This seems to show a genuine unfamiliarity in the whole point of view. It also shows, I think, that the second stage of opposition, which has already begun to express itself in the stock phrase that 'what is new is not true, and what is true not new,' in pragmatism, is insincere. If we said nothing in any degree new, why was our meaning so desperately hard to catch? The blame ,cannot be laid wholly upon our obscurity of speech, for in other subjects we have attained to making ourselves understood. But recriminations are tasteless; and, as far as I personally am concerned, I am sure that some of the misconception I complain of is due to my doctrine of truth being surrounded in that volume of popular lectures by a lot of other opinions not necessarily implicated with it, so that a reader may very naturally have grown confused. For this I am to blame, — likewise for omitting certain explicit cautions, which the pages that follow will now in part supply.

First misunderstanding: Pragmatism is only a re-editing of positivism.

This seems the commonest mistake. Scepticism, positivism, and agnosticism agree with ordinary dogmatic rationalism in presupposing that everybody knows what the word 'truth' means, without further explanation. But the former doctrines then either suggest or declare that real truth, absolute truth, is inaccessible to us, and that we must fain put up with relative or phenomenal truth as its next best substitute. By scepticism this is treated as an unsatisfactory state Of affairs,, while positivism and agnosticism are cheerful about it, call real truth sour grapes, and consider phenomenal truth quite sufficient for all our 'practical' purposes.

In point of fact, nothing could be farther from all this than what pragmatism has to say of truth. Its thesis is an altogether previous one. It leaves off where these other theories begin, having contented itself with the word truth's definition. 'No matter whether any mind extant in the universe possess truth or not,' it asks, 'what does the notion of truth signify ideally?' 'What kind of things would

true judgments be in case they existed?' The answer which pragmatism offers is intended to cover the most complete truth that can be conceived of, I absolute' truth if you like, as well as truth of the most relative and imperfect description. This question of what truth would be like if it did exist, belongs obviously to a purely speculative field of inquiry. It is not a theory about any sort of reality, or about what kind of knowledge is actually possible; it abstracts from particular terms altogether, and defines the nature of a possible relation between two of them.

As Kant's question about synthetic judgments had escaped previous philosophers, so the pragmatist question is not only so subtle as to have escaped attention hitherto, but even so subtle, it would seem, that when openly broached now, dogmatists and sceptics alike fail to apprehend it, and deem the pragmatist to be treating of something wholly different. He insists, they say (I quote an actual critic), 'that the greater problems are insoluble by human intelligence, that our need of knowing truly is artificial and illusory, and that our reason, incapable of reaching the foundations Of reality, must turn itself exclusively towards action.' There could not be a worse misapprehension.

Second misunderstanding: Pragmatism is primarily an appeal to action.

The name 'pragmatism,' with its suggestions Of action, has been an unfortunate choice, I have to admit, and has played into the hands of this mistake. But no word could protect the doctrine from critics so blind to the nature of the inquiry that, when Dr. Schiller speaks of ideas 'working' well, the only thing they think of is their immediate workings in the physical environment, their enabling us to make money, or gain some similar 'practical' advantage. Ideas do work thus, of course, immediately or remotely; but they work indefinitely inside of the mental world also. Not crediting us with this rudimentary insight, our critics treat our view as offering itself exclusively to engineers, doctors, financiers, and men Of action generally, who need some sort of a rough and ready Weltanschauung, but have no time or wit to study genuine philosophy. It is usually described as a characteristically American movement, a sort of bobtailed scheme of thought, excellently fitted for the man on the street., who naturally hates theory and wants cash returns immediately.

It is quite true that, when the refined theoretic question that pragmatism begins with is once answered, secondary corollaries of a practical sort follow. Investigation shows that, in the function called truth, previous realities are not the only independent variables. To a certain extent our ideas, being realities, are also independent variables, and, just as they follow other reality and fit it, so, in a measure, does other reality follow and fit them. When they add themselves to being, they partly redetermine the existent, so that reality as a whole appears incompletely definable unless ideas also are kept account of. This pragmatist doctrine,, exhibiting our ideas as complemental factors of reality., throws open (since our ideas are instigators of our action) a wide window upon human action, as well as a wide license to originality in thought. But few things could be sillier than to ignore the prior epistemological edifice in which the window is built, or to talk as if pragmatism began and ended at the window. This, nevertheless, is what our critics do almost without exception. They ignore our primary step and its motive, and make the relation to action, which is our secondary achievement, primary.

Third misunderstanding: Pragmatists cut themselves off from the right to believe in ejective realities.

They do so, according to the critics, by making the truth of our beliefs consist in their verifiability, and their verifiability in the way in which they do work for us. Professor Stout, in his otherwise admirable and hopeful review of Schiller in Mind for October, 1897, considers that this ought to lead Schiller (could he sincerely realize the effects of his own doctrine) to the absurd consequence of being unable to believe genuinely in another man's headache, even were the headache there. He can only 'postulate' it for the sake of the working value of the postulate to himself. The postulate guides certain of his acts and leads to advantageous consequences; but the moment he understands fully that the postulate is true only (!) in this sense, it ceases (or should cease) to be true for him that the other man really has a headache. All that makes the postulate most precious then evaporates: his interest in his fellow-man 'becomes a veiled form of self-interest, and his world grows cold, dull, and heartless.'

Such an objection makes a curious muddle of the pragmatist's universe of discourse. Within that universe the pragmatist finds some one with a headache or other feeling, and some one else who postulates that feeling. Asking on what condition the postulate is 'true,' the pragmatist replies that, for the postulator at any rate, it is true just in proportion as to believe in it works in him the fuller sum of satisfactions. What is it that is satisfactory here? Surely to believe in the postulated object, namely, in the really existing feeling of the other man. But how (especially if the postulator were himself a thoroughgoing pragmatist) could it ever be satisfactory to him not to believe in that feeling, so long as, in Professor Stout's words, disbelief 'made the world seem to him cold, dull, and heartless'? Disbelief would seem, on pragmatist principles, quite out of the question under such conditions, unless the heartlessness of the world were made probable already on other grounds. And since the belief in the headache, true for the subject assumed in the pragmatist's universe of discourse, is also true for the pragmatist who for his epitemologizing purposes has assumed that entire universe, why is it not true in that universe absolutely? The headache believed in is a reality there, and no extant mind disbelieves it, neither the critic's mind nor his subject's! Have our opponents any better brand of truth in this real universe of ours that they can show us?[2]

So much for the third misunderstanding, which is but one specification of the following still wider one.

Fourth misunderstanding: No pragmatist can be a realist in his epistemology.

This is supposed to follow from his statement that the truth of our beliefs consists in general in their giving satisfaction. Of course satisfaction per se is a subjective condition; so the conclusion is drawn that truth falls wholly inside of the subject, who then may manufacture it at his pleasure. True beliefs become thus wayward affections, severed from all responsibility to other parts of experience.

It is difficult to excuse such a parody of the pragmatist's opinion, ignoring as it does every element but one of his universe of discourse. The terms of which that universe consists positively forbid any non-realistic interpretation of the function of knowledge defined there. The pragmatizing epistemologist posits there a reality and a mind with ideas. What, now, he asks, can make those ideas true of that reality? Ordinary epistemology contents itself with the vague statement that the ideas must 'correspond' or 'agree; the pragmatist insists on being more concrete, and asks what such 'agreement' may mean in detail. He finds first that the ideas must point to or lead towards that reality and no other, and then that the pointings and leadings must yield satisfaction as their result. So far the pragmatist is hardly less abstract than the ordinary slouchy epistemologist; but as he defines himself farther, he grows more concrete. The entire quarrel of the intellectualist with him is over his concreteness, intellectualism contending that the vaguer and more abstract account is here the more profound. The concrete pointing and leading are conceived by the pragmatist to be the work of other portions of the same universe to which the reality and the mind belong, intermediary verifying bits of experience with which the mind at one end, and the reality at the other, are joined. The 'satisfaction,' in turn, is no abstract satisfaction überhaupt, felt by an unspecified being, but is assumed to consist of such satisfactions (in the plural) as concretely existing men actually do find in their beliefs. As we humans are constituted in point of fact, we find that to believe in other men's minds, in independent physical realities, in past events, in eternal logical relations, is satisfactory. We find hope satisfactory. We often find it satisfactory to cease to doubt. Above all we find consistency satisfactory, consistency between the present idea and the entire rest of our mental equipment, including the whole order of our sensations, and that of our intuitions of likeness and difference, and our whole stock of previously acquired truths.

The pragmatist, being himself a man, and imagining in general no contrary lines of truer belief than ours about the 'reality' which he has laid at the base of his epistemological discussion, is willing to treat our satisfactions as possibly really true guides to it, not as guides true solely for us. It would seem here to be the duty of his critics to show with some explicitness why, being our subjective feelings, these satisfactions can not yield I objective' truth. The beliefs which they accompany posit' the assumed reality, I correspond' and 'agree' with it, and 'fit' it in perfectly definite and assignable ways, through the sequent trains of thought and action which form their verification, so merely to insist on using these words abstractly instead of concretely is no way of driving the pragmatist from the field, —his more concrete account virtually includes his critic's. If our critics have any definite idea of a truth more objectively grounded than the kind we propose, why do they not show it more articulately? As they stand, they remind one of Hegel's man who wanted 'fruit,' but rejected cherries, pears, and grapes, because they were not fruit in the abstract. We offer them the full quart-pot, and they cry for the empty quart-capacity.

But here I think I hear some critic retort as follows: 'If satisfactions are all that is needed to make truth, how about the notorious fact that errors are so often satisfactory? And how about the equally notorious fact that certain true beliefs may cause the bitterest dissatisfaction? Isn't it clear that not the satisfaction which it gives, but the relation of the belief to the reality is all that makes it true? Suppose there were no such reality, and that the satisfactions yet remained: would they not then effectively work falsehood? Can they consequently be treated distinctively as the truthbuilders? It is the inherent relation to reality of a belief that gives us that specific truthsatisfaction, compared with which all other satisfactions are the hollowest humbug. The satisfaction of knowing truly is thus the only one which the pragmatist ought to have considered. As a psychological sentiment, the anti-pragmatist gladly concedes it to him, but then only as a concomitant of truth, not as a constituent. What constitutes truth is not the sentiment, but the purely logical or objective function of rightly cognizing the reality, and the pragmatist's failure to reduce this function to lower values is patent.'

Such anti-pragmatism as this seems to me a tissue of confusion. To begin with, when the pragmatist says 'indispensable,' it confounds this with 'sufficient.' The pragmatist calls satisfactions indispensable for truth-building, but I have everywhere called them insufficient unless reality be also incidentally led to. If the reality assumed were cancelled from the pragmatist's universe of discourse, he would straightway give the name of falsehoods to the beliefs remaining, in spite of all their satisfactoriness. For him, as for his critic, there can be no truth if there is nothing to be true about. Ideas are so much flat psychological surface unless some mirrored matter gives them cognitive lustre. This is why as a pragmatist I have so carefully posited 'reality' ab initio, and why, throughout my whole discussion, I remain an epistemological realist.[3]

The anti-pragmatist is guilty of the further confusion of imagining that, in undertaking to give him an account of what truth formally means, we are assuming at the same time to provide a warrant for it, trying to define the occasions when he can be sure of materially possessing it. Our making it hinge on a reality so independent' that when it comes, truth comes, and when it goes, truth goes with it, disappoints this naive expectation, so he deems our description unsatisfactory. I suspect that under this confusion lies the still deeper one of not discriminating sufficiently between the two notions, truth and reality. Realities are not true, they are; and beliefs are true of them. But I suspect that in the anti-pragmatist mind the two notions sometimes swap their attributes. The reality itself, I fear, is treated as if 'true,' and conversely. Whoso tells us of the one, it is then supposed, must also be telling us of the other; and a true idea must in a manner be, or at least yield without extraneous aid, the reality it cognitively is possessed of.

To this absolute-idealistic demand pragmatism simply opposes its non possumus. If there is to be truth, it says, both realities and beliefs about them must conspire to make it; but whether there ever is such a thing, or how anyone can be sure that his own beliefs possess it, it never pretends to determine. That truth-satisfaction par excellence which may tinge a belief unsatisfactory in other ways, it easily explains as the feeling of consistency with the stock of previous truths, or supposed truths, of which one's whole past experience may have left one in possession.

But are not all pragmatists sure that their own belief is right? their enemies will ask at this point; and this leads me to the

Fifth misunderstanding: What pragmatists say is inconsistent with their saying so.

A correspondent puts this objection as follows: 'When you say to your audience, "pragmatism is the truth concerning truth,," the first truth is different from the second. About the first you and they are not to be at odds; you are not giving them liberty to take or leave it according as it works satisfactorily or not for their private uses. Yet the second truth, which ought to describe and include the first, affirms this liberty. Thus the intent of your utterance seems to contradict the content of it.'

General scepticism has always received this same classic refutation. 'You have to dogmatize,' the rationalists say to the sceptics, ' whenever you express the sceptical position; so your lives keep contradicting your thesis.' One would suppose that the impotence of so hoary an argument to abate in the slightest degree the amount of general scepticism in the world might have led some rationalists themselves to doubt whether these instantaneous logical refutations are such fatal ways, after all, of killing off live mental attitudes. General scepticism is the live mental attitude of refusing to conclude. It is a permanent torpor of the will, renewing itself in detail towards each successive thesis that offers, and you can no more kill it off by logic than you can kill off obstinacy or practical joking. This is why it is so irritating. Your consistent sceptic never puts his scepticism into a formal proposition, — he simply chooses it as a habit. He provokingly hangs back when he might so easily join us in saying yes, but he is not illogical or stupid, — on the contrary, he often impresses us by his intellectual superiority. This is the real scepticism that rationalists have to meet, and their logic does not even touch it.

No more can logic kill the pragmatist's behavior: his act of utterance, so far from contradicting, accurately exemplifies the matter which he utters. What is the matter which he utters? In part, it is this, that truth, concretely considered, is an attribute of our beliefs, and that these are attitudes that follow satisfactions. The ideas around which the satisfactions cluster are primarily only hypotheses that challenge or summon a belief to come and take its stand upon them. The pragmatist's idea of truth is just such a challenge. He finds it ultra-satisfactory to accept it, and takes his own stand accordingly. But, being gregarious as they are, men seek to spread their beliefs, to awaken imitation, to infect others. Why should not you also find the same belief satisfactory? thinks the pragmatist, and forthwith endeavors to convert you. You and he will then believe similarly; you will hold up your subject—end of a truth, which will be a truth objective and irreversible if the reality holds up the object-end by being itself present simultaneously. What there is of self-contradiction in all this I confess I cannot discover. The pragmatist's conduct in his own case seems to me on the contrary admirably to illustrate his universal formula; and of all epistemologists, he is perhaps the only one who is irreproachably self-consistent.

Sixth misunderstanding: Pragmatism explains not what truth is, but only how it is arrived at.

In point of fact it tells us both, tells us what it is incidentally to telling us how it is arrived at, —for what is arrived at except just what the truth is? If I tell you how to get to the railroad station, don't I implicitly introduce you to the what, to the being and nature of that edifice? It is quite true that the abstract word 'how' has n't the same meaning as the abstract word 'what,' but in this universe of concrete facts you cannot keep hows and whats asunder. The reasons why I find it satisfactory to believe that any idea is true, the how of my arriving at that belief, may be among the very reasons why the idea is true in reality. If not, I summon the anti-pragmatist to explain the impossibility articulately.

His trouble seems to me mainly to arise from his fixed inability to understand how a concrete statement can possibly mean as much, or be as valuable, as an abstract one. I said above that the main quarrel between us and our critics was that of concreteness versus abstractness. This is the place to develop that point farther.

In the present question, the links of experience sequent upon an idea, which mediate between it and a reality, form and for the pragmatist indeed are, the concrete relation of truth that may obtain between the idea and that reality. They, he says, are all that we mean when we speak of the idea 'pointing' to the reality, 'fitting' it, 'corresponding' with it, or 'agreeing' with it, — they or other similar mediating trains of verification. Such mediating events make the idea 'true.' The idea itself, if it exists at all, is also a concrete event: so pragmatism insists that truth in the singular is only a collective name for truths in the plural, these consisting always of series of definite events; and that what intellectualism calls the truth, the inherent truth, of any one such series is only the abstract name for its truthfulness in act, for the fact that the ideas there do lead to the supposed reality in a way that we consider satisfactory.

The pragmatist himself has no objection to abstractions. Elliptically, and 'for short,' he relies on them as much as any one, finding upon innumerable occasions that their comparative emptiness makes of them useful substitutes for the overfulness of the facts he meets with. But he never ascribes to them a higher grade of reality. The full reality of a truth for him is always some process of verification, in which the abstract property of connecting ideas with objects truly is workingly embodied. Meanwhile it is endlessly serviceable to be able to talk of properties abstractly and apart from their working, to find them the same in innumerable cases, to take them 'out of time,' and to treat of their relations to other similar abstractions. We thus form whole universes of platonic ideas ante rem, universes in posse, tho none of them exists effectively except in rebus. Countless relations obtain there which nobody experiences as obtaining, —as, in the eternal universe of musical relations, for example, the notes of Aennchen von Tharau were a lovely melody long ere mortal ears ever heard them. Even so the music of the future sleeps now, to be awakened hereafter. Or, if we take the world of geometrical relations, the thousandth decimal of sleeps there, tho no one may ever try to compute it. Or, if we take the universe of 'fitting,' countless coats 'fit' backs, and countless boots "fit' feet, on which they are not practically fitted; countless stones 'fit' gaps in walls into which no one seeks to fit them actually. In the same way countless opinions 'fat' realities, and countless truths are valid, tho no thinker ever thinks them.

For the anti-pragmatist these prior timeless relations are the presupposition of the concrete ones, and possess the profounder dignity and value. The actual workings of our ideas in verification-processes are as naught in comparison with the 'obtainings' of this discarnate truth within them.

For the pragmatist, on the contrary, all discarnate truth is static, impotent, and relatively spectral, full truth being the truth that energizes and does battle. Can any one suppose that the sleeping quality of truth would ever have been abstracted or have received a name, if truths had remained forever in that storagevault of essential timeless 'agreements' and had never been embodied in any panting struggle of men's live ideas for verification? Surely no more than the abstract property of 'fitting' would have received a name, if in our world there had been no backs or feet or gaps in walls to be actually fitted. Existential truth is incidental to the actual competition of opinions. Essential truth, the truth of the intellectualists, the truth with no one thinking it, is like the coat that fits tho no one has ever tried it on, like the music that no ear has listened to. It is less real, not more real, than the verified article; and to attribute a superior degree of glory to it seems little more than a piece of perverse abstraction-worship. As well might a pencil insist that the outline is the essential thing in all pictorial representation, and chide the paint-brush and the camera for omit. ting it, forgetting that their pictures not only contain the whole outline, but a hundred other things in addition. Pragmatist truth contains the whole of intellectualist truth and a hundred other things in addition. Intellectualist truth is then only pragmatist truth in posse. That on innumerable occasions men do substitute truth in posse or verifiability, for verification or truth in act, is a fact to which no one at. tributes more importance than the pragmatist: he emphasizes the practical utility of such a habit. But he does not on that account consider truth in posse, —truth not alive enough ever to have been asserted or questioned or contradicted, —to be the metaphysically prior thing, to which truths in act are tributary and subsidiary. When intellectualists do this, pragmatism charges them with inverting the real relation. Truth in posse means only truths in act; and he insists that these latter take precedence in the order of logic as well as in that of being.

Seventh misunderstanding: Pragmatism ignores the theoretic interest.

This would seem to be an absolutely wanton slander, were not a certain excuse to be found in the linguistic affinities of the word 'pragmatism,' and in certain offhand habits of speech of ours which assumed too great a generosity on our reader's part. When we spoke of the meaning of ideas consisting in their 'practical' consequences, or of the 'practical' differences which our beliefs make to us; when we said that the truth of a belief consists in its 'working' value, etc.; our language evidently was too careless, for by 'practical' we were almost unanimously held to mean opposed to theoretical or genuinely cognitive, and the consequence was punctually drawn that a truth in our eyes could have no relation to any independent reality, or to any other truth, or to anything whatever but the acts which we might ground on it or the satisfactions they might bring. The mere existence of the idea, all by itself, if only its results were satisfactory, would give full truth to it, it was charged, in our absurd pragmatist epistemology. The solemn attribution of this rubbish to us was also encouraged by two other circumstances. First, ideas are practically useful in the narrow sense, false ideas sometimes, but most often ideas which we can verify by the sum total of all their leadings, and the reality of whose objects may thus be considered established beyond doubt. That these ideas should be true in advance of and apart from their utility, that, in other words, their objects should be really there, is the very condition of their having that kind of utility, — the objects they connect us with are so important that the ideas which serve as the objects' substitutes grow important also. This manner of their practical working was the first thing that made truths good in the eyes of primitive men; and buried among all the other good workings by which true beliefs are characterized, this kind of subsequential utility remains.

The second misleading circumstance was the emphasis laid by Schiller and Dewey on the fact that, unless a truth be relevant to the mind's momentary predicament, unless it be germane to the 'practical' situation, — meaning by this the quite particular perplexity, — it is no good to urge it. It does n't meet our interests any better than a falsehood would under the same circumstances. But why our predicaments and perplexities might not be theoretical here as well as narrowly practical, I wish that our critics would explain. They simply assume that no pragmatist can admit a genuinely theoretic interest. Having used the phrase 'cash-value' of an idea, I am implored by one correspondent to alter it, 'for every one thinks you mean only pecuniary profit and loss.' Having said that the true is 'the expedient in our thinking,' I am rebuked in this wise by another learned correspondent: 'The word expedient has no other meaning than that of self-interest. The pursuit of this has ended by landing a number of officers of national banks in penitentiaries. A philosophy that leads to such results must be unsound.'

But the word 'practical' is so habitually loosely used that more indulgence might have been expected. When one says that a sick man has now practically recovered, or that an enterprise has practically failed, one usually means just the opposite of practically in the literal sense. One means that, altho untrue in strict practice, what one says is true in theory, true virtually, certain to be true. Again, by the practical one often means the distinctively concrete, the individual, particular, and effective, as opposed to the abstract, general, and inert. To speak for myself, whenever I have emphasized the practical nature of truth, this is mainly what has been in my mind. 'Pragmata' are things in their plurality; and in that early California address, when I described pragmatism as holding that 'the meaning of any proposition can always be brought down to some particular consequence in our future practical experience, whether passive or active,' I expressly added these qualifying words: 'the point lying rather in the fact that the experience must be particular than in the fact that it must be active,'— by 'active' meaning here 'practical' in the narrow literal sense.[4] But particular consequences can perfectly well be of a theoretic nature. Every remote fact which we infer from an idea is a particular theoretic consequence which our mind practically works towards. The loss of every old opinion of ours which we see that we shall have to give up if a new opinion be true, is a particular theoretic as well as a particular practical consequence. After man's interest in breathing freely, the greatest of all his interests (because it never fluctuates or remits, as most of his physical interests do), is his interest in consistency, in feeling that what he now thinks goes with what he thinks on other occasions. We tirelessly compare truth with truth for this sole purpose. Is the present candidate for belief perhaps contradicted by principle number one? Is it compatible with fact number two? and so forth. The particular operations here are the purely logical ones of analysis, deduction, comparison, etc.; and altho general terms may be used ad libitum, the satisfactory practical working of the candidate-idea consists in the consciousness yielded by each successive theoretic consequence in particular. It is therefore simply idiotic to repeat that pragmatism takes no account of purely theoretic interests. All it insists on is that verity in act means verification, and that these are always particulars. Even in exclusively theoretic matters, it insists that vagueness and generality serve to verify nothing.

Eighth misunderstanding: Pragmatism is shut up to solipsism.

I have already said something about this misconception under the third and fourth heads, above, but a little more may be helpful. The objection is apt to clothe itself in words like these: 'You make truth to consist in every value except the cognitive value proper; you always leave your knower at many removes (or, at the uttermost, at one remove) from his real object; the best you do is to let his ideas carry him towards it; it remains forever outside of him,' etc.

I think that the leaven working here is the rooted intellectualist persuasion that, to know a reality, an idea must in some inscrutable fashion possess or be it.[5] For pragmatism this kind of coalescence is inessential. As a rule our cognitions are only processes of mind off their balance and in motion towards real termini; and the reality of the termini, believed in by the states of mind in question, can be guaranteed only by some wider knower.[6] But if there is no reason extant in the universe why they should be doubted, the beliefs are true in the only sense in which anything can be true anyhow: they are practically and concretely true, namely. True in the mystical mongrel sense of an Identitätsphilosophie they need not be; nor is there any intelligible reason why they ever need be true otherwise than verifiably and practically. It is reality's part to possess its own existence; it is thought's part to get into 'touch' with it by innumerable paths of verification.

I fear that the 'humanistic' developments of pragmatism may cause a certain difficulty here. We get at one truth only through the rest of truth; and the reality, everlastingly postulated as that which all our truth must keep in touch with, may never be given to us save in the form of truth other than that which we are now testing. But since Dr. Schiller has shown that all our truths, even the most elemental, are affected by race-inheritance with a human coefficient, reality per se thus may appear only as a sort of limit; it may be held to shrivel to the mere place for an object, and what is known may be held to be only matter of our psyche that we fill the place with.

It must be confessed that pragmatism, worked in this humanistic way, is compatible with solipsism. It joins friendly hands with the agnostic part of kantism, with contemporary agnosticism, and with idealism generally. But worked thus, it is a metaphysical theory about the matter of reality, and flies far beyond pragmatism's own modest analysis of the nature of the knowing function, which analysis may just as harmoniously be combined with less humanistic accounts of reality. One of pragmatism's merits is that it is so purely epistemological. It must assume realities; but it prejudges nothing as to their constitution, and the most diverse metaphysics can use it as their foundation. It certainly has no special affinity with solipsism.

As I look back over what I have written, much of it gives me a queer impression, as if the obvious were set forth so condescendingly that readers might well laugh at my pomposity. It may be, however, that concreteness as radical as ours is not so obvious. The whole originality of pragmatism, the whole point in it, is its use of the concrete way of seeing. It begins with concreteness, and returns and ends with it. Dr. Schiller, with his two 'Practical' aspects of truth, (1) relevancy to situation, and (2) subsequential utility, is only filling the cup of concreteness to the brim for us. Once seize that cup, and you cannot misunderstand pragmatism. It seems as if the power of imagining the world concretely might have been common enough to let our readers apprehend us better, as if they might have read between our lines, and, in spite of all our infelicities of expression, guessed a little more correctly what our thought was. But alas! this was not on fate's programme, so we can only think, with the German ditty:

"Es wär' zu schön gewesen,
Es hat nicht sollen sein.
"

Endnotes

1. Reprint from the Philosophical Review, January, 1908 (vol. xvii, p. 1).

2. I see here a chance to forestall a criticism which some one may make on Lecture III of my Pragmatism, where I said that 'God' and 'Matter' might be regarded as synonymous terms, so long as no differing future consequences were deducible from the two conceptions. The passage was transcribed from my address at the California Philosophical Union, reprinted in the Journal of Philosophy, vol. i, p. 673. I had no sooner given the address than I perceived a flaw in that part of it; but I have left the passage unaltered ever since, because the flaw did not spoil its illustrative value. The flaw was evident when, as a case analogous to that of a godless universe, I thought of what I called an 'automatic sweetheart meaning a soulless body which should be absolutely indistinguishable from a spiritually animated maiden, laughing, talking, blushing, nursing us, and performing all feminine offices as tactfully and sweetly as if a soul were in her. Would any one regard her as a full equivalent? Certainly not, and why? Because, framed as we are, our egoism craves above all things inward sympathy and recognition, love and admiration. The outward treatment is valued mainly as an expression, as a manifestation of the accompanying consciousness believed in. Pragmatically,

then, belief in the automatic sweetheart would not work, and in point of fact no one treats it as a serious hypothesis. The godless universe would be exactly similar. Even if matter could do every outward thing that God does, the idea of it would not work as satisfactorily, because the chief call for a God on modern men's put is for a being who will inwardly recognize them and judge them sympathetically. Matter disappoints this craving of our ego, so God remains for most men the truer hypothesis, and indeed remains so for definite pragmatic reasons.

3. I need hardly remind the reader that both sense-percepts and percepts of ideal relation (comparisons, etc.) should be classed among the realities. The bulk of our mental 'stock' consists of truths concerning these terms.

4. The ambiguity of the word 'practical' comes out well in these words of a recent would-be reporter of our views: 'Pragmatism is an Anglo-Saxon reaction against the intellectualism and rationalism of the Latin mind. . . . Man, each individual man is the measure of things. He is able to conceive none but relative truths, that is to say, illusions. What these illusions are worth is revealed to him, not by general theory, but by individual practice. Pragmatism, which consists in experiencing these illusions of the mind and obeying them by acting them out, is a philosophy without words, a philosophy of gestures and of acts, which abandons what is general and holds only to what is particular., (Bourdeau, in Journal des Débats, October 29, 1907.)

5. Sensations may, indeed, possess their objects or coalesce with them, as common sense supposes that they do; and intuited differences between concepts may coalesce with the 'eternal' objective differences; but to simplify our discussion here we can afford to abstract from these very special cases of knowing.

6. The transcendental idealist thinks that, in some inexplicable way, the finite states of mind are identical with the transfinite all-knower which he finds himself obliged to postulate in order to supply a fundamentum for the relation of knowing, as he apprehends it. Pragmatists can leave the question of identity open; but they cannot do without the wider knower any more than they can do without the reality, if they want to prove a case of knowing. They themselves play the part of the absolute knower for the universe of discourse which serves them as material for epistemologizing. They warrant the reality there, and the subject's true knowledge, there, of it. But whether what they themselves say about that whole universe is objectively true, i. e., whether the pragmatic theory of truth is true really, they cannot warrant, — they can only believe it. To their hearers they can only propose it, as I propose it to my readers, as something to be verified ambulando, or by the way in which its consequences may confirm it.

THE MEANING OF THE WORD TRUTH[1]

My account of truth is realistic, and follows the epistemological dualism of common sense. Suppose I say to you 'The thing exists' — is that true or not? How can you tell? Not till my statement has developed its meaning farther is it determined as being true, false, or irrelevant to reality altogether. But if now you ask 'what thing?' and I reply 'a desk'; if you ask 'where?' and I point to a place; if you ask 'does it exist materially, or only in imagination?' and I say 'materially'; if moreover I say 'I mean that desk,' and then grasp and shake a desk which you see just as I have described it, you are willing to call my statement true. But you and I are commutable here; we can exchange places; and, as you go bail for my desk, so I can go bail for yours.

This notion of a reality independent of either of us, taken from ordinary social experience, lies at the base of the pragmatist definition of truth. With some such reality any statement, in order to be counted true, must agree. Pragmatism defines 'agreeing' to mean certain ways of 'working,' be they actual or potential. Thus, for my statement 'the desk exists' to be true of a desk recognized as real by you, it must be able to lead me to shake your desk, to explain myself by words that suggest that desk to your mind, to make a drawing that is like the desk you see, etc. Only in such ways as this is there sense in saying it agrees with that reality, only thus does it gain for me the satisfaction of hearing you corroborate me. Reference then to something determinate, and some sort of adaptation to it worthy of the name of agreement, are thus constituent elements in the definition of any statement of mine as 'true.'

You cannot get at either the reference or the adaptation without using the notion of the workings. That the thing is, what it is, and which it is (of all the possible things with that what) are points determinable only by the pragmatic method. The 'which' means a possibility of pointing, or of otherwise singling out the special object; the 'what' means choice on our part of an essential aspect to conceive it by (and this is always relative to what Dewey calls our own situation'); and the 'that' means our assumption of the attitude of belief, the reality recognizing attitude. Surely for understanding what the word 'true' means as applied to a statement, the mention of such workings is indispensable. Surely if we leave them out the subject and the object of the cognitive relation float — in the same universe, 't is true — but vaguely and ignorantly and without mutual contact or mediation.

Our critics nevertheless call the workings inessential. No functional possibilities 'make' our beliefs true, they say; they are true inherently, true positively, born 'true' as the Count of Chambord was born 'Henri-Cinq.' Pragmatism insists, on the contrary, that statements and beliefs are thus inertly and statically true only by courtesy: they practically pass for true; but you cannot define what you mean by calling them true without referring to their functional possibilities. These give its whole logical content to that relation to reality on a belief's part to which the name 'truth' is applied, a relation which otherwise remains one of mere coexistence or bare witness.

The foregoing statements reproduce the essential content of the lecture on Truth in my book Pragmatism. Schiller's doctrine of 'humanism,' Dewey's 'Studies in logical theory,' and my own 'radical empiricism,' all involve this general notion of truth as 'working,' either actual or conceivable. But they envelop it as only one detail in the midst of much wider theories that aim eventually at determining the notion of what 'reality' at large is in its ultimate nature and constitution.

Endnotes

1. Remarks at the meeting of the American Philosophical Association, Cornell University, December, 1907.

THE EXISTENCE OF JULIUS CAESAR[1]

My account of truth is purely logical and relates to its definition only. I contend that you cannot tell what the word 'true' means, as applied to a statement, without invoking the concept of the statement's workings.

Assume, to fix our ideas, a universe composed of two things only: imperial Caesar dead and turned to clay, and me, saying 'Caesar really existed.' Most persons would naively deem truth to be thereby uttered, and say that by a sort of actio in distans my statement had taken direct hold of the other fact.

But have my words so certainly denoted that Caesar? — or so certainly connoted his individual attributes? To fill out the complete measure of what the epithet 'true' may ideally mean, my thought ought to bear a fully determinate and unambiguous 'one-to-one-relation' to its own particular object. In the ultrasimple universe imagined the reference is uncertified. Were there two Caesars we should n't know which was meant. The conditions of truth thus seem incomplete in this universe of discourse so that it must be enlarged.

Transcendentalists enlarge it by invoking an absolute mind which, as it owns all the facts, can sovereignly correlate them. If it intends that my statement shall refer to that identical Caesar, and that the attributes I have in mind shall mean his attributes, that intention suffices to make the statement true.

I, in turn, enlarge the universe by admitting finite intermediaries between the two original facts. Caesar had, and my statement has, effects; and if these effects in any way run together, a concrete medium and bottom is provided for the determinate cognitive relation, which, as a pure actio in distans, seemed to float too vaguely and unintelligibly.

The real Caesar, for example, wrote a manuscript of which I see a real reprint, and say 'the Caesar I mean is the author of that.' The workings of my thought thus determine both its denotative and its connotative significance more fully. It now defines itself as neither irrelevant to the real Caesar, nor false in what it suggests of him. The absolute mind, seeing me thus working towards Caesar through the cosmic intermediaries, might well say: 'Such workings only specify in detail what I meant myself by the statement being true. I decree the cognitive relation between the two original facts to mean that just that kind of concrete chain of intermediaries exists or can exist.'

But the chain involves facts prior to the statement the logical conditions of whose truth we are defining, and facts subsequent to it; and this circumstance, coupled with the vulgar employment of the terms truth and fact as synonyms, has laid my account open to misapprehension. 'How,' it is confusedly asked, 'can Caesar's existence, a truth already 2000 years old, depend for its truth on anything about to happen now? How can my acknowledgment of it be made true by the acknowledgment's own effects? The effects may indeed confirm my belief, but the belief was made true already by the fact that Caesar really did exist.'

Well, be it so, for if there were no Caesar, there could, of course, be no positive truth about him — but then distinguish between 'true' as being positively and completely so established, and 'true' as being so only 'practically,' elliptically, and by courtesy, in the sense of not being positively irrelevant or untrue. Remember also that Caesar's having existed in fact may make a present statement false or irrelevant as well as it may make it true, and that in neither case does it itself have to alter. It being given, whether truth, untruth, or irrelevancy shall be also given depends on something coming from the statement itself. What pragmatism contends for is that you cannot adequately define the something if you leave the notion of the statement's functional workings out of your account. Truth meaning agreement with reality, the mode of the agreeing is a practical problem which the subjective term of the relation alone can solve.

Note. This paper was originally followed by a couple of paragraphs meant to conciliate the intellectualist opposition. Since you love the word 'true' go, and since you despise so the concrete working of our ideas, I said, keep the word 'truth' for the saltatory and incomprehensible relation you care so much for, and I will say of thoughts that know their objects in an intelligible sense that they are 'truthful.'

Like most offerings, this one has been spurned, so I revoke it, repenting of my generosity. Professor Pratt, in his recent book, calls any objective state of facts 'a truth,' and uses the word 'trueness' in the sense of 'truth' as proposed by me. Mr. Hawtrey uses 'correctness' in the same sense. Apart from the general evil of ambiguous vocabularies, we may really forsake all hope, if the term 'truth' is officially to lose its status as a property of our beliefs and opinions, and become recognized as a technical synonym for 'fact.'

Endnotes

1. Originally printed under the title of 'Truth versus Truthfulness,' in the Journal of Philosophy.

THE ABSOLUTE AND THE STRENUOUS LIFE[1]

Professor W. A. Brown, in the Journal for August 15, approves my pragmatism for allowing that a belief in the absolute may give holidays to the spirit, but takes me to task for the narrowness of this concession, and shows by striking examples how great a power the same belief may have in letting loose the strenuous life.

I have no criticism whatever to make upon his excellent article, but let me explain why 'moral holidays' were the only gift of the absolute which I picked out for emphasis. I was primarily concerned in my lectures with contrasting the belief that the world is still in process of making with the belief that there is an 'eternal' edition of it ready-made and complete. The former, or 'pluralistic' belief, was the one that my pragmatism favored. Both beliefs confirm our strenuous moods. Pluralism actually demands them, since it makes the world's salvation depend upon the energizing of its several parts, among which we are. Monism permits them, for however furious they may be, we can always justify ourselves in advance for indulging them by the thought that they will have been expressions of the absolute's perfect life. By escaping from your finite perceptions to the conception of the eternal whole, you can hallow any tendency whatever. Tho the absolute dictates nothing, it will sanction anything and everything after the fact, for whatever is once there will have to be regarded as an integral member of the universe's perfection. Quietism and frenzy thus alike receive the absolute's permit to exist. Those of us who are naturally inert may abide in our resigned passivity; those whose energy is excessive may grow more reckless still. History shows how easily both quietists and fanatics have drawn inspiration from the absolutistic scheme. It suits sick souls and strenuous ones equally well.

One cannot say thus of pluralism. Its world is always vulnerable, for some part may go astray; and having no 'eternal' edition of it to draw comfort from, its partisans must always feel to some degree insecure. If, as pluralists, we grant ourselves moral holidays, they can only be provisional breathing-spells, intended to refresh us for the morrow's fight. This forms one permanent inferiority of pluralism from the pragmatic point of view. It has no saving message for incurably sick souls. Absolutism, among its other messages, has that message, and is the only scheme that has it necessarily. That constitutes its chief superiority and is the source of its religious power. That is why, desiring to do it full justice, I valued its aptitude for moral-holiday giving so highly. Its claims in that way are unique, whereas its affinities with strenuousness are less emphatic than those of the pluralistic scheme.

In the last lecture of my book I candidly admitted this inferiority of pluralism. It lacks the wide indifference that absolutism shows. It is bound to disappoint many sick souls whom absolutism can console. It seems therefore poor tactics for absolutists to make little of this advantage. The needs of sick souls are surely the most urgent; and believers in the absolute should rather hold it to be great merit in their philosophy that it can meet them so well.

The pragmatism or pluralism which I defend has to fall back on a certain ultimate hardihood, a certain willingness to live without assurances or guarantees. To minds thus willing to live on possibilities that are not certainties, quietistic religion, sure of salvation any how, has a slight flavor of fatty degeneration about it which has caused it to be looked askance on, even in the church. Which side is right here, who can say? Within religion, emotion is apt to be tyrannical; but philosophy must favor the emotion that allies itself best with the whole body and drift of all the truths in sight. I conceive this to be the more strenuous type of emotion; but I have to admit that its inability to let loose quictistic raptures is a serious deficiency in the pluralistic philosophy which I profess.

Endnotes

1. Reprinted from the Journal of Philosophy, etc., 1906.

PROFESSOR HÉBERT ON PRAGMATISM[1]

Professor Marcel Hébert is a singularly erudite and liberal thinker (a seceder, I believe, from the Catholic priesthood) and an uncommonly direct and clear writer. His book Le Divin is one of the ablest reviews of the general subject of religious philosophy which recent years have produced; and in the small volume the title of which is copied above he has, perhaps, taken more pains not to do injustice to pragmatism than any of its numerous critics. Yet the usual fatal misapprehension of its purposes vitiates his exposition and his critique. His pamphlet seems to me to form a worthy hook, as it were, on which to hang one more attempt to tell the reader what the pragmatist account of truth really means.

M. Hébert takes it to mean what most people take it to mean, the doctrine, namely, that whatever proves subjectively expedient in the way of our thinking is 'true' in the absolute and unrestricted sense of the word, whether it corresponds to any objective state of things outside of our thought or not. Assuming this to be the pragmatist thesis, M. Hébert opposes it at length. Thought that proves itself to be thus expedient may, indeed, have every other kind of value for the thinker, he says, but cognitive value, representative value, valeur de connaissance proprement dite, it has not; and when it does have a high degree of general utility value, this is in every case derived from its previous value in the way of correctly representing independent objects that have an important influence on our lives. Only by thus representing things truly do we reap the useful fruits. But the fruits follow on the truth, they do not constitute it; so M. Hébert accuses pragmatism of telling us everything about truth except what it essentially is. He admits, indeed, that the world is so framed that when men have true ideas of realities, consequential utilities ensue in abundance; and no one of our critics, I think, has shown as concrete a sense of the variety of these utilities as he has; but he reiterates that, whereas such utilities are secondary, we insist on treating them as primary, and that the connaissance objective from which they draw all their being is something which we neglect, exclude, and destroy. The utilitarian value and the strictly cognitive value of our ideas may perfectly well harmonize, he says — and in the main he allows that they do harmonize — but they are not logically identical for that. He admits that subjective interests, desires, impulses may even have the active 'primacy' in our intellectual life. Cognition awakens only at their spur, and follows their cues and aims; yet, when it is awakened, it is objective cognition proper and not merely another name for the impulsive tendencies themselves in the state of satisfaction. The owner of a picture ascribed to Corot gets uneasy when its authenticity is doubted. He looks up its origin and is reassured. But his uneasiness does not make the proposition false, any more than his relief makes the proposition true, that the actual Corot was the painter.

Pragmatism, which, according to M. Hébart, claims that our sentiments make truth and falsehood, would oblige us to conclude that our minds exert no genuinely cognitive function whatever.

This subjectivist interpretation of our position seems to follow from my having happened. to write (without supposing it necessary to explain that I was treating of cognition solely on its subjective side) that in the long run the true is the expedient in the way of our thinking, much as the good is the expedient in the way of our behavior! Having previously written that truth means 'agreement with reality,' and insisted that the chief part of the expediency of any one opinion is its agreement with the rest of acknowledged truth, I apprehended no exclusively subjectivistic reading of my mean ing. My mind was so filled with the notion of objective reference that I never dreamed that my hearers would let go of it; and the very last accusation I expected was that in speaking of ideas and their satisfactions, I was denying realities outside. My only wonder now is that critics should have found so silly a personage as I must have seemed in their eyes, worthy of explicit refutation.

The object, for me, is just as much one part of reality as the idea is another part. The truth of the idea is one relation of it to the reality, just as its date and its place are other relations. All three relations consist of intervening parts of the universe which can in every particular case be assigned and catalogued, and which differ in every instance of truth, just as they differ with every date and place.

The pragmatist thesis, as Dr. Schiller and I hold it, —I prefer to let Professor Dewey speak for himself, —is that the relation called 'truth' is thus concretely definable. Ours is the only articulate attempt in the field to say positively what truth actually consists of. Our denouncers have literally nothing to oppose to it as an alternative. For them, when an idea is true, it is true, and there the matter terminates, the word 'true' being indefinable. The relation of the true idea to its object, being, as they think, unique, it can be expressed in terms of nothing else, and needs only to be named for any one to recognize and understand it. Moreover it is invariable and universal, the same in every single instance of truth, however diverse the ideas, the realities, and the other relations between them may be.

Our pragmatist view, on the contrary, is that the truth-relation is a definitely experienceable relation, and therefore describable as well as namable; that it is not unique in kind, and neither invariable nor universal. The relation to its object that makes an idea true in any given instance, is, we say, embodied in intermediate details of reality which lead towards the object, which vary in every instance, and which in every instance can be concretely traced. The chain of workings which an opinion sets up is the opinion's truth, falsehood, or irrelevancy, as the case may be. Every idea that a man has works some consequences in him, in the shape either of bodily actions or of other ideas. Through these consequences the man's relations to surrounding realities are modified. He is carried nearer to some of them and farther from others, and gets now the feeling that the idea has worked satisfactorily, now that it has not. The idea has put him into touch with something that fulfils its intent, or it has not.

This something is the man's object, primarily. Since the only realities we can talk about are such objects-believed-in, the pragma. tist, whenever he says 'reality,' means in the first instance what may count for the man himself as a reality, what he believes at the moment to be such. Sometimes the reality is a concrete sensible —presence. The idea, for example, may be that a certain door opens into a room where a glass of beer may be bought. If opening the door leads to the actual sight and taste of the beer, the man calls the idea true. Or his idea may be that of an abstract relation, say of that between the sides and the hypothenuse of a triangle, such a relation being, of course, a reality quite as much as a glass of beer is. If the thought of such a relation leads him to draw auxiliary lines and to compare the figures they make, he may at last, perceiving one equality after another, see the relation thought of, by a vision quite as particular and direct as was the taste of the beer. If he does so, he calls that idea, also, true. His idea has, in each case, brought him into closer touch with a reality felt at the moment to just that idea. Each reality verifies and validates its own idea exclusively; and in each case the verification consists in the satisfactorily-ending consequences, mental or physical, which the idea was able to set up. These 'workings' differ in every single instance, they never transcend experience, they consist of particulars, mental or sensible, and they admit of concrete description in every individual case. Pragmatists are unable to see what you can possibly mean by calling an idea true, unless you mean that between it as a terminus a quo in some one's mind and some particular reality as a terminus ad quem, such concrete workings do or may intervene. Their direction constitutes the idea's reference to that reality, their satisfactoriness constitutes its adaptation thereto, and the two things together constitute the 'truth' of the idea for its possessor. Without such intermediating portions of concretely real experience the pragmatist sees no materials out of which the adaptive relation called truth can be built up.

The anti-pragmatist view is that the workings are but evidences of the truth's previous inherent presence in the idea, and that you can wipe the very possibility of them out of existence and still leave the truth of the idea as solid as ever. But surely this is not a countertheory of truth to ours. It is the renunciation of all articulate theory. It is but a claim to the right to call certain ideas true anyhow; and this is what I meant above by saying that the anti-pragmatists offer us no real alternative, and that our account is literally the only positive theory extant. What meaning, indeed, can an idea's truth have save its power of adapting us either mentally or physically to a reality?

How comes it, then, that our critics so uniformly accuse us of subjectivism, of denying the reality's existence? It comes, I think, from the necessary predominance of subjective language in our analysis. However independent and ejective realities may be, we can talk about them, in framing our accounts of truth, only as so many objects believed-in. But the process of experience leads men so continually to supersede their older objects by newer ones which they find it more satisfactory to believe in, that the notion of an absolute reality inevitably arises as a grenzbegriff, equivalent to that of an object that shall never be superseded, and belief in which shall be endgultig. Cognitively we thus live under a sort of rule of three: as our private concepts represent the senseobjects to which they lead us, these being public realities independent of the individual, so these sense-realities may, in turn, represent realities of a hypersensible order, electrons, mind-stuff, God, or what not, existing independently of all human thinkers. The notion of such final realities, knowledge of which would be absolute truth, is an outgrowth of our cognitive experience from which neither pragmatists nor anti-pragmatists escape. They form an inevitable regulative postulate in every one's thinking. Our notion of them is the most abundantly suggested and satisfied of all our beliefs, the last to suffer doubt. The difference is that our critics use this belief as their sole paradigm, and treat any one who talks of human realities as if he thought the notion of reality 'in itself 'illegitimate. Meanwhile, reality-in-itself, so far as by them talked of, is only a human object; they postulate it just as we postulate it; and if we are subjectivists they are so no less. Realities in themselves can be there for any one, whether pragmatist or anti-pragmatist, only by being believed; they are believed only by their notions appearing true; and their notions appear true only because they work satisfactorily. Satisfactorily, moreover, for the particular thinker's purpose. There is no idea which is the true idea, of anything. Whose is the true idea of the absolute? Or to take M. Hébert's example, what is the true idea of a picture which you possess? It is the idea that most satisfactorily meets your Present interest. The interest may be in the picture's place, its age, its 'tone,' its subject, its dimensions, its authorship, its price, its merit, or what not. If its authorship by Corot have been doubted, what will satisfy the interest aroused in you at that moment will be to have your claim to own a Corot confirmed; but, if you have a normal human mind, merely calling it a Corot will not satisfy other demands of your mind at the same time. For then to be satisfied, what you learn of the picture must make smooth connection with what you know of the rest of the system of reality in which the actual Corot played his part. M. Hébert accuses us of holding that the proprietary satisfactions of themselves suffice to make the belief true, and that, so far as we are concerned, no actual Corot need ever have existed. Why we should be thus cut off from the more general and intellectual satisfactions, I know not; but whatever the satisfactions may be, intellectual or proprietary, they belong to the subjective side of the truth-relation. They found our beliefs; our beliefs are in realities; if no realities are there, the beliefs are false; but if realities are there, how they can ever be known without first being believed, or how believed except by our first having ideas of them that work satisfactorily, pragmatists find it impossible to imagine. They also find it impossible to imagine what makes the antipragmatists' dogmatic I ipse dixit' assurance of reality more credible than the pragmatists' conviction based on concrete verifications. M. Herbert will probably agree to this, when put in this way, so I do not see our inferiority to him in the matter of connaissance proprement dite.

Some readers will say that, altho I may possibly believe in realities beyond our ideas, Dr. Schiller, at any rate, does not. This is a great misunderstanding, for Schiller's doctrine and mine are identical, only our expositions follow different directions. He starts from the subjective pole of the chain, the individual with his beliefs, as the more concrete and immediately given phenomenon. 'An individual claims his belief to be true,' Schiller says, I but what does he mean by true? and bow does he establish the claim?' With these questions we embark on a psychological inquiry. To be true, it appears, means, for that individual, to work satisfactorily for him; and the working and the satisfaction, since they vary from case to case, admit of no universal description. What works is true and represents a reality, for the individual for whom it works. If he is infallible, the reality is 'really' there; if mistaken it is not there, or not there as he thinks it. We all believe, when our ideas work satisfactorily; but we don't yet know who of us is infallible; so that the problem of truth and that of error are ebenburtig and arise out of the same situations. Schiller, remaining with the fallible individual, and treating only of reality for him, seems to many of his readers to ignore reality-in-itself altogether. But that is because he seeks only to tell us how truths are attained, not what the content of those truths, when attained, shall be. It may be that the truest of all beliefs shall be that in transsubjective realities. It certainly seems the truest, for no rival belief is as voluminously satisfactory, and it is probably Dr. Schiller's own belief; but he is not required, for his immediate purpose, to profess it. Still less is he obliged to assume it in advance as the basis of his discussion.

I, however, warned by the ways of critics, adopt different tactics. I start from the objectpole of the idea-reality chain and follow it in the opposite direction from Schiller's. Anticipating the results of the general truth-processes of mankind, I begin with the abstract notion of an objective reality. I postulate it, and ask on my own account, I vouching for this reality, what would make any one else's idea of it true for me as well as for him. But I find no different answer from that which Schiller gives. If the other man's idea leads him, not only to believe that the reality is there, but to use it as the reality's temporary substitute, by letting it evoke adaptive thoughts and acts similar to those which the reality itself would provoke, then it is true in the only intelligible sense, true through its particular consequences, and true for me as well as for the man.

My account is more of a logical definition; Schiller's is more of a psychological description. Both treat an absolutely identical matter of experience, only they traverse it in opposite ways.

Possibly these explanations may satisfy M. Hébert, whose little book, apart from the false accusation of subjectivism, gives a fairly instructive account of the pragmatist epistemology.

Endnotes

1. Reprint from the Journal of Philosophy for December 3,1908 (vol. v, p. 689), of a review of Le pragmatism et set diverses formes anglo-américaines, by Marcel Hébert. (Paris: Librairie critique Emile Nourry. 1908. Pp. 105.)

ABSTRACTIONISM AND 'RELATIVISMUS'

Abstract concepts, such as elasticity, voluminousness, disconnectedness, are salient aspects of our concrete experiences which we find it useful to single out. Useful, because we are then reminded of other things that offer those same aspects; and, if the aspects carry consequences in those other things, we can return to our first things, expecting those same consequences to accrue.

To be helped to anticipate consequences is always a gain, and such being the help that abstract concepts give us, it is obvious that their use is fulfilled only when we get back again into concrete particulars by their means, bearing the consequences in our minds, and enriching our notion of the original objects therewithal.

Without abstract concepts to handle our perceptual particulars by, we are like men hopping on one foot. Using concepts along with the particulars, we become bipedal. We throw our concept forward, get a foothold on the consequence, hitch our line to this, and draw our percept up, travelling thus with a hop, skip and jump over the surface of life at a vastly rapider rate than if we merely waded through the thickness of the particulars as accident rained them down upon our heads. Animals have to do this, but men raise their heads higher and breathe freely in the upper conceptual air.

The enormous esteem professed by all philosophers for the conceptual form of consciousness is easy to understand. From Plato's time downwards it has been held to be our sole avenue to essential truth. Concepts are universal, changeless, pure; their relations are eternal; they are spiritual, while the concrete particulars which they enable us to handle are corrupted by the flesh. They are precious in themselves, then, apart from their original use, and confer new dignity upon our life.

One can find no fault with this way of feeling about concepts so long as their original function does not get swallowed up in the admiration and lost. That function is of course to enlarge mentally our momentary experiences by adding to them the consequences conceived; but unfortunately, that function is not only too often forgotten by philosophers in their reasonings, but is often converted into its exact opposite, and made a means of diminishing the original experience by denying (implicitly or explicitly) all its features save the one specially abstracted to conceive it by.

This itself is a highly abstract way of stating my complaint, and it needs to be redeemed from obscurity by showing instances of what is meant. Some beliefs very dear to my own heart have been conceived in this viciously abstract way by critics. One is the 'will to believe,' so called; another is the indeterminism of certain futures; a third is the notion that truth may vary with the standpoint of the man who holds it. I believe that the perverse abuse Of the abstracting function has led critics to employ false arguments against these doctrines, and often has led their readers too to false conclusions. I should like to try to save the situation, if possible, by a few counter-critical remarks.

Let me give the name of 'vicious abstractionism' to a way of using concepts which may be thus described: We conceive a concrete situation by singling out some salient or important feature in it, and classing it under that; then, instead of adding to its previous characters all the positive consequences which the new way of conceiving it may bring, we proceed to use our concept privatively; reducing the originally rich phenomenon to the naked suggestions of that name abstractly taken, treating it as a case of 'nothing but' that concept, and acting as if all the other characters from out of which the concept is abstracted were expunged.[1] Abstraction, functioning in this way, becomes a means of arrest far more than a means of advance in thought. It mutilates things; it creates difficulties and finds impossibilities; and more than half the trouble that metaphysicians and logicians give themselves over the paradoxes and dialectic puzzles of the universe may, I am convinced, be traced to this relatively simple source. The viciously privative employment of abstract characters and class names is, I am persuaded, one of the great original sins of the rationalistic mind.

To proceed immediately to concrete examples, cast a glance at the belief in 'free will,' demolished with such specious persuasiveness recently by the skilful hand of Professor Fullerton.[2] When a common man says that his will is free, what does he mean? He means that there are situations of bifurcation inside of his life in which two futures seem to him equally possible, for both have their roots equally planted in his present and his past. Either., if realized, will grow out of his previous motives, character and circumstances, and will continue uninterruptedly the pulsations of his personal life. But sometimes both at once are incompatible with physical nature, and then it seems to the naive observer as if he made a choice between them now, and that the question of which future is to be, instead of having been decided at the foundation of the world, were decided afresh at every passing moment in which fact seems livingly to grow, and possibility seems, in turning itself towards one act, to exclude all others.

He who takes things at their face-value here may indeed be deceived. He may far too often mistake his private ignorance of what is predetermined for a real indetermination of what is to be. Yet, however imaginary it may be, his picture of the situation offers no appearance of breach between the past and future. A train. is the same train, its passengers are the same passengers, its momentum is the same momentum, no matter which way the switch which fixes its direction is placed. For the indeterminist there is at all times enough past for all the different futures in sight, and more besides, to find their reasons in it, and whichever future comes will slide out of that past as easily as the train slides by the switch. The world, in short, is just as continuous with itself for the believers in free will as for the rigorous determinists, only the latter are unable to believe in points of bifurcation as spots of really indifferent equilibrium or as containing shunts which there —and there only, not before — direct existing motions without altering their amount.

Were there such spots of indifference, the rigorous determinists think, the future and the past would be separated absolutely, for, abstractly taken, the word 'indifferent' suggests disconnection solely. Whatever is indifferent is in so far forth unrelated and detached. Take the term thus strictly, and you see, they tell us, that if any spot of indifference is found upon the broad highway between the past and the future, then no connection of any sort whatever, no continuous momentum, no identical passenger, no common aim or agent, can be found on both sides of the shunt or switch which there is moved. The place is an impassable chasm.

Mr. Fullerton writes as follows:

'In so far as my action is free, what I have been, what I am, what I have always done or striven to do, what I most earnestly wish or resolve to do at the present moment — these things can have no more to do with its future realization than if they had no existence.... The possibility is a hideous one; and surely even the most ardent free willist will, when he contemplates it frankly, excuse me for hoping that if I am free I am at least not very free, and that I may reasonably expect to find some degree of consistency in my life and actions.... Suppose that I have given a dollar to a blind beggar. Can I, if it is really an act of free-will, be properly said to have given the money? Was it given because I was a man of tender heart, etc., etc.?... What has all this to do with acts of free-will? If they are free, they must not be conditioned by antecedent circumstances of any sort, by the misery of the beggar, by the pity in the heart of the passer by. They must be causeless, not determined. They must drop from a clear sky out Of the void, for just in so far as they can be accounted for, they are not free.'[3]

Heaven forbid that I should get entangled here in a controversy about the rights and wrongs of the free-will question at large, for I am only trying to illustrate vicious abstractionism by the conduct of some of the doctrine's assailants. The moments Of bifurcation, as the indeterminist seems to himself to experience them, are moments both of re-direction and of continuation. But because in the 'either — or' of the re-direction we hesitate, the determinist abstracts this little element of discontinuity from the superabundant continuities of the experience, and cancels in its behalf all the connective characters with which the latter is filled. Choice, for him, means henceforward disconnection pure and simple, something undetermined in advance in any respect whatever, and a life of choices must be a raving chaos, at no two moments of which could we be treated as one and the same man. If Nero were 'free' at the moment of ordering his mother's murder, Mr. McTaggart[4] assures us that no one would have the right at any other moment to call him a bad man, for he would then be an absolutely other Nero.

A polemic author ought not merely to destroy his victim. He ought to try a bit to make him feel his error —perhaps not enough to convert him, but enough to give him a bad conscience and to weaken the energy of his defence. These violent caricatures of men's beliefs arouse only contempt for the incapacity of their authors to see the situations out of which the problems grow. To treat the negative character of one abstracted element as annulling all the positive features with which it coexists, is no way to change any actual indeterminist's way of looking on the matter, tho it may make the gallery applaud.

Turn now to some criticisms of the 'will to believe,' as another example of the vicious way in which abstraction is currently employed. The right to believe in things for the truth of which complete objective proof is yet lacking is defended by those who apprehend certain human situations in their concreteness. In those situations the mind has alternatives before it so vast that the full evidence for either branch is missing, and yet so significant that simply to wait for proof, and to doubt while waiting, might often in practical respects be the same thing as weighing down the negative side. Is life worth while at all? Is there any general meaning in all this cosmic weather? Is anything being permanently bought by all this suffering? Is there perhaps a transmundane experience in Being, something corresponding to a 'fourth dimension,' which, if we had access to it, might patch up some of this world's zerrissenheit and make things look more rational than they at first appear? Is there a superhuman consciousness of which our minds are parts, and from which inspiration and help may come? Such are the questions in which the right to take sides practically for yes or no is affirmed by some of us, while others hold that this is methodologically inadmissible, and summon us to die professing ignorance and proclaiming the duty of every one to refuse to believe.

I say nothing of the personal inconsistency of some of these critics, whose printed works furnish exquisite illustrations of the will to believe, in spite of their denunciations of it as a phrase and as a recommended thing. Air. McTaggart, whom I will once more take as an example, is sure that 'reality is rational and righteous' and 'destined subspecie temporis to become perfectly good'; and his calling this belief a result of necessary logic has surely never deceived any reader as to its real genesis in the gifted author's mind. Mankind is made on too uniform a pattern for any of us to escape successfully from acts of faith. We have a lively vision of what a certain view of the universe would mean for us. We kindle or we shudder at the thought, and our feeling rung through our whole logical nature and animates its workings. It can't be that, we feel; it must be this. It must be what it ought to be, and it ought to be this; and then we seek for every reason, good or bad, to make this which so deeply ought to be, seem objectively the probable thing. We show the arguments against it to be insufficient, so that it may be true; we represent its appeal to be to our whole nature's loyalty and not to any emaciated faculty of syllogistic proof. We reinforce it by remembering the enlargement of our world by music, by thinking of the promises of sunsets and the impulses from vernal woods. And the essence of the whole experience, when the individual swept through it says finally 'I believe,' is the intense concreteness of his vision, the individuality of the hypothesis before him, and the complexity of the various concrete motives and perceptions that issue in his final state.

But see now how the abstractionist treats this rich and intricate vision that a certain state of things must be true. He accuses the believer of reasoning by the following syllogism: —

All good desires must be fulfilled;

The desire to believe this proposition is a good desire;

Ergo, this proposition must be believed.

He substitutes this abstraction for the concrete state of mind of the believer, pins the naked absurdity of it upon him, and easily proves that any one who defends him must be the greatest fool on earth. As if any real believer ever thought in this preposterous way, or as if any defender of the legitimacy of men's concrete ways of concluding ever used the abstract and general premise, ' All desires must be fulfilled'! Nevertheless, Mr. McTaggart solemnly and laboriously refutes the syllogism in sections 47 to 57 of the above-cited book. He shows that there is no fixed link in the dictionary between the abstract concepts 'desire," 'goodness' and 'reality'; and he ignores all the links which in the single concrete case the believer feels and perceives to be there! He adds:—

'When the reality of a thing is uncertain, the argument encourages us to suppose that our approval of a thing can determine its reality. And when this unhallowed link has once been established, retribution overtakes us. For when the reality of the thing is independently certain, we [then] have to admit that the reality of the thing should determine our approval of that thing. I find it difficult to imagine a more degraded position.'

One here feels tempted to quote ironically Hegel's famous equation of the real with the rational to his english disciple, who ends his chapter with the heroic words:

'For those who do not pray, there remains the resolve that, so far as their strength may permit, neither the pains of death nor the pains of life shall drive them to any comfort in that which they hold to be false,, or drive them from any comfort [discomfort?] in that which they hold to be true.'

How can so ingenious-minded a writer fail to see how far over the heads of the enemy all his arrows pass? When Mr. McTaggart himself believes that the universe is run by the dialectic energy of the absolute idea, his insistent desire to have a world of that sort is felt by him to be no chance example of desire in general, but an altogether peculiar insight-giving passion to which, in this if in no other instance, he would be stupid not to yield— He obeys its concrete singularity, not the bare abstract feature in it of being a 'desire.' His situation is as particular as that of an actress who resolves that it is best for her to marry and leave the stage, of a priest who becomes secular, of a politician who abandons public life. What sensible man would seek to refute the concrete decisions of such persons by tracing them to abstract

premises, such as that 'all actresses must marry,' 'all clergymen must be laymen,' 'all politicians should resign their posts'? Yet this type of refutation, absolutely unavailing though it be for purposes of conversion, is spread by Mr. McTaggart through many pages of his book. For the aboundingness of our real reasons he substitutes one narrow point. For men's real probabilities he gives a skeletonized abstraction which no man was ever tempted to believe.

The abstraction in my next example is less simple, but is quite as flimsy as a weapon of attack. Empiricists think that truth in general is distilled from single men's beliefs; and the so-called pragmatists 'go them one better' by trying to define what it consists in when it comes. It consists, I have elsewhere said, in such a working on the part of the beliefs as may bring the man into satisfactory relations with objects to which these latter point. The working is of course a concrete working in the actual experience of human beings, among their ideas, feelings, perceptions, beliefs and acts, as well as among the physical things of their environment, and the relations must be understood as being possible as well as actual. In the chapter on truth of my book Pragmatism I have taken pains to defend energetically this view. Strange indeed have been the misconceptions of it by its enemies, and many have these latter been. Among the most formidable sounding onslaughts on the attempt to introduce some concreteness into our notion of what the truth of an idea may mean, is one that has been raised in many quarters to the effect that to make truth grow in any way out of human opinion is but to reproduce that protagorean doctrine that the individual man is 'the measure of all things,' which Plato in his immortal dialogue, the Thaeatetus, is unanimously said to have laid away so comfortably in its grave two thousand years ago. The two cleverest brandishers of this objection to make truth concrete, Professors Rickert and Munsterberg, write in German,[5] and 'relativismus' is the name they give to the heresy which they endeavor to uproot.

The first step in their campaign against 'relativismus' is entirely in the air. They accuse relativists — and we pragmatists axe typical relativists — of being debarred by their self-adopted principles, not only from the privilege which rationalist philosophers enjoy, of believing that these principles of their own are truth impersonal and absolute, but even of framing the abstract notion of such a truth, in the pragmatic sense, of an ideal opinion in which all men might agree, and which no man should ever wish to change. Both charges fall wide of their mark. I myself, as a pragmatist, believe in my own account of truth as firmly as any rationalist can possibly believe in his. And I believe in it for the very reason that I have the idea of truth which my learned adversaries contend that no pragmatist can frame. I expect, namely, that the more fully men discuss and test my account, the more they will agree that it fits, and the less will they desire a change. I may of course be premature in this confidence, and the glory of being truth final and absolute may fall upon some later revision and correction of my scheme, which latter will then be judged untrue in just the measure in which it departs from that finally satisfactory formulation. To admit, as we pragmatists do, that we are liable to correction (even tho we may not expect it) involves the use on our part of an ideal standard. Rationalists themselves are., as individuals, sometimes sceptical enough to admit the abstract possibility of their own present opinions being corrigible and revisable to some degree, so the fact that the mere notion of an absolute standard should seem to them so important a thing to claim for themselves and to deny to us is not easy to explain. if, along with the notion of the standard, they could also claim its exclusive warrant for their own fulminations now., it would be important to them indeed. But absolutists like Rickert freely admit the sterility of the notion, even in their own hands. Truth is what we ought to believe, they say, even tho no man ever did or shall believe it, and even tho we have no way of getting at it save by the usual empirical processes of testing our opinions by one another and by facts. Pragmatically, then, this part of the dispute is idle. No relativist who ever actually walked the earth,[6] has denied the regulative character in his own thinking of the notion of absolute truth. What is challenged by relativists is the pretence on any one's part to have found for certain at any given moment what the shape of that truth is. Since the better absolutists agree in this, admitting that the proposition ' There is absolute truth' is the only absolute truth of which we can be sure,[7] further debate is practically unimportant, so we may pass to their next charge.

It is in this charge that the vicious abstractionism becomes most apparent. The antipragmatist, in postulating absolute truth, refuses to give any account of what the words may mean. For him they form a self-explanatory term. The pragmatist, on the contrary, articulately defines their meaning. Truth absolute, he says, means an ideal set of formulations towards which all opinions may in the long run of experience be expected to converge. In this definition of absolute truth he not only postulates that there is a tendency to such convergence of opinions, to such ultimate consensus, but he postulates the other factors of his definition equally, borrowing them by anticipation from the true conclusions expected to be reached. He postulates the existence of opinions, he postulates the experience that will sift them, and the consistency which that experience will show. He justifies himself in these assumptions by saying that they are not postulates in the strict sense but simple inductions from the past extended to the future by analogy; and he insists that human opinion has already reached a pretty stable equilibrium regarding them, and that if its future development fails to alter them, the definition itself, with all its terms included, will be part of the very absolute truth which it defines. The hypothesis will, in short, have worked successfully all round the circle and proved self-corroborative, and the circle will be closed.

The anti-pragmatist, however, immediately falls foul of the word 'opinion' here, abstracts it from the universe of life, and uses it as a bare dictionary-substantive, to deny the rest of the assumptions which it coexists withal. Ile dictionary says that an opinion is 'what some one thinks or believes.' This definition leaves every one's opinion free to be autogenous, or unrelated either to what any one else may think or to what the truth may be. Therefore, continue our abstractionists, we must conceive it as essentially thus unrelated, so that even were a billion men to sport the same opinion, and only one man to differ, we could admit no collateral circumstances which might presumptively make it more probable that he, not they, should be wrong. Truth, they say, follows not the counting of noses, nor is it only another name for a majority vote. It is a relation that ante-dates experience, between our opinions and an independent something which the pragmatist account ignores, a relation which, tho the opinions of individuals should to all eternity deny it, would still remain to qualify them as false. To talk of opinions without referring to this independent something, the anti-pragmatist assures us, is to play Hamlet with Hamlet's part left out.

But when the pragmatist speaks of opinions, does he mean any such insulated and unmotived abstractions as are here supposed? Of course not, he means men's opinions in the flesh, as they have really formed themselves, opinions surrounded by their causes and the influences they obey and exert, and along with the whole environment of social communication of which they are a part and out of which they take their rise. Moreover the "experience' which the pragmatic definition postulates is the independent something which the anti-pragmatist accuses him of ignoring. Already have men grown unanimous in the opinion that such experience is 'of' an independent reality, the existence of which all opinions must acknowledge, in order to be true. Already do they agree that in the long run it is useless to resist experience's pressure; that the more of it a man has, the better position he stands in, in respect of truth; that some men, having had more experience, are therefore better authorities than others; that some are also wiser by nature and better able to interpret the experience they have had; that it is one part of such wisdom to compare notes, discuss, and follow the opinion of our betters; and that the more systematically and thoroughly such comparison and weighing of opinions is pursued, the truer the opinions that survive are likely to be. When the pragmatist talks of opinions, it is opinions as they thus concretely and livingly and interactingly and correlatively exist that he has in mind; and when the anti-pragmatist tries to floor him because the word opinion' can also be taken abstractly and as if it had no environment, he simply ignores the soil out of which the whole discussion grows. His weapons cut the air and strike no blow. No one gets wounded in the war against caricatures of belief and skeletons of opinion of which the German onslaughts upon 'relativismus' consists. Refuse to use the word 'opinion' abstractly, keep it in its real environment, and the withers of pragmatism remain unwrung.

That men do exist who are 'opinionated,' in the sense that their opinions are self-willed, is unfortunately a fact that must be admitted, no matter what one's notion of truth in general may be. But that this fact should make it impossible for truth to form itself authentically out of the life of opinion is what no critic has yet proved. Truth may well consist of certain opinions, and does indeed consist of nothing but opinions, tho not every opinion need be. true. No pragmatist needs to dogmatize about the consensus of opinion in the future being right —he need only postulate that it will probably contain more of truth than any one's opinion now.

Endnotes

1 Let not the reader confound the fallacy here described with legitimately negative inferences such as those drawn in the mood 'celarent' of the logic-books.

2.Popular Science Monthly, N. Y., vols. lviii and lix.

3. Loc. cit., vol. lviii, pp. 189, 188.

4. Some Dogmas of Religion.

5. Munsterberg's book has just appeared in an english version: The Eternal Values, Boston, 1909.

6. Of course the bugaboo creature called 'the sceptic' in the logic-books, who dogmatically makes the statement that no statement, not even the one he now makes, is true, is a mere mechanical toy-target for the rationalist shooting-gallery — bit him and he turns a summersault — yet he is the only sort of relativist whom my colleagues appear able to imagine to exist.

7. Compare Rickert's Gegenstand der Erkentniss, pp. 137, 138. Munsterberg's version of this first truth is that 'Es gibt eine Welt,, —see his Philosophie der Werte, pp. 38 and 74 And, after all, both these philosophers confess in the end that the primal truth of which they consider our supposed

denial so irrational is not properly an insight at all, but a dogma adopted by the will which any one who turns his back on duty may disregard! But if it all reverts to I the will to believe,' pragmatists have that privilege as well as their critics.

TWO ENGLISH CRITICS

Mr. Bertrand Russell's article entitled "Transatlantic Truth,"[1] has all the clearness, dialectic subtlety, and wit which one expects from his pen, but it entirely fails to hit the right point of view for apprehending our position. When, for instance, we say that a true proposition is one the consequences of believing which are good, he assumes us to mean that any one who believes a proposition to be true must first have made out clearly that its consequences are good, and that his belief must primarily be in that fact, — an obvious absurdity, for that fact is the deliverance of a new proposition, quite different from the first one and is, moreover, a fact usually very hard to verify, it being 'far easier,' as Mr. Russell justly says, "to settle the plain question of fact: "Have popes always been infallible?" than to settle the question whether the effects of thinking them infallible are on the whole good.'

We affirm nothing as silly as Mr. Russell supposes. Good consequences are not proposed by us merely as a sure sign, mark, or criterion, by which truth's presence is habitually ascertained, tho they may indeed serve on occasion as such a sign; they are proposed rather as the lurking motive inside of every truth-claim, whether the 'trower' be conscious of such motive, or whether he obey it blindly. They are proposed as the causa existendi of our beliefs, not as their logical cue or premise, and still less as their objective deliverance or content. They assign the only intelligible practical meaning to that difference in our beliefs which our habit of calling them true or false comports.

No truth-claimer except the pragmatist himself need ever be aware of the part played in his own mind by consequences, and he himself is aware of it only abstractly and in general, and may at any moment be quite oblivious of it with respect to his own beliefs.

Mr. Russell next joins the army of those who inform their readers that according to the pragmatist definition of the word 'truth' the belief that A exists may be 'true,' even when A does not exist. This is the usual slander, repeated to satiety by our critics. They forget that in any concrete account of what is denoted by 'truth' in human life, the word can only be used relatively to some particular trower. Thus, I may hold it true that Shakespere wrote the plays that bear his name, and may express my opinion to a critic. If the critic be both a pragmatist and a baconian, he will in his capacity of pragmatist see plainly that the workings of my opinion, I being what I am, make it perfectly true for me, while in his capacity of baconian he still believes that Shakespere never wrote the plays in question. But most anti-pragmatist critics take the word 'truth' as something absolute, and easily play on their reader's readiness to treat his own truths as the absolute ones. If the reader whom they address believes that A does not exist, while we pragmatists show that those for whom the belief that it exists works satisfactorily will always call it true, he easily sneers at the naïveté of our contention, for is not then the belief in question 'true,' tho what it declares as fact has, as the reader so well knows, no existence? Mr. Russell speaks of our statement as an 'attempt to get rid of fact' and naturally enough considers it 'a failure.' 'The old notion of truth reappears,'he adds —that notion being, of course, that when a belief is true, its object does exist.

It is, of course, bound to exist, on sound pragmatic principles. Concepts signify consequences. How is the world made different for me by my conceiving an opinion of mine under the concept 'true'? First, an object must be findable there (or sure signs of such an object must be found) which shall agree with the opinion. Second, such an opinion must not be contradicted by anything else I am aware of. But in spite of the obvious pragmatist requirement that when I have said truly that something exists, it shall exist, the slander which Mr. Russell repeats has gained the widest currency.

Mr. Russell himself is far too witty and athletic a ratiocinator simply to repeat the slander dogmatically. Being nothing if not mathematical and logical, he must prove the accusation secundum arten, and convict us not so much of error as of absurdity. I have sincerely tried to follow the windings of his mind in this procedure, but for the life of me I can only see in it another example of what I have called vicious abstractionism. The abstract world of mathematics and pure logic is so native to Mr. Russell that he thinks that we describers of the functions of concrete fact must also mean fixed mathematical terms and functions. A mathematical term, as a, b, c, x, y, sin., log., is self-sufficient, and terms of this sort, once equated, can be substituted for one another in endless series without error. Mr. Russell, and also Mr. Hawtrey, of whom I shall speak presently, seem to think that in our mouth also such terms as 'meaning,' ' truth,' 'belief,' 'object,' 'definition,' are self-sufficients with no context of varying relation that might be further asked about. What a word means is expressed by its definition, is n't it? The definition claims to be exact and adequate, does n't it? Then it can be substituted for the word —since the two are identical — can't it? Then two words with the same definition can be substituted for one "other, n'est- ce pas? Likewise two definitions of the same word, nicht wahr, etc., etc., till it will be indeed strange if you can't convict some one of self-contradiction and absurdity.

The particular application of this rigoristic treatment to my own little account of truth as working seems to be something like what follows. I say 'working' is what the 'truth' of our ideas means, and call it a definition. But since meanings and things meant, definitions and things defined, are equivalent and interchangeable, and nothing extraneous to its definition can be meant when a term is used, it follows that whoso calls an idea true, and means by that word that it works, cannot mean anything else, can believe nothing but that it does work, and in particular can neither imply nor allow anything about its object or deliverance. ' According to the pragmatists,' Mr. Russell writes, 'to say —it is true that other people exist" means "it is useful to believe that other people exist." But if so, then these two phrases are merely different words for the same proposition; therefore when I believe the one I believe the other.' [Logic, I may say in passing, would seem to require Mr. Russell to believe them both at once, but he ignores this consequence, and considers that 'other people exist' and 'it is useful to believe that they do even if they don't,' must be identical and therefore substitutable propositions in the pragmatist mouth.]

But may not real terms, I now ask, have accidents not expressed in their definitions? and when a real value is finally substituted for the result of an algebraic series of substituted definitions, do not all these accidents creep back? Beliefs have their objective 'content' or 'deliverance' as well as their truth, and truth has its implications as well as its workings. If any one believe that other men exist, it is both a content of his belief and an implication of its truth, that they should exist in fact. Mr. Russell's logic would seem to exclude, 'by definition,' all such accidents as contents, implications, and associates, and would represent us as translating all belief into a sort of belief in pragmatism itself — of all things! If I say that a speech is eloquent, and explain 'eloquent' as meaning the power to work in certain ways upon the audience; or if I say a book is original, and define 'original' to mean differing from other books, Russell's logic, if I follow it at all, would seem to doom me to agreeing that the speech is about eloquence, and the book about other books. When I call a belief true, and define its truth to mean its workings, I certainly do not mean that the belief is a belief about the workings. It is a belief about the object, and I who talk about the workings am a different subject, with a different universe of discourse, from that of the believer of whose concrete thinking I profess to give an account.

The social proposition 'other men exist' and the pragmatist proposition 'it is expedient to believe that other men exist' come from different universes of discourse. One can believe the second without being logically compelled to believe the first; one can believe the first without having ever heard of the second; or one can believe them both. The first expresses the object of a belief, the second tells of one condition of the belief's power to maintain itself. There is no identity of any kind, save the term 'other men' which they contain in common, in the two propositions; and to treat them as mutually substitutable, or to insist that we shall do so, is to give up dealing with realities altogether.

Mr. Ralph Hawtrey, who seems also to serve under the banner of abstractionist logic, convicts us pragmatists of absurdity by arguments similar to Mr. Russell's.[2]

As a favor to us and for the sake of the argument, he abandons the word 'true' to our fury, allowing it to mean nothing but the fact at certain beliefs are expedient; and he uses the word 'correctness' (as Mr. Pratt uses the word 'trueness') to designate a fact, not about the belief, but about the belief's object, namely that it is as the belief declares it. 'When therefore,' he writes, 'I say it is correct to say that Caesar is dead, I mean " Caesar is dead." This must be regarded as the definition of correctness.' And Mr. Hawtrey then goes on to demolish me by the conflict of the definitions. What is 'true' for the pragmatist cannot be what is 'correct,' he says, for the definitions are not logically interchangeable; or if we interchange them, we reach the tautology: "Caesar is dead" means "it is expedient to believe that Caesar is dead." But what is it expedient to believe? Why, "that Caesar is dead."' A precious definition indeed of 'Caesar is dead.'

Mr. Hawtrey's conclusion would seem to be that the pragmatic definition of the truth of a belief in no way implies — what? — that the believer shall believe in his own belief's deliverance? — or that the pragmatist who is talking about him shall believe in that deliverance? The two cases are quite different. For the believer, Caesar must of course really exist; for the pragmatist critic he need not, for the pragmatic deliverance belongs, as I have just said, to another universe of discourse altogether. When one argues by substituting definition for definition, one needs to stay in the same universe.

The great shifting of universes in this discussion occurs when we carry the word 'truth' from the subjective into the objective realm, applying it sometimes to a property of opinions, sometimes to the facts which the opinions assert. A number of writers, as Mr. Russell himself, Mr. G. E. Moore, and others, favor the unlucky word 'proposition,' which seems expressly invented to foster this confusion, for they speak of truth as a property of 'propositions.' But in naming propositions it is almost impossible not to use the word 'that.' That Caesar is dead, that virtue is its own reward, are propositions.

I do not say that for certain logical purposes it may not be useful to treat propositions as absolute entities, with truth or falsehood inside of them respectively, or to make of a complex like 'that-Caesar-is-dead' a single term and call it a 'truth.' But the 'that' here has the extremely convenient ambiguity for those who wish to make trouble for us pragmatists, that sometimes it means the fact that, and sometimes the belief that, Caesar is no longer living. When I then call the belief true, I am told that the truth means the fact; when I claim the fact also, I am told that my definition has excluded the fact, being a definition only of a certain peculiarity in the belief — so that in the end I have no truth to talk about left in my possession.

The only remedy for this intolerable ambiguity is, it seems to me, to stick to terms consistently. 'Reality,' 'idea' or 'belief,' and the 'truth of the idea or belief,' which are the terms I have consistently held to, seem to be free from all objection.

Whoever takes terms abstracted from all their natural settings, identifies them with definitions, and treats the latter more algebraico, not only risks mixing universes, but risks fallacies which the man in the street easily detects. To prove 'by definition' that the statement ' Caesar exists' is identical with a statement about 'expediency' because the one statement is 'true' and the other is about 'true statements,' is like proving that an omnibus is a boat because both are vehicles. A horse may be defined as a beast that walks on the nails of his middle digits. Whenever we see a horse we see such a beast, just as whenever we believe a 'truth' we believe something expedient. Messrs. Russell and Hawtrey, if they followed their antipragmatist logic, would have to say here that we see that it is such a beast, a fact which notoriously no one sees who is not a comparative anatomist.

It almost reconciles one to being no logician that one thereby escapes so much abstractionism. Abstractionism of the worst sort dogs Mr. Russell in his own trials to tell positively what the word 'truth' means. In the third of his articles on Meinong, in Mind, vol. xiii, p. 509 (1904), he attempts this feat by limiting the discussion to three terms only, a proposition, its content, and an object, abstracting from the whole context of associated realities in which such terms are found in every case of actual knowing. He puts the terms, thus taken in a vacuum, and made into bare logical entities, through every possible permutation and combination, tortures them on the rack until nothing is left of them, and after all this logical gymnastic, comes out with the following portentous conclusion as what he believes to be 'the correct view: that there is no problem at all in truth and falsehood, that some propositions are true and some false, just as some roses are red and some white, that belief is a certain attitude towards propositions, which is called knowledge when they are true, error when they are false' —and he seems to think that when once this insight is reached the question may be considered closed forever!

In spite of my admiration of Mr. Russell's analytic powers, I wish, after reading such an article, that pragmatism, even had it no other function, might result in making him and other similarly gifted men ashamed of having used such powers in such abstraction from reality. Pragmatism saves us at any rate from such diseased abstractionism as those pages show.

P. S. Since the foregoing rejoinder was written an article on Pragmatism which I believe to be by Mr. Russell has appeared in the Edinburgh Review for April, 1909. As far as his discussion of the truth-problem goes, altho he has evidently taken great pains to be fair, it seems to me that he has in no essential respect improved upon his former arguments. I will therefore add nothing further, but simply refer readers who may be curious to pp. 272-280 of the said article.

Endnotes

1. In the Albany Review for January, 1908.
2. See The New Quarterly, for March, 1908.

A DIALOGUE

After correcting the proof of all that precedes I imagine a residual state of mind on the part of my reader which may still keep him unconvinced, and which it may be my duty to try at least to dispel. I can perhaps be briefer if I put what I have to say in dialogue form. Let then the anti-pragmatist begin:—

Anti-Pragmatist: — You say that the truth of an idea is constituted by its workings. Now suppose a certain stat of facts, facts for example of antediluvian planetary history, concerning which the question may be asked: 'Shall the truth about ever be known?' And suppose (leaving the hypothesis of an omniscient absolute out of the account) that we assume that the truth is never to be known. I ask you now, brother pragmatist, whether according to you there can be said to be any truth at all about such a state of facts. Is?there a truth, or is there not a truth, in cases where at any rate it never comes to be known?

Pragmatist: — Why do you ask me such a question?

Anti-Prag.: — Because I think it puts you in a bad dilemma.

Prag.: — How so?

Anti-Prag.: —Why, because if on the one hand you elect to say that there is a truth, you thereby surrender your whole pragmatist theory. According to that theory, truth requires ideas and workings to constitute it; but in the present instance there is supposed to be no knower, and consequently neither ideas nor workings can exist. What then remains for you to make your truth of?

Prag.: —Do you wish, like so many of my enemies, to force me to make the truth out of the reality itself? I cannot: the truth is something known, thought or said about the reality, and consequently numerically additional to it. But probably your intent is something different; so before I say which horn of your dilemma I choose, I ask you to let me hear what the other horn may be.

Anti-Prag.: — The other horn is this, that if you elect to say that there is no truth under the conditions assumed, because there are no ideas or workings, then you fly in the face of common sense. Does n't common sense believe that every state of facts must in the nature of things be truly statable in some kind of a proposition, even tho in point of fact the proposition should never be propounded by a living soul?

Prag.: — Unquestionably common sense believes this, and so do I. There have been innumerable events in the history of our planet of which nobody ever has been or ever will be able to give an account, yet of which it can already be said abstractly that only one sort of possible account can ever be true. The truth about any such event is thus already generically predetermined by the event's nature; and one may accordingly say with a perfectly good conscience that it virtually pre-exists. Common sense is thus right in its instinctive contention.

Anti-Prag.: — Is this then the horn of the dilemma which you stand for? Do you say that there is a truth even in cases where it shall never be known?

Prag-: — Indeed I do, provided you let me hold consistently to my own conception of truth, and do not ask me to abandon it for something which I find impossible to comprehend. —You also believe, do you not, that there is a truth, even in cases where it never shall be known?

Anti-Prag.: — I do indeed believe so.

Prag.: — Pray then inform me in what, according to you, this truth regarding the unknown consists.

Anti-Prag.:— Consists? —pray what do you mean by 'consists'? It consists in nothing but itself, or more properly speaking it has neither consistence nor existence, it obtains, it holds.

Prag.: — Well, what relation does it bear to the reality of which it holds?

Anti-Prag.: — How do you mean, 'what relation'? It holds of it, of course; it knows it, it represents it.

Prag.: — Who knows it? What represents it?

Anti-Prag.: —The truth does; the truth knows it; or rather not exactly that, but any one knows it who possesses the truth. Any true idea of the reality represents the truth concerning it.

Prag.: — But I thought that we had agreed that no knower of it, nor any idea representing it was to be supposed.

Anti-Prag.: — Sure enough!

Prag.: — Then I beg you again to tell me in what this truth consists, all by itself, this tertium quid intermediate between the facts per se, on the one hand, and all knowledge of them, actual or potential, on the other. What is the shape of it in this third estate? Of what stuff, mental, physical, or 'epistemological,' isitbuiltP What metaphysical region of reality does it inhabit?

Anti-Prag.: — What absurd questions! Isn't it enough to say that it is true that the facts are so-and-so, and false that they are otherwise?

Prag.: — 'It' is true that the facts are so-and-so — I won't yield to the temptation of asking you what is true; but I do ask you whether your phrase that 'it is true that' the facts are so-and-so really means anything really additional to the bare being so-and-so of the facts themselves.

Anti-Prag.: — It seems to mean more than the bare being of the facts. It is a sort of mental equivalent for them, their epistemological function, their value in noetic terms.

Prag.:—A sort of spiritual double or ghost of them, apparently! If so, may I ask you where this truth is found.

Anti-Prag.: —Where? where? There is no 'where'— it simply obtains, absolutely obtains.

Prag.: —Not in any one's mind?

Anti-Prag.: —No, for we agreed that no actual knower of the truth should be assumed.

Prag.:—No actual knower, I agree. But are you sure that no notion of a potential or ideal knower has anything to do with forming this strangely elusive idea of the truth of the facts in your mind?

Anti-Prag.: — Of course if there be a truth concerning the facts, that truth is what the ideal knower would know. To that extent you can't keep the notion of it and the notion of him separate. But it is not him first and then it; it is it first and then him, in my opinion.

Prag.: — But you still leave me terribly puzzled as to the status of this so-called truth, hanging as it does between earth and heaven, between reality and knowledge, grounded in the reality, yet numerically additional to it, and at the same time antecedent to any knower's opinion and entirely independent thereof. Is it as independent of the knower as you suppose? It looks to me terribly dubious, as if it might be only another name for a potential as distinguished from an actual knowledge of the reality. Is n't your truth, after all, simply what any successful knower would have to know in case he existed? And in a universe where no knowers were even conceivable would any truth about the facts there as something numerically distinguishable from the facts themselves, find a place to exist in? To me such truth would not only be non-existent, it would be unimaginable, inconceivable.

Anti-Prag.: —But I thought you said a while ago that there is a truth of past events, even tho no one shall ever know it.

Prag.: — Yes, but you must remember that I also stipulated for permission to define the word in my own fashion. The truth of an event, past, present, or future, is for me only another name for the fact that if the event ever doe8get known, the nature of the knowledge is already to some degree predetermined. The truth which precedes actual knowledge of a fact means only what any possible knower of the fact will eventually find himself necessitated to believe about it. He must believe something that will bring him into satisfactory relations with it, that will prove a decent mental substitute for it. What this something may be is of course partly fixed already by the nature of the fact and by the sphere of its associations.

This seems to me all that you can clearly mean when you say that truth pre-exists to knowledge. It is knowledge anticipated, knowledge in the form of possibility merely.

Anti-Prag.: — But what does the knowledge know when it comes? Does n't it know the truth? And, if so, mustn't the truth be distinct from either the fact or the knowledge?

Prag-: — It seems to me that what the knowledge knows is the fact itself, the event., or whatever the reality may be. Where you see three distinct entities in the field, the reality, the knowing, and the truth, I see only two. Moreover, I can see what each of my two entities is known-as, but when I ask myself what your third entity, the truth, is known-as, I can find nothing distinct from the reality on the one hand, and the ways in which it may be known on the other. Are you not probably misled by common language, which has found it convenient to introduce a hybrid name, meaning sometimes a kind of knowing and sometimes a reality known, to apply to either of these things interchangeably? And has philosophy anything to gain by perpetuating and consecrating the ambiguity? If you call the object of knowledge 'reality,' and call the manner of its being cognized 'truth,' cognized moreover on particular occasions, and variously, by particular human beings who have their various businesses with it, and if you hold consistently to this nomenclature, it seems to me that you escape all sorts of trouble.

Anti-Prag.: — Do you mean that you think you escape from my dilemma?

Prag.: — Assuredly I escape; for if truth and knowledge are terms correlative and interdependent, as I maintain they are, then wherever knowledge is conceivable truth is conceivable, wherever knowledge is possible truth is possible, wherever knowledge is actual truth is actual. Therefore when you point your first horn at me, I think of truth actual, and say it does n't exist. It does n't; for by hypothesis there is no knower, no ideas, no workings. I agree, however, that truth possible or virtual might exist, for a knower might possibly be brought to birth; and truth conceivable, certainly exists, for, abstractly taken, there is nothing in the nature of antediluvian events that should make the application of knowledge to them inconceivable. Therefore when you try to impale me on your second horn, I think of the truth in question as a mere abstract possibility, so I say it does exist, and side with common sense.

Do not these distinctions rightly relieve me from embarrassment? And don't you think it might help you to make them yourself?

Anti-Prag.: — Never ! — so avaunt with your abominable hair-splitting and sophistry! Truth is truth; and never will I degrade it by identifying it with low pragmatic particulars in the way you propose.

Prag.: — Well, my dear antagonist, I hardly hoped to convert an eminent intellectualist and logician like you; so enjoy, as long as you live, your own ineffable conception. Perhaps the rising generation will grow up more accustomed than you are to that concrete and empirical interpretation of terms in which the pragmatic method consists. Perhaps they may then wonder how so harmless and natural an account of truth as mine could have found such difficulty in entering the minds of men far more intelligent than I can ever hope to become, but wedded by education and tradition to the abstractionist manner of thought.

What is an Emotion?

First published in Mind, 9.

The physiologists who, during the past few years, have been so industriously exploring the functions of the brain, have limited their attempts at explanation to its cognitive and volitional performances. Dividing the brain into sensorial and motor centres, they have found their division to be exactly paralleled by the analysis made by empirical psychology, of the perceptive and volitional parts of the mind into their simplest elements. But the aesthetic sphere of the mind, its longings, its pleasures and pains, and its emotions, have been so ignored in all these researches that one is tempted to suppose that if either Dr. Ferrier or Dr. Munk were asked for a theory in brain-terms of the latter mental facts, they might both reply, either that they had as yet bestowed no thought upon the subject, or that they had found it so difficult to make distinct hypotheses, that the matter lay for them among the problems of the future, only to be taken up after the simpler ones of the present should have been definitively solved.

And yet it is even now certain that of two things concerning the emotions, one must be true. Either separate and special centres, affected to them alone, are their brain-seat, or else they correspond to processes occurring in the motor and sensory centres, already assigned, or in others like them, not yet mapped out. If the former be the case we must deny the current view, and hold the cortex to be something more than the surface of "projection" for every sensitive spot and every muscle in the body. If the latter be the case, we must ask whether the emotional "process" in the sensory or motor centre be an altogether peculiar one, or whether it resembles the ordinary perceptive processes of which those centres are already recognised to be the seat. The purpose of the following pages is to show that the last alternative comes nearest to the truth, and that the emotional brain-processes no only resemble the ordinary sensorial brain-processes, but in very truth are nothing but such processes variously combined. The main result of this will be to simplify our notions of the possible complications of brain-physiology, and to make us see that we have already a brain-scheme in our hands whose applications are much wider than its authors dreamed. But although this seems to be the chief result of the arguments I am to urge, I should say that they were not originally framed for the sake of any such result. They grew out of fragmentary introspective observations, and it was only when these had already combined into a theory that the thought of the simplification the theory might bring to cerebral physiology occurred to me, and made it seem more important than before.

I should say first of all that the only emotions I propose expressly to consider here are those that have a distinct bodily expression. That there are feelings of pleasure and displeasure, of interest and excitement, bound up with mental operations, but having no obvious bodily expression for their consequence, would, I suppose, be held true by most readers. Certain arrangements of sounds, of lines, of colours, are agreeable, and others the reverse, without the degree of the feeling being sufficient to quicken the pulse or breathing, or to prompt to movements of either the body or the face. Certain sequences of ideas charm us as much as others tire us. It is a real intellectual delight to get a problem solved, and a real intellectual torment to have to leave it unfinished. The first set of examples, the sounds, lines, and colours, are either bodily sensations, or the images of such. The second set seem to depend on processes in the ideational centres exclusively. Taken together, they appear to prove that there are pleasures and pains inherent in certain forms of nerve-action as such, wherever that action occur. The case of these feelings we will at present leave entirely aside, and confine our attention to the more complicated cases in which a wave of bodily disturbance of some kind accompanies the perception of the interesting sights or sounds, or the passage of the exciting train of ideas. Surprise, curiosity, rapture, fear, anger, lust, greed, and the like, become then the names of the mental states with which the person is possessed. The bodily disturbances are said to be the "manifestation" of these several emotions, their "expression" or "natural language"; and these emotions themselves, being so strongly characterized both from within and without, may be called the standard emotions.

Our natural way of thinking about these standard emotions is that the mental perception of some fact excites the mental affection called the emotion, and that this latter state of mind gives rise to the bodily expression. My thesis on the contrary is that the bodily changes follow directly the PERCEPTION of the exciting fact, and that our feeling of the same changes as they occur IS the emotion. Common sense says, we lose our fortune, are sorry and weep; we meet a bear, are frightened and run; we are insulted by a rival, are angry and strike. The hypothesis here to be defended says that this order of sequence is incorrect, that the one mental state is not immediately induced by the other, that the bodily manifestations must first be interposed between, and that the more rational statement is that we feel sorry because we cry, angry because we strike, afraid because we tremble, and not that we cry, strike, or tremble, because we are sorry, angry, or fearful, as the case may be. Without the bodily states following on the perception, the latter would be purely cognitive in form, pale, colourless, destitute of emotional warmth. We might then see the bear, and judge it best to run, receive the insult and deem it right to strike, but we could not actually feel afraid or angry.

Stated in this crude way, the hypothesis is pretty sure to meet with immediate disbelief. And yet neither many nor far-fetched considerations are required to mitigate its paradoxical character, and possibly to produce conviction of its truth.

To begin with, readers of the Journal do not need to be reminded that the nervous system of every living thing is but a bundle of predispositions to react in particular ways upon the contact of particular features of the environment. As surely as the hermit-crab's abdomen presupposes the existence of empty whelk-shells somewhere to be found, so surely do the hound's olfactories imply the existence, on the one hand, of deer's or foxes' feet, and on the other, the tendency to follow up their tracks. The neural machinery is but a hyphen between determinate arrangements of matter ourtside the body and determinate impulses to inhibition or discharge within its organs. When the hen sees a white oval object on the ground, she cannot leave it; she must keep upon it and return to it, until at last its transformation into a little mass of moving chirping down elicits from her machinery an entirely new set of performances. The love of man for woman, or of the human mother for her babe, our wrath at snakes and our fear of precipices, may all be described similarly, as instances of the way in which peculiarly conformed pieces of the world's furniture will fatally call forth most particular mental and bodily reactions, in advance of, and often in direct opposition to, the verdict of our deliberate reason concerning them. The labours of Darwin and his successors are only just beginning to reveal the universal parasitism of each creature upon other special things, and the way in which each creature brings the signature of its special relations stampted on its nervous system with it upon the scene.

Every living creature is in fact a sort of lock, whose wards and springs presuppose special forms of key, — which keys however are not born attached to the locks, but are sure to be found in the world near by as life goes on. And the locks are indifferent to any but their own keys. The egg fails to fascinate the hound, the bird does not fear the precipice, the snake waxes not wroth at his kind, the deer cares nothing for the woman or the human babe. Those who wish for a full development of this point of view, should read Schneider's Der thierische Wille, — no other book shows how accurately anticipatory are the actions of animals, of the specific features of the environment in which they are to live.

Now among these nervous anticipations are of course to be reckoned the emotions, so far as these may be called forth directly by the perception of certain facts. In advance of all experience of elephants no child can but be frightened if he suddenly find one trumpeting and charging upon him. No woman can see a handsome little naked baby without delight, no man in the wilderness see a human form in the distance without excitement and curiosity. I said I should consider these emotions only so far as they have bodily movements of some sort for their accompaniments. But my first point is to show that their bodily accompaniments are much more far-reaching and complicated than we ordinarily suppose.

In the earlier books on Expression, written mostly from the artistic point of view, the signs of emotion visible from without were the only ones taken account of. Sir Charles Bell's celebrated Anatomy of Expression noticed the respiratory changes; and Bain's and Darwin's treatises went more thoroughly still into the study of the visceral factors involved,— changes in the functioning of glands and muscles, and in that of the circulatory apparatus. But not even a Darwin has exhaustively enumerated all the bodily affections characteristic of any one of the standard emotions. More and more, as physiology advances, we begin to discern how almost infinitely numerous and subtle they must be. The researches of Mosso with the plethysmograph have shown that not only the heart, but the entire circulatory system, forms a sort of sounding-board, which every change of our consciousness, however slight, may make reverberate. Hardly a sensation comes to us without sending waves of alternate constriction and dilatation down the arteries of our arms. The blood-vessels of the abdomen act reciprocally with those of the more outward parts. The bladder and bowels, the glands of the mouth, throat, and skin, and the liver, are known to be affected gravely in certain severe emotions, and are unquestionably affected transiently when the emotions are of a lighter sort. That the heart-beats and the rhythm of breathing play a leading part in all emotions whatsoever, is a matter too notorious for proof. And what is really equally prominent, but less likely to be admitted until special attention is drawn to the fact, is the continuous co-operation of the voluntary muscles in our emotional states. Even when no change of outward attitude is produced, their inward tension alters to suit each varying mood, and is felt as a difference of tone or of strain. In depression the flexors tend to prevail; in elation or belligerent excitement the extensors take the lead. And the various permutations and combinations of which these organic activities are susceptible, make it abstractly possible that no shade of emotion, however slight, should be without a bodily reverberation as unique, when taken in its totality, as is the mental mood itself.

The immense number of parts modified in each emotion is what makes it so difficult for us to reproduce in cold blood the total and integral expression of any one of them. We may catch the trick with the voluntary muscles, but fail with the skin, glands, heart, and other viscera. Just as an artificially imitated sneeze lacks something of the reality, so the attempt to imitate an emotion in the absence of its normal instigating cause is apt to be rather "hollow".

The next thing to be noticed is this, that every one of the bodily changes, whatsoever it be, is felt, acutely or obscurely, the moment it occurs. If the reader has never paid attention to this matter, he will be both interested and astonished to learn how many different local bodily feelings he can detect in himself as characteristic of his various emotional moods. It would be perhaps too much to expect him to arrest the tide of any strong gust of passion for the sake of any such curious analysis as this; but he can observe more tranquil states, and that may be assumed here to be true of the greater which is shown to be true of the less. Our whole cubic capacity is sensibly alive; and each morsel of it contributes its pulsations of feeling, dim or sharp, pleasant, painful, or dubious, to that sense of personality that every one of us unfailingly carries with him. It is surprising what little items give accent to these complexes of sensibility.

When worried by any slight trouble, one may find that the focus of one's bodily consciousness is the contraction, often quite inconsiderable, of the eyes and brows. When momentarily embarrassed, it is something in the pharynx that compels either a swallow, a clearing of the throat, or a slight cough; and so on for as many more instances as might be named. Our concern here being with the general view rather than with the details, I will not linger to discuss these but, assuming the point admitted that every change that occurs must be felt, I will pass on.[1]

I now proceed to urge the vital point of my whole theory, which is this. If we fancy some strong emotion, and then try to abstract from our consciousness of it all the feelings of its characteristic bodily symptoms, we find we have nothing left behind, no "mind-stuff" out of which the emotion can be constituted, and that a cold and neutral state of intellectual perception is all that remains. It is true, that although most people, when asked say that their introspection verifies this statement, some persist in saying theirs does not.

Many cannot be made to understand the question. When you beg them to imagine away every feeling of laughter and of tendency to laugh from their consciousness of the ludicrousness of an object, and then to tell you what the feeling of its ludicrousness would be like, whether it be anything more than the perception that the object belongs to the class "funny," they persist in replying that the thing proposed is a physical impossibility, and that they always must laugh, if they see a funny object. Of course the task proposed is not the practical one of seeing a ludicrous object and annihilating one's tendency to laugh. It is the purely speculative one of subtracting certain elements of feeling from an emotional state supposed to exist in its fulness, and saying what the residual elements are. I cannot help thinking that all who rightly apprehend this problem will agree with the proposition above laid down. What kind of an emotion of fear would be left, if the feelings neither of quickened heart-beats nor of shallow breathing, neither of trembling lips nor of weakened limbs, neither of goose-flesh nor of visceral stirrings, were present, it is quite impossible to think. Can one fancy the state of rage and picture no ebullition of it in the chest, no flushing of the face, no dilatation of the nostrils, no clenching of the teeth, no impulse to vigorous action, but in their stead limp muscles, calm breathing, and a placid face? The present writer, for one, certainly cannot. The rage is as completely evaporated as the sensation of its so-called manifestations, and the only thing that can possibly be supposed to take its place is some cold-blooded and dispassionate judicial sentence, confined entirely to the intellectual realm, to the effect that a certain person or persons merit chastisement for their sins. In like manner of grief: what would it be without its tears, its sobs, its suffocation of the heart, its pang in the breast-bone? A feelingless cognition that certain circumstances are deplorable, and nothing more. Every passion in turn tells the same story. A purely disembodied human emotion is a nonentity. I do not say that it is a contradiction in the nature of things, or that pure spirits are necessarily condemned to cold intellectual lives; but I say that for us, emotion dissociated from all bodily feeling is inconceivable. The more closely I scrutinise my states, the more persuaded I become, that whatever moods, affections, and passions I have, are in very truth constituted by, and made up of, those bodily changes we ordinarily call their expression or consequence; and the more it seems to me that if I were to become corporeally anaesthetic, I should be excluded from the life of the affections, harsh and tender alike, and drag out an existence of merely cognitive or intellectual form. Such an existence, although it seems to have been the ideal of ancient sages, is too apathetic to be keenly sought after by those born after the revival of the worship of sensibility, a few generations ago.

But if the emotion is nothing but the feeling of the reflex bodily effects of what we call its "objects," effects due to the connate adaptation of the nervous system to that object, we seem immediately faced by this objection: most of the objects of civilised men's emotions are things to which it would be preposterous to suppose their nervous systems connately adapted. Most occasions of shame and many insults are purely conventional, and vary with the social environment. The same is true of many matters of dread and of desire, and of many occasions of melancholy and regret. In these cases, at least, it would seem that the ideas of shame, desire, regret, &c., must first have been attached by education and association to these conventional objects before the bodily changes could possibly be awakened. And if in these cases the bodily changes follow the ideas, instead of giving rise to them, why not then in all cases?

To discuss thoroughly this objection would carry us deep into the study of purely intellectual Aesthetics. A few words must here suffice. We will say nothing of the argument's failure to distinguish between the idea of an emotion and the emotion itself. We will only recall the well-known evolutionary principle that when a certain power has once been fixed in an animal by virtue of its utility in presence of certain features of the environment, it may turn out to be useful in presence of other features of the environment that had originally nothing to do with either producing or preserving it. A nervous tendency to discharge being once there, all sorts of unforeseen things may pull the trigger and let loose the effects. That among these things should be conventionalities of man's contriving is a matter of no psychological consequence whatever. The most important part of my environment is my fellow-man. The consciousness of his attitude towards me is the perception that normally unlocks most of my shames and indignations and fears. The extraordinary sensitiveness of this consciousness is shown by the bodily modifications wrought in us by the awareness that our fellow-man is noticing us at all. No one can walk across the platform at a public meeting with just the same muscular innervation he uses to walk across his room at home. No one can give a message to such a meeting without organic excitement. "Stage-fright" is only the extreme degree of that wholly irrational personal self-consciousness which every one gets in some measure, as soon as he feels the eyes of a number of strangers fixed upon him, even though he be inwardly convinced that their feeling towards him is of no practical account[2]. This being so, it is not surprising that the additional persuasion that my fellow-man's attitude means either well or ill for me, should awaken stronger emotions still. In primitive societies "Well" may mean handing me a piece of beef, and "Ill" may mean aiming a blow at my skull. In our "cultured age," "Ill" may mean cutting me in the street, and "Well," giving me an honorary degree. What the action itself may be is quite insignificant, so long as I can perceive in it intent or animus. That is the emotion-arousing perception; and may give rise to as strong bodily convulsions in me, a civilised man experiencing the treatment of an artificial society, as in any savage prisoner of war, learning whether his captors are about to eat him or to make him a member of their tribe.

But now, this objection disposed of, there arises a more general doubt. Is there any evidence, it may be asked, for the assumption that particular perceptions do produce widespread bodily effects by a sort of immediate physical influence, antecedent to the arousal of an emotion or emotional idea?

The only possible reply is, that there is most assuredly such evidence. In listening to poetry, drama, or heroic narrative, we are often surprised at the cutaneous shiver which like a sudden wave flows over us, and at the heart-swelling and the lachrymal effusion that unexpectedly catch us at intervals. In listening to music, the same is even more strikingly true. If we abruptly see a dark moving form in the woods, our heart stops beating, and we catch our breath instantly and before any articulate idea of danger can arise. If our friend goes near to the edge of a precipice, we get the well-known feeling of "all-overishness," and we shrink back, although we positively know him to be safe, and have no distinct imagination of his fall. The writer well remembers his astonishment, when a boy of seven or eight, at fainting when he saw a horse bled. The blood was in a bucket, with a stick in it, and, if memory does not deceive him, he stirred it round and saw it drip from the stick with no feeling save that of childish curiosity. Suddenly the world grew black before his eyes, his ears began to buzz, and he knew no more. He had never heard of the sight of blood producing faintness or sickness, and he had so little repugnance to it, and so little apprehension of any other sort of danger from it, that even at that tender age, as he well remembers, he could not help wondering how the mere physical presence of a pailful of crimson fluid occasion in him such formidable bodily effects.

Imagine two steel knife-blades with their keen edges crossing each other at right-angles, and moving too and fro. Our whole nervous organisation is "on-edge" at the thought; and yet what emotion can be there except the unpleasant nervous feeling itself, or the dread that more of it may come?

The entire fund and capital of the emotion here is the senseless bodily effect the blades immediately arouse. This case is typical of a class: where an ideal emotion seems to precede the bodily symptoms, it is often nothing but a representation of the symptoms themselves. One who has already fainted at the sight of blood may witness the preparations for a surgical operation with uncontrollable heart-sinking and anxiety. He anticipates certain feelings, and the anticipation precipitates their arrival. I am told of a case of morbid terror, of which the subject confessed that what possessed her seemed, more than anything, to be the fear of fear itself. In the various forms of what Professor Bain calls "tender emotion," although the appropriate object must usually be directly contemplated before the emotion can be aroused, yet sometimes thinking of the symptoms of the emotion itself may have the same effect. In sentimental natures, the thought of "yearning" will produce real "yearning". And, not to speak of coarser examples, a mother's imagination of the caresses she bestows on her child may arouse a spasm of parental longing.

In such cases as these, we see plainly how the emotion both begins and ends with what we call its effects or manifestations. It has no mental status except as either the presented feeling, or the idea, of the manifestations; which latter thus constitute its entire material, its sum and substance, and its stock-in-trade. And these cases ought to make us see how in all cases the feeling of the manifestations may play a much deeper part in the constitution of the emotion than we are wont to suppose.

If our theory be true, a necessary corollary of it ought to be that any voluntary arousal of the so-called manifestations of a special emotion ought to give us the emotion itself. Of course in the majority of emotions, this test is inapplicable; for many of the manifestations are in organs over which we have no volitional control. Still, within the limits in which it can be verified, experience fully corroborates this test. Everyone knows how panic is increased by flight, and how the giving way to the symptoms of grief or anger increases those passions themselves. Each fit of sobbing makes the sorrow more acute, and calls forth another fit stronger still, until at last repose only ensues with lassitude and with the apparent exhaustion of the machinery. In rage, it is notorious how we "work ourselves up" to a climax by repeated outbreaks of expression. Refuse to express a passion, and it dies. Count ten before venting your anger, and it occasion seems ridiculous.

Whistling to keep up courage is no mere figure of speech. On the other hand, sit all day in a moping posture, sigh, and reply to everything with a dismal voice, and your melancholy lingers. There is no more valuable precept in moral education than this, as all who have experience know: if we wish to conquer undesirable emotional tendencies in ourselves, we must assiduously, and in the first instance cold-bloodedly, go through the outward motions of those contrary dispositions we prefer to cultivate. The reward of persistency will infallibly come, in the fading out of the sullenness or depression, and the advent of real cheerfulness and kindliness in their stead. Smooth the brow, brighten the eye, contract the dorsal rather than the ventral aspect of the frame, and speak in a major key, pass the genial compliment, and your heart must be frigid indeed if it do not gradually thaw!

The only exception to this are apparent, not real. The great emotional expressiveness and mobility of certain persons often lead us to say "They would feel more if they talked less". And in another class of persons, the explosive energy with which passion manifests itself on critical occasions, seems correlated with the way in which they bottle it up during the intervals. But these are only eccentric types of character, and within each type the law of the last paragraph prevails. The sentimentalist is so constructed that "gushing" is his or her normal mode of expression. Putting a stopper on the "gush" will only to a limited extent cause more "real" activities to take its place; in the main it will simply produce listlessness. On the other hand the ponderous and bilious "slumbering volcano," let him repress the expression of his passions as he will, will find them expire if they get no vent at all; whilst if the rare occasions multiply which he deems worthy of their outbreak, he will find them grow in intensity as life proceeds.

I feel persuaded there is no real exception to the law. The formidable effects of suppressed tears might be mentioned, and the calming results of speaking out your mind when angry and having done with it. But these are also but specious wanderings from the rule. Every perceptions must lead to some nervous result. If this be the normal emotional expression, it soon expends itself, and in the natural course of things a calm succeeds. But if the normal issue be blocked from any cause, the currents may under certain circumstances invade other tracts, and there work different and worse effects. Thus vengeful brooding may replace a burst of indignation; a dry heat may consume the frame of one who fain would weep, or he may, as Dante says, turn to stone within; and then tears or a storming-fit may bring a grateful relief. When we teach children to repress their emotions, it is not that they may feel more, quite the reverse. It is that they may think more; for to a certain extent whatever nerve-currents are diverted from the regions below, must swell the activity of the thought-tracts of the brain.[3]

The last great argument in favour of the priority of the bodily symptoms to the felt emotion, is the ease with which we formulate by its means pathological cases and normal cases under a common scheme. In every asylum we find examples of absolutely unmotived fear, anger, melancholy, or conceit; and others of an equally unmotived apathy which persists in spite of the best of outward reasons why it should give way. In the former cases we must suppose the nervous machinery to be so "labile" in some one emotional direction, that almost every stimulus, however inappropriate, will cause it to upset in that way, and as a consequence to engender the particular complex of feelings of which the psychic body of the emotion consists. Thus, to take one special instance, if inability to draw deep breath, fluttering of the heart, and that peculiar epigastric change felt as "precordial anxiety," with an irresistible tendency to take a somewhat crouching attitude and to sit still, and with perhaps other visceral processes not now known, all spontaneously occur together in a certain person; his feeling of their combination is the emotion of dread, and he is the victim of what is known as morbid fear. A friend who has had occasional attacks of this most distressing of all maladies, tells me that in his case the whole drama seems to centre about the region of the heart and respiratory apparatus, that his main effort during the attacks is to get control of his inspirations and to slow his heart, and that the moment he attains to breathing deeply and to holding himself erect, the dread, ipso facto, seems to depart[4]

The account given to Brachet by one of his own patients of her opposite condition, that of emotional insensibility, has been often quoted, and deserves to be quoted again:—

"I still continue (she says) to suffer constantly ; I have not a moment of comfort, and no human sensations. Surrounded by all that can render life happy and agreeable, still to me the faculty of enjoyment and of feeling is wanting — both have become physical impossibilities. In everything, even in the most tender caresses of my children, I find only bitterness. I cover them with kisses, but there is something between their lips and mine; and this horrid something is between me and all the enjoyments of life. My existence is incomplete. The functions and acts of ordinary life, it is true, still remain to me; but in every one of them there is something wanting-to wit, the feeling which is proper to them, and the pleasure which follows them...Each of my senses, each part of my proper self, is as it were separated from me and can no longer afford me any feeling; this impossibility seems to depend upon a void which I feel in the front of my head, and to be due to the diminution of the sensibility over the whole surface of my body, for it seems to me that I never actually reach the objects which I touch...I feel well enough the changes of temperature on my skin, but I no longer experience the internal feeling of the air when I breathe...All this would be a small matter enough, but for its frightful result, which is that of the impossibility of any other kind of feeling and of any sort of enjoyment, although I experience a need and desire of them that render my life an incomprehensible torture. Every function, every action of my life remains, but deprived of the feeling that belongs to it, of the enjoyment that should follow it. My feet are cold, I warm them, but gain no pleasure from the warmth. I recognise the taste of all I eat, without getting any pleasure from it....My children are growing handsome and healthy, everyone tells me so, I see it myself, but the delight, the inward comfort I ought to feel, I fail to get. Music has lost all charm for me, I used to love it dearly. My daughter plays very well, but for me it is mere noise. That lively interest which a year ago made me hear a delicious concert in the smallest air their fingers played,—that thrill, that general vibration which made me shed such tender tears,—all that exists no more".[5]

Other victims describe themselves as closed in walls of ice or covered with an india-rubber integument, through which no impression penetrates to the sealed-up sensibility.

If our hypothesis is true, it makes us realise more deeply than ever how much our mental life is knit up with our corporeal frame, in the strictest sense of the term. Rapture, love , ambition, indignation, and pride, considered as feelings, are fruits of the same soil with the grossest bodily sensations of pleasure and of pain. But it was said at the outset that this would be affirmed only of what we then agreed to call the "standard" emotions; and that those inward sensibilities that appeared devoid at first sight of bodily results should be left out of our account. We had better, before closing, say a word or two about these latter feelings.

They are, the reader will remember, the moral, intellectual, and aesthetic feelings. Concords of sounds, of colours, of lines, logical consistencies, teleological fitnesses, affect us with a pleasure that seems ingrained in the very form of the representation itself, and to borrow nothing from any reverberation surging up from the parts below the brain. The Herbartian psychologists have tried to distinguish feelings due to the form in which ideas may be arranged. A geometrical demonstration may be as "pretty," and an act of justice as "neat" as a drawing or a tune, although the prettiness and neatness seem here to be a pure matter of sensation, and there to have nothing to do with sensation. We have then, or some of us seem to have, genuinely cerebral forms of pleasure and displeasure, apparently not agreeing in their mode of production with the so-called "standard" emotions we have been analysing. And it is certain that readers whom our reasons have hitherto failed to convince, will now start up at this admission, and consider that by it we give up our whole case. Since musical perceptions, since logical ideas, can immediately arouse a form of emotional feeling, they will say, is it not more natural to suppose that in the case of the so-called "standard" emotions, prompted by the presence of objects or the experience of events, the emotional feeling is equally immediate, and the bodily expression something that comes later and is added on?

But a sober scrutiny of the cases of pure cerebral emotion gives little force to this assimilation. Unless in them there actually be coupled with the intellectual feeling a bodily reverberation of some kind, unless we actually laugh at the neatness of the mechanical device, thrill at the justice of the act, or tingle at the perfection of the musical form, our mental condition is more allied to a judgment of right than to anything else. And such a judgment is rather to be classed among awarenesses of truth: it is a cognitive act. But as a matter of fact the intellectual feeling hardly ever does exist thus unaccompanied. The bodily sounding-board is at work, as careful introspection will show, far more than we usually suppose. Still, where long familiarity with a certain class of effects has blunted emotional sensibility thereto as much as it has sharpened the taste and judgment, we do get the intellectual emotion, if such it can be called, pure and undefiled. And the dryness of it, the paleness, the absence of all glow, as it may exist in a thoroughly expert critic's mind, not only shows us what an altogether different thing it is from the "standard" emotions we considered first, but makes us suspect that almost the entire difference lies in the fact that the bodily sounding-board, vibrating in the one case, is in the other mute. "Not so very bad" is, in a person of consummate taste, apt to be the highest limit of approving expression. "Rien ne me choque" is said to have been Chopin's superlative of praise of new music. A sentimental layman would feel, and ought to feel, horrified, on being admitted into such a critic's mind, to see how cold, how thin, how void of human significance, are the motives for favour or disfavour that there prevail. The capacity to make a nice spot on the wall will outweigh a picture's whole content; a foolish trick of words will preserve a poem; an utterly meaningless fitness of sequence in one musical composition set at naught any amount of "expressiveness" in another.

I remember seeing an English couple sit for more than an hour on a piercing February day in the Academy at Venice before the celebrated "Assumption" by Titian; and when I, after being chased from room to room by the cold, concluded to get into the sunshine as fast as possible and let the pictures go, but before leaving drew reverently near to them to learn with what superior forms of susceptibility they might be endowed, all I overheard was the woman's voice murmuring : "What a deprecatory expression her face wears! What a self-abnegation! How unworthy she feels of the honour she is receiving!" Their honest hearts had been kept warm all the time by a glow of spurious sentiment that would have fairly made old Titian sick. Mr. Ruskin somewhere makes the (for him) terrible admission that religious people as a rule care little for pictures, and that when they do care for them they generally prefer the worst ones to the best. Yes! In every art, in every science, there is the keen perception of certain relations being right or not, and there is the emotional flush and thrill consequent thereupon. And these are two things, not one. In the former of them it is that experts and masters are at home. The latter accompaniments are bodily commotions that they may hardly feel, but that may be experienced in their fulness by Crétins and Philistines in whom the critical judgment is at its lowest ebb. The "marvels" of Science, about which so much edifying popular literature is written, are apt to be "caviare" to the men in the laboratories. Cognition and emotion are parted even in this last retreat, — who shall say that their antagonism may not just be one phase of the world-old struggle known as that between the spirit and the flesh? — a struggle in which it seems pretty certain that neither party will definitively drive the other off the field.

To return to our starting point, the physiology of the brain. If we suppose its cortex t contain centres for the perception of changes in each special sense-organ, in each portion of the skin, in each muscle, each joint, and each viscus, and to contain absolutely nothing else, we still have a scheme perfectly capable of representing the process of the emotions. An object falls on a sense-organ and is apperceived by the appropriate cortical centre; or else the latter, excited in some other way, gives rise to an idea of the same object. Quick as a flash, the reflex currents pass down through their pre-ordained channels, alter the condition of muscle, skin and viscus; and these alterations, apperceived like the original object, in as many specific portions of the cortex, combine with it in consciousness and transform it from an object-simply-apprehended into an object-emotionally-felt. No new principles have to be invoked, nothing is postulated beyond the ordinary reflex circuit, and the topical centres admitted in one shape or another by all to exist.

It must be confessed that a crucial test of the truth of the hypothesis is quite as hard to obtain as its decisive refutation. A case of complete internal and external corporeal anaesthesia, without motor alteration or alteration of intelligence except emotional apathy, would afford, if not a crucial test, at least a strong presumption, in favour of the truth of the view we have set forth; whilst the persistence of strong emotional feeling in such a case would completely overthrow our case. Hysterical anaesthesias seem never to be complete enough to cover the ground. Complete anaesthesias from organic disease, on the other hand, are excessibely rare. In the famous case of Remigius Leims, no mention is made by the reporters of his emotional condition, a circumstance which by itself affords no presumption that it was normal, since as a rule nothing ever is noticed without a pre-existing question in the mind. Dr. Georg Winter has recently described a case somewhat similar,[6] and in reply to a question, kindly writes to me as follows:—"The case has been for a year and a half entirely removed from my observation. But so far as I am able to state, the man was characterised by a certain mental inertia and indolence. He was tranquil, and had on the whole the temperament of a phlegmatic. He was not irritable, not quarrelsome, went quietly about his farm-work, and left the care of his business and housekeeping to other people. In short, he gave one the impression of a placid countryman, who has no interests beyond his work." Dr. Winter adds that in studying the case he paid no particular attention to the man's psychic condition, as this seemed "nebensächlich" to his main purpose. I should add that the form of my question to Dr. Winter could give him no clue as to the kind of answer I expected.

Of course, this case proves nothing, but it is to be hoped that asylum-physicians and nervous specialists may begin methodically to study the relation between anaesthesia and emotional apathy. If the hypothesis here suggested is ever to be definitively confirmed or disproved it seems as if it must be by them, for they alone have the data in their hands.

P.S.— By an unpardonable forgetfulness at the time of despatching my MS. to the Editor, I ignored the existence of the extraordinary case of total anaesthesia published by Professor Strümpell in Ziemssen's Deutsches Archiv für klinische Medicin xxii., 321, of which I had nevertheless read reports at the time of its publication. [Cf. first report of the case in Mind X., 263, translated from Pflüger's Archiv.Ed.] I believe that it constitutes the only remaining case of the sort in medical literature, so that with is our survey is complete. On referring to the original, which is important in many connexions, I found that the patient, a shoemaker's apprentice of 15, entirely anaesthetic, inside and out, with the exception of one eye and one ear, had shown shame on the occasion of soiling his bed, and grief, when a formerly favourite dish was set before him, at the thought that he could no longer taste its flavour. As Dr. Strümpell seemed however to have paid no special attention to his psychic states, so far as these are matter for our theory, I wrote to him in a few words what the essence of the theory was, and asked him to say whether he felt sure the grief and shame mentioned were real feelings in the boy's mind, or only the reflex manifestations provoked by certain perceptions, manifestations that an outside observer might note, but to which the boy himself might be insensible.

Dr. Strümpell has sent me a very obliging reply, of which I translate the most important passage.

"I must indeed confess that I naturally failed to institute with my Anoesthetiker observations as special as the sense of your theory would require. Nevertheless I think I can decidedly make the statement, that he was by no means completely lacking in emotional affections. In addition to the feelings of grief and shame mentioned in my paper, I recall distinctly that he showed e.f., anger, and frequently quarrelled with the hospital attendants. He also manifested fear lest I should punish him. In short, I do not think that my case speaks exactly in favour of your theory. On the other hand, I will not affirm that it positively refutes your theory. For my case was certainly one of a very centrally conditioned anaesthesia (perception-anaesthesia, like that of hysterics) and therefore the conduction of outward impressions may in him have been undisturbed."

I confess that I do not see the relevancy of the last consideration, and this makes me suspect that my own letter was too briefly or obscurely expressed to put my correspondent fully in possession of my own thought. For his reply still makes no explicit reference to anything but the outward manifestations of emotion in the boy. Is it not at least conceivable that, just as a stranger, brought into the boy's presence for the first time, and seeing him eat and drink and satisfy other natural necessities, would suppose him to have the feelings of hunger, thirst, &c., until informed by the boy himself that he did all these things with no feeling at all but that of sight and sound—is it not, I say, at least possible that Dr. Strümpell, addressing no direct introspective questions to his patient, and the patient not being of a class from which one could expect voluntary revelations of that sort, should have similarly omitted to discriminate between a feeling and its habitual motor accompaniment, and erroneously taken the latter as proof that the former was there? Such a mistake is of course possible, and I must therefore repeat Dr. Strümpell's own words, that his case does not yet refute my theory. Should a similar case recur, it ought to be interrogated as to the inward emotional state that co-existed with the outward expressions of shame, anger, &c. And if it then turned out that the patient recognised explicitly the same mood of feeling known under those names in his former normal state, my theory would of course fall. It is, however, to me incredible that the patient should have an identical feeling, for the dropping out of the organic sounding-board would necessarily diminish its volume in some way. The teacher of Dr. Strümpell's patient found a mental deficiency in him during his anaesthesia, that may possibly have been due to the consequences resulting to his general intellectual vivacity from the subtraction of so important a mass of feelings, even though they were not the whole of his emotional life. Whoever wishes to extract from the next case of total anaesthesia the maximum of knowledge about the emotions, will have to interrogate the patient with some such notion as that of my article in his mind. We can define the pure psychic emotions far better by starting from such an hypothesis and modifying it in the way of restriction and subtraction, than by having no definite hypothesis at all. Thus will the publication of my article have been justified, even thought the theory it advocates, rigorously taken, be erroneous. The best thing I can say for it is, that in writing it, I have almost persuaded myself it may be true.

Footnotes

[1] Of course the physiological question arises, how are the changes felt? —after they are produced, by the sensory nerves of the organs bringing back to the brain a report of the modifications that have occurred? or before they are produced, by our being conscious of the outgoing nerve-currents starting on their way downward towards the parts they are to excite? I believe all the evidence we have to be in favour of the former alternative. The question is too minute for discussion here, but I have said something about it in a paper entitled "The Feeling of Effort," in the Anniversary Memoirs of the Boston Natural History Society, 1880 (translated in La Critique Philosophique for that year, and summarised in MIND XX., 582). See also G.E. Müller's Grundlegung der Psychophysik, 110.

[2] Let it be noted in passing that this personal self-consciousness seems an altogether bodily affair, largely a consciousness of our attitude, and that, like other emotions, it reacts on its physical condition, and leads to modifications of the attitude,—to a certain rigidity in most men, but in children to a regular twisting and squirming fit, and in women to various gracefully shy poses.

[3] This is the opposite of what happens in injuries to the brain, whether from outward violence, inward rupture or tumor, or mere starvation from disease. The cortical permeability seems reduced, so that excitement, instead of propagating itself laterally through the ideational channels as before, tends to take the downward track into the organs of the body. The consequences is that we have tears, laughter, and temper-fits, on the most insignificant provocation, accompanying a proportional feebleness in logical thought and the power of volitional attention and decision.

[4] It must be confessed that there are cases of morbid fear in which objectively the heart is not much perturbed. These however fail to prove anything against our theory, for it is of course possible that the cortical centres normally percipient of dread as a complex of cardiac and other organic sensations due to real bodily change, should become primarily excited in brain-disease, and give rise to an hallucination of the changes being there,—an hallucination of dread, consequently, coexistent with a comparatively calm pulse, &c. I say it is possible, for I am ignorant of observations which might test the fact. Trance, ecstasy, &c., offer analogous examples,—not to speak of ordinary dreaming. Under all these conditions one may have the liveliest subjective feelings, either of eye or ear, or of the more

visceral and emotional sort, as a result of pure nerve-central activity, with complete peripheral repose. Whether the subjective strength of the feeling be due in these cases to the actual energy of the central disturbance, or merely to the narrowing of the field of consciousness, need not concern us. In the asylum cases of melancholy, there is usually a narrowing of the field.

[5] Quoted by Semal: De la Sensibilité générale dans les Affections mélancoliques, Paris, 1876, pp. 130-135.

[6] "Ein Fall von allgemeiner Anaesthesie," Inaugural-Dissertation. Heidelberg, Winter, 1882.

The Varieties of Religious Experience

A Study in Human Nature
Gifford Lectures on Natural Religion
Delivered at Edinburgh in 1901-1902

PREFACE

This book would never have been written had I not been honored with an appointment as Gifford Lecturer on Natural Religion at the University of Edinburgh. In casting about me for subjects of the two courses of ten lectures each for which I thus became responsible, it seemed to me that the first course might well be a descriptive one on 'Man's Religious Appetites,' and the second a metaphysical one on 'Their Satisfaction through Philosophy.' But the unexpected growth of the psychological matter as I came to write it out has resulted in the second subject being postponed entirely, and the description of man's religious constitution now fills the twenty lectures. In Lecture XX I have suggested rather than stated my own philosophic conclusions, and the reader who desires immediately to know them should turn to the 'Conclusions,' and to the 'Postscript' of the book. I hope to be able at some later day to express them in more explicit form.

In my belief that a large acquaintance with particulars often makes us wiser than the possession of abstract formulas, however deep, I have loaded the lectures with concrete examples, and I have chosen these among the extremer expressions of the religious temperament. To some readers I may consequently seem, before they get beyond the middle of the book, to offer a caricature of the subject. Such convulsions of piety, they will say, are not sane. If, however, they will have the patience to read to the end, I believe that this unfavorable impression will disappear; for I there combine the religious impulses with other principles of common sense which serve as correctives of exaggeration, and allow the individual reader to draw as moderate conclusions as he will.

My thanks for help in writing these lectures are due to Edwin D. Starbuck, of Stanford University, who made
over to me his large collection of manuscript material; to Henry W. Rankin, of East Northfield, a friend unseen but proved, to whom I owe precious information; to Theodore Flournoy, of Geneva, to Canning Schiller, of Oxford, and to my colleague Benjamin Rand, for documents; to my colleague Dickinson S. Miller, and to my friends, Thomas Wren Ward, of New York, and Wincenty Lutoslawski, late of Cracow, for important suggestions and advice. Finally, to conversations with the lamented Thomas Davidson and to the use of his books, at Glenmore, above Keene Valley, I owe more obligations than I can well express.

Harvard University,
March, 1902.

TABLE OF CONTENTS

LECTURE I: RELIGION AND NEUROLOGY

It is with no small amount of trepidation that I take my place behind this desk, and face this learned audience. To us Americans, the experience of receiving instruction from the living voice, as well as from the books, of European scholars, is very familiar. At my own University of Harvard, not a winter passes without its harvest, large or small, of lectures from Scottish, English, French, or German representatives of the science or literature of their respective countries whom we have either induced to cross the ocean to address us, or captured on the wing as they were visiting our land. It seems the natural thing for us to listen whilst the Europeans talk. The contrary habit, of talking whilst the Europeans listen, we have not yet acquired; and in him who first makes the adventure it begets a certain sense of apology being due for so presumptuous an act. Particularly must this be the case on a soil as sacred to the American imagination as that of Edinburgh. The glories of the philosophic chair of this university were deeply impressed on my imagination in boyhood. Professor Fraser's Essays in Philosophy, then just published, was the first philosophic book I ever looked into, and I well remember the awe-struck feeling I received from the account of Sir William Hamilton's class-room therein contained. Hamilton's own lectures were the first philosophic writings I ever forced myself to study, and after that I was immersed in Dugald Stewart and Thomas Brown. Such juvenile emotions of reverence never get outgrown; and I confess that to find my humble self promoted from my native wilderness to be actually for the time an official here, and transmuted into a colleague of these illustrious names, carries with it a sense of dreamland quite as much as of reality.

But since I have received the honor of this appointment I have felt that it would never do to decline. The academic career also has its heroic obligations, so I stand here without further deprecatory words. Let me say only this, that now that the current, here and at Aberdeen, has begun to run from west to east, I hope it may continue to do so. As the years go by, I hope that many of my countrymen may be asked to lecture in the Scottish universities, changing places with Scotsmen lecturing in the United States; I hope that our people may become in all these higher matters even as one people; and that the peculiar philosophic temperament, as well as the peculiar political temperament, that goes with our English speech may more and more pervade and influence the world.

As regards the manner in which I shall have to administer this lectureship, I am neither a theologian, nor a scholar learned in the history of religions, nor an anthropologist. Psychology is the only branch of learning in which I am particularly versed. To the psychologist the religious propensities of man must be at least as interesting as any other of the facts pertaining to his mental constitution. It would seem, therefore, that, as a psychologist, the natural thing for me would be to invite you to a descriptive survey of those religious propensities.

If the inquiry be psychological, not religious institutions, but rather religious feelings and religious impulses must be its subject, and I must confine myself to those more developed subjective phenomena recorded in literature produced by articulate and fully self-conscious men, in works of piety and autobiography. Interesting as the origins and early stages of a subject always are, yet when one seeks earnestly for its full significance, one must always look to its more completely evolved and perfect forms. It follows from this that the documents that will most concern us will be those of the men who were most accomplished in the religious life and best able to give an intelligible account of their ideas and motives. These men, of course, are either comparatively modern writers, or else such earlier ones as have become religious classics. The documents humains which we shall find most instructive need not then be sought for in the haunts of special erudition— they lie along the beaten highway; and this circumstance, which flows so naturally from the character of our problem, suits admirably also your lecturer's lack of special theological learning. I may take my citations, my sentences and paragraphs of personal confession, from books that most of you at some time will have had already in your hands, and yet this will be no detriment to the value of my conclusions. It is true that some more adventurous reader and investigator, lecturing here in future, may unearth from the shelves of libraries documents that will make a more delectable and curious entertainment to listen to than mine. Yet I doubt whether he will necessarily, by his control of so much more out-of-the-way material, get much closer to the essence of the matter in hand.

The question, What are the religious propensities? and the question, What is their philosophic significance? are two entirely different orders of question from the logical point of view; and, as a failure to recognize this fact distinctly may breed confusion, I wish to insist upon the point a little before we enter into the documents and materials to which I have referred.

In recent books on logic, distinction is made between two orders of inquiry concerning anything. First, what is the nature of it? how did it come about? what is its constitution, origin, and history? And second, What is its importance, meaning, or significance, now that it is once here? The answer to the one question is given in an existential judgment or proposition. The answer to the other is a proposition of value, what the Germans call a Werthurtheil, or what we may, if we like, denominate a spiritual judgment. Neither judgment can be deduced immediately from the other. They proceed from diverse intellectual preoccupations, and the mind combines them only by making them first separately, and then adding them together.

In the matter of religions it is particularly easy to distinguish the two orders of question. Every religious phenomenon has its history and its derivation from natural antecedents. What is nowadays called the higher criticism of the Bible is only a study of the Bible from this existential point of view, neglected too much by the earlier church. Under just what biographic conditions did the sacred writers bring forth their various contributions to the holy volume? And what had they exactly in their several individual minds, when they delivered their utterances? These are manifestly questions of historical fact, and one does not see how the answer to them can decide offhand the still further question: of what use should such a volume, with its manner of coming into existence so defined, be to us as a guide to life and a revelation? To answer this other question we must have already in our mind some sort of a general theory as to what the peculiarities in a thing should be which give it value for purposes of revelation; and this theory itself would be what I just called a spiritual judgment. Combining it with our existential judgment, we might indeed deduce another spiritual judgment as to the Bible's worth. Thus if our theory of revelation-value were to affirm that any book, to possess it, must have been composed automatically or not by the free caprice of the writer, or that it must exhibit no scientific and historic errors and express no local or personal passions, the Bible would probably fare ill at our hands. But if, on the other hand, our theory should allow that a book may well be a revelation in spite of errors and passions and deliberate human composition, if only it be a true record of the inner experiences of great-souled persons wrestling with the crises of their fate, then the verdict would be much more favorable. You see that the existential facts by themselves are insufficient for determining the value; and the best adepts of the higher criticism accordingly never confound the existential with the spiritual problem. With the same conclusions of fact before them, some take one view, and some another, of the Bible's value as a revelation, according as their spiritual judgment as to the foundation of values differs.

I make these general remarks about the two sorts of judgment, because there are many religious persons-some of you now present, possibly, are among them— who do not yet make a working use of the distinction, and who may therefore feel at first a little startled at the purely existential point of view from which in the following lectures the phenomena of religious experience must be considered. When I handle them biologically and psychologically as if they were mere curious facts of individual history, some of you may think it a degradation of so sublime a subject, and may even suspect me, until my purpose gets more fully expressed, of deliberately seeking to discredit the religious side of life.

Such a result is of course absolutely alien to my intention; and since such a prejudice on your part would seriously obstruct the due effect of much of what I have to relate, I will devote a few more words to the point.

There can be no doubt that as a matter of fact a religious life, exclusively pursued, does tend to make the person exceptional and eccentric. I speak not now of your ordinary religious believer, who follows the conventional observances of his country, whether it be Buddhist, Christian, or Mohammedan. His religion has been made for him by others, communicated to him by tradition, determined to fixed forms by imitation, and retained by habit. It would profit us little to study this second-hand religious life. We must make search rather for the original experiences which were the pattern-setters to all this mass of suggested feeling and imitated conduct. These experiences we can only find in individuals for whom religion exists not as a dull habit, but as an acute fever rather. But such individuals are 'geniuses' in the religious line; and like many other geniuses who have brought forth fruits effective enough for commemoration in the pages of biography, such religious geniuses have often shown symptoms of nervous instability. Even more perhaps than other kinds of genius, religious leaders have been subject to abnormal psychical visitations. Invariably they have been creatures of exalted emotional sensibility. Often they have led a discordant inner life, and had melancholy during a part of their career. They have known no measure, been liable to obsessions and fixed ideas; and frequently they have fallen into trances, heard voices, seen visions, and presented all sorts of peculiarities which are ordinarily classed as pathological. Often, moreover, these pathological features in their career have helped to give them their religious authority and influence.

If you ask for a concrete example, there can be no better one than is furnished by the person of George Fox. The Quaker religion which he founded is something which it is impossible to overpraise. In a day of shams, it was a religion of veracity rooted in spiritual inwardness, and a return to something more like the original gospel truth than men had ever known in England. So far as our Christian sects today are evolving into liberality, they are simply reverting in essence to the position which Fox and the early Quakers so long ago assumed. No one can pretend for a moment that in point of spiritual sagacity and capacity, Fox's mind was unsound. Every one who confronted him personally, from Oliver Cromwell down to county magistrates and jailers, seems to have acknowledged his superior power. Yet from the point of view of his nervous constitution, Fox was a psychopath or detraque of the deepest dye. His Journal abounds in entries of this sort:—

"As I was walking with several friends, I lifted up my head, and saw three steeple-house spires, and they struck at my life. I asked them what place that was? They said, Lichfield. Immediately the word of the Lord came to me, that I must go thither. Being come to the house we were going to, I wished the friends to walk into the house, saying nothing to them of whither I was to go. As soon as they were gone I stept away, and went by my eye over hedge and ditch till I came within a mile of Lichfield; where, in a great field, shepherds were keeping their sheep. Then was I commanded by the Lord to pull off my shoes. I stood still, for it was winter: but the word of the Lord was like a fire in me. So I put off my shoes, and left them with the shepherds; and the poor shepherds trembled, and were astonished. Then I walked on about a mile, and as soon as I was got within the city, the word of the Lord came to me again, saying: Cry, 'Wo to the bloody city of Lichfield!' So I went up and down the streets, crying with a loud voice, Wo to the bloody city of Lichfield! It being market day, I went into the market-place, and to and fro in the several parts of it, and made stands, crying as before, Wo to the bloody city of Lichfield! And no one laid hands on me. As I went thus crying through the streets, there seemed to me to be a channel of blood running down the streets, and the market-place appeared like a pool of blood. When I had declared what was upon me, and felt myself clear, I went out of the town in peace: and returning to the shepherds gave them some money, and took my shoes of them again. But the fire of the Lord was so on my feet, and all over me, that I did not matter to put on my shoes again, and was at a stand whether I should or no, till I felt freedom from the Lord so to do: then, after I had washed my feet, I put on my shoes again. After this a deep consideration came upon me, for what reason I should be sent to cry against that city, and call it The bloody city! For though the parliament had the minister one while, and the king another, and much blood had been shed in the town during the wars between them, yet there was no more than had befallen many other places. But afterwards I came to understand, that in the Emperor Diocletian's time a thousand Christians were martyr'd in Lichfield. So I was to go, without my shoes, through the channel of their blood, and into the pool of their blood in the market-place, that I might raise up the memorial of the blood of those martyrs, which had been shed above a thousand years before, and lay cold in their streets. So the sense of this blood was upon me, and I obeyed the word of the Lord."

Bent as we are on studying religion's existential conditions, we cannot possibly ignore these pathological aspects of the subject. We must describe and name them just as if they occurred in non-religious men. It is true that we instinctively recoil from seeing an object to which our emotions and affections are committed handled by the intellect as any other object is handled. The first thing the intellect does with an object is to class it along with something else. But any object that is infinitely important to us and awakens our devotion feels to us also as if it must be sui generis and unique. Probably a crab would be filled with a sense of personal outrage if it could hear us class it without ado or apology as a crustacean, and thus dispose of it. "I am no such thing," it would say; "I am MYSELF, MYSELF alone."

The next thing the intellect does is to lay bare the causes in which the thing originates. Spinoza says: "I will analyze the actions and appetites of men as if it were a question of lines, of planes, and of solids." And elsewhere he remarks that he will consider our passions and their properties with the same eye with which he looks on all other natural things, since the consequences of our affections flow from their nature with the same necessity as it results from the nature of a triangle that its three angles should be equal to two right angles. Similarly M. Taine, in the introduction to his history of English literature, has written: "Whether facts be moral or physical, it makes no matter. They always have their causes. There are causes for ambition, courage, veracity, just as there are for digestion, muscular movement, animal heat. Vice and virtue are products like vitriol and sugar." When we read such proclamations of the intellect bent on showing the existential conditions of absolutely everything, we feel— quite apart from our legitimate impatience at the somewhat ridiculous swagger of the program, in view of what the authors are actually able to perform— menaced and negated in the springs of our innermost life. Such cold-blooded assimilations threaten, we think, to undo our soul's vital secrets, as if the same breath which should succeed in explaining their origin would simultaneously explain away their significance, and make them appear of no more preciousness, either, than the useful groceries of which M. Taine speaks.

Perhaps the commonest expression of this assumption that spiritual value is undone if lowly origin be asserted is seen in those comments which unsentimental people so often pass on their more sentimental acquaintances. Alfred believes in immortality so strongly because his temperament is so emotional. Fanny's extraordinary conscientiousness is merely a matter of over-instigated nerves. William's melancholy about the universe is due to bad digestion— probably his liver is torpid. Eliza's delight in her church is a symptom of her hysterical constitution. Peter would be less troubled about his soul if he would take more exercise in the open air, etc. A more fully developed example of the same kind of reasoning is the fashion, quite common nowadays among certain writers, of criticising the religious emotions by showing a connection between them and the sexual life. Conversion is a crisis of puberty and adolescence. The macerations of saints, and the devotion of missionaries, are only instances of the parental instinct of self-sacrifice gone astray. For the hysterical nun, starving for natural life, Christ is but an imaginary substitute for a more earthly object of affection. And the like.

As with many ideas that float in the air of one's time, this notion shrinks from dogmatic general statement and expresses itself only partially and by innuendo. It seems to me that few conceptions are less instructive than this re-interpretation of religion as perverted sexuality. It reminds one, so crudely is it often employed, of the famous Catholic taunt, that the Reformation may be best understood by remembering that its fons et origo was Luther's wish to marry a nun:— the effects are infinitely wider than the alleged causes, and for the most part opposite in nature. It is true that in the vast collection of religious phenomena, some are undisguisedly amatory— e.g., sex-deities and obscene rites in polytheism, and ecstatic feelings of union with the Saviour in a few Christian mystics. But then why not equally call religion an aberration of the digestive function, and prove one's point by the worship of Bacchus and Ceres, or by the ecstatic feelings of some other saints about the Eucharist? Religious language clothes itself in such poor symbols as our life affords, and the whole organism gives overtones of comment whenever the mind is strongly stirred to expression. Language drawn from eating and drinking is probably as common in religious literature as is language drawn from the sexual life. We 'hunger and thirst' after righteousness; we 'find the Lord a sweet savor;' we 'taste and see that he is good.' 'Spiritual milk for American babes, drawn from the breasts of both testaments,' is a sub-title of the once famous New England Primer, and Christian devotional literature indeed quite floats in milk, thought of from the point of view, not of the mother, but of the greedy babe.

Saint Francois de Sales, for instance, thus describes the 'orison of quietude': "In this state the soul is like a little child still at the breast, whose mother, to caress him whilst he is still in her arms, makes her milk distill into his mouth without his even moving his lips. So it is here.... Our Lord desires that our will should be satisfied with sucking the milk which His Majesty pours into our mouth, and that we should relish the sweetness without even knowing that it cometh from the Lord." And again: "Consider the little infants, united and joined to the breasts of their nursing mothers, you will see that from time to time they press themselves closer by little starts to which the pleasure of sucking prompts them. Even so, during its orison, the heart united to its God oftentimes makes attempts at closer union by movements during which it presses closer upon the divine sweetness." Chemin de la Perfection, ch. xxxi.; Amour de Dieu, vii. ch. i.

In fact, one might almost as well interpret religion as a perversion of the respiratory function. The Bible is full of the language of respiratory oppression: "Hide not thine ear at my breathing; my groaning is not hid from thee; my heart panteth, my strength faileth me; my bones are hot with my roaring all the night long; as the hart panteth after the water-brooks, so my soul panteth after thee, O my God." God's Breath in Man is the title of the chief work of our best known American mystic (Thomas Lake Harris); and in certain non-Christian countries the foundation of all religious discipline consists in regulation of the inspiration and expiration.

These arguments are as good as much of the reasoning one hears in favor of the sexual theory. But the champions of the latter will then say that their chief argument has no analogue elsewhere. The two main phenomena of religion, namely, melancholy and conversion, they will say, are essentially phenomena of adolescence, and therefore synchronous with the development of sexual life. To which the retort again is easy. Even were the asserted synchrony unrestrictedly true as a fact (which it is not), it is not only the sexual life, but the entire higher mental life which awakens during adolescence. One might then as well set up the thesis that the interest in mechanics, physics, chemistry, logic, philosophy, and sociology, which springs up during adolescent years along with that in poetry and religion, is also a perversion of the sexual instinct:— but that would be too absurd. Moreover, if the argument from synchrony is to decide, what is to be done with the fact that the religious age par excellence would seem to be old age, when the uproar of the sexual life is past?

The plain truth is that to interpret religion one must in the end look at the immediate content of the religious consciousness. The moment one does this, one sees how wholly disconnected it is in the main from the content of the sexual consciousness. Everything about the two things differs, objects, moods, faculties concerned, and acts impelled to. Any general assimilation is simply impossible: what we find most often is complete hostility and contrast. If now the defenders of the sex-theory say that this makes no difference to their thesis; that without the chemical contributions which the sex-organs make to the blood, the brain would not be nourished so as to carry on religious activities, this final proposition may be true or not true; but at any rate it has become profoundly uninstructive: we can deduce no consequences from it which help us to interpret religion's meaning or value. In this sense the religious life depends just as much upon the spleen, the pancreas, and the kidneys as on the sexual apparatus, and the whole theory has lost its point in evaporating into a vague, general assertion of the dependence, somehow, of the mind upon the body.

We are surely all familiar in a general way with this method of discrediting states of mind for which we have an antipathy. We all use it to some degree in criticising persons whose states of mind we regard as overstrained. But when other people criticise our own more exalted soul-flights by calling them 'nothing but' expressions of our organic disposition, we feel outraged and hurt, for we know that, whatever be our organism's peculiarities, our mental states have their substantive value as revelations of the living truth; and we wish that all this medical materialism could be made to hold its tongue.

Medical materialism seems indeed a good appellation for the too simple-minded system of thought which we are considering. Medical materialism finishes up Saint Paul by calling his vision on the road to Damascus a discharging lesion of the occipital cortex, he being an epileptic. It snuffs out Saint Teresa as an hysteric, Saint Francis of Assisi as an hereditary degenerate. George Fox's discontent with the shams of his age, and his pining for spiritual veracity, it treats as a symptom of a disordered colon. Carlyle's organ-tones of misery it accounts for by a gastro-duodenal catarrh. All such mental over-tensions, it says, are, when you come to the bottom of the matter, mere affairs of diathesis (auto-intoxications most probably), due to the perverted action of various glands which physiology will yet discover.

And medical materialism then thinks that the spiritual authority of all such personages is successfully undermined. [For a first-rate example of medical-materialist reasoning, see an article on 'les Varietes du Type devot,' by Dr. Binet-Sangle, in the Revue de l'Hypnotisme, xiv. 161.]

Let us ourselves look at the matter in the largest possible way. Modern psychology, finding definite psycho-physical connections to hold good, assumes as a convenient hypothesis that the dependence of mental states upon bodily conditions must be thorough-going and complete. If we adopt the assumption, then of course what medical materialism insists on must be true in a general way, if not in every detail: Saint Paul certainly had once an epileptoid, if not an epileptic seizure; George Fox was an hereditary degenerate; Carlyle was undoubtedly auto-intoxicated by some organ or other, no matter which,— and the rest. But now, I ask you, how can such an existential account of facts of mental history decide in one way or another upon their spiritual significance? According to the general postulate of psychology just referred to, there is not a single one of our states of mind, high or low, healthy or morbid, that has not some organic process as its condition. Scientific theories are organically conditioned just as much as religious emotions are; and if we only knew the facts intimately enough, we should doubtless see 'the liver' determining the dicta of the sturdy atheist as decisively as it does those of the Methodist under conviction anxious about his soul. When it alters in one way the blood that percolates it, we get the methodist, when in another way, we get the atheist form of mind. So of all our rapturer, and our drynesses, our longings and pantings, our questions and beliefs. They are equally organically founded, be they of religious or of non-religious content.

To plead the organic causation of a religious state of mind, then, in refutation of its claim to possess superior spiritual value, is quite illogical and arbitrary, unless one have already worked out in advance some psycho-physical theory connecting spiritual values in general with determinate sorts of physiological change. Otherwise none of our thoughts and feelings, not even our scientific doctrines, not even our dis-beliefs, could retain any value as revelations of the truth, for every one of them without exception flows from the state of their possessor's body at the time.

It is needless to say that medical materialism draws in point of fact no such sweeping skeptical conclusion. It is sure, just as every simple man is sure, that some states of mind are inwardly superior to others, and reveal to us more truth, and in this it simply makes use of an ordinary spiritual judgment. It has no physiological theory of the production of these its favorite states, by which it may accredit them; and its attempt to discredit the states which it dislikes, by vaguely associating them with nerves and liver, and connecting them with names connoting bodily affliction, is altogether illogical and inconsistent.

Let us play fair in this whole matter, and be quite candid with ourselves and with the facts. When we think certain states of mind superior to others, is it ever because of what we know concerning their organic antecedents? No! it is always for two entirely different reasons. It is either because we take an immediate delight in them; or else it is because we believe them to bring us good consequential fruits for life. When we speak disparagingly of 'feverish fancies,' surely the fever-process as such is not the ground of our disesteem— for aught we know to the contrary, 103 degrees or 104 degrees Fahrenheit might be a much more favorable temperature for truths to germinate and sprout in, than the more ordinary blood-heat of 97 or 98 degrees. It is either the disagreeableness itself of the fancies, or their inability to bear the criticisms of the convalescent hour. When we praise the thoughts which health brings, health's peculiar chemical metabolisms have nothing to do with determining our judgment. We know in fact almost nothing about these metabolisms. It is the character of inner happiness in the thoughts which stamps them as good, or else their consistency with our other opinions and their serviceability for our needs, which make them pass for true in our esteem.

Now the more intrinsic and the more remote of these criteria do not always hang together. Inner happiness and serviceability do not always agree. What immediately feels most 'good' is not always most 'true,' when measured by the verdict of the rest of experience. The difference between Philip drunk and Philip sober is the classic instance in corroboration. If merely 'feeling good' could decide, drunkenness would be the supremely valid human experience. But its revelations, however acutely satisfying at the moment, are inserted into an environment which refuses to bear them out for any length of time. The consequence of this discrepancy of the two criteria is the uncertainty which still prevails over so many of our spiritual judgments. There are moments of sentimental and mystical experience— we shall hereafter hear much of them— that carry an enormous sense of inner authority and illumination with them when they come. But they come seldom, and they do not come to every one; and the rest of life makes either no connection with them, or tends to contradict them more than it confirms them. Some persons follow more the voice of the moment in these cases, some prefer to be guided by the average results. Hence the sad discordancy of so many of the spiritual judgments of human beings; a discordancy which will be brought home to us acutely enough before these lectures end.

It is, however, a discordancy that can never be resolved by any merely medical test. A good example of the impossibility of holding strictly to the medical tests is seen in the theory of the pathological causation of genius promulgated by recent authors. "Genius," said Dr. Moreau, "is but one of the many branches of the neuropathic tree." "Genius," says Dr. Lombroso, "is a symptom of hereditary degeneration of the epileptoid variety, and is allied to moral insanity." "Whenever a man's life," writes Mr. Nisbet, "is at once sufficiently illustrious and recorded with sufficient fullness to be a subject of profitable study, he inevitably falls into the morbid category.... And it is worthy of remark that, as a rule, the greater the genius, the greater the unsoundness." [J.F. NISBET: The Insanity of Genius, 3d. ed., London, 1893, pp. xvi, xxiv.]

Now do these authors, after having succeeded in establishing to their own satisfaction that the works of genius are fruits of disease, consistently proceed thereupon to impugn the value of the fruits? Do they deduce a new spiritual judgment from their new doctrine of existential conditions? Do they frankly forbid us to admire the productions of genius from now onwards? and say outright that no neuropath can ever be a revealer of new truth?

No! their immediate spiritual instincts are too strong for them here, and hold their own against inferences which, in mere love of logical consistency, medical materialism ought to be only too glad to draw. One disciple of the school, indeed, has striven to impugn the value of works of genius in a wholesale way (such works of contemporary art, namely, as he himself is unable to enjoy, and they are many) by using medical arguments. But for the most part the masterpieces are left unchallenged; and the medical line of attack either confines itself to such secular productions as every one admits to be intrinsically eccentric, or else addresses itself exclusively to religious manifestations. And then it is because the religious manifestations have been already condemned because the critic dislikes them on internal or spiritual grounds.

In the natural sciences and industrial arts it never occurs to any one to try to refute opinions by showing up their author's neurotic constitution. Opinions here are invariably tested by logic and by experiment, no matter what may be their author's neurological type. It should be no otherwise with religious opinions. Their value can only be ascertained by spiritual judgments directly passed upon them, judgments based on our own immediate feeling primarily; and secondarily on what we can ascertain of their experiential relations to our moral needs and to the rest of what we hold as true.

Immediate luminousness, in short, philosophical reasonableness, and moral helpfulness are the only available criteria. Saint Teresa might have had the nervous system of the placidest cow, and it would not now save her theology, if the trial of the theology by these other tests should show it to be contemptible. And conversely if her theology can stand these other tests, it will make no difference how hysterical or nervously off her balance Saint Teresa may have been when she was with us here below.

You see that at bottom we are thrown back upon the general principles by which the empirical philosophy has always contended that we must be guided in our search for truth. Dogmatic philosophies have sought for tests for truth which might dispense us from appealing to the future. Some direct mark, by noting which we can be protected immediately and absolutely, now and forever, against all mistake-such has been the darling dream of philosophic dogmatists. It is clear that the origin of the truth would be an admirable criterion of this sort, if only the various origins could be discriminated from one another from this point of view, and the history of dogmatic opinion shows that origin has always been a favorite test. Origin in immediate intuition; origin in pontifical authority; origin in supernatural revelation, as by vision, hearing, or unaccountable impression; origin in direct possession by a higher spirit, expressing itself in prophecy and warning; origin in automatic utterance generally,— these origins have been stock warrants for the truth of one opinion after another which we find represented in religious history. The medical materialists are therefore only so many belated dogmatists, neatly turning the tables on their predecessors by using the criterion of origin in a destructive instead of an accreditive way.

They are effective with their talk of pathological origin only so long as supernatural origin is pleaded by the other side, and nothing but the argument from origin is under discussion. But the argument from origin has seldom been used alone, for it is too obviously insufficient. Dr. Maudsley is perhaps the cleverest of the rebutters of supernatural religion on grounds of origin. Yet he finds himself forced to write:—

"What right have we to believe Nature under any obligation to do her work by means of complete minds only? She may find an incomplete mind a more suitable instrument for a particular purpose. It is the work that is done, and the quality in the worker by which it was done, that is alone of moment; and it may be no great matter from a cosmical standpoint, if in other qualities of character he was singularly defective- if indeed he were hypocrite, adulterer, eccentric, or lunatic.... Home we come again, then, to the old and last resort of certitude,— namely the common assent of mankind, or of the competent by instruction and training among mankind." [H. MAUDSLEY: Natural Causes and Supernatural Seemings, 1886, pp. 257, 256.]

In other words, not its origin, but the way in which it works on the whole, is Dr. Maudsley's final test of a belief. This is our own empiricist criterion; and this criterion the stoutest insisters on supernatural origin have also been forced to use in the end. Among the visions and messages some have always been too patently silly, among the trances and convulsive seizures some have been too fruitless for conduct and character, to pass themselves off as significant, still less as divine. In the history of Christian mysticism the problem how to discriminate between such messages and experiences as were really divine miracles, and such others as the demon in his malice was able to counterfeit, thus making the religious person twofold more the child of hell he was before, has always been a difficult one to solve, needing all the sagacity and experience of the best directors of conscience. In the end it had to come to our empiricist criterion: By their fruits ye shall know them, not by their roots. Jonathan Edwards's Treatise on Religious Affections is an elaborate working out of this thesis. The roots of a man's virtue are inaccessible to us. No appearances whatever are infallible proofs of grace. Our practice is the only sure evidence, even to ourselves, that we are genuinely Christians.

"In forming a judgment of ourselves now," Edwards writes, "we should certainly adopt that evidence which our supreme Judge will chiefly make use of when we come to stand before him at the last day.... There is not one grace of the Spirit of God, of the existence of which, in any professor of religion, Christian practice is not the most decisive evidence.... The degree in which our experience is productive of practice shows the degree in which our experience is spiritual and divine."

Catholic writers are equally emphatic. The good dispositions which a vision, or voice, or other apparent heavenly favor leave behind them are the only marks by which we may be sure they are not possible deceptions of the tempter. Says Saint Teresa:—

"Like imperfect sleep which, instead of giving more strength to the head, doth but leave it the more exhausted, the result of mere operations of the imagination is but to weaken the soul. Instead of nourishment and energy she reaps only lassitude and disgust: whereas a genuine heavenly vision yields to her a harvest of ineffable spiritual riches, and an admirable renewal of bodily strength. I alleged these reasons to those who so often accused my visions of being the work of the enemy of mankind and the sport of my imagination.... I showed them the jewels which the divine hand had left with me:— they were my actual dispositions. All those who knew me saw that I was changed; my confessor bore witness to the fact; this improvement, palpable in all respects, far from being hidden, was brilliantly evident to all men. As for myself, it was impossible to believe that if the demon were its author, he could have used, in order to lose me and lead me to hell, an expedient so contrary to his own interests as that of uprooting my vices, and filling me with masculine courage and other virtues instead, for I saw clearly that a single one of these visions was enough to enrich me with all that wealth." [Autobiography, ch. xxviii.]

I fear I may have made a longer excursus than was necessary, and that fewer words would have dispelled the uneasiness which may have arisen among some of you as I announced my pathological programme. At any rate you must all be ready now to judge the religious life by its results exclusively, and I shall assume that the bugaboo of morbid origin will scandalize your piety no more.

Still, you may ask me, if its results are to be the ground of our final spiritual estimate of a religious phenomenon, why threaten us at all with so much existential study of its conditions? Why not simply leave pathological questions out?

To this I reply in two ways: First, I say, irrepressible curiosity imperiously leads one on; and I say, secondly, that it always leads to a better understanding of a thing's significance to consider its exaggerations and perversions, its equivalents and substitutes and nearest relatives elsewhere. Not that we may thereby swamp the thing in the wholesale condemnation which we pass on its inferior congeners, but rather that we may by contrast ascertain the more precisely in what its merits consist, by learning at the same time to what particular dangers of corruption it may also be exposed.

Insane conditions have this advantage, that they isolate special factors of the mental life, and enable us to inspect them unmasked by their more usual surroundings. They play the part in mental anatomy which the scalpel and the microscope play in the anatomy of the body. To understand a thing rightly we need to see it both out of its environment and in it, and to have acquaintance with the whole range of its variations. The study of hallucinations has in this way been for psychologists the key to their comprehension of normal sensation, that of illusions has been the key to the right comprehension of perception. Morbid impulses and imperative conceptions, 'fixed ideas,' so called, have thrown a flood of light on the psychology of the normal will; and obsessions and delusions have performed the same service for that of the normal faculty of belief.

Similarly, the nature of genius has been illuminated by the attempts, of which I already made mention, to class it with psychopathical phenomena. Borderland insanity, crankiness, insane temperament, loss of mental balance, psychopathic degeneration (to use a few of the many synonyms by which it has been called), has certain peculiarities and liabilities which, when combined with a superior quality of intellect in an individual, make it more probable that he will make his mark and affect his age, than if his temperament were less neurotic. There is of course no special affinity between crankiness as such and superior intellect, for most psychopaths have feeble intellects, and superior intellects more commonly have normal nervous systems. But the psychopathic temperament, whatever be the intellect with which it finds itself paired, often brings with it ardor and excitability of character. The cranky person has extraordinary emotional susceptibility. He is liable to fixed ideas and obsessions. His conceptions tend to pass immediately into belief and action; and when he gets a new idea, he has no rest till he proclaims it, or in some way 'works it off.' "What shall I think of it?" a common person says to himself about a vexed question but in a 'cranky' mind "What must I do about it?" is the form the question tends to take. In the autobiography of that high-souled woman, Mrs. Annie Besant, I read the following passage: "Plenty of people wish well to any good cause, but very few care to exert themselves to help it, and still fewer will risk anything in its support. 'Some one ought to do it, but why should I?' is the ever re-echoed phrase of weak-kneed amiability. 'Some one ought to do it, so why not I?' is the cry of some earnest servant of man, eagerly forward springing to face some perilous duty. Between these two sentences lie whole centuries of moral evolution." True enough! and between these two sentences lie also the different destinies of the ordinary sluggard and the psychopathic man. Thus, when a superior intellect and a psychopathic temperament coalesce— as in the endless permutations and combinations of human faculty, they are bound to coalesce often enough— in the same individual, we have the best possible condition for the kind of effective genius that gets into the biographical dictionaries. Such men do not remain mere critics and understanders with their intellect. Their ideas possess them, they inflict them, for better or worse, upon their companions or their age. It is they who get counted when Messrs Lombroso, Nisbet, and others invoke statistics to defend their paradox.

Superior intellect, as Professor Bain has admirably shown, seems to consist in nothing so much as in a large development of the faculty of association by similarity.

To pass now to religious phenomena, take the melancholy which, as we shall see, constitutes an essential moment in every complete religious evolution. Take the happiness which achieved religious belief confers. Take the trance-like states of insight into truth which all religious mystics report. These are each and all of them special cases of kinds of human experience of much wider scope. Religious melancholy, whatever peculiarities it may have qua religious, is at any rate melancholy. Religious happiness is happiness. Religious trance is trance. And the moment we renounce the absurd notion that a thing is exploded away as soon as it is classed with others, or its origin is shown; the moment we agree to stand by experimental results and inner quality, in judging of values,— who does not see that we are likely to ascertain the distinctive significance of religious melancholy and happiness, or of religious trances, far better by comparing them as conscientiously as we can with other varieties of melancholy, happiness, and trance, than by refusing to consider their place in any more general series, and treating them as if they were outside of nature's order altogether? [I may refer to a criticism of the insanity theory of genius in the Psychological Review, ii. 287 (1895).]

I hope that the course of these lectures will confirm us in this supposition. As regards the psychopathic origin of so many religious phenomena, that would not be in the least surprising or disconcerting, even were such phenomena certified from on high to be the most precious of human experiences. No one organism can possibly yield to its owner the whole body of truth. Few of us are not in some way infirm, or even diseased; and our very infirmities help us unexpectedly. In the psychopathic temperament we have the emotionality which is the sine qua non of moral perception; we have the intensity and tendency to emphasis which are the essence of practical moral vigor; and we have the love of metaphysics and mysticism which carry one's interests beyond the surface of the sensible world. What, then, is more natural than that this temperament should introduce one to regions of religious truth, to corners of the universe, which your robust Philistine type of nervous system, forever offering its biceps to be felt, thumping its breast, and thanking Heaven that it hasn't a single morbid fibre in its composition, would be sure to hide forever from its self-satisfied possessors?

If there were such a thing as inspiration from a higher realm, it might well be that the neurotic temperament would furnish the chief condition of the requisite receptivity. And having said thus much, I think that I may let the matter of religion and neuroticism drop.

The mass of collateral phenomena, morbid or healthy, with which the various religious phenomena must be compared in order to understand them better, forms what in the slang of pedagogics is termed 'the apperceiving mass' by which we comprehend them. The only novelty that I can imagine this course of lectures to possess lies in the breadth of the apperceiving mass. I may succeed in discussing religious experiences in a wider context than has been usual in university courses.

LECTURE II: CIRCUMSCRIPTION OF THE TOPIC

Most books on the philosophy of religion try to begin with a precise definition of what its essence consists of. Some of these would-be definitions may possibly come before us in later portions of this course, and I shall not be pedantic enough to enumerate any of them to you now. Meanwhile the very fact that they are so many and so different from one another is enough to prove that the word 'religion' cannot stand for any single principle or essence, but is rather a collective name. The theorizing mind tends always to the over-simplification of its materials. This is the root of all that absolutism and one-sided dogmatism by which both philosophy and religion have been infested. Let us not fall immediately into a one-sided view of our subject, but let us rather admit freely at the outset that we may very likely find no one essence, but many characters which may alternately be equally important in religion. If we should inquire for the essence of 'government,' for example, one man might tell us it was authority, another submission, another police, another an army, another an assembly, another a system of laws; yet all the while it would be true that no concrete government can exist without all these things, one of which is more important at one moment and others at another. The man who knows governments most completely is he who troubles himself least about a definition which shall give their essence. Enjoying an intimate acquaintance with all their particularities in turn, he would naturally regard an abstract conception in which these were unified as a thing more misleading than enlightening. And why may not religion be a conception equally complex? [I can do no better here than refer my readers to the extended and admirable remarks on the futility of all these definitions of religion, in an article by Professor Leuba, published in the Monist for January, 1901, after my own text was written.]

Consider also the 'religious sentiment' which we see referred to in so many books, as if it were a single sort of mental entity.

In the psychologies and in the philosophies of religion, we find the authors attempting to specify just what entity it is. One man allies it to the feeling of dependence; one makes it a derivative from fear; others connect it with the sexual life; others still identify it with the feeling of the infinite; and so on. Such different ways of conceiving it ought of themselves to arouse doubt as to whether it possibly can be one specific thing; and the moment we are willing to treat the term 'religious sentiment' as a collective name for the many sentiments which religious objects may arouse in alternation, we see that it probably contains nothing whatever of a psychologically specific nature. There is religious fear, religious love, religious awe, religious joy, and so forth. But religious love is only man's natural emotion of love directed to a religious object; religious fear is only the ordinary fear of commerce, so to speak, the common quaking of the human breast, in so far as the notion of divine retribution may arouse it; religious awe is the same organic thrill which we feel in a forest at twilight, or in a mountain gorge; only this time it comes over us at the thought of our supernatural relations; and similarly of all the various sentiments which may be called into play in the lives of religious persons. As concrete states of mind, made up of a feeling plus a specific sort of object, religious emotions of course are psychic entities distinguishable from other concrete emotions; but there is no ground for assuming a simple abstract 'religious emotion' to exist as a distinct elementary mental affection by itself, present in every religious experience without exception.

As there thus seems to be no one elementary religious emotion, but only a common storehouse of emotions upon which religious objects may draw, so there might conceivably also prove to be no one specific and essential kind of religious object, and no one specific and essential kind of religious act.

The field of religion being as wide as this, it is manifestly impossible that I should pretend to cover it. My lectures must be limited to a fraction of the subject. And, although it would indeed be foolish to set up an abstract definition of religion's essence, and then proceed to defend that definition against all comers, yet this need not prevent me from taking my own narrow view of what religion shall consist in for the purpose of these lectures, or, out of the many meanings of the word, from choosing the one meaning in which I wish to interest you particularly, and proclaiming arbitrarily that when I say 'religion' I mean that. This, in fact, is what I must do, and I will now preliminarily seek to mark out the field I choose.

One way to mark it out easily is to say what aspects of the subject we leave out. At the outset we are struck by one great partition which divides the religious field. On the one side of it lies institutional, on the other personal religion. As M.P. Sabatier says, one branch of religion keeps the divinity, another keeps man most in view. Worship and sacrifice, procedures for working on the dispositions of the deity, theology and ceremony and ecclesiastical organization, are the essentials of religion in the institutional branch. Were we to limit our view to it, we should have to define religion as an external art, the art of winning the favor of the gods. In the more personal branch of religion it is on the contrary the inner dispositions of man himself which form the centre of interest, his conscience, his deserts, his helplessness, his incompleteness. And although the favor of the God, as forfeited or gained, is still an essential feature of the story, and theology plays a vital part therein, yet the acts to which this sort of religion prompts are personal not ritual acts, the individual transacts the business by himself alone, and the ecclesiastical organization, with its priests and sacraments and other go-betweens, sinks to an altogether secondary place. The relation goes direct from heart to heart, from soul to soul, between man and his maker.

Now in these lectures I propose to ignore the institutional branch entirely, to say nothing of the ecclesiastical organization, to consider as little as possible the systematic theology and the ideas about the gods themselves, and to confine myself as far as I can to personal religion pure and simple. To some of you personal religion, thus nakedly considered, will no doubt seem too incomplete a thing to wear the general name. "It is a part of religion," you will say, "but only its unorganized rudiment; if we are to name it by itself, we had better call it man's conscience or morality than his religion. The name 'religion' should be reserved for the fully organized system of feeling, thought, and institution, for the Church, in short, of which this personal religion, so called, is but a fractional element."

But if you say this, it will only show the more plainly how much the question of definition tends to become a dispute about names. Rather than prolong such a dispute, I am willing to accept almost any name for the personal religion of which I propose to treat. Call it conscience or morality, if you yourselves prefer, and not religion— under either name it will be equally worthy of our study. As for myself, I think it will prove to contain some elements which morality pure and simple does not contain, and these elements I shall soon seek to point out; so I will myself continue to apply the word 'religion' to it; and in the last lecture of all, I will bring in the theologies and the ecclesiasticisms, and say something of its relation to them.

In one sense at least the personal religion will prove itself more fundamental than either theology or ecclesiasticism. Churches, when once established, live at second hand upon tradition; but the founders of every church owed their power originally to the fact of their direct personal communion with the divine. Not only the superhuman founders, the Christ, the Buddha, Mahomet, but all the originators of Christian sects have been in this case;— so personal religion should still seem the primordial thing, even to those who continue to esteem it incomplete.

There are, it is true, other things in religion chronologically more primordial than personal devoutness in the moral sense. Fetishism and magic seem to have preceded inward piety historically— at least our records of inward piety do not reach back so far. And if fetishism and magic be regarded as stages of religion, one may say that personal religion in the inward sense and the genuinely spiritual ecclesiasticisms which it founds are phenomena of secondary or even tertiary order. But, quite apart from the fact that many anthropologists— for instance, Jevons and Frazer— expressly oppose 'religion' and 'magic' to each other, it is certain that the whole system of thought which leads to magic, fetishism, and the lower superstitions may just as well be called primitive science as called primitive religion. The question thus becomes a verbal one again; and our knowledge of all these early stages of thought and feeling is in any case so conjectural and imperfect that farther discussion would not be worth while.

Religion, therefore, as I now ask you arbitrarily to take it, shall mean for us the feelings, acts, and experiences of individual men in their solitude, so far as they apprehend themselves to stand in relation to whatever they may consider the divine. Since the relation may be either moral, physical, or ritual, it is evident that out of religion in the sense in which we take it, theologies, philosophies, and ecclesiastical organizations may secondarily grow. In these lectures, however, as I have already said, the immediate personal experiences will amply fill our time, and we shall hardly consider theology or ecclesiasticism at all.

We escape much controversial matter by this arbitrary definition of our field. But, still, a chance of controversy comes up over the word 'divine,' if we take it in the definition in too narrow a sense. There are systems of thought which the world usually calls religious, and yet which do not positively assume a God. Buddhism is in this case. Popularly, of course, the Buddha himself stands in place of a God; but in strictness the Buddhistic system is atheistic. Modern transcendental idealism, Emersonianism, for instance, also seems to let God evaporate into abstract Ideality. Not a deity in concreto, not a superhuman person, but the immanent divinity in things, the essentially spiritual structure of the universe, is the object of the transcendentalist cult. In that address to the graduating class at Divinity College in 1838 which made Emerson famous, the frank expression of this worship of mere abstract laws was what made the scandal of the performance.

"These laws," said the speaker, "execute themselves. They are out of time, out of space, and not subject to circumstance: Thus, in the soul of man there is a justice whose retributions are instant and entire. He who does a good deed is instantly ennobled. He who does a mean deed is by the action itself contracted. He who puts off impurity thereby puts on purity. If a man is at heart just, then in so far is he God; the safety of God, the immortality of God, the majesty of God, do enter into that man with justice. If a man dissemble, deceive, he deceives himself, and goes out of acquaintance with his own being. Character is always known. Thefts never enrich; alms never impoverish; murder will speak out of stone walls. The least admixture of a lie- for example, the taint of vanity, any attempt to make a good impression, a favorable appearance— will instantly vitiate the effect. But speak the truth, and all things alive or brute are vouchers, and the very roots of the grass underground there do seem to stir and move to bear your witness. For all things proceed out of the same spirit, which is differently named love, justice, temperance, in its different applications, just as the ocean receives different names on the several shores which it washes. In so far as he roves from these ends, a man bereaves himself of power, of auxiliaries. His being shrinks... he becomes less and less, a mote, a point, until absolute badness is absolute death. The perception of this law awakens in the mind a sentiment which we call the religious sentiment, and which makes our highest happiness. Wonderful is its power to charm and to command. It is a mountain air. It is the embalmer of the world. It makes the sky and the hills sublime, and the silent song of the stars is it. It is the beatitude of man. It makes him illimitable. When he says 'I ought'; when love warns him; when he chooses, warned from on high, the good and great deed; then, deep melodies wander through his soul from supreme wisdom. Then he can worship, and be enlarged by his worship; for he can never go behind this sentiment. All the expressions of this sentiment are sacred and permanent in proportion to their purity. [They] affect us more than all other compositions. The sentences of the olden time, which ejaculate this piety, are still fresh and fragrant. And the unique impression of Jesus upon mankind, whose name is not so much written as ploughed into the history of this world, is proof of the subtle virtue of this infusion."

Such is the Emersonian religion. The universe has a divine soul of order, which soul is moral, being also the soul within the soul of man. But whether this soul of the universe be a mere quality like the eye's brilliancy or the skin's softness, or whether it be a self-conscious life like the eye's seeing or the skin's feeling, is a decision that never unmistakably appears in Emerson's pages. It quivers on the boundary of these things, sometimes leaning one way, sometimes the other, to suit the literary rather than the philosophic need. Whatever it is, though, it is active. As much as if it were a God, we can trust it to protect all ideal interests and keep the world's balance straight. The sentences in which Emerson, to the very end, gave utterance to this faith are as fine as anything in literature: "If you love and serve men, you cannot by any hiding or stratagem escape the remuneration. Secret retributions are always restoring the level, when disturbed, of the divine justice. It is impossible to tilt the beam. All the tyrants and proprietors and monopolists of the world in vain set their shoulders to heave the bar. Settles forevermore the ponderous equator to its line, and man and mote, and star and sun, must range to it, or be pulverized by the recoil." [Lectures and Biographical Sketches, 1868, p. 186.]

Now it would be too absurd to say that the inner experiences that underlie such expressions of faith as this and impel the writer to their utterance are quite unworthy to be called religious experiences. The sort of appeal that Emersonian optimism, on the one hand, and Buddhistic pessimism, on the other, make to the individual and the sort of response which he makes to them in his life are in fact indistinguishable from, and in many respects identical with, the best Christian appeal and response. We must therefore, from the experiential point of view, call these godless or quasi-godless creeds 'religions'; and accordingly when in our definition of religion we speak of the individual's relation to 'what he considers the divine,' we must interpret the term 'divine' very broadly, as denoting any object that is godlike, whether it be a concrete deity or not.

But the term 'godlike,' if thus treated as a floating general quality, becomes exceedingly vague, for many gods have flourished in religious history, and their attributes have been discrepant enough. What then is that essentially godlike quality— be it embodied in a concrete deity or not— our relation to which determines our character as religious men? It will repay us to seek some answer to this question before we proceed farther.

For one thing, gods are conceived to be first things in the way of being and power. They overarch and envelop, and from them there is no escape. What relates to them is the first and last word in the way of truth. Whatever then were most primal and enveloping and deeply true might at this rate be treated as godlike, and a man's religion might thus be identified with his attitude, whatever it might be, towards what he felt to be the primal truth.

Such a definition as this would in a way be defensible. Religion, whatever it is, is a man's total reaction upon life, so why not say that any total reaction upon life is a religion? Total reactions are different from casual reactions, and total attitudes are different from usual or professional attitudes. To get at them you must go behind the foreground of existence and reach down to that curious sense of the whole residual cosmos as an everlasting presence, intimate or alien, terrible or amusing, lovable or odious, which in some degree every one possesses. This sense of the world's presence, appealing as it does to our peculiar individual temperament, makes us either strenuous or careless, devout or blasphemous, gloomy or exultant, about life at large; and our reaction, involuntary and inarticulate and often half unconscious as it is, is the completest of all our answers to the question, "What is the character of this universe in which we dwell?" It expresses our individual sense of it in the most definite way. Why then not call these reactions our religion, no matter what specific character they may have? Non-religious as some of these reactions may be, in one sense of the word 'religious,' they yet belong to the general sphere of the religious life, and so should generically be classed as religious reactions. "He believes in No-God, and he worships him," said a colleague of mine of a student who was manifesting a fine atheistic ardor; and the more fervent opponents of Christian doctrine have often enough shown a temper which, psychologically considered, is indistinguishable from religious zeal.

But so very broad a use of the word 'religion' would be inconvenient, however defensible it might remain on logical grounds. There are trifling, sneering attitudes even towards the whole of life; and in some men these attitudes are final and systematic. It would strain the ordinary use of language too much to call such attitudes religious, even though, from the point of view of an unbiased critical philosophy, they might conceivably be perfectly reasonable ways of looking upon life. Voltaire, for example, writes thus to a friend, at the age of seventy-three: "As for myself," he says, "weak as I am, I carry on the war to the last moment, I get a hundred pike-thrusts, I return two hundred, and I laugh. I see near my door Geneva on fire with quarrels over nothing, and I laugh again; and, thank God, I can look upon the world as a farce even when it becomes as tragic as it sometimes does. All comes out even at the end of the day, and all comes out still more even when all the days are over."

Much as we may admire such a robust old gamecock spirit in a valetudinarian, to call it a religious spirit would be odd. Yet it is for the moment Voltaire's reaction on the whole of life. Je m'en fiche is the vulgar French equivalent for our English ejaculation 'Who cares?' And the happy term je m'en fichisme recently has been invented to designate the systematic determination not to take anything in life too solemnly. 'All is vanity' is the relieving word in an difficult crises for this mode of thought, which that exquisite literary genius Renan took pleasure, in his later days of sweet decay, in putting into coquettishly sacrilegious forms which remain to us as excellent expressions of the 'all is vanity' state of mind. Take the following passage, for example,- we must hold to duty, even against the evidence, Renan says,— but he then goes on:—

"There are many chances that the world may be nothing but a fairy pantomime of which no God has care. We must therefore arrange ourselves so that on neither hypothesis we shall be completely wrong. We must listen to the superior voices, but in such a way that if the second hypothesis were true we should not have been too completely duped. If in effect the world be not a serious thing, it is the dogmatic people who will be the shallow ones, and the worldly minded whom the theologians now call frivolous will be those who are really wise.

"In utrumque paratus, then. Be ready for anything— that perhaps is wisdom. Give ourselves up, according to the hour, to confidence, to skepticism, to optimism, to irony, and we may be sure that at certain moments at least we shall be with the truth.... Good-humor is a philosophic state of mind; it seems to say to Nature that we take her no more seriously than she takes us. I maintain that one should always talk of philosophy with a smile. We owe it to the Eternal to be virtuous; but we have the right to add to this tribute our irony as a sort of personal reprisal. In this way we return to the right quarter jest for jest; we play the trick that has been played on us. Saint Augustine's phrase: Lord, if we are deceived, it is by thee! remains a fine one, well suited to our modern feeling. Only we wish the Eternal to know that if we accept the fraud, we accept it knowingly and willingly. We are resigned in advance to losing the interest on our investments of virtue, but we wish not to appear ridiculous by having counted on them too securely." [Feuilles detachees, pp. 394-398 (abridged).]

Surely all the usual associations of the word 'religion' would have to be stripped away if such a systematic parti pris of irony were also to be denoted by the name. For common men 'religion,' whatever more special meanings it may have, signifies always a serious state of mind. If any one phrase could gather its universal message, that phrase would be, 'All is not vanity in this Universe, whatever the appearances may suggest.' If it can stop anything, religion as commonly apprehended can stop just such chaffing talk as Renan's. It favors gravity, not pertness; it says 'hush' to all vain chatter and smart wit.

But if hostile to light irony, religion is equally hostile to heavy grumbling and complaint. The world appears tragic enough in some religions, but the tragedy is realized as purging, and a way of deliverance is held to exist. We shall see enough of the religious melancholy in a future lecture; but melancholy, according to our ordinary use of language, forfeits all title to be called religious when, in Marcus Aurelius's racy words, the sufferer simply lies kicking and screaming after the fashion of a sacrificed pig. The mood of a Schopenhauer or a Nietzsche,— and in a less degree one may sometimes say the same of our own sad Carlyle,— though often an ennobling sadness, is almost as often only peevishness running away with the bit between its teeth. The sallies of the two German authors remind one, half the time, of the sick shriekings of two dying rats. They lack the purgatorial note which religious sadness gives forth.

There must be something solemn, serious, and tender about any attitude which we denominate religious. If glad, it must not grin or snicker; if sad, it must not scream or curse. It is precisely as being solemn experiences that I wish to interest you in religious experiences. So I propose— arbitrarily again, if you please— to narrow our definition once more by saying that the word 'divine,' as employed therein, shall mean for us not merely the primal and enveloping and real, for that meaning if taken without restriction might well prove too broad. The divine shall mean for us only such a primal reality as the individual feels impelled to respond to solemnly and gravely, and neither by a curse nor a jest.

But solemnity, and gravity, and all such emotional attributes, admit of various shades; and, do what we will with our defining, the truth must at last be confronted that we are dealing with a field of experience where there is not a single conception that can be sharply drawn. The pretension, under such conditions, to be rigorously 'scientific' or 'exact' in our terms would only stamp us as lacking in understanding of our task. Things are more or less divine, states of mind are more or less religious, reactions are more or less total, but the boundaries are always misty, and it is everywhere a question of amount and degree. Nevertheless, at their extreme of development, there can never be an question as to what experiences are religious. The divinity of the object and the solemnity of the reaction are too well marked for doubt. Hesitation as to whether a state of mind is 'religious,' or 'moral,' or 'philosophical,' is only likely to arise when the state of mind is weakly characterized, but in that case it will be hardly worthy of our study at all. With states that can only by courtesy be called religious we need have nothing to do, our only profitable business being with what nobody can possibly feel tempted to call anything else. I said in my former lecture that we learn most about a thing when we view it under a microscope, as it were, or in its most exaggerated form. This is as true of religious phenomena as of any other kind of fact. The only cases likely to be profitable enough to repay our attention will therefore be cases where the religious spirit is unmistakable and extreme. Its fainter manifestations we may tranquilly pass by. Here, for example, is the total reaction upon life of Frederick Locker Lampson, whose autobiography, entitled 'Confidences,' proves him to have been a most amiable man.

"I am so far resigned to my lot that I feel small pain at the thought of having to part from what has been called the pleasant habit of existence, the sweet fable of life. I would not care to live my wasted life over again, and so to prolong my span. Strange to say, I have but little wish to be younger. I submit with a chill at my heart. I humbly submit because it is the Divine Will, and my appointed destiny. I dread the increase of infirmities that will make me a burden to those around me, those dear to me. No! let me slip away as quietly and comfortably as I can. Let the end come, if peace come with it.

"I do not know that there is a great deal to be said for this world, or our sojourn here upon it; but it has pleased God so to place us, and it must please me also. I ask you, what is human life? Is not it a maimed happiness- care and weariness, weariness and care, with the baseless expectation, the strange cozenage of a brighter tomorrow? At best it is but a froward child, that must be played with and humored, to keep it quiet till it falls asleep, and then the care is over."

This is a complex, a tender, a submissive, and a graceful state of mind. For myself, I should have no objection to calling it on the whole a religious state of mind, although I dare say that to many of you it may seem too listless and half-hearted to merit so good a name. But what matters it in the end whether we call such a state of mind religious or not? It is too insignificant for our instruction in any case; and its very possessor wrote it down in terms which he would not have used unless he had been thinking of more energetically religious moods in others, with which he found himself unable to compete. It is with these more energetic states that our sole business lies, and we can perfectly well afford to let the minor notes and the uncertain border go.

It was the extremer cases that I had in mind a little while ago when I said that personal religion, even without theology or ritual, would prove to embody some elements that morality pure and simple does not contain. You may remember that I promised shortly to point out what those elements were. In a general way I can now say what I had in mind.

"I accept the universe" is reported to have been a favorite utterance of our New England transcendentalist, Margaret Fuller; and when some one repeated this phrase to Thomas Carlyle, his sardonic comment is said to have been: "Gad! she'd better!" At bottom the whole concern of both morality and religion is with the manner of our acceptance of the universe. Do we accept it only in part and grudgingly, or heartily and altogether? Shall our protests against certain things in it be radical and unforgiving, or shall we think that, even with evil, there are ways of living that must lead to good? If we accept the whole, shall we do so as if stunned into submission,— as Carlyle would have us— "Gad! we'd better!"— or shall we do so with enthusiastic assent? Morality pure and simple accepts the law of the whole which it finds reigning, so far as to acknowledge and obey it, but it may obey it with the heaviest and coldest heart, and never cease to feel it as a yoke. But for religion, in its strong and fully developed manifestations, the service of the highest never is felt as a yoke. Dull submission is left far behind, and a mood of welcome, which may fill any place on the scale between cheerful serenity and enthusiastic gladness, has taken its place.

It makes a tremendous emotional and practical difference to one whether one accept the universe in the drab discolored way of stoic resignation to necessity, or with the passionate happiness of Christian saints. The difference is as great as that between passivity and activity, as that between the defensive and the aggressive mood. Gradual as are the steps by which an individual may from one state into the other, many as are the intermediate stages which different individuals represent, yet when you place the typical extremes beside each other for comparison, you feel that two discontinuous psychological universes confront you, and that in passing from one to the other a 'critical point' has been overcome.

If we compare stoic with Christian ejaculations we see much more than a difference of doctrine; rather is it a difference of emotional mood that parts them. When Marcus Aurelius reflects on the eternal reason that has ordered things, there is a frosty chill about his words which you rarely find in a Jewish, and never in a Christian piece of religious writing. The universe is 'accepted' by all these writers; but how devoid of passion or exultation the spirit of the Roman Emperor is! Compare his fine sentence "If gods care not for me or my children, here is a reason for it," with Job's cry: "Though he slay me, yet will I trust in him!" and you immediately see the difference I mean. The anima mundi, to whose disposal of his own personal destiny the Stoic consents, is there to be respected and submitted to, but the Christian God is there to be loved and the difference of emotional atmosphere is like that between an arctic climate and the tropics, though the outcome in the way of accepting actual conditions uncomplainingly may seem in abstract terms to be much the same.

"It is a man's duty," says Marcus Aurelius, "to comfort himself and wait for the natural dissolution, and not to be vexed, but to find refreshment solely in these thoughts- first that nothing will happen to me which is not conformable to the nature of the universe; and secondly that I need do nothing contrary to the God and deity within me; for there is no man who can compel me to transgress. [Book V., ch. x. (abridged).] He is an abscess on the universe who withdraws and separates himself from the reason of our common nature, through being displeased with the things which happen. For the same nature produces these, and has produced thee too. And so accept everything which happens, even if it seem disagreeable, because it leads to this, the health of the universe and to the prosperity and felicity of Zeus. For he would not have brought on any man what he has brought, if it were not useful for the whole. The integrity of the whole is mutilated if thou cuttest off anything. And thou dost cut off, as far as it is in thy power, when thou art dissatisfied, and in a manner triest to put anything out of the way." [Book V., ch. ix. (abridged).]

Compare now this mood with that of the old Christian author of the Theologia Germanica:—

"Where men are enlightened with the true light, they renounce all desire and choice, and commit and commend themselves and all things to the eternal Goodness, so that every enlightened man could say: 'I would fain be to the Eternal Goodness what his own hand is to a man.' Such men are in a state of freedom, because they have lost the fear of pain or hell, and the hope of reward or heaven, and are living in pure submission to the eternal Goodness, in the perfect freedom of fervent love. When a man truly perceiveth and considereth himself, who and what he is, and findeth himself utterly vile and wicked and unworthy, he falleth into such a deep abasement that it seemeth to him reasonable that all creatures in heaven and earth should rise up against him. And therefore he will not and dare not desire any consolation and release; but he is willing to be unconsoled and unreleased; and he doth not grieve over his sufferings, for they are right in his eyes, and he hath nothing to say against them. This is what is meant by true repentance for sin; and he who in this present time entereth into this hell, none may console him. Now God hath not forsaken a man in this hell, but He is laying his hand upon him, that the man may not desire nor regard anything but the eternal Good only. And then, when the man neither careth for nor desireth anything but the eternal Good alone, and seeketh not himself nor his own things, but the honour of God only, he is made a partaker of all manner of joy, bliss, peace, rest, and consolation, and so the man is henceforth in the kingdom of heaven. This hell and this heaven are two good safe ways for a man, and happy is he who truly findeth them." [Chaps. x., xi. (abridged): Winkworth's translation.]

How much more active and positive the impulse of the Christian writer to accept his place in the universe is! Marcus Aurelius agrees to the scheme— the German theologian agrees with it. He literally abounds in agreement, he runs out to embrace the divine decrees.

Occasionally, it is true, the Stoic rises to something like a Christian warmth of sentiment, as in the often quoted passage of Marcus Aurelius:—

"Everything harmonizes with me which is harmonious to thee, O Universe. Nothing for me is too early nor too late, which is in due time for thee.

Everything is fruit to me which thy seasons bring, O Nature: from thee are all things, in thee are all things, to thee all things return. The poet says, Dear City of Cecrops; and wilt thou not say, Dear City of Zeus?" [Book IV., SS 23.]

But compare even as devout a passage as this with a genuine Christian outpouring, and it seems a little cold. Turn, for instance, to the Imitation of Christ:—

"Lord, thou knowest what is best; let this or that be according as thou wilt. Give what thou wilt, so much as thou wilt, when thou wilt. Do with me as thou knowest best, and as shall be most to thine honour. Place me where thou wilt, and freely work thy will with me in all things.... When could it be evil when thou wert near? I had rather be poor for thy sake than rich without thee. I choose rather to be a pilgrim upon the earth with thee, than without thee to possess heaven. Where thou art, there is heaven; and where thou art not, behold there death and hell." [Benham's translation: Book III., chaps. xv., lix. Compare Mary Moody Emerson: "Let me be a blot on this fair world, the obscurest, the loneliest sufferer, with one proviso,— that I know it is His agency. I will love Him though He shed frost and darkness on every way of mine." R.W. EMERSON: Lectures and Biographical Sketches, p. 188.]

It is a good rule in physiology, when we are studying the meaning of an organ, to ask after its most peculiar and characteristic sort of performance, and to seek its office in that one of its functions which no other organ can possibly exert. Surely the same maxim holds good in our present quest. The essence of religious experiences, the thing by which we finally must judge them, must be that element or quality in them which we can meet nowhere else. And such a quality will be of course most prominent and easy to notice in those religious experiences which are most one-sided, exaggerated, and intense.

Now when we compare these intenser experiences with the experiences of tamer minds, so cool and reasonable that we are tempted to call them philosophical rather than religious, we find a character that is perfectly distinct. That character, it seems to me, should be regarded as the practically important differentia of religion for our purpose; and just what it is can easily be brought out by comparing the mind of an abstractly conceived Christian with that of a moralist similarly conceived.

A life is manly, stoical, moral, or philosophical, we say, in proportion as it is less swayed by paltry personal considerations and more by objective ends that call for energy, even though that energy bring personal loss and pain. This is the good side of war, in so far as it calls for 'volunteers.' And for morality life is a war, and the service of the highest is a sort of cosmic patriotism which also calls for volunteers. Even a sick man, unable to be militant outwardly, can carry on the moral warfare. He can willfully turn his attention away from his own future, whether in this world or the next. He can train himself to indifference to his present drawbacks and immerse himself in whatever objective interests still remain accessible. He can follow public news, and sympathize with other people's affairs. He can cultivate cheerful manners, and be silent about his miseries. He can contemplate whatever ideal aspects of existence his philosophy is able to present to him, and practice whatever duties, such as patience, resignation, trust, his ethical system requires. Such a man lives on his loftiest, largest plane. He is a high-hearted freeman and no pining slave. And yet he lacks something which the Christian par excellence, the mystic and ascetic saint, for example, has in abundant measure, and which makes of him a human being of an altogether different denomination.

The Christian also spurns the pinched and mumping sick-room attitude, and the lives of saints are full of a kind of callousness to diseased conditions of body which probably no other human records show. But whereas the merely moralistic spurning takes an effort of volition, the Christian spurning is the result of the excitement of a higher kind of emotion, in the presence of which no exertion of volition is required. The moralist must hold his breath and keep his muscles tense; and so long as this athletic attitude is possible all goes well— morality suffices. But the athletic attitude tends ever to break down, and it inevitably does break down even in the most stalwart when the organism begins to decay, or when morbid fears invade the mind. To suggest personal will and effort to one all sicklied o'er with the sense of irremediable impotence is to suggest the most impossible of things. What he craves is to be consoled in his very powerlessness, to feel that the spirit of the universe recognizes and secures him, all decaying and failing as he is. Well, we are all such helpless failures in the last resort. The sanest and best of us are of one clay with lunatics and prison inmates, and death finally runs the robustest of us down. And whenever we feel this, such a sense of the vanity and provisionality of our voluntary career comes over us that all our morality appears but as a plaster hiding a sore it can never cure, and all our well-doing as the hollowest substitute for that well-being that our lives ought to be grounded in, but, alas! are not.

And here religion comes to our rescue and takes our fate into her hands. There is a state of mind, known to religious men, but to no others, in which the will to assert ourselves and hold our own has been displaced by a willingness to close our mouths and be as nothing in the floods and waterspouts of God. In this state of mind, what we most dreaded has become the habitation of our safety, and the hour of our moral death has turned into our spiritual birthday. The time for tension in our soul is over, and that of happy relaxation, of calm deep breathing, of an eternal present, with no discordant future to be anxious about, has arrived. Fear is not held in abeyance as it is by mere morality, it is positively expunged and washed away.

We shall see abundant examples of this happy state of mind in later lectures of this course. We shall see how infinitely passionate a thing religion at its highest flights can be. Like love, like wrath, like hope, ambition, jealousy, like every other instinctive eagerness and impulse, it adds to life an enchantment which is not rationally or logically deducible from anything else. This enchantment, coming as a gift when it does come,— a gift of our organism, the physiologists will tell us, a gift of God's grace, the theologians say,— is either there or not there for us, and there are persons who can no more become possessed by it than they can fall in love with a given woman by mere word of command. Religious feeling is thus an absolute addition to the Subject's range of life. It gives him a new sphere of power. When the outward battle is lost, and the outer world disowns him, it redeems and vivifies an interior world which otherwise would be an empty waste.

If religion is to mean anything definite for us, it seems to me that we ought to take it as meaning this added dimension of emotion, this enthusiastic temper of espousal, in regions where morality strictly so called can at best but bow its head and acquiesce. It ought to mean nothing short of this new reach of freedom for us, with the struggle over, the keynote of the universe sounding in our ears, and everlasting possession spread before our eyes. [Once more, there are plenty of men, constitutionally sombre men, in whose religious life this rapturousness is lacking. They are religious in the wider sense; yet in this acutest of all senses they are not so, and it is religion in the acutest sense that I wish, without disputing about words, to study first, so as to get at its typical differentia.]

This sort of happiness in the absolute and everlasting is what we find nowhere but in religion. It is parted off from all mere animal happiness, all mere enjoyment of the present, by that element of solemnity of which I have already made so much account. Solemnity is a hard thing to define abstractly, but certain of its marks are patent enough. A solemn state of mind is never crude or simple— it seems to contain a certain measure of its own opposite in solution. A solemn joy preserves a sort of bitter in its sweetness; a solemn sorrow is one to which we intimately consent. But there are writers who, realizing that happiness of a supreme sort is the prerogative of religion, forget this complication, and call all happiness, as such, religious. Mr. Havelock Ellis, for example, identifies religion with the entire field of the soul's liberation from oppressive moods.

"The simplest functions of physiological life," he writes, "may be its ministers. Every one who is at all acquainted with the Persian mystics knows how wine may be regarded as an instrument of religion. Indeed, in all countries and in all ages, some form of physical enlargement— singing, dancing, drinking, sexual excitement— has been intimately associated with worship. Even the momentary expansion of the soul in laughter is, to however slight an extent, a religious exercise.... Whenever an impulse from the world strikes against the organism, and the resultant is not discomfort or pain, not even the muscular contraction of strenuous manhood, but a joyous expansion or aspiration of the whole soul— there is religion. It is the infinite for which we hunger, and we ride gladly on every little wave that promises to bear us towards it." [The New Spirit, p. 232.]

But such a straight identification of religion with any and every form of happiness leaves the essential peculiarity of religious happiness out. The more commonplace happinesses which we get are 'reliefs,' occasioned by our momentary escapes from evils either experienced or threatened. But in its most characteristic embodiments, religious happiness is no mere feeling of escape. It cares no longer to escape. It consents to the evil outwardly as a form of sacrifice- inwardly it knows it to be permanently overcome. If you ask how religion thus falls on the thorns and faces death, and in the very act annuls annihilation, I cannot explain the matter, for it is religion's secret, and to understand it you must yourself have been a religious man of the extremer type. In our future examples, even of the simplest and healthiest-minded type of religious consciousness, we shall find this complex sacrificial constitution, in which a higher happiness holds a lower unhappiness in check. In the Louvre there is a picture, by Guido Reni, of St. Michael with his foot on Satan's neck. The richness of the picture is in large part due to the fiend's figure being there. The richness of its allegorical meaning also is due to his being there— that is, the world is all the richer for having a devil in it, so long as we keep our foot upon his neck. In the religious consciousness, that is just the position in which the fiend, the negative or tragic principle, is found; and for that very reason the religious consciousness is so rich from the emotional point of view. We shall see how in certain men and women it takes on a monstrously ascetic form. There are saints who have literally fed on the negative principle, on humiliation and privation, and the thought of suffering and death,— their souls growing in happiness just in proportion as their outward state grew more intolerable. No other emotion than religious emotion can bring a man to this peculiar pass. And it is for that reason that when we ask our question about the value of religion for human life, I think we ought to look for the answer among these violenter examples rather than among those of a more moderate hue.

Having the phenomenon of our study in its acutest possible form to start with, we can shade down as much as we please later. And if in these cases, repulsive as they are to our ordinary worldly way of judging, we find ourselves compelled to acknowledge religion's value and treat it with respect, it will have proved in some way its value for life at large. By subtracting and toning down extravagances we may thereupon proceed to trace the boundaries of its legitimate sway.

To be sure, it makes our task difficult to have to deal so much with eccentricities and extremes. "How can religion on the whole be the most important of all human functions," you may ask, "if every several manifestation of it in turn have to be corrected and sobered down and pruned away?" Such a thesis seems a paradox impossible to sustain reasonably,— yet I believe that something like it will have to be our final contention. That personal attitude which the individual finds himself impelled to take up towards what he apprehends to be the divine and you will remember that this was our definition will prove to be both a helpless and a sacrificial attitude. That is, we shall have to confess to at least some amount of dependence on sheer mercy, and to practice some amount of renunciation, great or small, to save our souls alive. The constitution of the world we live in requires it:

"Entbehren sollst du! sollst entbehren!
Das ist der ewige Gesang
Der jedem an die Ohren klingt,
Den, unser ganzes Leben lang
Uns heiser jede Stunde singt."

For when all is said and done, we are in the end absolutely dependent on the universe; and into sacrifices and surrenders of some sort, deliberately looked at and accepted, we are drawn and pressed as into our only permanent positions of repose. Now in those states of mind which fall short of religion, the surrender is submitted to as an imposition of necessity, and the sacrifice is undergone at the very best without complaint. In the religious life, on the contrary, surrender and sacrifice are positively espoused: even unnecessary givings-up are added in order that the happiness may increase. Religion thus makes easy and felicitous what in any case is necessary; and if it be the only agency that can accomplish this result, its vital importance as a human faculty stands vindicated beyond dispute. It becomes an essential organ of our life, performing a function which no other portion of our nature can so successfully fulfill. From the merely biological point of view, so to call it, this is a conclusion to which, so far as I can now see, we shall inevitably be led, and led moreover by following the purely empirical method of demonstration which I sketched to you in the first lecture. Of the farther office of religion as a metaphysical revelation I will say nothing now.

But to foreshadow the terminus of one's investigations is one thing, and to arrive there safely is another. In the next lecture, abandoning the extreme generalities which have engrossed us hitherto, I propose that we begin our actual journey by addressing ourselves directly to the concrete facts.

LECTURE III: THE REALITY OF THE UNSEEN

Were one asked to characterize the life of religion in the broadest and most general terms possible, one might say that it consists of the belief that there is an unseen order, and that our supreme good lies in harmoniously adjusting ourselves thereto. This belief and this adjustment are the religious attitude in the soul. I wish during this hour to call your attention to some of the psychological peculiarities of such an attitude as this, of belief in an object which we cannot see. All our attitudes, moral, practical, or emotional, as well as religious, are due to the 'objects' of our consciousness, the things which we believe to exist, whether really or ideally, along with ourselves. Such objects may be present to our senses, or they may be present only to our thought. In either case they elicit from us a reaction; and the reaction due to things of thought is notoriously in many cases as strong as that due to sensible presences. It may be even stronger. The memory of an insult may make us angrier than the insult did when we received it. We are frequently more ashamed of our blunders afterwards than we were at the moment of making them; and in general our whole higher prudential and moral life is based on the fact that material sensations actually present may have a weaker influence on our action than ideas of remoter facts.

The more concrete objects of most men's religion, the deities whom they worship, are known to them only in idea. It has been vouchsafed, for example, to very few Christian believers to have had a sensible vision of their Saviour; though enough appearances of this sort are on record, by way of miraculous exception, to merit our attention later. The whole force of the Christian religion, therefore, so far as belief in the divine personages determines the prevalent attitude of the believer, is in general exerted by the instrumentality of pure ideas, of which nothing in the individual's past experience directly serves as a model.

But in addition to these ideas of the more concrete religious objects, religion is full of abstract objects which prove to have an equal power. God's attributes as such, his holiness, his justice, his mercy, his absoluteness, his infinity, his omniscience, his tri-unity, the various mysteries of the redemptive process, the operation of the sacraments, etc., have proved fertile wells of inspiring meditation for Christian believers. We shall see later that the absence of definite sensible images is positively insisted on by the mystical authorities in all religions as the sine qua non of a successful orison, or contemplation of the higher divine truths. Such contemplations are expected (and abundantly verify the expectation, as we shall also see) to influence the believer's subsequent attitude very powerfully for good.

Example: "I have had much comfort lately in meditating on the passages which show the personality of the Holy Ghost, and his distinctness from the Father and the Son. It is a subject that requires searching into to find out, but, when realized, gives one so much more true and lively a sense of the fullness of the Godhead, and its work in us and to us, than when only thinking of the Spirit in its effect on us." Augustus Hare: Memorials, i. 244, Maria Hare to Lucy H. Hare.

Immanuel Kant held a curious doctrine about such objects of belief as God, the design of creation, the soul, its freedom, and the life hereafter. These things, he said, are properly not objects of knowledge at all. Our conceptions always require a sense-content to work with, and as the words 'soul,' 'God,' 'immortality,' cover no distinctive sense-content whatever, it follows that theoretically speaking they are words devoid of any significance. Yet strangely enough they have a definite meaning for our practice. We can act as if there were a God; feel as if we were free; consider Nature as if she were full of special designs; lay plans as if we were to be immortal; and we find then that these words do make a genuine difference in our moral life. Our faith that these unintelligible objects actually exist proves thus to be a full equivalent in praktischer Hinsicht, as Kant calls it, or from the point of view of our action, for a knowledge of what they might be, in case we were permitted positively to conceive them. So we have the strange phenomenon, as Kant assures us, of a mind believing with all its strength in the real presence of a set of things of no one of which it can form any notion whatsoever.

My object in thus recalling Kant's doctrine to your mind is not to express any opinion as to the accuracy of this particularly uncouth part of his philosophy, but only to illustrate the characteristic of human nature which we are considering, by an example so classical in its exaggeration. The sentiment of reality can indeed attach itself so strongly to our object of belief that our whole life is polarized through and through, so to speak, by its sense of the existence of the thing believed in, and yet that thing, for purpose of definite description, can hardly be said to be present to our mind at all. It is as if a bar of iron, without touch or sight, with no representative faculty whatever, might nevertheless be strongly endowed with an inner capacity for magnetic feeling; and as if, through the various arousals of its magnetism by magnets coming and going in its neighborhood, it might be consciously determined to different attitudes and tendencies. Such a bar of iron could never give you an outward description of the agencies that had the power of stirring it so strongly; yet of their presence, and of their significance for its life, it would be intensely aware through every fibre of its being.

It is not only the Ideas of pure Reason, as Kant styled them, that have this power of making us vitally feel presences that we are impotent articulately to describe. All sorts of higher abstractions bring with them the same kind of impalpable appeal. Remember those passages from Emerson which I read at my last lecture. The whole universe of concrete objects, as we know them, swims, not only for such a transcendentalist writer, but for all of us, in a wider and higher universe of abstract ideas, that lend it its significance. As time, space, and the ether soak through all things, so (we feel) do abstract and essential goodness, beauty, strength, significance, justice, soak through all things good, strong, significant, and just.

Such ideas, and others equally abstract, form the background for all our facts, the fountain-head of all the possibilities we conceive of. They give its 'nature,' as we call it, to every special thing. Everything we know is 'what' it is by sharing in the nature of one of these abstractions. We can never look directly at them, for they are bodiless and featureless and footless, but we grasp all other things by their means, and in handling the real world we should be stricken with helplessness in just so far forth as we might lose these mental objects, these adjectives and adverbs and predicates and heads of classification and conception.

This absolute determinability of our mind by abstractions is one of the cardinal facts in our human constitution. Polarizing and magnetizing us as they do, we turn towards them and from them, we seek them, hold them, hate them, bless them, just as if they were so many concrete beings. And beings they are, beings as real in the realm which they inhabit as the changing things of sense are in the realm of space.

Plato gave so brilliant and impressive a defense of this common human feeling, that the doctrine of the reality of abstract objects has been known as the platonic theory of ideas ever since. Abstract Beauty, for example, is for Plato a perfectly definite individual being, of which the intellect is aware as of something additional to all the perishing beauties of the earth. "The true order of going," he says, in the often quoted passage in his 'Banquet,' "is to use the beauties of earth as steps along which one mounts upwards for the sake of that other Beauty, going from one to two, and from two to all fair forms, and from fair forms to fair actions, and from fair actions to fair notions, until from fair notions he arrives at the notion of absolute Beauty, and at last knows what the essence of Beauty is." [Symposium, Jowett, 1871, i. 527.] In our last lecture we had a glimpse of the way in which a platonizing writer like Emerson may treat the abstract divineness of things, the moral structure of the universe, as a fact worthy of worship. In those various churches without a God which today are spreading through the world under the name of ethical societies, we have a similar worship of the abstract divine, the moral law believed in as an ultimate object. 'Science' in many minds is genuinely taking the place of a religion. Where this is so, the scientist treats the 'Laws of Nature' as objective facts to be revered. A brilliant school of interpretation of Greek mythology would have it that in their origin the Greek gods were only half-metaphoric personifications of those great spheres of abstract law and order into which the natural world falls apart— the sky-sphere, the ocean-sphere, the earth-sphere, and the like; just as even now we may speak of the smile of the morning, the kiss of the breeze, or the bite of the cold, without really meaning that these phenomena of nature actually wear a human face. [Example: "Nature is always so interesting, under whatever aspect she shows herself, that when it rains, I seem to see a beautiful woman weeping. She appears the more beautiful, the more afflicted she is." B. de St. Pierre.]

As regards the origin of the Greek gods, we need not at present seek an opinion. But the whole array of our instances leads to a conclusion something like this: It is as if there were in the human consciousness a sense of reality, a feeling of objective presence, a perception of what we may call 'something there,' more deep and more general than any of the special and particular 'senses' by which the current psychology supposes existent realities to be originally revealed. If this were so, we might suppose the senses to waken our attitudes and conduct as they so habitually do, by first exciting this sense of reality; but anything else, any idea, for example, that might similarly excite it, would have that same prerogative of appearing real which objects of sense normally possess. So far as religious conceptions were able to touch this reality-feeling, they would be believed in in spite of criticism, even though they might be so vague and remote as to be almost unimaginable, even though they might be such non-entities in point of whatness, as Kant makes the objects of his moral theology to be.

The most curious proofs of the existence of such an undifferentiated sense of reality as this are found in experiences of hallucination. It often happens that an hallucination is imperfectly developed: the person affected will feel a 'presence' in the room, definitely localized, facing in one particular way, real in the most emphatic sense of the word, often coming suddenly, and as suddenly gone; and yet neither seen, heard, touched, nor cognized in any of the usual 'sensible' ways. Let me give you an example of this, before I pass to the objects with whose presence religion is more peculiarly concerned.

An intimate friend of mine, one of the keenest intellects I know, has had several experiences of this sort. He writes as follows in response to my inquiries:—

"I have several times within the past few years felt the so-called 'consciousness of a presence.' The experiences which I have in mind are clearly distinguishable from another kind of experience which I have had very frequently, and which I fancy many persons would also call the 'consciousness of a presence.' But the difference for me between the two sets of experience is as great as the difference between feeling a slight warmth originating I know not where, and standing in the midst of a conflagration with all the ordinary senses alert.

"It was about September, 1884, when I had the first experience. On the previous night I had had, after getting into bed at my rooms in College, a vivid tactile hallucination of being grasped by the arm, which made me get up and search the room for an intruder; but the sense of presence properly so called came on the next night. After I had got into bed and blown out the candle, I lay awake awhile thinking on the previous night's experience, when suddenly I felt something come into the room and stay close to my bed. It remained only a minute or two. I did not recognize it by any ordinary sense, and yet there was a horribly unpleasant 'sensation' connected with it. It stirred something more at the roots of my being than any ordinary perception. The feeling had something of the quality of a very large tearing vital pain spreading chiefly over the chest, but within the organism— and yet the feeling was not pain so much as abhorrence. At all events, something was present with me, and I knew its presence far more surely than I have ever known the presence of any fleshly living creature. I was conscious of its departure as of its coming: an almost instantaneously swift going through the door, and the 'horrible sensation' disappeared.

"On the third night when I retired my mind was absorbed in some lectures which I was preparing, and I was still absorbed in these when I became aware of the actual presence (though not of the coming) of the thing that was there the night before, and of the 'horrible sensation.' I then mentally concentrated all my effort to charge this 'thing,' if it was evil, to depart, if it was not evil, to tell me who or what it was, and if it could not explain itself, to go, and that I would compel it to go. It went as on the previous night, and my body quickly recovered its normal state.

"On two other occasions in my life I have had precisely the same 'horrible sensation.' Once it lasted a full quarter of an hour. In all three instances the certainty that there in outward space there stood something was indescribably stronger than the ordinary certainty of companionship when we are in the close presence of ordinary living people. The something seemed close to me, and intensely more real than any ordinary perception. Although I felt it to be like unto myself, so to speak, or finite, small, and distressful, as it were, I didn't recognize it as any individual being or person."

Of course such an experience as this does not connect itself with the religious sphere. Yet it may upon occasion do so; and the same correspondent informs me that at more than one other conjuncture he had the sense of presence developed with equal intensity and abruptness, only then it was filled with a quality of joy.

"There was not a mere consciousness of something there, but fused in the central happiness of it, a startling awareness of some ineffable good. Not vague either, not like the emotional effect of some poem, or scene, or blossom, of music, but the sure knowledge of the close presence of a sort of mighty person, and after it went, the memory persisted as the one perception of reality. Everything else might be a dream, but not that."

My friend, as it oddly happens, does not interpret these latter experiences theistically, as signifying the presence of God. But it would clearly not have been unnatural to interpret them as a revelation of the deity's existence. When we reach the subject of mysticism, we shall have much more to say upon this head.

Lest the oddity of these phenomena should disconcert you, I will venture to read you a couple of similar narratives, much shorter, merely to show that we are dealing with a well-marked natural kind of fact. In the first case, which I take from the Journal of the Society for Psychical Research, the sense of presence developed in a few moments into a distinctly visualized hallucination,— but I leave that part of the story out.

"I had read," the narrator says, "some twenty minutes or so, was thoroughly absorbed in the book, my mind was perfectly quiet, and for the time being my friends were quite forgotten, when suddenly without a moment's warning my whole being seemed roused to the highest state of tension or aliveness, and I was aware, with an intenseness not easily imagined by those who had never experienced it, that another being or presence was not only in the room, but quite close to me. I put my book down, and although my excitement was great, I felt quite collected, and not conscious of any sense of fear. Without changing my position, and looking straight at the fire, I knew somehow that my friend A.H. was standing at my left elbow, but so far behind me as to be hidden by the armchair in which I was leaning back. Moving my eyes round slightly without otherwise changing my position, the lower portion of one leg became visible, and I instantly recognized the gray-blue material of trousers he often wore, but the stuff appeared semi-transparent, reminding me of tobacco smoke in consistency," and hereupon the visual hallucination came. [Journal of the S.P.R., February, 1895, p. 26.]

Another informant writes:—

"Quite early in the night I was awakened.... I felt as if I had been aroused intentionally, and at first thought some one was breaking into the house.... I then turned on my side to go to sleep again, and immediately felt a consciousness of a presence in the room, and singular to state, it was not the consciousness of a live person, but of a spiritual presence. This may provoke a smile, but I can only tell you the facts as they occurred to me. I do not know how to better describe my sensations than by simply stating that I felt a consciousness of a spiritual presence.... I felt also at the same time a strong feeling of superstitious dread, as if something strange and fearful were about to happen." [E. Gurney: Phantasms of the Living, i. 384.]

Professor Flournoy of Geneva gives me the following testimony of a friend of his, a lady, who has the gift of automatic or involuntary writing:

"Whenever I practice automatic writing, what makes me feel that it is not due to a subconscious self is the feeling I always have of a foreign presence, external to my body. It is sometimes so definitely characterized that I could point to its exact position. This impression of presence is impossible to describe. It varies in intensity and clearness according to the personality from whom the writing professes to come. If it is some one whom I love, I feel it immediately, before any writing has come. My heart seems to recognize it."

In an earlier book of mine I have cited at full length a curious case of presence felt by a blind man. The presence was that of the figure of a gray-bearded man dressed in a pepper and salt suit, squeezing himself under the crack of the door and moving across the floor of the room towards a sofa. The blind subject of this quasi-hallucination is an exceptionally intelligent reporter. He is entirely without internal visual imagery and cannot represent light or colors to himself, and is positive that his other senses, hearing, etc., were not involved in this false perception. It seems to have been an abstract conception rather, with the feelings of reality and spatial outwardness directly attached to it— in other words, a fully objectified and exteriorized idea.

Such cases, taken along with others which would be too tedious for quotation, seem sufficiently to prove the existence in our mental machinery of a sense of present reality more diffused and general than that which our special senses yield. For the psychologists the tracing of the organic seat of such a feeling would form a pretty problem— nothing could be more natural than to connect it with the muscular sense, with the feeling that our muscles were innervating themselves for action.

Whatsoever thus innervated our activity, or 'made our flesh creep,'— our senses are what do so oftenest,— might then appear real and present, even though it were but an abstract idea. But with such vague conjectures we have no concern at present, for our interest lies with the faculty rather than with its organic seat.

Like all positive affections of consciousness, the sense of reality has its negative counterpart in the shape of a feeling of unreality by which persons may be haunted, and of which one sometimes hears complaint:—

"When I reflect on the fact that I have made my appearance by accident upon a globe itself whirled through space as the sport of the catastrophes of the heavens," says Madame Ackermann; "when I see myself surrounded by beings as ephemeral and incomprehensible as I am myself, and all excitedly pursuing pure chimeras, I experience a strange feeling of being in a dream. It seems to me as if I have loved and suffered and that erelong I shall die, in a dream. My last word will be, 'I have been dreaming.'" [Pensees d'un Solitaire, p. 66.]

In another lecture we shall see how in morbid melancholy this sense of the unreality of things may become a carking pain, and even lead to suicide.

We may now lay it down as certain that in the distinctively religious sphere of experience, many persons (how many we cannot tell) possess the objects of their belief, not in the form of mere conceptions which their intellect accepts as true, but rather in the form of quasi-sensible realities directly apprehended. As his sense of the real presence of these objects fluctuates, so the believer alternates between warmth and coldness in his faith. Other examples will bring this home to one better than abstract description, so I proceed immediately to cite some. The first example is a negative one, deploring the loss of the sense in question. I have extracted it from an account given me by a scientific man of my acquaintance, of his religious life. It seems to me to show clearly that the feeling of reality may be something more like a sensation than an intellectual operation properly so-called.

"Between twenty and thirty I gradually became more and more agnostic and irreligious, yet I cannot say that I ever lost that 'indefinite consciousness' which Herbert Spencer describes so well, of an Absolute Reality behind phenomena. For me this Reality was not the pure Unknowable of Spencer's philosophy, for although I had ceased my childish prayers to God, and never prayed to It in a formal manner, yet my more recent experience shows me to have been in a relation to It which practically was the same thing as prayer. Whenever I had any trouble, especially when I had conflict with other people, either domestically or in the way of business, or when I was depressed in spirits or anxious about affairs, I now recognize that I used to fall back for support upon this curious relation I felt myself to be in to this fundamental cosmical It. It was on my side, or I was on Its side, however you please to term it, in the particular trouble, and it always strengthened me and seemed to give me endless vitality to feel its underlying and supporting presence. In fact, it was an unfailing fountain of living justice, truth, and strength, to which I instinctively turned at times of weakness, and it always brought me out. I know now that it was a personal relation I was in to it, because of late years the power of communicating with it has left me, and I am conscious of a perfectly definite loss. I used never to fail to find it when I turned to it. Then came a set of years when sometimes I found it, and then again I would be wholly unable to make connection with it. I remember many occasions on which at night in bed, I would be unable to get to sleep on account of worry. I turned this way and that in the darkness, and groped mentally for the familiar sense of that higher mind of my mind which had always seemed to be close at hand as it were, closing the passage, and yielding support, but there was no electric current. A blank was there instead of It: I couldn't find anything. Now, at the age of nearly fifty, my power of getting into connection with it has entirely left me; and I have to confess that a great help has gone out of my life. Life has become curiously dead and indifferent; and I can now see that my old experience was probably exactly the same thing as the prayers of the orthodox, only I did not call them by that name. What I have spoken of as 'It' was practically not Spencer's Unknowable, but just my own instinctive and individual God, whom I relied upon for higher sympathy, but whom somehow I have lost."

Nothing is more common in the pages of religious biography than the way in which seasons of lively and of difficult faith are described as alternating. Probably every religious person has the recollection of particular crises in which a directer vision of the truth, a direct perception, perhaps, of a living God's existence, swept in and overwhelmed the languor of the more ordinary belief. In James Russell Lowell's correspondence there is a brief memorandum of an experience of this kind:—

"I had a revelation last Friday evening. I was at Mary's, and happening to say something of the presence of spirits (of whom, I said, I was often dimly aware), Mr. Putnam entered into an argument with me on spiritual matters. As I was speaking, the whole system rose up before me like a vague destiny looming from the Abyss. I never before so clearly felt the Spirit of God in me and around me. The whole room seemed to me full of God. The air seemed to waver to and fro with the presence of Something I knew not what. I spoke with the calmness and clearness of a prophet. I cannot tell you what this revelation was. I have not yet studied it enough. But I shall perfect it one day, and then you shall hear it and acknowledge its grandeur." [Letters of Lowell, i. 75.]

Here is a longer and more developed experience from a manuscript communication by a clergyman,— I take it from Starbuck's manuscript collection:

"I remember the night, and almost the very spot on the hill-top, where my soul opened out, as it were, into the Infinite, and there was a rushing together of the two worlds, the inner and the outer. It was deep calling unto deep,— the deep that my own struggle had opened up within being answered by the unfathomable deep without, reaching beyond the stars. I stood alone with Him who had made me, and all the beauty of the world, and love, and sorrow, and even temptation. I did not seek Him, but felt the perfect unison of my spirit with His. The ordinary sense of things around me faded. For the moment nothing but an ineffable joy and exaltation remained. It is impossible fully to describe the experience. It was like the effect of some great orchestra when all the separate notes have melted into one swelling harmony that leaves the listener conscious of nothing save that his soul is being wafted upwards, and almost bursting with its own emotion. The perfect stillness of the night was thrilled by a more solemn silence. The darkness held a presence that was all the more felt because it was not seen. I could not any more have doubted that He was there than that I was. Indeed, I felt myself to be, if possible, the less real of the two.

"My highest faith in God and truest idea of him were then born in me. I have stood upon the Mount of Vision since, and felt the Eternal round about me. But never since has there come quite the same stirring of the heart. Then, if ever, I believe, I stood face to face with God, and was born anew of his spirit. There was, as I recall it, no sudden change of thought or of belief, except that my early crude conception had, as it were, burst into flower. There was no destruction of the old, but a rapid, wonderful unfolding. Since that time no discussion that I have heard of the proofs of God's existence has been able to shake my faith. Having once felt the presence of God's spirit, I have never lost it again for long. My most assuring evidence of his existence is deeply rooted in that hour of vision, in the memory of that supreme experience, and in the conviction, gained from reading and reflection, that something the same has come to all who have found God. I am aware that it may justly be called mystical. I am not enough acquainted with philosophy to defend it from that or any other charge. I feel that in writing of it I have overlaid it with words rather than put it clearly to your thought. But, such as it is, I have described it as carefully as I now am able to do."

Here is another document, even more definite in character, which, the writer being a Swiss, I translate from the French original. [I borrow it, with Professor Flournoy's permission, from his rich collection of psychological documents.]

"I was in perfect health: we were on our sixth day of tramping, and in good training. We had come the day before from Sixt to Trient by Buet. I felt neither fatigue, hunger, nor thirst, and my state of mind was equally healthy. I had had at Forlaz good news from home; I was subject to no anxiety, either near or remote, for we had a good guide, and there was not a shadow of uncertainty about the road we should follow. I can best describe the condition in which I was by calling it a state of equilibrium. When all at once I experienced a feeling, of being raised above myself, I felt the presence of God- I tell of the thing just as I was conscious of it— as if his goodness and his power were penetrating me altogether. The throb of emotion was so violent that I could barely tell the boys to pass on and not wait for me. I then sat down on a stone, unable to stand any longer, and my eyes overflowed with tears. I thanked God that in the course of my life he had taught me to know him, that he sustained my life and took pity both on the insignificant creature and on the sinner that I was. I begged him ardently that my life might be consecrated to the doing of his will. I felt his reply, which was that I should do his will from day to day, in humility and poverty, leaving him, the Almighty God, to be judge of whether I should some time be called to bear witness more conspicuously. Then, slowly, the ecstasy left my heart; that is, I felt that God had withdrawn the communion which he had granted, and I was able to walk on, but very slowly, so strongly was I still possessed by the interior emotion. Besides, I had wept uninterruptedly for several minutes, my eyes were swollen, and I did not wish my companions to see me. The state of ecstasy may have lasted four or five minutes, although it seemed at the time to last much longer. My comrades waited for me ten minutes at the cross of Barine, but I took about twenty-five or thirty minutes to join them, for as well as I can remember, they said that I had kept them back for about half an hour. The impression had been so profound that in climbing slowly the slope I asked myself if it were possible that Moses on Sinai could have had a more intimate communication with God. I think it well to add that in this ecstasy of mine God had neither form, color, odor, nor taste; moreover, that the feeling of his presence was accompanied with no determinate localization. It was rather as if my personality had been transformed by the presence of a spiritual spirit. But the more I seek words to express this intimate intercourse, the more I feel the impossibility of describing the thing by any of our usual images. At bottom the expression most apt to render what I felt is this: God was present, though invisible; he fell under no one of my senses, yet my consciousness perceived him."

The adjective 'mystical' is technically applied, most often, to states that are of brief duration. Of course such hours of rapture as the last two persons describe are mystical experiences, of which in a later lecture I shall have much to say. Meanwhile here is the abridged record of another mystical or semi-mystical experience, in a mind evidently framed by nature for ardent piety. I owe it to Starbuck's collection. The lady who gives the account is the daughter of a man well known in his time as a writer against Christianity. The suddenness of her conversion shows well how native the sense of God's presence must be to certain minds. She relates that she was brought up in entire ignorance of Christian doctrine, but, when in Germany, after being talked to by Christian friends, she read the Bible and prayed, and finally the plan of salvation flashed upon her like a stream of light.

"To this day," she writes, "I cannot understand dallying with religion and the commands of God. The very instant I heard my Father's cry calling unto me, my heart bounded in recognition. I ran, I stretched forth my arms, I cried aloud, 'Here, here I am, my Father.' Oh, happy child, what should I do? 'Love me,' answered my God. 'I do, I do,' I cried passionately. 'Come unto me,' called my Father. 'I will,' my heart panted. Did I stop to ask a single question? Not one. It never occurred to me to ask whether I was good enough, or to hesitate over my unfitness, or to find out what I thought of his church, or... to wait until I should be satisfied.

Satisfied! I was satisfied. Had I not found my God and my Father? Did he not love me? Had he not called me? Was there not a Church into which I might enter?... Since then I have had direct answers to prayer— so significant as to be almost like talking with God and hearing his answer. The idea of God's reality has never left me for one moment."

Here is still another case, the writer being a man aged twenty-seven, in which the experience, probably almost as characteristic, is less vividly described:

"I have on a number of occasions felt that I had enjoyed a period of intimate communion with the divine. These meetings came unasked and unexpected, and seemed to consist merely in the temporary obliteration of the conventionalities which usually surround and cover my life.... Once it was when from the summit of a high mountain I looked over a gashed and corrugated landscape extending to a long convex of ocean that ascended to the horizon, and again from the same point when I could see nothing beneath me but a boundless expanse of white cloud, on the blown surface of which a few high peaks, including the one I was on, seemed plunging about as if they were dragging their anchors. What I felt on these occasions was a temporary loss of my own identity, accompanied by an illumination which revealed to me a deeper significance than I had been wont to attach to life. It is in this that I find my justification for saying that I have enjoyed communication with God. Of course the absence of such a being as this would be chaos. I cannot conceive of life without its presence."

Of the more habitual and so to speak chronic sense of God's presence the following sample from Professor Starbuck's manuscript collection may serve to give an idea. It is from a man aged forty-nine,— probably thousands of unpretending Christians would write an almost identical account.

"God is more real to me than any thought or thing or person. I feel his presence positively, and the more as I live in closer harmony with his laws as written in my body and mind. I feel him in the sunshine or rain; and awe mingled with a delicious restfulness most nearly describes my feelings. I talk to him as to a companion in prayer and praise, and our communion is delightful. He answers me again and again, often in words so clearly spoken that it seems my outer ear must have carried the tone, but generally in strong mental impressions. Usually a text of Scripture, unfolding some new view of him and his love for me, and care for my safety. I could give hundreds of instances, in school matters, social problems, financial difficulties, etc. That he is mine and I am his never leaves me, it is an abiding joy. Without it life would be a blank, a desert, a shoreless, trackless waste."

I subjoin some more examples from writers of different ages and sexes. They are also from Professor Starbuck's collection, and their number might be greatly multiplied. The first is from a man twenty-seven years old:—

"God is quite real to me. I talk to him and often get answers. Thoughts sudden and distinct from any I have been entertaining come to my mind after asking God for his direction. Something over a year ago I was for some weeks in the direst perplexity. When the trouble first appeared before me I was dazed, but before long (two or three hours) I could hear distinctly a passage of Scripture: 'My grace is sufficient for thee.' Every time my thoughts turned to the trouble I could hear this quotation. I don't think I ever doubted the existence of God, or had him drop out of my consciousness. God has frequently stepped into my affairs very perceptibly, and I feel that he directs many little details all the time. But on two or three occasions he has ordered ways for me very contrary to my ambitions and plans."

Another statement (none the less valuable psychologically for being so decidedly childish) is that of a boy of seventeen:

"Sometimes as I go to church, I sit down, join in the service, and before I go out I feel as if God was with me, right side of me, singing and reading the Psalms with me.... And then again I feel as if I could sit beside him, and put my arms around him, kiss him, etc. When I am taking Holy Communion at the altar, I try to get with him and generally feel his presence.

I let a few other cases follow at random:

"God surrounds me like the physical atmosphere. He is closer to me than my own breath. In him literally I live and move and have my being."

"There are times when I seem to stand in his very presence, to talk with him. Answers to prayer have come, sometimes direct and overwhelming in their revelation of his presence and powers. There are times when God seems far off, but this is always my own fault."

"I have the sense of a presence, strong, and at the same time soothing, which hovers over me. Sometimes it seems to enwrap me with sustaining arms."

Such is the human ontological imagination, and such is the convincingness of what it brings to birth. Unpicturable beings are realized, and realized with an intensity almost like that of an hallucination. They determine our vital attitude as decisively as the vital attitude of lovers is determined by the habitual sense, by which each is haunted, of the other being in the world. A lover has notoriously this sense of the continuous being of his idol, even when his attention is addressed to other matters and he no longer represents her features. He cannot forget her; she uninterruptedly affects him through and through.

I spoke of the convincingness of these feelings of reality, and I must dwell a moment longer on that point. They are as convincing to those who have them as any direct sensible experiences can be, and they are, as a rule, much more convincing than results established by mere logic ever are. One may indeed be entirely without them; probably more than one of you here present is without them in any marked degree; but if you do have them, and have them at all strongly, the probability is that you cannot help regarding them as genuine perceptions of truth, as revelations of a kind of reality which no adverse argument, however unanswerable by you in words, can expel from your belief. The opinion opposed to mysticism in philosophy is sometimes spoken of as rationalism.

Rationalism insists that all our beliefs ought ultimately to find for themselves articulate grounds. Such grounds, for rationalism, must consist of four things: (1) definitely statable abstract principles; (2) definite facts of sensation; (3) definite hypotheses based on such facts; and (4) definite inferences logically drawn. Vague impressions of something indefinable have no place in the rationalistic system, which on its positive side is surely a splendid intellectual tendency, for not only are all our philosophies fruits of it, but physical science (amongst other good things) is its result.

Nevertheless, if we look on man's whole mental life as it exists, on the life of men that lies in them apart from their learning and science, and that they inwardly and privately follow, we have to confess that the part of it of which rationalism can give an account is relatively superficial. It is the part that has the prestige undoubtedly, for it has the loquacity, it can challenge you for proofs, and chop logic, and put you down with words. But it will fail to convince or convert you all the same, if your dumb intuitions are opposed to its conclusions. If you have intuitions at all, they come from a deeper level of your nature than the loquacious level which rationalism inhabits. Your whole subconscious life, your impulses, your faiths, your needs, your divinations, have prepared the premises, of which your consciousness now feels the weight of the result; and something in you absolutely knows that that result must be truer than any logic-chopping rationalistic talk, however clever, that may contradict it. This inferiority of the rationalistic level in founding belief is just as manifest when rationalism argues for religion as when it argues against it. That vast literature of proofs of God's existence drawn from the order of nature, which a century ago seemed so overwhelmingly convincing, today does little more than gather dust in libraries, for the simple reason that our generation has ceased to believe in the kind of God it argued for. Whatever sort of a being God may be, we know today that he is nevermore that mere external inventor of 'contrivances' intended to make manifest his 'glory' in which our great-grandfathers took such satisfaction, though just how we know this we cannot possibly make clear by words either to others or to ourselves. I defy any of you here fully to account for your persuasion that if a God exist he must be a more cosmic and tragic personage than that Being.

The truth is that in the metaphysical and religious sphere, articulate reasons are cogent for us only when our inarticulate feelings of reality have already been impressed in favor of the same conclusion. Then, indeed, our intuitions and our reason work together, and great world-ruling systems, like that of the Buddhist or of the Catholic philosophy, may grow up. Our impulsive belief is here always what sets up the original body of truth, and our articulately verbalized philosophy is but its showy translation into formulas. The unreasoned and immediate assurance is the deep thing in us, the reasoned argument is but a surface exhibition. Instinct leads, intelligence does but follow. If a person feels the presence of a living God after the fashion shown by my quotations, your critical arguments, be they never so superior, will vainly set themselves to change his faith.

Please observe, however, that I do not yet say that it is better that the subconscious and non-rational should thus hold primacy in the religious realm. I confine myself to simply pointing out that they do so hold it as a matter of fact.

So much for our sense of the reality of the religious objects. Let me now say a brief word more about the attitudes they characteristically awaken.

We have already agreed that they are solemn; and we have seen reason to think that the most distinctive of them is the sort of joy which may result in extreme cases from absolute self-surrender. The sense of the kind of object to which the surrender is made has much to do with determining the precise complexion of the joy; and the whole phenomenon is more complex than any simple formula allows. In the literature of the subject, sadness and gladness have each been emphasized in turn. The ancient saying that the first maker of the Gods was fear receives voluminous corroboration from every age of religious history; but none the less does religious history show the part which joy has evermore tended to play. Sometimes the joy has been primary; sometimes secondary, being the gladness of deliverance from the fear. This latter state of things, being the more complex, is also the more complete; and as we proceed, I think we shall have abundant reason for refusing to leave out either the sadness or the gladness, if we look at religion with the breadth of view which it demands. Stated in the completest possible terms, a man's religion involves both moods of contraction and moods of expansion of his being. But the quantitative mixture and order of these moods vary so much from one age of the world, from one system of thought, and from one individual to another, that you may insist either on the dread and the submission, or on the peace and the freedom as the essence of the matter, and still remain materially within the limits of the truth. The constitutionally sombre and the constitutionally sanguine onlooker are bound to emphasize opposite aspects of what lies before their eyes.

The constitutionally sombre religious person makes even of his religious peace a very sober thing. Danger still hovers in the air about it. Flexion and contraction are not wholly checked. It were sparrowlike and childish after our deliverance to explode into twittering laughter and caper-cutting, and utterly to forget the imminent hawk on bough. Lie low, rather, lie low; for you are in the hands of a living God. In the Book of Job, for example, the impotence of man and the omnipotence of God is the exclusive burden of its author's mind. "It is as high as heaven; what canst thou do?— deeper than hell; what canst thou know?" There is an astringent relish about the truth of this conviction which some men can feel, and which for them is as near an approach as can be made to the feeling of religious joy.

"In Job," says that coldly truthful writer, the author of Mark Rutherford, "God reminds us that man is not the measure of his creation. The world is immense, constructed on no plan or theory which the intellect of man can grasp. It is transcendent everywhere. This is the burden of every verse, and is the secret, if there be one, of the poem. Sufficient or insufficient, there is nothing more.... God is great, we know not his ways. He takes from us all we have, but yet if we possess our souls in patience, we may pass the valley of the shadow, and come out in sunlight again. We may or we may not!... What more have we to say now than God said from the whirlwind over two thousand five hundred years ago?" [Mark Rutherford's Deliverance, London, 1885, pp. 196, 198.]

If we turn to the sanguine onlooker, on the other hand, we find that deliverance is felt as incomplete unless the burden be altogether overcome and the danger forgotten. Such onlookers give us definitions that seem to the sombre minds of whom we have just been speaking to leave out all the solemnity that makes religious peace so different from merely animal joys. In the opinion of some writers an attitude might be called religious, though no touch were left in it of sacrifice or submission, no tendency to flexion, no bowing of the head. Any "habitual and regulated admiration," says Professor J.R. Seeley, "is worthy to be called a religion"; and accordingly he thinks that our Music, our Science, and our so-called 'Civilization,' as these things are now organized and admiringly believed in, form the more genuine religions of our time. [In his book (too little read, I fear), Natural Religion, 3d edition, Boston, 1886, pp. 91, 122.] Certainly the unhesitating and unreasoning way in which we feel that we must inflict our civilization upon 'lower' races, by means of Hotchkiss guns, etc., reminds one of nothing so much as of the early spirit of Islam spreading its religion by the sword.

In my last lecture I quoted to you the ultra-radical opinion of Mr. Havelock Ellis, that laughter of any sort may be considered a religious exercise, for it bears witness to the soul's emancipation. I quoted this opinion in order to deny its adequacy. But we must now settle our scores more carefully with this whole optimistic way of thinking. It is far too complex to be decided off-hand. I propose accordingly that we make of religious optimism the theme of the next two lectures.

LECTURES IV AND V: THE RELIGION OF HEALTHY-MINDEDNESS

If we were to ask the question: 'What is human life's chief concern?' one of the answers we should receive would be: 'It is happiness.' How to gain, how to keep, how to recover happiness, is in fact for most men at all times the secret motive of all they do, and of all they are willing to endure. The hedonistic school in ethics deduces the moral life wholly from the experiences of happiness and unhappiness which different kinds of conduct bring; and, even more in the religious life than in the moral life, happiness and unhappiness seem to be the poles round which the interest revolves. We need not go so far as to say with the author whom I lately quoted that any persistent enthusiasm is, as such, religion, nor need we call mere laughter a religious exercise; but we must admit that any persistent enjoyment may produce the sort of religion which consists in a grateful admiration of the gift of so happy an existence; and we must also acknowledge that the more complex ways of experiencing religion are new manners of producing happiness, wonderful inner paths to a supernatural kind of happiness, when the first gift of natural existence is unhappy, as it so often proves itself to be.

With such relations between religion and happiness, it is perhaps not surprising that men come to regard the happiness which a religious belief affords as a proof of its truth. If a creed makes a man feel happy, he almost inevitably adopts it. Such a belief ought to be true; therefore it is true— such, rightly or wrongly, is one of the 'immediate inferences' of the religious logic used by ordinary men.

"The near presence of God's spirit," says a German writer, "may be experienced in its reality— indeed only experienced. And the mark by which the spirit's existence and nearness are made irrefutably clear to those who have ever had the experience is the utterly incomparable feeling of happiness which is connected with the nearness, and which is therefore not only a possible and altogether proper feeling for us to have here below, but is the best and most indispensable proof of God's reality. No other proof is equally convincing, and therefore happiness is the point from which every efficacious new theology should start." [C. Hilty: Gluck, dritter Theil, 1900, p. 18.]

In the hour immediately before us, I shall invite you to consider the simpler kinds of religious happiness, leaving the more complex sorts to be treated on a later day.

In many persons, happiness is congenital and irreclaimable. 'Cosmic emotion' inevitably takes in them the form of enthusiasm and freedom. I speak not only of those who are animally happy. I mean those who, when unhappiness is offered or proposed to them, positively refuse to feel it, as if it were something mean and wrong. We find such persons in every age, passionately flinging themselves upon their sense of the goodness of life, in spite of the hardships of their own condition, and is spite of the sinister theologies into which they may be born. From the outset their religion is one of union with the divine. The heretics who went before the reformation are lavishly accused by the church writers of antinomian practices, just as the first Christians were accused of indulgence in orgies by the Romans. It is probable that there never has been a century in which the deliberate refusal to think ill of life has not been idealized by a sufficient number of persons to form sects, open or secret, who claimed all natural things to be permitted. Saint Augustine's maxim, Dilige et quod vis fac,— if you but love [God], you may do as you incline,— is morally one of the profoundest of observations, yet it is pregnant, for such persons, with passports beyond the bounds of conventional morality. According to their characters they have been refined or gross; but their belief has been at all times systematic enough to constitute a definite religious attitude. God was for them a giver of freedom, and the sting of evil was overcome. Saint Francis and his immediate disciples were, on the whole, of this company of spirits, of which there are of course infinite varieties. Rousseau in the earlier years of his writing, Diderot, B. de Saint Pierre, and many of the leaders of the eighteenth century anti-christian movement were of this optimistic type. They owed their influence to a certain authoritativeness in their feeling that Nature, if you will only trust her sufficiently, is absolutely good.

It is to be hoped that we all have some friend, perhaps more often feminine than masculine, and young than old, whose soul is of this sky-blue tint, whose affinities are rather with flowers and birds and all enchanting innocencies than with dark human passions, who can think no ill of man or God, and in whom religious gladness, being in possession from the outset, needs no deliverance from any antecedent burden.

"God has two families of children on this earth," says Francis W. Newman, [The Soul; its Sorrows and its Aspirations, 3d edition, 1852, pp. 89, 91.] "the once-born and the twice-born," and the once-born he describes as follows: "They see God, not as a strict Judge, not as a Glorious Potentate; but as the animating Spirit of a beautiful harmonious world, Beneficent and Kind, Merciful as well as Pure. The same characters generally have no metaphysical tendencies: they do not look back into themselves. Hence they are not distressed by their own imperfections: yet it would be absurd to call them self-righteous; for they hardly think of themselves at all. This childlike quality of their nature makes the opening of religion very happy to them: for they no more shrink from God, than a child from an emperor, before whom the parent trembles: in fact, they have no vivid conception of any of the qualities in which the severer Majesty of God consists. He is to them the impersonation of Kindness and Beauty. They read his character, not in the disordered world of man, but in romantic and harmonious nature. Of human sin they know perhaps little in their own hearts and not very much in the world; and human suffering does but melt them to tenderness. Thus, when they approach God, no inward disturbance ensues; and without being as yet spiritual, they have a certain complacency and perhaps romantic sense of excitement in their simple worship." [I once heard a lady describe the pleasure it gave her to think that she "could always cuddle up to God."]

In the Romish Church such characters find a more congenial soil to grow in than in Protestantism, whose fashions of feeling have been set by minds of a decidedly pessimistic order. But even in Protestantism they have been abundant enough; and in its recent 'liberal' developments of Unitarianism and latitudinarianism generally, minds of this order have played and still are playing leading and constructive parts. Emerson himself is an admirable example. Theodore Parker is another,— here are a couple of characteristic passages from Parker's correspondence. [John Weiss: Life of Theodore Parker, i. 152, 32.]

"Orthodox scholars say: 'In the heathen classics you find no consciousness of sin.' It is very true- God be thanked for it. They were conscious of wrath, of cruelty, avarice, drunkenness, lust, sloth, cowardice, and other actual vices, and struggled and got rid of the deformities, but they were not conscious of 'enmity against God,' and didn't sit down and whine and groan against non-existent evil. I have done wrong things enough in my life, and do them now; I miss the mark, draw bow, and try again. But I am not conscious of hating God, or man, or right, or love, and I know there is much 'health in me'; and in any body, even now, there dwelleth many a good thing, spite of consumption and Saint Paul." In another letter Parker writes: "I have swum in clear sweet waters all my days; and if sometimes they were a little cold, and the stream ran adverse and something rough, it was never too strong to be breasted and swum through. From the days of earliest boyhood, when I went stumbling through the grass,... up to the gray-bearded manhood of this time, there is none but has left me honey in the hive of memory that I now feed on for present delight, When I recall the years... I am filled with a sense of sweetness and wonder that such little things can make a mortal so exceedingly rich. But I must confess that the chiefest of all my delights is still the religious."

Another good expression of the 'once-born' type of consciousness, developing straight and natural, with no element of morbid compunction or crisis, is contained in the answer of Dr. Edward Everett Hale, the eminent Unitarian preacher and writer, to one of Dr. Starbuck's circulars. I quote a part of it:

"I observe, with profound regret, the religious struggles which come into many biographies, as if almost essential to the formation of the hero. I ought to speak of these, to say that any man has an advantage, not to be estimated, who is born, as I was, into a family where the religion is simple and rational; who is trained in the theory of such a religion, so that he never knows, for an hour, what these religious or irreligious struggles are. I always knew God loved me, and I was always grateful to him for the world he placed me in. I always liked to tell him so, and was always glad to receive his suggestions to me.... I can remember perfectly that when I was coming to manhood, the half-philosophical novels of the time had a deal to say about the young men and maidens who were facing the 'problem of life.' I had no idea whatever what the problem of life was. To live with all my might seemed to me easy; to learn where there was so much to learn seemed pleasant and almost of course; to lend a hand, if one had a chance, natural; and if one did this, why, he enjoyed life because he could not help it, and without proving to himself that he ought to enjoy it.... A child who is early taught that he is God's child, that he may live and move and have his being in God, and that he has, therefore, infinite strength at hand for the conquering of any difficulty, will take life more easily, and probably will make more of it, than one who is told that he is born the child of wrath and wholly incapable of good." [Starbuck: Psychology of Religion, pp. 305, 306.]

One can but recognize in such writers as these the presence of a temperament organically weighted on the side of cheer and fatally forbidden to linger, as those of opposite temperament linger, over the darker aspects of the universe. In some individuals optimism may become quasi-pathological. The capacity for even a transient sadness or a momentary humility seems cut off from them as by a kind of congenital anaesthesia.

"I know not to what physical laws philosophers will some day refer the feelings of melancholy. For myself, I find that they are the most voluptuous of all sensations," writes Saint Pierre, and accordingly he devotes a series of sections of his work on Nature to the Plaisirs de la Ruine, Plaisirs des Tombeaux, Ruines de la Nature, Plaisirs de la Solitude— each of them more optimistic than the last.

This finding of a luxury in woe is very common during adolescence. The truth-telling Marie Bashkirtseff expresses it well:

"In this depression and dreadful uninterrupted suffering, I don't condemn life. On the contrary, I like it and find it good. Can you believe it? I find everything good and pleasant, even my tears, my grief. I enjoy weeping, I enjoy my despair. I enjoy being exasperated and sad. I feel as if these were so many diversions, and I love life in spite of them all. I want to live on. It would be cruel to have me die when I am so accommodating. I cry, I grieve, and at the same time I am pleased— no, not exactly that— I know not how to express it. But everything in life pleases me. I find everything agreeable, and in the very midst of my prayers for happiness, I find myself happy at being miserable. It is not I who undergo all this— my body weeps and cries; but something inside of me which is above me is glad of it all." Journal de Marie Bashkirtseff, i. 67.

The supreme contemporary example of such an inability to feel evil is of course Walt Whitman.

"His favorite occupation," writes his disciple, Dr. Bucke, seemed to be strolling or sauntering about outdoors by himself, looking at the grass, the trees, the flowers, the vistas of light, the varying aspects of the sky, and listening to the birds, the crickets, the tree frogs, and all the hundreds of natural sounds. It was evident that these things gave him a pleasure far beyond what they give to ordinary people. Until I knew the man," continues Dr. Bucke, "it had not occurred to me that any one could derive so much absolute happiness from these things as be did. He was very fond of flowers, either wild or cultivated; liked all sorts. I think he admired lilacs and sunflowers just as much as roses. Perhaps, indeed, no man who ever lived liked so many things and disliked so few as Walt Whitman. All natural objects seemed to have a charm for him. All sights and sounds seemed to please him. He appeared to like (and I believe he did like) all the men, women, and children he saw (though I never knew him to say that he liked any one), but each who knew him felt that he liked him or her, and that he liked others also. I never knew him to argue or dispute, and he never spoke about money. He always justified, sometimes playfully, sometimes quite seriously, those who spoke harshly of himself or his writings, and I often thought he even took pleasure in the opposition of enemies. When I first knew [him], I used to think that he watched himself, and would not allow his tongue to give expression to fretfulness, antipathy, complaint, and remonstrance. It did not occur to me as possible that these mental states could be absent in him. After long observation, however, I satisfied myself that such absence or unconsciousness was entirely real. He never spoke deprecatingly of any nationality or class of men, or time in the world's history, or against any trades or occupations— not even against any animals, insects, or inanimate things, nor any of the laws of nature, nor any of the results of those laws, such as illness, deformity, and death. He never complained or grumbled either at the weather, pain, illness, or anything else. He never swore. He could not very well, since he never spoke in anger and apparently never was angry. He never exhibited fear, and I do not believe he ever felt It." [R.M. Bucke: Cosmic Consciousness, pp. 182-186, abridged.]

Walt Whitman owes his importance in literature to the systematic expulsion from his writings of all contractile elements. The only sentiments he allowed himself to express were of the expansive order; and he expressed these in the first person, not as your mere monstrously conceited individual might so express them, but vicariously for all men, so that a passionate and mystic ontological emotion suffuses his words, and ends by persuading the reader that men and women, life and death, and all things are divinely good.

Thus it has come about that many persons today regard Walt Whitman as the restorer of the eternal natural religion. He has infected them with his own love of comrades, with his own gladness that he and they exist. Societies are actually formed for his cult; a periodical organ exists for its propagation, in which the lines of orthodoxy and heterodoxy are already beginning to be drawn; hymns are written by others in his peculiar prosody; and he is even explicitly compared with the founder of the Christian religion, not altogether to the advantage of the latter.

Whitman is often spoken of as a 'pagan.' The word nowadays means sometimes the mere natural animal man without a sense of sin; sometimes it means a Greek or Roman with his own peculiar religious consciousness. In neither of these senses does it fitly define this poet. He is more than your mere animal man who has not tasted of the tree of good and evil. He is aware enough of sin for a swagger to be present in his indifference towards it, a conscious pride in his freedom from flexions and contractions, which your genuine pagan in the first sense of the word would never show.

"I could turn and live with animals, they are so placid and self-contained,

I stand and look at them long and long;

They do not sweat and whine about their condition.

They do not lie awake in the dark and weep for their sins.

Not one is dissatisfied, not one is demented with the mania of owning things,

Not one kneels to another, nor to his kind that lived thousands of years ago

Not one is respectable or unhappy over the whole earth." [Song of Myself.]

No natural pagan could have written these well-known lines. But on the other hand Whitman is less than a Greek or Roman; for their consciousness, even in Homeric times, was full to the brim of the sad mortality of this sunlit world, and such a consciousness Walt Whitman resolutely refuses to adopt. When, for example, Achilles, about to slay Lycaon, Priam's young son, hears him sue for mercy, he stops to say:

"Ah, friend, thou too must die: why thus lamentest thou? Patroclos too is dead, who was better far than thou.... Over me too hang death and forceful fate. There cometh morn or eve or some noonday when my life too some man shall take in battle, whether with spear he smite, or arrow from the string." [Iliad, XXI., E. Myers's translation.]

Then Achilles savagely severs the poor boy's neck with his sword, heaves him by the foot into the Scamander, and calls to the fishes of the river to eat the white fat of Lycaon. Just as here the cruelty and the sympathy each ring true, and do not mix or interfere with one another, so did the Greeks and Romans keep all their sadnesses and gladnesses unmingled and entire. Instinctive good they did not reckon sin; nor had they any such desire to save the credit of the universe as to make them insist, as so many of us insist, that what immediately appears as evil must be 'good in the making,' or something equally ingenious. Good was good, and bad just bad, for the earlier Greeks. They neither denied the ills of nature,— Walt Whitman's verse, 'What is called good is perfect and what is called bad is just as perfect,' would have been mere silliness to them,— nor did they, in order to escape from those ills, invent 'another and a better world' of the imagination, in which, along with the ills, the innocent goods of sense would also find no place. This integrity of the instinctive reactions, this freedom from all moral sophistry and strain, gives a pathetic dignity to ancient pagan feeling. And this quality Whitman's outpourings have not got. His optimism is too voluntary and defiant; his gospel has a touch of bravado and an affected twist, and this diminishes its effect on many readers who yet are well disposed towards optimism, and on the whole quite willing to admit that in important respects Whitman is of the genuine lineage of the prophets.

"God is afraid of me!" remarked such a titanic-optimistic friend in my presence one morning when he was feeling particularly hearty and cannibalistic. The defiance of the phrase showed that a Christian education in humility still rankled in his breast.

If, then, we give the name of healthy-mindedness to the tendency which looks on all things and sees that they are good, we find that we must distinguish between a more involuntary and a more voluntary or systematic way of being healthy-minded. In its involuntary variety, healthy mindedness is a way of feeling happy about things immediately. In its systematical variety, it is an abstract way of conceiving things as good. Every abstract way of conceiving things selects some one aspect of them as their essence for the time being, and disregards the other aspects. Systematic healthy-mindedness, conceiving good as the essential and universal aspect of being, deliberately excludes evil from its field of vision; and although, when thus nakedly stated, this might seem a difficult feat to perform for one who is intellectually sincere with himself and honest about facts, a little reflection shows that the situation is too complex to lie open to so simple a criticism.

In the first place, happiness, like every other emotional state, has blindness and insensibility to opposing facts given it as its instinctive weapon for self-protection against disturbance. When happiness is actually in possession, the thought of evil can no more acquire the feeling of reality than the thought of good can gain reality when melancholy rules. To the man actively happy, from whatever cause, evil simply cannot then and there be believed in. He must ignore it; and to the bystander he may then seem perversely to shut his eyes to it and hush it up.

But more than this: the hushing of it up may, in a perfectly candid and honest mind, grow into a deliberate religious policy, or parti pris. Much of what we call evil is due entirely to the way men take the phenomenon. It can so often be converted into a bracing and tonic good by a simple change of the sufferer's inner attitude from one of fear to one of fight; its sting so often departs and turns into a relish when, after vainly seeking to shun it, we agree to face about and bear it cheerfully, that a man is simply bound in honor, with reference to many of the facts that seem at first to disconcert his peace, to adopt this way of escape. Refuse to admit their badness; despise their power; ignore their presence; turn your attention the other way; and so far as you yourself are concerned at any rate, though the facts may still exist, their evil character exists no longer. Since you make them evil or good by your own thoughts about them, it is the ruling of your thoughts which proves to be your principal concern.

The deliberate adoption of an optimistic turn of mind thus makes its entrance into philosophy. And once in, it is hard to trace its lawful bounds. Not only does the human instinct for happiness, bent on self-protection by ignoring, keep working in its favor, but higher inner ideals have weighty words to say. The attitude of unhappiness is not only painful, it is mean and ugly. What can be more base and unworthy than the pining, puling, mumping mood, no matter by what outward ills it may have been engendered? What is more injurious to others? What less helpful as a way out of the difficulty? It but fastens and perpetuates the trouble which occasioned it, and increases the total evil of the situation. At all costs, then, we ought to reduce the sway of that mood; we ought to scout it in ourselves and others, and never show it tolerance. But it is impossible to carry on this discipline in the subjective sphere without zealously emphasizing the brighter and minimizing the darker aspects of the objective sphere of things at the same time. And thus our resolution not to indulge in misery, beginning at a comparatively small point within ourselves, may not stop until it has brought the entire frame of reality under a systematic conception optimistic enough to be congenial with its needs.

In all this I say nothing of any mystical insight or persuasion that the total frame of things absolutely must be good. Such mystical persuasion plays an enormous part in the history of the religious consciousness, and we must look at it later with some care. But we need not go so far at present. More ordinary non-mystical conditions of rapture suffice for my immediate contention. All invasive moral states and passionate enthusiasms make one feelingless to evil in some direction. The common penalties cease to deter the patriot, the usual prudences are flung by the lover to the winds. When the passion is extreme, suffering may actually be gloried in, provided it be for the ideal cause, death may lose its sting, the grave its victory. In these states, the ordinary contrast of good and ill seems to be swallowed up in a higher denomination, an omnipotent excitement which engulfs the evil, and which the human being welcomes as the crowning experience of his life. This, he says, is truly to live, and I exult in the heroic opportunity and adventure.

The systematic cultivation of healthy-mindedness as a religious attitude is therefore consonant with important currents in human nature, and is anything but absurd. In fact, we all do cultivate it more or less, even when our professed theology should in consistency forbid it. We divert our attention from disease and death as much as we can; and the slaughter-houses and indecencies without end on which our life is founded are huddled out of sight and never mentioned, so that the world we recognize officially in literature and in society is a poetic fiction far handsomer and cleaner and better than the world that really is.

"As I go on in this life, day by day, I become more of a bewildered child; I cannot get used to this world, to procreation, to heredity, to sight, to hearing; the commonest things are a burthen. The prim, obliterated, polite surface of life, and the broad, bawdy, and orgiastic— or monadic foundations, form a spectacle to which no habit reconciles me." [R.L. Stevenson: Letters, ii. 355.]

The advance of liberalism, so-called, in Christianity, during the past fifty years, may fairly be called a victory of healthy-mindedness within the church over the morbidness with which the old hell-fire theology was more harmoniously related. We have now whole congregations whose preachers, far from magnifying our consciousness of sin, seem devoted rather to making little of it. They ignore, or even deny, eternal punishment, and insist on the dignity rather than on the depravity of man. They look at the continual preoccupation of the old-fashioned Christian with the salvation of his soul as something sickly and reprehensible rather than admirable; and a sanguine and 'muscular' attitude, which to our forefathers would have seemed purely heathen, has become in their eyes an ideal element of Christian character. I am not asking whether or not they are right, I am only pointing out the change.

The persons to whom I refer have still retained for the most part their nominal connection with Christianity, in spite of their discarding of its more pessimistic theological elements. But in that 'theory of evolution' which, gathering momentum for a century, has within the past twenty-five years swept so rapidly over Europe and America, we see the ground laid for a new sort of religion of Nature, which has entirely displaced Christianity from the thought of a large part of our generation. The idea of a universal evolution lends itself to a doctrine of general meliorism and progress which fits the religious needs of the healthy-minded so well that it seems almost as if it might have been created for their use. Accordingly we find 'evolutionism' interpreted thus optimistically and embraced as a substitute for the religion they were born in, by a multitude of our contemporaries who have either been trained scientifically, or been fond of reading popular science, and who had already begun to be inwardly dissatisfied with what seemed to them the harshness and irrationality of the orthodox Christian scheme. As examples are better than descriptions, I will quote a document received in answer to Professor Starbuck's circular of questions. The writer's state of mind may by courtesy be called a religion, for it is his reaction on the whole nature of things, it is systematic and reflective, and it loyally binds him to certain inner ideals. I think you will recognize in him, coarse-meated and incapable of wounded spirit as he is, a sufficiently familiar contemporary type.

Q. What does Religion mean to you?

A. It means nothing; and it seems, so far as I can observe, useless to others. I am sixty-seven years of age and have resided in X. fifty years, and have been in business forty-five, consequently I have some little experience of life and men, and some women too, and I find that the most religious and pious people are as a rule those most lacking in uprightness and morality. The men who do not go to church or have any religious convictions are the best. Praying, singing of hymns, and sermonizing are pernicious— they teach us to rely on some supernatural power, when we ought to rely on ourselves. I teetotally disbelieve in a God. The God-idea was begotten in ignorance, fear, and a general lack of any knowledge of Nature. If I were to die now, being in a healthy condition for my age, both mentally and physically, I would just as lief, yes, rather, die with a hearty enjoyment of music, sport, or any other rational pastime. As a timepiece stops, we die— there being no immortality in either case.

Q. What comes before your mind corresponding to the words God, Heaven, Angels, etc.?

A. Nothing whatever. I am a man without a religion. These words mean so much mythic bosh.

Q. Have you had any experience which appeared providential?

A. None whatever. There is no agency of the superintending kind. A little judicious observation as well as knowledge of scientific law will convince any one of this fact.

Q. What things work most strongly on your emotions?

A. Lively songs and music; Pinafore instead of an Oratorio. I like Scott, Burns, Byron, Longfellow, especially Shakespeare, etc., etc. Of songs, the Star-spangled Banner, America, Marseillaise, and all moral and soul-stirring songs, but wishy-washy hymns are my detestation. I greatly enjoy nature, especially fine weather, and until within a few years used to walk Sundays into the country, twelve miles often, with no fatigue, and bicycle forty or fifty. I have dropped the bicycle. I never go to church, but attend lectures when there are any good ones. All of my thoughts and cogitations have been of a healthy and cheerful kind, for instead of doubts and fears I see things as they are, for I endeavor to adjust myself to my environment. This I regard as the deepest law. Mankind is a progressive animal. I am satisfied he will have made a great advance over his present status a thousand years hence.

Q. What is your notion of sin?

A. It seems to me that sin is a condition, a disease, incidental to man's development not being yet advanced enough. Morbidness over it increases the disease. We should think that a million of years hence equity, justice, and mental and physical good order will be so fixed and organized that no one will have any idea of evil or sin.

Q. What is your temperament?

A. Nervous, active, wide-awake, mentally and physically. Sorry that Nature compels us to sleep at all.

If we are in search of a broken and a contrite heart, clearly we need not look to this brother. His contentment with the finite incases him like a lobster-shell and shields him from all morbid repining at his distance from the Infinite. We have in him an excellent example of the optimism which may be encouraged by popular science.

To my mind a current far more important and interesting religiously than that which sets in from natural science towards healthy-mindedness is that which has recently poured over America and seems to be gathering force every day,— I am ignorant what foothold it may yet have acquired in Great Britain,— and to which, for the sake of having a brief designation, I will give the title of the 'Mind-cure movement.' There are various sects of this 'New Thought,' to use another of the names by which it calls itself; but their agreements are so profound that their differences may be neglected for my present purpose, and I will treat the movement, without apology, as if it were a simple thing.

It is a deliberately optimistic scheme of life, with both a speculative and a practical side. In its gradual development during the last quarter of a century, it has taken up into itself a number of contributory elements, and it must now be reckoned with as a genuine religious power. It has reached the stage, for example, when the demand for its literature is great enough for insincere stuff mechanically produced for the market, to be to a certain extent supplied by publishers,— a phenomenon never observed, I imagine, until a religion has got well past its earliest insecure beginnings.

One of the doctrinal sources of Mind-cure is the four Gospels; another is Emersonianism or New England transcendentalism; another is Berkeleyan idealism; another is spiritism, with its messages of 'law' and 'progress' and 'development'; another the optimistic popular science evolutionism of which I have recently spoken; and, finally, Hinduism has contributed a strain. But the most characteristic feature of the mind-cure movement is an inspiration much more direct. The leaders in this faith have had an intuitive belief in the all-saving power of healthy-minded attitudes as such, in the conquering efficacy of courage, hope, and trust, and a correlative contempt for doubt, fear, worry, and all nervously precautionary states of mind. Their belief has in a general way been corroborated by the practical experience of their disciples; and this experience forms today a mass imposing in amount. ['Cautionary Verses for Children': this title of a much used work, published early in the nineteenth century, shows how far the muse of evangelical protestantism in England, with her mind fixed on the idea of danger, had at last drifted away from the original gospel freedom. Mind-care might be briefly called a reaction against all that religion of chronic anxiety which marked the earlier part of our century in the evangelical circles of England and America.]

The blind have been made to see, the halt to walk; lifelong invalids have had their health restored. The moral fruits have been no less remarkable. The deliberate adoption of a healthy-minded attitude has proved possible to many who never supposed they had it in them; regeneration of character has gone on on an extensive scale; and cheerfulness has been restored to countless homes. The indirect influence of this has been great. The mind-cure principles are beginning so to pervade the air that one catches their spirit at second-hand. One hears of the 'Gospel of Relaxation' of the 'Don't Worry Movement,' of people who repeat to themselves, 'Youth, health, vigor!' when dressing in the morning, as their motto for the day. Complaints of the weather are getting to be forbidden in many households; and more and more people are recognizing it to be bad form to speak of disagreeable sensations, or to make much of the ordinary inconveniences and ailments of life. These general tonic effects on public opinion would be good even if the more striking results were non-existent. But the latter abound so that we can afford to overlook the innumerable failures and self-deceptions that are mixed in with them (for in everything human failure is a matter of course), and we can also overlook the verbiage of a good deal of the mind-cure literature, some of which is so moonstruck with optimism and so vaguely expressed that an academically trained intellect finds it almost impossible to read it at all.

The plain fact remains that the spread of the movement has been due to practical fruits, and the extremely practical turn of character of the American people has never been better shown than by the fact that this,

their only decidedly original contribution to the systematic philosophy of
life, should be so intimately knit up with concrete therapeutics. To the
importance of mind-cure the medical and clerical professions in the
United States are beginning, though with much recalcitrancy and
protesting, to open their eyes. It is evidently bound to develop still farther,
both speculatively and practically, and its latest writers are far and away
the ablest of the group. [I refer to Mr. Horatio W. Dresser and Mr. Henry
Wood, especially the former. Mr. Dresser's works are published by G.P.
Putnam's Sons, New York and London; Mr. Wood's by Lee & Shepard,
Boston.] It matters nothing that, just as there are hosts of persons who
cannot pray, so there are greater hosts who cannot by any possibility be
influenced by the mind-curers' ideas. For our immediate purpose, the
important point is that so large a number should exist who can be so
influenced. They form a psychic type to be studied with respect.

Lest my own testimony be suspected, I will quote another reporter, Dr.
H.H. Goddard, of Clark University, whose thesis on "the Effects of Mind
on Body as evidenced by Faith Cures" is published in the American
Journal of Psychology for 1899 (vol. x.). This critic, after a wide study of
the facts, concludes that the cures by mind-cure exist, but are in no
respect different from those now officially recognized in medicine as cures
by suggestion; and the end of his essay contains an interesting
physiological speculation as to the way in which the suggestive ideas may
work. As regards the general phenomenon of mental cure itself, Dr.
Goddard writes: "In spite of the severe criticism we have made of reports
of cure, there still remains a vast amount of material, showing a powerful
influence of the mind in disease. Many cases are of diseases that have
been diagnosed and treated by the best physicians of the country, or
which prominent hospitals have tried their hand at curing, but without
success. People of culture and education have been treated by this method
with satisfactory results. Diseases of long standing have been
ameliorated, and even cured.... We have traced the mental element
through primitive medicine and folk-medicine of today, patent medicine,
and witchcraft. We are convinced that it is impossible to account for the
existence of these practices, if they did not cure disease, and that if they
cured disease, it must have been the mental element that was effective.
The same argument applies to those modern schools of mental
therapeutics— Divine Healing and Christian Science. It is hardly
conceivable that the large body of intelligent people who comprise the
body known distinctively as Mental Scientists should continue to exist if
the whole thing were a delusion. It is not a thing of a day; it is not
confined to a few; it is not local. It is true that many failures are recorded,
but that only adds to the argument. There must be many and striking
successes to counterbalance the failures, otherwise the failures would
have ended the delusion.... Christian Science, Divine Healing, or Mental
Science do not, and never can in the very nature of things, cure all
diseases; nevertheless, the practical applications of the general principles
of the broadest mental science will tend to prevent disease.... We do find
sufficient evidence to convince us that the proper reform in mental

attitude would relieve many a sufferer of ills that the ordinary physician cannot touch; would even delay the approach of death to many a victim beyond the power of absolute cure, and the faithful adherence to a truer philosophy of life will keep many a man well, and give the doctor time to devote to alleviating ills that are unpreventable."

To come now to a little closer quarters with their creed. The fundamental pillar on which it rests is nothing more than the general basis of all religious experience, the fact that man has a dual nature, and is connected with two spheres of thought, a shallower and a profounder sphere, in either of which he may learn to live more habitually. The shallower and lower sphere is that of the fleshly sensations, instincts, and desires, of egotism, doubt, and the lower personal interests. But whereas Christian theology has always considered frowardness to be the essential vice of this part of human nature, the mind-curers say that the mark of the beast in it is fear; and this is what gives such an entirely new religious turn to their persuasion.

"Fear," to quote a writer of the school, "has had its uses in the evolutionary process, and seems to constitute the whole of forethought in most animals; but that it should remain any part of the mental equipment of human civilized life is an absurdity. I find that the fear element of forethought is not stimulating to those more civilized persons to whom duty and attraction are the natural motives, but is weakening and deterrent. As soon as it becomes unnecessary, fear becomes a positive deterrent, and should be entirely removed, as dead flesh is removed from living tissue. To assist in the analysis of fear, and in the denunciation of its expressions, I have coined the word fearthought to stand for the unprofitable element of forethought, and have defined the word 'worry' as fearthought in contradistinction to forethought. I have also defined fearthought as the self-imposed or self-permitted suggestion of inferiority, in order to place it where it really belongs, in the category of harmful, unnecessary, and therefore not respectable things." [Horace Fletcher: Happiness as found in Forethought minus Fearthought, Menticulture Series, ii. Chicago and New York, Stone, 1897, pp. 21-25, abridged.]

The 'misery-habit,' the 'martyr-habit,' engendered by the prevalent 'fearthought,' get pungent criticism from the mind-cure writers:

"Consider for a moment the habits of life into which we are born. There are certain social conventions or customs and alleged requirements, there is a theological bias, a general view of the world. There are conservative ideas in regard to our early training, our education, marriage, and occupation in life. Following close upon this, there is a long series of anticipations, namely, that we shall suffer certain children's diseases, diseases of middle life,, and of old age; the thought that we shall grow old, lose our faculties, and again become childlike; while crowning all is the fear of death. Then there is a long line of particular fears and trouble-bearing expectations, such, for example, as ideas associated with certain articles of food, the dread of the east wind, the terrors of hot weather, the aches and pains associated with cold weather, the fear of catching cold if one sits in a draught, the coming of hay-fever upon the

14th of August in the middle of the day, and so on through a long list of
fears, dreads, worriments, anxieties, anticipations, expectations,
pessimisms, morbidities, and the whole ghostly train of fateful shapes
which our fellow-men, and especially physicians, are ready to help us
conjure up, an array worthy to rank with Bradley's 'unearthly ballet of
bloodless categories.'

"Yet this is not all. This vast array is swelled by innumerable
volunteers from daily life,— the fear of accident, the possibility of
calamity, the loss of property, the chance of robbery, of fire, or the
outbreak of war. And it is not deemed sufficient to fear for ourselves.
When a friend is taken ill, we must forthwith fear the worst and
apprehend death. If one meets with sorrow... sympathy means to enter
into and increase the suffering." [H.W. Dresser: Voices of Freedom, New
York, 1899, p. 38.]

"Man," to quote another writer, "often has fear stamped upon him
before his entrance into the outer world; he is reared in fear; all his life is
passed in bondage to fear of disease and death, and thus his whole
mentality becomes cramped, limited, and depressed, and his body follows
its shrunken pattern and specification.... Think of the millions of sensitive
and responsive souls among our ancestors who have been under the
dominion of such a perpetual nightmare! Is it not surprising that health
exists at all? Nothing but the boundless divine love, exuberance, and
vitality, constantly poured in, even though unconsciously to us, could in
some degree neutralize such an ocean of morbidity." [HENRY WOOD:
Ideal Suggestion through Mental Photography, Boston, 1899, p. 54.]

Although the disciples of the mind-cure often use Christian
terminology, one sees from such quotations how widely their notion of the
fall of man diverges from that of ordinary Christians.

Whether it differs so much from Christ's own notion is for the exegetists
to decide. According to Harnack, Jesus felt about evil and disease much
as our mind-curers do. "What is the answer which Jesus sends to John the
Baptist?" asks Harnack, and says it is this: "'The blind see, and the lame
walk, the lepers are cleansed, and the deaf hear, the dead rise up, and the
gospel is preached to the poor.' That is the 'coming of the kingdom,' or
rather in these saving works the kingdom is already there. By the
overcoming and removal of misery, of need, of sickness, by these actual
effects John is to see that the new time has arrived. The casting out of
devils is only a part of this work of redemption, but Jesus points to that
as the sense and seal of his mission. Thus to the wretched, sick, and poor
did he address himself, but not as a moralist, and without a trace of
sentimentalism. He never makes groups and departments of the ills; he
never spends time in asking whether the sick one 'deserves' to be cured;
and it never occurs to him to sympathize with the pain or the death. He
nowhere says that sickness is a beneficent infliction, and that evil has a
healthy use. No, he calls sickness sickness and health health. All evil, all
wretchedness, is for him something dreadful; it is of the great kingdom of
Satan; but he feels the power of the Saviour within him. He knows that

advance is possible only when weakness is overcome when sickness is made well." Das Wesen des Christenthums, 1900, p. 39.

Their notion of man's higher nature is hardly less divergent, being decidedly pantheistic. The spiritual in man appears in the mind-cure philosophy as partly conscious, but chiefly subconscious; and through the subconscious part of it we are already one with the Divine without any miracle of grace, or abrupt creation of a new inner man. As this view is variously expressed by different writers, we find in it traces of Christian mysticism, of transcendental idealism, of vedantism, and of the modern psychology of the subliminal self. A quotation or two will put us at the central point of view:

"The great central fact of the universe is that spirit of infinite life and power that is back of all, that manifests itself in and through all. This spirit of infinite life and power that is back of all is what I call God. I care not what term you may use, be it Kindly Light, Providence, the Over-Soul, Omnipotence, or whatever term may be most convenient, so long as we are agreed in regard to the great central fact itself. God then fills the universe alone, so that all is from Him and in Him, and there is nothing that is outside. He is the life of our life, our very life itself. We are partakers of the life of God; and though we differ from Him in that we are individualized spirits, while He is the Infinite Spirit, including us, as well as all else beside, yet in essence the life of God and the life of man are identically the same, and so are one. They differ not in essence or quality; they differ in degree.

"The great central fact in human life is the coming into a conscious vital realization of our oneness with this Infinite Life. and the opening of ourselves fully to this divine inflow. In just the degree that we come into a conscious realization of our oneness with the Infinite Life, and open ourselves to this divine inflow, do we actualize in ourselves the qualities and powers of the Infinite Life, do we make ourselves channels through which the Infinite Intelligence and Power can work. In just the degree in which you realize your oneness with the Infinite Spirit, you will exchange disease for ease, inharmony for harmony, suffering and pain for abounding health and strength. To recognize our own divinity, and our intimate relation to the Universal, is to attach the belts of our machinery to the power. house of the Universe. One need remain in hell no longer than one chooses to; we can rise to any heaven we ourselves choose; and when we choose so to rise, all the higher powers of the Universe combine to help us heavenward." [R.W. Trine: In Tune with the Infinite, 26th thousand, N. Y., 1899. I have strung scattered passages together.]

Let me now pass from these abstracter statements to some more concrete accounts of experience with the mind-cure religion. I have many answers from correspondents— the only difficulty is to choose. The first two whom I shall quote are my personal friends. One of them, a woman, writing as follows, expresses well the feeling of continuity with the Infinite Power, by which all mind-cure disciples are inspired.

"The first underlying cause of all sickness, weakness, or depression is the human sense of separateness from that Divine Energy which we call

God. The soul which can feel and affirm in serene but jubilant confidence, as did the Nazarene: 'I and my Father are one,' has no further need of healer, or of healing. This is the whole truth in a nutshell, and other foundation for wholeness can no man lay than this fact of impregnable divine union. Disease can no longer attack one whose feet are planted on this rock, who feels hourly, momently, the influx of the Deific Breath. If one with Omnipotence, how can weariness enter the consciousness, how illness assail that indomitable spark?

"This possibility of annulling forever the law of fatigue has been abundantly proven in my own case; for my earlier life bears a record of many, many years of bedridden invalidism, with spine and lower limbs paralyzed. My thoughts were no more impure than they are today, although my belief in the necessity of illness was dense and unenlightened; but since my resurrection in the flesh, I have worked as a healer unceasingly for fourteen years without a vacation, and can truthfully assert that I have never known a moment of fatigue or pain, although coming in touch constantly with excessive weakness, illness, and disease of all kinds. For how can a conscious part of Deity be sick?— since 'Greater is he that is with us than all that can strive against us.'"

My second correspondent, also a woman, sends me the following statement:

"Life seemed difficult to me at one time. I was always breaking down, and had several attacks of what is called nervous prostration, with terrible insomnia, being on the verge of insanity; besides having many other troubles, especially of the digestive organs. I had been sent away from home in charge of doctors, had taken all the narcotics, stopped all work, been fed up, and in fact knew all the doctors within reach. But I never recovered permanently till this New Thought took possession of me.

"I think that the one thing which impressed me most was learning the fact that we must be in absolutely constant relation or mental touch (this word is to me very expressive) with that essence of life which permeates all and which we call God. This is almost unrecognizable unless we live it into ourselves actually, that is, by a constant turning to the very innermost, deepest consciousness of our real selves or of God in us, for illumination from within, just as we turn to the sun for light, warmth, and invigoration without. When you do this consciously, realizing that to turn inward to the light within you is to live in the presence of God or your divine self, you soon discover the unreality of the objects to which you have hitherto been turning and which have engrossed you without.

"I have come to disregard the meaning of this attitude for bodily health as such, because that comes of itself, as an incidental result, and cannot be found by any special mental act or desire to have it, beyond that general attitude of mind I have referred to above. That which we usually make the object of life, those outer things we are all so wildly seeking, which we so often live and die for, but which then do not give us peace and happiness, they should all come of themselves as accessory, and as the mere outcome or natural result of a far higher life sunk deep in the bosom of the spirit. This life is the real seeking of the kingdom of God, the desire for his supremacy in our hearts, so that all else comes as that which shall be 'added unto you'— as quite incidental and as a surprise to us, perhaps; and yet it is the proof of the reality of the perfect poise in the very centre of our being.

"When I say that we commonly make the object of our life that which we should not work for primarily, I mean many things which the world considers praiseworthy and excellent, such as success in business, fame as author or artist, physician or lawyer, or renown in philanthropic undertakings. Such things should be results, not objects. I would also include pleasures of many kinds which seem harmless and good at the time, and are pursued because many accept them— I mean conventionalities, sociabilities, and fashions in their various development, these being mostly approved by the masses, although they may be unreal and even unhealthy superfluities."

Here is another case, more concrete, also that of a woman. I read you these cases without comment,— they express so many varieties of the state of mind we are studying.

"I had been a sufferer from my childhood till my fortieth year. [Details of ill-health are given which I omit.] I had been in Vermont several months hoping for good from the change of air, but steadily growing weaker, when one day during the latter part of October, while resting in the afternoon, I suddenly heard as it were these words: 'You will be healed and do a work you never dreamed of.' These words were impressed upon my mind with such power I said at once that only God could have put them there. I believed them in spite of myself and of my suffering and weakness, which continued until Christmas, when I returned to Boston. Within two days a young friend offered to take me to a mental healer (this was January 7, 1881). The healer said: 'There is nothing but Mind; we are expressions of the One Mind; body is only a mortal belief; as a man thinketh so is he.' I could not accept all she said, but I translated all that was there for me in this way; 'There is nothing but God; I am created by Him, and am absolutely dependent upon Him; mind is given me to use; and by just so much of it as I will put upon the thought of right action in body I shall be lifted out of bondage to my ignorance and fear and past experience.' That day I commenced accordingly to take a little of every food provided for the family, constantly saying to myself: 'The Power that created the stomach must take care of what I have eaten.' By holding these suggestions through the evening I went to bed and fell asleep, saying: 'I am soul, spirit, just one with God's Thought of me,' and slept all night without waking, for the first time in several years [the distress-turns had usually recurred about two o'clock in the night]. I felt the next day like an escaped prisoner, and believed I had found the secret that would in time give me perfect health. Within ten days I was able to eat anything provided for others, and after two weeks I began to have my own positive mental suggestions of Truth, which were to me like stepping-stones. I will note a few of them; they came about two weeks apart.

"1st. I am Soul, therefore it is well with me.

"2d. I am Soul, therefore I am well.

"3d. A sort of inner vision of myself as a four-footed beast with a protuberance on every part of my body where I had suffering, with my own face, begging me to acknowledge it as myself. I resolutely fixed my attention on being well, and refused to even look at my old self in this form.

"4th. Again the vision of the beast far in the background, with faint voice. Again refusal to acknowledge.

"5th. Once more the vision, but only of my eyes with the longing look; and again the refusal. Then came the conviction, the inner consciousness, that I was perfectly well and always had been, for I was Soul, an expression of God's Perfect Thought. That was to me the perfect and completed separation between what I was and what I appeared to be. I succeeded in never losing sight after this of my real being, by constantly affirming this truth, and by degrees (though it took me two years of hard work to get there) I expressed health continuously throughout my whole body.

"In my subsequent nineteen years' experience I have never known this Truth to fail when I applied it, though in my ignorance I have often failed to apply it, but through my failures I have learned the simplicity and trustfulness of the little child."

But I fear that I risk tiring you by so many examples, and I must lead you back to philosophic generalities again. You see already by such records of experience how impossible it is not to class mind-cure as primarily a religious movement. Its doctrine of the oneness of our life with God's life is in fact quite indistinguishable from an interpretation of Christ's message which in these very Gifford lectures has been defended by some of your very ablest Scottish religious philosophers. [The Cairds, for example. In Edward Caird's Glasgow Lectures of 1890-92 passages like this abound:]

"The declaration made in the beginning of the ministry of Jesus that 'the time is fulfilled, and the kingdom of heaven is at hand,' passes with scarce a break into the announcement that the kingdom of God is among you and the importance of this announcement is asserted to be such that it makes, so to speak, a difference in kind between the greatest saints and prophets who lived under the previous reign of division, and 'the least in the kingdom of heaven.' The highest ideal is brought close to men and declared to be within their reach, they are called on to be 'perfect as their Father in heaven is perfect.' The sense of alienation and distance from God which had grown upon the pious in Israel must in proportion as they had learned to look upon Him as no mere national divinity, but as a God of justice who would punish Israel for its sin as certainly as Edom or Moab, is declared to be no longer in place; and the typical form of Christian prayer points to the abolition of the contrast between this world and the next which thought all the history of the Jews had continually been growing wider: 'As in heaven, so on earth.' The sense of the division of man from God, as a finite being from the Infinite, as weak and sinful from the Omnipotent Goodness, is not indeed lost; but it can no longer overpower the consciousness of oneness. The terms 'Son' and 'Father' at once state the opposition and mark its limit. They show that it is not an absolute opposition, but one which presupposes an indestructible principle of unity, that can and must become a principle of reconciliation." The Evolution of Religion, ii. pp. 146, 147.

But philosophers usually profess to give a quasi-logical explanation of the existence of evil, whereas of the general fact of evil in the world, the existence of the selfish, suffering, timorous finite consciousness, the mind-curers, so far as I am acquainted with them, profess to give no speculative explanation. Evil is empirically there for them as it is for everybody, but the practical point of view predominates, and it would ill agree with the spirit of their system to spend time in worrying over it as a 'mystery' or 'problem,' or in 'laying to heart' the lesson of its experience, after the manner of the Evangelicals. Don't reason about it, as Dante says, but give a glance and pass beyond! It is Avidhya, ignorance! something merely to be outgrown and left behind, transcended and forgotten. Christian Science so-called, the sect of Mrs. Eddy, is the most radical branch of mind-cure in its dealings with evil. For it evil is simply a lie, and any one who mentions it is a liar. The optimistic ideal of duty forbids us to pay it the compliment even of explicit attention. Of course, as our next lectures will show us, this is a bad speculative omission, but it is intimately linked with the practical merits of the system we are examining. Why regret a philosophy of evil, a mind-curer would ask us, if I can put you in possession of a life of good?

After all, it is the life that tells; and mind-cure has developed a living system of mental hygiene which may well claim to have thrown all previous literature of the Diatetik der Seele into the shade. This system is wholly and exclusively compacted of optimism: 'Pessimism leads to weakness. Optimism leads to power.' 'Thoughts are things,' as one of the most vigorous mind-cure writers prints in bold type at the bottom of each of his pages; and if your thoughts are of health, youth, vigor, and success, before you know it these things will also be your outward portion. No one can fail of the regenerative influence of optimistic thinking, pertinaciously pursued. Every man owns indefeasibly this inlet to the divine. Fear, on the contrary, and all the contracted and egoistic modes of thought, are inlets to destruction. Most mind-curers here bring in a doctrine that thoughts are 'forces,' and that, by virtue of a law that like attracts like, one man's thoughts draw to themselves as allies all the thoughts of the same character that exist the world over. Thus one gets, by one's thinking, reinforcements from elsewhere for the realization of one's desires; and the great point in the conduct of life is to get the heavenly forces on one's side by opening one's own mind to their influx.

On the whole, one is struck by a psychological similarity between the mind-cure movement and the Lutheran and Wesleyan movements. To the believer in moralism and works, with his anxious query, 'What shall I do to be saved?' Luther and Wesley replied: 'You are saved now, if you would but believe it.' And the mind-curers come with precisely similar words of emancipation. They speak, it is true, to persons for whom the conception of salvation has lost its ancient theological meaning, but who labor nevertheless with the same eternal human difficulty. Things are wrong with them; and 'What shall I do to be clear, right, sound, whole, well?' is the form of their question. And the answer is: 'You are well, sound, and clear already, if you did but know it.' "The whole matter may be summed up in one sentence," says one of the authors whom I have already quoted, "God is well, and so are you. You must awaken to the knowledge of your real being."

The adequacy of their message to the mental needs of a large fraction of mankind is what gave force to those earlier gospels. Exactly the same adequacy holds in the case of the mind-cure message, foolish as it may sound upon its surface; and seeing its rapid growth in influence, and its therapeutic triumphs, one is tempted to ask whether it may not be destined (probably by very reason of the crudity and extravagance of many of its manifestations) to play a part almost as great in the evolution of the popular religion of the future as did those earlier movements in their day.

It remains to be seen whether the school of Mr. Dresser, which assumes more and more the form of mind-cure experience and academic philosophy mutually impregnating each other, will score the practical triumphs of the less critical and rational sects.

But I here fear that I may begin to 'jar upon the nerves' of some of the members of this academic audience. Such contemporary vagaries, you may think, should hardly take so large a place in dignified Gifford lectures. I can only beseech you to have patience. The whole outcome of these lectures will, I imagine, be the emphasizing to your mind of the enormous diversities which the spiritual lives of different men exhibit. Their wants, their susceptibilities, and their capacities all vary and must be classed under different heads. The result is that we have really different types of religious experience; and, seeking in these lectures closer acquaintance with the healthy-minded type, we must take it where we find it in most radical form. The psychology of individual types of character has hardly begun even to be sketched as yet— our lectures may possibly serve as a crumb-like contribution to the structure. The first thing to bear in mind (especially if we ourselves belong to the clerico-academic-scientific type, the officially and conventionally 'correct' type, 'the deadly respectable' type, for which to ignore others is a besetting temptation) is that nothing can be more stupid than to bar out phenomena from our notice, merely because we are incapable of taking part in anything like them ourselves.

Now the history of Lutheran salvation by faith, of methodistic conversions, and of what I call the mind-cure movement seems to prove the existence of numerous persons in whom— at any rate at a certain stage in their development— a change of character for the better, so far from being facilitated by the rules laid down by official moralists, will take place all the more successfully if those rules be exactly reversed. Official moralists advise us never to relax our strenuousness. "Be vigilant, day and night," they adjure us; "hold your passive tendencies in check; shrink from no effort; keep your will like a bow always bent." But the persons I speak of find that all this conscious effort leads to nothing but failure and vexation in their hands, and only make them twofold more the children of hell they were before. The tense and voluntary attitude becomes in them an impossible fever and torment. Their machinery refuses to run at all when the bearings are made so hot and the belts so tight.

Under these circumstances the way to success, as vouched for by innumerable authentic personal narrations, is by an anti-moralistic method, by the 'surrender' of which I spoke in my second lecture. Passivity, not activity; relaxation, not intentness, should be now the rule. Give up the feeling of responsibility, let go your hold, resign the care of your destiny to higher powers, be genuinely indifferent as to what becomes of it all, and you will find not only that you gain a perfect inward relief, but often also, in addition, the particular goods you sincerely thought you were renouncing. This is the salvation through self-despair, the dying to be truly born, of Lutheran theology, the passage into nothing of which Jacob Behmen writes. To get to it, a critical point must usually be passed, a corner turned within one. Something must give way, a native hardness must break down and liquefy; and this event (as we shall abundantly see hereafter) is frequently sudden and automatic, and leaves on the Subject an impression that he has been wrought on by an external power.

Whatever its ultimate significance may prove to be, this is certainly one fundamental form of human experience. Some say that the capacity or incapacity for it is what divides the religious from the merely moralistic character. With those who undergo it in its fullness, no criticism avails to cast doubt on its reality. They know; for they have actually felt the higher powers, in giving up the tension of their personal will.

A story which revivalist preachers often tell is that of a man who found himself at night slipping down the side of a precipice. At last he caught a branch which stopped his fall, and remained clinging to it in misery for hours. But finally his fingers had to loose their hold, and with a despairing farewell to life, he let himself drop. He fell just six inches. If he had given up the struggle earlier, his agony would have been spared. As the mother earth received him, so, the preachers tell us, will the everlasting arms receive us if we confide absolutely in them, and give up the hereditary habit of relying on our personal strength, with its precautions that cannot shelter and safeguards that never save.

The mind-curers have given the widest scope to this sort of experience. They have demonstrated that a form of regeneration by relaxing, by letting go, psychologically indistinguishable from the Lutheran justification by faith and the Wesleyan acceptance of free grace, is within the reach of persons who have no conviction of sin and care nothing for the Lutheran theology. It is but giving your little private convulsive self a rest, and finding that a greater Self is there. The results, slow or sudden, or great or small, of the combined optimism and expectancy, the regenerative phenomena which ensue on the abandonment of effort, remain firm facts of human nature, no matter whether we adopt a theistic, a pantheistic-idealistic, or a medical-materialistic view of their ultimate causal explanation.

The theistic explanation is by divine grace, which creates a new nature within one the moment the old nature is sincerely given up. The pantheistic explanation (which is that of most mind-curers) is by the merging of the narrower private self into the wider or greater self, the spirit of the universe (which is your own 'subconscious' self), the moment the isolating barriers of mistrust and anxiety are removed. The medico-materialistic explanation is that simpler cerebral processes act more freely where they are left to act automatically by the shunting-out of physiologically (though in this instance not spiritually) 'higher' ones which, seeking to regulate, only succeed in inhibiting results.— Whether this third explanation might, in a psycho-physical account of the universe, be combined with either of the others may be left an open question here.

When we take up the phenomena of revivalistic conversion, we shall learn something more about all this. Meanwhile I will say a brief word about the mind-curer's methods.

They are of course largely suggestive. The suggestive influence of environment plays an enormous part in all spiritual education. But the word 'suggestion,' having acquired official status, is unfortunately already beginning to play in many quarters the part of a wet blanket upon investigation, being used to fend off all inquiry into the varying susceptibilities of individual cases. 'Suggestion' is only another name for the power of ideas, so far as they prove efficacious over belief and conduct. Ideas efficacious over some people prove inefficacious over others. Ideas efficacious at some times and in some human surroundings are not so at other times and elsewhere. The ideas of Christian churches are not efficacious in the therapeutic direction today, whatever they may have been in earlier centuries; and when the whole question is as to why the salt has lost its savor here or gained it there, the mere blank waving of the word 'suggestion' as if it were a banner gives no light. Dr. Goddard, whose candid psychological essay on Faith Cures ascribes them to nothing but ordinary suggestion, concludes by saying that "Religion [and by this he seems to mean our popular Christianity] has in it all there is in mental therapeutics, and has it in its best form. Living up to [our religious] ideas will do anything for us that can be done." And this in spite of the actual fact that the popular Christianity does absolutely nothing, or did nothing until mind-cure came to the rescue.

Within the churches a disposition has always prevailed to regard sickness as a visitation; something sent by God for our good, either as chastisement, as warning, or as opportunity for exercising virtue, and, in the Catholic Church, of earning 'merit.' "Illness," says a good Catholic writer (P. Lejeune: Introd. a la Vie Mystique, 1899, p. 218), "is the most excellent of corporeal mortifications, the mortification which one has not one's self chosen, which is imposed directly by God, and is the direct expression of his will. 'If other mortifications are of silver,' Mgr. Gay says, 'this one is of gold; since although it comes of ourselves, coming as it does of original sin, still on its greater side, as coming (like all that happens) from the providence of God, it is of divine manufacture. And how just are its blows! And how efficacious it is!... I do not hesitate to say that patience in a long illness is mortification's very masterpiece, and consequently the triumph of mortified souls.'" According to this view, disease should in any case be submissively accepted, and it might under certain circumstances even be blasphemous to wish it away.

Of course there have been exceptions to this, and cures by special miracle have at all times been recognized within the church's pale, almost all the great saints having more or less performed them. It was one of the heresies of Edward Irving, to maintain them still to be possible. An extremely pure faculty of healing after confession and conversion on the patient's part, and prayer on the priest's, was quite spontaneously developed in the German pastor, Joh. Christoph Blumhardt, in the early forties and exerted during nearly thirty years. Blumhardt's Life by Zundel gives in chapters ix., x., xi., and xvii. a pretty full account of his healing activity, which he invariably ascribed to direct divine inter-position. Blumhardt was a singularly pure, simple, and non-fanatical character, and in this part of his work followed no previous model. In Chicago today we have the case of Dr. J.A. Dowie, a Scottish Baptist preacher, whose weekly 'Leaves of Healing' were in the year of grace 1900 in their sixth volume, and who, although he denounces the cares wrought in other sects as 'diabolical counterfeits' of his own exclusively 'Divine Healing,' must on the whole be counted into the mind-cure movement. In mind-cure circles the fundamental article of faith is that disease should never be accepted. It is wholly of the pit. God wants us to be absolutely healthy, and we should not tolerate ourselves on any lower terms.

An idea, to be suggestive, must come to the individual with the force of a revelation. The mind-cure with its gospel of healthy-mindedness has come as a revelation to many whose hearts the church Christianity had left hardened. It has let loose their springs of higher life. In what can the originality of any religious movement consist, save in finding a channel, until then sealed up, through which those springs may be set free in some group of human beings?

The force of personal faith, enthusiasm, and example, and above all the force of novelty, are always the prime suggestive agency in this kind of success. If mind-cure should ever become official, respectable, and intrenched, these elements of suggestive efficacy will be lost. In its acuter stages every religion must be a homeless Arab of the desert. The church knows this well enough, with its everlasting inner struggle of the acute religion of the few against the chronic religion of the many, indurated into an obstructiveness worse than that which irreligion opposes to the movings of the Spirit. "We may pray," says Jonathan Edwards, "concerning all those saints that are not lively Christians, that they may either be enlivened, or taken away; if that be true that is often said by some at this day, that these cold dead saints do more hurt than natural men, and lead more souls to hell, and that it would be well for mankind if they were all dead." [Edwards, from whose book on the Revival in New England I quote these words, dissuades from such a use of prayer, but it is easy to see that he enjoys making his thrust at the cold dead church members.]

The next condition of success is the apparent existence, in large numbers, of minds who unite healthy-mindedness with readiness for regeneration by letting go. Protestantism has been too pessimistic as regards the natural man, Catholicism has been too legalistic and moralistic, for either the one or the other to appeal in any generous way to the type of character formed of this peculiar mingling of elements. However few of us here present may belong to such a type, it is now evident that it forms a specific moral combination, well represented in the world.

Finally, mind-cure has made what in our protestant countries is an unprecedentedly great use of the subconscious life. To their reasoned advice and dogmatic assertion, its founders have added systematic exercise in passive relaxation, concentration, and meditation, and have even invoked something like hypnotic practice. I quote some passages at random:

"The value, the potency of ideals is the great practical truth on which the New Thought most strongly insists,— the development namely from within outward, from small to great. [H.W. Dresser: Voices of Freedom, 46.] Consequently one's thought should be centred on the ideal outcome, even though this trust be literally like a step in the dark. [Dresser: Living by the Spirit, 58.] To attain the ability thus effectively to direct the mind, the New Thought advises the practice of concentration, or in other words, the attainment of self-control. One is to learn to marshal the tendencies of the mind, so that they may be held together as a unit by the chosen ideal. To this end, one should set apart times for silent meditation, by one's self, preferably in a room where the surroundings are favorable to spiritual thought. In New Thought terms, this is called 'entering the silence.'" [Dresser: Voices of Freedom, 33.]

"The time will come when in the busy office or on the noisy street you can enter into the silence by simply drawing the mantle of your own thoughts about you and realizing that there and everywhere the Spirit of Infinite Life, Love, Wisdom, Peace, Power, and Plenty is guiding, keeping, protecting, leading you. This is the spirit of continual prayer. [Trine: In Tune with the Infinite, p. 214.] One of the most intuitive men we ever met had a desk at a city office where several other gentlemen were doing business constantly, and often talking loudly. Entirely undisturbed by the many various sounds about him, this self-centred faithful man would, in any moment of perplexity, draw the curtains of privacy so completely about him that he would be as fully inclosed in his own psychic aura, and thereby as effectually removed from all distractions, as though he were alone in some primeval wood. Taking his difficulty with him into the mystic silence in the form of a direct question, to which he expected a certain answer, he would remain utterly passive until the reply came, and never once through many years' experience did he find himself disappointed or misled." [Trine: p. 117.]

Wherein, I should like to know, does this intrinsically differ from the practice of 'recollection' which plays so great a part in Catholic discipline? Otherwise called the practice of the presence of God (and so known among ourselves, as for instance in Jeremy Taylor), it is thus defined by the eminent teacher Alvarez de Paz in his work on Contemplation.

"It is the recollection of God, the thought of God, which in all places and circumstances makes us see him present, lets us commune respectfully and lovingly with him, and fills us with desire and affection for him.... Would you escape from every ill? Never lose this recollection of God, neither in prosperity nor in adversity, nor on any occasion whichsoever it be. Invoke not, to excuse yourself from this duty, either the difficulty or the importance of your business, for you can always remember that God sees you, that you are under his eye. If a thousand times an hour you forget him, reanimate a thousand times the recollection. If you cannot practice this exercise continuously, at least make yourself as familiar with it as possible; and, like unto those who in a rigorous winter draw near the fire as often as they can, go as often as you can to that ardent fire which will warm your soul." [Quoted by Lejeune: Introd. a la Vie Mystique, 1899, p. 66.]

All the external associations of the Catholic discipline are of course unlike anything in mind-cure thought, but the purely spiritual part of the exercise is identical in both communions, and in both communions those who urge it write with authority, for they have evidently experienced in their own persons that whereof they tell. Compare again some mind-cure utterances:

"High, healthful, pure thinking can be encouraged, promoted, and strengthened. Its current can be turned upon grand ideals until it forms a habit and wears a channel. By means of such discipline the mental horizon can be flooded with the sunshine of beauty, wholeness, and harmony. To inaugurate pure and lofty thinking may at first seem difficult, even almost mechanical, but perseverance will at length render it easy, then pleasant, and finally delightful.

"The soul's real world is that which it has built of its thoughts, mental states, and imaginations. If we will, we can turn our backs upon the lower and sensuous plane, and lift ourselves into the realm of the spiritual and Real, and there gain a residence. The assumption of states of expectancy and receptivity will attract spiritual sunshine, and it will flow in as naturally as air inclines to a vacuum.... Whenever the thought is not occupied with one's daily duty or profession, it should be sent aloft into the spiritual atmosphere. There are quiet leisure moments by day, and wakeful hours at night, when this wholesome and delightful exercise may be engaged in to great advantage. If one who has never made any systematic effort to lift and control the thought-forces will, for a single month, earnestly pursue the course here suggested, he will be surprised and delighted at the result, and nothing will induce him to go back to careless, aimless, and superficial thinking. At such favorable seasons the outside world, with all its current of daily events, is barred out, and one goes into the silent sanctuary of the inner temple of soul to commune and aspire. The spiritual hearing becomes delicately sensitive, so that the 'still, small voice' is audible, the tumultuous waves of external sense are hushed, and there is a great calm. The ego gradually becomes conscious that it is face to face with the Divine Presence; that mighty, healing, loving, Fatherly life which is nearer to us than we are to ourselves. There is soul-contact with the Parent-Soul, and an influx of life, love, virtue, health, and happiness from the Inexhaustible Fountain." [Henry Wood: Ideal Suggestion through Mental Photography.]

When we reach the subject of mysticism, you will undergo so deep an immersion into these exalted states of consciousness as to be wet all over, if I may so express myself; and the cold shiver of doubt with which this little sprinkling may affect you will have long since passed away- doubt, I mean, as to whether all such writing be not mere abstract talk and rhetoric set down pour encourager les autres. You Will then be convinced, I trust, that these states of consciousness of 'union' form a perfectly definite class of experiences, of which the soul may occasionally partake, and which certain persons may live by in a deeper sense than they live by anything else with which they have acquaintance. This brings me to a general philosophical reflection with which I should like to pass from the subject of healthy-mindedness, and close a topic which I fear is already only too long drawn out. It concerns the relation of all this systematized healthy-mindedness and mind-cure religion to scientific method and the scientific life.

In a later lecture I shall have to treat explicitly of the relation of religion to science on the one hand, and to primeval savage thought on the other. There are plenty of persons today 'scientists' or 'positivists,' they are fond of calling themselves— who will tell you that religious thought is a mere survival, an atavistic reversion to a type of consciousness which humanity in its more enlightened examples has long since left behind and outgrown. If you ask them to explain themselves more fully, they will probably say that for primitive thought everything is conceived of under the form of personality. The savage thinks that things operate by personal forces, and for the sake of individual ends. For him, even external nature obeys individual needs and claims, just as if these were so many elementary powers. Now science, on the other hand, these positivists say, has proved that personality, so far from being an elementary force in nature, is but a passive resultant of the really elementary forces, physical, chemical, physiological, and psycho-physical, which are all impersonal and general in character. Nothing individual accomplishes anything in the universe save in so far as it obeys and exemplifies some universal law. Should you then inquire of them by what means science has thus supplanted primitive thought, and discredited its personal way of looking at things, they would undoubtedly say it has been by the strict use of the method of experimental verification. Follow out science's conceptions practically, they will say, the conceptions that ignore personality altogether, and you will always be corroborated. The world is so made that all your expectations will be experientially verified so long, and only so long, as you keep the terms from which you infer them impersonal and universal.

But here we have mind-cure, with her diametrically opposite philosophy, setting up an exactly identical claim. Live as if I were true, she says, and every day will practically prove you right. That the controlling energies of nature are personal, that your own personal thoughts are forces, that the powers of the universe will directly respond to your individual appeals and needs, are propositions which your whole bodily and mental experience will verify. And that experience does largely verify these primeval religious ideas is proved by the fact that the mind-cure movement spreads as it does, not by proclamation and assertion simply, but by palpable experiential results. Here, in the very heyday of science's authority, it carries on an aggressive warfare against the scientific philosophy, and succeeds by using science's own peculiar methods and weapons. Believing that a higher power will take care of us in certain ways better than we can take care of ourselves, if we only genuinely throw ourselves upon it and consent to use it, it finds the belief, not only not impugned, but corroborated by its observation.

How conversions are thus made, and converts confirmed, is evident enough from the narratives which I have quoted. I will quote yet another couple of shorter ones to give the matter a perfectly concrete turn. Here is one:

"One of my first experiences in applying my teaching was two months after I first saw the healer. I fell, spraining my right ankle, which I had done once four years before, having then had to use a crutch and elastic anklet for some months, and carefully guarding it ever since. As soon as I was on my feet I made the positive suggestion (and felt it through all my being): 'There is nothing but God, all life comes from him perfectly. I cannot be sprained or hurt, I will let him take care of it.' Well, I never had a sensation in it, and I walked two miles that day."

The next case not only illustrates experiment and verification, but also the element of passivity and surrender of which awhile ago I made such account.

"I went into town to do some shopping one morning, and I had not been gone long before I began to feel ill. The ill feeling increased rapidly, until I had pains in an my bones, nausea and faintness, headache, all the symptoms in short that precede an attack of influenza. I thought that I was going to have the grippe, epidemic then in Boston, or something worse. The mind-cure teachings that I had been listening to all the winter thereupon came into my mind, and I thought that here was an opportunity to test myself. On my way home I met a friend, and I refrained with some effort from telling her how I felt. That was the first step gained. I went to bed immediately, and my husband wished to send for the doctor. But I told him that I would rather wait until morning and see how I felt. Then followed one of the most beautiful experiences of my life.

"I cannot express it in any other way than to say that I did 'lie down in the stream of life and let it flow over me.' I gave up all fear of any impending disease; I was perfectly willing and obedient. There was no intellectual effort, or train of thought. My dominant idea was: 'Behold the handmaid of the Lord: be it unto me even as thou wilt,' and a perfect confidence that all would be well, that all was well. The creative life was flowing into me every instant, and I felt myself allied with the Infinite, in harmony, and full of the peace that passeth understanding. There was no place in my mind for a jarring body. I had no consciousness of time or space or persons; but only of love and happiness and faith.

"I do not know how long this state lasted, nor when I fell asleep; but when I woke up in the morning, I was well."

These are exceedingly trivial instances, but in them, if we have anything at all, we have the method of experiment and verification. For the point I am driving at now, it makes no difference whether you consider the patients to be deluded victims of their imagination or not. That they seemed to themselves to have been cured by the experiments tried was enough to make them converts to the system. And although it is evident that one must be of a certain mental mould to get such results (for not every one can get thus cured to his own satisfaction any more than every one can be cured by the first regular practitioner whom he calls in), yet it would surely be pedantic and over-scrupulous for those who can get their savage and primitive philosophy of mental healing verified in such experimental ways as this, to give them up at word of command for more scientific therapeutics. What are we to think of all this? Has science made too wide a claim?

I believe that the claims of the sectarian scientist are, to say the least, premature. The experiences which we have been studying during this hour (and a great many other kinds of religious experiences are like them) plainly show the universe to be a more many-sided affair than any sect, even the scientific sect, allows for. What, in the end, are all our verifications but experiences that agree with more or less isolated systems of ideas (conceptual systems) that our minds have framed? But why in the name of common sense need we assume that only one such system of ideas can be true? The obvious outcome of our total experience is that the world can be handled according to many systems of ideas, and is so handled by different men, and will each time give some characteristic kind of profit, for which he cares, to the handler, while at the same time some other kind of profit has to be omitted or postponed. Science gives to all of us telegraphy, electric lighting, and diagnosis, and succeeds in preventing and curing a certain amount of disease. Religion in the shape of mind-cure gives to some of us serenity, moral poise, and happiness, and prevents certain forms of disease as well as science does, or even better in a certain class of persons. Evidently, then, the science and the religion are both of them genuine keys for unlocking the world's treasure-house to him who can use either of them practically. Just as evidently neither is exhaustive or exclusive of the other's simultaneous use. And why, after all, may not the world be so complex as to consist of many interpenetrating spheres of reality, which we can thus approach in alternation by using different conceptions and assuming different attitudes, just as mathematicians handle the same numerical and spatial facts by geometry, by analytical geometry, by algebra, by the calculus, or by quaternions, and each time come out right? On this view religion and science, each verified in its own way from hour to hour and from life to life, would be co-eternal. Primitive thought, with its belief in individualized personal forces, seems at any rate as far as ever from being driven by science from the field today. Numbers of educated people still find it the directest experimental channel by which to carry on their intercourse with reality.

Whether the various spheres or systems are ever to fuse integrally into one absolute conception, as most philosophers assume that they must, and how, if so, that conception may best be reached, are questions that only the future can answer. What is certain now is the fact of lines of disparate conception, each corresponding to some part of the world's truth, each verified in some degree, each leaving out some part of real experience.

The case of mind-cure lay so ready to my hand that I could not resist the temptation of using it to bring these last truths home to your attention, but I must content myself today with this very brief indication. In a later lecture the relations of religion both to science and to primitive thought will have to receive much more explicit attention.

LECTURES IV & V APPENDIX

CASE 1. "My own experience is this: I had long been ill, and one of the first results of my illness, a dozen years before, had been a diplopia which deprived me of the use of my eyes for reading and writing almost entirely, while a later one had been to shut me out from exercise of any kind under penalty of immediate and great exhaustion. I had been under the care of doctors of the highest standing both in Europe and America, men in whose power to help me I had had great faith, with no or ill result. Then, at a time when I seemed to be rather rapidly losing ground, I heard some things that gave me interest enough in mental healing to make me try it; I had no great hope of getting any good from it— it was a chance I tried, partly because my thought was interested by the new possibility it seemed to open, partly because it was the only chance I then could see. I went to X. in Boston, from whom some friends of mine had got, or thought that they had got, great help; the treatment was a silent one; little was said, and that little carried no conviction to my mind; whatever influence was exerted was that of another person's thought or feeling silently projected on to my unconscious mind, into my nervous system as it were, as we sat still together. I believed from the start in the possibility of such action, for I knew the power of the mind to shape, helping or hindering the body's nerve-activities, and I thought telepathy probable, although unproved, but I had no belief in it as more than a possibility, and no strong conviction nor any mystic or religious faith connected with my thought of it that might have brought imagination strongly into play.

"I sat quietly with the healer for half an hour each day, at first with no result; then, after ten days or so, I became quite suddenly and swiftly conscious of a tide of new energy rising within me, a sense of power to pass beyond old halting-places, of power to break the bounds that, though often tried before, had long been veritable walls about my life, too high to climb. I began to read and walk as I had not done for years, and the change was sudden, marked, and unmistakable. This tide seemed to mount for some weeks, three or four perhaps, when, summer having come, I came away, taking the treatment up again a few months later. The lift I got proved permanent, and left me slowly gaining ground instead of losing it, but with this lift the influence seemed in a way to have spent itself, and, though my confidence in the reality of the power had gained immensely from this first experience, and should have helped me to make further gain in health and strength if my belief in it had been the potent factor there, I never after this got any result at all as striking or as clearly marked as this which came when I made trial of it first, with little faith and doubtful expectation. It is difficult to put all the evidence in such a matter into words, to gather up into a distinct statement all that one bases one's conclusions on, but I have always felt that I had abundant evidence to justify (to myself, at least) the conclusion that I came to then, and since have held to, that the physical change which came at that time was, first, the result of a change wrought within me by a change of mental state; and, secondly, that that change of mental state was not, save in a very secondary way, brought about through the influence of an excited imagination, or a consciously received suggestion of an hypnotic sort. Lastly, I believe that this change was the result of my receiving telepathically, and upon a mental stratum quite below the level of immediate consciousness, a healthier and more energetic attitude, receiving it from another person whose thought was directed upon me with the intention of impressing the idea of this attitude upon me. In my case the disease was distinctly what would be classed as nervous, not organic; but from such opportunities as I have had of observing, I have come to the conclusion that the dividing line that has been drawn is an arbitrary one, the nerves controlling the internal activities and the nutrition of the body throughout; and I believe that the central nervous system, by starting and inhibiting local centres, can exercise a vast influence upon disease of any kind, if it can be brought to bear. In my judgment the question is simply how to bring it to bear, and I think that the uncertainty and remarkable differences in the results obtained through mental healing do but show how ignorant we are as yet of the forces at work and of the means we should take to make them effective. That these results are not due to chance coincidences my observation of myself and others makes me sure; that the conscious mind, the imagination, enters into them as a factor in many cases is doubtless true, but in many others, and sometimes very extraordinary ones, it hardly seems to enter in at all. On the whole I am inclined to think that as the healing action, like the morbid one, springs from the plane of the normally unconscious mind, so the strongest and most effective impressions are those which it receives, in some as yet unknown, subtle way, directly from a healthier mind whose state, through a hidden law of sympathy, it reproduces."

CASE II. "At the urgent request of friends, and with no faith and hardly any hope (possibly owing to a previous unsuccessful experience with a Christian Scientist), our little daughter was placed under the care of a healer, and cured of a trouble about which the physician had been very discouraging in his diagnosis. This interested me, and I began studying earnestly the method and philosophy of this method of healing. Gradually an inner peace and tranquility came to me in so positive a way that my manner changed greatly. My children and friends noticed the change and commented upon it. All feelings of irritability disappeared. Even the expression of my face changed noticeably.

"I had been bigoted, aggressive, and intolerant in discussion, both in public and private. I grew broadly tolerant and receptive toward the views of others. I had been nervous and irritable, coming home two or three times a week with a sick headache induced, as I then supposed, by dyspepsia and catarrh. I grew serene and gentle, and the physical troubles entirely disappeared. I had been in the habit of approaching every business interview with an almost morbid dread. I now meet every one with confidence and inner calm.

"I may say that the growth has all been toward the elimination of selfishness. I do not mean simply the grosser, more sensual forms, but those subtler and generally unrecognized kinds, such as express themselves in sorrow, grief, regret, envy, etc. It has been in the direction of a practical, working realization of the immanence of God and the Divinity of man's true, inner self."

LECTURES VI AND VII: THE SICK SOUL

At our last meeting, we considered the healthy-minded temperament, the temperament which has a constitutional incapacity for prolonged suffering, and in which the tendency to see things optimistically is like a water of crystallization in which the individual's character is set. We saw how this temperament may become the basis for a peculiar type of religion, a religion in which good, even the good of this world's life, is regarded as the essential thing for a rational being to attend to. This religion directs him to settle his scores with the more evil aspects of the universe by systematically declining to lay them to heart or make much of them by ignoring them in his reflective calculations, or even, on occasion, by denying outright that they exist. Evil is a disease; and worry over disease is itself an additional form of disease, which only adds to the original complaint. Even repentance and remorse, affections which come in the character of ministers of good, may be but sickly and relaxing impulses, The best repentance is to up and act for righteousness, and forget that you ever had relations with sin.

Spinoza's philosophy has this sort of healthy-mindedness woven into the heart of it, and this has been one secret of its fascination. He whom Reason leads, according to Spinoza, is led altogether by the influence over his mind of good. Knowledge of evil is an 'inadequate' knowledge, fit only for slavish minds. So Spinoza categorically condemns repentance. When men make mistakes, he says,—

"One might perhaps expect gnawings of conscience and repentance to help to bring them on the right path, and might thereupon conclude (as every one does conclude) that these affections are good things. Yet when we look at the matter closely, we shall find that not only are they not good, but on the contrary deleterious and evil passions. For it is manifest that we can always get along better by reason and love of truth than by worry of conscience and remorse. Harmful are these and evil, inasmuch as they form a particular kind of sadness; and the disadvantages of sadness," he continues, "I have already proved, and shown that we should strive to keep it from our life. Just so we should endeavor, since uneasiness of conscience and remorse are of this kind of complexion, to flee and shun these states of mind." [Tract on God, Man, and Happiness, Book ii. ch. x.]

Within the Christian body, for which repentance of sins has from the beginning been the critical religious act, healthy-mindedness has always come forward with its milder interpretation. Repentance according to such healthy-minded Christians means getting away from the sin, not groaning and writhing over its commission. The Catholic practice of confession and absolution is in one of its aspects little more than a systematic method of keeping healthy-mindedness on top. By it a man's accounts with evil are periodically squared and audited, so that he may start the clean page with no old debts inscribed. Any Catholic will tell us how clean and fresh and free he feels after the purging operation. Martin Luther by no means belonged to the healthy-minded type in the radical sense in which we have discussed it, and be repudiated priestly absolution for sin. Yet in this matter of repentance he had some very healthy-minded ideas, due in the main to the largeness of his conception of God.

"When I was a monk," he says, "I thought that I was utterly cast away, if at any time I felt the lust of the flesh: that is to say, if I felt any evil motion, fleshly lust, wrath, hatred, or envy against any brother. I assayed many ways to help to quiet my conscience, but it would not be; for the concupiscence and lust of my flesh did always return, so that I could not rest, but was continually vexed with these thoughts: This or that sin thou hast committed: thou art infected with envy, with impatiency, and such other sins: therefore thou art entered into this holy order in vain, and all thy good works are unprofitable. But if then I had rightly understood these sentences of Paul: 'The flesh lusteth contrary to the Spirit, and the Spirit contrary to the flesh; and these two are one against another, so that ye cannot do the things that ye would do,' I should not have so miserably tormented myself, but should have thought and said to myself, as now commonly I do, 'Martin, thou shalt not utterly be without sin, for thou hast flesh; thou shalt therefore feel the battle thereof.' I remember that Staupitz was wont to say, 'I have vowed unto God above a thousand times that I would become a better man: but I never performed that which I vowed. Hereafter I will make no such vow: for I have now learned by experience that I am not able to perform it. Unless, therefore, God be favorable and merciful unto me for Christ's sake, I shall not be able, with all my vows and all my good deeds, to stand before him.' This (of Staupitz's) was not only a true, but also a godly and a holy desperation; and this must they all confess, both with mouth and heart, who will be saved. For the godly trust not to their own righteousness. They look unto Christ their reconciler, who gave his life for their sins. Moreover, they know that the remnant of sin which is in their flesh is not laid to their charge, but freely pardoned. Notwithstanding, in the mean while they fight in spirit against the flesh, lest they should fulfill the lusts thereof; and although they feel the flesh to rage and rebel, and themselves also do fan sometimes into sin through infirmity, yet are they not discouraged, nor think therefore that their state and kind of life, and the works which are done according to their calling, displease God; but they raise up themselves by faith." [Commentary on Galatians, Philadelphia, 1891.]

One of the heresies for which the Jesuits got that spiritual genius, Molinos, the founder of Quietism, so abominably condemned was his healthy-minded opinion of repentance:—

"When thou fallest into a fault, in what matter soever it be, do not trouble nor afflict thyself for it. For they are effects of our frail Nature, stained by Original Sin. The common enemy will make thee believe, as soon as thou fallest into any fault, that thou walkest in error, and therefore art out of God and his favor, and herewith would he make thee distrust of the divine Grace, telling thee of thy misery, and making a giant of it; and putting it into thy head that every day thy soul grows worse instead of better, whilst it so often repeats these failings. O blessed Soul, open thine eyes; and shut the gate against these diabolical suggestions, knowing thy misery, and trusting in the mercy divine. Would not he be a mere fool who, running at tournament with others, and falling in the best of the career, should lie weeping on the ground and afflicting himself with discourses upon his fall? Man (they would tell him), lose no time, get up and take the course again, for he that rises again quickly and continues his race is as if he had never fallen. If thou seest thyself fallen once and a thousand times, thou oughtest to make use of the remedy which I have given thee, that is, a loving confidence in the divine mercy. These are the weapons with which thou must fight and conquer cowardice and vain thoughts. This is the means thou oughtest to use— not to lose time, not to disturb thyself, and reap no good." [Molinos: Spiritual Guide.]

Now in contrast with such healthy-minded views as these, if we treat them as a way of deliberately minimizing evil, stands a radically opposite view, a way of maximizing evil, if you please so to call it, based on the persuasion that the evil aspects of our life are of its very essence, and that the world's meaning most comes home to us when we lay them most to heart. We have now to address ourselves to this more morbid way of looking at the situation. But as I closed our last hour with a general philosophical reflection on the healthy-minded way of taking life, I should like at this point to make another philosophical reflection upon it before turning to that heavier task. You will excuse the brief delay.

If we admit that evil is an essential part of our being and the key to the interpretation of our life, we load ourselves down with a difficulty that has always proved burdensome in philosophies of religion. Theism, whenever it has erected itself into a systematic philosophy of the universe, has shown a reluctance to let God be anything less than All-in-All. In other words, philosophic theism has always shown a tendency to become pantheistic and monistic, and to consider the world as one unit of absolute fact; and this has been at variance with popular or practical theism, which latter has ever been more or less frankly pluralistic, not to say polytheistic, and shown itself perfectly well satisfied with a universe composed of many original principles, provided we be only allowed to believe that the divine principle remains supreme, and that the others are subordinate. In this latter case God is not necessarily responsible for the existence of evil; he would only be responsible if it were not finally overcome. But on the monistic or pantheistic view, evil, like everything else, must have its foundation in God; and the difficulty is to see how this can possibly be the case if God be absolutely good. This difficulty faces us in every form of philosophy in which the world appears as one flawless unit of fact. Such a unit is an Individual, and in it the worst parts must be as essential as the best, must be as necessary to make the individual what he is; since if any part whatever in an individual were to vanish or alter, it would no longer be that individual at all. The philosophy of absolute idealism, so vigorously represented both in Scotland and America today, has to struggle with this difficulty quite as much as scholastic theism struggled in its time; and although it would be premature to say that there is no speculative issue whatever from the puzzle, it is perfectly fair to say that there is no clear or easy-issue, and that the only obvious escape from paradox here is to cut loose from the monistic assumption altogether, and to allow the world to have existed from its origin in pluralistic form, as an aggregate or collection of higher and lower things and principles, rather than an absolutely unitary fact. For then evil would not need to be essential; it might be, and may always have been, an independent portion that had no rational or absolute right to live with the rest, and which we might conceivably hope to see got rid of at last.

Now the gospel of healthy-mindedness, as we have described it, casts its vote distinctly for this pluralistic view. Whereas the monistic philosopher finds himself more or less bound to say, as Hegel said, that everything actual is rational, and that evil, as an element dialectically required, must be pinned in and kept and consecrated and have a function awarded to it in the final system of truth, healthy-mindedness refuses to say anything of the sort. Evil, it says, is emphatically irrational, and not to be pinned in, or preserved, or consecrated in any final system of truth. It is a pure abomination to the Lord, an alien unreality, a waste element, to be sloughed off and negated, and the very memory of it, if possible, wiped out and forgotten. The ideal, so far from being co-extensive with the whole actual, is a mere extract from the actual, marked by its deliverance from all contact with this diseased, inferior, and excrementitious stuff.

I say this in spite of the monistic utterances of many mind-cure writers; for these utterances are really inconsistent with their attitude towards disease, and can easily be shown not to be logically involved in the experiences of union with a higher Presence with which they connect themselves. The higher Presence, namely, need not be the absolute whole of things, it is quite sufficient for the life of religious experience to regard it as a part, if only it be the most ideal part.

Here we have the interesting notion fairly and squarely presented to us, of there being elements of the universe which may make no rational whole in conjunction with the other elements, and which, from the point of view of any system which those other elements make up, can only be considered so much irrelevance and accident— so much 'dirt,' as it were, and matter out of place. I ask you now not to forget this notion; for although most philosophers seem either to forget it or to disdain it too much ever to mention it, I believe that we shall have to admit it ourselves in the end as containing an element of truth. The mind-cure gospel thus once more appears to us as having dignity and importance. We have seen it to be a genuine religion, and no mere silly appeal to imagination to cure disease; we have seen its method of experimental verification to be not unlike the method of all science; and now here we find mind-cure as the champion of a perfectly definite conception of the metaphysical structure of the world. I hope that, in view of all this, you will not regret my having pressed it upon your attention at such length.

Let us now say good-by for a while to all this way of thinking, and turn towards those persons who cannot so swiftly throw off the burden of the consciousness of evil, but are congenitally fated to suffer from its presence. Just as we saw that in healthy-mindedness there are shallower and profounder levels, happiness like that of the mere animal, and more regenerate of happiness, so also are there different levels of the morbid mind, and the one is much more formidable than the other. There are people for whom evil means only a mal-adjustment with things, a wrong correspondence of one's life with the environment. Such evil as this is curable, in principle at least, upon the natural plane, for merely by modifying either the self or the things, or both at once, the two terms may be made to fit, and all go merry as a marriage bell again. But there are others for whom evil is no mere relation of the subject to particular outer things, but something more radical and general, a wrongness or vice in his essential nature, which no alteration of the environment, or any superficial rearrangement of the inner self, can cure, and which requires a supernatural remedy. On the whole, the Latin races have leaned more towards the former way of looking upon evil, as made up of ills and sins in the plural, removable in detail; while the Germanic races have tended rather to think of Sin in the singular, and with a capital S, as of something ineradicably ingrained in our natural subjectivity, and never to be removed by any superficial piecemeal operations. These comparisons of races are always open to exception, but undoubtedly the northern tone in religion has inclined to the more intimately pessimistic persuasion, and this way of feeling, being the more extreme, we shall find by far the more instructive for our study. [Cf., J. Milsand: Luther et le Serf-Arbitre, 1884, passim.]

Recent psychology has found great use for the word 'threshold' as a symbolic designation for the point at which one state of mind passes into another. Thus we speak of the threshold of a man's consciousness in general, to indicate the amount of noise, pressure, or other outer stimulus which it takes to arouse his attention at all. One with a high threshold will doze through an amount of racket by which one with a low threshold would be immediately waked. Similarly, when one is sensitive to small differences in any order of sensation we say he has a low 'difference-threshold'— his mind easily steps over it into the consciousness of the differences in question. And just so we might speak of a 'pain-threshold,' a 'fear-threshold,' a 'misery-threshold,' and find it quickly overpassed by the consciousness of some individuals, but lying too high in others to be often reached by their consciousness. The sanguine and healthy-minded live habitually on the sunny side of their misery-line, the depressed and melancholy live beyond it, in darkness and apprehension. There are men who seem to have started in life with a bottle or two of champagne inscribed to their credit; whilst others seem to have been born close to the pain-threshold, which the slightest irritants fatally send them over.

Does it not appear as if one who lived more habitually on one side of the pain-threshold might need a different sort of religion from one who habitually lived on the other? This question, of the relativity of different types of religion to different types of need, arises naturally at this point, and will become a serious problem ere we have done. But before we confront it in general terms, we must address ourselves to the unpleasant task of hearing what the sick souls, as we may call them in contrast to the healthy-minded, have to say of the secrets of their prison-house, their own peculiar form of consciousness. Let us then resolutely turn our backs on the once-born and their sky-blue optimistic gospel; let us not simply cry out, in spite of all appearances, "Hurrah for the Universe!— God's in his Heaven, all's right with the world." Let us see rather whether pity, pain, and fear, and the sentiment of human helplessness may not open a profounder view and put into our hands a more complicated key to the meaning of the situation.

To begin with, how can things so insecure as the successful experiences of this world afford a stable anchorage? A chain is no stronger than its weakest link, and life is after all a chain. In the healthiest and most prosperous existence, how many links of illness, danger, and disaster are always interposed? Unsuspectedly from the bottom of every fountain of pleasure, as the old poet said, something bitter rises up: a touch of nausea, a falling dead of the delight, a whiff of melancholy, things that sound a knell, for fugitive as they may be, they bring a feeling of coming from a deeper region and often have an appalling convincingness. The buzz of life ceases at their touch as a piano-string stops sounding when the damper falls upon it.

Of course the music can commence again;— and again and again,— at intervals. But with this the healthy-minded consciousness is left with an irremediable sense of precariousness. It is a bell with a crack; it draws its breath on sufferance and by an accident.

Even if we suppose a man so packed with healthy-mindedness as never to have experienced in his own person any of these sobering intervals, still, if he is a reflecting being, he must generalize and class his own lot with that of others; and, doing so, he must see that his escape is just a lucky chance and no essential difference. He might just as well have been born to an entirely different fortune. And then indeed the hollow security! What kind of a frame of things is it of which the best you can say is, "Thank God, it has let me off clear this time!" Is not its blessedness a fragile fiction? Is not your joy in it a very vulgar glee, not much unlike the snicker of any rogue at his success? If indeed it were an success, even on such terms as that! But take the happiest man, the one most envied by the world, and in nine cases out of ten his inmost consciousness is one of failure. Either his ideals in the line of his achievements are pitched far higher than the achievements themselves, or else he has secret ideals of which the world knows nothing, and in regard to which he inwardly knows himself to be found wanting.

When such a conquering optimist as Goethe can express himself in this wise, how must it be with less successful men?

"I will say nothing," writes Goethe in 1824, "against the course of my existence. But at bottom it has been nothing but pain and burden, and I can affirm that during the whole of my 75 years, I have not had four weeks of genuine well-being. It is but the perpetual rolling of a rock that must be raised up again forever."

What single-handed man was ever on the whole as successful as Luther? yet when he had grown old, he looked back on his life as if it were an absolute failure.

"I am utterly weary of life. I pray the Lord will come forthwith and carry me hence. Let him come, above all, with his last Judgment: I will stretch out my neck, the thunder will burst forth, and I shall be at rest."— And having a necklace of white agates in his hand at the time he added: "O God, grant that it may come without delay. I would readily eat up this necklace today, for the Judgment to come tomorrow."— The Electress Dowager, one day when Luther was dining with her, said to him: "Doctor, I wish you may live forty years to come." "Madam," replied he, "rather than live forty years more, I would give up my chance of Paradise."

Failure, then, failure! so the world stamps us at every turn. We strew it with our blunders, our misdeeds, our lost opportunities, with all the memorials of our inadequacy to our vocation. And with what a damning emphasis does it then blot us out! No easy fine, no mere apology or formal expiation, will satisfy the world's demands, but every pound of flesh exacted is soaked with all its blood. The subtlest forms of suffering known to man are connected with the poisonous humiliations incidental to these results.

And they are pivotal human experiences. A process so ubiquitous and everlasting is evidently an integral part of life. "There is indeed one element in human destiny," Robert Louis Stevenson writes, "that not blindness itself can controvert. Whatever else we are intended to do, we are not intended to succeed; failure is the fate allotted. "Our business is to continue to fail in good spirits." And our nature being thus rooted in failure, is it any wonder that theologians should have held it to be essential, and thought that only through the personal experience of humiliation which it engenders the deeper sense of life's significance is reached?

The God of many men is little more than their court of appeal against the damnatory judgment passed on their failures by the opinion of this world. To our own consciousness there is usually a residuum of worth left over after our sins and errors have been told off- our capacity of acknowledging and regretting them is the germ of a better self in posse at least. But the world deals with us in actu and not in posse: and of this bidden germ, not to be guessed at from without, it never takes account. Then we turn to the All-knower, who knows our bad, but knows this good in us also, and who is just. We cast ourselves with our repentance on his mercy: only by an All-knower can we finally be judged. So the need of a God very definitely emerges from this sort of experience of life.

But this is only the first stage of the world-sickness. Make the human being's sensitiveness a little greater, carry him a little farther over the misery-threshold, and the good quality of the successful moments themselves when they occur is spoiled and vitiated. All natural goods perish. Riches take wings; fame is a breath; love is a cheat; youth and health and pleasure vanish. Can things whose end is always dust and disappointment be the real goods which our souls require? Back of everything is the great spectre of universal death, the all-encompassing blackness:—

"What profit hath a man of all his labour which he taketh under the Sun? I looked on all the works that my hands had wrought, and behold, all was vanity and vexation of spirit. For that which befalleth the sons of men befalleth beasts; as the one dieth, so dieth the other; all are of the dust, and all turn to dust again.... The dead know not anything, neither have they any more a reward; for the memory of them is forgotten. Also their love and their hatred and their envy is now perished; neither have they any more a portion for ever in anything that is done under the Sun.... Truly the light is sweet, and a pleasant thing it is for the eyes to behold the Sun: but if a man live many years and rejoice in them all, yet let him remember the days of darkness; for they shall be many."

In short, life and its negation are beaten up inextricably together. But if the life be good, the negation of it must be bad. Yet the two are equally essential facts of existence; and all natural happiness thus seems infected with a contradiction. The breath of the sepulchre surrounds it.

To a mind attentive to this state of things and rightly subject to the joy-destroying chill which such a contemplation engenders, the only relief that healthy-mindedness can give is by saying: 'Stuff and nonsense, get out into the open air!' or 'Cheer up, old fellow, you'll be all right erelong, if you will only drop your morbidness!' But in all seriousness, can such bald animal talk as that be treated as a rational answer? To ascribe religious value to mere happy-go-lucky contentment with one's brief chance at natural good is but the very consecration of forgetfulness and superficiality. Our troubles lie indeed too deep for that cure. The fact that we can die, that we can be ill at all, is what perplexes us; the fact that we now for a moment live and are well is irrelevant to that perplexity. We need a life not correlated with death, a health not liable to illness, a kind of good that will not perish, a good in fact that flies beyond the Goods of nature.

It all depends on how sensitive the soul may become to discords. "The trouble with me is that I believe too much in common happiness and goodness," said a friend of mine whose consciousness was of this sort, "and nothing can console me for their transiency. I am appalled and disconcerted at its being possible." And so with most of us: a little cooling down of animal excitability and instinct, a little loss of animal toughness, a little irritable weakness and descent of the pain-threshold, will bring the worm at the core of all our usual springs of delight into full view, and turn us into melancholy metaphysicians. The pride of life and glory of the world will shrivel. It is after all but the standing quarrel of hot youth and hoary eld. Old age has the last word: the purely naturalistic look at life, however enthusiastically it may begin, is sure to end in sadness.

This sadness lies at the heart of every merely positivistic, agnostic, or naturalistic scheme of philosophy. Let sanguine healthy-mindedness do its best with its strange power of living in the moment and ignoring and forgetting, still the evil background is really there to be thought of, and the skull will grin in at the banquet. In the practical life of the individual, we know how his whole gloom or glee about any present fact depends on the remoter schemes and hopes with which it stands related. Its significance and framing give it the chief part of its value. Let it be known to lead nowhere, and however agreeable it may be in its immediacy, its glow and gilding vanish. The old man, sick with an insidious internal disease, may laugh and quaff his wine at first as well as ever, but he knows his fate now, for the doctors have revealed it; and the knowledge knocks the satisfaction out of all these functions. They are partners of death and the worm is their brother, and they turn to a mere flatness.

The lustre of the present hour is always borrowed from the background of possibilities it goes with. Let our common experiences be enveloped in an eternal moral order; let our suffering have an immortal significance; let Heaven smile upon the earth, and deities pay their visits; let faith and hope be the atmosphere which man breathes in;— and his days pass by with zest; they stir with prospects, they thrill with remoter values. Place round them on the contrary the curdling cold and gloom and absence of all permanent meaning which for pure naturalism and the popular science evolutionism of our time are all that is visible ultimately, and the thrill stops short, or turns rather to an anxious trembling.

For naturalism, fed on recent cosmological speculations, mankind is in a position similar to that of a set of people living on a frozen lake, surrounded by cliffs over which there is no escape, yet knowing that little by little the ice is melting, and the inevitable day drawing near when the last film of it will disappear, and to be drowned ignominiously will be the human creature's portion. The merrier the skating, the warmer and more sparkling the sun by day, and the ruddier the bonfires at night, the more poignant the sadness with which one must take in the meaning of the total situation.

The early Greeks are continually held up to us in literary works as models of the healthy-minded joyousness which the religion of nature may engender. There was indeed much joyousness among the Greeks— Homer's flow of enthusiasm for most things that the sun shines upon is steady. But even in Homer the reflective passages are cheerless, [E.g., Iliad, XVII. 446: "Nothing then is more wretched anywhere than man of all that breathes and creeps upon this earth."] and the moment the Greeks grew systematically pensive and thought of ultimates, they became unmitigated pessimists. The jealousy of the gods, the nemesis that follows too much happiness, the all-encompassing death, fate's dark opacity, the ultimate and unintelligible cruelty, were the fixed background of their imagination. The beautiful joyousness of their polytheism is only a poetic modern fiction. They knew no joys comparable in quality of preciousness to those which we shall erelong see that Brahmans, Buddhists, Christians, Mohammedans, twice-born people whose religion is non-naturalistic, get from their several creeds of mysticism and renunciation. [E.g., Theognis, 425-428: "Best of all for all things upon earth is it not to be born nor to behold the splendors of the Sun; next best to traverse as soon as possible the gates of Hades." See also the almost identical passage in Oedipus in Colonus, 1225.— The Anthology is full of pessimistic utterances: "Naked came I upon the earth, naked I go below the ground— why then do I vainly toil when I see the end naked before me?"— "How did I come to be? Whence am I? Wherefore did I come? To pass away. How can I learn aught when naught I know? Being naught I came to life: once more shall I be what I was. Nothing and nothingness is the whole race of mortals."— "For death we are all cherished and fattened like a herd of hogs that is wantonly butchered."]

The difference between Greek pessimism and the oriental and modern variety is that the Greeks had not made the discovery that the pathetic mood may be idealized, and figure as a higher form of sensibility. Their spirit was still too essentially masculine for pessimism to be elaborated or lengthily dwelt on in their classic literature. They would have despised a life set wholly in a minor key, and summoned it to keep within the proper bounds of lachrymosity. The discovery that the enduring emphasis, so far as this world goes, may be laid on its pain and failure, was reserved for races more complex, and (so to speak) more feminine than the Hellenes had attained to being in the classic period. But all the same was the outlook of those Hellenes blackly pessimistic.

Stoic insensibility and Epicurean resignation were the farthest advance which the Greek mind made in that direction. The Epicurean said: "Seek not to be happy, but rather to escape unhappiness; strong happiness is always linked with pain; therefore hug the safe shore, and do not tempt the deeper raptures. Avoid disappointment by expecting little, and by aiming low; and above all do not fret." The Stoic said: "The only genuine good that life can yield a man is the free possession of his own soul; all other goods are lies." Each of these philosophies is in its degree a philosophy of despair in nature's boons. Trustful self-abandonment to the joys that freely offer has entirely departed from both Epicurean and Stoic; and what each proposes is a way of rescue from the resultant dust-and-ashes state of mind. The Epicurean still awaits results from economy of indulgence and damping of desire. The Stoic hopes for no results, and gives up natural good altogether. There is dignity in both these forms of resignation. They represent distinct stages in the sobering process which man's primitive intoxication with sense-happiness is sure to undergo. In the one the hot blood has grown cool, in the other it has become quite cold; and although I have spoken of them in the past tense, as if they were merely historic, yet Stoicism and Epicureanism will probably be to all time typical attitudes, marking a certain definite stage accomplished in the evolution of the world-sick soul. They mark the conclusion of what we call the once-born period, and represent the highest flights of what twice-born religion would call the purely natural man— Epicureanism, which can only by great courtesy be called a religion, showing his refinement, and Stoicism exhibiting his moral will. They leave the world in the shape of an unreconciled contradiction, and seek no higher unity. Compared with the complex ecstasies which the supernaturally regenerated Christian may enjoy, or the oriental pantheist indulge in, their receipts for equanimity are expedients which seem almost crude in their simplicity.

For instance, on the very day on which I write this page, the post brings me some aphorisms from a worldly-wise old friend in Heidelberg which may serve as a good contemporaneous expression of Epicureanism: "By the word 'happiness' every human being understands something different. It is a phantom pursued only by weaker minds. The wise man is satisfied with the more modest but much more definite term contentment. What education should chiefly aim at is to save us from a discontented life. Health is one favoring condition, but by no means an indispensable one, of contentment. Woman's heart and love are a shrewd device of Nature, a trap which she sets for the average man, to force him into working. But the wise man will always prefer work chosen by himself."

Please observe, however, that I am not yet pretending finally to judge any of these attitudes. I am only describing their variety.

The securest way to the rapturous sorts of happiness of which the twice-born make report has as an historic matter of fact been through a more radical pessimism than anything that we have yet considered. We have seen how the lustre and enchantment may be rubbed off from the goods of nature. But there is a pitch of unhappiness so great that the goods of nature may be entirely forgotten, and all sentiment of their existence vanish from the mental field. For this extremity of pessimism to be reached, something more is needed than observation of life and reflection upon death. The individual must in his own person become the prey of a pathological melancholy. As the healthy-minded enthusiast succeeds in ignoring evil's very existence, so the subject of melancholy is forced in spite of himself to ignore that of all good whatever: for him it may no longer have the least reality. Such sensitiveness and susceptibility to mental pain is a rare occurrence where the nervous constitution is entirely normal; one seldom finds it in a healthy subject even where he is the victim of the most atrocious cruelties of outward fortune. So we note here the neurotic constitution, of which I said so much in my first lecture, making its active entrance on our scene, and destined to play a part in much that follows. Since these experiences of melancholy are in the first instance absolutely private and individual, I can now help myself out with personal documents. Painful indeed they will be to listen to, and there is almost an indecency in handling them in public. Yet they lie right in the middle of our path; and if we are to touch the psychology of religion at all seriously, we must be willing to forget conventionalities, and dive below the smooth and lying official conversational surface.

One can distinguish many kinds of pathological depression. Sometimes it is mere passive joylessness and dreariness, discouragement, dejection, lack of taste and zest and spring. Professor Ribot has proposed the name anhedonia to designate this condition.

"The state of anhedonia, if I may coin a new word to pair off with analgesia," he writes, "has been very little studied, but it exists. A young girl was smitten with a liver disease which for some time altered her constitution. She felt no longer any affection for her father and mother. She would have played with her doll, but it was impossible to find the least pleasure in the act. The same things which formerly convulsed her with laughter entirely failed to interest her now. Esquirol observed the case of a very intelligent magistrate who was also a prey to hepatic disease. Every emotion appeared dead within him. He manifested neither perversion nor violence, but complete absence of emotional reaction. If he went to the theatre, which he did out of habit, he could find no pleasure there. The thought of his house, of his home, of his wife, and of his absent children moved him as little, he said, as a theorem of Euclid." [ribot: Psychologie des sentiments, p. 54.]

Prolonged seasickness will in most persons produce a temporary condition of anhedonia. Every good, terrestrial or celestial, is imagined only to be turned from with disgust. A temporary condition of this sort, connected with the religious evolution of a singularly lofty character, both intellectual and moral, is well described by the Catholic philosopher, Father Gratry, in his autobiographical recollections. In consequence of mental isolation and excessive study at the Polytechnic school, young Gratry fell into a state of nervous exhaustion with symptoms which he thus describes:—

"I had such a universal terror that I woke at night with a start, thinking that the Pantheon was tumbling on the Polytechnic school, or that the school was in flames, or that the Seine was pouring into the Catacombs, and that Paris was being swallowed up. And when these impressions were past, all day long without respite I suffered an incurable and intolerable desolation, verging on despair. I thought myself, in fact, rejected by God, lost, damned! I felt something like the suffering of hell. Before that I had never even thought of hell. My mind had never turned in that direction. Neither discourses nor reflections had impressed me in that way. I took no account of hell. Now, and all at once, I suffered in a measure what is suffered there.

"But what was perhaps still more dreadful is that every idea of heaven was taken away from me: I could no longer conceive of anything of the sort. Heaven did not seem to me worth going to. It was like a vacuum; a mythological elysium, an abode of shadows less real than the earth. I could conceive no joy, no pleasure in inhabiting it. Happiness, joy, light, affection, love— all these words were now devoid of sense. Without doubt I could still have talked of all these things, but I had become incapable of feeling anything in them, of understanding anything about them, of hoping anything from them, or of believing them to exist. There was my great and inconsolable grief! I neither perceived nor conceived any longer the existence of happiness or perfection. An abstract heaven over a naked rock. Such was my present abode for eternity." [A. Gratry: Sonvenirs de ma jeunesse, 1880, pp. 119-121, abridged. Some persons are affected with anhedonia permanently, or at any rate with a loss of the usual appetite for life. The annals of suicide supply such examples as the following:]

An uneducated domestic servant, aged nineteen, poisons herself, and leaves two letters expressing her motive for the act. To her parents she writes:

"Life is sweet perhaps to some, but I prefer what is sweeter than life, and that is death. So good-by forever, my dear parents. It is nobody's fault, but a strong desire of my own which I have longed to fulfill for three or four years. I have always had a hope that some day I might have all opportunity of fulfilling it, and now it has come.... It is a wonder I have put this off so long, but I thought perhaps I should cheer up a bit and put all thought out of my head." To her brother she writes: "Good-by forever, my own dearest brother. By the time you get this I shall be gone forever. I know, dear love, there is no forgiveness for what I am going to do.... I am tired of living, so am willing to die.... Life may be sweet to some, but death to me is sweeter." [S.A.K. Strahan: Suicide and Insanity, 2d edition, London, 1894, p. 131.]

So much for melancholy in the sense of incapacity for joyous feeling. A much worse form of it is positive and active anguish, a sort of psychical neuralgia wholly unknown to healthy life. Such anguish may partake of various characters, having sometimes more the quality of loathing; sometimes that of irritation and exasperation; or again of self-mistrust and self-despair; or of suspicion, anxiety, trepidation, fear. The patient may rebel or submit; may accuse himself, or accuse outside powers; and he may or he may not be tormented by the theoretical mystery of why he should so have to suffer. Most case are mixed cases, and we should not treat our classifications with too much respect. Moreover, it is only a relatively small proportion of cases that connect themselves with the religious sphere of experience at all. Exasperated cases, for instance, as a rule do not. I quote now literally from the first case of melancholy on which I lay my hand. It is a letter from a patient in a French asylum.

"I suffer too much in this hospital, both physically and morally. Besides the burnings and the sleeplessness (for I no longer sleep since I am shut up here, and the little rest I get is broken by bad dreams, and I am waked with a jump by nightmares, dreadful visions, lightning, thunder, and the rest), fear, atrocious fear, presses me down, holds me without respite, never lets me go. Where is the justice in it all! What have I done to deserve this excess of severity? Under what form will this fear crush me? What would I not owe to any one who would rid me of my life! Eat, drink, lie awake all night, suffer without interruption— such is the fine legacy I have received from my mother! What I fail to understand is this abuse of power. There are limits to everything, there is a middle way. But God knows neither middle way nor limits. I say God, but why? All I have known so far has been the devil. After all, I am afraid of God as much as of the devil, so I drift along, thinking of nothing but suicide, but with neither courage nor means here to execute the act. As you read this, it will easily prove to you my insanity. The style and the ideas are incoherent enough— I can see that myself. But I cannot keep myself from being either crazy or an idiot; and, as things are, from whom should I ask pity? I am defenseless against the invisible enemy who is tightening his coils around me. I should be no better armed against him even if I saw him, or had seen him. Oh, if he would but kill me, devil take him! Death, death, once for all! But I stop. I have raved to you long enough. I say raved, for I can write no otherwise, having neither brain nor thoughts left. O God! what a misfortune to be born! Born like a mushroom, doubtless between an evening and a morning; and how true and right I was when in our philosophy-year in college I chewed the cud of bitterness with the pessimists. Yes, indeed, there is more pain in life than gladness— it is one long agony until the grave. Think how gay it makes me to remember that this horrible misery of mine, coupled with this unspeakable fear, may last fifty, one hundred, who knows how many more years!" [Roubinovitch et Toulouse: La Melancolie, 1897, p. 170, abridged.]

This letter shows two things. First, you see how the entire consciousness of the poor man is so choked with the feeling of evil that the sense of there being any good in the world is lost for him altogether. His attention excludes it, cannot admit it: the sun has left his heaven. And secondly you see how the querulous temper of his misery keeps his mind from taking a religious direction. Querulousness of mind tends in fact rather towards irreligion; and it has played, so far as I know, no part whatever in the construction of religious systems.

Religious melancholy must be cast in a more melting mood. Tolstoy has left us, in his book called My Confession, a wonderful account of the attack of melancholy which led him to his own religious conclusions. The latter in some respects are peculiar; but the melancholy presents two characters which make it a typical document for our present purpose. First it is a well-marked case of anhedonia, of passive loss of appetite for all life's values; and second, it shows how the altered and estranged aspect which the world assumed in consequence of this stimulated Tolstoy's intellect to a gnawing, carking questioning and effort for philosophic relief. I mean to quote Tolstoy at some length; but before doing so, I will make a general remark on each of these two points.

First on our spiritual judgments and the sense of value in general.

It is notorious that facts are compatible with opposite emotional comments, since the same fact will inspire entirely different feelings in different persons, and at different times in the same person; and there is no rationally deducible connection between any outer fact and the sentiments it may happen to provoke. These have their source in another sphere of existence altogether, in the animal and spiritual region of the subject's being. Conceive yourself, if possible, suddenly stripped of all the emotion with which your world now inspires you, and try to imagine it as it exists, purely by itself, without your favorable or unfavorable, hopeful or apprehensive comment. It will be almost impossible for you to realize such a condition of negativity and deadness. No one portion of the universe would then have importance beyond another; and the whole collection of its things and series of its events would be without significance, character, expression, or perspective. Whatever of value, interest, or meaning our respective worlds may appear endued with are thus pure gifts of the spectator's mind. The passion of love is the most familiar and extreme example of this fact. If it comes, it comes; if it does not come, no process of reasoning can force it. Yet it transforms the value of the creature loved as utterly as the sunrise transforms Mont Blanc from a corpse-like gray to a rosy enchantment; and it sets the whole world to a new tune for the lover and gives a new issue to his life. So with fear, with indignation, jealousy, ambition, worship. If they are there, life changes. And whether they shall be there or not depends almost always upon non-logical, often on organic conditions. And as the excited interest which these passions put into the world is our gift to the world, just so are the passions themselves gifts,— gifts to us, from sources sometimes low and sometimes high; but almost always non-logical and beyond our control. How can the moribund old man reason back to himself the romance, the mystery, the imminence of great things with which our old earth tingled for him in the days when he was young and well? Gifts, either of the flesh or of the spirit; and the spirit bloweth where it listeth; and the world's materials lend their surface passively to all the gifts alike, as the stage-setting receives indifferently whatever alternating colored lights may be shed upon it from the optical apparatus in the gallery.

Meanwhile the practically real world for each one of us, the effective world of the individual, is the compound world, the physical facts and emotional values in indistinguishable combination. Withdraw or pervert either factor of this complex resultant, and the kind of experience we call pathological ensues.

In Tolstoy's case the sense that life had any meaning whatever was for a time wholly withdrawn. The result was a transformation in the whole expression of reality. When we come to study the phenomenon of conversion or religious regeneration, we shall see that a not infrequent consequence of the change operated in the subject is a transfiguration of the face of nature in his eyes. A new heaven seems to shine upon a new earth. In melancholiacs there is usually a similar change, only it is in the reverse direction. The world now looks remote, strange, sinister, uncanny. Its color is gone, its breath is cold, there is no speculation in the eyes it glares with. "It is as if I lived in another century," says one asylum patient.— "I see everything through a cloud," says another, "things are not as they were, and I am changed."— "I see," says a third, "I touch, but the things do not come near me, a thick veil alters the hue and look of everything."— "Persons move like shadows, and sounds seem to come from a distant world."— "There is no longer any past for me; people appear so strange; it is as if I could not see any reality, as if I were in a theatre; as if people were actors, and everything were scenery; I can no longer find myself; I walk, but why? Everything floats before my eyes, but leaves no impression."— "I weep false tears, I have unreal hands: the things I see are not real things."— Such are expressions that naturally rise to the lips of melancholy subjects describing their changed state. [I cull these examples from the work of G. Dumas: La Tristesse et la Joie, 1900.]

Now there are some subjects whom all this leaves a prey to the profoundest astonishment. The strangeness is wrong. The unreality cannot be. A mystery is concealed, and a metaphysical solution must exist. If the natural world is so double-faced and unhomelike, what world what thing is real? An urgent wondering and questioning is set up, a poring theoretic activity, and in the desperate effort to get into right relations with the matter, the sufferer is often led to what becomes for him a satisfying religious solution.

At about the age of fifty, Tolstoy relates that he began to have moments of perplexity, of what he calls arrest, as if he knew not 'how to live,' or what to do. It is obvious that these were moments in which the excitement and interest which our functions naturally bring had ceased. Life had been enchanting, it was now flat sober, more than sober, dead. Things were meaningless whose meaning had always been self-evident. The questions 'Why?' and 'What next?' began to beset him more and more frequently. At first it seemed as if such questions must be answerable, and as if he could easily find the answers if he would take the time; but as they ever became more urgent, he perceived that it was like those first discomforts of a sick man, to which he pays but little attention till they run into one continuous suffering, and then he realizes that what he took for a passing disorder means the most momentous thing in the world for him, means his death.

These questions 'Why?' 'Wherefore?' 'What for?' found no response.

"I felt," says Tolstoy, "that something had broken within me on which my life had always rested, that I had nothing left to hold on to, and that morally my life had stopped. An invincible force impelled me to get rid of my existence, in one way or another. It cannot be said exactly that I wished to kill myself, for the force which drew me away from life was fuller, more powerful, more general than any mere desire. It was a force like my old aspiration to live, only it impelled me in the opposite direction. It was an aspiration of my whole being to get out of life.

"Behold me then, a man happy and in good health, hiding the rope in order not to hang myself to the rafters of the room where every night I went to sleep alone; behold me no longer going shooting, lest I should yield to the too easy temptation of putting an end to myself with my gun.

"I did not know what I wanted. I was afraid of life; I was driven to leave it; and in spite of that I still hoped something from it.

"All this took place at a time when so far as all my outer circumstances went, I ought to have been completely happy. I had a good wife who loved me and whom I loved; good children and a large property which was increasing with no pains taken on my part. I was more respected by my kinsfolk and acquaintance than I had ever been; I was loaded with praise by strangers; and without exaggeration I could believe my name already famous. Moreover I was neither insane nor ill. On the contrary, I possessed a physical and mental strength which I have rarely met in persons of my age. I could mow as well as the peasants, I could work with my brain eight hours uninterruptedly and feel no bad effects.

"And yet I could give no reasonable meaning to any actions of my life. And I was surprised that I had not understood this from the very beginning. My state of mind was as if some wicked and stupid jest was being played upon me by some one. One can live only so long as one is intoxicated, drunk with life; but when one grows sober one cannot fail to see that it is all a stupid cheat. What is truest about it is that there is nothing even funny or silly in it; it is cruel and stupid, purely and simply.

"The oriental fable of the traveler surprised in the desert by a wild beast is very old.

"Seeking to save himself from the fierce animal, the traveler jumps into a well with no water in it; but at the bottom of this well he sees a dragon waiting with open mouth to devour him. And the unhappy man, not daring to go out lest he should be the prey of the beast, not daring to jump to the bottom lest he should be devoured by the dragon, clings to the branches of a wild bush which grows out of one of the cracks of the well. His hands weaken, and he feels that he must soon give way to certain fate; but still he clings, and sees two mice, one white, the other black, evenly moving round the bush to which he hangs, and gnawing off its roots.

"The traveler sees this and knows that he must inevitably perish; but while thus hanging he looks about him and finds on the leaves of the bush some drops of honey. These he reaches with his tongue and licks them off with rapture.

"Thus I hang upon the boughs of life, knowing that the inevitable dragon of death is waiting ready to tear me, and I cannot comprehend why I am thus made a martyr. I try to suck the honey which formerly consoled me; but the honey pleases me no longer, and day and night the white mouse and the black mouse gnaw the branch to which I cling. I can see but one thing: the inevitable dragon and the mice— I cannot turn my gaze away from them.

"This is no fable, but the literal incontestable truth which every one may understand. What will be the outcome of what I do today? Of what I shall do tomorrow? What will be the outcome of all my life? Why should I live? Why should I do anything? Is there in life any purpose which the inevitable death which awaits me does not undo and destroy?

"These questions are the simplest in the world. From the stupid child to the wisest old man, they are in the soul of every human being. Without an answer to them, it is impossible, as I experienced, for life to go on.

"'But perhaps,' I often said to myself, 'there may be something I have failed to notice or to comprehend. It is not possible that the condition of despair should be natural to mankind.' And I sought for an explanation in all the branches of knowledge acquired by men. I questioned painfully and protractedly and with no idle curiosity. I sought, not with indolence, but laboriously and obstinately for days and nights together. I sought like a man who is lost and seeks to save himself,— and I found nothing. I became convinced, moreover, that all those who before me had sought for an answer in the sciences have also found nothing. And not only this, but that they have recognized that the very thing which was leading me to despair— the meaningless absurdity of life— is the only incontestable knowledge accessible to man."

To prove this point, Tolstoy quotes the Buddha, Solomon, and Schopenhauer. And he finds only four ways in which men of his own class and society are accustomed to meet the situation. Either mere animal blindness, sucking the honey without seeing the dragon or the mice,— "and from such a way," he says, "I can learn nothing, after what I now know;" or reflective epicureanism, snatching what it can while the day lasts,— which is only a more deliberate sort of stupefaction than the first; or manly suicide; or seeing the mice and dragon and yet weakly and plaintively clinging to the bush of life.

Suicide was naturally the consistent course dictated by the logical intellect.

"Yet," says Tolstoy, "whilst my intellect was working, something else in me was working too, and kept me from the deed— a consciousness of life, as I may call it, which was like a force that obliged my mind to fix itself in another direction and draw me out of my situation of despair.... During the whole course of this year, when I almost unceasingly kept asking myself how to end the business, whether by the rope or by the bullet, during all that time, alongside of all those movements of my ideas and observations, my heart kept languishing with another pining emotion. I can call this by no other name than that of a thirst for God. This craving for God had nothing to do with the movement of my ideas,— in fact, it was the direct contrary of that movement,— but it came from my heart. It was like a feeling of dread that made me seem like an orphan and isolated in the midst of all these things that were so foreign. And this feeling of dread was mitigated by the hope of finding the assistance of some one." [My extracts are from the French translation by 'Zonia.' In abridging I have taken the liberty of transposing one passage.]

Of the process, intellectual as well as emotional, which, starting from this idea of God, led to Tolstoy's recovery, I will say nothing in this lecture, reserving it for a later hour. The only thing that need interest us now is the phenomenon of his absolute disenchantment with ordinary life, and the fact that the whole range of habitual values may, to a man as powerful and full of faculty as he was, come to appear so ghastly a mockery.

When disillusionment has gone as far as this, there is seldom a restitutio ad integrum. One has tasted of the fruit of the tree, and the happiness of Eden never comes again. The happiness that comes, when any does come,— and often enough it fails to return in an acute form, though its form is sometimes very acute,— is not the simple ignorance of ill, but something vastly more complex, including natural evil as one of its elements, but finding natural evil no such stumbling-block and terror because it now sees it swallowed up in supernatural good. The process is one of redemption, not of mere reversion to natural health, and the sufferer, when saved, is saved by what seems to him a second birth, a deeper kind of conscious being than he could enjoy before.

We find a somewhat different type of religious melancholy enshrined in literature in John Bunyan's autobiography. Tolstoy's preoccupations were largely objective, for the purpose and meaning of life in general was what so troubled him; but poor Bunyan's troubles were over the condition of his own personal self. He was a typical case of the psychopathic temperament, sensitive of conscience to a diseased degree, beset by doubts, fears, and insistent ideas, and a victim of verbal automatisms, both motor and sensory. These were usually texts of Scripture which, sometimes damnatory and sometimes favorable, would come in a half-hallucinatory form as if they were voices, and fasten on his mind and buffet it between them like a shuttlecock. Added to this were a fearful melancholy self-contempt and despair.

"Nay, thought I, now I grow worse and worse; now I am farther from conversion than ever I was before. If now I should have burned at the stake, I could not believe that Christ had love for me; alas, I could neither hear him, nor see him, nor feel him, nor savor any of his things. Sometimes I would tell my condition to the people of God, which, when they heard, they would pity me, and would tell of the Promises. But they had as good have told me that I must reach the Sun with my finger as have bidden me receive or rely upon the Promise [Yet] all this while as to the act of sinning, I never was more tender than now; I durst not take a pin or stick, though but so big as a straw, for my conscience now was sore, and would smart at every touch; I could not tell how to speak my words, for fear I should misplace them. Oh, how gingerly did I then go, in all I did or said! I found myself as on a miry bog that shook if I did but stir; and was as there left both by God and Christ, and the spirit, and all good things.

"But my original and inward pollution, that was my plague and my affliction. By reason of that, I was more loathsome in my own eyes than was a toad; and I thought I was so in God's eyes too. Sin and corruption, I said, would as naturally bubble out of my heart as water would bubble out of a fountain. I could have changed heart with anybody. I thought none but the Devil himself could equal me for inward wickedness and pollution of mind. Sure, thought I, I am forsaken of God; and thus I continued a long while, even for some years together.

"And now I was sorry that God had made me a man. The beasts, birds, fishes, etc., I blessed their condition, for they had not a sinful nature; they were not obnoxious to the wrath of God; they were not to go to hell-fire after death. I could therefore have rejoiced, had my condition been as any of theirs. Now I blessed the condition of the dog and toad, yea, gladly would I have been in the condition of the dog or horse, for I knew they had no soul to perish under the everlasting weight of Hell or Sin, as mine was like to do. Nay, and though I saw this, felt this, and was broken to pieces with it, yet that which added to my sorrow was, that I could not find with all my soul that I did desire deliverance. My heart was at times exceedingly hard. If I would have given a thousand pounds for a tear, I could not shed one; no, nor sometimes scarce desire to shed one.

"I was both a burthen and a terror to myself; nor did I ever so know, as now, what it was to be weary of my life, and yet afraid to die. How gladly would I have been anything but myself! Anything but a man! and in any condition but my own." [Grace abounding to the Chief of Sinners: I have printed a number of detached passages continuously.]

Poor patient Bunyan, like Tolstoy, saw the light again, but we must also postpone that part of his story to another hour. In a later lecture I will also give the end of the experience of Henry Alline, a devoted evangelist who worked in Nova Scotia a hundred years ago, and who thus vividly describes the high-water mark of the religious melancholy which formed its beginning. The type was not unlike Bunyan's.

"Everything I saw seemed to be a burden to me; the earth seemed accursed for my sake: all trees, plants, rocks, bills, and vales seemed to be dressed in mourning and groaning, under the weight of the curse, and everything around me seemed to be conspiring my ruin. My sins seemed to be laid open; so that I thought that every one I saw knew them, and sometimes I was almost ready to acknowledge many things, which I thought they knew: yea sometimes it seemed to me as if every one was pointing me out as the most guilty wretch upon earth. I had now so great a sense of the vanity and emptiness of all things here below, that I knew the whole world could not possibly make me happy, no, nor the whole system of creation. When I waked in the morning, the first thought would be, Oh, my wretched soul, what shall I do, where shall I go? And when I laid down, would say, I shall be perhaps in hell before morning. I would many times look on the beasts with envy, wishing with all my heart I was in their place, that I might have no soul to lose; and when I have seen birds flying over my head, have often thought within myself, Oh, that I could fly away from my danger and distress! Oh, how happy should I be, if I were in their place!" [The Life and Journal of the Rev. Mr. Henry Alline, Boston, 1806, pp. 25, 26. I owe my acquaintance with this book to my colleague, Dr. Benjamin Rand.]

Envy of the placid beasts seems to be a very widespread affection in this type of sadness.

The worst kind of melancholy is that which takes the form of panic fear. Here is an excellent example, for permission to print which I have to thank the sufferer. The original is in French, and though the subject was evidently in a bad nervous condition at the time of which he writes, his case has otherwise the merit of extreme simplicity. I translate freely.

"Whilst in this state of philosophic pessimism and general depression of spirits about my prospects, I went one evening into a dressing-room in the twilight to procure some article that was there; when suddenly there fell upon me without any warning, just as if it came out of the darkness, a horrible fear of my own existence. Simultaneously there arose in my mind the image of an epileptic patient whom I had seen in the asylum, a black-haired youth with greenish skin, entirely idiotic, who used to sit all day on one of the benches, or rather shelves against the wall, with his knees drawn up against his chin, and the coarse gray undershirt, which was his only garment, drawn over them inclosing his entire figure. He sat there like a sort of sculptured Egyptian cat or Peruvian mummy, moving nothing but his black eyes and looking absolutely non-human. This image and my fear entered into a species of combination with each other. That shape am I, I felt, potentially. Nothing that I possess can defend me against that fate, if the hour for it should strike for me as it struck for him. There was such a horror of him, and such a perception of my own merely momentary discrepancy from him, that it was as if something hitherto solid within my breast gave way entirely, and I became a mass of quivering fear. After this the universe was changed for me altogether. I awoke morning after morning with a horrible dread at the pit of my stomach, and with a sense of the insecurity of life that I never knew before, and that I have never felt since. It was like a revelation; and although the immediate feelings passed away, the experience has made me sympathetic with the morbid feelings of others ever since. It gradually faded, but for months I was unable to go out into the dark alone.

Compare Bunyan: "There was I struck into a very great trembling, insomuch that at some times I could, for days together, feel my very body, as well as my mind, to shake and totter under the sense of the dreadful judgment of God, that should fall on those that have sinned that most fearful and unpardonable sin. I felt also such clogging and beat at my stomach, by reason of this my terror, that I was, especially at some times, as if my breast-bone would have split asunder.... Thus did I wind, and twine, and shrink, under the burden that was upon me; which burden also did so oppress me that I could neither stand, nor go, nor lie, either at rest or quiet."

"In general I dreaded to be left alone. I remember wondering how other people could live, how I myself had ever lived, so unconscious of that pit of insecurity beneath the surface of life. My mother in particular, a very cheerful person, seemed to me a perfect paradox in her unconsciousness of danger, which you may well believe I was very careful not to disturb by revelations of my own state of mind. I have always thought that this experience of melancholia of mine had a religious bearing."

On asking this correspondent to explain more fully what he meant by these last words, the answer he wrote was this:

"I mean that the fear was so invasive and powerful that if I had not clung to scripture—texts like 'The eternal God is my refuge,' etc., 'Come unto me, all ye that labor and are heavy-laden,' etc., 'I am the resurrection and the life,' etc., I think I should have grown really insane." [For another case of fear equally sudden, see Henry James: Society the Redeemed Form of Man, Boston, 1879, pp. 43 ff.]

There is no need of more examples. The cases we have looked at are enough. One of them gives us the vanity of mortal things; another the sense of sin; and the remaining one describes the fear of the universe; and in one or other of these three ways it always is that man's original optimism and self-satisfaction get leveled with the dust.

In none of these cases was there any intellectual insanity or delusion about matters of fact; but were we disposed to open the chapter of really insane melancholia, with its hallucinations and delusions, it would be a worse story still— desperation absolute and complete, the whole universe coagulating about the sufferer into a material of overwhelming horror, surrounding him without opening or end. Not the conception or intellectual perception of evil, but the grisly blood-freezing heart-palsying sensation of it close upon one, and no other conception or sensation able to live for a moment in its presence. How irrelevantly remote seem all our usual refined optimisms and intellectual and moral consolations in presence of a need of help like this! Here is the real core of the religious problem: Help! help! No prophet can claim to bring a final message unless he says things that will have a sound of reality in the ears of victims such as these. But the deliverance must come in as strong a form as the complaint, if it is to take effect; and that seems a reason why the coarser religions, revivalistic, orgiastic, with blood and miracles and supernatural operations, may possibly never be displaced. Some constitutions need them too much.

Arrived at this point, we can see how great an antagonism may naturally arise between the healthy-minded way of viewing life and the way that takes all this experience of evil as something essential. To this latter way, the morbid-minded way, as we might call it, healthy-mindedness pure and simple seems unspeakably blind and shallow. To the healthy-minded way, on the other hand, the way of the sick soul seems unmanly and diseased. With their grubbing in rat-holes instead of living in the light; with their manufacture of fears, and preoccupation with every unwholesome kind of misery, there is something almost obscene about these children of wrath and cravers of a second birth. If religious intolerance and hanging and burning could again become the order of the day, there is little doubt that, however it may have been in the past, the healthy-minded would at present show themselves the less indulgent party of the two.

In our own attitude, not yet abandoned, of impartial onlookers, what are we to say of this quarrel? It seems to me that we are bound to say that morbid-mindedness ranges over the wider scale of experience, and that its survey is the one that overlaps. The method of averting one's attention from evil, and living simply in the light of good is splendid as long as it will work. It will work with many persons; it will work far more generally than most of us are ready to suppose; and within the sphere of its successful operation there is nothing to be said against it as a religious solution. But it breaks down impotently as soon as melancholy comes; and even though one be quite free from melancholy one's self, there is no doubt that healthy-mindedness is inadequate as a philosophical doctrine, because the evil facts which it refuses positively to account for are a genuine portion of reality; and they may after all be the best key to life's significance, and possibly the only openers of our eyes to the deepest levels of truth.

The normal process of life contains moments as bad as any of those which insane melancholy is filled with, moments in which radical evil gets its innings and takes its solid turn. The lunatic's visions of horror are all drawn from the material of daily fact. Our civilization is founded on the shambles, and every individual existence goes out in a lonely spasm of helpless agony. If you protest, my friend, wait till you arrive there yourself! To believe in the carnivorous reptiles of geologic times is hard for our imagination— they seem too much like mere museum specimens. Yet there is no tooth in any one of those museum-skulls that did not daily through long years of the foretime hold fast to the body struggling in despair of some fated living victim. Forms of horror just as dreadful to their victims, if on a smaller spatial scale, fill the world about us today. Here on our very hearths and in our gardens the infernal cat plays with the panting mouse, or holds the hot bird fluttering in her jaws. Crocodiles and rattlesnakes and pythons are at this moment vessels of life as real as we are; their loathsome existence fills every minute of every day that drags its length along; and whenever they or other wild beasts clutch their living prey, the deadly horror which an agitated melancholiac feels is the literally right reaction on the situation.

Example: "It was about eleven o'clock at night... but I strolled on still with the people.... Suddenly upon the left side of our road, a crackling was heard among the bushes; all of us were alarmed, and in an instant a tiger, rushing out of the jungle, pounced upon the one of the party that was foremost, and carried him off in the twinkling of an eye. The rush of the animal, and the crush of the poor victim's bones in his mouth, and his last cry of distress, 'Ho hai!' involuntarily reechoed by all of us, was over in three seconds; and then I know not what happened till I returned to my senses, when I found myself and companions lying down on the ground as if prepared to be devoured by our enemy, the sovereign of the forest. I find my pen incapable of describing the terror of that dreadful moment. Our limbs stiffened, our power of speech ceased, and our hearts beat violently, and only a whisper of the same 'Ho hai!' was heard from us. In this state we crept on all fours for some distance back, and then ran for life with the speed of an Arab horse for about half an hour, and fortunately happened to come to a small village.... After this every one of us was attacked with fever, attended with shivering, in which deplorable state we remained till morning." [Autobiography of Lutfullah, a Mohammedan Gentleman, Leipzig, 1857, p. 112.]

It may indeed be that no religious reconciliation with the absolute totality of things is possible. Some evils, indeed, are ministerial to higher forms of good; but it may be that there are forms of evil so extreme as to enter into no good system whatsoever, and that, in respect of such evil, dumb submission or neglect to notice is the only practical resource. This question must confront us on a later day. But provisionally, and as a mere matter of program and method, since the evil facts are as genuine parts of nature as the good ones, the philosophic presumption should be that they have some rational significance, and that systematic healthy-mindedness, failing as it does to accord to sorrow, pain, and death any positive and active attention whatever, is formally less complete than systems that try at least to include these elements in their scope.

The completest religions would therefore seem to be those in which the pessimistic elements are best developed. Buddhism, of course, and Christianity are the best known to us of these. They are essentially religions of deliverance: the man must die to an unreal life before he can be born into the real life. In my next lecture, I will try to discuss some of the psychological conditions of this second birth. Fortunately from now onward we shall have to deal with more cheerful subjects than those which we have recently been dwelling on.

LECTURE VIII: THE DIVIDED SELF, AND THE PROCESS OF ITS UNIFICATION

The last lecture was a painful one, dealing as it did with evil as a pervasive element of the world we live in. At the close of it we were brought into full view of the contrast between the two ways of looking at life which are characteristic respectively of what we called the healthy-minded, who need to be born only once, and of the sick souls, who must be twice-born in order to be happy. The result is two different conceptions of the universe of our experience. In the religion of the once-born the world is a sort of rectilinear or one-storied affair, whose accounts are kept in one denomination, whose parts have just the values which naturally they appear to have, and of which a simple algebraic sum of pluses and minuses will give the total worth. Happiness and religious peace consist in living on the plus side of the account. In the religion of the twice-born, on the other hand, the world is a double-storied mystery. Peace cannot be reached by the simple addition of pluses and elimination of minuses from life. Natural good is not simply insufficient in amount and transient, there lurks a falsity in its very being. Cancelled as it all is by death if not by earlier enemies, it gives no final balance, and can never be the thing intended for our lasting worship. It keeps us from our real good, rather; and renunciation and despair of it are our first step in the direction of the truth. There are two lives, the natural and the spiritual, and we must lose the one before we can participate in the other.

In their extreme forms, of pure naturalism and pure salvationism, the two types are violently contrasted; though here as in most other current classifications, the radical extremes are somewhat ideal abstractions, and the concrete human beings whom we oftenest meet are intermediate varieties and mixtures. Practically, however, you all recognize the difference: you understand, for example, the disdain of the methodist convert for the mere sky-blue healthy-minded moralist; and you likewise enter into the aversion of the latter to what seems to him the diseased subjectivism of the Methodist, dying to live, as he calls it, and making of paradox and the inversion of natural appearances the essence of God's truth. [E.g., "Our young people are diseased with the theological problems of original sin, origin of evil, predestination, and the like. These never presented a practical difficulty to any man— never darkened across any man's road, who did not go out of his way to seek them. These are the soul's mumps, and measles, and whooping-coughs," etc. Emerson: 'Spiritual Laws.']

The psychological basis of the twice-born character seems to be a certain discordancy or heterogeneity in the native temperament of the subject, an incompletely unified moral and intellectual constitution.

"Homo duplex, homo duplex!" writes Alphonse Daudet. "The first time that I perceived that I was two was at the death of my brother Henri, when my father cried out so dramatically, 'He is dead, he is dead!' While my first self wept, my second self thought, 'How truly given was that cry, how fine it would be at the theatre.' I was then fourteen years old.

"This horrible duality has often given me matter for reflection. Oh, this terrible second me, always seated whilst the other is on foot, acting, living, suffering, bestirring itself. This second me that I have never been able to intoxicate, to make shed tears, or put to sleep. And how it sees into things, and how it mocks!" [Notes sur la Vie, p. 1.]

Recent works on the psychology of character have had much to say upon this point. Some persons are born with an inner constitution which is harmonious and well balanced from the outset. Their impulses are consistent with one another, their will follows without trouble the guidance of their intellect, their passions; are not excessive, and their lives are little haunted by regrets. Others are oppositely constituted; and are so in degrees which may vary from something so slight as to result in a merely odd or whimsical inconsistency, to a discordancy of which the consequences may be inconvenient in the extreme. Of the more innocent kinds of heterogeneity I find a good example in Mrs. Annie Besant's autobiography. [See, for example, F. Paulhan, in his book Les Caracteres, 1894, who contrasts les Equilibres, les Unifies, with les Inquiets, les Contrariants, les Incoherents, les Emiettes, as so many diverse psychic types.]

"I have ever been the queerest mixture of weakness and strength, and have paid heavily for the weakness. As a child I used to suffer tortures of shyness, and if my shoe-lace was untied would feel shamefacedly that every eye was fixed on the unlucky string; as a girl I would shrink away from strangers and think myself unwanted and unliked, so that I was full of eager gratitude to any one who noticed me kindly; as the young mistress of a house I was afraid of my servants, and would let careless work pass rather than bear the pain of reproving the ill-doer; when I have been lecturing and debating with no lack of spirit on the platform, I have preferred to go without what I wanted at the hotel rather than to ring and make the waiter fetch it. Combative on the platform in defense of any cause I cared for, I shrink from quarrel or disapproval in the house, and am a coward at heart in private while a good fighter in public. How often have I passed unhappy quarters of an hour screwing up my courage to find fault with some subordinate whom my duty compelled me to reprove, and how often have I jeered at myself for a fraud as the doughty platform combatant, when shrinking from blaming some lad or lass for doing their work badly. An unkind look or word has availed to make me shrink into myself as a snail into its shell, while, on the platform, opposition makes me speak my best." [Annie Besant: an Autobiography, p. 82.]

This amount of inconsistency will only count as amiable weakness; but a stronger degree of heterogeneity may make havoc of the subject's life. There are persons whose existence is little more than a series of zig-zags, as now one tendency and now another gets the upper hand. Their spirit wars with their flesh, they wish for incompatibles, wayward impulses interrupt their most deliberate plans, and their lives are one long drama of repentance and of effort to repair misdemeanors and mistakes.

Heterogeneous personality has been explained as the result of inheritance— the traits of character of incompatible and antagonistic ancestors are supposed to be preserved alongside of each other. [Smith Baker, in Journal of Nervous and Mental Diseases, September, 1893.] This explanation may pass for what it is worth— it certainly needs corroboration. But whatever the cause of heterogeneous personality may be, we find the extreme examples of it in the psychopathic temperament, of which I spoke in my first lecture. All writers about that temperament make the inner heterogeneity prominent in their descriptions. Frequently, indeed, it is only this trait that leads us to ascribe that temperament to a man at all. A 'degenere superieur' is simply a man of sensibility in many directions, who finds more difficulty than is common in keeping his spiritual house in order and running his furrow straight, because his feelings and impulses are too keen and too discrepant mutually. In the haunting and insistent ideas, in the irrational impulses, the morbid scruples, dreads, and inhibitions which beset the psychopathic temperament when it is thoroughly pronounced, we have exquisite examples of heterogeneous personality. Bunyan had an obsession of the words, "Sell Christ for this, sell him for that, sell him, sell him!" which would run through his mind a hundred times together, until one day out of breath with retorting, "I will not, I will not," he impulsively said, "Let him go if he will," and this loss of the battle kept him in despair for over a year. The lives of the saints are full of such blasphemous obsessions, ascribed invariably to the direct agency of Satan. The phenomenon connects itself with the life of the subconscious self, so-called, of which we must erelong speak more directly.

Now in all of us, however constituted, but to a degree the greater in proportion as we are intense and sensitive and subject to diversified temptations, and to the greatest possible degree if we are decidedly psychopathic, does the normal evolution of character chiefly consist in the straightening out and unifying of the inner self. The higher and the lower feelings, the useful and the erring impulses, begin by being a comparative chaos within us— they must end by forming a stable system of functions in right subordination. Unhappiness is apt to characterize the period of order-making and struggle. If the individual be of tender conscience and religiously quickened, the unhappiness will take the form of moral remorse and compunction, of feeling inwardly vile and wrong, and of standing in false relations to the author of one's being and appointer of one's spiritual fate. This is the religious melancholy and 'conviction of sin' that have played so large a part in the history of Protestant Christianity. The man's interior is a battle-ground for what he feels to be two deadly hostile selves, one actual, the other ideal. As Victor Hugo makes his Mahomet say:

"Je suis le champ vil des sublimes combats:
Tantot l'homme d'en haut, et tantot l'homme d'en bas;

Et le mal dans ma bouche avec le bien alterne,
Comme dans le desert le sable et la citerne."

Wrong living, impotent aspirations; "What I would, that do I not; but what I hate, that do I," as Saint Paul says; self-loathing, self-despair; an unintelligible and intolerable burden to which one is mysteriously the heir.

Let me quote from some typical cases of discordant personality, with melancholy in the form of self-condemnation and sense of sin. Saint Augustine's case is a classic example. You all remember his half-pagan, half-Christian bringing up at Carthage, his emigration to Rome and Milan, his adoption of Manicheism and subsequent skepticism, and his restless search for truth and purity of life; and finally how, distracted by the struggle between the two souls in his breast, and ashamed of his own weakness of will, when so many others whom he knew and knew of had thrown off the shackles of sensuality and dedicated themselves to chastity and the higher life, he heard a voice in the garden say, "Sume, lege" (take and read), and opening the Bible at random, saw the text, "not in chambering and wantonness," etc., which seemed directly sent to his address, and laid the inner storm to rest forever. Augustine's psychological genius has given an account of the trouble of having a divided self which has never been surpassed. [Louis Gourdon (Essai sur la Conversion de Saint Augustine, Paris, Fischbacher, 1900) has shown by an analysis of Augustine's writings immediately after the date of his conversion (A.D. 386) that the account he gives in the Confessions is premature. The crisis in the garden marked a definitive conversion from his former life, but it was to the neo-platonic spiritualism and only a halfway stage toward Christianity. The latter he appears not fully and radically to have embraced until four years more had passed.]

"The new will which I began to have was not yet strong enough to overcome that other will, strengthened by long indulgence. So these two wills, one old, one new, one carnal, the other spiritual, contended with each other and disturbed my soul. I understood by my own experience what I had read, 'flesh lusteth against spirit, and spirit against flesh.' It was myself indeed in both the wills, yet more myself in that which I approved in myself than in that which I disapproved in myself. Yet it was through myself that habit had attained so fierce a mastery over me, because I had willingly come whither I willed not. Still bound to earth, I refused, O God, to fight on thy side, as much afraid to be freed from all bonds, as I ought to have feared being trammeled by them.

"Thus the thoughts by which I meditated upon thee were like the efforts of one who would awake, but being overpowered with sleepiness is soon asleep again. Often does a man when heavy sleepiness is on his limbs defer to shake it off, and though not approving it, encourage it; even so I was sure it was better to surrender to thy love than to yield to my own lusts, yet, though the former course convinced me, the latter pleased and held me bound. There was naught in me to answer thy call, 'Awake, thou sleeper,' but only drawling, drowsy words, 'Presently; yes, presently; wait a little while.' But the 'presently' had no 'present,' and the 'little while' grew long.... For I was afraid thou wouldst hear me too soon, and heal me at once of my disease of lust, which I wished to satiate rather than to see extinguished. With what lashes of words did I not scourge my own soul. Yet it shrank back; it refused, though it had no excuse to offer.... I said within myself: 'Come, let it be done now,' and as I said it, I was on the point of the resolve. I all but did it, yet I did not do it. And I made another effort, and almost succeeded, yet I did not reach it, and did not grasp it, hesitating to die to death, and live to life; and the evil to which I was so wonted held me more than the better life I had not tried." [Confessions, Book VIII., chaps. v., vii., xi., abridged.]

There could be no more perfect description of the divided will, when the higher wishes lack just that last acuteness, that touch of explosive intensity, of dynamogenic quality (to use the slang of the psychologists), that enables them to burst their shell, and make irruption efficaciously into life and quell the lower tendencies forever. In a later lecture we shall have much to say about this higher excitability.

I find another good description of the divided will in the autobiography of Henry Alline, the Nova Scotian evangelist, of whose melancholy I read a brief account in my last lecture. The poor youth's sins were, as you will see, of the most harmless order, yet they interfered with what proved to be his truest vocation, so they gave him great distress.

"I was now very moral in my life, but found no rest of conscience. I now began to be esteemed in young company, who knew nothing of my mind all this while, and their esteem began to be a snare to my soul, for I soon began to be fond of carnal mirth, though I still flattered myself that if I did not get drunk, nor curse, nor swear, there would be no sin in frolicking and carnal mirth, and I thought God would indulge young people with some (what I called simple or civil) recreation. I still kept a round of duties, and would not suffer myself to run into any open vices, and so got along very well in time of health and prosperity, but when I was distressed or threatened by sickness, death, or heavy storms of thunder, my religion would not do, and I found there was something wanting, and would begin to repent my going so much to frolics, but when the distress was over, the devil and my own wicked heart, with the solicitations of my associates, and my fondness for young company, were such strong allurements, I would again give way, and thus I got to be very wild and rude, at the same time kept up my rounds of secret prayer and reading; but God, not willing I should destroy myself, still followed me with his calls, and moved with such power upon my conscience, that I could not satisfy myself with my diversions, and in the midst of my mirth sometimes would have such a sense of my lost and undone condition, that I would wish myself from the company, and after it was over, when I went home, would make many promises that I would attend no more on these frolics, and would beg forgiveness for hours and hours; but when I came to have the temptation again, I would give way: no sooner would I hear the music and drink a glass of wine, but I would find my mind elevated and soon proceed to any sort of merriment or diversion, that I thought was not debauched or openly vicious; but when I returned from my carnal mirth I felt as guilty as ever, and could sometimes not close my eyes for some hours after I had gone to my bed. I was one of the most unhappy creatures on earth.

"Sometimes I would leave the company (often speaking to the fiddler to cease from playing, as if I was tired), and go out and walk about crying and praying, as if my very heart would break, and beseeching God that he would not cut me off, nor give me up to hardness of heart. Oh, what unhappy hours and nights I thus wore away! When I met sometimes with merry companions, and my heart was ready to sink, I would labor to put on as cheerful a countenance as possible, that they might not distrust anything, and sometimes would begin some discourse with young men or young women on purpose, or propose a merry song, lest the distress of my soul would be discovered, or mistrusted, when at the same time I would then rather have been in a wilderness in exile, than with them or any of their pleasures or enjoyments. Thus for many months when I was in company, I would act the hypocrite and feign a merry heart, but at the same time would endeavor as much as I could to shun their company, oh wretched and unhappy mortal that I was! Everything I did, and wherever I went, I was still in a storm, and yet I continued to be the chief contriver and ring-leader of the frolics for many months after; though it was a toil and torment to attend them; but the devil and my own wicked heart drove me about like a slave, telling me that I must do this and do that, and bear this and bear that, and turn here and turn there, to keep my credit up, and retain the esteem of my associates: and all this while I continued as strict as possible in my duties, and left no stone unturned to pacify my conscience, watching even against my thoughts, and praying continually wherever I went: for I did not think there was any sin in my conduct, when I was among carnal company, because I did not take any satisfaction there, but only followed it, I thought, for sufficient reasons.

"But still, all that I did or could do, conscience would roar night and day."

Saint Augustine and Alline both emerged into the smooth waters of inner unity and peace, and I shall next ask you to consider more closely some of the peculiarities of the process of unification, when it occurs. It may come gradually, or it may occur abruptly; it may come through altered feelings, or through altered powers of action; or it may come through new intellectual insights, or through experiences which we shall later have to designate as 'mystical.' However it come, it brings a characteristic sort of relief; and never such extreme relief as when it is cast into the religious mould. Happiness! happiness! religion is only one of the ways in which men gain that gift. Easily, permanently, and successfully, it often transforms the most intolerable misery into the profoundest and most enduring happiness.

But to find religion is only one out of many ways of reaching unity; and the process of remedying inner incompleteness and reducing inner discord is a general psychological process, which may take place with any sort of mental material, and need not necessarily assume the religious form. In judging of the religious types of regeneration which we are about to study, it is important to recognize that they are only one species of a genus that contains other types as well. For example, the new birth may be away from religion into incredulity; or it may be from moral scrupulosity into freedom and license; or it may be produced by the irruption into the individual's life of some new stimulus or passion, such as love, ambition, cupidity, revenge, or patriotic devotion. In all these instances we have precisely the same psychological form of event,— a firmness, stability, and equilibrium succeeding a period of storm and stress and inconsistency. In these non-religious cases the new man may also be born either gradually or suddenly.

The French philosopher Jouffroy has left an eloquent memorial of his own 'counter-conversion,' as the transition from orthodoxy to infidelity has been well styled by Mr. Starbuck. Jouffroy's doubts had long harassed him; but he dates his final crisis from a certain night when his disbelief grew fixed and stable, and where the immediate result was sadness at the illusions he had lost.

"I shall never forget that night of December," writes Jouffroy, "in which the veil that concealed from me my own incredulity was torn. I hear again my steps in that narrow naked chamber where long after the hour of sleep had come I had the habit of walking up and down. I see again that moon, half-veiled by clouds, which now and again illuminated the frigid window-panes. The hours of the night flowed on and I did not note their passage. Anxiously I followed my thoughts, as from layer to layer they descended towards the foundation of my consciousness, and, scattering one by one all the illusions which until then had screened its windings from my view, made them every moment more clearly visible.

"Vainly I clung to these last beliefs as a shipwrecked sailor clings to the fragments of his vessel; vainly, frightened at the unknown void in which I was about to float, I turned with them towards my childhood, my family, my country, all that was dear and sacred to me: the inflexible current of my thought was too strong,— parents, family, memory, beliefs, it forced me to let go of everything. The investigation went on more obstinate and more severe as it drew near its term, and did not stop until the end was reached. I knew then that in the depth of my mind nothing was left that stood erect.

"This moment was a frightful one; and when towards morning I threw myself exhausted on my bed, I seemed to feel my earlier life, so smiling and so full, go out like a fire, and before me another life opened, sombre and unpeopled, where in future I must live alone, alone with my fatal thought which had exiled me thither, and which I was tempted to curse. The days which followed this discovery were the saddest of my life." [TH. Jouffroy: Nouveaux Melanges philosophiques, 2me edition, p. 83. I add two other cases of counter-conversion dating from a certain moment. The first is from Professor Starbuck's manuscript collection, and the narrator is a woman.]

"Away down in the bottom of my heart, I believe I was always more or less skeptical about 'God;' skepticism grew as an undercurrent, all through my early youth, but it was controlled and covered by the emotional elements in my religious growth. When I was sixteen I joined the church and was asked if I loved God. I replied 'Yes,' as was customary and expected. But instantly with a flash something spoke within me, 'No, you do not.' I was haunted for a long time with shame and remorse for my falsehood and for my wickedness in not loving God, mingled with fear that there might be an avenging God who would punish me in some terrible way.... At nineteen, I had an attack of tonsilitis. Before I had quite recovered, I heard told a story of a brute who had kicked his wife downstairs, and then continued the operation until she became insensible. I felt the horror of the thing keenly. Instantly this thought flashed through my mind: 'I have no use for a God who permits such things.' This experience was followed by months of stoical indifference to the God of my previous life, mingled with feelings of positive dislike and a somewhat proud defiance of him. I still thought there might be a God. If so he would probably damn me, but I should have to stand it. I felt very little fear and no desire to propitiate him. I have never had any personal relation with him since this painful experience."

The second case exemplifies how small an additional stimulus will overthrow the mind into a new state of equilibrium when the process of preparation and incubation has proceeded far enough. It is like the proverbial last straw added to the camel's burden, or that touch of a needle which makes the salt in a supersaturated fluid suddenly begin to crystallize out.

Tolstoy writes: "S., a frank and intelligent man, told me as follows how he ceased to believe:

"He was twenty-six years old when one day on a hunting expedition, the time for sleep having come, he set himself to pray according to the custom he had held from childhood.

"His brother, who was hunting with him, lay upon the hay and looked at him. When S. had finished his prayer and was turning to sleep, the brother said, 'Do you still keep up that thing?' Nothing more was said. But since that day, now more than thirty years ago, S. has never prayed again; he never takes communion, and does not go to church. All this, not because he became acquainted with convictions of his brother which he then and there adopted; not because he made any new resolution in his soul, but merely because the words spoken by his brother were like the light push of a finger against a leaning wall already about to tumble by its own weight. These words but showed him that the place wherein he supposed religion dwelt in him had long been empty, and that the sentences he uttered, the crosses and bows which he made during his prayer, were actions with no inner sense. Having once seized their absurdity, he could no longer keep them up." Ma Confession, p. 8.

In John Foster's Essay on Decision of Character, there is an account of a case of sudden conversion to avarice, which is illustrative enough to quote:

A young man, it appears, "wasted, in two or three years, a large patrimony in profligate revels with a number of worthless associates who called themselves his friends, and who, when his last means were exhausted, treated him of course with neglect or contempt. Reduced to absolute want, he one day went out of the house with an intention to put an end to his life; but wandering awhile almost unconsciously, he came to the brow of an eminence which overlooked what were lately his estates. Here he sat down, and remained fixed in thought a number of hours, at the end of which he sprang from the ground with a vehement, exulting emotion. He had formed his resolution, which was, that all these estates should be his again; he had formed his plan, too, which he instantly began to execute. He walked hastily forward, determined to seize the first opportunity, of however humble a kind, to gain any money, though it were ever so despicable a trifle, and resolved absolutely not to spend, if he could help it, a farthing of whatever he might obtain. The first thing that drew his attention was a heap of coals shot out of carts on the pavement before a house. He offered himself to shovel or wheel them into the place where they were to be laid, and was employed. He received a few pence for the labor; and then, in pursuance of the saving part of his plan, requested some small gratuity of meat and drink, which was given him. He then looked out for the next thing that might chance; and went, with indefatigable industry, through a succession of servile employments in different places, of longer and shorter duration, still scrupulous in avoiding, as far as possible, the expense of a penny. He promptly seized every opportunity which could advance his design, without regarding the meanness of occupation or appearance. By this method he had gained, after a considerable time, money enough to purchase in order to sell again a few cattle, of which he had taken pains to understand the value. He speedily but cautiously turned his first gains into second advantages; retained without a single deviation his extreme parsimony; and thus advanced by degrees into larger transactions and incipient wealth. I did not hear, or have forgotten, the continued course of his life, but the final result was, that he more than recovered his lost possessions, and died an inveterate miser, worth £60,000 (pounds)." [Op. cit., Letter III., abridged.]

I subjoin an additional document which has come into my possession, and which represents in a vivid way what is probably a very frequent sort of conversion, if the opposite of 'falling in love,' falling out of love, may be so termed. Falling in love also conforms frequently to this type, a latent process of unconscious preparation often preceding a sudden awakening to the fact that the mischief is irretrievably done. The free and easy tone in this narrative gives it a sincerity that speaks for itself.

"For two years of this time I went through a very bad experience, which almost drove me mad. I had fallen violently in love with a girl who, young as she was, had a spirit of coquetry like a cat. As I look back on her now, I hate her, and wonder how I could ever have fallen so low as to be worked upon to such an extent by her attractions. Nevertheless, I fell into a regular fever, could think of nothing else; whenever I was alone, I pictured her attractions, and spent most of the time when I should have been working, in recalling our previous interviews, and imagining future conversations. She was very pretty, good humored, and jolly to the last degree, and intensely pleased with my admiration. Would give me no decided answer yes or no, and the queer thing about it was that whilst pursuing her for her hand, I secretly knew all along that she was unfit to be a wife for me, and that she never would say yes. Although for a year we took our meals at the same boarding-house, so that I saw her continually and familiarly, our closer relations had to be largely on the sly, and this fact, together with my jealousy of another one of her male admirers, and my own conscience despising me for my uncontrollable weakness, made me so nervous and sleepless that I really thought I should become insane. I understand well those young men murdering their sweethearts, which appear so often in the papers. Nevertheless I did love her passionately, and in some ways she did deserve it.

"The queer thing was the sudden and unexpected way in which it all stopped. I was going to my work after breakfast one morning, thinking as usual of her and of my misery, when, just as if some outside power laid hold of me, I found myself turning round and almost running to my room, where I immediately got out all the relics of her which I possessed, including some hair, all her notes and letters, and ambrotypes on glass. The former I made a fire of, the latter I actually crushed beneath my heel, in a sort of fierce joy of revenge and punishment. I now loathed and despised her altogether, and as for myself I felt as if a load of disease had suddenly been removed from me. That was the end. I never spoke to her or wrote to her again in all the subsequent years, and I have never had a single moment of loving thought towards one who for so many months entirely filled my heart. In fact, I have always rather hated her memory, though now I can see that I had gone unnecessarily far in that direction. At any rate, from that happy morning onward I regained possession of my own proper soul, and have never since fallen into any similar trap.

This seems to me an unusually clear example of two different levels of personality, inconsistent in their dictates, yet so well balanced against each other as for a long time to fill the life with discord and dissatisfaction. At last, not gradually, but in a sudden crisis, the unstable equilibrium is resolved, and this happens so unexpectedly that it is as if, to use the writer's words, "some outside power laid hold."

Professor Starbuck gives an analogous case, and a converse case of hatred suddenly turning into love, in his Psychology of Religion, p. 141. Compare the other highly curious instances which he gives on pp. 137-144, of sudden non-religious alterations of habit or character. He seems right in conceiving all such sudden changes as results of special cerebral functions unconsciously developing until they are ready to play a controlling part, when they make irruption into the conscious life. When we treat of sudden 'conversion,' I shall make as much use as I can of this hypothesis of subconscious incubation.

Let me turn now to the kind of case, the religious case, namely, that immediately concerns us. Here is one of the simplest possible type, an account of the conversion to the systematic religion of healthy-mindedness of a man who must already have been naturally of the healthy-minded type. It shows how, when the fruit is ripe, a touch will make it fall.

Mr. Horace Fletcher, in his little book called Menticulture, relates that a friend with whom he was talking of the self-control attained by the Japanese through their practice of the Buddhist discipline said:

"'You must first get rid of anger and worry.' 'But,' said I, 'is that possible?' 'Yes,' replied he; 'it is possible to the Japanese, and ought to be possible to us.'

"On my way back I could think of nothing else but the words 'get rid, get rid'; and the idea must have continued to possess me during my sleeping hours, for the first consciousness in the morning brought back the same thought, with the revelation of a discovery, which framed itself into the reasoning, 'If it is possible to get rid of anger and worry, why is it necessary to have them at all?' I felt the strength of the argument, and at once accepted the reasoning. The baby had discovered that it could walk. It would scorn to creep any longer.

"From the instant I realized that these cancer spots of worry and anger were removable, they left me. With the discovery of their weakness they were exorcised. From that time life has had an entirely different aspect.

"Although from that moment the possibility and desirability of freedom from the depressing passions has been a reality to me, it took me some months to feel absolute security in my new position; but, as the usual occasions for worry and anger have presented themselves over and over again, and I have been unable to feel them in the slightest degree, I no longer dread or guard against them, and I am amazed at my increased energy and vigor of mind; at my strength to meet situations of all kinds, and at my disposition to love and appreciate everything.

"I have had occasion to travel more than ten thousand miles by rail since that morning. The same Pullman porter, conductor, hotel-waiter, peddler, book-agent, cabman, and others who were formerly a source of annoyance and irritation have been met, but I am not conscious of a single incivility. All at once the whole world has turned good to me. I have become, as it were, sensitive only to the rays of good.

"I could recount many experiences which prove a brand-new condition of mind, but one will be sufficient. Without the slightest feeling of annoyance or impatience, I have seen a train that I had planned to take with a good deal of interested and pleasurable anticipation move out of the station without me, because my baggage did not arrive. The porter from the hotel came running and panting into the station just as the train pulled out of sight. When he saw me, he looked as if he feared a scolding, and began to tell of being blocked in a crowded street and unable to get out. When he had finished, I said to him: 'It does n't matter at all, you could n't help it, so we will try again tomorrow. Here is your fee, I am sorry you had all this trouble in earning it.' The look of surprise that came over his face was so filled with pleasure that I was repaid on the spot for the delay in my departure. Next day he would not accept a cent for the service, and he and I are friends for life.

"During the first weeks of my experience I was on guard only against worry and anger; but, in the mean time, having noticed the absence of the other depressing and dwarfing passions, I began to trace a relationship, until I was convinced that they are all growths from the two roots I have specified. I have felt the freedom now for so long a time that I am sure of my relation toward it; and I could no more harbor any of the thieving and depressing influences that once I nursed as a heritage of humanity than a fop would voluntarily wallow in a filthy gutter.

"There is no doubt in my mind that pure Christianity and pure Buddhism, and the Mental Sciences and all Religions, fundamentally teach what has been a discovery to me; but none of them have presented it in the light of a simple and easy process of elimination. At one time I wondered if the elimination would not yield to indifference and sloth. In my experience, the contrary is the result. I feel such an increased desire to do something useful that it seems as if I were a boy again and the energy for play had returned. I could fight as readily as (and better than) ever, if there were occasion for it. It does not make one a coward. It can't, since fear is one of the things eliminated. I notice the absence of timidity in the presence of any audience. When a boy, I was standing under a tree which was struck by lightning, and received a shock from the effects of which I never knew exemption until I had dissolved partnership with worry. Since then, lightning and thunder have been encountered under conditions which would formerly have caused great depression and discomfort, without [my] experiencing a trace of either. Surprise is also greatly modified, and one is less liable to become startled by unexpected sights or noises.

"As far as I am individually concerned, I am not bothering myself at present as to what the results of this emancipated condition may be. I have no doubt that the perfect health aimed at by Christian Science may be one of the possibilities, for I note a marked improvement in the way my stomach does its duty in assimilating the food I give it to handle, and I am sure it works better to the sound of a song than under the friction of a frown. Neither am I wasting any of this precious time formulating an idea of a future existence or a future Heaven. The Heaven that I have within myself is as attractive as any that has been promised or that I can imagine; and I am willing to let the growth lead where it will, as long as the anger and their brood have no part in misguiding it." [H. Fletcher: Menticulture, or the A-B-C of True Living, New York and Chicago, 1899, pp. 26-36, abridged.]

The older medicine used to speak of two ways, lysis and crisis, one gradual, the other abrupt, in which one might recover from a bodily disease. In the spiritual realm there are also two ways, one gradual, the other sudden, in which inner unification may occur. Tolstoy and Bunyan may again serve us as examples, as it happens, of the gradual way, though it must be confessed at the outset that it is hard to follow these windings of the hearts of others, and one feels that their words do not reveal their total secret.

Howe'er this be, Tolstoy, pursuing his unending questioning, seemed to come to one insight after another. First he perceived that his conviction that life was meaningless took only this finite life into account. He was looking for the value of one finite term in that of another, and the whole result could only be one of those indeterminate equations in mathematics which end with 0=0. Yet this is as far as the reasoning intellect by itself can go, unless irrational sentiment or faith brings in the infinite. Believe in the infinite as common people do, and life grows possible again.

"Since mankind has existed, wherever life has been, there also has been the faith that gave the possibility of living. Faith is the sense of life, that sense by virtue of which man does not destroy himself, but continues to live on. It is the force whereby we live. If Man did not believe that he must live for something, he would not live at all. The idea of an infinite God, of the divinity of the soul, of the union of men's actions with God— these are ideas elaborated in the infinite secret depths of human thought. They are ideas without which there would be no life, without which I myself," said Tolstoy, "would not exist. I began to see that I had no right to rely on my individual reasoning and neglect these answers given by faith, for they are the only answers to the question."

Yet how believe as the common people believe, steeped as they are in grossest superstition? It is impossible,— but yet their life! their life! It is normal. It is happy! It is an answer to the question!

Little by little, Tolstoy came to the settled conviction— he says it took him two years to arrive there— that his trouble had not been with life in general, not with the common life of common men, but with the life of the upper, intellectual, artistic classes, the life which he had personally always led, the cerebral life, the life of conventionality, artificiality, and personal ambition. He had been living wrongly and must change. To work for animal needs, to abjure lies and vanities, to relieve common wants, to be simple, to believe in God, therein lay happiness again.

"I remember," he says, "one day in early spring, I was alone in the forest, lending my ear to its mysterious noises. I listened,. and my thought went back to what for these three years it always was busy with— the quest of God. But the idea of him, I said, how did I ever come by the idea?

"And again there arose in me, with this thought, glad aspirations towards life. Everything in me awoke and received a meaning.... Why do I look farther? a voice within me asked. He is there: he, without whom one cannot live. To acknowledge God and to live are one and the same thing. God is what life is. Well, then I live, seek God, and there will be no life without him....

"After this, things cleared up within me and about me better than ever, and the light has never wholly died away. I was saved from suicide. Just how or when the change took place I cannot tell. But as insensibly and gradually as the force of life had been annulled within me, and I had reached my moral death-bed, just as gradually and imperceptibly did the energy of life come back. And what was strange was that this energy that came back was nothing new. It was my ancient juvenile force of faith, the belief that the sole purpose of my life was to be better. I gave up the life of the conventional world, recognizing it to be no life, but a parody on life, which its superfluities simply keep us from comprehending,"— and Tolstoy thereupon embraced the life of the peasants, and has felt right and happy, or at least relatively so, ever since. [I have considerably abridged Tolstoy's words in my translation.]

As I interpret his melancholy, then, it was not merely an accidental vitiation of his humors, though it was doubtless also that. It was logically called for by the clash between his inner character and his outer activities and aims. Although a literary artist, Tolstoy was one of those primitive oaks of men to whom the superfluities and insincerities, the cupidities, complications, and cruelties of our polite civilization are profoundly unsatisfying, and for whom the eternal veracities lie with more natural and animal things. His crisis was the getting of his soul in order, the discovery of its genuine habitat and vocation, the escape from falsehoods into what for him were ways of truth. It was a case of heterogeneous personality tardily and slowly finding its unity and level. And though not many of us can imitate Tolstoy, not having enough, perhaps, of the aboriginal human marrow in our bones, most of us may at least feel as if it might be better for us if we could.

Bunyan's recovery seems to have been even slower. For years together he was alternately haunted with texts of Scripture, now up and now down, but at last with an ever growing relief in his salvation through the blood of Christ.

"My peace would be in and out twenty times a day; comfort now and trouble presently; peace now and before I could go a furlong as full of guilt and fear as ever heart could hold." When a good text comes home to him, "This," he writes, "gave me good encouragement for the space of two or three hours"; or "This was a good day to me, I hope I shall not forget it"; or "The glory of these words was then so weighty on me that I was ready to swoon as I sat; yet not with grief and trouble, but with solid joy and peace"; or "This made a strange seizure on my spirit; it brought light with it, and commanded a silence in my heart of all those tumultuous thoughts that before did use, like masterless hell-hounds, to roar and bellow and make a hideous noise within me. It showed me that Jesus Christ had not quite forsaken and cast off my Soul."

Such periods accumulate until he can write: "And now remained only the hinder part of the tempest, for the thunder was gone beyond me, only some drops would still remain, that now and then would fall upon me";— and at last: "Now did my chains fall off my legs indeed; I was loosed from my afflictions and irons; my temptations also fled away; so that from that time, those dreadful Scriptures of God left off to trouble me; now went I also home rejoicing, for the grace and love of God.... Now could I see myself in Heaven and Earth at once; in Heaven by my Christ, by my Head, by my Righteousness and Life, though on Earth by my body or person.... Christ was a precious Christ to my soul that night; I could scarce lie in my bed for joy and peace and triumph through Christ."

Bunyan became a minister of the gospel, and in spite of his neurotic constitution, and of the twelve years he lay in prison for his non-conformity, his life was turned to active use. He was a peacemaker and doer of good, and the immortal Allegory which he wrote has brought the very spirit of religious patience home to English hearts.

But neither Bunyan nor Tolstoy could become what we have called healthy-minded. They had drunk too deeply of the cup of bitterness ever to forget its taste, and their redemption is into a universe two stories deep. Each of them realized a good which broke the effective edge of his sadness; yet the sadness was preserved as a minor ingredient in the heart of the faith by which it was overcome. The fact of interest for us is that as a matter of fact they could and did find something welling up in the inner reaches of their consciousness, by which such extreme sadness could be overcome. Tolstoy does well to talk of it as that by which men live; for that is exactly what it is, a stimulus, an excitement, a faith, a force that re-infuses the positive willingness to live, even in full presence of the evil perceptions that erewhile made life seem unbearable. For Tolstoy's perceptions of evil appear within their sphere to have remained unmodified. His later works show him implacable to the whole system of official values: the ignobility of fashionable life; the infamies of empire; the spuriousness of the church, the vain conceit of the professions; the meannesses and cruelties that go with great success; and every other pompous crime and lying institution of this world. To all patience with such things his experience has been for him a permanent ministry of death.

Bunyan also leaves this world to the enemy.

"I must first pass a sentence of death," he says, "upon everything that can properly be called a thing of this life, even to reckon myself, my wife, my children, my health, my enjoyments, and all, as dead to me, and myself as dead to them; to trust in God through Christ, as touching the world to come; and as touching this world, to count the grave my house, to make my bed in darkness, and to say to corruption, Thou art my father, and to the worm, Thou art my mother and sister.... The parting with my wife and my poor children hath often been to me as the pulling of my flesh from my bones, especially my poor blind child who lay nearer my heart than all I had besides. Poor child, thought I, what sorrow art thou like to have for thy portion in this world! Thou must be beaten, must beg, suffer hunger, cold, nakedness, and a thousand calamities, though I cannot now endure that the wind should blow upon thee. But yet I must venture you all with God, though it goeth to the quick to leave you." [In my quotations from Bunyan I have omitted certain intervening portions of the text.

The 'hue of resolution' is there, but the full flood of ecstatic liberation seems never to have poured over poor John Bunyan's soul.]

These examples may suffice to acquaint us in a general way with the phenomenon technically called 'Conversion.' In the next lecture I shall invite you to study its peculiarities and concomitants in some detail.

LECTURE IX: CONVERSION

To be converted, to be regenerated, to receive grace, to experience religion, to gain an assurance, are so many phrases which denote the process, gradual or sudden, by which a self hitherto divided, and consciously wrong inferior and unhappy, becomes unified and consciously right superior and happy, in consequence of its firmer hold upon religious realities. This at least is what conversion signifies in general terms, whether or not we believe that a direct divine operation is needed to bring such a moral change about.

Before entering upon a minuter study of the process, let me enliven our understanding of the definition by a concrete example. I choose the quaint case of an unlettered man, Stephen H. Bradley, whose experience is related in a scarce American pamphlet. [A sketch of the life of Stephen H. Bradley, from the age of five to twenty-four years, including his remarkable experience of the power of the Holy Spirit on the second evening of November, 1829. Madison, Connecticut, 1830.]

I select this case because it shows how in these inner alterations one may find one unsuspected depth below another, as if the possibilities of character lay disposed in a series of layers or shells, of whose existence we have no premonitory knowledge.

Bradley thought that he had been already fully converted at the age of fourteen.

"I thought I saw the Saviour, by faith, in human shape, for about one second in the room, with arms extended, appearing to say to me, Come. The next day I rejoiced with trembling; soon after, my happiness was so great that I said that I wanted to die; this world had no place in my affections, as I knew of, and every day appeared as solemn to me as the Sabbath. I had an ardent desire that all mankind might feel as I did; I wanted to have them all love God supremely. Previous to this time I was very selfish and self-righteous; but now I desired the welfare of all mankind, and could with a feeling heart forgive my worst enemies, and I felt as if I should be willing to bear the scoffs and sneers of any person, and suffer anything for His sake, if I could be the means in the hands of God, of the conversion of one soul."

Nine years later, in 1829, Mr. Bradley heard of a revival of religion that had began in his neighborhood. "Many of the young converts," he says, "would come to me when in meeting and ask me if I had religion, and my reply generally was, I hope I have. This did not appear to satisfy them; they said they knew they had it. I requested them to pray for me, thinking with myself, that if I had not got religion now, after so long a time professing to be a Christian, that it was time I had, and hoped their prayers would be answered in my behalf.

"One Sabbath, I went to hear the Methodist at the Academy. He spoke of the ushering in of the day of general judgment; and he set it forth in such a solemn and terrible manner as I never heard before. The scene of that day appeared to be taking place, and so awakened were all the powers of my mind that, like Felix, I trembled involuntarily on the bench where I was sitting, though I felt nothing at heart. The next day evening I went to hear him again. He took his text from Revelation: 'And I saw the dead, small and great, stand before God.' And he represented the terrors of that day in such a manner that it appeared as if it would melt the heart of stone. When he finished his discourse, an old gentleman turned to me and said, 'This is what I call preaching.' I thought the same; but my feelings were still unmoved by what he said, and I did not enjoy religion, but I believe he did.

"I will now relate my experience of the power of the Holy Spirit which took place on the same night. Had any person told me previous to this that I could have experienced the power of the Holy Spirit in the manner which I did, I could not have believed it, and should have thought the person deluded that told me so. I went directly home after the meeting, and when I got home I wondered what made me feel so stupid. I retired to rest soon after I got home, and felt indifferent to the things of religion until I began to be exercised by the Holy Spirit, which began in about five minutes after, in the following manner:

"At first, I began to feel my heart beat very quick all on a sudden, which made me at first think that perhaps something is going to ail me, though I was not alarmed, for I felt no pain. My heart increased in its beating, which soon convinced me that it was the Holy Spirit from the effect it had on me. I began to feel exceedingly happy and humble, and such a sense of unworthiness as I never felt before. I could not very well help speaking out, which I did, and said, Lord, I do not deserve this happiness, or words to that effect, while there was a stream (resembling air in feeling) came into my mouth and heart in a more sensible manner than that of drinking anything, which continued, as near as I could judge, five minutes or more, which appeared to be the cause of such a palpitation of my heart. It took complete possession of my soul, and I am certain that I desired the Lord, while in the midst of it, not to give me any more happiness, for it seemed as if I could not contain what I had got. My heart seemed as if it would burst but it did not stop until I felt as if I was unutterably full of the love and grace of God. In the mean time while thus exercised, a thought arose in my mind, what can it mean? and all at once, as if to answer it, my memory became exceedingly clear, and it appeared to me just as if the New Testament was placed open before me, eighth chapter of Romans, and as light as if some candle lighted was held for me to read the 26th and 27th verses of that chapter, and I read these words: 'The Spirit helpeth our infirmities with groanings which cannot be uttered.' And all the time that my heart was a-beating, it made me groan like a person in distress, which was not very easy to stop, though I was in no pain at all, and my brother being in bed in another room came and opened the door, and asked me if I had got the toothache. I told him no, and that he might get to sleep. I tried to stop. I felt unwilling to go to sleep myself, I was so happy, fearing I should loose it— thinking within myself

'My willing soul would stay

In such a frame as this.'

And while I lay reflecting, after my heart stopped beating, feeling as if my soul was full of the Holy Spirit, I thought that perhaps there might be angels hovering round my bed. I felt just as if I wanted to converse with them, and finally I spoke, saying, 'O ye affectionate angels! how is it that ye can take so much interest in our welfare, and we take so little interest in our own.' After this, with difficulty I got to sleep; and when I awoke in the morning my first thoughts were: What has become of my happiness? and, feeling a degree of it in my heart, I asked for more, which was given to me as quick as thought. I then got up to dress myself, and found to my surprise that I could but just stand. It appeared to me as if it was a little heaven upon earth. My soul felt as completely raised above the fears of death as of going to sleep; and like a bird in a cage, I had a desire, if it was the will of God, to get released from my body and to dwell with Christ, though willing to live to do good to others, and to warn sinners to repent. I went downstairs feeling as solemn as if I had lost all my friends, and thinking with myself, that I would not let my parents know it until I had first looked into the Testament. I went directly to the shelf and looked into it, at the eighth chapter of Romans, and every verse seemed to almost speak and to confirm it to be truly the Word of God, and as if my feelings corresponded with the meaning of the word. I then told my parents of it, and told them that I thought that they must see that when I spoke, that it was not my own voice, for it appeared so to me. My speech seemed entirely under the control of the Spirit within me; I do not mean that the words which I spoke were not my own, for they were. I thought that I was influenced similar to the Apostles on the day of Pentecost (with the exception of having power to give it to others, and doing what they did). After breakfast I went round to converse with my neighbors on religion, which I could not have been hired to have done before this, and at their request I prayed with them, though I had never prayed in public before.

"I now feel as if I had discharged my duty by telling the truth, and hope by the blessing of God, it may do some good to all who shall read it. He has fulfilled his promise in sending the Holy Spirit down into our hearts, or mine at least, and I now defy all the Deists and Atheists in the world to shake my faith in Christ."

So much for Mr. Bradley and his conversion, of the effect of which upon his later life we gain no information. Now for a minuter survey of the constituent elements of the conversion process.

If you open the chapter on Association, of any treatise on Psychology, you will read that a man's ideas, aims, and objects form diverse internal groups and systems, relatively independent of one another. Each 'aim' which he follows awakens a certain specific kind of interested excitement, and gathers a certain group of ideas together in subordination to it as its associates; and if the aims and excitements are distinct in kind, their groups of ideas may have little in common. When one group is present and engrosses the interest, all the ideas connected with other groups may be excluded from the mental field. The President of the United States when with paddle, gun, and fishing-rod, he goes camping in the wilderness for a vacation, changes his system of ideas from top to bottom. The presidential anxieties have lapsed into the background entirely; the official habits are replaced by the habits of a son of nature, and those who knew the man only as the strenuous magistrate would not 'know him for the same person' if they saw him as the camper.

If now he should never go back, and never again suffer political interests to gain dominion over him, he would be for practical intents and purposes a permanently transformed being. Our ordinary alterations of character, as we pass from one of our aims to another, are not commonly called transformations, because each of them is so rapidly succeeded by another in the reverse direction; but whenever one aim grows so stable as to expel definitively its previous rivals from the individual's life, we tend to speak of the phenomenon, and perhaps to wonder at it, as a 'transformation.'

These alternations are the completest of the ways in which a self may be divided. A less complete way is the simultaneous coexistence of two or more different groups of aims, of which one practically holds the right of way and instigates activity, whilst the others are only pious wishes, and never practically come to anything. Saint Augustine's aspirations to a purer life, in our last lecture, were for a while an example. Another would be the President in his full pride of office, wondering whether it were not all vanity, and whether the life of a wood-chopper were not the wholesomer destiny. Such fleeting aspirations are mere velleitates, whimsies. They exist on the remoter outskirts of the mind, and the real self of the man, the centre of his energies, is occupied with an entirely different system. As life goes on, there is a constant change of our interests, and a consequent change of place in our systems of ideas, from more central to more peripheral, and from more peripheral to more central parts of consciousness. I remember, for instance, that one evening when I was a youth, my father read aloud from a Boston newspaper that part of Lord Gifford's will which founded these four lectureships. At that time I did not think of being a teacher of philosophy: and what I listened to was as remote from my own life as if it related to the planet Mars. Yet here I am, with the Gifford system part and parcel of my very self, and all my energies, for the time being, devoted to successfully identifying myself with it. My soul stands now planted in what once was for it a practically unreal object, and speaks from it as from its proper habitat and centre.

When I say 'Soul,' you need not take me in the ontological sense unless you prefer to; for although ontological language is instinctive in such matters, yet Buddhists or Humians can perfectly well describe the facts in the phenomenal terms which are their favorites. For them the soul is only a succession of fields of consciousness: yet there is found in each field a part, or sub-field, which figures as focal and contains the excitement, and from which, as from a centre, the aim seems to be taken. Talking of this part, we involuntarily apply words of perspective to distinguish it from the rest, words like 'here,' 'this,' 'now,' 'mine,' or 'me'; and we ascribe to the other parts the positions 'there,' 'then,' 'that,' 'his' or 'thine,' 'it,' 'not me.' But a 'here' can change to a 'there,' and a 'there' become a 'here,' and what was 'mine' and what was 'not mine' change their places.

What brings such changes about is the way in which emotional excitement alters. Things hot and vital to us today are cold tomorrow. It is as if seen from the hot parts of the field that the other parts appear to us, and from these hot parts personal desire and volition make their sallies. They are in short the centres of our dynamic energy, whereas the cold parts leave us indifferent and passive in proportion to their coldness.

Whether such language be rigorously exact is for the present of no importance. It is exact enough, if you recognize from your own experience the facts which I seek to designate by it.

Now there may be great oscillation in the emotional interest, and the hot places may shift before one almost as rapidly as the sparks that run through burnt-up paper. Then we have the wavering and divided self we heard so much of in the previous lecture. Or the focus of excitement and heat, the point of view from which the aim is taken, may come to lie permanently within a certain system; and then, if the change be a religious one, we call it a conversion, especially if it be by crisis, or sudden.

Let us hereafter, in speaking of the hot place in a man's consciousness, the group of ideas to which he devotes himself, and from which he works, call it the habitual centre of his personal energy. It makes a great difference to a man whether one set of his ideas, or another, be the centre of his energy; and it makes a great difference, as regards any set of ideas which he may possess, whether they become central or remain peripheral in him. To say that a man is 'converted' means, in these terms, that religious ideas, previously peripheral in his consciousness, now take a central place, and that religious aims form the habitual centre of his energy.

Now if you ask of psychology just how the excitement shifts in a man's mental system, and why aims that were peripheral become at a certain moment central, psychology has to reply that although she can give a general description of what happens, she is unable in a given case to account accurately for all the single forces at work. Neither an outside observer nor the Subject who undergoes the process can explain fully how particular experiences are able to change one's centre of energy so decisively, or why they so often have to bide their hour to do so. We have a thought, or we perform an act, repeatedly, but on a certain day the real meaning of the thought peals through us for the first time, or the act has suddenly turned into a moral impossibility. All we know is that there are dead feelings, dead ideas, and cold beliefs, and there are hot and live ones; and when one grows hot and alive within us, everything has to re-crystallize about it. We may say that the heat and liveliness mean only the 'motor efficacy,' long deferred but now operative, of the idea; but such talk itself is only circumlocution, for whence the sudden motor efficacy? And our explanations then get so vague and general that one realizes all the more the intense individuality of the whole phenomenon.

In the end we fall back on the hackneyed symbolism of a mechanical equilibrium. A mind is a system of ideas, each with the excitement it arouses, and with tendencies impulsive and inhibitive, which mutually check or reinforce one another. The collection of ideas alters by subtraction or by addition in the course of experience, and the tendencies alter as the organism gets more aged. A mental system may be undermined or weakened by this interstitial alteration just as a building is, and yet for a time keep upright by dead habit. But a new perception, a sudden emotional shock, or an occasion which lays bare the organic alteration, will make the whole fabric fall together; and then the centre of gravity sinks into an attitude more stable, for the new ideas that reach the centre in the rearrangement seem now to be locked there, and the new structure remains permanent.

Formed associations of ideas and habits are usually factors of retardation in such changes of equilibrium. New information, however acquired, plays an accelerating part in the changes; and the slow mutation of our instincts and propensities, under the 'unimaginable touch of time' has an enormous influence. Moreover, all these influences may work subconsciously or half unconsciously. And when you get a Subject in whom the subconscious life— of which I must speak more fully soon— is largely developed, and in whom motives habitually ripen in silence, you get a case of which you can never give a full account, and in which, both to the Subject and the onlookers, there may appear an element of marvel. Emotional occasions, especially violent ones, are extremely potent in precipitating mental rearrangements. The sudden and explosive ways in which love, jealousy, guilt, fear, remorse, or anger can seize upon one are known to everybody. Hope, happiness, security, resolve, emotions characteristic of conversion, can be equally explosive. And emotions that come in this explosive way seldom leave things as they found them.

Jouffroy is an example: "Down this slope it was that my intelligence had glided, and little by little it had got far from its first faith. But this melancholy revolution had not taken place in the broad daylight of my consciousness; too many scruples, too many guides and sacred affections had made it dreadful to me, so that I was far from avowing to myself the progress it had made. It had gone on in silence, by an involuntary elaboration of which I was not the accomplice; and although I had in reality long ceased to be a Christian, yet, in the innocence of my intention, I should have shuddered to suspect it, and thought it calumny had I been accused of such a falling away." Then follows Jouffroy's account of his counter-conversion, quoted above in Lecture VIII.

One hardly needs examples; but for love, see Lecture VIII note [Op. cit., Letter III...], for fear, see Lecture VI and VII, for remorse, see Othello after the murder; for anger, see Lear after Cordelia's first speech to him; for resolve, see Lecture VIII (J. Foster case). Here is a pathological case in which guilt was the feeling that suddenly exploded: "One night I was seized on entering bed with a rigor, such as Swedenborg describes as coming over him with a sense of holiness, but over me with a sense of guilt. During that whole night I lay under the influence of the rigor, and from its inception I felt that I was under the curse of God. I have never done one act of duty in my life- sins against God and man, beginning as far as my memory goes back— a wildcat in human shape."

In his recent work on the Psychology of Religion, Professor Starbuck of California has shown by a statistical inquiry how closely parallel in its manifestations the ordinary 'conversion' which occurs in young people brought up in evangelical circles is to that growth into a larger spiritual life which is a normal phase of adolescence in every class of human beings. The age is the same falling usually between fourteen and seventeen. The symptoms are the same,— sense of incompleteness and imperfection; brooding, depression, morbid introspection, and sense of sin; anxiety about the hereafter; distress over doubts, and the like. And the result is the same,— a happy relief and objectivity, as the confidence in self gets greater through the adjustment of the faculties to the wider outlook. In spontaneous religious awakening, apart from revivalistic examples, and in the ordinary storm and stress and moulting-time of adolescence, we also may meet with mystical experiences, astonishing the subjects by their suddenness, just as in revivalistic conversion. The analogy, in fact, is complete; and Starbuck's conclusion as to these ordinary youthful conversions would seem to be the only sound one: Conversion is in its essence a normal adolescent phenomenon, incidental to the passage from the child's small universe to the wider intellectual and spiritual life of maturity.

"Theology," says Dr. Starbuck, "takes the adolescent tendencies and builds upon them; it sees that the essential thing in adolescent growth is bringing the person out of childhood into the new life of maturity and personal insight. It accordingly brings those means to bear which will intensify the normal tendencies. It shortens up the period of duration of storm and stress." The conversion phenomena of 'conviction of sin' last, by this investigator's statistics, about one fifth as long as the periods of adolescent storm and stress phenomena of which he also got statistics, but they are very much more intense. Bodily accompaniments, loss of sleep and appetite, for example, are much more frequent in them. "The essential distinction appears to be that conversion intensifies but shortens the period by bringing the person to a definite crisis." [E.D. Starbuck: The Psychology of Religion, pp. 224, 262.]

The conversions which Dr. Starbuck here has in mind are of course mainly those of very commonplace persons, kept true to a pre-appointed type by instruction, appeal, and example. The particular form which they affect is the result of suggestion and imitation. If they went through their growth-crisis in other faiths and other countries, although the essence of the change would be the same (since it is one in the main so inevitable), its accidents would be different. In Catholic lands, for example, and in our own Episcopalian sects, no such anxiety and conviction of sin is usual as in sects that encourage revivals. The sacraments being more relied on in these more strictly ecclesiastical bodies, the individual's personal acceptance of salvation needs less to be accentuated and led up to.

No one understands this better than Jonathan Edwards understood it already. Conversion narratives of the more commonplace sort must always be taken with the allowances which he suggests: "A rule received and established by common consent has a very great, though to many persons an insensible influence in forming their notions of the process of their own experience. I know very well how they proceed as to this matter, for I have had frequent opportunities of observing their conduct. Very often their experience at first appears like a confused chaos, but then those parts are selected which bear the nearest resemblance to such particular steps as are insisted on; and these are dwelt upon in their thoughts, and spoken of from time to time, till they grow more and more conspicuous in their view, and other parts which are neglected grow more and more obscure. Thus what they have experienced is insensibly strained, so as to bring it to an exact conformity to the scheme already established in their minds. And it becomes natural also for ministers, who have to deal with those who insist upon distinctness and clearness of method, to do so too." Treatise on Religious Affections.

But every imitative phenomenon must once have had its original, and I propose that for the future we keep as close as may be to the more first-hand and original forms of experience. These are more likely to be found in sporadic adult cases.

Professor Leuba, in a valuable article on the psychology of conversion, subordinates the theological aspect of the religious life almost entirely to its moral aspect. The religious sense he defines as "the feeling of unwholeness, of moral imperfection, of sin, to use the technical word, accompanied by the yearning after the peace of unity." "The word 'religion,'" he says, "is getting more and more to signify the conglomerate of desires and emotions springing from the sense of sin and its release"; and he gives a large number of examples, in which the sin ranges from drunkenness to spiritual pride, to show that the sense of it may beset one and crave relief as urgently as does the anguish of the sickened flesh or any form of physical misery. [Studies in the Psychology of Religious Phenomena, American Journal of Psychology, vii. 309 (1896).]

Undoubtedly this conception covers an immense number of cases. A good one to use as an example is that of Mr. S.H. Hadley, who after his conversion became an active and useful rescuer of drunkards in New York. His experience runs as follows:

"One Tuesday evening I sat in a saloon in Harlem, a homeless, friendless, dying drunkard. I had pawned or sold everything that would bring a drink. I could not sleep unless I was dead drunk. I had not eaten for days, and for four nights preceding I had suffered with delirium tremens, or the horrors, from midnight till morning. I had often said, 'I will never be a tramp. I will never be cornered, for when that time comes, if ever it comes, I will find a home in the bottom of the river.' But the Lord so ordered it that when that time did come I was not able to walk one quarter of the way to the river. As I sat there thinking, I seemed to feel some great and mighty presence. I did not know then what it was. I did learn afterwards that it was Jesus, the sinner's friend. I walked up to the bar and pounded it with my fist till I made the glasses rattle. Those who stood by drinking looked on with scornful curiosity. I said I would never take another drink, if I died on the street, and really I felt as though that would happen before morning. Something said, 'If you want to keep this promise, go and have yourself locked up.' I went to the nearest station-house and had myself locked up.

"I was placed in a narrow cell, and it seemed as though all the demons that could find room came in that place with me. This was not all the company I had, either. No, praise the Lord; that dear Spirit that came to me in the saloon was present, and said, Pray. I did pray, and though I did not feel any great help, I kept on praying. As soon as I was able to leave my cell I was taken to the police court and remanded back to the cell. I was finally released, and found my way to my brother's house, where every care was given me. While lying in bed the admonishing Spirit never left me, and when I arose the following Sabbath morning I felt that day would decide my fate, and toward evening it came into my head to go to Jerry M'Auley's Mission. I went. The house was packed, and with great difficulty I made my way to the space near the platform. There I saw the apostle to the drunkard and the outcast— that man of God, Jerry M'Auley. He rose, and amid deep silence told his experience. There was a sincerity about this man that carried conviction with it, and I found myself saying, 'I wonder if God can save me?' I listened to the testimony of twenty-five or thirty persons, every one of whom had been saved from rum, and I made up my mind that I would be saved or die right there. When the invitation was given, I knelt down with a crowd of drunkards. Jerry made the first prayer. Then Mrs. M'Auley prayed fervently for us. Oh, what a conflict was going on for my poor soul! A blessed whisper said, 'Come'; the devil said, 'Be careful.' I halted but a moment, and then, with a breaking heart, I said, 'Dear Jesus, can you help me?' Never with mortal tongue can I describe that moment. Although up to that moment my soul had been filled with indescribable gloom, I felt the glorious brightness of the noonday sun shine into my heart. I felt I was a free man. Oh, the precious feeling of safety, of freedom, of resting on Jesus! I felt that Christ with all his brightness and power had come into my life; that, indeed, old things had passed away and all things had become new.

"From that moment till now I have never wanted a drink of whiskey, and I have never seen money enough to make me take one. I promised God that night that if he would take away the appetite for strong drink, I would work for him all my life. He has done his part, and I have been trying to do mine." [I have abridged Mr. Hadley's account. For other conversions of drunkards, see his pamphlet, Rescue Mission Work, published at the Old Jerry M'Auley Water Street Mission, New York city. A striking collection of cases also appears in the appendix to Professor Leuba's article.]

Dr. Leuba rightly remarks that there is little doctrinal theology in such an experience, which starts with the absolute need of a higher helper, and ends with the sense that he has helped us. He gives other cases of drunkards conversions which are purely ethical, containing, as recorded, no theological beliefs whatever. John B. Gough's case, for instance, is practically, says Dr. Leuba, the conversion of an atheist— neither God nor Jesus being mentioned. But in spite of the importance of this type of regeneration, with little or no intellectual readjustment, this writer surely makes it too exclusive. It corresponds to the subjectively centred form of morbid melancholy, of which Bunyan and Alline were examples. But we saw in our seventh lecture that there are objective forms of melancholy also, in which the lack of rational meaning of the universe, and of life anyhow, is the burden that weighs upon one— you remember Tolstoy's case. So there are distinct elements in conversion, and their relations to individual lives deserve to be discriminated.

A restaurant waiter served provisionally as Gough's 'Saviour.' General Booth, the founder of the Salvation Army, considers that the first vital step in saving outcasts consists in making them feel that some decent human being cares enough for them to take an interest in the question whether they are to rise or sink.

The crisis of apathetic melancholy— no use in life— into which J.S. Mill records that he fell, and from which he emerged by the reading of Marmontel's Memoirs (Heaven save the mark!) and Wordsworth's poetry, is another intellectual and general metaphysical case. [See Mill's Autobiography, New York, 1873, pp. 141, 148.]

Starbuck, in addition to 'escape from sin,' discriminates 'spiritual illumination' as a distinct type of conversion experience. [Psychology of Religion, p. 85.]

Some persons, for instance, never are, and possibly never under any circumstances could be, converted. Religious ideas cannot become the centre of their spiritual energy. They may be excellent persons, servants of God in practical ways, but they are not children of his kingdom. They are either incapable of imagining the invisible; or else, in the language of devotion, they are life-long subjects of 'barrenness' and 'dryness.' Such inaptitude for religious faith may in some cases be intellectual in its origin. Their religious faculties may be checked in their natural tendency to expand, by beliefs about the world that are inhibitive, the pessimistic and materialistic beliefs, for example, within which so many good souls, who in former times would have freely indulged their religious propensities, find themselves nowadays, as it were, frozen; or the agnostic vetoes upon faith as something weak and shameful, under which so many of us today lie cowering, afraid to use our instincts. In many persons such inhibitions are never overcome. To the end of their days they refuse to believe, their personal energy never gets to its religious centre, and the latter remains inactive in perpetuity.

In other persons the trouble is profounder. There are men anaesthetic on the religious side, deficient in that category of sensibility. Just as a bloodless organism can never, in spite of all its goodwill, attain to the reckless 'animal spirits' enjoyed by those of sanguine temperament; so the nature which is spiritually barren may admire and envy faith in others, but can never compass the enthusiasm and peace which those who are temperamentally qualified for faith enjoy. All this may, however, turn out eventually to have been a matter of temporary inhibition. Even late in life some thaw, some release may take place, some bolt be shot back in the barrenest breast, and the man's hard heart may soften and break into religious feeling. Such cases more than any others. suggest the idea that sudden conversion is by miracle. So long as they exist, we must not imagine ourselves to deal with irretrievably fixed classes.

Now there are two forms of mental occurrence in human beings, which lead to a striking difference in the conversion process, a difference to which Professor Starbuck has called attention. You know how it is when you try to recollect a forgotten name. Usually you help the recall by working for it, by mentally running over the places, persons, and things with which the word was connected. But sometimes this effort fails: you feel then as if the harder you tried the less hope there would be, as though the name were jammed, and pressure in its direction only kept it all the more from rising. And then the opposite expedient often succeeds. Give up the effort entirely; think of something altogether different, and in half an hour the lost name comes sauntering into your mind, as Emerson says, as carelessly as if it had never been invited. Some hidden process was started in you by the effort, which went on after the effort ceased, and made the result come as if it came spontaneously. A certain music teacher, says Dr. Starbuck, says to her pupils after the thing to be done has been clearly pointed out, and unsuccessfully attempted: "Stop trying and it will do itself!" [Psychology of Religion, p. 117.]

There is thus a conscious and voluntary way and an involuntary and unconscious way in which mental results may get accomplished; and we find both ways exemplified in the history of conversion, giving us two types, which Starbuck calls the volitional type and the type by self-surrender respectively.

In the volitional type the regenerative change is usually gradual, and consists in the building up, piece by piece, of a new set of moral and spiritual habits. But there are always critical points here at which the movement forward seems much more rapid. This psychological fact is abundantly illustrated by Dr. Starbuck. Our education in any practical accomplishment proceeds apparently by jerks and starts, just as the growth of our physical bodies does.

"An athlete... sometimes awakens suddenly to an understanding of the fine points of the game and to a real enjoyment of it, just as the convert awakens to an appreciation of religion. If he keeps on engaging in the sport, there may come a day when all at once the game plays itself through him— when he loses himself in some great contest. In the same way, a musician may suddenly reach a point at which pleasure in the technique of the art entirely falls away, and in some moment of inspiration he becomes the instrument through which music flows. The writer has chanced to hear two different married persons, both of whose wedded lives had been beautiful from the beginning, relate that not until a year or more after marriage did they awake to the full blessedness of married life. So it is with the religious experience of these persons we are studying." [Psychology of Religion, p. 385. Compare, also, pp. 137-144 and 262.]

We shall erelong hear still more remarkable illustrations of subconsciously maturing processes eventuating in results of which we suddenly grow conscious. Sir William Hamilton and Professor Laycock of Edinburgh were among the first to call attention to this class of effects; but Dr. Carpenter first, unless I am mistaken, introduced the term 'unconscious cerebration,' which has since then been a popular phrase of explanation. The facts are now known to us far more extensively than he could know them, and the adjective 'unconscious,' being for many of them almost certainly a misnomer, is better replaced by the vaguer term 'subconscious' or 'subliminal.'

Of the volitional type of conversion it would be easy to give examples, but they are as a rule less interesting than those of the self-surrender type, in which the subconscious effects are more abundant and often startling. I will therefore hurry to the latter, the more so because the difference between the two types is after all not radical. Even in the most voluntarily built-up sort of regeneration there are passages of partial self-surrender interposed; and in the great majority of all cases, when the will has done its uttermost towards bringing one close to the complete unification aspired after, it seems that the very last step must be left to other forces and performed without the help of its activity. In other words, self-surrender becomes then indispensable. "The personal will," says Dr. Starbuck, "must be given up. In many cases relief persistently refuses to come until the person ceases to resist, or to make an effort in the direction he desires to go."

For instance, C.G. Finney italicizes the volitional element: "Just at this point the whole question of Gospel salvation opened to my mind in a manner most marvelous to me at the time. I think I then saw, as clearly an I ever have in my life, the reality and fullness of the atonement of Christ. Gospel salvation seemed to me to be an offer of something to be accepted, and all that was necessary on my part was to get my own consent to give up my sins and accept Christ. After this distinct revelation had stood for some little time before my mind, the question seemed to be put, 'Will you accept it now, today?' I replied, 'Yes; I will accept it today, or I will die in the attempt!'" He then went into the woods, where he describes his struggles. He could not pray, his heart was hardened in its pride. "I then reproached myself for having promised to give my heart to God before I left the woods. When I came to try I found I could not.... My inward soul hung back, and there was no going out of my heart to God. The thought was pressing me, of the rashness of my promise that I would give my heart to God that day, or die in the attempt. It seemed to me as if that was binding on my soul; and yet I was going to break my vow. A great sinking and discouragement came over me, and I felt almost too weak to stand upon my knees. Just at this moment I again thought I heard some one approach me, and I opened my eyes to see whether it were so. But right there the revelation of my pride of heart, as the great difficulty that stood in the way, was distinctly shown to me. An overwhelming sense of my wickedness in being ashamed to have a human being see me on my knees before God took such powerful possession of me, that I cried at the top of my voice, and exclaimed that I would not leave that place if all the men on earth and all the devils in hell surrounded me. 'What!' I said, 'such a degraded sinner as I am, on my knees confessing my sins to the great and holy God; and ashamed to have any human being, and a sinner like myself, find me on my knees endeavoring to make my peace with my offended God!' The sin appeared awful, infinite. It broke me down before the Lord." Memoirs, pp. 14-16, abridged.

"I had said I would not give up; but when my will was broken, it was all over," writes one of Starbuck's correspondents.— Another says: "I simply said: 'Lord, I have done all I can; I leave the whole matter with Thee;' and immediately there came to me a great peace."— Another: "All at once it occurred to me that I might be saved, too, if I would stop trying to do it all myself, and follow Jesus: somehow I lost my load."— Another: "I finally ceased to resist, and gave myself up, though it was a hard struggle. Gradually the feeling came over me that I had done my part, and God was willing to do his." [Starbuck: Op. cit., pp. 91, 114.] "Lord, Thy will be done; damn or save!" cries John Nelson, exhausted with the anxious struggle to escape damnation; and at that moment his soul was filled with peace. [Extracts from the Journal of Mr. John Nelson, London, no date, p. 24.]

Dr. Starbuck gives an interesting, and it seems to me a true, account— so far as conceptions so schematic can claim truth at all— of the reasons why self-surrender at the last moment should be so indispensable. To begin with, there are two things in the mind of the candidate for conversion first, the present incompleteness or wrongness, the 'sin' which he is eager to escape from; and, second, the positive ideal which he longs to compass. Now with most of us the sense of our present wrongness is a far more distinct piece of our consciousness than is the imagination of any positive ideal we can aim at. In a majority of cases, indeed, the 'sin' almost exclusively engrosses the attention, so that conversion is "a process of struggling away from sin rather than of striving towards righteousness." A man's conscious wit and will, so far as they strain towards the ideal, are aiming at something only dimly and inaccurately imagined. Yet all the while the forces of mere organic ripening within him are going on towards their own prefigured result, and his conscious strainings are letting loose subconscious allies behind the scenes, which in their way work towards rearrangement; and the rearrangement towards which all these deeper forces tend is pretty surely definite, and definitely different from what he consciously conceives and determines. It may consequently be actually interfered with (jammed, as it were, like the lost word when we seek too energetically to recall it), by his voluntary efforts slanting from the true direction. [Starbuck, p. 64.]

Starbuck seems to put his finger on the root of the matter when he says that to exercise the personal will is still to live in the region where tho imperfect self is the thing most emphasized. Where, on the contrary, the subconscious forces take the lead, it is more probably the better self in posse which directs the operation. Instead of being clumsily and vaguely aimed at from with. out, it is then itself the organizing centre. What then must the person do? "He must relax," says Dr. Starbuck,— "that is, he must fall back on the larger Power that makes for righteousness, which has been welling up in his own being, and let it finish in its own way the work it has begun.... The act of yielding, in this point of view, is giving one's self over to the new life, making it the centre of a new personality, and living, from within, the truth of it which had before been viewed objectively." [Starbuck, p. 115.]

"Man's extremity is God's opportunity" is the theological way of putting this fact of the need of self-surrender; whilst the physiological way of stating it would be, "Let one do all in one's power, and one's nervous system will do the rest." Both statements acknowledge the same fact. [Starbuck, p. 113.]

To state it in terms of our own symbolism: When the new centre of personal energy has been subconsciously incubated so long as to be just ready to open into flower, 'hands off' is the only word for us, it must burst forth unaided!

We have used the vague and abstract language of psychology. But since, in any terms, the crisis described is the throwing of our conscious selves upon the mercy of powers which, whatever they may be, are more ideal than we are actually, and make for our redemption, you see why self-surrender has been and always must be regarded as the vital turning-point of the religious life, so far as the religious life is spiritual and no affair of outer works and ritual and sacraments. One may say that the whole development of Christianity in inwardness has consisted in little more than the greater and greater emphasis attached to this crisis of self-surrender. From Catholicism to Lutheranism, and then to Calvinism; from that to Wesleyanism; and from this, outside of technical Christianity altogether, to pure 'liberalism' or transcendental idealism, whether or not of the mind-cure type, taking in the medieval mystics, the quietists, the pietists, and quakers by the way, we can trace the stages of progress towards the idea of an immediate spiritual help, experienced by the individual in his forlornness and standing in no essential need of doctrinal apparatus or propitiatory machinery.

Psychology and religion are thus in perfect harmony up to this point, since both admit that there are forces seemingly outside of the conscious individual that bring redemption to his life. Nevertheless psychology, defining these forces as 'subconscious,' and speaking of their effects as due to 'incubation,' or 'cerebration,' implies that they do not transcend the individual's personality; and herein she diverges from Christian theology, which insists that they are direct supernatural operations of the Deity. I propose to you that we do not yet consider this divergence final, but leave the question for a while in abeyance— continued inquiry may enable us to get rid of some of the apparent discord.

Revert, then, for a moment more to the psychology of self-surrender.

When you find a man living on the ragged edge of his consciousness, pent in to his sin and want and incompleteness, and consequently inconsolable, and then simply tell him that all is well with him, that he must stop his worry, break with his discontent, and give up his anxiety, you seem to him to come with pure absurdities. The only positive consciousness he has tells him that all is not well, and the better way you offer sounds simply as if you proposed to him to assert cold-blooded falsehoods. 'The will to believe' cannot be stretched as far as that. We can make ourselves more faithful to a belief of which we have the rudiments, but we cannot create a belief out of whole cloth when our perception actively assures us of its opposite. The better mind proposed to us comes in that case in the form of a pure negation of the only mind we have, and we cannot actively will a pure negation.

There are only two ways in which it is possible to get rid of anger, worry, fear, despair, or other undesirable affections. One is that an opposite affection should overpoweringly break over us, and the other is by getting so exhausted with the struggle that we have to stop,— so we drop down, give up, and don't care any longer. Our emotional brain-centres strike work, and we lapse into a temporary apathy. Now there is documentary proof that this state of temporary exhaustion not infrequently forms part of the conversion crisis. So long as the egoistic worry of the sick soul guards the door, the expansive confidence of the soul of faith gains no presence. But let the former faint away, even but for a moment, and the latter can profit by the opportunity, and, having once acquired possession, may retain it. Carlyle's Teufelsdroeckh passes from the everlasting No to the everlasting Yes through a 'Centre of Indifference.'

Let me give you a good illustration of this feature in the conversion process. That genuine saint, David Brainerd, describes his own crisis in the following words:

"One morning, while I was walking in a solitary place as usual, I at once saw that all my contrivances and projects to effect or procure deliverance and salvation for myself were utterly in vain; I was brought quite to a stand, as finding myself totally lost. I saw that it was forever impossible for me to do anything towards helping or delivering myself, that I had made all the pleas I ever could have made to all eternity; and that all my pleas were vain, for I saw that self-interest had led me to pray, and that I had never once prayed from any respect to the glory of God. I saw that there was no necessary connection between my prayers and the bestowment of divine mercy; that they laid not the least obligation upon God to bestow his grace upon me; and that there was no more virtue or goodness in them than there would be in my paddling with my hand in the water. I saw that I had been heaping up my devotions before God, fasting, praying, etc., pretending, and indeed really thinking sometimes that I was aiming at the glory of God; whereas I never once truly intended it, but only my own happiness. I saw that as I had never done anything for God, I had no claim on anything from him but perdition, on account of my hypocrisy and mockery. When I saw evidently that I had regard to nothing but self-interest, then my duties appeared a vile mockery and a continual course of lies, for the whole was nothing but self-worship, and an horrid abuse of God.

"I continued, as I remember, in this state of mind, from Friday morning till the Sabbath evening following (July 12, 1739), when I was walking again in the same solitary place. Here, in a mournful melancholy state [I was attempting to pray; but found no heart to engage in that or any other duty; my former concern, exercise, and religious affections were now gone. I thought that the Spirit of God had quite left me; but still was not distressed; yet disconsolate, as if there was nothing in heaven or earth could make me happy. Having been thus endeavoring to pray— though, as I thought, very stupid and senseless]— for near half an hour; then, as I was walking in a thick grove, unspeakable glory seemed to open to the apprehension of my soul. I do not mean any external brightness, nor any imagination of a body of light, but it was a new inward apprehension or view that I had of God, such as I never had before, nor anything which had the least resemblance to it. I had no particular apprehension of any one person in the Trinity, either the Father, the Son, or the Holy Ghost; but it appeared to be Divine glory. My soul rejoiced with joy unspeakable. to see such a God, such a glorious Divine Being; and I was inwardly pleased and satisfied that he should be God over all for ever and ever. My soul was so captivated and delighted with the excellency of God that I was even swallowed up in him; at least to that degree that I had no thought about my own salvation, and scarce reflected that there was such a creature as myself. I continued in this state of inward joy, peace, and astonishing, till near dark without any sensible abatement; and then began to think and examine what I had seen; and felt sweetly composed in my mind all the evening following. I felt myself in a new world, and everything about me appeared with a different aspect from what it was wont to do. At this time, the way of salvation opened to me with such infinite wisdom, suitableness, and excellency, that I wondered I should ever think of any other way of salvation; was amazed that I had not dropped my own contrivances, and complied with this lovely, blessed, and excellent way before. If I could have been saved by my own duties or any other way that I had formerly contrived, my whole soul would now have refused it. I wondered that all the world did not see and comply with this way of salvation, entirely by the righteousness of Christ." [Edward's and Dwight's Life of Brainerd, New Haven, 1822, pp. 45-47, abridged.]

I have the passage which records the exhaustion of the anxious emotion hitherto habitual. In a large proportion, perhaps the majority, of reports, the writers speak as if the exhaustion of the lower and the entrance of the higher emotion were simultaneous, yet often again they speak as if the higher actively drove the lower out. This is undoubtedly true in a great many instances, as we shall presently see. But often there seems little doubt that both conditions— subconscious ripening of the one affection and exhaustion of the other— must simultaneously have conspired, in order to produce the result.

Describing the whole phenomenon as a change of equilibrium, we might say that the movement of new psychic energies towards the personal centre and the recession of old ones towards the margin (or the rising of some objects above, and the sinking of others below the conscious threshold) were only two ways of describing an indivisible event. Doubtless this is often absolutely true, and Starbuck is right when he says that 'self-surrender' and 'new determination,' though seeming at first sight to be such different experiences, are "really the same thing. Self-surrender sees the change in terms of the old self; determination sees it in terms of the new."

T.W.B., a convert of Nettleton's, being brought to an acute paroxysm of conviction of sin, ate nothing all day, locked himself in his room in the evening in complete despair, crying aloud, "How long, O Lord, how long?" "After repeating this and similar language," he says, "several times, I seemed to sink away into a state of insensibility. When I came to myself again I was on my knees, praying not for myself but for others. I felt submission to the will of God, willing that he should do with me as should seem good in his sight. My concern seemed all lost in concern for others." [A.A. Bonar: Nettleton and his Labors, Edinburgh, 1854, p. 261.]

Our great American revivalist Finney writes: "I said to myself: 'What is this? I must have grieved the Holy Ghost entirely away. I have lost all my conviction. I have not a particle of concern about my soul; and it must be that the Spirit has left me.' 'Why!' thought I, 'I never was so far from being concerned about my own salvation in my life.'... I tried to recall my convictions, to get back again the load of sin under which I had been laboring. I tried in vain to make myself anxious. I was so quiet and peaceful that I tried to feel concerned about that, lest it should be the result of my having grieved the Spirit away." [Charles G. Finney: Memoirs written by Himself, 1876, pp. 17, 18.]

But beyond all question there are persons in whom, quite independently of any exhaustion in the Subject's capacity for feeling, or even in the absence of any acute previous feeling, the higher condition, having reached the due degree of energy, bursts through all barriers and sweeps in like a sudden flood. These are the most striking and memorable cases, the cases of instantaneous conversion to which the conception of divine grace has been most peculiarly attached. I have given one of them at length— the case of Mr. Bradley. But I had better reserve the other cases and my comments on the rest of the subject for the following lecture.

LECTURE IX: CONVERSION

To be converted, to be regenerated, to receive grace, to experience religion, to gain an assurance, are so many phrases which denote the process, gradual or sudden, by which a self hitherto divided, and consciously wrong inferior and unhappy, becomes unified and consciously right superior and happy, in consequence of its firmer hold upon religious realities. This at least is what conversion signifies in general terms, whether or not we believe that a direct divine operation is needed to bring such a moral change about.

Before entering upon a minuter study of the process, let me enliven our understanding of the definition by a concrete example. I choose the quaint case of an unlettered man, Stephen H. Bradley, whose experience is related in a scarce American pamphlet. [A sketch of the life of Stephen H. Bradley, from the age of five to twenty-four years, including his remarkable experience of the power of the Holy Spirit on the second evening of November, 1829. Madison, Connecticut, 1830.]

I select this case because it shows how in these inner alterations one may find one unsuspected depth below another, as if the possibilities of character lay disposed in a series of layers or shells, of whose existence we have no premonitory knowledge.

Bradley thought that he had been already fully converted at the age of fourteen.

"I thought I saw the Saviour, by faith, in human shape, for about one second in the room, with arms extended, appearing to say to me, Come. The next day I rejoiced with trembling; soon after, my happiness was so great that I said that I wanted to die; this world had no place in my affections, as I knew of, and every day appeared as solemn to me as the Sabbath. I had an ardent desire that all mankind might feel as I did; I wanted to have them all love God supremely. Previous to this time I was very selfish and self-righteous; but now I desired the welfare of all mankind, and could with a feeling heart forgive my worst enemies, and I felt as if I should be willing to bear the scoffs and sneers of any person, and suffer anything for His sake, if I could be the means in the hands of God, of the conversion of one soul."

Nine years later, in 1829, Mr. Bradley heard of a revival of religion that had began in his neighborhood. "Many of the young converts," he says, "would come to me when in meeting and ask me if I had religion, and my reply generally was, I hope I have. This did not appear to satisfy them; they said they knew they had it. I requested them to pray for me, thinking with myself, that if I had not got religion now, after so long a time professing to be a Christian, that it was time I had, and hoped their prayers would be answered in my behalf.

"One Sabbath, I went to hear the Methodist at the Academy. He spoke of the ushering in of the day of general judgment; and he set it forth in such a solemn and terrible manner as I never heard before. The scene of that day appeared to be taking place, and so awakened were all the powers of my mind that, like Felix, I trembled involuntarily on the bench where I was sitting, though I felt nothing at heart. The next day evening I went to hear him again. He took his text from Revelation: 'And I saw the dead, small and great, stand before God.' And he represented the terrors of that day in such a manner that it appeared as if it would melt the heart of stone. When he finished his discourse, an old gentleman turned to me and said, 'This is what I call preaching.' I thought the same; but my feelings were still unmoved by what he said, and I did not enjoy religion, but I believe he did.

"I will now relate my experience of the power of the Holy Spirit which took place on the same night. Had any person told me previous to this that I could have experienced the power of the Holy Spirit in the manner which I did, I could not have believed it, and should have thought the person deluded that told me so. I went directly home after the meeting, and when I got home I wondered what made me feel so stupid. I retired to rest soon after I got home, and felt indifferent to the things of religion until I began to be exercised by the Holy Spirit, which began in about five minutes after, in the following manner:

"At first, I began to feel my heart beat very quick all on a sudden, which made me at first think that perhaps something is going to ail me, though I was not alarmed, for I felt no pain. My heart increased in its beating, which soon convinced me that it was the Holy Spirit from the effect it had on me. I began to feel exceedingly happy and humble, and such a sense of unworthiness as I never felt before. I could not very well help speaking out, which I did, and said, Lord, I do not deserve this happiness, or words to that effect, while there was a stream (resembling air in feeling) came into my mouth and heart in a more sensible manner than that of drinking anything, which continued, as near as I could judge, five minutes or more, which appeared to be the cause of such a palpitation of my heart. It took complete possession of my soul, and I am certain that I desired the Lord, while in the midst of it, not to give me any more happiness, for it seemed as if I could not contain what I had got. My heart seemed as if it would burst but it did not stop until I felt as if I was unutterably full of the love and grace of God. In the mean time while thus exercised, a thought arose in my mind, what can it mean? and all at once, as if to answer it, my memory became exceedingly clear, and it appeared to me just as if the New Testament was placed open before me, eighth chapter of Romans, and as light as if some candle lighted was held for me to read the 26th and 27th verses of that chapter, and I read these words: 'The Spirit helpeth our infirmities with groanings which cannot be uttered.' And all the time that my heart was a-beating, it made me groan like a person in distress, which was not very easy to stop, though I was in no pain at all, and my

brother being in bed in another room came and opened the door, and asked me if I had got the toothache. I told him no, and that he might get to sleep. I tried to stop. I felt unwilling to go to sleep myself, I was so happy, fearing I should loose it— thinking within myself
'My willing soul would stay
In such a frame as this.'
And while I lay reflecting, after my heart stopped beating, feeling as if my soul was full of the Holy Spirit, I thought that perhaps there might be angels hovering round my bed. I felt just as if I wanted to converse with them, and finally I spoke, saying, 'O ye affectionate angels! how is it that ye can take so much interest in our welfare, and we take so little interest in our own.' After this, with difficulty I got to sleep; and when I awoke in the morning my first thoughts were: What has become of my happiness? and, feeling a degree of it in my heart, I asked for more, which was given to me as quick as thought. I then got up to dress myself, and found to my surprise that I could but just stand. It appeared to me as if it was a little heaven upon earth. My soul felt as completely raised above the fears of death as of going to sleep; and like a bird in a cage, I had a desire, if it was the will of God, to get released from my body and to dwell with Christ, though willing to live to do good to others, and to warn sinners to repent. I went downstairs feeling as solemn as if I had lost all my friends, and thinking with myself, that I would not let my parents know it until I had first looked into the Testament. I went directly to the shelf and looked into it, at the eighth chapter of Romans, and every verse seemed to almost speak and to confirm it to be truly the Word of God, and as if my feelings corresponded with the meaning of the word. I then told my parents of it, and told them that I thought that they must see that when I spoke, that it was not my own voice, for it appeared so to me. My speech seemed entirely under the control of the Spirit within me; I do not mean that the words which I spoke were not my own, for they were. I thought that I was influenced similar to the Apostles on the day of Pentecost (with the exception of having power to give it to others, and doing what they did). After breakfast I went round to converse with my neighbors on religion, which I could not have been hired to have done before this, and at their request I prayed with them, though I had never prayed in public before.

"I now feel as if I had discharged my duty by telling the truth, and hope by the blessing of God, it may do some good to all who shall read it. He has fulfilled his promise in sending the Holy Spirit down into our hearts, or mine at least, and I now defy all the Deists and Atheists in the world to shake my faith in Christ."

So much for Mr. Bradley and his conversion, of the effect of which upon his later life we gain no information. Now for a minuter survey of the constituent elements of the conversion process.

If you open the chapter on Association, of any treatise on Psychology, you will read that a man's ideas, aims, and objects form diverse internal groups and systems, relatively independent of one another. Each 'aim' which he follows awakens a certain specific kind of interested excitement, and gathers a certain group of ideas together in subordination to it as its associates; and if the aims and excitements are distinct in kind, their groups of ideas may have little in common. When one group is present and engrosses the interest, all the ideas connected with other groups may be excluded from the mental field. The President of the United States when with paddle, gun, and fishing-rod, he goes camping in the wilderness for a vacation, changes his system of ideas from top to bottom. The presidential anxieties have lapsed into the background entirely; the official habits are replaced by the habits of a son of nature, and those who knew the man only as the strenuous magistrate would not 'know him for the same person' if they saw him as the camper.

If now he should never go back, and never again suffer political interests to gain dominion over him, he would be for practical intents and purposes a permanently transformed being. Our ordinary alterations of character, as we pass from one of our aims to another, are not commonly called transformations, because each of them is so rapidly succeeded by another in the reverse direction; but whenever one aim grows so stable as to expel definitively its previous rivals from the individual's life, we tend to speak of the phenomenon, and perhaps to wonder at it, as a 'transformation.'

These alternations are the completest of the ways in which a self may be divided. A less complete way is the simultaneous coexistence of two or more different groups of aims, of which one practically holds the right of way and instigates activity, whilst the others are only pious wishes, and never practically come to anything. Saint Augustine's aspirations to a purer life, in our last lecture, were for a while an example. Another would be the President in his full pride of office, wondering whether it were not all vanity, and whether the life of a wood-chopper were not the wholesomer destiny. Such fleeting aspirations are mere velleitates, whimsies. They exist on the remoter outskirts of the mind, and the real self of the man, the centre of his energies, is occupied with an entirely different system. As life goes on, there is a constant change of our interests, and a consequent change of place in our systems of ideas, from more central to more peripheral, and from more peripheral to more central parts of consciousness. I remember, for instance, that one evening when I was a youth, my father read aloud from a Boston newspaper that part of Lord Gifford's will which founded these four lectureships. At that time I did not think of being a teacher of philosophy: and what I listened to was as remote from my own life as if it related to the planet Mars. Yet here I am, with the Gifford system part and parcel of my very self, and all my energies, for the time being, devoted to successfully identifying myself with it. My soul stands now planted in what once was for it a practically unreal object, and speaks from it as from its proper habitat and centre.

When I say 'Soul,' you need not take me in the ontological sense unless you prefer to; for although ontological language is instinctive in such matters, yet Buddhists or Humians can perfectly well describe the facts in the phenomenal terms which are their favorites. For them the soul is only a succession of fields of consciousness: yet there is found in each field a part, or sub-field, which figures as focal and contains the excitement, and from which, as from a centre, the aim seems to be taken. Talking of this part, we involuntarily apply words of perspective to distinguish it from the rest, words like 'here,' 'this,' 'now,' 'mine,' or 'me'; and we ascribe to the other parts the positions 'there,' 'then,' 'that,' 'his' or 'thine,' 'it,' 'not me.' But a 'here' can change to a 'there,' and a 'there' become a 'here,' and what was 'mine' and what was 'not mine' change their places.

What brings such changes about is the way in which emotional excitement alters. Things hot and vital to us today are cold tomorrow. It is as if seen from the hot parts of the field that the other parts appear to us, and from these hot parts personal desire and volition make their sallies. They are in short the centres of our dynamic energy, whereas the cold parts leave us indifferent and passive in proportion to their coldness.

Whether such language be rigorously exact is for the present of no importance. It is exact enough, if you recognize from your own experience the facts which I seek to designate by it.

Now there may be great oscillation in the emotional interest, and the hot places may shift before one almost as rapidly as the sparks that run through burnt-up paper. Then we have the wavering and divided self we heard so much of in the previous lecture. Or the focus of excitement and heat, the point of view from which the aim is taken, may come to lie permanently within a certain system; and then, if the change be a religious one, we call it a conversion, especially if it be by crisis, or sudden.

Let us hereafter, in speaking of the hot place in a man's consciousness, the group of ideas to which he devotes himself, and from which he works, call it the habitual centre of his personal energy. It makes a great difference to a man whether one set of his ideas, or another, be the centre of his energy; and it makes a great difference, as regards any set of ideas which he may possess, whether they become central or remain peripheral in him. To say that a man is 'converted' means, in these terms, that religious ideas, previously peripheral in his consciousness, now take a central place, and that religious aims form the habitual centre of his energy.

Now if you ask of psychology just how the excitement shifts in a man's mental system, and why aims that were peripheral become at a certain moment central, psychology has to reply that although she can give a general description of what happens, she is unable in a given case to account accurately for all the single forces at work. Neither an outside observer nor the Subject who undergoes the process can explain fully how particular experiences are able to change one's centre of energy so decisively, or why they so often have to bide their hour to do so. We have a thought, or we perform an act, repeatedly, but on a certain day the real meaning of the thought peals through us for the first time, or the act has suddenly turned into a moral impossibility. All we know is that there are dead feelings, dead ideas, and cold beliefs, and there are hot and live ones; and when one grows hot and alive within us, everything has to re-crystallize about it. We may say that the heat and liveliness mean only the 'motor efficacy,' long deferred but now operative, of the idea; but such talk itself is only circumlocution, for whence the sudden motor efficacy?

And our explanations then get so vague and general that one realizes all the more the intense individuality of the whole phenomenon.

In the end we fall back on the hackneyed symbolism of a mechanical equilibrium. A mind is a system of ideas, each with the excitement it arouses, and with tendencies impulsive and inhibitive, which mutually check or reinforce one another. The collection of ideas alters by subtraction or by addition in the course of experience, and the tendencies alter as the organism gets more aged. A mental system may be undermined or weakened by this interstitial alteration just as a building is, and yet for a time keep upright by dead habit. But a new perception, a sudden emotional shock, or an occasion which lays bare the organic alteration, will make the whole fabric fall together; and then the centre of gravity sinks into an attitude more stable, for the new ideas that reach the centre in the rearrangement seem now to be locked there, and the new structure remains permanent.

Formed associations of ideas and habits are usually factors of retardation in such changes of equilibrium. New information, however acquired, plays an accelerating part in the changes; and the slow mutation of our instincts and propensities, under the 'unimaginable touch of time' has an enormous influence. Moreover, all these influences may work subconsciously or half unconsciously. And when you get a Subject in whom the subconscious life— of which I must speak more fully soon— is largely developed, and in whom motives habitually ripen in silence, you get a case of which you can never give a full account, and in which, both to the Subject and the onlookers, there may appear an element of marvel. Emotional occasions, especially violent ones, are extremely potent in precipitating mental rearrangements. The sudden and explosive ways in which love, jealousy, guilt, fear, remorse, or anger can seize upon one are known to everybody. Hope, happiness, security, resolve, emotions characteristic of conversion, can be equally explosive. And emotions that come in this explosive way seldom leave things as they found them.

Jouffroy is an example: "Down this slope it was that my intelligence had glided, and little by little it had got far from its first faith. But this melancholy revolution had not taken place in the broad daylight of my consciousness; too many scruples, too many guides and sacred affections had made it dreadful to me, so that I was far from avowing to myself the progress it had made. It had gone on in silence, by an involuntary elaboration of which I was not the accomplice; and although I had in reality long ceased to be a Christian, yet, in the innocence of my intention, I should have shuddered to suspect it, and thought it calumny had I been accused of such a falling away." Then follows Jouffroy's account of his counter-conversion, quoted above in Lecture VIII.

One hardly needs examples; but for love, see Lecture VIII note [Op. cit., Letter III...], for fear, see Lecture VI and VII, for remorse, see Othello after the murder; for anger, see Lear after Cordelia's first speech to him; for resolve, see Lecture VIII (J. Foster case). Here is a pathological case in which guilt was the feeling that suddenly exploded: "One night I was seized on entering bed with a rigor, such as Swedenborg describes as coming over him with a sense of holiness, but over me with a sense of guilt. During that whole night I lay under the influence of the rigor, and from its inception I felt that I was under the curse of God. I have never done one act of duty in my life- sins against God and man, beginning as far as my memory goes back— a wildcat in human shape."

In his recent work on the Psychology of Religion, Professor Starbuck of California has shown by a statistical inquiry how closely parallel in its manifestations the ordinary 'conversion' which occurs in young people brought up in evangelical circles is to that growth into a larger spiritual life which is a normal phase of adolescence in every class of human beings. The age is the same falling usually between fourteen and seventeen. The symptoms are the same,— sense of incompleteness and imperfection; brooding, depression, morbid introspection, and sense of sin; anxiety about the hereafter; distress over doubts, and the like. And the result is the same,— a happy relief and objectivity, as the confidence in self gets greater through the adjustment of the faculties to the wider outlook. In spontaneous religious awakening, apart from revivalistic examples, and in the ordinary storm and stress and moulting-time of adolescence, we also may meet with mystical experiences, astonishing the subjects by their suddenness, just as in revivalistic conversion. The analogy, in fact, is complete; and Starbuck's conclusion as to these ordinary youthful conversions would seem to be the only sound one: Conversion is in its essence a normal adolescent phenomenon, incidental to the passage from the child's small universe to the wider intellectual and spiritual life of maturity.

"Theology," says Dr. Starbuck, "takes the adolescent tendencies and builds upon them; it sees that the essential thing in adolescent growth is bringing the person out of childhood into the new life of maturity and personal insight. It accordingly brings those means to bear which will intensify the normal tendencies. It shortens up the period of duration of storm and stress." The conversion phenomena of 'conviction of sin' last, by this investigator's statistics, about one fifth as long as the periods of adolescent storm and stress phenomena of which he also got statistics, but they are very much more intense. Bodily accompaniments, loss of sleep and appetite, for example, are much more frequent in them. "The essential distinction appears to be that conversion intensifies but shortens the period by bringing the person to a definite crisis." [E.D. Starbuck: The Psychology of Religion, pp. 224, 262.]

The conversions which Dr. Starbuck here has in mind are of course mainly those of very commonplace persons, kept true to a pre-appointed type by instruction, appeal, and example. The particular form which they affect is the result of suggestion and imitation. If they went through their growth-crisis in other faiths and other countries, although the essence of the change would be the same (since it is one in the main so inevitable), its accidents would be different. In Catholic lands, for example, and in our own Episcopalian sects, no such anxiety and conviction of sin is usual as in sects that encourage revivals. The sacraments being more relied on in these more strictly ecclesiastical bodies, the individual's personal acceptance of salvation needs less to be accentuated and led up to.

No one understands this better than Jonathan Edwards understood it already. Conversion narratives of the more commonplace sort must always be taken with the allowances which he suggests: "A rule received and established by common consent has a very great, though to many persons an insensible influence in forming their notions of the process of their own experience. I know very well how they proceed as to this matter, for I have had frequent opportunities of observing their conduct. Very often their experience at first appears like a confused chaos, but then those parts are selected which bear the nearest resemblance to such particular steps as are insisted on; and these are dwelt upon in their thoughts, and spoken of from time to time, till they grow more and more conspicuous in their view, and other parts which are neglected grow more and more obscure. Thus what they have experienced is insensibly strained, so as to bring it to an exact conformity to the scheme already established in their minds. And it becomes natural also for ministers, who have to deal with those who insist upon distinctness and clearness of method, to do so too." Treatise on Religious Affections.

But every imitative phenomenon must once have had its original, and I propose that for the future we keep as close as may be to the more first-hand and original forms of experience. These are more likely to be found in sporadic adult cases.

Professor Leuba, in a valuable article on the psychology of conversion, subordinates the theological aspect of the religious life almost entirely to its moral aspect. [Studies in the Psychology of Religious Phenomena, American Journal of Psychology, vii. 309 (1896).] The religious sense he defines as "the feeling of unwholeness, of moral imperfection, of sin, to use the technical word, accompanied by the yearning after the peace of unity." "The word 'religion,'" he says, "is getting more and more to signify the conglomerate of desires and emotions springing from the sense of sin and its release"; and he gives a large number of examples, in which the sin ranges from drunkenness to spiritual pride, to show that the sense of it may beset one and crave relief as urgently as does the anguish of the sickened flesh or any form of physical misery.

Undoubtedly this conception covers an immense number of cases. A good one to use as an example is that of Mr. S.H. Hadley, who after his conversion became an active and useful rescuer of drunkards in New York. His experience runs as follows:

"One Tuesday evening I sat in a saloon in Harlem, a homeless, friendless, dying drunkard. I had pawned or sold everything that would bring a drink. I could not sleep unless I was dead drunk. I had not eaten for days, and for four nights preceding I had suffered with delirium tremens, or the horrors, from midnight till morning. I had often said, 'I will never be a tramp. I will never be cornered, for when that time comes, if ever it comes, I will find a home in the bottom of the river.' But the Lord so ordered it that when that time did come I was not able to walk one quarter of the way to the river. As I sat there thinking, I seemed to feel

some great and mighty presence. I did not know then what it was. I did
learn afterwards that it was Jesus, the sinner's friend. I walked up to the
bar and pounded it with my fist till I made the glasses rattle. Those who
stood by drinking looked on with scornful curiosity. I said I would never
take another drink, if I died on the street, and really I felt as though that
would happen before morning. Something said, 'If you want to keep this
promise, go and have yourself locked up.' I went to the nearest
station-house and had myself locked up.

"I was placed in a narrow cell, and it seemed as though all the demons
that could find room came in that place with me. This was not all the
company I had, either. No, praise the Lord; that dear Spirit that came to
me in the saloon was present, and said, Pray. I did pray, and though I did
not feel any great help, I kept on praying. As soon as I was able to leave
my cell I was taken to the police court and remanded back to the cell. I
was finally released, and found my way to my brother's house, where
every care was given me. While lying in bed the admonishing Spirit never
left me, and when I arose the following Sabbath morning I felt that day
would decide my fate, and toward evening it came into my head to go to
Jerry M'Auley's Mission. I went. The house was packed, and with great
difficulty I made my way to the space near the platform. There I saw the
apostle to the drunkard and the outcast— that man of God, Jerry
M'Auley. He rose, and amid deep silence told his experience. There was
a sincerity about this man that carried conviction with it, and I found
myself saying, 'I wonder if God can save me?' I listened to the testimony
of twenty-five or thirty persons, every one of whom had been saved from
rum, and I made up my mind that I would be saved or die right there.
When the invitation was given, I knelt down with a crowd of drunkards.
Jerry made the first prayer. Then Mrs. M'Auley prayed fervently for us.
Oh, what a conflict was going on for my poor soul! A blessed whisper said,
'Come'; the devil said, 'Be careful.' I halted but a moment, and then, with
a breaking heart, I said, 'Dear Jesus, can you help me?' Never with mortal
tongue can I describe that moment. Although up to that moment my soul
had been filled with indescribable gloom, I felt the glorious brightness of
the noonday sun shine into my heart. I felt I was a free man. Oh, the
precious feeling of safety, of freedom, of resting on Jesus! I felt that Christ
with all his brightness and power had come into my life; that, indeed, old
things had passed away and all things had become new.

"From that moment till now I have never wanted a drink of whiskey,
and I have never seen money enough to make me take one. I promised
God that night that if he would take away the appetite for strong drink,
I would work for him all my life. He has done his part, and I have been
trying to do mine." [I have abridged Mr. Hadley's account. For other
conversions of drunkards, see his pamphlet, Rescue Mission Work,
published at the Old Jerry M'Auley Water Street Mission, New York city.
A striking collection of cases also appears in the appendix to Professor
Leuba's article.]

Dr. Leuba rightly remarks that there is little doctrinal theology in such
an experience, which starts with the absolute need of a higher helper, and

ends with the sense that he has helped us. He gives other cases of drunkards conversions which are purely ethical, containing, as recorded, no theological beliefs whatever. John B. Gough's case, for instance, is practically, says Dr. Leuba, the conversion of an atheist— neither God nor Jesus being mentioned. But in spite of the importance of this type of regeneration, with little or no intellectual readjustment, this writer surely makes it too exclusive. It corresponds to the subjectively centred form of morbid melancholy, of which Bunyan and Alline were examples. But we saw in our seventh lecture that there are objective forms of melancholy also, in which the lack of rational meaning of the universe, and of life anyhow, is the burden that weighs upon one— you remember Tolstoy's case. [The crisis of apathetic melancholy— no use in life— into which J.S. Mill records that he fell, and from which he emerged by the reading of Marmontel's Memoirs (Heaven save the mark!) and Wordsworth's poetry, is another intellectual and general metaphysical case. See Mill's Autobiography, New York, 1873, pp. 141, 148.] So there are distinct elements in conversion, and their relations to individual lives deserve to be discriminated. [Starbuck, in addition to 'escape from sin,' discriminates 'spiritual illumination' as a distinct type of conversion experience. Psychology of Religion, p. 85.]

Some persons, for instance, never are, and possibly never under any circumstances could be, converted. Religious ideas cannot become the centre of their spiritual energy. They may be excellent persons, servants of God in practical ways, but they are not children of his kingdom. They are either incapable of imagining the invisible; or else, in the language of devotion, they are life-long subjects of 'barrenness' and 'dryness.' Such inaptitude for religious faith may in some cases be intellectual in its origin. Their religious faculties may be checked in their natural tendency to expand, by beliefs about the world that are inhibitive, the pessimistic and materialistic beliefs, for example, within which so many good souls, who in former times would have freely indulged their religious propensities, find themselves nowadays, as it were, frozen; or the agnostic vetoes upon faith as something weak and shameful, under which so many of us today lie cowering, afraid to use our instincts. In many persons such inhibitions are never overcome. To the end of their days they refuse to believe, their personal energy never gets to its religious centre, and the latter remains inactive in perpetuity.

In other persons the trouble is profounder. There are men anaesthetic on the religious side, deficient in that category of sensibility. Just as a bloodless organism can never, in spite of all its goodwill, attain to the reckless 'animal spirits' enjoyed by those of sanguine temperament; so the nature which is spiritually barren may admire and envy faith in others, but can never compass the enthusiasm and peace which those who are temperamentally qualified for faith enjoy. All this may, however, turn out eventually to have been a matter of temporary inhibition. Even late in life some thaw, some release may take place, some bolt be shot back in the barrenest breast, and the man's hard heart may soften and break into religious feeling. Such cases more than any others. suggest the idea that sudden conversion is by miracle. So long as they exist, we must not imagine ourselves to deal with irretrievably fixed classes.

Now there are two forms of mental occurrence in human beings, which lead to a striking difference in the conversion process, a difference to which Professor Starbuck has called attention. You know how it is when you try to recollect a forgotten name. Usually you help the recall by working for it, by mentally running over the places, persons, and things with which the word was connected. But sometimes this effort fails: you feel then as if the harder you tried the less hope there would be, as though the name were jammed, and pressure in its direction only kept it all the more from rising. And then the opposite expedient often succeeds. Give up the effort entirely; think of something altogether different, and in half an hour the lost name comes sauntering into your mind, as Emerson says, as carelessly as if it had never been invited. Some hidden process was started in you by the effort, which went on after the effort ceased, and made the result come as if it came spontaneously. A certain music teacher, says Dr. Starbuck, says to her pupils after the thing to be done has been clearly pointed out, and unsuccessfully attempted: "Stop trying and it will do itself!" [Psychology of Religion, p. 117.]

There is thus a conscious and voluntary way and an involuntary and unconscious way in which mental results may get accomplished; and we find both ways exemplified in the history of conversion, giving us two types, which Starbuck calls the volitional type and the type by self-surrender respectively.

In the volitional type the regenerative change is usually gradual, and consists in the building up, piece by piece, of a new set of moral and spiritual habits. But there are always critical points here at which the movement forward seems much more rapid. This psychological fact is abundantly illustrated by Dr. Starbuck. Our education in any practical accomplishment proceeds apparently by jerks and starts, just as the growth of our physical bodies does.

"An athlete... sometimes awakens suddenly to an understanding of the fine points of the game and to a real enjoyment of it, just as the convert awakens to an appreciation of religion. If he keeps on engaging in the sport, there may come a day when all at once the game plays itself through him— when he loses himself in some great contest. In the same way, a musician may suddenly reach a point at which pleasure in the technique of the art entirely falls away, and in some moment of inspiration he becomes the instrument through which music flows. The writer has chanced to hear two different married persons, both of whose wedded lives had been beautiful from the beginning, relate that not until a year or more after marriage did they awake to the full blessedness of married life. So it is with the religious experience of these persons we are studying." [Psychology of Religion, p. 385. Compare, also, pp. 137-144 and 262.]

We shall erelong hear still more remarkable illustrations of subconsciously maturing processes eventuating in results of which we suddenly grow conscious. Sir William Hamilton and Professor Laycock of

Edinburgh were among the first to call attention to this class of effects; but Dr. Carpenter first, unless I am mistaken, introduced the term 'unconscious cerebration,' which has since then been a popular phrase of explanation. The facts are now known to us far more extensively than he could know them, and the adjective 'unconscious,' being for many of them almost certainly a misnomer, is better replaced by the vaguer term 'subconscious' or 'subliminal.'

Of the volitional type of conversion it would be easy to give examples, but they are as a rule less interesting than those of the self-surrender type, in which the subconscious effects are more abundant and often startling. I will therefore hurry to the latter, the more so because the difference between the two types is after all not radical. Even in the most voluntarily built-up sort of regeneration there are passages of partial self-surrender interposed; and in the great majority of all cases, when the will has done its uttermost towards bringing one close to the complete unification aspired after, it seems that the very last step must be left to other forces and performed without the help of its activity. In other words, self-surrender becomes then indispensable. "The personal will," says Dr. Starbuck, "must be given up. In many cases relief persistently refuses to come until the person ceases to resist, or to make an effort in the direction he desires to go."

For instance, C.G. Finney italicizes the volitional element: "Just at this point the whole question of Gospel salvation opened to my mind in a manner most marvelous to me at the time. I think I then saw, as clearly an I ever have in my life, the reality and fullness of the atonement of Christ. Gospel salvation seemed to me to be an offer of something to be accepted, and all that was necessary on my part was to get my own consent to give up my sins and accept Christ. After this distinct revelation had stood for some little time before my mind, the question seemed to be put, 'Will you accept it now, today?' I replied, 'Yes; I will accept it today, or I will die in the attempt!'" He then went into the woods, where he describes his struggles. He could not pray, his heart was hardened in its pride. "I then reproached myself for having promised to give my heart to God before I left the woods. When I came to try I found I could not.... My inward soul hung back, and there was no going out of my heart to God. The thought was pressing me, of the rashness of my promise that I would give my heart to God that day, or die in the attempt. It seemed to me as if that was binding on my soul; and yet I was going to break my vow. A great sinking and discouragement came over me, and I felt almost too weak to stand upon my knees. Just at this moment I again thought I heard some one approach me, and I opened my eyes to see whether it were so. But right there the revelation of my pride of heart, as the great difficulty that stood in the way, was distinctly shown to me. An overwhelming sense of my wickedness in being ashamed to have a human being see me on my knees before God took such powerful possession of me, that I cried at the top of my voice, and exclaimed that I would not leave that place if all the men on earth and all the devils in hell surrounded me. 'What!' I said, 'such a degraded sinner as I am, on my knees confessing my sins to the great and holy God; and ashamed to have any human being, and a sinner like myself, find me on my knees endeavoring to make my peace with my offended God!' The sin appeared awful, infinite. It broke me down before the Lord." [Memoirs, pp. 14-16, abridged.]

"I had said I would not give up; but when my will was broken, it was all over," writes one of Starbuck's correspondents.— Another says: "I simply said: 'Lord, I have done all I can; I leave the whole matter with Thee;' and immediately there came to me a great peace."— Another: "All at once it occurred to me that I might be saved, too, if I would stop trying to do it all myself, and follow Jesus: somehow I lost my load."— Another: "I finally ceased to resist, and gave myself up, though it was a hard struggle. Gradually the feeling came over me that I had done my part, and God was willing to do his." [Starbuck: Op. cit., pp. 91, 114.] "Lord, Thy will be done; damn or save!" cries John Nelson, exhausted with the anxious struggle to escape damnation; and at that moment his soul was filled with peace. [Extracts from the Journal of Mr. John Nelson, London, no date, p. 24.]

Dr. Starbuck gives an interesting, and it seems to me a true, account— so far as conceptions so schematic can claim truth at all— of the reasons why self-surrender at the last moment should be so indispensable. To begin with, there are two things in the mind of the candidate for conversion first, the present incompleteness or wrongness, the 'sin' which he is eager to escape from; and, second, the positive ideal which he longs to compass. Now with most of us the sense of our present wrongness is a far more distinct piece of our consciousness than is the imagination of any positive ideal we can aim at. In a majority of cases, indeed, the 'sin' almost exclusively engrosses the attention, so that conversion is "a process of struggling away from sin rather than of striving towards righteousness." A man's conscious wit and will, so far as they strain towards the ideal, are aiming at something only dimly and inaccurately imagined. [Starbuck, p. 64.] Yet all the while the forces of mere organic ripening within him are going on towards their own prefigured result, and his conscious strainings are letting loose subconscious allies behind the scenes, which in their way work towards rearrangement; and the rearrangement towards which all these deeper forces tend is pretty surely definite, and definitely different from what he consciously conceives and determines. It may consequently be actually interfered with (jammed, as it were, like the lost word when we seek too energetically to recall it), by his voluntary efforts slanting from the true direction.

Starbuck seems to put his finger on the root of the matter when he says that to exercise the personal will is still to live in the region where tho imperfect self is the thing most emphasized. Where, on the contrary, the subconscious forces take the lead, it is more probably the better self in posse which directs the operation. Instead of being clumsily and vaguely aimed at from with. out, it is then itself the organizing centre. What then must the person do? "He must relax," says Dr. Starbuck,— "that is, he must fall back on the larger Power that makes for righteousness, which has been welling up in his own being, and let it finish in its own way the work it has begun.... The act of yielding, in this point of view, is giving one's self over to the new life, making it the centre of a new personality, and living, from within, the truth of it which had before been viewed objectively." [Starbuck, p. 115.]

"Man's extremity is God's opportunity" is the theological way of putting this fact of the need of self-surrender; whilst the physiological way of stating it would be, "Let one do all in one's power, and one's nervous system will do the rest." Both statements acknowledge the same fact. [Starbuck, p. 113.]

To state it in terms of our own symbolism: When the new centre of personal energy has been subconsciously incubated so long as to be just ready to open into flower, 'hands off' is the only word for us, it must burst forth unaided!

We have used the vague and abstract language of psychology. But since, in any terms, the crisis described is the throwing of our conscious selves upon the mercy of powers which, whatever they may be, are more ideal than we are actually, and make for our redemption, you see why self-surrender has been and always must be regarded as the vital turning-point of the religious life, so far as the religious life is spiritual and no affair of outer works and ritual and sacraments. One may say that the whole development of Christianity in inwardness has consisted in little more than the greater and greater emphasis attached to this crisis of self-surrender. From Catholicism to Lutheranism, and then to Calvinism; from that to Wesleyanism; and from this, outside of technical Christianity altogether, to pure 'liberalism' or transcendental idealism, whether or not of the mind-cure type, taking in the medieval mystics, the quietists, the pietists, and quakers by the way, we can trace the stages of progress towards the idea of an immediate spiritual help, experienced by the individual in his forlornness and standing in no essential need of doctrinal apparatus or propitiatory machinery.

Psychology and religion are thus in perfect harmony up to this point, since both admit that there are forces seemingly outside of the conscious individual that bring redemption to his life. Nevertheless psychology, defining these forces as 'subconscious,' and speaking of their effects as due to 'incubation,' or 'cerebration,' implies that they do not transcend the individual's personality; and herein she diverges from Christian theology, which insists that they are direct supernatural operations of the Deity. I propose to you that we do not yet consider this divergence final, but leave the question for a while in abeyance— continued inquiry may enable us to get rid of some of the apparent discord.

Revert, then, for a moment more to the psychology of self-surrender.

When you find a man living on the ragged edge of his consciousness, pent in to his sin and want and incompleteness, and consequently inconsolable, and then simply tell him that all is well with him, that he must stop his worry, break with his discontent, and give up his anxiety, you seem to him to come with pure absurdities. The only positive consciousness he has tells him that all is not well, and the better way you offer sounds simply as if you proposed to him to assert cold-blooded falsehoods. 'The will to believe' cannot be stretched as far as that. We can make ourselves more faithful to a belief of which we have the rudiments, but we cannot create a belief out of whole cloth when our perception actively assures us of its opposite. The better mind proposed to us comes in that case in the form of a pure negation of the only mind we have, and we cannot actively will a pure negation.

There are only two ways in which it is possible to get rid of anger, worry, fear, despair, or other undesirable affections. One is that an opposite affection should overpoweringly break over us, and the other is by getting so exhausted with the struggle that we have to stop,— so we drop down, give up, and don't care any longer. Our emotional brain-centres strike work, and we lapse into a temporary apathy. Now there is documentary proof that this state of temporary exhaustion not infrequently forms part of the conversion crisis. So long as the egoistic worry of the sick soul guards the door, the expansive confidence of the soul of faith gains no presence. But let the former faint away, even but for a moment, and the latter can profit by the opportunity, and, having once acquired possession, may retain it. Carlyle's Teufelsdrockh passes from the everlasting No to the everlasting Yes through a 'Centre of Indifference.'

Let me give you a good illustration of this feature in the conversion process. That genuine saint, David Brainerd, describes his own crisis in the following words:

"One morning, while I was walking in a solitary place as usual, I at once saw that all my contrivances and projects to effect or procure deliverance and salvation for myself were utterly in vain; I was brought quite to a stand, as finding myself totally lost. I saw that it was forever impossible for me to do anything towards helping or delivering myself, that I had made all the pleas I ever could have made to all eternity; and that all my pleas were vain, for I saw that self-interest had led me to pray, and that I had never once prayed from any respect to the glory of God. I saw that there was no necessary connection between my prayers and the bestowment of divine mercy; that they laid not the least obligation upon God to bestow his grace upon me; and that there was no more virtue or goodness in them than there would be in my paddling with my hand in the water. I saw that I had been heaping up my devotions before God, fasting, praying, etc., pretending, and indeed really thinking sometimes that I was aiming at the glory of God; whereas I never once truly intended it, but only my own happiness. I saw that as I had never done anything for God, I had no claim on anything from him but perdition, on account of my hypocrisy and mockery. When I saw evidently that I had regard to nothing but self-interest, then my duties appeared a vile mockery and a continual course of lies, for the whole was nothing but self-worship, and an horrid abuse of God.

"I continued, as I remember, in this state of mind, from Friday morning till the Sabbath evening following (July 12, 1739), when I was walking again in the same solitary place. Here, in a mournful melancholy state [I was attempting to pray; but found no heart to engage in that or any other duty; my former concern, exercise, and religious affections were now gone.

I thought that the Spirit of God had quite left me; but still was not distressed; yet disconsolate, as if there was nothing in heaven or earth could make me happy. Having been thus endeavoring to pray— though, as I thought, very stupid and senseless]— for near half an hour; then, as I was walking in a thick grove, unspeakable glory seemed to open to the apprehension of my soul. I do not mean any external brightness, nor any imagination of a body of light, but it was a new inward apprehension or view that I had of God, such as I never had before, nor anything which had the least resemblance to it. I had no particular apprehension of any one person in the Trinity, either the Father, the Son, or the Holy Ghost; but it appeared to be Divine glory. My soul rejoiced with joy unspeakable. to see such a God, such a glorious Divine Being; and I was inwardly pleased and satisfied that he should be God over all for ever and ever. My soul was so captivated and delighted with the excellency of God that I was even swallowed up in him; at least to that degree that I had no thought about my own salvation, and scarce reflected that there was such a creature as myself. I continued in this state of inward joy, peace, and astonishing, till near dark without any sensible abatement; and then began to think and examine what I had seen; and felt sweetly composed in my mind all the evening following. I felt myself in a new world, and everything about me appeared with a different aspect from what it was wont to do. At this time, the way of salvation opened to me with such infinite wisdom, suitableness, and excellency, that I wondered I should ever think of any other way of salvation; was amazed that I had not dropped my own contrivances, and complied with this lovely, blessed, and excellent way before. If I could have been saved by my own duties or any other way that I had formerly contrived, my whole soul would now have refused it. I wondered that all the world did not see and comply with this way of salvation, entirely by the righteousness of Christ." [Edward's and Dwight's Life of Brainerd, New Haven, 1822, pp. 45-47, abridged.]

In a large proportion, perhaps the majority, of reports, the writers speak as if the exhaustion of the lower and the entrance of the higher emotion were simultaneous, yet often again they speak as if the higher actively drove the lower out. This is undoubtedly true in a great many instances, as we shall presently see. But often there seems little doubt that both conditions— subconscious ripening of the one affection and exhaustion of the other- must simultaneously have conspired, in order to produce the result. [Describing the whole phenomenon as a change of equilibrium, we might say that the movement of new psychic energies towards the personal centre and the recession of old ones towards the margin (or the rising of some objects above, and the sinking of others below the conscious threshold) were only two ways of describing an indivisible event. Doubtless this is often absolutely true, and Starbuck is right when he says that 'self-surrender' and 'new determination,' though seeming at first sight to be such different experiences, are "really the same thing. Self-surrender sees the change in terms of the old self; determination sees it in terms of the new." Op. cit.]

T.W.B., a convert of Nettleton's, being brought to an acute paroxysm of conviction of sin, ate nothing all day, locked himself in his room in the evening in complete despair, crying aloud, "How long, O Lord, how long?" "After repeating this and similar language," he says, "several times, I seemed to sink away into a state of insensibility. When I came to myself again I was on my knees, praying not for myself but for others. I felt submission to the will of God, willing that he should do with me as should seem good in his sight. My concern seemed all lost in concern for others."[A.A. Bonar: Nettleton and his Labors, Edinburgh, 1854, p. 261.]

Our great American revivalist Finney writes: "I said to myself: 'What is this? I must have grieved the Holy Ghost entirely away. I have lost all my conviction. I have not a particle of concern about my soul; and it must be that the Spirit has left me.' 'Why!' thought I, 'I never was so far from being concerned about my own salvation in my life.'... I tried to recall my convictions, to get back again the load of sin under which I had been laboring. I tried in vain to make myself anxious. I was so quiet and peaceful that I tried to feel concerned about that, lest it should be the result of my having grieved the Spirit away." [Charles G. Finney: Memoirs written by Himself, 1876, pp. 17, 18.]

But beyond all question there are persons in whom, quite independently of any exhaustion in the Subject's capacity for feeling, or even in the absence of any acute previous feeling, the higher condition, having reached the due degree of energy, bursts through all barriers and sweeps in like a sudden flood. These are the most striking and memorable cases, the cases of instantaneous conversion to which the conception of divine grace has been most peculiarly attached. I have given one of them at length— the case of Mr. Bradley. But I had better reserve the other cases and my comments on the rest of the subject for the following lecture.

LECTURE X: CONVERSION

Concluded

In this lecture we have to finish the subject of Conversion, considering at first those striking instantaneous instances of which Saint Paul's is the most eminent, and in which, often amid tremendous emotional excitement or perturbation of the senses, a complete division is established in the twinkling of an eye between the old life and the new. Conversion of this type is an important phase of religious experience, owing to the part which it has played in Protestant theology, and it behooves us to study it conscientiously on that account.

I think I had better cite two or three of these cases before proceeding to a more generalized account. One must know concrete instances first; for, as Professor Agassiz used to say, one can see no farther into a generalization than just so far as one's previous acquaintance with particulars enables one to take it in. I will go back, then, to the case of our friend Henry Alline, and quote his report of the 26th of March, 1775, on which his poor divided mind became unified for good

"As I was about sunset wandering in the fields lamenting my miserable lost and undone condition, and almost ready to sink under my burden, I thought I was in such a miserable case as never any man was before. I returned to the house, and when I got to the door, just as I was stepping off the threshold, the following impressions came into my mind like a powerful but small still voice. You have been seeking, praying, reforming, laboring, reading, hearing, and meditating, and what have you done by it towards your salvation? Are you any nearer to conversion now than when you first began? Are you any more prepared for heaven, or fitter to appear before the impartial bar of God, than when you first began to seek?

"It brought such conviction on me that I was obliged to say that I did not think I was one step nearer than at first, but as much condemned, as much exposed, and as miserable as before. I cried out within myself, O Lord God, I am lost, and if thou, O Lord, dost not find out some new way, I know nothing of, I shall never be saved, for the ways and methods I have prescribed to myself have all failed me, and I am willing they should fail. O Lord, have mercy! O Lord, have mercy!"

"These discoveries continued until I went into the house and sat down. After I sat down, being all in confusion, like a drowning man that was just giving up to sink, and almost in an agony, I turned very suddenly round in my chair, and seeing part of an old Bible lying in one of the chairs, I caught hold of it in great haste; and opening it without any premeditation, cast my eyes on the 38th Psalm, which was the first time I ever saw the word of God: it took hold of me with such power that it seemed to go through my whole soul, so that it seemed as if God was praying in, with, and for me. About this time my father called the family to attend prayers; I attended, but paid no regard to what he said in his prayer, but continued praying in those words of the Psalm. Oh, help me, help me! cried I, thou Redeemer of souls, and save me, or I am gone forever; thou canst this night, if thou pleasest, with one drop of thy blood atone for my sins, and appease the wrath of an angry God. At that instant of time when I gave all up to him to do with me as he pleased, and was willing that God should rule over me at his pleasure, redeeming love broke into my soul with repeated scriptures, with such power that my whole soul seemed to be melted down with love; the burden of guilt and condemnation was gone, darkness was expelled, my heart humbled and filled with gratitude, and my whole soul, that was a few minutes ago groaning under mountains of death, and crying to an unknown God for help, was now filled with immortal love, soaring on the wings of faith, freed from the chains of death and darkness, and crying out, My Lord and my God; thou art my rock and my fortress, my shield and my high tower, my life, my joy, my present and my everlasting portion. Looking up, I thought I saw that same light [he had on more than one previous occasion seen subjectively a bright blaze of light], though it appeared different; and as soon as I saw it, the design was opened to me, according to his promise, and I was obliged to cry out: Enough, enough, O blessed God! The work of conversion, the change, and the manifestations of it are no more disputable than that light which I see, or anything that ever I saw.

"In the midst of all my joys, in less than half an hour after my soul was set at liberty, the Lord discovered to me my labor in the ministry and call to preach the gospel. I cried out, Amen, Lord, I'll go; send me, send me. I spent the greatest part of the night in ecstasies of joy, praising and adoring the Ancient of Days for his free and unbounded grace. After I had been so long in this transport and heavenly frame that my nature seemed to require sleep, I thought to close my eyes for a few moments; then the devil stepped in, and told me that if I went to sleep, I should lose it all, and when I should awake in the morning I would find it to be nothing but a fancy and delusion. I immediately cried out, O Lord God, if I am deceived, undeceive me.

"I then closed my eyes for a few minutes, and seemed to be refreshed with sleep; and when I awoke, the first inquiry was, Where is my God? And in an instant of time, my soul seemed awake in and with God, and surrounded by the arms of everlasting love. About sunrise I arose with joy to relate to my parents what God had done for my soul, and declared to them the miracle of God's unbounded grace. I took a Bible to show them the words that were impressed by God on my soul the evening before; but when I came to open the Bible, it appeared all new to me.

"I so longed to be useful in the cause of Christ, in preaching the gospel, that it seemed as if I could not rest any longer, but go I must and tell the wonders of redeeming love. I lost all taste for carnal pleasures, and carnal company, and was enabled to forsake them." [Life and Journals, Boston, 1806, pp. 31-40, abridged.]

Young Mr. Alline, after the briefest of delays, and with no book-learning but his Bible, and no teaching save that of his own experience, became a Christian minister, and thenceforward his life was fit to rank, for its austerity and single-mindedness, with that of the most devoted saints. But happy as he became in his strenuous way, he never got his taste for even the most innocent carnal pleasures back. We must class him, like Bunyan and Tolstoy, amongst those upon whose soul the iron of melancholy left a permanent imprint. His redemption was into another universe than this mere natural world, and life remained for him a sad and patient trial. Years later we can find him making such an entry as this in his diary: "On Wednesday the 12th I preached at a wedding, and had the happiness thereby to be the means of excluding carnal mirth."

The next case I will give is that of a correspondent of Professor Leuba, printed in the latter's article, already cited, in vol. vi. of the American Journal of Psychology. This subject was an Oxford graduate, the son of a clergyman, and the story resembles in many points the classic case of Colonel Gardiner, which everybody may be supposed to know. Here it is, somewhat abridged:

"Between the period of leaving Oxford and my conversion I never darkened the door of my father's church, although I lived with him for eight years, making what money I wanted by journalism, and spending it in high carousal with any one who would sit with me and drink it away. So I lived, sometimes drunk for a week together, and then a terrible repentance, and would not touch a drop for a whole month.

"In all this period, that is, up to thirty-three years of age, I never had a desire to reform on religious grounds. But all my pangs were due to some terrible remorse I used to feel after a heavy carousal, the remorse taking the shape of regret after my folly in wasting my life in such a way— a man of superior talents and education. This terrible remorse turned me gray in one night, and whenever it came upon me I was perceptibly grayer the next morning. What I suffered in this way is beyond the expression of words. It was hell-fire in all its most dreadful tortures. Often did I vow that if I got over 'this time' I would reform. Alas, in about three days I fully recovered, and was as happy as ever. So it went on for years, but, with a physique like a rhinoceros, I always recovered, and as long as I let drink alone, no man was as capable of enjoying life as I was.

"I was converted in my own bedroom in my father's rectory house at precisely three o'clock in the afternoon of a hot July day (July 18, 1886). I was in perfect health, having been off from the drink for nearly a month. I was in no way troubled about my soul. In fact, God was not in my thoughts that day. A young lady friend sent me a copy of Professor Drummond's Natural Law in the Spiritual World, asking me my opinion of it as a literary work only. Being proud of my critical talents and wishing to enhance myself in my new friend's esteem, I took the book to my bedroom for quiet, intending to give it a thorough study, and then write her what I thought of it. It was here that God met me face to face, and I shall never forget the meeting. 'He that hath the Son hath life eternal, he that hath not the Son hath not life.' I had read this scores of times before, but this made all the difference. I was now in God's presence and my attention was absolutely 'soldered' on to this verse, and I was not allowed to proceed with the book till I had fairly considered what these words really involved. Only then was I allowed to proceed, feeling all the while that there was another being in my bedroom, though not seen by me. The stillness was very marvelous, and I felt supremely happy. It was most unquestionably shown me, in one second of time, that I had never touched the Eternal: and that if I died then, I must inevitably be lost. I was undone. I knew it as well as I now know I am saved. The Spirit of God showed it me in ineffable love; there was no terror in it; I felt God's love so powerfully upon me that only a mighty sorrow crept over me that I had lost all through my own folly and what was I to do? What could I do? I did not repent even; God never asked me to repent. All I felt was 'I am undone,' and God cannot help it, although he loves me. No fault on the part of the Almighty. All the time I was supremely happy: I felt like a little child before his father. I had done wrong, but my Father did not scold me, but loved me most wondrously. Still my doom was sealed. I was lost to a certainty, and being naturally of a brave disposition I did not quail under it, but deep sorrow for the past, mixed with regret for what I had lost, took hold upon me, and my soul thrilled within me to think it was all over. Then there crept in upon me so gently, so lovingly, so unmistakably, a way of escape, and what was it after all? The old, old story over again, told in the simplest way: 'There is no name under heaven whereby ye can be saved except that of the Lord Jesus Christ.' No words were spoken to me; my soul seemed to see my Saviour in the spirit, and from that hour to this, nearly nine years now, there has never been in my life one doubt that the Lord Jesus Christ and God the Father both worked upon me that afternoon in July, both differently, and both in the most perfect love conceivable, and I rejoiced there and then in a conversion so astounding that the whole village heard of it in less than twenty-four hours.

"But a time of trouble was yet to come. The day after my conversion I went into the hay-field to lend a hand with the harvest, and not having made any promise to God to abstain or drink in moderation only, I took too much and came home drunk. My poor sister was heart-broken; and I felt ashamed of myself and got to my bedroom at once, where she followed me, weeping copiously. She said I had been converted and fallen away instantly. But although I was quite full of drink (not muddled, however), I knew that God's work begun in me was not going to be wasted. About midday I made on my knees the first prayer before God for twenty years. I did not ask to be forgiven; I felt that was no good, for I would be sure to fall again. Well what did I do? I committed myself to him in the profoundest belief that my individuality was going to be destroyed, that he would take all from me, and I was willing. In such a surrender lies the secret of a holy life. From that hour drink has had no terrors for me: I never touch it, never want it. The same thing occurred with my pipe: after being a regular smoker from my twelfth year the desire for it went at once, and has never returned. So with every known sin, the deliverance in each case being permanent and complete. I have had no temptation since conversion, God seemingly having shut out Satan from that course with me. He gets a free hand in other ways, but never on sins of the flesh. Since I gave up to God all ownership in my own life, he has guided me in a thousand ways, and has opened my path in a way almost incredible to those who do not enjoy the blessing of a truly surrendered life."

So much for our graduate of Oxford, in whom you notice the complete abolition of an ancient appetite as one of the conversion's fruits.

The most curious record of sudden conversion with which I am acquainted is that of M. Alphonse Ratisbonne, a freethinking French Jew, to Catholicism, at Rome in 1842. In a letter to a clerical friend, written a few months later, the convert gives a palpitating account of the circumstances. The predisposing conditions appear to have been slight. He had an elder brother who had been converted and was a Catholic priest. He was himself irreligious, and nourished an antipathy to the apostate brother and generally to his 'cloth.' Finding himself at Rome in his twenty-ninth year, he fell in with a French gentleman who tried to make a proselyte of him, but who succeeded no farther after two or three conversations than to get him to hang (half jocosely) a religious medal round his neck, and to accept and read a copy of a short prayer to the Virgin. M. Ratisbonne represents his own part in the conversations as having been of a light and chaffing order; but he notes the fact that for some days he was unable to banish the words of the prayer from his mind, and that the night before the crisis he had a sort of nightmare, in the imagery of which a black cross with no Christ upon it figured. Nevertheless, until noon of the next day he was free in mind and spent the time in trivial conversations. I now give his own words. "My quotations are made from an Italian translation of this letter in the Biografia del Sig. M.A. Ratisbonne, Ferrara, 1843, which I have to thank Monsignore D. O'Connell of Rome for bringing to my notice. I abridge the original."

"If at this time any one had accosted me, saying: 'Alphonse, in a quarter of an hour you shall be adoring Jesus Christ as your God and Saviour; you shall lie prostrate with your face upon the ground in a humble church; you shall be smiting your breast at the foot of a priest; you shall pass the carnival in a college of Jesuits to prepare yourself to receive baptism, ready to give your life for the Catholic faith; you shall renounce the world and its pomps and pleasures; renounce your fortune, your hopes, and if need be, your betrothed; the affections of your family, the esteem of your friends, and your attachment to the Jewish people; you shall have no other aspiration than to follow Christ and bear his cross till death;'— if, I say a prophet had come to me with such a prediction, I should have judged that only one person could be more mad than he,— whosoever, namely, might believe in the possibility of such senseless folly becoming true. And yet that folly is at present my only wisdom, my sole happiness.

"Coming out of the cafe I met the carriage of Monsieur B. [the proselyting friend]. He stopped and invited me in for a drive, but first asked me to wait for a few minutes whilst he attended to some duty at the church of San Andrea delle Fratte. Instead of waiting in the carriage, I entered the church myself to look at it. The church of San Andres was poor, small and empty; I believe that I found myself there almost alone. No work of art attracted my attention; and I passed my eyes mechanically over its interior without being arrested by any particular thought. I can only remember an entirely black dog which went trotting and turning before me as I mused. In an instant the dog had disappeared, the whole church had vanished, I no longer saw anything,... or more truly I saw, O my God, one thing alone.

"Heavens, how can I speak of it? Oh no! human words cannot attain to expressing the inexpressible. Any description, however sublime it might be, could be but a profanation of the unspeakable truth.

"I was there prostrate on the ground, bathed in my tears, with my heart beside itself, when M.B. called me back to life. I could not reply to the questions which followed from him one upon the other. But finally I took the medal which I had on my breast, and with all the effusion of my soul I kissed the image of the Virgin, radiant with grace, which it bore. Oh, indeed, it was She! It was indeed She! [What he had seen had been a vision of the Virgin.]

"I did not know where I was: I did not know whether I was Alphonse or another. I only felt myself changed and believed myself another me; I looked for myself in myself and did not find myself. In the bottom of my soul I felt an explosion of the most ardent joy; I could not speak; I had no wish to reveal what had happened. But I felt something solemn and sacred within me which made me ask for a priest. I was led to one; and there, alone, after he had given me the positive order, I spoke as best I could, kneeling, and with my heart still trembling. I could give no account to myself of the truth of which I had acquired a knowledge and a faith. All that I can say is that in an instant the bandage had fallen from my eyes; and not one bandage only, but the whole manifold of bandages in which I had been brought up. One after another they rapidly disappeared, even as the mud and ice disappear under the rays of the burning sun.

"I came out as from a sepulchre, from an abyss of darkness; and I was living, perfectly living. But I wept, for at the bottom of that gulf I saw the extreme of misery from which I had been saved by an infinite mercy; and I shuddered at the sight of my iniquities, stupefied, melted, overwhelmed with wonder and with gratitude. You may ask me how I came to this new insight, for truly I had never opened a book of religion nor even read a single page of the Bible, and the dogma of original sin is either entirely denied or forgotten by the Hebrews of today, so that I had thought so little about it that I doubt whether I ever knew its name. But how came I, then, to this perception of it? I can answer nothing save this, that on entering that church I was in darkness altogether, and on coming out of it I saw the fullness of the light. I can explain the change no better than by the simile of a profound sleep or the analogy of one born blind who should suddenly open his eyes to the day. He sees, but cannot define the light which bathes him and by means of which he sees the objects which excite his wonder. If we cannot explain physical light, how can we explain the light which is the truth itself? And I think I remain within the limits of veracity when I say that without having any knowledge of the letter of religious doctrine, I now intuitively perceived its sense and spirit. Better than if I saw them, I felt those hidden things; I felt them by the inexplicable effects they produced in me. It all happened in my interior mind and those impressions, more rapid than thought, shook my soul, revolved and turned it, as it were, in another direction, towards other aims, by other paths. I express myself badly. But do you wish, Lord, that I should inclose in poor and barren words sentiments which the heart alone can understand?"

I might multiply cases almost indefinitely, but these will suffice to show you how real, definite, and memorable an event a sudden conversion may be to him who has the experience. Throughout the height of it he undoubtedly seems to himself a passive spectator or undergoer of an astounding process performed upon him from above. There is too much evidence of this for any doubt of it to be possible. Theology, combining this fact with the doctrines of election and grace, has concluded that the spirit of God is with us at these dramatic moments in a peculiarly miraculous way, unlike what happens at any other juncture of our lives. At that moment, it believes, an absolutely new nature is breathed into us, and we become partakers of the very substance of the Deity.

That the conversion should be instantaneous seems called for on this view, and the Moravian Protestants appear to have been the first to see this logical consequence. The Methodists soon followed suit, practically if not dogmatically, and a short time ere his death, John Wesley wrote:

"In London alone I found 652 members of our Society who were exceeding clear in their experience, and whose testimony I could see no reason to doubt. And every one of these (without a single exception) has declared that his deliverance from sin was instantaneous; that the change was wrought in a moment. Had half of these, or one third, or one in twenty, declared it was gradually wrought in them, I should have believed this, with regard to them, and thought that some were gradually sanctified and some instantaneously. But as I have not found, in so long a space of time, a single person speaking thus, I cannot but believe that sanctification is commonly, if not always, an instantaneous work." [Tyerman's Life of Wesley, I. 463.]

All this while the more usual sects of Protestantism have set no such store by instantaneous conversion. For them as for the Catholic Church, Christ's blood, the sacraments, and the individual's ordinary religious duties are practically supposed to suffice to his salvation, even though no acute crisis of self-despair and surrender followed by relief should be experienced. For Methodism, on the contrary, unless there have been a crisis of this sort, salvation is only offered, not effectively received, and Christ's sacrifice in so far forth is incomplete. Methodism surely here follows, if not the healthier-minded, yet on the whole the profounder spiritual instinct. The individual models which it has set up as typical and worthy of imitation are not only the more interesting dramatically, but psychologically they have been the more complete.

In the fully evolved Revivalism of Great Britain and America we have, so to speak, the codified and stereotyped procedure to which this way of thinking has led. In spite of the unquestionable fact that saints of the once-born type exist, that there may be a gradual growth in holiness without a cataclysm; in spite of the obvious leakage (as one may say) of much mere natural goodness into the scheme of salvation; revivalism has always assumed that only its own type of religious experience can be perfect; you must first be nailed on the cross of natural despair and agony, and then in the twinkling of an eye be miraculously released.

It is natural that those who personally have traversed such an experience should carry away a feeling of its being a miracle rather than a natural process. Voices are often heard, lights seen, or visions witnessed; automatic motor phenomena occur; and it always seems, after the surrender of the personal will, as if an extraneous higher power had flooded in and taken possession. Moreover the sense of renovation, safety, cleanness, rightness, can be so marvelous and jubilant as well to warrant one's belief in a radically new substantial nature.

"Conversion," writes the New England Puritan, Joseph Alleine," is not the putting in a patch of holiness; but with the true convert holiness is woven into all his powers, principles, and practice. The sincere Christian is quite a new fabric, from the foundation to the top-stone. He is a new man, a new creature."

And Jonathan Edwards says in the same strain: "Those gracious influences which are the effects of the Spirit of God are altogether supernatural— are quite different from anything that unregenerate men experience. They are what no improvement, or composition of natural qualifications or principles will ever produce; because they not only differ from what is natural, and from everything that natural men experience in degree and circumstances, but also in kind, and are of a nature far more excellent. From hence it follows that in gracious affections there are [also] new perceptions and sensations entirely different in their nature and kind from anything experienced by the [same] saints before they were sanctified.... The conceptions which the saints have of the loveliness of God, and that kind of delight which they experience in it, are quite peculiar, and entirely different from anything which a natural man can possess, or of which he can form any proper notion."

And that such a glorious transformation as this ought of necessity to be preceded by despair is shown by Edwards in another passage.

"Surely it cannot be unreasonable," he says, "that before God delivers us from a state of sin and liability to everlasting woe, he should give us some considerable sense of the evil from which he delivers us, in order that we may know and feel the importance of salvation, and be enabled to appreciate the value of what God is pleased to do for us. As those who are saved are successively in two extremely different states first in a state of condemnation and then in a state of justification and blessedness— and as God, in the salvation of men, deals with them as rational and intelligent creatures, it appears agreeable to this wisdom, that those who are saved should be made sensible of their Being, in those two different states. In the first place, that they should be made sensible of their state of condemnation; and afterwards, of their state of deliverance and happiness."

Such quotations express sufficiently well for our purpose the doctrinal interpretation of these changes. Whatever part suggestion and imitation may have played in producing them in men and women in excited assemblies, they have at any rate been in countless individual instances an original and unborrowed experience. Were we writing the story of the mind from the purely natural-history point of view, with no religious interest whatever, we should still have to write down man's liability to sudden and complete conversion as one of his most curious peculiarities.

What, now, must we ourselves think of this question? Is an instantaneous conversion a miracle in which God is present as he is present in no change of heart less strikingly abrupt? Are there two classes of human beings, even among the apparently regenerate, of which the one class really partakes of Christ's nature while the other merely seems to do so? Or, on the contrary, may the whole phenomenon of regeneration; even in these startling instantaneous examples, possibly be a strictly natural process, divine in its fruits, of course, but in one case more and in another less so, and neither more nor less divine in its mere causation and mechanism than any other process, high or low, of man's interior life?

Before proceeding to answer this question, I must ask you to listen to some more psychological remarks. At our last lecture, I explained the shifting of men's centres of personal energy within them and the lighting up of new crises of emotion. I explained the phenomena as partly due to explicitly conscious processes of thought and will, but as due largely also to the subconscious incubation and maturing of motives deposited by the experiences of life. When ripe, the results hatch out, or burst into flower. I have now to speak of the subconscious region, in which such processes of flowering may occur, in a somewhat less vague way. I only regret that my limits of time here force me to be so short.

The expression 'field of consciousness' has but recently come into vogue in the psychology books. Until quite lately the unit of mental life which figured most was the single 'idea,' supposed to be a definitely outlined thing. But at present psychologists are tending, first, to admit that the actual unit is more probably the total mental state, the entire wave of consciousness or field of objects present to the thought at any time; and, second, to see that it is impossible to outline this wave, this field, with any definiteness.

As our mental fields succeed one another, each has its centre of interest, around which the objects of which we are less and less attentively conscious fade to a margin so faint that its limits are unassignable. Some fields are narrow fields and some are wide fields. Usually when we have a wide field we rejoice, for we then see masses of truth together, and often get glimpses of relations which we divine rather than see, for they shoot beyond the field into still remoter regions of objectivity, regions which we seem rather to be about to perceive than to perceive actually. At other times, of drowsiness, illness, or fatigue, our fields may narrow almost to a point, and we find ourselves correspondingly oppressed and contracted.

Different individuals present constitutional differences in this matter of width of field. Your great organizing geniuses are men with habitually vast fields of mental vision, in which a whole programme of future operations will appear dotted out at once, the rays shooting far ahead into definite directions of advance. In common people there is never this magnificent inclusive view of a topic. They stumble along, feeling their way, as it were, from point to point, and often stop entirely. In certain diseased conditions consciousness is a mere spark, without memory of the past or thought of the future, and with the present narrowed down to some one simple emotion or sensation of the body.

The important fact which this 'field' formula commemorates is the indetermination of the margin. Inattentively realized as is the matter which the margin contains, it is nevertheless there, and helps both to guide our behavior and to determine the next movement of our attention. It lies around us like a 'magnetic field,' inside of which our centre of energy turns like a compass-needle, as the present phase of consciousness alters into its successor. Our whole past store of memories floats beyond this margin, ready at a touch to come in; and the entire mass of residual powers, impulses, and knowledges that constitute our empirical self stretches continuously beyond it. So vaguely drawn are the outlines between what is actual and what is only potential at any moment of our conscious life, that it is always hard to say of certain mental elements whether we are conscious of them or not.

The ordinary psychology, admitting fully the difficulty of tracing the marginal outline, has nevertheless taken for granted, first, that all the consciousness the person now has, be the same focal or marginal, inattentive or attentive, is there in the 'field' of the moment, all dim and impossible to assign as the latter's outline may be; and, second, that what is absolutely extra-marginal is absolutely non-existent, and cannot be a fact of consciousness at all.

And having reached this point, I must now ask you to recall what I said in my last lecture about the subconscious life. I said, as you may recollect, that those who first laid stress upon these phenomena could not know the facts as we now know them. My first duty now is to tell you what I meant by such a statement.

I cannot but think that the most important step forward that has occurred in psychology since I have been a student of that science is the discovery, first made in 1886, that, in certain subjects at least, there is not only the consciousness of the ordinary field, with its usual centre and margin, but an addition thereto in the shape of a set of memories, thoughts, and feelings which are extra-marginal and outside of the primary consciousness altogether, but yet must be classed as conscious facts of some sort, able to reveal their presence by unmistakable signs. I call this the most important step forward because, unlike the other advances which psychology has made, this discovery has revealed to us an entirely unsuspected peculiarity in the constitution of human nature. No other step forward which psychology has made can proffer any such claim as this.

In particular this discovery of a consciousness existing beyond the field, or subliminally as Mr. Myers terms it, casts light on many phenomena of religious biography. That is why I have to advert to it now, although it is naturally impossible for me in this place to give you any account of the evidence on which the admission of such a consciousness is based. You will find it set forth in many recent books, Binet's Alterations of Personality being perhaps as good a one as any to recommend.[Published in the International Scientific Series.]

The human material on which the demonstration has been made has so far been rather limited and, in part at least, eccentric, consisting of unusually suggestible hypnotic subjects, and of hysteric patients. Yet the elementary mechanisms of our life are presumably so uniform that what is shown to be true in a marked degree of some persons is probably true in some degree of all, and may in a few be true in an extraordinarily high degree.

The most important consequence of having a strongly developed ultra-marginal life of this sort is that one's ordinary fields of consciousness are liable to incursions from it of which the subject does not guess the source, and which, therefore, take for him the form of unaccountable impulses to act, or inhibitions of action, of obsessive ideas, or even of hallucinations of sight or hearing. The impulses may take the direction of automatic speech or writing, the meaning of which the subject himself may not understand even while he utters it; and generalizing this phenomenon, Mr. Myers has given the name of automatism, sensory or motor, emotional or intellectual, to this whole sphere of effects due to 'uprushes' into the ordinary consciousness of energies originating in the subliminal parts of the mind.

The simplest instance of an automatism is the phenomenon of post-hypnotic suggestion, so-called. You give to a hypnotized subject, adequately susceptible, an order to perform some designated act— usual or eccentric, it makes no difference— after he wakes from his hypnotic sleep. Punctually, when the signal comes or the time elapses upon which you have told him that the act must ensue, he performs it; — but in so doing he has no recollection of your suggestion, and he always trumps up an improvised pretext for his behavior if the act be of an eccentric kind. It may even be suggested to a subject to have a vision or to hear a voice at a certain interval after waking, and when the time comes the vision is seen or the voice heard, with no inkling on the subject's part of its source. In the wonderful explorations by Binet, Janet, Breuer, Freud, Mason, Prince, and others, of the subliminal consciousness of patients with hysteria, we have revealed to us whole systems of underground life, in the shape of memories of a painful sort which lead a parasitic existence, buried outside of the primary field of consciousness, and making irruptions thereinto with hallucinations, pains, convulsions, paralyses of feeling and of motion, and the whole procession of symptoms of hysteric disease of body and of mind. Alter or abolish by suggestion these subconscious memories, and the patient immediately gets well. His symptoms were automatisms, in Mr. Myers's sense of the word. These clinical records sound like fairy-tales when one first reads them, yet it is impossible to doubt their accuracy; and, the path having been once opened by these first observers, similar observations have been made elsewhere. They throw, as I said, a wholly new light upon our natural constitution.

And it seems to me that they make a farther step inevitable. Interpreting the unknown after the analogy of the known, it seems to me that hereafter, wherever we meet with a phenomenon of automatism, be it motor impulses, or obsessive idea, or unaccountable caprice, or delusion, or hallucination, we are bound first of all to make search whether it be not an explosion, into the fields of ordinary consciousness, of ideas elaborated outside of those fields in subliminal regions of the mind. We should look, therefore, for its source in the Subject's subconscious life. In the hypnotic cases, we ourselves create the source by our suggestion, so we know it directly. In the hysteric cases, the lost memories which are the source have to be extracted from the patient's Subliminal by a number of ingenious methods, for an account of which you must consult the books. In other pathological cases, insane delusions, for example, or psychopathic obsessions, the source is yet to seek, but by analogy it also should be in subliminal regions which improvements in our methods may yet conceivably put on tap. There lies the mechanism logically to be assumed,— but the assumption involves a vast program of work to be done in the way of verification, in which the religious experiences of man must play their part.

The reader will here please notice that in my exclusive reliance in the last lecture on the subconscious 'incubation' of motives deposited by a growing experience, I followed the method of employing accepted principles of explanation as far as one can. The subliminal region, whatever else it may be, is at any rate a place now admitted by psychologists to exist for the accumulation of vestiges of sensible experience (whether inattentively or attentively registered), and for their elaboration according to ordinary psychological or logical laws into results that end by attaining such a 'tension' that they may at times enter consciousness with something like a burst. It thus is 'scientific' to interpret all otherwise unaccountable invasive alterations of consciousness as results of the tension of subliminal memories reaching the bursting-point. But candor obliges me to confess that there are occasional bursts into consciousness of results of which it is not easy to demonstrate any prolonged subconscious incubation. Some of the cages I used to illustrate the sense of presence of the unseen in Lecture III were of this order; and we shall see other experiences of the kind when we come to the subject of mysticism. The case of Mr. Bradley, that of M. Ratisbonne, possibly that of Colonel Gardiner, possibly that of Saint Paul, might not be so easily explained in this simple way. The result, then, would have to be ascribed either to a merely physiological nerve storm, a 'discharging lesion' like that of epilepsy; or, in case it were useful and rational, as in the two latter cases named, to some more mystical or theological hypothesis. I make this remark in order that the reader may realize that the subject is really complex. But I shall keep myself as far as possible at present to the more 'scientific' view; and only as the plot thickens in subsequent lectures shall I consider the question of its absolute sufficiency as an explanation of all the facts. That subconscious incubation explains a great number of them, there can be no doubt.

And thus I return to our own specific subject of instantaneous conversions. You remember the cases of Alline, Bradley, Brainerd, and the graduate of Oxford converted at three in the afternoon. Similar occurrences abound, some with and some without luminous visions, all with a sense of astonished happiness, and of being wrought on by a higher control. If, abstracting altogether from the question of their value for the future spiritual life of the individual, we take them on their psychological side exclusively, so many peculiarities in them remind us of what we find outside of conversion that we are tempted to class them along with other automatisms, and to suspect that what makes the difference between a sudden and a gradual convert is not necessarily the presence of divine miracle in the care of one and of something less divine in that of the other, but rather a simple psychological peculiarity, the fact, namely, that in the recipient of the more instantaneous grace we have one of those Subjects who are in possession of a large region in which mental work can go on subliminally, and from which invasive experiences, abruptly upsetting the equilibrium of the primary consciousness, may come.

I do not see why Methodists need object to such a view. Pray go back and recollect one of the conclusions to which I sought to lead you in my very first lecture. You may remember how I there argued against the notion that the worth of a thing can be decided by its origin. Our spiritual judgment, I said, our opinion of the significance and value of a human event or condition, must be decided on empirical grounds exclusively. If the fruits for life of the state of conversion are good, we ought to idealize and venerate it, even though it be a piece of natural psychology; if not, we ought to make short work with it, no matter what supernatural being may have infused it.

Well, how is it with these fruits? If we except the class of preeminent saints of whom the names illumine history, and consider only the usual run of 'saints,' the shopkeeping church-members and ordinary youthful or middle-aged recipients of instantaneous conversion, whether at revivals or in the spontaneous course of methodistic, growth, you will probably agree that no splendor worthy of a wholly supernatural creature fulgurates from them, or sets them apart from the mortals who have never experienced that favor. Were it true that a suddenly converted man as such is, as Edwards says, of an entirely different kind from a natural man, partaking as he does directly of Christ's substance, there surely ought to be some exquisite class-mark, some distinctive radiance attaching even to the lowliest specimen of this genus, to which no one of us could remain insensible, and which, so far as it went, would prove him more excellent than ever the most highly gifted among mere natural men. But notoriously there is no such radiance. Converted men as a class are indistinguishable from natural men; some natural men even excel some converted men in their fruits; and no one ignorant of doctrinal theology could guess by mere every-day inspection of the 'accidents' of the two groups of persons before him, that their substance differed as much as divine differs from human substance.

Edwards says elsewhere: "I am bold to say that the work of God in the conversion of one soul, considered together with the source, foundation, and purchase of it, and also the benefit, end, and eternal issue of it, is a more glorious work of God than the creation of the whole material universe."

The believers in the non-natural character of sudden conversion have had practically to admit that there is no unmistakable class-mark distinctive of all true converts. The super-normal incidents, such as voices and visions and overpowering impressions of the meaning of suddenly presented scripture texts, the melting emotions and tumultuous affections connected with the crisis of change, may all come by way of nature, or worse still, be counterfeited by Satan. The real witness of the spirit to the second birth is to be found only in the disposition of the genuine child of God, the permanently patient heart, the love of self eradicated. And this, it has to be admitted, is also found in those who pass no crisis, and may even be found outside of Christianity altogether.

Throughout Jonathan Edwards's admirably rich and delicate description of the supernaturally infused condition, in his Treatise on Religious Affections, there is not one decisive trait, not one mark, that unmistakably parts it off from what may possibly be only an exceptionally high degree of natural goodness. In fact, one could hardly read a clearer argument than this book unwittingly offers in favor of the thesis that no chasm exists between the orders of human excellence, but that here as elsewhere, nature shows continuous differences, and generation and regeneration are matters of degree.

All which denial of two objective classes of human beings separated by a chasm must not leave us blind to the extraordinary momentousness of the fact of his conversion to the individual himself who gets converted. There are higher and lower limits of possibility set to each personal life. If a flood but goes above one's head, its absolute elevation becomes a matter of small importance; and when we touch our own upper limit and live in our own highest centre of energy, we may call ourselves saved, no matter how much higher some one else's centre may be. A small man's salvation will always be a great salvation and the greatest of all facts for him, and we should remember this when the fruits of our ordinary evangelicism look discouraging. Who knows how much less ideal still the lives of these spiritual grubs and earthworms, these Crumps and Stigginses, might have been, if such poor grace as they have received had never touched them at all?

Emerson writes: "When we see a soul whose acts are regal, graceful, and pleasant as roses, we must thank God that such things can be and are, and not turn sourly on the angel and say: Crump is a better man, with his grunting resistance to all his native devils." True enough. Yet Crump may really be the better Crump, for his inner discords and second birth; and your once-born 'regal' character, though indeed always better than poor Crump, may fall far short of what he individually might be had he only some Crump-like capacity for compunction over his own peculiar diabolisms, graceful and pleasant and invariably gentlemanly as these may be.

If we roughly arrange human beings in classes, each class standing for a grade of spiritual excellence, I believe we shall find natural men and converts both sudden and gradual in all the classes. The forms which regenerative change effects have, then, no general spiritual significance, but only a psychological significance. We have seen how Starbuck's laborious statistical studies tend to assimilate conversion to ordinary spiritual growth. Another American psychologist, Prof. George A. Coe, [In his book, The Spiritual Life, New York, 1900.] has analyzed the cases of seventy-seven converts or ex-candidates for conversion, known to him, and the results strikingly confirm the view that sudden conversion is connected with the possession of an active subliminal self. Examining his subjects with reference to their hypnotic sensibility and to such automatisms as hypnagogic hallucinations, odd impulses, religious dreams about the time of their conversion, etc., he found these relatively much more frequent in the group of converts whose transformation had been 'striking,' 'striking' transformation being defined as a change which, though not necessarily instantaneous, seems to the subject of it to be distinctly different from a process of growth, however rapid." Candidates for conversion at revivals are, as you know, often disappointed: they experience nothing striking. Professor Coe had a number of persons of this class among his seventy-seven subjects, and they almost all, when tested by hypnotism, proved to belong to a subclass which he calls 'spontaneous,' that is, fertile in self-suggestions, as distinguished from a 'passive' subclass, to which most of the subjects of striking transformation belonged. His inference is that self-suggestion of impossibility had prevented the influence upon these persons of an environment which, on the more 'passive' subjects, had easily brought forth the effects they looked for. Sharp distinctions are difficult in these regions, and Professor Coe's numbers are small. But his methods were careful and the results tally with what one might expect; and they seem, on the whole, to justify his practical conclusion, which is that if you should expose to a converting influence a subject in whom three factors unite: first, pronounced emotional sensibility; second, tendency to automatisms; and third, suggestibility of the passive type; you might then safely predict the result: there would be a sudden conversion, a transformation of the striking kind.

Does this temperamental origin diminish the significance of the sudden conversion when it has occurred? Not in the least, as Professor Coe well says; for "the ultimate test of religious values is nothing psychological, nothing definable in terms of how it happens, but something ethical, definable only in terms of what is attained."

As we proceed farther in our inquiry we shall see that what is attained is often an altogether new level of spiritual vitality, a relatively heroic level, in which impossible things have become possible, and new energies and endurances are shown. The personality is changed, the man is born anew, whether or not his psychological idiosyncrasies are what give the particular shape to his metamorphosis. 'Sanctification' is the technical name of this result; and erelong examples of it shall be brought before you. In this lecture I have still only to add a few remarks on the assurance and peace which fill the hour of change itself.

One word more, though, before proceeding to that point, lest the final purpose of my explanation of suddenness by subliminal activity be misunderstood. I do indeed believe that if the Subject have no liability to such subconscious activity, or if his conscious fields have a hard rind of a margin that resists incursions from beyond it, his conversion must be gradual if it occur, and must resemble any simple growth into new habits. His possession of a developed subliminal self, and of a leaky or pervious margin, is thus a conditio sine qua non of the Subject's becoming converted in the instantaneous way. But if you, being orthodox Christians, ask me as a psychologist whether the reference of a phenomenon to a subliminal self does not exclude the notion of the direct presence of the Deity altogether, I have to say frankly that as a psychologist I do not see why it necessarily should. The lower manifestations of the Subliminal, indeed, fall within the resources of the personal subject: his ordinary sense-material, inattentively taken in and subconsciously remembered and combined, will account for all his usual automatisms. But just as our primary wide-awake consciousness throws open our senses to the touch of things material, so it is logically conceivable that if there be higher spiritual agencies that can directly touch us, the psychological condition of their doing so might be our possession of a subconscious region which alone should yield access to them. The hubbub of the waking life might close a door which in the dreamy Subliminal might remain ajar or open.

Thus that perception of external control which is so essential a feature in conversion might, in some cases at any rate, be interpreted as the orthodox interpret it: forces transcending the finite individual might impress him, on condition of his being what we may call a subliminal human specimen. But in any case the value of these forces would have to be determined by their effects, and the mere fact of their transcendency would of itself establish no presumption that they were more divine than diabolical.

I confess that this is the way in which I should rather see the topic left lying in your minds until I come to a much later lecture, when I hope once more to gather these dropped threads together into more definitive conclusions. The notion of a subconscious self certainly ought not at this point of our inquiry to be held to exclude all notion of a higher penetration. If there be higher powers able to impress us, they may get access to us only through the subliminal door.

Let us turn now to the feelings which immediately fill the hour of the conversion experience. The first one to be noted is just this sense of higher control. It is not always, but it is very often present. We saw examples of it in Alline, Bradley, Brainerd, and elsewhere. The need of such a higher controlling agency is well expressed in the short reference which the eminent French Protestant Adolphe Monod makes to the crisis of his own conversion. It was at Naples in his early manhood, in the summer of 1827.

"My sadness," he says, "was without limit, and having got entire possession of me, it filled my life from the most indifferent external acts to the most secret thoughts, and corrupted at their source my feelings, my judgment, and my happiness. It was then that I saw that to expect to put a stop to this disorder by my reason and my will, which were themselves diseased, would be to act like a blind man who should pretend to correct one of his eyes by the aid of the other equally blind one. I had then no resource save in some influence from without. I remembered the promise of the Holy Ghost; and what the positive declarations of the Gospel had never succeeded in bringing home to me, I learned at last from necessity, and believed, for the first time in my life, in this promise, in the only sense in which it answered the needs of my soul, in that, namely, of a real external supernatural action, capable of giving me thoughts, and taking them away from me, and exerted on me by a God as truly master of my heart as he is of the rest of nature. Renouncing then all merit, all strength, abandoning all my personal resources, and acknowledging no other title to his mercy than my own utter misery, I went home and threw myself on my knees, and prayed as I never yet prayed in my life. From this day onwards a new interior life began for me: not that my melancholy had disappeared, but it had lost its sting. Hope had entered into my heart, and once entered on the path. the God of Jesus Christ, to whom I then had learned to give myself up, little by little did the rest." [I piece together a quotation made by W. Monod, in his book la Vie, and a letter printed in the work: Adolphe Monod: I., Souvenirs de sa Vie, 1885, p. 433.]

It is needless to remind you once more of the admirable congruity of Protestant theology with the structure of the mind as shown in such experiences. In the extreme of melancholy the self that consciously is can do absolutely nothing. It is completely bankrupt and without resource, and no works it can accomplish will avail. Redemption from such subjective conditions must be a free gift or nothing, and grace through Christ's accomplished sacrifice is such a gift.

"God," says Luther, "is the God of the humble, the miserable, the oppressed, and the desperate, and of those that are brought even to nothing; and his nature is to give sight to the blind, to comfort the broken-hearted, to justify sinners, to save the very desperate and damned. Now that pernicious and pestilent opinion of man's own righteousness, which will not be a sinner, unclean, miserable, and damnable, but righteous and holy, suffereth not God to come to his own natural and proper work. Therefore God must take this maul in hand (the law, I mean) to beat in pieces and bring to nothing this beast with her vain confidence, that she may so learn at length by her own misery that she is utterly forlorn and damned. But here lieth the difficulty, that when a man is terrified and cast down, he is so little able to raise himself up again and say, 'Now I am bruised and afflicted enough; now is the time of grace; now is the time to hear Christ.' The foolishness of man's heart is so great that then he rather seeketh to himself more laws to satisfy his conscience. 'If I live,' saith he, 'I will amend my life: I will do this, I will do that.' But here, except thou do the quite contrary, except thou send Moses away with his law, and in these terrors and this anguish lay hold upon Christ who died for thy sins, look for no salvation. Thy cowl, thy shaven crown, thy chastity, thy obedience, thy poverty, thy works, thy merits? what shall all these do? what shall the law of Moses avail? If I, wretched and damnable sinner, through works or merits could have loved the Son of God, and so come to him, what needed be to deliver himself for me? If I, being a wretch and damned sinner, could be redeemed by any other price, what needed the Son of God to be given? But because there was no other price, therefore he delivered neither sheep, ox, gold, nor silver, but even God himself, entirely and wholly 'for me,' even 'for me,' I say, a miserable, wretched sinner. Now, therefore, I take comfort and apply this to myself. And this manner of applying is the very true force and power of faith. For he died not to justify the righteous, but the un-righteous, and to make them the children of God." [Commentary on Galatians, ch. iii. verse 19, and ch. ii. verse 20, abridged.]

That is, the more literally lost you are, the more literally you are the very being whom Christ's sacrifice has already saved. Nothing in Catholic theology, I imagine, has ever spoken to sick souls as straight as this message from Luther's personal experience. As Protestants are not all sick souls, of course reliance on what Luther exults in calling the dung of one's merits, the filthy puddle of one's own righteousness, has come to the front again in their religion; but the adequacy of his view of Christianity to the deeper parts of our human mental structure is shown by its wildfire contagiousness when it was a new and quickening thing.

Faith that Christ has genuinely done his work was part of what Luther meant by faith, which so far is faith in a fact intellectually conceived of. But this is only one part of Luther's faith, the other part being far more vital. This other part is something not intellectual but immediate and intuitive, the assurance, namely, that I, this individual I, just as I stand, without one plea, etc., am saved now and forever. [In some conversions, both steps are distinct; in this one, for example:]

"Whilst I was reading the evangelical treaties, I was soon struck by an expression: 'the finished work of Christ.' 'Why,' I asked of myself, 'does the author use these terms? Why does he not say "the atoning work"? Then these words, 'It is finished,' presented themselves to my mind. 'What is it that is finished?' I asked, and in an instant my mind replied: 'A perfect expiation for sin; entire satisfaction has been given; the debt has been paid by the Substitute. Christ has died for our sins; not for ours only, but for those of all men. If, then, the entire work is finished, all the debt paid, what remains for me to do?' In another instant the light was shed through my mind by the Holy Ghost, and the joyous conviction was given me that nothing more was to be done, save to fall on my knees, to accept this Saviour and his love, to praise God forever." Autobiography of Hudson Taylor. I translate back into English from the French translation of Challand (Geneva, no date), the original not being accessible.

Professor Leuba is undoubtedly right in contending that the conceptual belief about Christ's work, although so often efficacious and antecedent, is really accessory and nonessential, and that the 'joyous conviction' can also come by far other channels than this conception. It is to the joyous conviction itself, the assurance that all is well with one, that he would give the name of faith par excellence.

"When the sense of estrangement," he writes, "fencing man about in a narrowly limited ego, breaks down, the individual finds himself 'at one with all creation.' He lives in the universal life; he and man, he and nature, he and God, are one. That state of confidence, trust, union with all things, following upon the achievement of moral unity, is the Faith-state. Various dogmatic beliefs suddenly, on the advent of the faith-state, acquire a character of certainty, assume a new reality, become an object of faith. As the ground of assurance here is not rational, argumentation is irrelevant. But such conviction being a mere casual offshoot of the faith-state, it is a gross error to imagine that the chief practical value of the faith-state is its power to stamp with the seal of reality certain particular theological conceptions. [Tolstoy's case was a good comment on those words. There was almost no theology in his conversion. His faith-state was the sense come back that life was infinite in its moral significance.] On the contrary, its value lies solely in the fact that it is the psychic correlate of a biological growth reducing contending desires to one direction; a growth which expresses itself in new affective states and new reactions; in larger, nobler, more Christ-like activities. The ground of the specific assurance in religious dogmas is then an affective experience. The objects of faith may even be preposterous; the affective stream will float them along, and invest them with unshakable certitude. The more startling the affective experience, the less explicable it seems, the easier it is to make it the carrier of unsubstantiated notions." [American Journal of Psychology, vii. 345-347, abridged.]

The characteristics of the affective experience which, to avoid ambiguity, should, I think, be called the state of assurance rather than the faith-state, can be easily enumerated, though it is probably difficult to realize their intensity, unless one have been through the experience one's self.

The central one is the loss of all the worry, the sense that all is ultimately well with one, the peace, the harmony, the willingness to be, even though the outer conditions should remain the same. The certainty of God's 'grace,' of 'justification,' 'salvation,' is an objective belief that usually accompanies the change in Christians; but this may be entirely lacking and yet the affective peace remain the same— you will recollect the case of the Oxford graduate: and many might be given where the assurance of personal salvation was only a later result. A passion of willingness, of acquiescence, of admiration, is the glowing centre of this state of mind.

The second feature is the sense of perceiving truths not known before. The mysteries of life become lucid, as Professor Leuba says; and often, nay usually, the solution is more or less unutterable in words. But these more intellectual phenomena may be postponed until we treat of mysticism.

A third peculiarity of the assurance state is the objective change which the world often appears to undergo. 'An appearance of newness beautifies every object,' the precise opposite of that other sort of newness, that dreadful unreality and strangeness in the appearance of the world, which is experienced by melancholy patients, and of which you may recall my relating some examples. This sense of clean and beautiful newness within and without is one of the commonest entries in conversion records. Jonathan Edwards thus describes it in himself: [Above, Lecture VI and VII.]

"After this my sense of divine things gradually increased and became more and more lively, and had more of that inward sweetness. The appearance of everything was altered; there seemed to be, as it were, a calm, sweet cast, or appearance of divine glory, in almost everything. God's excellency, his wisdom, his purity and love, seemed to appear in everything; in the sun, moon, and stars; in the clouds and blue sky; in the grass, flowers, and trees; in the water and all nature; which used greatly to fix my mind. And scarce anything, among all the works of nature, was so sweet to me as thunder and lightning; formerly nothing had been so terrible to me. Before, I used to be uncommonly terrified with thunder, and to be struck with terror when I saw a thunderstorm rising; but now, on the contrary, it rejoices me." [Dwight: Life of Edwards, New York, 1830, p. 61, abridged.]

Billy Bray, an excellent little illiterate English evangelist, records his sense of newness thus:

"I said to the Lord: 'Thou hast said, they that ask shall receive, they that seek shall find, and to them that knock the door shall be opened, and I have faith to believe it.' In an instant the Lord made me so happy that I cannot express what I felt. I shouted for joy. I praised God with my whole heart.... I think this was in November, 1823, but what day of the month I do not know. I remember this, that everything looked new to me, the people, the fields, the cattle, the trees. I was like a new man in a new world. I spent the greater part of my time in praising the Lord." [W.F. Bourne: The King's Son, a Memoir of Billy Bray, London Hamilton, Adams & Co., 1887, p. 9.]

Starbuck and Leuba both illustrate this sense of newness by quotations. I take the two following from Starbuck's manuscript collection. One, a woman, says:

"I was taken to a camp-meeting, mother and religious friends seeking and praying for my conversion. My emotional nature was stirred to its depths; confessions of depravity and pleading with God for salvation from sin made me oblivious of all surroundings. I plead for mercy, and had a vivid realization of forgiveness and renewal of my nature. When rising from my knees I exclaimed, 'Old things have passed away, all things have become new.' It was like entering another world, a new state of existence. Natural objects were glorified, my spiritual vision was so clarified that I saw beauty in every material object in the universe, the woods were vocal with heavenly music; my soul exulted in the love of God, and I wanted everybody to share in my joy."

The next case is that of a man:

"I know not how I got back into the encampment, but found myself staggering up to Rev. __'s Holiness tent— and as it was full of seekers and a terrible noise inside, some groaning, some laughing, and some shouting, and by a large oak, ten feet from the tent, I fell on my face by a bench, and tried to pray, and every time I would call on God, something like a man's hand would strangle me by choking. I don't know whether there were any one around or near me or not. I thought I should surely die if I did not get help, but just as often as I would pray, that unseen hand was felt on my throat and my breath squeezed off. Finally something said: 'Venture on the atonement, for you will die anyway if you don't.' So I made one final struggle to call on God for mercy, with the same choking and strangling, determined to finish the sentence of prayer for Mercy, if I did strangle and die, and the last I remember that time was falling back on the ground with the same unseen hand on my throat. I don't know how long I lay there or what was going on. None of my folks were present. When I came to myself, there were a crowd around me praising God. The very heavens seemed to open and pour down rays of light and glory. Not for a moment only, but all day and night, floods of light and glory seemed to pour through my soul, and oh, how I was changed, and everything became new. My horses and hogs and even everybody seemed changed."

This man's case introduces the feature of automatisms, which in suggestible subjects have been so startling a feature at revivals since, in Edwards's, Wesley's, and Whitfield's time, these became a regular means of gospel-propagation. They were at first supposed to be semi-miraculous proofs of 'power' on the part of the Holy Ghost; but great divergence of opinion quickly arose concerning them. Edwards, in his Thoughts on the Revival of Religion in New England, has to defend them against their critics; and their value has long been matter of debate even within the revivalistic denominations. They undoubtedly have no essential spiritual significance, and although their presence makes his conversion more memorable to the convert, it has never been proved that converts who show them are more persevering or fertile in good fruits than those whose change of heart has had less violent accompaniments. On the whole, unconsciousness, convulsions, visions, involuntary vocal utterances, and suffocation, must be simply ascribed to the subject's having a large subliminal region, involving nervous instability. This is often the subject's own view of the matter afterwards. One of Starbuck's correspondents writes, for instance: [Consult William B. Sprague: Lectures on Revivals of Religion, New York, 1832, in the long Appendix to which the opinions of a large number of ministers are given.]

"I have been through the experience which is known as conversion. My explanation of it is this: the subject works his emotions up to the breaking point, at the same time resisting their physical manifestations, such as quickened pulse, etc., and then suddenly lets them have their full sway over his body. The relief is something wonderful, and the pleasurable effects of the emotions are experienced to the highest degree."

There is one form of sensory automatism which possibly deserves special notice on account of its frequency. I refer to hallucinatory or pseudo-hallucinatory luminous phenomena, photisms, to use the term of the psychologists. Saint Paul's blinding heavenly vision seems to have been a phenomen of this sort; so does Constantine's cross in the sky. The last case but one which I quoted mentions floods of light and glory. Henry Alline mentions a light, about whose externality he seems uncertain. Colonel Gardiner sees a blazing light. President Finney writes:

"All at once the glory of God shone upon and round about me in a manner almost marvelous.... A light perfectly ineffable shone in my soul, that almost prostrated me on the ground. This light seemed like the brightness of the sun in every direction. It was too intense for the eyes.... I think I knew something then, by actual experience, of that light that prostrated Paul on the way to Damascus. It was surely a light such as I could not have endured long." [Memoirs, p. 34.]

Such reports of photisms are indeed far from uncommon. Here is another from Starbuck's collection, where the light appeared evidently external:

"I had attended a series of revival services for about two weeks off and on. Had been invited to the altar several times, all the time becoming more deeply impressed, when finally I decided I must do this, or I should be lost. Realization of conversion was very vivid, like a ton's weight being lifted from my heart; a strange light which seemed to light up the whole room (for it was dark); a conscious supreme bliss which caused me to repeat 'Glory to God' for a long time. Decided to be God's child for life, and to give up my pet ambition, wealth and social position. My former habits of life hindered my growth somewhat, but I set about overcoming these systematically, and in one year my whole nature was changed, i. e., my ambitions were of a different order."

Here is another one of Starbuck's cases, involving a luminous element:

"I had been clearly converted twenty-three years before, or rather reclaimed. My experience in regeneration was then clear and spiritual, and I had not backslidden. But I experienced entire sanctification on the 15th day of March, 1893, about eleven o'clock in the morning. The particular accompaniments of the experience were entirely unexpected. I was quietly sitting at home singing selections out of Pentecostal Hymns. Suddenly there seemed to be a something sweeping into me and inflating my entire being— such a sensation as I had never experienced before. When this experience came, I seemed to be conducted around a large, capacious, well-lighted room. As I walked with my invisible conductor and looked around, a clear thought was coined in my mind, 'They are not here, they are gone.' As soon as the thought was definitely formed in my mind, though no word was spoken, the Holy Spirit impressed me that I was surveying my own soul. Then, for the first time in all my life, did I know that I was cleansed from all sin, and filled with the fullness of God."

Leuba quotes the case of a Mr. Peck, where the luminous affection reminds one of the chromatic hallucinations produced by the intoxicant cactus buds called mescal by the Mexicans:

"When I went in the morning into the fields to work, the glory of God appeared in all his visible creation. I well remember we reaped oats, and how every straw and head of the oats seemed, as it were, arrayed in a kind of rainbow glory, or to glow, if I may so express it, in the glory of God."

These reports of sensorial photism shade off into what are evidently only metaphorical accounts of the sense of new spiritual illumination, as, for instance, in Brainerd's statement: "As I was walking in a thick grove, unspeakable glory seemed to open to the apprehension of my soul. I do not mean any external brightness, for I saw no such thing, nor any imagination of a body of light in the third heavens, or anything of that nature, but it was a new inward apprehension or view that I had of God."

In a case like this next one from Starbuck's manuscript collection, the lighting up of the darkness is probably also metaphorical:

"One Sunday night, I resolved that when I got home to the ranch where I was working, I would offer myself with my faculties and all to God to be used only by and for him. It was raining and the roads were muddy; but this desire grew so strong that I kneeled down by the side of the road and told God all about it, intending then to get up and go on. Such a thing as any special answer to my prayer never entered my mind, having been converted by faith, but still being most undoubtedly saved. Well, while I was praying, I remember holding out my hands to God and telling him they should work for him, my feet walk for him, my tongue speak for him, etc., etc., if he would only use me as his instrument and give me a satisfying experience— when suddenly the darkness of the night seemed lit up— I felt, realized, knew, that God heard and answered my prayer. Deep happiness came over me; I felt I was accepted into the inner circle of God's loved ones."

In the following case also the flash of light is metaphorical:

"A prayer meeting had been called for at close of evening service. The minister supposed me impressed by his discourse (a mistake— he was dull). He came and, placing his hand upon my shoulder, said: 'Do you not want to give your heart to God?' I replied in the affirmative. Then said he, 'Come to the front seat.' They sang and prayed and talked with me. I experienced nothing but unaccountable wretchedness. They declared that the reason why I did not 'obtain peace' was because I was not willing to give up all to God. After about two hours the minister said we would go home. As usual, on retiring, I prayed. In great distress, I at this time simply said, I Lord, I have done all I can, I leave the whole matter with thee.' Immediately, like a flash of light, there came to me a great peace, and I arose and went into my parents' bedroom and said, 'I do feel so wonderfully happy.' This I regard as the hour of conversion. It was the hour in which I became assured of divine acceptance and favor. So far as my life was concerned, it made little immediate change."

The most characteristic of all the elements of the conversion crisis, and the last one of which I shall speak, is the ecstasy of happiness produced. We have already heard several accounts of it, but I will add a couple more. President Finney's is so vivid that I give it at length:

"All my feelings seemed to rise and flow out; and the utterance of my heart was, 'I want to pour my whole soul out to God.' The rising of my soul was so great that I rushed into the back room of the front office, to pray. There was no fire and no light in the room; nevertheless it appeared to me as if it were perfectly light. As I went in and shut the door after me, it seemed as if I met the Lord Jesus Christ face to face. It did not occur to me then, nor did it for some time afterwards, that it was wholly a mental state. On the contrary, it seemed to me that I saw him as I would see any other man. He said nothing, but looked at me in such a manner as to break me right down at his feet. I have always since regarded this as a most remarkable state of mind; for it seemed to me a reality that he stood before me, and I fell down at his feet and poured out my soul to him. I wept aloud like a child, and made such confessions as I could with my choked utterance. It seemed to me that I bathed his feet with my tears; and yet I had no distinct impression that I touched him, that I recollect. I must have continued in this state for a good while; but my mind was too much absorbed with the interview to recollect anything that I said. But I know, as soon as my mind became calm enough to break off from the interview, I returned to the front office, and found that the fire that I had made of large wood was nearly burned out. But as I turned and was about to take a seat by the fire, I received a mighty baptism of the Holy Ghost. Without any expectation of it, without ever having the thought in my mind that there was any such thing for me, without any recollection that I had ever heard the thing mentioned by any person in the world, the Holy Spirit descended upon me in a manner that seemed to go through me, body and soul. I could feel the impression, like a wave of electricity, going through and through me. Indeed, it seemed to come in waves and waves of liquid love; for I could not express it in any other way. It seemed like the very breath of God. I can recollect distinctly that it seemed to fan me, like immense wings.

"No words can express the wonderful love that was shed abroad in my heart. I wept aloud with joy and love; and I do not know but I should say I literally bellowed out the unutterable gushings of my heart. These waves came over me, and over me, and over me, one after the other, until I recollect I cried out, 'I shall die if these waves continue to pass over me.' I said, 'Lord, I cannot bear any more;' yet I had no fear of death.

"How long I continued in this state, with this baptism continuing to roll over me and go through me, I do not know. But I know it was late in the evening when a member of my choir— for I was the leader of the choir— came into the office to see me. He was a member of the church. He found me in this state of loud weeping, and said to me, 'Mr. Finney, what ails you?' I could make him no answer for some time. He then said, 'Are you in pain?' I gathered myself up as best I could, and replied, 'No, but so happy that I cannot live.'"

I just now quoted Billy Bray; I cannot do better than give his own brief account of his post-conversion feelings:

"I can't help praising the Lord. As I go along the street, I lift up one foot, and it seems to say 'Glory'; and I lift up the other, and it seems to say 'Amen'; and so they keep up like that all the time I am walking." [I add in a note a few more records:]

"One morning, being in deep distress, fearing every moment I should drop into hell, I was constrained to cry in earnest for mercy, and the Lord came to my relief, and delivered my soul from the burden and guilt of sin. My whole frame was in a tremor from head to foot, and my soul enjoyed sweet peace. The pleasure I then felt was indescribable, The happiness lasted about three days, during which time I never spoke to any person about my feelings." [Autobiography of Dan Young, edited by W.P. Strickland, New York, 1860.]

"In an instant there rose up in me such a sense of God's taking care of those who put their trust in him that for an hour all the world was crystalline, the heavens were lucid, and I sprang to my feet and began to cry and laugh." [H.W. Beecher, quoted by Leuba.]

"My tears of sorrow changed to joy, and I lay there praising God in such ecstasy of joy as only the soul who experiences it can realize."— "I cannot express how I felt. It was as if I had been in a dark dungeon and lifted into the light of the sun. I shouted and I sang praise unto him who loved me and washed me from my sins. I was forced to retire into a secret place, for the tears did flow, and I did not wish my shopmates to see me, and yet I could not keep it a secret."— "I experienced joy almost to weeping."— "I felt my face must have shone like that of Moses. I had a general feeling of buoyancy. It was the greatest joy it was ever my lot to experience."— "I wept and laughed alternately. I was as light as if walking on air. I felt as if I had gained greater peace and happiness than I had ever expected to experience." Starbuck's correspondents.

One word, before I close this lecture, on the question of the transiency or permanence of these abrupt conversions. Some of you, I feel sure, knowing that numerous backslidings and relapses take place, make of these their apperceiving mass for interpreting the whole subject, and dismiss it with a pitying smile at so much 'hysterics.' Psychologically, as well as religiously, however, this is shallow. It misses the point of serious interest, which is not so much the duration as the nature and quality of these shiftings of character to higher levels. Men lapse from every level— we need no statistics to tell us that. Love is, for instance, well known not to be irrevocable, yet, constant or inconstant, it reveals new flights and reaches of ideality while it lasts. These revelations form its significance to men and women, whatever be its duration. So with the conversion experience: that it should for even a short time show a human being what the highwater mark of his spiritual capacity is, this is what constitutes its importance,— an importance which backsliding cannot diminish, although persistence might increase it. As a matter of fact, all the more striking instances of conversion, all those, for instance, which I have quoted, have been permanent. The case of which there might be most doubt, on account of its suggesting so strongly an epileptoid seizure, was the case of M. Ratisbonne. Yet I am informed that Ratisbonne's whole future was shaped by those few minutes. He gave up his project of marriage, became a priest, founded at Jerusalem, where he went to dwell, a mission of nuns for the conversion of the Jews, showed no tendency to use for egotistic purposes the notoriety given him by the peculiar circumstances of his conversion,— which, for the rest, he could seldom refer to without tears,— and in short remained an exemplary son of the Church until he died, late in the 80's, if I remember rightly.

The only statistics I know of, on the subject of the duration of conversions, are those collected for Professor Starbuck by Miss Johnston. They embrace only a hundred persons, evangelical church-members, more than half being Methodists. According to the statement of the subjects themselves, there had been backsliding of some sort in nearly all the cases, 93 per cent. of the women, 77 per cent. of the men. Discussing the returns more minutely, Starbuck finds that only 6 per cent. are relapses from the religious faith which the conversion confirmed, and that the backsliding complained of is in most only a fluctuation in the ardor of sentiment. Only six of the hundred cases report a change of faith. Starbuck's conclusion is that the effect of conversion is to bring with it "a changed attitude towards life, which is fairly constant and permanent, although the feelings fluctuate.... In other words, the persons who have passed through conversion, having once taken a stand for the religious life, tend to feel themselves identified with it, no matter how much their religious enthusiasm declines." [Psychology of Religion, pp. 360, 357.]

LECTURES XI, XII, AND XIII: SAINTLINESS

The last lecture left us in a state of expectancy. What may the practical fruits for life have been, of such movingly happy conversions as those we heard of? With this question the really important part of our task opens, for you remember that we began all this empirical inquiry not merely to open a curious chapter in the natural history of human consciousness, but rather to attain a spiritual judgment as to the total value and positive meaning of all the religious trouble and happiness which we have seen. We must, therefore, first describe the fruits of the religious life, and then we must judge them. This divides our inquiry into two distinct parts. Let us without further preamble proceed to the descriptive task.

It ought to be the pleasantest portion of our business in these lectures. Some small pieces of it, it is true, may be painful, or may show human nature in a pathetic light, but it will be mainly pleasant, because the best fruits of religious experience are the best things that history has to show. They have always been esteemed so; here if anywhere is the genuinely strenuous life; and to call to mind a succession of such examples as I have lately had to wander through, though it has been only in the reading of them, is to feel encouraged and uplifted and washed in better moral air.

The highest flights of charity, devotion, trust, patience, bravery to which the wings of human nature have spread themselves have been flown for religious ideals. I can do no better than quote, as to this, some remarks which Sainte-Beuve in his History of Port-Royal makes on the results of conversion or the state of grace.

"Even from the purely human point of view," Sainte-Beuve says, "the phenomenon of grace must still appear sufficiently extraordinary, eminent, and rare, both in its nature and in its effects, to deserve a closer study. For the soul arrives thereby at a certain fixed and invincible state, a state which is genuinely heroic, and from out of which the greatest deeds which it ever performs are executed. Through all the different forms of communion, and all the diversity of the means which help to produce this state, whether it be reached by a jubilee, by a general confession, by a solitary prayer and effusion, whatever in short be the place and the occasion, it is easy to recognize that it is fundamentally one state in spirit and in fruits. Penetrate a little beneath the diversity of circumstances, and it becomes evident that in Christians of different epochs it is always one and the same modification by which they are affected: there is veritably a single fundamental and identical spirit of piety and charity, common to those who have received grace; an inner state which before all things is one of love and humility, of infinite confidence in God, and of severity for one's self, accompanied with tenderness for others. The fruits peculiar to this condition of the soul have the same savor in all, under distant suns and in different surroundings, in Saint Teresa of Avila just as in any Moravian brother of Herrnhut." [Sainte Beuve: Port-Royal, vol. i. pp. 95 and 106, abridged.]

Sainte-Beuve has here only the more eminent instances of regeneration in mind, and these are of course the instructive ones for us also to consider. These devotees have often laid their course so differently from other men that, judging them by worldly law, we might be tempted to call them monstrous aberrations from the path of nature. I begin, therefore, by asking a general psychological question as to what the inner conditions are which may make one human character differ so extremely from another.

I reply at once that where the character, as something distinguished from the intellect, is concerned, the causes of human diversity lie chiefly in our differing susceptibilities of emotional excitement, and in the different impulses and inhibitions which these bring in their train. Let me make this more clear.

Speaking generally, our moral and practical attitude, at any given time, is always a resultant of two sets of forces within us, impulses pushing us one way and obstructions and inhibitions holding us back. "Yes! yes!" say the impulses; "No! no!" say the inhibitions. Few people who have not expressly reflected on the matter realize how constantly this factor of inhibition is upon us, how it contains and moulds us by its restrictive pressure almost as if we were fluids pent within the cavity of a jar. The influence is so incessant that it becomes subconscious. All of you, for example, sit here with a certain constraint at this moment, and entirely without express consciousness of the fact, because of the influence of the occasion. If left alone in the room, each of you would probably involuntarily rearrange himself, and make his attitude more 'free and easy.' But proprieties and their inhibitions snap like cobwebs if any great emotional excitement supervenes. I have seen a dandy appear in the street with his face covered with shaving-lather because a house across the way was on fire; and a woman will run among strangers in her nightgown if it be a question of saving her baby's life or her own. Take a self-indulgent woman's life in general. She will yield to every inhibition set by her disagreeable sensations, lie late in bed, live upon tea or bromides, keep indoors from the cold. Every difficulty finds her obedient to its 'no.' But make a mother of her, and what have you? Possessed by maternal excitement, she now confronts wakefulness, weariness, and toil without an instant of hesitation or a word of complaint. The inhibitive power of pain over her is extinguished wherever the baby's interests are at stake. The inconveniences which this creature occasions have become, as James Hinton says, the glowing heart of a great joy, and indeed are now the very conditions whereby the joy becomes most deep.

This is an example of what you have already heard of as the 'expulsive power of a higher affection.' But be the affection high or low, it makes no difference, so long as the excitement it brings be strong enough. In one of Henry Drummond's discourses he tells of an inundation in India where an eminence with a bungalow upon it remained unsubmerged, and became the refuge of a number of wild animals and reptiles in addition to the human beings who were there. At a certain moment a royal Bengal tiger appeared swimming towards it, reached it, and lay panting like a dog upon the ground in the midst of the people, still possessed by such an agony of terror that one of the Englishmen could calmly step up with a rifle and blow out its brains. The tiger's habitual ferocity was temporarily quelled by the emotion of fear, which became sovereign, and formed a new centre for his character.

Sometimes no emotional state is sovereign, but many contrary ones are mixed together. In that case one hears both 'yeses' and 'noes,' and the 'will' is called on then to solve the conflict. Take a soldier, for example, with his dread of cowardice impelling him to advance, his fears impelling him to run, and his Propensities to imitation pushing him towards various courses if his comrades offer various examples. His person becomes the seat of a mass of interferences; and he may for a time simply waver, because no one emotion prevails. There is a pitch of intensity, though, which, if any emotion reach it, enthrones that one as alone effective and sweeps its antagonists and all their inhibitions away. The fury of his comrades' charge, once entered on, will give this pitch of courage to the soldier; the panic of their rout will give this pitch of fear. In these sovereign excitements, things ordinarily impossible grow natural because the inhibitions are annulled. Their 'no! no!' not only is not heard, it does not exist. Obstacles are then like tissue-paper hoops to the circus rider— no impediment; the flood is higher than the dam they make. "Lass sie betteln gehn wenn sie hungrig sind!" cries the grenadier, frantic over his Emperor's capture, when his wife and babes are suggested; and men pent into a burning theatre have been known to cut their way through the crowd with knives.

"'Love would not be love,' says Bourget, 'unless it could carry one to crime.' And so one may say that no passion would be a veritable passion unless it could carry one to crime." [Sighele: Psychologie des Sectes, p. 136.] In other words, great passions annul the ordinary inhibitions set by 'conscience.' And conversely, of all the criminal human beings, the false, cowardly, sensual, or cruel persons who actually live, there is perhaps not one whose criminal impulse may not be at some moment overpowered by the presence of some other emotion to which his character is also potentially liable, provided that other emotion be only made intense enough. Fear is usually the most available emotion for this result in this particular class of persons. It stands for conscience, and may here be classed appropriately as a 'higher affection.' If we are soon to die, or if we believe a day of judgment to be near at hand, how quickly do we put our moral house in order— we do not see how sin can evermore exert temptation over us! Old-fashioned hell-fire Christianity well knew how to extract from fear its full equivalent in the way of fruits for repentance, and its full conversion value.

One mode of emotional excitability is exceedingly important in the composition of the energetic character, from its peculiarly destructive power over inhibitions. I mean what in its lower form is mere irascibility, susceptibility to wrath, the fighting temper; and what in subtler ways manifests itself as impatience, grimness, earnestness, severity of character. Earnestness means willingness to live with energy, though energy bring pain. The pain may be pain to other people or pain to one's self— it makes little difference; for when the strenuous mood is on one, the aim is to break something, no matter whose or what. Nothing annihilates an inhibition as irresistibly as anger does it; for, as Moltke says of war, destruction pure and simple is its essence. This is what makes it so invaluable an ally of every other passion. The sweetest delights are trampled on with a ferocious pleasure the moment they offer themselves as checks to a cause by which our higher indignations are elicited. It costs then nothing to drop friendships, to renounce long-rooted privileges and possessions, to break with social ties. Rather do we take a stern joy in the astringency and desolation; and what is called weakness of character seems in most cases to consist in the inaptitude for these sacrificial moods, of which one's own inferior self and its pet softnesses must often be the targets and the victims.

Example: Benjamin Constant was often marveled at as an extraordinary instance of superior intelligence with inferior character, He writes [Journal, Paris, 1895, p. 56], "I am tossed and dragged about by my miserable weakness. Never was anything so ridiculous as my indecision. Now marriage, now solitude; now Germany, now France, hesitation upon hesitation, and all because at bottom I am unable to give up anything." He can't 'get mad' at any of his alternatives; and the career of a man beset by such an all-round amiability is hopeless.

So far I have spoken of temporary alterations produced by shifting excitements in the same person. But the relatively fixed differences of character of different persons are explained in a precisely similar way. In a man with a liability to a special sort of emotion, whole ranges of inhibition habitually vanish, which in other men remain effective, and other sorts of inhibition take their place. When a person has an inborn genius for certain emotions, his life differs strangely from that of ordinary people, for none of their usual deterrents check him. Your mere aspirant to a type of character, on the contrary, only shows, when your natural lover, fighter, or reformer, with whom the passion is a gift of nature, comes along, the hopeless inferiority of voluntary to instinctive action. He has deliberately to overcome his inhibitions; the genius with the inborn passion seems not to feel them at all; he is free of all that inner friction and nervous waste. To a Fox, a Garibaldi, a General Booth, a John Brown, a Louise Michel, a Bradlaugh, the obstacles omnipotent over those around them are as if non-existent. Could the rest of us so disregard them, there might be many such heroes, for many have the wish to live for similar ideals, and only the adequate degree of inhibition-quenching fury is lacking.

The great thing which the higher excitabilities give is courage; and the addition or subtraction of a certain amount of this quality makes a different man, a different life. Various excitements let the courage loose. Trustful hope will do it; inspiring example will do it; love will do it; wrath will do it. In some people it is natively so high that the mere touch of danger does it, though danger is for most men the great inhibitor of action. 'Love of adventure' becomes in such persons a ruling passion. "I believe," says General Skobeleff, "that my bravery is simply the passion and at the same time the contempt of danger. The risk of life fills me with an exaggerated rapture. The fewer there are to share it, the more I like it. The participation of my body in the event is required to furnish me an adequate excitement. Everything intellectual appears to me to be reflex; but a meeting of man to man, a duel, a danger into which I can throw myself headforemost, attracts me, moves me, intoxicates me. I am crazy for it, I love it, I adore it. I run after danger as one runs after women; I wish it never to stop. Were it always the same, it would always bring me a new pleasure. When I throw myself into an adventure in which I hope to find it, my heart palpitates with the uncertainty; I could wish at once to have it appear and yet to delay. A sort of painful and delicious shiver shakes me; my entire nature runs to meet the peril with an impetus that my will would in vain try to resist." [Juliette Adam: Le General Skobeleff, Nouvelle Revue, 1886, abridged.] Skobeleff seems to have been a cruel egoist; but the disinterested Garibaldi, if one may judge by his 'Memorie,' lived in an unflagging emotion of similar danger-seeking excitement.

The difference between willing and merely wishing, between having ideals that are creative and ideals that are but pinings and regrets, thus depends solely either on the amount of steam-pressure chronically driving the character in the ideal direction, or on the amount of ideal excitement transiently acquired. Given a certain amount of love, indignation, generosity, magnanimity, admiration, loyalty, or enthusiasm of self-surrender, the result is always the same. That whole raft of cowardly obstructions, which in tame persons and dull moods are sovereign impediments to action, sinks away at once. Our conventionality, our shyness, laziness, and stinginess, our demands for precedent and permission, for guarantee and surety, our small suspicions, timidities, despairs, where are they now? Severed like cobwebs, broken like bubbles in the sun

"Wo sind die Sorge nun und Noth

Die mich noch gestern wollt' erschlaffen?

Ich scham' mich dess' im Morgenroth."

The flood we are borne on rolls them so lightly under that their very contact is unfelt. Set free of them, we float and soar and sing. This auroral openness and uplift gives to all creative ideal levels a bright and caroling quality, which is nowhere more marked than where the controlling emotion is religious. "The true monk," writes an Italian mystic, "takes nothing with him but his lyre." [See the case in Lecture III, above, where the writer describes his experiences of communion with the Divine as consisting "merely in the temporary obliteration of the conventionalities which usually cover my life."]

We may now turn from these psychological generalities to those fruits of the religious state which form the special subject of our present lecture. The man who lives in his religious centre of personal energy, and is actuated by spiritual enthusiasms, differs from his previous carnal self in perfectly definite ways. The new ardor which burns in his breast consumes in its glow the lower 'noes' which formerly beset him, and keeps him immune against infection from the entire groveling portion of his nature. Magnanimities once impossible are now easy; paltry conventionalities and mean incentives once tyrannical hold no sway. The stone wall inside of him has fallen, the hardness in his heart has broken down. The rest of us can, I think, imagine this by recalling our state of feeling in those temporary 'melting moods' into which either the trials of real life, or the theatre, or a novel sometimes throw us. Especially if we weep! For it is then as if our tears broke through an inveterate inner dam, and let all sorts of ancient peccancies and moral stagnancies drain away, leaving us now washed and soft of heart and open to every nobler leading. With most of us the customary hardness quickly returns, but not so with saintly persons. Many saints, even as energetic ones as Teresa and Loyola, have possessed what the church traditionally reveres as a special grace, the so-called gift of tears. In these persons the melting mood seems to have held almost uninterrupted control. And as it is with tears and melting moods, so it is with other exalted affections. Their reign may come by gradual growth or by a crisis; but in either case it may have 'come to stay.'

At the end of the last lecture we saw this permanence to be true of the general paramountcy of the higher insight, even though in the ebbs of emotional excitement meaner motives might temporarily prevail and backsliding might occur. But that lower temptations may remain completely annulled, apart from transient emotion and as if by alteration of the man's habitual nature, is also proved by documentary evidence in certain cases. Before embarking on the general natural history of the regenerate character, let me convince you of this curious fact by one or two examples. The most numerous are those of reformed drunkards. You recollect the case of Mr. Hadley in the last lecture; the Jerry McAuley Water Street Mission abounds in similar instances. You also remember the graduate of Oxford, converted at three in the afternoon, and getting drunk in the hay-field the next day, but after that permanently cured of his appetite. "From that hour drink has had no terrors for me: I never touch it, never want it. The same thing occurred with my pipe,... the desire for it went at once and has never returned. So with every known sin, the deliverance in each case being permanent and complete. I have had no temptations since conversion." [Above, Lecture IX. "The only radical remedy I know for dipsomania is religiomania," is a saying I have heard quoted from some medical man.]

Here is an analogous case from Starbuck's manuscript collection:

"I went into the old Adelphi Theatre, where there was a Holiness meeting,... and I began saying, 'Lord, Lord, I must have this blessing.' Then what was to me an audible voice said: 'Are you willing to give up everything to the Lord?' and question after question kept coming up, to all of which I said: 'Yes, Lord; yes, Lord!' until this came: 'Why do you not accept it now?' and I said: 'I do, Lord.'— I felt no particular joy, only a trust. Just then the meeting closed, and, as I went out on the street, I met a gentleman smoking a fine cigar, and a cloud of smoke came into my face, and I took a long, deep breath of it, and praise the Lord, all my appetite for it was gone. Then as I walked along the street, passing saloons where the fumes of liquor came out, I found that all my taste and longing for that accursed stuff was gone. Glory to God!... [But] for ten or eleven long years [after that] I was in the wilderness with its ups and downs. My appetite for liquor never came back."

The classic case of Colonel Gardiner is that of a man cured of sexual temptation in a single hour. To Mr. Spears the colonel said, "I was effectually cured of all inclination to that sin I was so strongly addicted to that I thought nothing but shooting me through the head could have cured me of it; and all desire and inclination to it was removed, as entirely as if I had been a sucking child; nor did the temptation return to this day." Mr. Webster's words on the same subject are these: "One thing I have heard the colonel frequently say, that he was much addicted to impurity before his acquaintance with religion; but that, so soon as he was enlightened from above, he felt the power of the Holy Ghost changing his nature so wonderfully that his sanctification in this respect seemed more remarkable than in any other." [Doddridge's Life of Colonel James Gardiner, London Religious Tract Society, pp. 23-32.]

Such rapid abolition of ancient impulses and propensities reminds us so strongly of what has been observed as the result of hypnotic suggestion that it is difficult not to believe that subliminal influences play the decisive part in these abrupt changes of heart, just as they do in hypnotism. Suggestive therapeutics abound in records of cure, after a few sittings, of inveterate bad habits with which the patient, left to ordinary moral and physical influences, had struggled in vain. Both drunkenness and sexual vice have been cured in this way, action through the subliminal seeming thus in many individuals to have the prerogative of inducing relatively stable change. If the grace of God miraculously operates, it probably operates through the subliminal door, then. But just how anything operates in this region is still unexplained, and we shall do well now to say good-by to the process of transformation altogether,— leaving it, if you like, a good deal of a psychological or theological mystery,— and to turn our attention to the fruits of the religious condition, no matter in what way they may have been produced.

Here, for example, is a case, from Starbuck's book, in which a 'sensory automatism' brought about quickly what prayers and resolves had been unable to effect. The subject is a woman. She writes:

"When I was about forty I tried to quit smoking, but the desire was on me, and had me in its power. I cried and prayed and promised God to quit, but could not. I had smoked for fifteen years. When I was fifty. three, as I sat by the fire one day smoking, a voice came to me. I did not hear it with my ears, but more as a dream or sort of double think. It said, 'Louisa, lay down smoking.' At once I replied, 'Will you take the desire away?' But it only kept saying: 'Louisa, lay down smoking.' Then I got up, laid my pipe on the mantel-shelf, and never smoked again or had any desire to.

The desire was gone as though I had never known it or touched tobacco. The sight of others smoking and the smell of smoke never gave me the least wish to touch it again." [The Psychology of Religion, p. 142.]

Professor Starbuck expresses the radical destruction of old influences physiologically, as a cutting off of the connection between higher and lower cerebral centres. "This condition," he says, "in which the association-centres connected with the spiritual life are cut off from the lower, is often reflected in the way correspondents describe their experiences.... For example: 'Temptations from without still assail me, but there is nothing within to respond to them.' The ego [here] is wholly identified with the higher centres, whose quality of feeling is that of withinness. Another of the respondents says: 'Since then, although Satan tempts me, there is as it were a wall of brass around me, so that his darts cannot touch me.'"— Unquestionably, functional exclusions of this sort must occur in the cerebral organ. But on the side accessible to introspection, their causal condition is nothing but the degree of spiritual excitement, getting at last so high and strong as to be sovereign; and it must be frankly confessed that we do not know just why or how such sovereignty comes about in one person and not in another. We can only give our imagination a certain delusive help by mechanical analogies.

If we should conceive, for example, that the human mind, with its different possibilities of equilibrium, might be like a many-sided solid with different surfaces on which it could lie flat, we might liken mental revolutions to the spatial revolutions of such a body. As it is pried up, say by a lever, from a position in which it lies on surface A, for instance, it will linger for a time unstably halfway up, and if the lever cease to urge it, it will tumble back or 'relapse' under the continued poll of gravity. But if at last it rotate far enough for its centre of gravity to pass beyond surface A altogether, the body will fall over, on surface B, say, and abide there permanently. The pulls of gravity towards A have vanished, and may now be disregarded. The polyhedron has become immune against farther attraction from their direction.

In this figure of speech the lever may correspond to the emotional influence making for a new life, and the initial pull of gravity to the ancient drawbacks and inhibitions. So long as the emotional influence fails to reach a certain pitch of efficacy, the changes it produces are unstable, and the man relapses into his original attitude. But when a certain intensity is attained by the new emotion, a critical point is passed, and there then ensues an irreversible revolution, equivalent to the production of a new nature.

The collective name for the ripe fruits of religion in a character is Saintliness. I use this word saintly in spite of a certain flavor of 'sanctimoniousness' which sometimes clings to it, because no other word suggests as well the exact combination of affections which the text goes on to describe.

The saintly character is the character for which spiritual emotions are the habitual centre of the personal energy; and there is a certain composite photograph of universal saintliness, the same in all religions, of which the features can easily be traced. "It will be found," says Dr. W.R. Inge (in his lectures on Christian Mysticism, London, 1899, p. 326), "that men of preeminent saintliness agree very closely in what they tell us. They tell us that they have arrived at an unshakable conviction, not based on inference but on immediate experience, that God is a spirit with whom the human spirit can hold intercourse; that in him meet all that they can imagine of goodness, truth, and beauty that they can see his footprints everywhere in nature, and feel his presence within them as the very life of their life, so that in proportion as they come to themselves they come to him. They tell us what separates us from him and from happiness is, first, self-seeking in all its forms; and, secondly, sensuality in all its forms; that these are the ways of darkness and death, which hide from us the face of God; while the path of the just is like a shining light, which shineth more and more unto the perfect day."

They are these:

1. A feeling of being in a wider life than that of this world's selfish little interests; and a conviction, not merely intellectual, but as it were sensible, of the existence of an Ideal Power. In Christian saintliness this power is always personified as God; but abstract moral ideals, civic or patriotic utopias, or inner visions of holiness or right may also be felt as the true lords and enlargers of our life, in ways which I described in the lecture on the Reality of the Unseen.

The 'enthusiasm of humanity' may lead to a life which coalesces in many respects with that of Christian saintliness. Take the following rules proposed to members of the Union pour l'Action morale, in the Bulletin de l'Union, April 1-15, 1894. See, also, Revue Bleue, August 13, 1892.

"We would make known in our own persons the usefulness, of rule, of discipline, of resignation and renunciation; we would teach the necessary perpetuity of suffering, and explain the creative part which it plays. We would wage war upon false optimism; on the base hope of happiness coming to us ready made; on the notion of a salvation by knowledge alone, or by material civilization alone, vain symbol as this is of civilization, precarious external arrangement, ill-fitted to replace the intimate union and consent of souls. We would wage war also on bad morals, whether in public or in private life; on luxury, fastidiousness, and over-refinement; on all that tends to increase the painful, immoral, and anti-social multiplication of our wants; on all that excites envy and dislike in the soul of the common people, and confirms the notion that the chief end of life is freedom to enjoy. We would preach by our example the respect of superiors and equals, the respect of all men; affectionate simplicity in our relations with inferiors and insignificant persons; indulgence where our own claims only are concerned, but firmness in our demands where they relate to duties towards others or towards the public.

"For the common people are what we help them to become; their vices are our vices, gazed upon, envied, and imitated; and if they come back with all their weight upon us, it is but just.

"We forbid ourselves all seeking after popularity, all ambition to appear important. We pledge ourselves to abstain from falsehood, in all its degrees. We promise not to create or encourage illusions as to what is possible, by what we say or write. We promise to one another active sincerity, which strives to see truth clearly, and which never fears to declare what it sees.

"We promise deliberate resistance to the tidal waves of fashion, to the 'booms' and panics of the public mind, to all the forms of weakness and of fear.

"We forbid ourselves the use of sarcasm. Of serious things we will speak seriously and unsmilingly, without banter and without the appearance of banter;— and even so of all things, for there are serious ways of being light of heart.

"We will put ourselves forward always for what we are, simply and without false humility, as well as without pedantry, affectation, or pride."

2. A sense of the friendly continuity of the ideal power with our own life, and a willing self-surrender to its control.

3. An immense elation and freedom, as the outlines of the confining selfhood melt down.

4. A shifting of the emotional centre towards loving and harmonious affections, towards 'yes, yes,' and away from 'no,' where the claims of the non-ego are concerned.

These fundamental inner conditions have characteristic practical consequences, as follows:

a. Asceticism.— The self-surrender may become so passionate as to turn into self-immolation. It may then so overrule the ordinary inhibitions of the flesh that the saint finds positive pleasure in sacrifice and asceticism, measuring and expressing as they do the degree of his loyalty to the higher power.

b. Strength of Soul.— The sense of enlargement of life may be so uplifting that personal motives and inhibitions, commonly omnipotent, become too insignificant for notice, and new reaches of patience and fortitude open out. Fears and anxieties go, and blissful equanimity takes their place. Come heaven, come hell, it makes no difference now!

c. Purity.— The shifting of the emotional centre brings with it, first, increase of purity. The sensitiveness to spiritual discords is enhanced, and the cleansing of existence from brutal and sensual elements becomes imperative. Occasions of contact with such elements are avoided: the saintly life must deepen its spiritual consistency and keep unspotted from the world. In some temperaments this need of purity of spirit takes an ascetic turn, and weaknesses of the flesh are treated with relentless severity.

d. Charity.— The shifting of the emotional centre brings, secondly, increase of charity, tenderness for fellow-creatures. The ordinary motives to antipathy, which usually set such close bounds to tenderness among human beings, are inhibited. The saint loves his enemies, and treats loathsome beggars as his brothers.

I now have to give some concrete illustrations of these fruits of the spiritual tree. The only difficulty is to choose, for they are so abundant.

Since the sense of Presence of a higher and friendly Power seems to be the fundamental feature in the spiritual life, I will begin with that.

In our narratives of conversion we saw how the world might look shining and transfigured to the convert, and, apart from anything acutely religious, we all have moments when the universal life seems to wrap us round with friendliness. In youth and health, in summer, in the woods or on the mountains, there come days when the weather seems all whispering with peace, hours when the goodness and beauty of existence enfold us like a dry warm climate, or chime through us as if our inner ears were subtly ringing with the world's security. Thoreau writes:

"Once, a few weeks after I came to the woods, for an hour I doubted whether the near neighborhood of man was not essential to a serene and healthy life. To be alone was somewhat unpleasant. But, in the midst of a gentle rain, while these thoughts prevailed, I was suddenly sensible of such sweet and beneficent society in Nature, in the very pattering of the drops, and in every sight and sound around my house, an infinite and unaccountable friendliness all at once, like an atmosphere, sustaining me, as made the fancied advantages of human neighborhood insignificant, and I have never thought of them since. Every little pine-needle expanded and swelled with sympathy and befriended me. I was so distinctly made aware of the presence of something kindred to me, that I thought no place could ever be strange to me again." [H. Thoreau: Walden, Riverside edition, p. 206, abridged.]

In the Christian consciousness this sense of the enveloping friendliness becomes most personal and definite. "The compensation," writes a German author, "for the loss of that sense of personal independence which man so unwillingly gives up, is the disappearance of all fear from one's life, the quite indescribable and inexplicable feeling of an inner security, which one can only experience, but which, once it has been experienced, one can never forget." [C.H. Hilty: Gluck, vol. i. p. 85.]

I find an excellent description of this state of mind in a sermon by Mr. Voysey:

"It is the experience of myriads of trustful souls, that this sense of God's unfailing presence with them in their going out and in their coming in, and by night and day, is a source of absolute repose and confident calmness. It drives away all fear of what may befall them. That nearness of God is a constant security against terror and anxiety. It is not that they are at all assured of physical safety, or deem themselves protected by a love which is denied to others, but that they are in a state of mind equally ready to be safe or to meet with injury. If injury befall them, they will be content to bear it because the Lord is their keeper, and nothing can befall them without his will. If it be his will, then injury is for them a blessing and no calamity at all. Thus and thus only is the trustful man protected and shielded from harm. And I for one— by no means a thick-skinned or hard-nerved man— am absolutely satisfied with this arrangement, and do not wish for any other kind of immunity from danger and catastrophe. Quite as sensitive to pain as the most highly strung organism, I yet feel that the worst of it is conquered, and the sting taken out of it altogether, by the thought that God is our loving and sleepless keeper, and that nothing can hurt us without his will." [The Mystery of Pain and Death, London, 1892, p. 258.]

More excited expressions of this condition are abundant in religious literature. I could easily weary you with their monotony. Here is an account from Mrs. Jonathan Edwards:

"Last night," Mrs. Edwards writes, "was the sweetest night I ever had in my life. I never before, for so long a time together, enjoyed so much of the light and rest and sweetness of heaven in my soul, but without the least agitation of body during the whole time. Part of the night I lay awake, sometimes asleep, and sometimes between sleeping and waking. But all night I continued in a constant, clear, and lively sense of the heavenly sweetness of Christ's excellent love, of his nearness to me, and of my dearness to him; with an inexpressibly sweet calmness of soul in an entire rest in him. I seemed to myself to perceive a glow of divine love come down from the heart of Christ in heaven into my heart in a constant stream, like a stream or pencil of sweet light. At the same time my heart and soul all flowed out in love to Christ, so that there seemed to be a constant flowing and reflowing of heavenly love, and I appeared to myself to float or swim, in these bright, sweet beams, like the motes swimming in the beams of the sun, or the streams of his light which come in at the window. I think that what I felt each minute was worth more than all the outward comfort and pleasure which I had enjoyed in my whole life put together. It was pleasure, without the least sting, or any interruption. It was a sweetness, which my soul was lost in; it seemed to be all that my feeble frame could sustain. There was but little difference, whether I was asleep or awake, but if there was any difference, the sweetness was greatest while I was asleep. As I awoke early the next morning, it seemed to me that I had entirely done with myself. I felt that the opinions of the world concerning me were nothing, and that I had no more to do with any outward interest of my own than with that of a person whom I never saw. The glory of God seemed to swallow up every wish and desire of my heart.... After retiring to rest and sleeping a little while, I awoke, and was led to reflect on God's mercy to me, in giving me, for many years, a willingness to die; and after that, in making me willing to live, that I might do and suffer whatever he called me to here. I also thought how God had graciously given me an entire resignation to his will, with respect to the kind and manner of death that I should die; having been made willing to die on the rack, or at the stake, and if it were God's will, to die in darkness. But now it occurred to me, I used to think of living no longer than to the ordinary age of man. Upon this I was led to ask myself, whether I was not willing to be kept out of heaven even longer; and my whole heart seemed immediately to reply: Yes, a thousand years, and a thousand in horror, if it be most for the honor of God, the torment of my body being so great, awful, and overwhelming that none could bear to live in the country where the spectacle was seen, and the torment of my mind being vastly greater. And it seemed to me that I found a perfect willingness, quietness, and alacrity of soul in consenting that it should be so, if it were most for the glory of God, so that there was no hesitation, doubt, or darkness in my mind. The glory of God seemed to overcome me and swallow me up, and every conceivable suffering, and everything that was terrible to my nature, seemed to shrink to nothing before it. This resignation continued in its clearness and brightness the rest of the night, and all the next day, and the night following, and on Monday in the forenoon, without interruption or abatement." [I have considerably abridged the words of the original, which is given in Edwards's Narrative of the Revival in New England.]

Compare Madame Guyon: "It was my practice to arise at midnight for purposes of devotion.... It seemed to me that God came at the precise time and woke me from sleep in order that I might enjoy him. When I was out of health or greatly fatigued, he did not awake me, but at such times I felt, even in my sleep, a singular possession of God. He loved me so much that he seemed to pervade my being, at a time when I could be only imperfectly conscious of his presence. My sleep is sometimes broken,— a sort of half sleep; but my soul seems to be awake enough to know God, when it is hardly capable of knowing anything else." [T.C. Upham: The Life and Religious Experiences of Madame de la Mothe Guyon, New York, 1877, vol. i. p. 260.]

The annals of Catholic saintship abound in records as ecstatic or more ecstatic than this. "Often the assaults of the divine love," it is said of the Sister Seraphique de la Martiniere, "reduced her almost to the point of death. She used tenderly to complain of this to God. 'I cannot support it,' she used to say. 'Bear gently with my weakness, or I shall expire under the violence of your love.'" [Bougaud: Hist. de la Bienheureuse Marguerite Marie, 1894, p. 125.]

Let me pass next to the Charity and Brotherly Love which are a usual fruit of saintliness, and have always been reckoned essential theological virtues, however limited may have been the kinds of service which the particular theology enjoined. Brotherly love would follow logically from the assurance of God's friendly presence, the notion of our brotherhood as men being an immediate inference from that of God's fatherhood of us all. When Christ utters the precepts: "Love your enemies, bless them that curse you, do good to them that hate you, and pray for them which despitefully use you, and persecute you," he gives for a reason: "That ye may be the children of your Father which is in heaven: for he maketh his sun to rise on the evil and on the good, and sendeth rain on the just and on the unjust." One might therefore be tempted to explain both the humility as to one's self and the charity towards others which characterize spiritual excitement, as results of the all-leveling character of theistic belief. But these affections are certainly not mere derivatives of theism. We find them in Stoicism, in Hinduism, and in Buddhism in the highest possible degree. They harmonize with paternal theism beautifully; but they harmonize with all reflection whatever upon the dependence of mankind on general causes; and we must, I think, consider them not subordinate but coordinate parts of that great complex excitement in the study of which we are engaged. Religious rapture, moral enthusiasm, ontological wonder, cosmic emotion, are all unifying states of mind, in which the sand and grit of the selfhood incline to disappear, and tenderness to rule. The best thing is to describe the condition integrally as a characteristic affection to which our nature is liable, a region in which we find ourselves at home, a sea in which we swim; but not to pretend to explain its parts by deriving them too cleverly from one another. Like love or fear, the faith-state is a natural psychic complex, and carries charity with it by organic consequence. Jubilation is an expansive affection, and all expansive affections are self-forgetful and kindly so long as they endure.

We find this the case even when they are pathological in origin. In his instructive work, la Tristesse et la Joie, [Paris, 1900.] M. Georges Dumas compares together the melancholy and the joyous phase of circular insanity, and shows that, while selfishness characterizes the one, the other is marked by altruistic impulses. No human being so stingy and useless as was Marie in her melancholy period! But the moment the happy period begins, "sympathy and kindness become her characteristic sentiments. She displays a universal goodwill, not only of intention, but in act.... She becomes solicitous of the health of other patients, interested in getting them out, desirous to procure wool to knit socks for some of them. Never since she has been under my observation have I heard her in her joyous period utter any but charitable opinions." And later, Dr. Dumas says of all such joyous conditions that "unselfish sentiments and tender emotions are the only affective states to be found in them. The subject's mind is closed against envy, hatred, and vindictiveness, and wholly transformed into benevolence, indulgence, and mercy."

There is thus an organic affinity between joyousness and tenderness, and their companionship in the saintly life need in no way occasion surprise. Along with the happiness, this increase of tenderness is often noted in narratives of conversion. "I began to work for others";—"I had more tender feeling for my family and friends";— "I spoke at once to a person with whom I had been angry";— "I felt for every one, and loved my friends better";— "I felt every one to be my friend"; — these are so many expressions from the records collected by Professor Starbuck.

"When," says Mrs. Edwards, continuing the narrative from which I made quotation a moment ago, "I arose on the morning of the Sabbath, I felt a love to all mankind, wholly peculiar in its strength and sweetness, far beyond all that I had ever felt before. The power of that love seemed inexpressible. I thought, if I were surrounded by enemies, who were venting their malice and cruelty upon me, in tormenting me, it would still be impossible that I should cherish any feelings towards them but those of love, and pity, and ardent desires for their happiness. I never before felt so far from a disposition to judge and censure others, as I did that morning. I realized also, in an unusual and very lively manner, how great a part of Christianity lies in the performance of our social and relative duties to one another. The same joyful sense continued throughout the day— a sweet love to God and all mankind."

Whatever be the explanation of the charity, it may efface all usual human barriers.

The barrier between men and animals also. We read of Towianski, an eminent Polish patriot and mystic, that "one day one of his friends met him in the rain, caressing a big dog which was jumping upon him and covering him horribly with mud. On being asked why he permitted the animal thus to dirty his clothes, Towianski replied: 'This dog, whom I am now meeting for the first time, has shown a great fellow-feeling for me, and a great joy in my recognition and acceptance of his greetings. Were I to drive him off, I should wound his feelings and do him a moral injury. It would be an offense not only to him, but to all the spirits of the other world who are on the same level with him. The damage which he does to my coat is as nothing in comparison with the wrong which I should inflict upon him, in case I were to remain indifferent to the manifestations of his friendship. We ought,' he added, 'both to lighten the condition of animals, whenever we can, and at the same time to facilitate in ourselves that union of the world of all spirits, which the sacrifice of Christ has made possible.'" Andre Towianski, Traduction de l'Italien, Turin, 1897 (privately printed). I owe my knowledge of this book and of Towianski to my friend Professor W. Lutoslawski, author of 'Plato's Logic.'

Here, for instance, is an example of Christian non-resistance from Richard Weaver's autobiography. Weaver was a collier, a semi-professional pugilist in his younger days, who became a much beloved evangelist. Fighting, after drinking, seems to have been the sin to which he originally felt his flesh most perversely inclined. After his first conversion he had a backsliding, which consisted in pounding a man who had insulted a girl. Feeling that, having once fallen, he might as well be hanged for a sheep as for a lamb, he got drunk and went and broke the jaw of another man who had lately challenged him to fight and taunted him with cowardice for refusing as a Christian man;— I mention these incidents to show how genuine a change of heart is implied in the later conduct which he describes as follows:

"I went down the drift and found the boy crying because a fellow-workman was trying to take the wagon from him by force. I said to him:

"'Tom, you must n't take that wagon.'

"He swore at me, and called me a Methodist devil. I told him that God did not tell me to let him rob me. He cursed again, and said he would push the wagon over me.

"'Well,' I said, 'let us see whether the devil and thee are stronger than the Lord and me.'

"And the Lord and I proving stronger than the devil and he, he had to get out of the way, or the wagon would have gone over him. So I gave the wagon to the boy. Then said Tom:

"'I've a good mind to smack thee on the face.'

"'Well,' I said, 'if that will do thee any good, thou canst do it.' So he struck me on the face.

"I turned the other cheek to him, and said, 'Strike again.'

"He struck again and again, till he had struck me five times. I turned my cheek for the sixth stroke; but he turned away cursing. I shouted after him: 'The Lord forgive thee, for I do, and the Lord save thee.'

"This was on a Saturday; and when I went home from the coal-pit my wife saw my face was swollen, and asked what was the matter with it. I said: 'I've been fighting, and I've given a man a good thrashing.'

"She burst out weeping, and said, 'O Richard, what made you fight?' Then I told her all about it; and she thanked the Lord I had not struck back.

"But the Lord had struck, and his blows have more effect than man's. Monday came. The devil began to tempt me, saying: 'The other men will laugh at thee for allowing Tom to treat thee as he did on Saturday.' I cried, 'Get thee behind me, Satan;'— and went on my way to the coal-pit.

"Tom was the first man I saw. I said 'Good-morning,' but got no reply.

"He went down first. When I got down, I was surprised to see him sitting on the wagon-road waiting for me. When I came to him he burst into tears and said: 'Richard, will you forgive me for striking you?'

'I have forgiven thee,' said I; 'ask God to forgive thee. The Lord bless thee.' I gave him my hand, and we went each to his work." [J. Patterson's Life of Richard Weaver, pp. 66-68, abridged.]

'Love your enemies!' Mark you, not simply those who happen not to be your friends, but your enemies, your positive and active enemies. Either this is a mere Oriental hyperbole, a bit of verbal extravagance, meaning only that we should, as far as we can, abate our animosities, or else it is sincere and literal. Outside of certain cases of intimate individual relation, it seldom has been taken literally. Yet it makes one ask the question: Can there in general be a level of emotion so unifying, so obliterative of differences between man and man, that even enmity may come to be an irrelevant circumstance and fail to inhibit the friendlier interests aroused? If positive well-wishing could attain so supreme a degree of excitement, those who were swayed by it might well seem superhuman beings. Their life would be morally discrete from the life of other men, and there is no saying, in the absence of positive experience of an authentic kind,— for there are few active examples in our scriptures, and the Buddhistic examples are legendary,— what the effects might be: they might conceivably transform the world.

As where the future Buddha, incarnated as a hare, jumps into the fire to cook himself for a meal for a beggar— having previously shaken himself three times, so that none of the insects in his fur should perish with him.

Psychologically and in principle, the precept 'Love your enemies' is not self-contradictory. It is merely the extreme limit of a kind of magnanimity with which, in the shape of pitying tolerance of our oppressors, we are fairly familiar. Yet if radically followed, it would involve such a breach with our instinctive springs of action as a whole, and with the present world's arrangements, that a critical point would practically be passed, and we should be born into another kingdom of being. Religious emotion makes us feel that other kingdom to be close at hand, within our reach.

The inhibition of instinctive repugnance is proved not only by the showing of love to enemies, but by the showing of it to any one who is personally loathsome. In the annals of saintliness we find a curious mixture of motives impelling in this direction. Asceticism plays its part; and along with charity pure and simple, we find humility or the desire to disclaim distinction and to grovel on the common level before God. Certainly all three principles were at work when Francis of Assisi and Ignatius Loyola exchanged their garments with those of filthy beggars. All three are at work when religious persons consecrate their lives to the care of leprosy or other peculiarly unpleasant diseases. The nursing of the sick is a function to which the religious seem strongly drawn, even apart from the fact that church traditions set that way. But in the annals of this sort of charity we find fantastic excesses of devotion recorded which are only explicable by the frenzy of self-immolation simultaneously aroused. Francis of Assisi kisses his lepers; Margaret Mary Alacoque, Francis Xavier, St. John of God, and others are said to have cleansed the sores and ulcers of their patients with their respective tongues; and the lives of such saints as Elizabeth of Hungary and Madame de Chantal are full of a sort of reveling in hospital purulence, disagreeable to read of, and which makes us admire and shudder at the same time.

So much for the human love aroused by the faith-state. Let me next speak of the Equanimity, Resignation, Fortitude, and Patience which it brings.

'A paradise of inward tranquillity' seems to be faith's usual result; and it is easy, even without being religious one's self, to understand this. A moment back, in treating of the sense of God's presence, I spoke of the unaccountable feeling of safety which one may then have. And, indeed, how can it possibly fail to steady the nerves, to cool the fever, and appease the fret, if one be sensibly conscious that, no matter what one's difficulties for the moment may appear to be, one's life as a whole is in the keeping of a power whom one can absolutely trust? In deeply religious men the abandonment of self to this power is passionate. Whoever not only says, but feels, 'God's will be done,' is mailed against every weakness; and the whole historic array of martyrs, missionaries, and religious reformers is there to prove the tranquil-mindedness, under naturally agitating or distressing circumstances, which self-surrender brings.

The temper of the tranquil-mindedness differs, of course, according as the person is of a constitutionally sombre or of a constitutionally cheerful cast of mind. In the sombre it partakes more of resignation and submission; in the cheerful it is a joyous consent. As an example of the former temper, I quote part of a letter from Professor Lagneau, a venerated teacher of philosophy who lately died, a great invalid, at Paris:

"My life, for the success of which you send good wishes, will be what it is able to be. I ask nothing from it, I expect nothing from it. For long years now I exist, think, and act, and am worth what I am worth, only through the despair which is my sole strength and my sole foundation. May it preserve for me, even in these last trials to which I am coming, the courage to do without the desire of deliverance. I ask nothing more from the Source whence all strength cometh, and if that is granted, your wishes will have been accomplished." [Bulletin l'Union pour l'Action Morale, September, 1894.]

There is something pathetic and fatalistic about this, but the power of such a tone as a protection against outward shocks is manifest. Pascal is another Frenchman of pessimistic natural temperament. He expresses still more amply the temper of self-surrendering submissiveness:

"Deliver me, Lord," he writes in his prayers, "from the sadness at my proper suffering which self-love might give, but put into me a sadness like your own. Let my sufferings appease your choler. Make them an occasion for my conversion and salvation. I ask you neither for health nor for sickness, for life nor for death; but that you may dispose of my health and my sickness, my life and my death, for your glory, for my salvation, and for the use of the Church and of your saints, of whom I would by your grace be one. You alone know what is expedient for me; you are the sovereign master; do with me according to your will. Give to me, or take away from me, only conform my will to yours. I know but one thing, Lord, that it is good to follow you, and bad to offend you. Apart from that, I know not what is good or bad in anything. I know not which is most profitable to me, health or sickness, wealth or poverty, nor anything else in the world. That discernment is beyond the power of men or angels, and is hidden among the secrets of your Providence, which I adore, but do not seek to fathom." [B. Pascal: Prieres pour les Maladies, SS SS xiii., xiv., abridged.]

When we reach more optimistic temperaments, the resignation grows less passive. Examples are sown so broadcast throughout history that I might well pass on without citation. As it is, I snatch at the first that occurs to my mind. Madame Guyon, a frail creature physically, was yet of a happy native disposition. She went through many perils with admirable serenity of soul. After being sent to prison for heresy,

"Some of my friends," she writes, "wept bitterly at the hearing of it, but such was my state of acquiescence and resignation that it failed to draw any tears from me.... There appeared to be in me then, as I find it to be in me now, such an entire loss of what regards myself, that any of my own interests gave me little pain or pleasure; ever wanting to will or wish for myself only the very thing which God does." In another place she writes: "We all of us came near perishing in a river which we found it necessary to pass. The carriage sank in the quicksand. Others who were with us threw themselves out in excessive fright. But I found my thoughts so much taken up with God that I had no distinct sense of danger. It is true that the thought of being drowned passed across my mind, but it cost no other sensation or reflection in me than this— that I felt quite contented and willing it were so, if it were my heavenly Father's choice." Sailing from Nice to Genoa, a storm keeps her eleven days at sea. "As the irritated waves dashed round us," she writes, "I could not help experiencing a certain degree of satisfaction in my mind. I pleased myself with thinking that those mutinous billows, under the command of Him who does all things rightly, might probably furnish me with a watery grave. Perhaps I carried the point too far, in the pleasure which I took in thus seeing myself beaten and bandied by the swelling waters. Those who were with me took notice of my intrepidity." [From Thomas C. Upham's Life and Religious Opinions and Experiences of Madame de la Mothe Guyon, New York, 1877, ii. 48, i. 141, 413, abridged.]

The contempt of danger which religious enthusiasm produces may be even more buoyant still. I take an example from that charming recent autobiography, "With Christ at Sea," by Frank Bullen. A couple of days after he went through the conversion on shipboard of which he there gives an account,

"It was blowing stiffly," he writes, "and we were carrying a press of canvas to get north out of the bad weather. Shortly after four bells we hauled down the flying-jib, and I sprang out astride the boom to furl it. I was sitting astride the boom when suddenly it gave way with me. The sail slipped through my fingers, and I fell backwards, hanging head downwards over the seething tumult of shining foam under the ship's bows, suspended by one foot. But I felt only high exultation in my certainty of eternal life. Although death was divided from me by a hair's breadth, and I was acutely conscious of the fact, it gave me no sensation but joy. I suppose I could have hung there no longer than five seconds, but in that time I lived a whole age of delight. But my body asserted itself, and with a desperate gymnastic effort I regained the boom. How I furled the sail I don't know, but I sang at the utmost pitch of my voice praises to God that went pealing out over the dark waste of waters." [Op. cit., London, 1901, p. 130.]

The annals of martyrdom are of course the signal field of triumph for religious imperturbability. Let me cite as an example the statement of a humble sufferer, persecuted as a Huguenot under Louis XIV.:

"They shut all the doors," Blanche Gamond writes, "and I saw six women, each with a bunch of willow rods as thick as the hand could hold, and a yard long. He gave me the order, 'Undress yourself,' which I did. He said, 'You are leaving on your shift; you must take it off.' They had so little patience that they took it off themselves, and I was naked from the waist up. They brought a cord with which they tied me to a beam in the kitchen. They drew the cord tight with all their strength and asked me, 'Does it hurt you?' and then they discharged their fury upon me, exclaiming as they struck me, 'Pray now to your God.' It was the Roulette woman who held this language. But at this moment I received the greatest consolation that I can ever receive in my life, since I had the honor of being whipped for the name of Christ, and in addition of being crowned with his mercy and his consolations. Why can I not write down the inconceivable influences, consolations, and peace which I felt interiorly? To understand them one must have passed by the same trial; they were so great that I was ravished, for there where afflictions abound grace is given superabundantly. In vain the women cried, 'We must double our blows; she does not feel them, for she neither speaks nor cries.' And how should I have cried, since I was swooning with happiness within?" [Claparede et Goty: Deux Heroines de la Foi, Paris, 1880, 112.]

The transition from tenseness, self-responsibility, and worry, to equanimity, receptivity, and peace, is the most wonderful of all those shiftings of inner equilibrium, those changes of the personal centre of energy, which I have analyzed so often; and the chief wonder of it is that it so often comes about, not by doing, but by simply relaxing and throwing the burden down. This abandonment of self-responsibility seems to be the fundamental act in specifically religious, as distinguished from moral practice. It antedates theologies and is independent of philosophies. Mind-cure, theosophy, stoicism, ordinary neurological hygiene, insist on it as emphatically as Christianity does, and it is capable of entering into closest marriage with every speculative creed. [Compare these three different statements of it: A.P. Call: As a Matter of Course, Boston, 1894; H.W. Dresser: Living by the Spirit, New York and London, 1900; H.W. Smith: The Christian's Secret of a Happy Life, published by the Willard Tract Repository, and now in thousands of hands.] Christians who have it strongly live in what is called 'recollection,' and are never anxious about the future, nor worry over the outcome of the day. Of Saint Catharine of Genoa it is said that "she took cognizance of things, only as they were presented to her in succession, moment by moment." To her holy soul, "the divine moment was the present moment,... and when the present moment was estimated in itself and in its relations, and when the duty that was involved in it was accomplished, it was permitted to pass away as if it had never been, and to give way to the facts and duties of the moment which came after." Hinduism, mind-cure, and theosophy all lay great emphasis upon this concentration of the consciousness upon the moment at hand. [T.C. Upham: Life of Madame Catharine Adorna, 3d ed., New York, 1864, pp. 158, 172-174.]

The next religious symptom which I will note is what I have called Purity of Life. The saintly person becomes exceedingly sensitive to inner inconsistency or discord, and mixture and confusion grow intolerable. All the mind's objects and occupations must be ordered with reference to the special spiritual excitement which is now its keynote. Whatever is unspiritual taints the pure water of the soul and is repugnant. Mixed with this exaltation of the moral sensibilities there is also an ardor of sacrifice, for the beloved deity's sake, of everything unworthy of him. Sometimes the spiritual ardor is so sovereign that purity is achieved at a stroke— we have seen examples. Usually it is a more gradual conquest. Billy Bray's account of his abandonment of tobacco is a good example of the latter form of achievement.

"I had been a smoker as well as a drunkard, and I used to love my tobacco as much as I loved my meat, and I would rather go down into the mine without my dinner than without my pipe. In the days of old, the Lord spoke by the mouths of his servants, the prophets; now he speaks to us by the spirit of his Son. I had not only the feeling part of religion, but I could hear the small, still voice within speaking to me. When I took the pipe to smoke, it would be applied within, 'It is an idol, a lust; worship the Lord with clean lips.' So, I felt it was not right to smoke. The Lord also sent a woman to convince me. I was one day in a house, and I took out my pipe to light it at the fire, and Mary Hawke— for that was the woman's name— said, 'Do you not feel it is wrong to smoke?' I said that I felt something inside telling me that it was an idol, a lust, and she said that was the Lord. Then I said, 'Now, I must give it up, for the Lord is telling me of it inside, and the woman outside, so the tobacco must go, love it as I may.' There and then I took the tobacco out of my pocket, and threw it into the fire, and put the pipe under my foot, 'ashes to ashes, dust to dust.' And I have not smoked since. I found it hard to break off old habits, but I cried to the Lord for help, and he gave me strength, for he has said, 'Call upon me in the day of trouble, and I will deliver thee.' The day after I gave up smoking I had the toothache so bad that I did not know what to do. I thought this was owing to giving up the pipe, but I said I would never smoke again, if I lost every tooth in my head. I said, 'Lord, thou hast told us My yoke is easy and my burden is light,' and when I said that, all the pain left me. Sometimes the thought of the pipe would come back to me very strong; but the Lord strengthened me against the habit, and, bless his name, I have not smoked since."

Bray's biographer writes that after he had given up smoking, he thought that he would chew a little, but he conquered this dirty habit, too. "On one occasion," Bray said, "when at a prayer-meeting at Hicks Mill, I heard the Lord say to me, 'Worship me with clean lips.' So, when we got up from our knees, I took the quid out of my mouth and I whipped 'en' [threw it] under the form. But, when we got on our knees again, I put another quid into my mouth. Then the Lord said to me again, 'Worship me with clean lips.' So I took the quid out of my mouth, and whipped 'en under the form again, and said, 'Yes, Lord, I will.' From that time I gave up chewing as well as smoking, and have been a free man."

The ascetic forms which the impulse for veracity and purity of life may take are often pathetic enough. The early Quakers, for example, had hard battles to wage against the worldliness and insincerity of the ecclesiastical Christianity of their time. Yet the battle that cost them most wounds was probably that which they fought in defense of their own right to social veracity and sincerity in their thee-ing and thou-ing, in not doffing the hat or giving titles of respect. It was laid on George Fox that these conventional customs were a lie and a sham, and the whole body of his followers thereupon renounced them, as a sacrifice to truth, and so that their acts and the spirit they professed might be more in accord.

"When the Lord sent me into the world," says Fox in his Journal, "he forbade me to put off my hat to any, high or low: and I was required to 'thee' and 'thou' all men and women, without any respect to rich or poor, great or small. And as I traveled up and down, I was not to bid people Good-morning, or Good-evening, neither might I bow or scrape with my leg to any one. This made the sects and professions rage. Oh! the rage that was in the priests, magistrates, professors, and people of all sorts: and especially in priests and professors: for though 'thou' to a single person was according to their accidence and grammar rules, and according to the Bible, yet they could not bear to hear it: and because I could not put off my hat to them, it set them all into a rage.... Oh! the scorn, heat, and fury that arose! Oh! the blows, punchings, beatings, and imprisonments that we underwent for not putting off our hats to men! Some had their hats violently plucked off and thrown away, so that they quite lost them. The bad language and evil usage we received on this account is hard to be expressed, besides the danger we were sometimes in of losing our lives for this matter, and that by the great professors of Christianity, who thereby discovered they were not true believers. And though it was but a small thing in the eye of man, yet a wonderful confusion it brought among all professors and priests: but, blessed be the Lord, many came to see the vanity of that custom of putting off hats to men, and felt the weight of Truth's testimony against it."

In the autobiography of Thomas Elwood, an early Quaker, who at one time was secretary to John Milton, we find an exquisitely quaint and candid account of the trials he underwent both at home and abroad, in following Fox's canons of sincerity. The anecdotes are too lengthy for citation; but Elwood sets down his manner of feeling about these things in a shorter passage, which I will quote as a characteristic utterance of spiritual sensibility:

"By this divine light, then," says Elwood, "I saw that though I had not the evil of the common uncleanliness, debauchery, profaneness, and pollutions of the world to put away, because I had, through the great goodness of God and a civil education, been preserved out of those grosser evils, yet I had many other evils to put away and to cease from; some of which were not by the world, which lies in wickedness (1 John v. 19), accounted evils, but by the light of Christ were made manifest to me to be evils, and as such condemned in me.

"As particularly those fruits and effects of pride that discover themselves in the vanity and superfluity of apparel; which I took too much delight in. This evil of my doings I was required to put away and cease from; and judgment lay upon me till I did so.

"I took off from my apparel those unnecessary trimmings of lace, ribbons, and useless buttons, which had no real service, but were set on only for that which was by mistake called ornament; and I ceased to wear rings.

"Again, the giving of flattering titles to men between whom and me there was not any relation to which such titles could be pretended to belong. This was an evil I had been much addicted to, and was accounted a ready artist in; therefore this evil also was I required to put away and cease from. So that thenceforward I durst not say, Sir, Master, My Lord, Madam (or My Dame); or say Your Servant to any one to whom I did not stand in the real relation of a servant, which I had never done to any.

"Again, respect of persons, in uncovering the head and bowing the knee or body in salutation, was a practice I had been much in the use of; and this, being one of the vain customs of the world, introduced by the spirit of the world, instead of the true honor which this is a false representation of, and used in deceit as a token of respect by persons one to another, who bear no real respect one to another; and besides this, being a type and a proper emblem of that divine honor which all ought to pay to Almighty

God, and which all of all sorts, who take upon them the Christian name, appear in when they offer their prayers to him, and therefore should not be given to men;— I found this to be one of those evils which I had been too long doing; therefore I was now required to put it away and cease from it.

"Again, the corrupt and unsound form of speaking in the plural number to a single person, you to one, instead of thou, contrary to the pure, plain, and single language of truth, thou to one, and you to more than one, which had always been used by God to men, and men to God, as well as one to another, from the oldest record of time till corrupt men, for corrupt ends, in later and corrupt times, to flatter, fawn, and work upon the corrupt nature in men, brought in that false and senseless way of speaking you to one, which has since corrupted the modern languages, and hath greatly debased the spirits and depraved the manners of men;— this evil custom I had been as forward in as others, and this I was now called out of and required to cease from.

"These and many more evil customs which had sprung up in the night of darkness and general apostasy from the truth and true religion were now, by the inshining of this pure my of divine light in my conscience, gradually discovered to me to be what I ought to cease from, shun, and stand a witness against." [The History of Thomas Elwood, written by Himself, London, 1885, pp. 32-34.]

These early Quakers were Puritans indeed. The slightest inconsistency between profession and deed jarred some of them to active protest. John Woolman writes in his diary:

"In these journeys I have been where much cloth hath been dyed; and have at sundry times walked over ground where much of their dyestuffs has drained away. This hath produced a longing in my mind that people might come into cleanness of spirit, cleanness of person, and cleanness about their houses and garments. Dyes being invented partly to please the eye, and partly to hide dirt, I have felt in this weak state, when traveling in dirtiness, and affected with unwholesome scents, a strong desire that the nature of dyeing cloth to hide dirt may be more fully considered.

"Washing our garments to keep them sweet is cleanly, but it is the opposite to real cleanliness to hide dirt in them. Through giving way to hiding dirt in our garments a spirit which would conceal that which is disagreeable is strengthened. Real cleanliness becometh a holy people; but hiding that which is not clean by coloring our garments seems contrary to the sweetness of sincerity. Through some sorts of dyes cloth is rendered less useful. And if the value of dyestuffs, and expense of dyeing, and the damage done to cloth, were all added together, and that cost applied to keeping all sweet and clean, how much more would real cleanliness prevail.

"Thinking often on these things, the use of bats and garments dyed with a dye hurtful to them, and wearing more clothes in summer than are useful, grew more uneasy to me; believing them to be customs which have not their foundation in pure wisdom. The apprehension of being singular from my beloved friends was a strait upon me; and thus I continued in the use of some things, contrary to my judgment, about nine months. Then I thought of getting a hat the natural color of the fur, but the apprehension of being looked upon as one affecting singularity felt uneasy to me. On this account I was under close exercise of mind in the time of our general spring meeting in 1762, greatly desiring to be rightly directed; when, being deeply bowed in spirit before the Lord, I was made willing to submit to what I apprehended was required of me; and when I returned home, got a hat of the natural color of the fur.

"In attending meetings, this singularity was a trial to me, and more especially at this time, as white hats were used by some who were fond of following the changeable modes of dress, and as some friends, who knew not from what motives I wore it, grew shy of me, I felt my way for a time shut up in the exercise of the ministry. Some friends were apprehensive that my wearing such a hat savored of an affected singularity: those who spoke with me in a friendly way, I generally informed in a few words, that I believed my wearing it was not in my own will."

When the craving for moral consistency and purity is developed to this degree, the subject may well find the outer world too full of shocks to dwell in, and can unify his life and keep his soul unspotted only by withdrawing from it. That law which impels the artist to achieve harmony in his composition by simply dropping out whatever jars, or suggests a discord, rules also in the spiritual life. To omit, says Stevenson, is the one art in literature: "If I knew how to omit, I should ask no other knowledge." And life, when full of disorder and slackness and vague superfluity, can no more have what we call character than literature can have it under similar conditions. So monasteries and communities of sympathetic devotees open their doors, and in their changeless order, characterized by omissions quite as much as constituted of actions, the holy-minded person finds that inner smoothness and cleanness which it is torture to him to feel violated at every turn by the discordancy and brutality of secular existence.

That the scrupulosity of purity may be carried to a fantastic extreme must be admitted. In this it resembles Asceticism, to which further symptom of saintliness we had better turn next. The adjective 'ascetic' is applied to conduct originating on diverse psychological levels, which I might as well begin by distinguishing from one another.

1. Asceticism may be a mere expression of organic hardihood, disgusted with too much ease.

2. Temperance in meat and drink, simplicity of apparel, chastity, and non-pampering of the body generally, may be fruits of the love of purity, shocked by whatever savors of the sensual.

3. They may also be fruits of love, that is, they may appeal to the subject in the light of sacrifices which he is happy in making to the Deity whom he acknowledges.

4. Again, ascetic mortifications and torments may be due to pessimistic feelings about the self, combined with theological beliefs concerning expiation. The devotee may feel that he is buying himself free, or escaping worse sufferings hereafter, by doing penance now.

5. In Psychopathic persons, mortifications may be entered on irrationally, by a sort of obsession or fixed idea which comes as a challenge and must be worked off, because only thus does the subject get his interior consciousness feeling right again.

6. Finally, ascetic exercises may in rarer instances be prompted by genuine perversions of the bodily sensibility, in consequence of which normally pain-giving stimuli are actually felt as pleasures.

I will try to give an instance under each of these heads in turn; but it is not easy to get them pure, for in cases pronounced enough to be immediately classed as ascetic, several of the assigned motives usually work together. Moreover, before citing any examples at all, I must invite you to some general psychological considerations which apply to all of them alike.

A strange moral transformation has within the past century swept over our Western world. We no longer think that we are called on to face physical pain with equanimity. It is not expected of a man that he should either endure it or inflict much of it, and to listen to the recital of cases of it makes our flesh creep morally as well as physically. The way in which our ancestors looked upon pain as an eternal ingredient of the world's order, and both caused and suffered it as a matter-of-course portion of their day's work, fills us with amazement. We wonder that any human beings could have been so callous. The result of this historic alteration is that even in the Mother Church herself, where ascetic discipline has such a fixed traditional prestige as a factor of merit, it has largely come into desuetude, if not discredit. A believer who flagellates or 'macerates' himself today arouses more wonder and fear than emulation. Many Catholic writers who admit that the times have changed in this respect do so resignedly; and even add that perhaps it is as well not to waste feelings in regretting the matter, for to return to the heroic corporeal discipline of ancient days might be an extravagance.

Where to seek the easy and the pleasant seems instinctive— and distinctive it appears to be in man; any deliberate tendency to pursue the hard and painful as such and for their own sakes might well strike one as purely abnormal. Nevertheless, in moderate degrees it is natural and even usual to human nature to court the arduous. It is only the extreme manifestations of the tendency that can be regarded as a paradox.

The psychological reasons for this lie near the surface. When we drop abstractions and take what we call our will in the act, we see that it is a very complex function. It involves both stimulations and inhibitions; it follows generalized habits; it is escorted by reflective criticisms; and it leaves a good or a bad taste of itself behind, according to the manner of the performance. The result is that, quite apart from the immediate pleasure which any sensible experience may give us, our own general moral attitude in procuring or undergoing the experience brings with it a secondary satisfaction or distaste. Some men and women, indeed, there are who can live on smiles and the word 'yes' forever. But for others (indeed for most), this is too tepid and relaxed a moral climate. Passive happiness is slack and insipid, and soon grows mawkish and intolerable.

Some austerity and wintry negativity, some roughness, danger, stringency, and effort, some 'no! no!' be mixed in, to produce the sense of an existence with character and texture and power. The range of individual differences in this respect is enormous; but whatever the mixture of yeses and noes may be, the person is infallibly aware when he has struck it in the right proportion for him. This, he feels, is my proper vocation, this is the optimum, the law, the life for me to live. Here I find the degree of equilibrium, safety calm, and leisure which I need, or here I find the challenge, passion, fight, and hardship without which my soul's energy expires.

Every individual soul, in short, like every individual machine or organism, has its own best conditions of efficiency. A given machine will run best under a certain steam-pressure, a certain amperage; an organism under a certain diet, weight, or exercise. You seem to do best, I heard a doctor say to a patient, at about 140 millimeters of arterial tension. And it is just so with our sundry souls: some are happiest in calm weather; some need the sense of tension, of strong volition, to make them feel alive and well. For these latter souls, whatever is gained from day to day must be paid for by sacrifice and inhibition, or else it comes too cheap and has no zest.

Now when characters of this latter sort become religious, they are apt to turn the edge of their need of effort and negativity against their natural self; and the ascetic life gets evolved as a consequence.

When Professor Tyndall in one of his lectures tells us that Thomas Carlyle put him into his bath-tub every morning of a freezing Berlin winter, proclaimed one of the lowest grades of asceticism. Even without Carlyle, most of us find it necessary to our soul's health to start the day with a rather cool immersion. A little farther along the scale we get such statements as this, from one of my correspondents, an agnostic:

"Often at night in my warm bed I would feel ashamed to depend so on the warmth, and whenever the thought would come over me I would have to get up, no matter what time of night it was, and stand for a minute in the cold, just so as to prove my manhood."

Such cases as these belong simply to our head 1. In the next case we probably have a mixture of heads 2 and 3— the asceticism becomes far more systematic and pronounced. The writer is a Protestant, whose sense of moral energy could doubtless be gratified on no lower terms, and I take his case from Starbuck's manuscript collection.

"I practiced fasting and mortification of the flesh. I secretly made burlap shirts, and put the burrs next the skin, and wore pebbles in my shoes. I would spend nights flat on my back on the floor without any covering."

The Roman Church has organized and codified all this sort of thing, and given it a market-value in the shape of 'merit.' But we see the cultivation of hardship cropping out under every sky and in every faith, as a spontaneous need of character. Thus we read of Channing, when first settled as a Unitarian minister, that

"He was now more simple than ever, and seemed to have become incapable of any form of self-indulgence. He took the smallest room in the house for his study, though he might easily have commanded one more light, airy, and in every way more suitable; and chose for his sleeping chamber an attic which he shared with a younger brother. The furniture of the latter might have answered for the cell of an anchorite, and consisted of a hard mattress on a cot-bedstead, plain wooden chairs and table, with matting on the floor. It was without fire, and to cold he was throughout life extremely sensitive; but he never complained or appeared in any way to be conscious of inconvenience. 'I recollect,' says his brother, 'after one most severe night, that in the morning he sportively thus alluded to his suffering: "If my bed were my country, I should be somewhat like Bonaparte: I have no control except over the part which I occupy; the instant I move, frost takes possession."' In sickness only would he change for the time his apartment and accept a few comforts. The dress too that he habitually adopted was of most inferior quality; and garments were constantly worn which the world would call mean, though an almost feminine neatness preserved him from the least appearance of neglect." [Memoirs of W.E. Channing, Boston, 1840, i. 196.]

Channing's asceticism, such as it was, was evidently a compound of hardihood and love of purity. The democracy which is an offshoot of the enthusiasm of humanity, and of which I will speak later under the head of the cult of poverty, doubtless bore also a share. Certainly there was no pessimistic element in his case. In the next case we have a strongly pessimistic element, so that it belongs under head 4. John Cennick was Methodism's first lay preacher. In 1735 he was convicted of sin, while walking in Cheapside,

"And at once left off song-singing, card-playing, and attending theatres. Sometimes he wished to go to a popish monastery, to spend his life in devout retirement. At other times he longed to live in a cave, sleeping on fallen leaves, and feeding on forest fruits. He fasted long and often, and prayed nine times a day.... Fancying dry bread too great an indulgence for so great a sinner as himself, he began to feed on potatoes, acorns, crabs, and grass; and often wished that he could live on roots and herbs. At length, in 1737, he found peace with God, and went on his way rejoicing." [L. Tyerman: The Life and Times of the Rev. John Wesley, i. 274.]

In this poor man we have morbid melancholy and fear, and the sacrifices made are to purge out sin, and to buy safety. The hopelessness of Christian theology in respect of the flesh and the natural man generally has, in systematizing fear, made of it one tremendous incentive to self-mortification. It would be quite unfair, however, in spite of the fact that this incentive has often been worked in a mercenary way for hortatory purposes, to call it a mercenary incentive. The impulse to expiate and do penance is, in its first intention, far too immediate and spontaneous an expression of self-despair and anxiety to be obnoxious to any such reproach. In the form of loving sacrifice, of spending all we have to show our devotion, ascetic discipline of the severest sort may be the fruit of highly optimistic religious feeling.

M. Vianney, the cure of Ars, was a French country priest, whose holiness was exemplary. We read in his life the following account of his inner need of sacrifice:

"'On this path,' M. Vianney said, 'it is only the first step that costs. There is in mortification a balm and a savor without which one cannot live when once one has made their acquaintance. There is but one way in which to give one's self to God,— that is, to give one's self entirely, and to keep nothing for one's self. The little that one keeps is only good to trouble one and make one suffer.' Accordingly he imposed it on himself that he should never smell a flower, never drink when parched with thirst, never drive away a fly, never show disgust before a repugnant object, never complain of anything that had to do with his personal comfort, never sit down, never lean upon his elbows when he was kneeling. The Cure of Ars was very sensitive to cold, but he would never take means to protect himself against it. During a very severe winter, one of his missionaries contrived a false floor to his confessional and placed a metal case of hot water beneath. The trick succeeded, and the Saint was deceived: 'God is very good,' he said with emotion. 'This year, through all the cold, my feet have always been warm.'" [A. Mounin: Le Cure d'Ars, Vie de M.J.B.M. Vianney, 1864, p. 545, abridged.]

In this case the spontaneous impulse to make sacrifices for the pure love of God was probably the uppermost conscious motive. We may class it, then, under our head 3. Some authors think that the impulse to sacrifice is the main religious phenomenon. It is a prominent, a universal phenomenon certainly, and lies deeper than any special creed. Here, for instance, is what seems to be a spontaneous example of it, simply expressing what seemed right at the time between the individual and his Maker. Cotton Mather, the New England Puritan divine, is generally reputed a rather grotesque pedant; yet what is more touchingly simple than his relation of what happened when his wife came to die?

"When I saw to what a point of resignation I was now called of the Lord." he says, "I resolved, with his help, therein to glorify him. So, two hours before my lovely consort expired, I kneeled by her bedside, and I took into my two hands a dear hand, the dearest in the world. With her thus in my hands, I solemnly and sincerely gave her up unto the Lord: and in token of my real Resignation, I gently put her out of my hands, and laid away a most lovely hand, resolving that I would never touch it more. This was the hardest, and perhaps the bravest action that ever I did. She... told me that she signed and sealed my act of resignation. And though before that she called for me continually, she after this never asked for me any more." [B. Wendell: Cotton Mather, New York, no date, p. 198.]

Father Vianney's asceticism taken in its totality was simply the result of a permanent flood of high spiritual enthusiasm, longing to make proof of itself. The Roman Church has, in its incomparable fashion, collected all the motives towards asceticism together, and so codified them that any one wishing to pursue Christian perfection may find a practical system mapped out for him in any one of a number of ready-made manuals. The dominant Church notion of perfection is of course the negative one of avoidance of sin. Sin proceeds from concupiscence, and concupiscence from our carnal passions and temptations, chief of which are pride, sensuality in all its forms, and the loves of worldly excitement and possession. All these sources of sin must be resisted; and discipline and austerities are a most efficacious mode of meeting them. Hence there are always in these books chapters on self-mortification. But whenever a procedure is codified, the more delicate spirit of it evaporates, and if we wish the undiluted ascetic spirit,— the passion of self-contempt wreaking itself on the poor flesh, the divine irrationality of devotion making a sacrificial gift of all it has (its sensibilities, namely) to the object of its adoration,— we must go to autobiographies, or other individual documents.

Saint John of the Cross, a Spanish mystic who flourished— or rather who existed, for there was little that suggested flourishing about him— in the sixteenth century, will supply a passage suitable for our purpose.

"First of all, carefully excite in yourself an habitual affectionate will in all things to imitate Jesus Christ. If anything agreeable offers itself to your senses, yet does not at the same time tend purely to the honor and glory of God, renounce it and separate yourself from it for the love of Christ, who all his life long had no other taste or wish than to do the will of his Father whom he called his meat and nourishment. For example, you take satisfaction in hearing of things in which the glory of God bears no part. Deny yourself this satisfaction, mortify your wish to listen. You take pleasure in seeing objects which do not raise your mind to God: refuse yourself this pleasure, and turn away your eyes. The same with conversations and all other things. Act similarly, so far as you are able, with all the operations of the senses, striving to make yourself free from their yokes.

"The radical remedy lies in the mortification of the four great natural passions, joy, hope, fear, and grief. You must seek to deprive these of every satisfaction and leave them as it were in darkness and the void. Let your soul therefore turn always:

"Not to what is most easy, but to what is hardest;

"Not to what tastes best, but to what is most distasteful;

"Not to what most pleases, but to what disgusts;

"Not to matter of consolation, but to matter for desolation rather;

"Not to rest, but to labor;

"Not to desire the more, but the less;

"Not to aspire to what is highest and most precious, but to what is lowest and most contemptible;

"Not to will anything, but to will nothing;

"Not to seek the best in everything, but to seek the worst, so that you may enter for the love of Christ into a complete destitution, a perfect poverty of spirit, and an absolute renunciation of everything in this world.

"Embrace these practices with all the energy of your soul and you will find in a short time great delights and unspeakable consolations.

"Despise yourself, and wish that others should despise you.

"Speak to your own disadvantage, and desire others to do the same;

"Conceive a low opinion of yourself, and find it good when others hold the same;

"To enjoy the taste of all things, have no taste for anything.

"To know all things, learn to know nothing.

"To possess all things, resolve to possess nothing.

"To be all things, be willing to be nothing.

"To get to where you have no taste for anything, go through whatever experiences you have no taste for.

"To learn to know nothing, go whither you are ignorant.

"To reach what you possess not, go whithersoever you own nothing.

"To be what you are not, experience what you are not."

These later verses play with that vertigo of self-contradiction which is so dear to mysticism. Those that come next are completely mystical, for in them Saint John passes from God to the more metaphysical notion of the All.

"When you stop at one thing, you cease to open yourself to the All.

"For to come to the All you must give up the All.

"And if you should attain to owning the All, you must own it, desiring Nothing.

"In this spoliation, the soul finds its tranquillity and rest. Profoundly established in the centre of its own nothingness, it can be assailed by naught that comes from below; and since it no longer desires anything, what comes from above cannot depress it; for its desires alone are the causes of its woes." [Saint Jean De La Croix, Vis et Oeuvres, Paris, 1893, ii. 94, 99, abridged.]

And now, as a more concrete example of heads 4 and 5, in fact of all our heads together, and of the irrational extreme to which a psychopathic individual may go in the line of bodily austerity, I will quote the sincere Suso's account of his own self-tortures. Suso, you will remember, was one of the fourteenth century German mystics; his autobiography, written in the third person, is a classic religious document.

"He was in his youth of a temperament full of fire and life; and when this began to make itself felt, it was very grievous to him; and he sought by many devices how he might bring his body into subjection. He wore for a long time a hair shirt and an iron chain, until the blood ran from him, so that he was obliged to leave them off. He secretly caused an undergarment to be made for him; and in the undergarment he had strips of leather fixed, into which a hundred and fifty brass nails, pointed and filed sharp, were driven, and the points of the nails were always turned towards the flesh. He had this garment made very tight, and so arranged as to go round him and fasten in front, in order that it might fit the closer to his body, and the pointed nails might be driven into his flesh; and it was high enough to reach upwards to his navel. In this he used to sleep at night. Now in summer, when it was hot, and he was very tired and ill from his journeyings, or when he held the office of lecturer, he would sometimes, as he lay thus in bonds, and oppressed with toil, and tormented also by noxious insects, cry aloud and give way to fretfulness, and twist round and round in agony, as a worm does when run through with a pointed needle. It often seemed to him as if he were lying upon an ant-hill, from the torture caused by the insects; for if he wished to sleep, or when he had fallen asleep, they vied with one another. Sometimes he cried to Almighty God in the fullness of his heart: Alas! Gentle God, what a dying is this! When a man is killed by murderers or strong beasts of prey it is soon over; but I lie dying here under the cruel insects, and yet cannot die. The nights in winter were never so long, nor was the summer so hot, as to make him leave off this exercise. On the contrary, he devised something farther— two leathern loops into which he put his hands, and fastened one on each side his throat, and made the fastenings so secure that even if his cell had been on fire about him, he could not have helped himself. This he continued until his hands and arms had become almost tremulous with the strain, and then he devised something else: two leather gloves; and he caused a brazier to fit them all over with sharp-pointed brass tacks, and he used to put them on at night, in order that if he should try while asleep to throw off the hair undergarment, or relieve himself from the gnawings of the vile insects, the tacks might then stick into his body. And so it came to pass. If ever he sought to help himself with his hands in his sleep, he drove the sharp tacks into his breast, and tore himself, so that his flesh festered. When after many weeks the wounds had healed, he tore himself again and made fresh wounds.

"He continued this tormenting exercise for about sixteen years. At the end of this time, when his blood was now chilled, and the fire of his temperament destroyed, there appeared to him in a vision on Whitsunday, a messenger from heaven, who told him that God required this of him no longer. Whereupon he discontinued it, and threw all these things away into a running stream."

Suso then tells how, to emulate the sorrows of his crucified Lord, he made himself a cross with thirty protruding iron needles and nails. This he bore on his bare back between his shoulders day and night. The first time that he stretched out this cross upon his back his tender frame was struck with terror at it, and blunted the sharp nails slightly against a stone. But soon, repenting of this womanly cowardice, he pointed them all again with a file, and placed once more the cross upon him. It made his back, where the bones are, bloody and seared. Whenever he sat down or stood up, it was as if a hedgehog-skin were on him. If any one touched him unawares, or pushed against his clothes, it tore him."

Suso next tells of his penitences by means of striking this cross and forcing the nails deeper into the flesh, and likewise of his self-scourgings,— a dreadful story,— and then goes on as follows: "At this same period the Servitor procured an old castaway door, and he used to lie upon it at night without any bedclothes to make him comfortable, except that he took of his shoes and wrapped a thick cloak round him. He thus secured for himself a most miserable bed; for hard pea-stalks lay in humps under his head, the cross with the sharp nails stuck into his back, his arms were locked fast in bonds, the horsehair undergarment was round his loins, and the cloak too was heavy and the door hard. Thus he lay in wretchedness, afraid to stir, just like a log, and he would send up many a sigh to God.

"In winter he suffered very much from the frost. If he stretched out his feet they lay bare on the floor and froze, if he gathered them up the blood became all on fire in his legs, and this was great pain. His feet were full of sores, his legs dropsical, his knees bloody and seared, his loins covered with sears from the horsehair, his body wasted, his mouth parched with intense thirst, and his hands tremulous from weakness. Amid these torments he spent his nights and days; and he endured them all out of the greatness of the love which he bore in his heart to the Divine and Eternal Wisdom, our Lord Jesus Christ, whose agonizing sufferings he sought to imitate. After a time he gave up this penitential exercise of the door, and instead of it he took up his abode in a very small cell, and used the bench, which was so narrow and short that he could not stretch himself upon it, as his bed. In this hole, or upon the door, he lay at night in his usual bonds, for about eight years. It was also his custom, during the space of twenty-five years, provided he was staying in the convent, never to go after compline in winter into any warm room, or to the convent stove to warm himself, no matter how cold it might be, unless he was obliged to do so for other reasons. Throughout all these years he never took a bath, either a water or a sweating bath; and this he did in order to mortify his comfort-seeking body. He practiced during a long time such rigid poverty that he would neither receive nor touch a penny, either with leave or without it. For a considerable time he strove to attain such a high degree of purity that he would neither scratch nor touch any part of his body, save only his hands and feet." [The Life of the Blessed Henry Suso, by Himself, translated by T.F. Knox, London, 1865, pp. 56-80, abridged.]

I spare you the recital of poor Suso's self-inflicted tortures from thirst. It is pleasant to know that after his fortieth year, God showed him by a series of visions that he had sufficiently broken down the natural man, and that he might leave these exercises off. His case is distinctly pathological, but he does not seem to have had the alleviation, which some ascetics have enjoyed, of an alteration of sensibility capable of actually turning torment into a perverse kind of pleasure. Of the founder of the Sacred Heart order, for example, we read that

"Her love of pain and suffering was insatiable.... She said that she could cheerfully live till the day of judgment, provided she might always have matter for suffering for God; but that to live a single day without suffering would be intolerable. She said again that she was devoured with two unassuageable fevers, one for the holy communion, the other for suffering, humiliation, and annihilation. 'Nothing but pain,' she continually said in her letters, 'makes my life supportable.'" [Bougaud: Hist. de la bienheureuse Marguerite Marie, Paris, 1894, pp. 265, 171. Compare, also, pp. 386, 387.]

So much for the phenomena to which the ascetic impulse will in certain persons give rise. In the ecclesiastically consecrated character three minor branches of self-mortification have been recognized as indispensable pathways to perfection. I refer to the chastity, obedience, and poverty which the monk vows to observe; and upon the heads of obedience and poverty I will make a few remarks.

First, of Obedience. The secular life of our twentieth century opens with this virtue held in no high esteem. The duty of the individual to determine his own conduct and profit or suffer by the consequences seems, on the contrary, to be one of our best rooted contemporary Protestant social ideals. So much so that it is difficult even imaginatively to comprehend how men possessed of an inner life of their own could ever have come to think the subjection of its will to that of other finite creatures recommendable. I confess that to myself it seems something of a mystery. Yet it evidently corresponds to a profound interior need of many persons, and we must do our best to understand it.

On the lowest possible plane, one sees how the expediency of obedience in a firm ecclesiastical organization must have led to its being viewed as meritorious. Next, experience shows that there are times in every one's life when one can be better counseled by others than by one's self. Inability to decide is one of the commonest symptoms of fatigued nerves; friends who see our troubles more broadly, often see them more wisely than we do; so it is frequently an act of excellent virtue to consult and obey a doctor, a partner, or a wife. But, leaving these lower prudential regions, we find, in the nature of some of the spiritual excitements which we have been studying, good reasons for idealizing obedience. Obedience may spring from the general religious phenomenon of inner softening and self-surrender and throwing one's self on higher powers. So saving are these attitudes felt to be that in themselves, apart from utility, they become ideally consecrated; and in obeying a man whose fallibility we see through thoroughly, we, nevertheless, may feel much as we do when we resign our will to that of infinite wisdom. Add self-despair and the passion of self-crucifixion to this, and obedience becomes an ascetic sacrifice, agreeable quite irrespective of whatever prudential uses it might have.

It is as a sacrifice, a mode of 'mortification,' that obedience is primarily conceived by Catholic writers, a "sacrifice which man offers to God, and of which he is himself both the priest and the victim. By poverty he immolates his exterior possessions; by chastity he immolates his body; by obedience he completes the sacrifice, and gives to God all that he yet holds as his own, his two most precious goods, his intellect and his will. The sacrifice is then complete and unreserved, a genuine holocaust, for the entire victim is now consumed for the honor of God." Accordingly, in Catholic discipline, we obey our superior not as mere man, but as the representative of Christ. Obeying God in him by our intention, obedience is easy. But when the text-book theologians marshal collectively all their reasons for recommending it, the mixture sounds to our ears rather odd. [Lejeune: Introduction a la Vie Mystique, 1899, p. 277. The holocaust simile goes back at least as far as Ignatius Loyola.]

"One of the great consolations of the monastic life," says a Jesuit authority, "is the assurance we have that in obeying we can commit no fault. The Superior may commit a fault in commanding you to do this thing or that, but you are certain that you commit no fault so long as you obey, because God will only ask you if you have duly performed what orders you received, and if you can furnish a clear account in that respect, you are absolved entirely. Whether the things you did were opportune, or whether there were not something better that might have been done, these are questions not asked of you, but rather of your Superior. The moment what you did was done obediently, God wipes it out of your account, and charges it to the Superior. So that Saint Jerome well exclaimed, in celebrating the advantages of obedience, 'Oh, sovereign liberty! Oh, holy and blessed security by which one becomes almost impeccable!'

"Saint John Climachus is of the same sentiment when he calls obedience an excuse before God. In fact, when God asks why you have done this or that, and you reply, it is because I was so ordered by my Superiors, God will ask for no other excuse. As a passenger in a good vessel with a good pilot need give himself no farther concern, but may go to sleep in peace, because the pilot has charge over all, and 'watches for him'; so a religious person who lives under the yoke of obedience goes to heaven as if while sleeping, that is, while leaning entirely on the conduct of his Superiors, who are the pilots of his vessel, and keep watch for him continually. It is no small thing, of a truth, to be able to cross the stormy sea of life on the shoulders and in the arms of another, yet that is just the grace which God accords to those who live under the yoke of obedience. Their Superior bears all their burdens.... A certain grave doctor said that he would rather spend his life in picking up straws by obedience, than by his own responsible choice busy himself with the loftiest works of charity, because one is certain of following the will of God in whatever one may do from obedience, but never certain in the same degree of anything which we may do of our own proper movement." [Alfonso Rodriguez. S.J.: Pratique de Perfection Chretienne, Part iii., Treatise v., ch. x.]

One should read the letters in which Ignatius Loyola recommends obedience as the backbone of his order, if one would gain insight into the full spirit of its cult. They are too long to quote; but Ignatius's belief is so vividly expressed in a couple of sayings reported by companions that, though they have been so often cited, I will ask your permission to copy them once more: [Letters li. and cxx. of the collection translated into French by Bouix, Paris, 1870.]

"I ought," an early biographer reports him as saying, "on entering religion, and thereafter, to place myself entirely in the hands of God, and of him who takes His place by His authority. I ought to desire that my Superior should oblige me to give up my own judgment, and conquer my own mind. I ought to set up no difference between one Superior and another,... but recognize them all as equal before God, whose place they fill. For if I distinguish persons, I weaken the spirit of obedience. In the hands of my Superior, I must be a soft wax, a thing, from which he is to require whatever pleases him, be it to write or receive letters, to speak or not to speak to such a person, or the like; and I must put all my fervor in executing zealously and exactly what I am ordered. I must consider myself as a corpse which has neither intelligence nor will; be like a mass of matter which without resistance lets itself be placed wherever it may please any one; like a stick in the hand of an old man, who uses it according to his needs and places it where it suits him. So must I be under the hands of the Order, to serve it in the way it judges most useful.

"I must never ask of the Superior to be sent to a particular place, to be employed in a particular duty.... I must consider nothing as belonging to me personally, and as regards the things I use, be like a statue which lets itself be stripped and never opposes resistance." [Bartoli-Michel, ii. 13.]

The other saying is reported by Rodriguez in the chapter from which I a moment ago made quotations. When speaking of the Pope's authority, Rodriguez writes:

"Saint Ignatius said, when general of his company, that if the Holy Father were to order him to set sail in the first bark which he might find in the port of Ostia, near Rome, and to abandon himself to the sea, without a mast, without sails, without oars or rudder or any of the things that are needful for navigation or subsistence, he would obey not only with alacrity, but without anxiety or repugnance, and even with a great internal satisfaction." [Rodriguez: Op. cit., Part iii., Treatise v., ch. vi.]

With a solitary concrete example of the extravagance to which the virtue we are considering has been carried, I will pass to the topic next in order.

"Sister Marie Claire [of Port Royal] had been greatly imbued with the holiness and excellence of M. de Langres. This prelate, soon after he came to Port Royal, said to her one day, seeing her so tenderly attached to Mother Angelique, that it would perhaps be better not to speak to her again. Marie Claire, greedy of obedience, took this inconsiderate word for an oracle of God, and from that day forward remained for several years without once speaking to her sister." [Sainte-Beuve: Histoire de Port Royal, i. 346.]

Our next topic shall be Poverty, felt at all times and under all creeds as one adornment of a saintly life. Since the instinct of ownership is fundamental in man's nature, this is one more example of the ascetic paradox. Yet it appears no paradox at all, but perfectly reasonable, the moment one recollects how easily higher excitements hold lower cupidities in check. Having just quoted the Jesuit Rodriguez on the subject of obedience, I will, to give immediately a concrete turn to our discussion of poverty, also read you a page from his chapter on this latter virtue. You must remember that he is writing instructions for monks of his own order, and bases them all on the text, "Blessed are the poor in spirit."

"If any one of you," he says, "will know whether or not he is really poor in spirit, let him consider whether he loves the ordinary consequences and effects of poverty, which are hunger, thirst, cold, fatigue, and the denudation of all conveniences. See if you are glad to wear a worn-out habit full of patches. See if you are glad when something is lacking to your meal, when you are passed by in serving it, when what you receive is distasteful to you, when your cell is out of repair. If you are not glad of these things, if instead of loving them you avoid them, then there is proof that you have not attained the perfection of poverty of spirit." Rodriguez then goes on to describe the practice of poverty in more detail. "The first point is that which Saint Ignatius proposes in his constitutions, when he says, 'Let no one use anything as if it were his private possession.' 'A religious person,' he says, 'ought in respect to all the things that he uses, to be like a statue which one may drape with clothing, but which feels no grief and makes no resistance when one strips it again. It is in this way that you should feel towards your clothes, your books, your cell, and everything else that you make use of; if ordered to quit them, or to exchange them for others, have no more sorrow than if you were a statue being uncovered. In this way you will avoid using them as if they were your private possession. But if, when you give up your cell, or yield possession of this or that object or exchange it for another, you feel repugnance and are not like a statue, that shows that you view these things as if they were your private property.'

"And this is why our holy founder wished the superiors to test their monks somewhat as God tested Abraham, and to put their poverty and their obedience to trial, that by this means they may become acquainted with the degree of their virtue, and gain a chance to make ever farther progress in perfection,... making the one move out of his room when he finds it comfortable and is attached to it; taking away from another a book of which he is fond; or obliging a third to exchange his garment for a worse one. Otherwise we should end by acquiring a species of property in all these several objects, and little by little the wall of poverty that surrounds us and constitutes our principal defense would be thrown down. The ancient fathers of the desert used often thus to treat their companions.... Saint Dositheus, being sick-nurse, desired a certain knife, and asked Saint Dorotheus for it, not for his private use, but for employment in the infirmary of which he had charge. Whereupon Saint Dorotheus answered him: 'Ha! Dositheus, so that knife pleases you so much! Will you be the slave of a knife or the slave of Jesus Christ? Do you not blush with shame at wishing that a knife should be your master? I will not let you touch it.' Which reproach and refusal had such an effect upon the holy disciple that since that time he never touched the knife again.''...

"Therefore, in our rooms," Father Rodriguez continues, "there must be no other furniture than a bed, a table, a bench, and a candlestick, things purely necessary, and nothing more. It is not allowed among us that our cells should be ornamented with pictures or aught else, neither armchairs, carpets, curtains, nor any sort of cabinet or bureau of any elegance. Neither is it allowed us to keep anything to eat, either for ourselves or for those who may come to visit us. We must ask permission to go to the refectory even for a glass of water; and finally we may not keep a book in which we can write a line, or which we may take away with us. One cannot deny that thus we are in great poverty. But this poverty is at the same time a great repose and a great perfection. For it would be inevitable, in case a religious person were allowed to own superfluous possessions, that these things would greatly occupy his mind, be it to acquire them, to preserve them, or to increase them; so that in not permitting us at all to own them, all these inconveniences are remedied. Among the various good reasons why the company forbids secular persons to enter our cells, the principal one is that thus we may the easier be kept in poverty. After all, we are all men, and if we were to receive people of the world into our rooms, we should not have the strength to remain within the bounds prescribed, but should at least wish to adorn them with some books to give the visitors a better opinion of our scholarship." [Rodriguez: Op. Cit., Part iii., Treatise iii., chaps. vi., vii.]

Since Hindu fakirs, Buddhist monks, and Mohammedan dervishes unite with Jesuits and Franciscans in idealizing poverty as the loftiest individual state, it is worth while to examine into the spiritual grounds for such a seemingly unnatural opinion. And first, of those which lie closest to common human nature.

The opposition between the men who have and the men who are is immemorial. Though the gentleman, in the old-fashioned sense of the man who is well born, has usually in point of fact been predaceous and reveled in lands and goods, yet he has never identified his essence with these possessions, but rather with the personal superiorities, the courage, generosity, and pride supposed to be his birthright. To certain huckstering kinds of consideration he thanked God he was forever inaccessible, and if in life's vicissitudes he should become destitute through their lack, he was glad to think that with his sheer valor he was all the freer to work out his salvation. "Wer nur selbst was hatte," says Lessing's Tempelherr, in Nathan the Wise, "mein Gott, mein Gott, ich habe nichts!" This ideal of the well-born man without possessions was embodied in knight-errantry and templardom; and, hideously corrupted as it has always been, it still dominates sentimentally, if not practically, the military and aristocratic view of life. We glorify the soldier as the man absolutely unincumbered. Owning nothing but his bare life, and willing to toss that up at any moment when the cause commands him, he is the representative of unhampered freedom in ideal directions. The laborer who pays with his person day by day, and has no rights invested in the future, offers also much of this ideal detachment. Like the savage, he may make his bed wherever his right arm can support him, and from his simple and athletic attitude of observation, the property-owner seems buried and smothered in ignoble externalities and trammels, "wading in straw and rubbish to his knees." The claims which things make are corrupters of manhood, mortgages on the soul, and a drag anchor on our progress towards the empyrean.

"Everything I meet with," writes Whitefield, "seems to carry this voice with it,— 'Go thou and preach the Gospel; be a pilgrim on earth; have no party or certain dwelling place.' My heart echoes back, 'Lord Jesus, help me to do or suffer thy will. When thou seest me in danger of nesting,— in pity— in tender pity,— put a thorn in my nest to prevent me from it.'" [R. Philip: The Life and Times of George Whitefield, London, 1842, p. 366.]

The loathing of 'capital' with which our laboring classes today are growing more and more infected seems largely composed of this sound sentiment of antipathy for lives based on mere having. As an anarchist poet writes:

"Not by accumulating riches, but by giving away that which you have,
"Shall you become beautiful;
"You must undo the wrappings, not case yourself in fresh ones;
"Not by multiplying clothes shall you make your body sound and healthy, but rather by discarding them...
"For a soldier who is going on a campaign does not seek what fresh furniture he can carry on his back, but rather what he can leave behind;
"Knowing well that every additional thing which he cannot freely use and handle is an impediment." [Edward Carpenter: Towards Democracy, p. 362, abridged.]

In short, lives based on having are less free than lives based either on doing or on being, and in the interest of action people subject to spiritual excitement throw away possessions as so many clogs. Only those who have no private interests can follow an ideal straight away. Sloth and cowardice creep in with every dollar or guinea we have to guard. When a brother novice came to Saint Francis, saying: "Father, it would be a great consolation to me to own a psalter, but even supposing that our general should concede to me this indulgence, still I should like also to have your consent," Francis put him off with the examples of Charlemagne, Roland, and Oliver, pursuing the infidels in sweat and labor, and finally dying on the field of battle. "So care not," he said, "for owning books and knowledge, but care rather for works of goodness." And when some weeks later the novice came again to talk of his craving for the psalter, Francis said: "After you have got your psalter you will crave a breviary; and after you have got your breviary you will sit in your stall like a grand prelate, and will say to your brother: 'Hand me my breviary.'... And thenceforward he denied all such requests, saying: A man possesses of learning only so much as comes out of him in action, and a monk is a good preacher only so far as his deeds proclaim him such, for every tree is known by its fruits." [Speculum Perfectionis, ed. P. Sabatier, Paris, 1898, pp. 10, 13.]

But beyond this more worthily athletic attitude involved in doing and being, there is, in the desire of not having, something profounder still, something related to that fundamental mystery of religious experience, the satisfaction found in absolute surrender to the larger power. So long as any secular safeguard is retained, so long as any residual prudential guarantee is clung to, so long the surrender is incomplete, the vital crisis is not passed, fear still stands sentinel, and mistrust of the divine obtains: we hold by two anchors, looking to God, it is true, after a fashion, but also holding by our proper machinations. In certain medical experiences we have the same critical point to overcome. A drunkard, or a morphine or cocaine maniac, offers himself to be cured. He appeals to the doctor to wean him from his enemy, but he dares not face blank abstinence. The tyrannical drug is still an anchor to windward: he hides supplies of it among his clothing; arranges secretly to have it smuggled in in case of need. Even so an incompletely regenerate man still trusts in his own expedients. His money is like the sleeping potion which the chronically wakeful patient keeps beside his bed; he throws himself on God, but if he should need the other help, there it will be also. Every one knows cases of this incomplete and ineffective desire for reform,— drunkards whom, with all their self-reproaches and resolves, one perceives to be quite unwilling seriously to contemplate never being drunk again! Really to give up anything on which we have relied, to give it up definitively, 'for good and all' and forever, signifies one of those radical alterations of character which came under our notice in the lectures on conversion. In it the inner man rolls over into an entirely different position of equilibrium, lives in a new centre of energy from this time on, and the turning-point and hinge of all such operations seems usually to involve the sincere acceptance of certain nakednesses and destitutions.

Accordingly, throughout the annals of the saintly life, we find this ever-recurring note: Fling yourself upon God's providence without making any reserve whatever,— take no thought for the morrow,— sell all you have and give it to the poor, only when the sacrifice is ruthless and reckless will the higher safety really arrive. As a concrete example let me read a page from the biography of Antoinette Bourignon, a good woman, much persecuted in her day by both Protestants and Catholics, because she would not take her religion at second hand. When a young girl, in her father's house,

"She spent whole nights in prayer, oft repeating: Lord, what wilt thou have me to do? And being one night in a most profound penitence, she said from the bottom of her heart: 'O my Lord! What must I do to please thee? For I have nobody to teach me. Speak to my soul and it will hear thee.' At that instant she heard, as if another had spoke within her: Forsake all earthly things. Separate thyself from the love of the creatures. Deny thyself. She was quite astonished, not understanding this language, and mused long on these three points, thinking how she could fulfill them. She thought she could not live without earthly things, nor without loving the creatures, nor without loving herself. Yet she said, 'By thy Grace I will do it, Lord!' But when she would perform her promise, she knew not where to begin. Having thought on the religious in monasteries, that they forsook all earthly things by being shut up in a cloister, and the love of themselves by subjecting of their wills, she asked leave of her father to enter into a cloister of the barefoot Carmelites, but he would not permit it, saying he would rather see her laid in her grave. This seemed to her a great cruelty, for she thought to find in the cloister the true Christians she had been seeking, but she found afterwards that he knew the cloisters better than she; for after he had forbidden her, and told her he would never permit her to be a religious, nor give her any money to enter there, yet she went to Father Laurens, the Director, and offered to serve in the monastery and work hard for her bread, and be content with little, if he would receive her. At which he smiled and said: That cannot be. We must have money to build; we take no maids without money; you must find the way to get it, else there is no entry here.

"This astonished her greatly, and she was thereby undeceived as to the cloisters, resolving to forsake all company and live alone till it should please God to show her what she ought to do and whither to go. She asked always earnestly, 'When shall I be perfectly thine, O my God?' And she thought he still answered her, 'When thou shalt no longer possess anything, and shalt die to thyself. 'And where shall I do that, Lord?' He answered her, In the desert. This made so strong an impression on her soul that she aspired after this; but being a maid of eighteen years only, she was afraid of unlucky chances, and was never used to travel, and knew no way. She laid aside all these doubts and said, 'Lord, thou wilt guide me how and where it shall please thee. It is for thee that I do it. I will lay aside my habit of a maid, and will take that of a hermit that I may pass unknown.' Having then secretly made ready this habit, while her parents thought to have married her, her father having promised her to a rich French merchant, she prevented the time, and on Easter evening, having cut her hair, put on the habit, and slept a little, she went out of her chamber about four in the morning, taking nothing but one penny to buy bread for that day. And it being said to her in the going out, Where is thy faith? in a penny? she threw it away, begging pardon of God for her fault, and saying, 'No, Lord, my faith is not in a penny, but in thee alone.' Thus she went away wholly delivered from the heavy burthen of the cares and good things of this world, and found her soul so satisfied that she no longer wished for anything upon earth, resting entirely upon God, with this only fear lest she should be discovered and be obliged to return home; for she felt already more content in this poverty than she had done for all her life in all the delights of the world." [An Apology for M. Antonia Bourignon, London, 1699, pp. 269, 270, abridged.]

Another example from Starbuck's MS. collection:

"At a meeting held at six the next morning, I heard a man relate his experience. He said: The Lord asked him if he would confess Christ among the quarrymen with whom he worked, and he said he would. Then he asked him if he would give up to be used of the Lord the four hundred dollars he had laid up, and he said he would, and thus the Lord saved him. The thought came to me at once that I had never made a real consecration either of myself or of my property to the Lord, but had always tried to serve the Lord in my way. Now the Lord asked me if I would serve him in his way, and go out alone and penniless if he so ordered. The question was pressed home, and I must decide: To forsake all and have him, or have all and lose him! I soon decided to take him; and the blessed assurance came, that he had taken me for his own, and my joy was full. I returned home from the meeting with feelings as simple as a child. I thought all would be glad to hear of the joy of the Lord that possessed me, and so I began to tell the simple story. But to my great surprise, the pastors (for I attended meetings in three churches) opposed the experience and said it was fanaticism, and one told the members of his church to shun those that professed it, and I soon found that my foes were those of my own household."

The penny was a small financial safeguard, but an effective spiritual obstacle. Not till it was thrown away could the character settle into the new equilibrium completely.

Over and above the mystery of self-surrender, there are in the cult of poverty other religious mysteries. There is the mystery of veracity: "Naked came I into the world," etc.,—whoever first said that, possessed this mystery. My own bare entity must fight the battle— shams cannot save me. There is also the mystery of democracy, or sentiment of the equality before God of all his creatures. This sentiment (which seems in general to have been more widespread in Mohammedan than in Christian lands) tends to nullify man's usual acquisitiveness. Those who have it spurn dignities and honors, privileges and advantages, preferring, as I said in a former lecture, to grovel on the common level before the face of God. It is not exactly the sentiment of humility, though it comes so close to it in practice. It is humanity, rather, refusing to enjoy anything that others do not share. A profound moralist, writing of Christ's saying, 'Sell all thou hast and follow me,' proceeds as follows:

"Christ may have meant: If you love mankind absolutely you will as a result not care for any possessions whatever, and this seems a very likely proposition. But it is one thing to believe that a proposition is probably true; it is another thing to see it as a fact. If you loved mankind as Christ loved them, you would see his conclusion as a fact. It would be obvious. You would sell your goods, and they would be no loss to you, These truths, while literal to Christ, and to any mind that has Christ's love for mankind, become parables to lesser natures. There are in every generation people who, beginning innocently, with no predetermined intention of becoming saints, find themselves drawn into the vortex by their interest in helping mankind, and by the understanding that comes from actually doing it. The abandonment of their old mode of life is like dust in the balance. It is done gradually, incidentally, imperceptibly. Thus the whole question of the abandonment of luxury is no question at all, but a mere incident to another question, namely, the degree to which we abandon ourselves to the remorseless logic of our love for others." [J.J. Chapman, in the Political Nursery, vol. iv. p. 4, April, 1900, abridged.]

But in all these matters of sentiment one must have 'been there' one's self in order to understand them. No American can ever attain to understanding the loyalty of a Briton towards his king, of a German towards his emperor; nor can a Briton or German ever understand the peace of heart of an American in having no king, no Kaiser, no spurious nonsense, between him and the common God of all. If sentiments as simple as these are mysteries which one must receive as gifts of birth, how much more is this the case with those subtler religious sentiments which we have been considering! One can never fathom an emotion or divine its dictates by standing outside of it. In the glowing hour of excitement, however, all incomprehensibilities are solved, and what was so enigmatical from without becomes transparently obvious. Each emotion obeys a logic of its own, and makes deductions which no other logic can draw. Piety and charity live in a different universe from worldly lusts and fears, and form another centre of energy altogether. As in a supreme sorrow lesser vexations may become a consolation; as a supreme love may turn minor sacrifices into gain; so a supreme trust may render common safeguards odious, and in certain glows of generous excitement it may appear unspeakably mean to retain one's hold of personal possessions. The only sound plan, if we are ourselves outside the pale of such emotions, is to observe as well as we are able those who feel them, and to record faithfully what we observe; and this, I need hardly say, is what I have striven to do in these last two descriptive lectures, which I now hope will have covered the ground sufficiently for our present needs.

LECTURES XIV AND XV: THE VALUE OF SAINTLINESS

We have now passed in review the more important of the phenomena which are regarded as fruits of genuine religion and characteristics of men who are devout. Today we have to change our attitude from that of description to that of appreciation; we have to ask whether the fruits in question can help us to judge the absolute value of what religion adds to human life. Were I to parody Kant, I should say that a 'Critique of pure Saintliness' must be our theme.

If, in turning to this theme, we could descend upon our subject from above like Catholic theologians, with our fixed definitions of man and man's perfection and our positive dogmas about God, we should have an easy time of it. Man's perfection would be the fulfillment of his end; and his end would be union with his Maker. That union could be pursued by him along three paths, active, purgative, and contemplative, respectively; and progress along either path would be a simple matter to measure by the application of a limited number of theological and moral conceptions and definitions. The absolute significance and value of any bit of religious experience we might hear of would thus be given almost mathematically into our hands.

If convenience were everything, we ought now to grieve at finding ourselves cut off from so admirably convenient a method as this. But we did cut ourselves off from it deliberately in those remarks which you remember we made, in our first lecture, about the empirical method; and it must be confessed that after that act of renunciation we can never hope for clean-cut and scholastic results. We cannot divide man sharply into an animal and a rational part. We cannot distinguish natural from supernatural effects; nor among the latter know which are favors of God, and which are counterfeit operations of the demon. We have merely to collect things together without any special a priori theological system, and out of an aggregate of piecemeal judgments as to the value of this and that experience- judgments in which our general philosophic prejudices, our instincts, and our common sense are our only guides— decide that on the whole one type of religion is approved by its fruits, and another type condemned. 'On the whole,'— I fear we shall never escape complicity with that qualification, so dear to your practical man, so repugnant to your systematizer!

I also fear that as I make this frank confession, I may seem to some of you to throw our compass overboard, and to adopt caprice as our pilot. Skepticism or wayward choice, you may think, can be the only results of such a formless method as I have taken up. A few remarks in deprecation of such an opinion, and in farther explanation of the empiricist principles which I profess, may therefore appear at this point to be in place.

Abstractly, it would seem illogical to try to measure the worth of a religion's fruits in merely human terms of value. How can you measure their worth without considering whether the God really exists who is supposed to inspire them? If he really exists, then all the conduct instituted by men to meet his wants must necessarily be a reasonable fruit of his religion,— it would be unreasonable only in case he did not exist. If, for instance, you were to condemn a religion of human or animal sacrifices by virtue of your subjective sentiments, and if all the while a deity were really there demanding such sacrifices, you would be making a theoretical mistake by tacitly assuming that the deity must be non-existent; you would be setting up a theology of your own as much as if you were a scholastic philosopher.

To this extent, to the extent of disbelieving peremptorily in certain types of deity, I frankly confess that we must be theologians. If disbeliefs can be said to constitute a theology, then the prejudices, instincts, and common sense which I chose as our guides make theological partisans of us whenever they make certain beliefs abhorrent.

But such common-sense prejudices and instincts are themselves the fruit of an empirical evolution. Nothing is more striking than the secular alteration that goes on in the moral and religious tone of men, as their insight into nature and their social arrangements progressively develop. After an interval of a few generations the mental climate proves unfavorable to notions of the deity which at an earlier date were perfectly satisfactory: the older gods have fallen below the common secular level, and can no longer be believed in. Today a deity who should require bleeding sacrifices to placate him would be too sanguinary to be taken seriously. Even if powerful historical credentials were put forward in his favor, we would not look at them. Once, on the contrary, his cruel appetites were of themselves credentials. They positively recommended him to men's imaginations in ages when such coarse signs of power were respected and no others could be understood. Such deities then were worshiped because such fruits were relished.

Doubtless historic accidents always played some later part, but the original factor in fixing the figure of the gods must always have been psychological. The deity to whom the prophets, seers, and devotees who founded the particular cult bore witness was worth something to them personally. They could use him. He guided their imagination, warranted their hopes, and controlled their will,— or else they required him as a safeguard against the demon and a curber of other people's crimes. In any case, they chose him for the value of the fruits he seemed to them to yield. So soon as the fruits began to seem quite worthless; so soon as they conflicted with indispensable human ideals, or thwarted too extensively other values; so soon as they appeared childish, contemptible, or immoral when reflected on, the deity grew discredited, and was erelong neglected and forgotten. It was in this way that the Greek and Roman gods ceased to be believed in by educated pagans; it is thus that we ourselves judge of the Hindu, Buddhist, and Mohammedan theologies; Protestants have so dealt with the Catholic notions of deity, and liberal Protestants with older Protestant notions; it is thus that Chinamen judge of us, and that all of us now living will be judged by our descendants. When we cease to admire or approve what the definition of a deity implies, we end by deeming that deity incredible.

Few historic changes are more curious than these mutations of theological opinion. The monarchical type of sovereignty was, for example, so ineradicably planted in the mind of our own forefathers that a dose of cruelty and arbitrariness in their deity seems positively to have been required by their imagination. They called the cruelty 'retributive justice,' and a God without it would certainly have struck them as not 'sovereign' enough. But today we abhor the very notion of eternal suffering inflicted; and that arbitrary dealing-out of salvation and damnation to selected individuals, of which Jonathan Edwards could persuade himself that he had not only a conviction, but a 'delightful conviction,' as of a doctrine 'exceeding pleasant, bright, and sweet,' appears to us, if sovereignly anything, sovereignly irrational and mean. Not only the cruelty, but the paltriness of character of the gods believed in by earlier centuries also strikes later centuries with surprise. We shall see examples of it from the annals of Catholic saintship which make us rub our Protestant eyes. Ritual worship in general appears to the modern transcendentalist, as well as to the ultra-puritanic type of mind, as if addressed to a deity of an almost absurdly childish character, taking delight in toy-shop furniture, tapers and tinsel, costume and mumbling and mummery, and finding his 'glory' incomprehensibly enhanced thereby;— just as on the other hand the formless spaciousness of pantheism appears quite empty to ritualistic natures, and the gaunt theism of evangelical sects seems intolerably bald and chalky and bleak. Luther, says Emerson, would have would have cut off his right hand rather than nail his theses to the door at Wittenberg, if he had supposed that they were destined to lead to the pale negations of Boston Unitarianism.

So far, then, although we are compelled, whatever may be our pretensions to empiricism, to employ some sort of a standard of theological probability of our own whenever we assume to estimate the fruits of other men's religion, yet this very standard has been begotten out of the drift of common life. It is the voice of human experience within us, judging and condemning all gods that stand athwart the pathway along which it feels itself to be advancing. Experience, if we take it in the largest sense, is thus the parent of those disbeliefs which, it was charged, were inconsistent with the experiential method. The inconsistency, you see, is immaterial, and the charge may be neglected.

If we pass from disbeliefs to positive beliefs, it seems to me that there is not even a formal inconsistency to be laid against our method. The gods we stand by are the gods we need and can use, the gods whose demands on us are reinforcements of our demands on ourselves and on one another. What I then propose to do is, briefly stated, to test saintliness by common sense, to use human standards to help us decide how far the religious life commends itself as an ideal kind of human activity. If it commends itself, then any theological beliefs that may inspire it, in so far forth will stand accredited. If not, then they will be discredited, and all without reference to anything but human working principles. It is but the elimination of the humanly unfit, and the survival of the humanly fittest, applied to religious beliefs; and if we look at history candidly and without prejudice, we have to admit that no religion has ever in the long run established or proved itself in any other way. Religions have approved themselves; they have ministered to sundry vital needs which they found reigning. When they violated other needs too strongly, or when other faiths came which served the same needs better, the first religions were supplanted.

The needs were always many, and the tests were never sharp. So the reproach of vagueness and subjectivity and 'on the whole'-ness, which can with perfect legitimacy be addressed to the empirical method as we are forced to use it, is after all a reproach to which the entire life of man in dealing with these matters is obnoxious. No religion has ever yet owed its prevalence to 'apodictic certainty.' In a later lecture I will ask whether objective certainty can ever be added by theological reasoning to a religion that already empirically prevails.

One word, also, about the reproach that in following this sort of an empirical method we are handing ourselves over to systematic skepticism.

Since it is impossible to deny secular alterations in our sentiments and needs, it would be absurd to affirm that one's own age of the world can be beyond correction by the next age. Skepticism cannot, therefore, be ruled out by any set of thinkers as a possibility against which their conclusions are secure; and no empiricist ought to claim exemption from this universal liability. But to admit one's liability to correction is one thing, and to embark upon a sea of wanton doubt is another. Of willfully playing into the hands of skepticism we cannot be accused. He who acknowledges the imperfectness of his instrument, and makes allowance for it in discussing his observations, is in a much better position for gaining truth than if he claimed his instrument to be infallible. Or is dogmatic or scholastic theology less doubted in point of fact for claiming, as it does, to be in point of right undoubtable? And if not, what command over truth would this kind of theology really lose if, instead of absolute certainty, she only claimed reasonable probability for her conclusions? If we claim only reasonable probability, it will be as much as men who love the truth can ever at any given moment hope to have within their grasp. Pretty surely it will be more than we could have had, if we were unconscious of our liability to err.

Nevertheless, dogmatism will doubtless continue to condemn us for this confession. The mere outward form of inalterable certainty is so precious to some minds that to renounce it explicitly is for them out of the question. They will claim it even where the facts most patently pronounce its folly. But the safe thing is surely to recognize that all the insights of creatures of a day like ourselves must be provisional. The wisest of critics is an altering being, subject to the better insight of the morrow, and right at any moment, only 'up to date' and 'on the whole.' When larger ranges of truth open, it is surely best to be able to open ourselves to their reception, unfettered by our previous pretensions. "Heartily know, when half-gods go, the gods arrive."

The fact of diverse judgments about religious phenomena is therefore entirely unescapable, whatever may be one's own desire to attain the irreversible. But apart from that fact, a more fundamental question awaits us, the question whether men's opinions ought to be expected to be absolutely uniform in this field. Ought all men to have the same religion? Ought they to approve the same fruits and follow the same leadings? Are they so like in their inner needs that, for hard and soft, for proud and humble, for strenuous and lazy, for healthy-minded and despairing, exactly the same religious incentives are required? Or are different functions in the organism of humanity allotted to different types of man, so that some may really be the better for a religion of consolation and reassurance, whilst others are better for one of terror and reproof? It might conceivably be so; and we shall, I think, more and more suspect it to be so as we go on. And if it be so, how can any possible judge or critic help being biased in favor of the religion by which his own needs are best met? He aspires to impartiality; but he is too close to the struggle not to be to some degree a participant, and he is sure to approve most warmly those fruits of piety in others which taste most good and prove most nourishing to him.

I am well aware of how anarchic much of what I say may sound. Expressing myself thus abstractly and briefly, I may seem to despair of the very notion of truth. But I beseech you to reserve your judgment until we see it applied to the details which lie before us. I do indeed disbelieve that we or any other mortal men can attain on a given day to absolutely incorrigible and unimprovable truth about such matters of fact as those with which religions deal. But I reject this dogmatic ideal not out of a perverse delight in intellectual instability. I am no lover of disorder and doubt as such. Rather do I fear to lose truth by this pretension to possess it already wholly. That we can gain more and more of it by moving always in the right direction, I believe as much as any one, and I hope to bring you all to my way of thinking before the termination of these lectures. Till then, do not, I pray you, harden your minds irrevocably against the empiricism which I profess.

I will waste no more words, then, in abstract justification of my method, but seek immediately to use it upon the facts.

In critically judging of the value of religious phenomena, it is very important to insist on the distinction between religion as an individual personal function, and religion as an institutional, corporate, or tribal product. I drew this distinction, you may remember, in my second lecture. The word 'religion,' as ordinarily used, is equivocal. A survey of history shows us that, as a rule, religious geniuses attract disciples, and produce groups of sympathizers. When these groups get strong enough to 'organize' themselves, they become ecclesiastical institutions with corporate ambitions of their own. The Spirit of politics and the lust of dogmatic rule are then apt to enter and to contaminate the originally innocent thing; so that when we hear the word 'religion' nowadays, we think inevitably of some 'church' or other; and to some persons the word 'church' suggests so much hypocrisy and tyranny and meanness and tenacity of superstition that in a wholesale undiscerning way they glory in saying that they are 'down' on religion altogether. Even we who belong to churches do not exempt other churches than our own from the general condemnation.

But in this course of lectures ecclesiastical institutions hardly concern us at all. The religious experience which we are studying is that which lives itself out within the private breast. First-hand individual experience of this kind has always appeared as a heretical sort of innovation to those who witnessed its birth. Naked comes it into the world and lonely; and it has always, for a time at least, driven him who had it into the wilderness, often into the literal wilderness out of doors, where the Buddha, Jesus, Mohammed, St. Francis, George Fox, and so many others had to go. George Fox expresses well this isolation; and I can do no better at this point than read to you a page from his Journal, referring to the period of his youth when religion began to ferment within him seriously.

"I fasted much," Fox says, "walked abroad in solitary places many days, and often took my Bible, and sat in hollow trees and lonesome places until night came on; and frequently in the night walked mournfully about by myself; for I was a man of sorrows in the time of the first workings of the Lord in me.

"During all this time I was never joined in profession of religion with any, but gave up myself to the Lord, having forsaken all evil company, taking leave of father and mother, and all other relations, and traveled up and down as a stranger on the earth, which way the Lord inclined my heart; taking a chamber to myself in the town where I came, and tarrying sometimes more, sometimes less in a place: for I durst not stay long in a place, being afraid both of professor and profane, lest, being a tender young man, I should be hurt by conversing much with either. For which reason I kept much as a stranger, seeking heavenly wisdom and getting knowledge from the Lord; and was brought off from outward things, to rely on the Lord alone. As I had forsaken the priests, so I left the separate preachers also, and those called the most experienced people; for I saw there was none among them all that could speak to my condition. And when all my hopes in them and in all men were gone so that I had nothing outwardly to help me, nor could tell what to do; then, oh then, I heard a voice which said, 'There is one, even Jesus Christ, that can speak to thy condition.' When I heard it, my heart did leap for joy. Then the Lord let me see why there was none upon the earth that could speak to my condition. I had not fellowship with any people, priests, nor professors, nor any sort of separated people. I was afraid of all carnal talk and talkers, for I could see nothing but corruptions. When I was in the deep, under all shut up, I could not believe that I should ever overcome; my troubles, my sorrows, and my temptations were so great that I often thought I should have despaired, I was so tempted. But when Christ opened to me how he was tempted by the same devil, and had overcome him, and had brushed his head; and that through him and his power, life, grace, and spirit, I should overcome also, I had confidence in him. If I had had a king's diet, palace, and attendance, all would have been as nothing; for nothing gave me comfort but the Lord by his power. I saw professors, priests, and people were whole and at ease in that condition which was my misery, and they loved that which I would have been rid of. But the Lord did stay my desires upon himself, and my care was cast upon him alone." [George Fox: Journal, Philadelphia, 1800, pp. 59-61, abridged.]

A genuine first-hand religious experience like this is bound to be a heterodoxy to its witnesses, the prophet appearing as a mere lonely madman. If his doctrine prove contagious enough to spread to any others, it becomes a definite and labeled heresy. But if it then still prove contagious enough to triumph over persecution, it becomes itself an orthodoxy; and when a religion has become an orthodoxy, its day of inwardness is over: the spring is dry; the faithful live at second hand exclusively and stone the prophets in their turn. The new church, in spite of whatever human goodness it may foster, can be henceforth counted on as a staunch ally in every attempt to stifle the spontaneous religious spirit, and to stop all later bubblings of the fountain from which in purer days it drew its own supply of inspiration. Unless, indeed, by adopting new movements of the spirit it can make capital out of them and use them for its selfish corporate designs! Of protective action of this politic sort, promptly or tardily decided on, the dealings of the Roman ecclesiasticism with many individual saints and prophets yield examples enough for our instruction.

The plain fact is that men's minds are built, as has been often said, in water-tight compartments. Religious after a fashion, they yet have many other things in them beside their religion, and unholy entanglements and associations inevitably obtain. The basenesses so commonly charged to religion's account are thus, almost all of them, not chargeable at all to religion proper, but rather to religion's wicked practical partner, the spirit of corporate dominion. And the bigotries are most of them in their turn chargeable to religion's wicked intellectual partner, the spirit of dogmatic dominion, the passion for laying down the law in the form of an absolutely closed-in theoretic system. The ecclesiastical spirit in general is the sum of these two spirits of dominion; and I beseech you never to confound the phenomena of mere tribal or corporate psychology which it presents with those manifestations of the purely interior life which are the exclusive object of our study. The baiting of Jews, the hunting of Albigenses and Waldenses, the stoning of Quakers and ducking of Methodists, the murdering of Mormons and the massacring of Armenians, express much rather that aboriginal human neophobia, that pugnacity of which we all share the vestiges, and that unborn hatred of the alien and of eccentric and non-conforming men as aliens, than they express the positive piety of the various perpetrators. Piety is the mask, the inner force is tribal instinct. You believe as little as I do, in spite of the Christian unction with which the German emperor addressed his troops upon their way to China, that the conduct which he suggested, and in which other Christian armies went beyond them, had anything whatever to do with the interior religious life of those concerned in the performance.

Well, no more for past atrocities than for this atrocity should we make piety responsible. At most we may blame piety for not availing to check our natural passions, and sometimes for supplying them with hypocritical pretexts. But hypocrisy also imposes obligations, and with the pretext usually couples some restriction; and when the passion gust is over, the piety may bring a reaction of repentance which the irreligious natural man would not have shown.

For many of the historic aberrations which have been laid to her charge, religion as such, then, is not to blame. Yet of the charge that over-zealousness or fanaticism is one of her liabilities we cannot wholly acquit her, so I will next make a remark upon that point. But I will preface it by a preliminary remark which connects itself with much that follows.

Our survey of the phenomena of saintliness has unquestionably produced in your minds an impression of extravagance. Is it necessary, some of you have asked, as one example after another came before us, to be quite so fantastically good as that? We who have no vocation for the extremer ranges of sanctity will surely be let off at the last day if our humility, asceticism, and devoutness prove of a less convulsive sort. This practically amounts to saying that much that it is legitimate to admire in this field need nevertheless not be imitated, and that religious phenomena, like all other human phenomena, are subject to the law of the golden mean. Political reformers accomplish their successive tasks in the history of nations by being blind for the time to other causes. Great schools of art work out the effects which it is their mission to reveal, at the cost of a one-sidedness for which other schools must make amends. We accept a John Howard, a Mazzini, a Botticelli, a Michael Angelo, with a kind of indulgence. We are glad they existed to show us that way, but we are glad there are also other ways of seeing and taking life. So of many of the saints whom we have looked at. We are proud of a human nature that could be so passionately extreme, but we shrink from advising others to follow the example. The conduct we blame ourselves for not following lies nearer to the middle line of human effort. It is less dependent on particular beliefs and doctrines. It is such as wears well in different ages, such as under different skies all judges are able to commend.

The fruits of religion, in other words, are, like all human products, liable to corruption by excess. Common sense must judge them. It need not blame the votary; but it may be able to praise him only conditionally, as one who acts faithfully according to his lights. He shows us heroism in one way, but the unconditionally good way is that for which no indulgence need be asked.

We find that error by excess is exemplified by every saintly virtue. Excess, in human faculties, means usually one-sidedness or want of balance; for it is hard to imagine an essential faculty too strong, if only other faculties equally strong be there to cooperate with it in action. Strong affections need a strong will; strong active powers need a strong intellect; strong intellect needs strong sympathies, to keep life steady. If the balance exist, no one faculty can possibly be too strong— we only get the stronger all-round character. In the life of saints, technically so called, the spiritual faculties are strong, but what gives the impression of extravagance proves usually on examination to be a relative deficiency of intellect. Spiritual excitement takes pathological forms whenever other interests are too few and the intellect too narrow. We find this exemplified by all the saintly attributes in turn— devout love of God, purity, charity, asceticism, all may lead astray. I will run over these virtues in succession.

First of all let us take Devoutness. When unbalanced, one of its vices is called Fanaticism. Fanaticism (when not a mere expression of ecclesiastical ambition) is only loyalty carried to a convulsive extreme. When an intensely loyal and narrow mind is once grasped by the feeling that a certain superhuman person is worthy of its exclusive devotion, one of the first things that happens is that it idealizes the devotion itself. To adequately realize the merits of the idol gets to be considered the one great merit of the worshiper; and the sacrifices and servilities by which savage tribesmen have from time immemorial exhibited their faithfulness to chieftains are now outbid in favor of the deity. Vocabularies are exhausted and languages altered in the attempt to praise him enough; death is looked on as gain if it attract his grateful notice; and the personal attitude of being his devotee becomes what one might almost call a new and exalted kind of professional specialty within the tribe. The legends that gather round the lives of holy persons are fruits of this impulse to celebrate and glorify, The Buddha [Compare H.C. Warren: Buddhism in Translation, Cambridge, U.S., 1898, passim.] and Mohammed [Compare J.L. Merrick: The Life and Religion of Mohammed, as contained in the Sheeah traditions of the Hyat-ul-Kuloob, Boston, 1850, passim.] and their companions and many Christian saints are incrusted with a heavy jewelry of anecdotes which are meant to be honorific, but are simply abgeschmackt and silly, and form a touching expression of man's misguided propensity to praise.

Christian saints have had their specialties of devotion, Saint Francis to Christ's wounds; Saint Anthony of Padua to Christ's childhood; Saint Bernard to his humanity; Saint Teresa to Saint Joseph, etc. The Shi-ite Mohammedans venerate Ali, the Prophet's son-in-law, instead of Abu-bekr, his brother-in-law. Vambery describes a dervish whom he met in Persia, "who had solemnly vowed, thirty years before, that he would never employ his organs of speech otherwise but in uttering, everlastingly, the name of his favorite, Ali, Ali. He thus wished to signify to the world that he was the most devoted partisan of that Ali who had been dead a thousand years. In his own home, speaking with his wife, children, and friends, no other word but 'Ali!' ever passed his lips. If he wanted food or drink or anything else, he expressed his wants still by repeating 'Ali!' Begging or buying at the bazaar, it was always 'Ali!' Treated ill or generously, he would still harp on his monotonous 'Ali!' Latterly his zeal assumed such tremendous proportions that, like a madman, he would race, the whole day, up and down the streets of the town, throwing his stick high up into the air, and shriek out, all the while, at the top of his voice, 'Ali!' This dervish was venerated by everybody as a saint, and received everywhere with the greatest distinction." [Arminius Vambery, his Life and Adventures, written by Himself, London, 1889, p. 69.] On the anniversary of the death of Hussein, Ali's son, the Shi-ite Moslems still make the air resound with cries of his name and Ali's.

An immediate consequence of this condition of mind is jealousy for the deity's honor. How can the devotee show his loyalty better than by sensitiveness in this regard? The slightest affront or neglect must be resented, the deity's enemies must be put to shame. In exceedingly narrow minds and active wills, such a care may become an engrossing preoccupation; and crusades have been preached and massacres instigated for no other reason than to remove a fancied slight upon the God. Theologies representing the gods as mindful of their glory, and churches with imperialistic policies, have conspired to fan this temper to a glow, so that intolerance and persecution have come to be vices associated by some of us inseparably with the saintly mind. They are unquestionably its besetting sins. The Saintly temper is a moral temper, and a moral temper has often to be cruel. It is a partisan temper, and that is cruel. Between his own and Jehovah's enemies a David knows no difference; a Catherine of Siena, panting to stop the warfare among Christians which was the scandal of her epoch, can think of no better method of union among them than a crusade to massacre the Turks; Luther finds no word of protest or regret over the atrocious tortures with which the Anabaptist leaders were put to death; and a Cromwell praises the Lord for delivering his enemies into his hands for 'execution.' Politics come in in all such cases; but piety finds the partnership not quite unnatural. So, when 'freethinkers' tell us that religion and fanaticism are twins, we cannot make an unqualified denial of the charge.

Fanaticism must then be inscribed on the wrong side of religion's account, so long as the religious person's intellect is on the stage which the despotic kind of God satisfies. But as soon as the God is represented as less intent on his own honor and glory, it ceases to be a danger.

Fanaticism is found only where the character is masterful and aggressive. In gentle characters, where devoutness is intense and the intellect feeble, we have an imaginative absorption in the love of God to the exclusion of all practical human interests, which, though innocent enough, is too one-sided to be admirable. A mind too narrow has room but for one kind of affection. When the love of God takes possession of such a mind, it expels all human loves and human uses. There is no English name for such a sweet excess of devotion, so I will refer to it as a theopathic condition.

The blessed Margaret Mary Alacoque may serve as an example.

"To be loved here upon the earth," her recent biographer exclaims: "to be loved by a noble, elevated, distinguished being; to be loved with fidelity, with devotion,— what enchantment! But to be loved by God! and loved by him to distraction [aime jusqu'a la folie]!— Margaret melted away with love at the thought of such a thing. Like Saint Philip of Neri in former times, or like Saint Francis Xavier, she said to God: 'Hold back, O my God, these torrents which overwhelm me, or else enlarge my capacity for their reception.'" [Bougaud: Hist. de la bienheureuse Marguerite Marie, Paris, 1894, p. 145.]

The most signal proofs of God's love which Margaret Mary received were her hallucinations of sight, touch, and hearing, and the most signal in turn of these were the revelations of Christ's sacred heart, "surrounded with rays more brilliant than the Sun, and transparent like a crystal. The wound which he received on the cross visibly appeared upon it. There was a crown of thorns round about this divine Heart, and a cross above it." At the same time Christ's voice told her that, unable longer to contain the flames of his love for mankind, he had chosen her by a miracle to spread the knowledge of them. He thereupon took out her mortal heart, placed it inside of his own and inflamed it, and then replaced it in her breast, adding: "Hitherto thou hast taken the name of my slave, hereafter thou shalt be called the well-beloved disciple of my Sacred Heart."

In a later vision the Saviour revealed to her in detail the 'great design' which he wished to establish through her instrumentality. "I ask of thee to bring it about that every first Friday after the week of holy Sacrament shall be made into a special holy day for honoring my Heart by a general communion and by services intended to make honorable amends for the indignities which it has received. And I promise thee that my Heart will dilate to shed with abundance the influences of its love upon all those who pay to it these honors, or who bring it about that others do the same."

"This revelation," says Mgr. Bougaud, "is unquestionably the most important of all the revelations which have illumined the Church since that of the Incarnation and of the Lord's Supper.... After the Eucharist, the supreme effort of the Sacred Heart." Well, what were its good fruits for Margaret Mary's life? Apparently little else but sufferings and prayers and absences of mind and swoons and ecstasies. She became increasingly useless about the convent, her absorption in Christ's love,— [Bougaud: Hist. de la bienheureuse Marguerite Marie, Paris, 1894, pp. 365, 241.]

"Which grew upon her daily, rendering her more and more incapable of attending to external duties. They tried her in the infirmary, but without much success, although her kindness, zeal, and devotion were without bounds, and her charity rose to acts of such a heroism that our readers would not bear the recital of them. They tried her in the kitchen, but were forced to give it up as hopeless— everything dropped out of her hands. The admirable humility with which she made amends for her clumsiness could not prevent this from being prejudicial to the order and regularity which must always reign in a community. They put her in the school, where the little girls cherished her, and cut pieces out of her clothes [for relics] as if she were already a saint, but where she was too absorbed inwardly to pay the necessary attention. Poor dear sister, even less after her visions than before them was she a denizen of earth, and they had to leave her in her heaven." [Bougaud: Op. cit., p. 267.]

Poor dear sister, indeed! Amiable and good, but so feeble of intellectual outlook that it would be too much to ask of us, with our Protestant and modern education, to feel anything but indulgent pity for the kind of saintship which she embodies. A lower example still of theopathic saintliness is that of Saint Gertrude, a Benedictine nun of the thirteenth century, whose 'Revelations,' a well-known mystical authority, consist mainly of proofs of Christ's partiality for her undeserving person. Assurances of his love, intimacies and caresses and compliments of the most absurd and puerile sort, addressed by Christ to Gertrude as an individual, form the tissue of this paltry-minded recital. In reading such a narrative, we realize the gap between the thirteenth and the twentieth century, and we feel that saintliness of character may yield almost absolutely worthless fruits if it be associated with such inferior intellectual sympathies. What with science, idealism, and democracy, our own imagination has grown to need a God of an entirely different temperament from that Being interested exclusively in dealing out personal favors, with whom our ancestors were so contented. Smitten as we are with the vision of social righteousness, a God indifferent to everything but adulation, and full of partiality for his individual favorites, lacks an essential element of largeness; and even the best professional sainthood of former centuries, pent in as it is to such a conception, seems to us curiously shallow and unedifying.

Examples: "Suffering from a headache, she sought, for the glory of God, to relieve herself by holding certain odoriferous substances in her mouth, when the Lord appeared to her to lean over towards her lovingly, and to find comfort Himself in these odors. After having gently breathed them in, He arose, and said with a gratified air to the Saints, as if contented with what He had done: 'See the new present which my betrothed has given Me!'

"One day, at chapel, she heard supernaturally sung the words, 'Sanctus, Sanctus, Sanctus.' The Son of God leaning towards her like a sweet lover, and giving to her soul the softest kiss, said to her at the second Sanctus: 'In this Sanctus addressed to my person, receive with this kiss all the sanctity of my divinity and of my humanity, and let it be to thee a sufficient preparation for approaching the communion table.' And the next following Sunday, while she was thanking God for this favor, behold the Son of God, more beauteous than thousands of angels, takes her in His arms as if He were proud of her, and presents her to God the Father, in that perfection of sanctity with which He had dowered her. And the Father took such delight in this soul thus presented by His only Son, that, as if unable longer to restrain Himself, He gave her, and the Holy Ghost gave her also, the Sanctity attributed to each by His own Sanctus— and thus she remained endowed with the plenary fullness of the blessing of Sanctity, bestowed on her by Omnipotence, by Wisdom, and by Love." Revelations de Sainte Gertrude, Paris, 1898, i. 44, 186.

Take Saint Teresa, for example, one of the ablest women, in many respects, of whose life we have the record. She had a powerful intellect of the practical order. She wrote admirable descriptive psychology, possessed a will equal to any emergency, great talent for politics and business, a buoyant disposition, and a first-rate literary style. She was tenaciously aspiring, and put her whole life at the service of her religious ideals. Yet so paltry were these, according to our present way of thinking, that (although I know that others have been moved differently) I confess that my only feeling in reading her has been pity that so much vitality of soul should have found such poor employment.

In spite of the sufferings which she endured, there is a curious flavor of superficiality about her genius. A Birmingham anthropologist, Dr. Jordan, has divided the human race into two types, whom he calls 'shrews' and 'non-shrews' respectively. The shrew-type is defined as possessing an 'active unimpassioned temperament.' In other words, shrews are the 'motors,' rather than the 'sensories,' and their expressions are as a rule more energetic than the feelings which appear to prompt them. Saint Teresa, paradoxical as such a judgment may sound, was a typical shrew, in this sense of the term. The bustle of her style, as well as of her life, proves it. Not only must she receive unheard-of personal favors and spiritual graces from her Saviour, but she must immediately write about them and exploiter them professionally, and use her expertness to give instruction to those less privileged. Her voluble egotism; her sense, not of radical bad being, as the really contrite have it, but of her 'faults' and 'imperfections' in the plural; her stereo-typed humility and return upon herself, as covered with 'confusion' at each new manifestation of God's singular partiality for a person so unworthy, are typical of shrewdom: a paramountly feeling nature would be objectively lost in gratitude, and silent. She had some public instincts, it is true; she hated the Lutherans, and longed for the church's triumph over them; but in the main her idea of religion seems to have been that of an endless amatory flirtation— if one may say so without irreverence—between the devotee and the deity; and apart from helping younger nuns to go in this direction by the inspiration of her example and instruction, there is absolutely no human use in her, or sign of any general human interest. Yet the spirit of her age, far from rebuking her, exalted her as superhuman.

We have to pass a similar judgment on the whole notion of saintship based on merits. Any God who, on the one hand, can care to keep a pedantically minute account of individual shortcomings, and on the other can feel such partialities, and load particular creatures with such insipid marks of favor, is too small-minded a God for our credence. When Luther, in his immense manly way, swept off by a stroke of his hand the very notion of a debit and credit account kept with individuals by the Almighty, he stretched the soul's imagination and saved theology from puerility.

So much for mere devotion, divorced from the intellectual conceptions which might guide it towards bearing useful human fruit.

The next saintly virtue in which we find excess is Purity. In theopathic characters, like those whom we have just considered, the love of God must not be mixed with any other love. Father and mother, sisters, brothers, and friends are felt as interfering distractions; for sensitiveness and narrowness, when they occur together, as they often do, require above all things a simplified world to dwell in. Variety and confusion are too much for their powers of comfortable adaptation. But whereas your aggressive pietist reaches his unity objectively, by forcibly stamping disorder and divergence out, your retiring pietist reaches his subjectively, leaving disorder in the world at large, but making a smaller world in which he dwells himself and from which he eliminates it altogether. Thus, alongside of the church militant with its prisons, dragonnades, and inquisition methods, we have the church fugient, as one might call it, with its hermitages, monasteries, and sectarian organizations, both churches pursuing the same object— to unify the life, and simplify the spectacle presented to the soul. A mind extremely sensitive to inner discords will drop one external relation after another, as interfering with the absorption of consciousness in spiritual things. Amusements must go first, then conventional 'society,' then business, then family duties, until at last seclusion, with a subdivision of the day into hours for stated religious acts, is the only thing that can be borne. The lives of saints are a history of successive renunciations of complication, one form of contact with the outer life being dropped after another, to save the purity of inner tone. "Is it not better," a young sister asks her Superior, "that I should not speak at all during the hour of recreation, so as not to run the risk, by speaking, of falling into some sin of which I might not be conscious?" If the life remains a social one at all, those who take part in it must follow one identical rule. Embosomed in this monotony, the zealot for purity feels clean and free once more. The minuteness of uniformity maintained in certain sectarian communities, whether monastic or not, is something almost inconceivable to a man of the world. Costume, phraseology, hours, and habits are absolutely stereotyped, and there is no doubt that some persons are so made as to find in this stability an incomparable kind of mental rest.

On this subject I refer to the work of M. Murisier (Les Maladies du Sentiment Religieux, Paris, 1901), who makes inner unification the mainspring of the whole religious life. But all strongly ideal interests, religious or irreligious, unify the mind and tend to subordinate everything to themselves. One would infer from M. Murisier's pages that this formal condition was peculiarly characteristic of religion, and that one might in comparison almost neglect material content, in studying the latter. I trust that the present work will convince the reader that religion has plenty of material content which is characteristic, and which is more important by far than any general psychological form. In spite of this criticism, I find M. Murisier's book highly instructive.

Example: "At the first beginning of the Servitor's [Suso's] interior life, after he had purified his soul properly by confession, he marked out for himself, in thought, three circles, within which he shut himself up, as in a spiritual intrenchment. The first circle was his cell, his chapel, and the choir. When he was within this circle, he seemed to himself in complete security. The second circle was the whole monastery as far as the outer gate. The third and outermost circle was the gate itself, and here it was necessary for him to stand well upon his guard. When he went outside these circles, it seemed to him that he was in the plight of some wild animal which is outside its hole, and surrounded by the hunt, and therefore in need of all its cunning and watchfulness." The Life of the Blessed Henry Suso, by Himself, translated by Knox, London, 1865, p. 168.

We have no time to multiply examples, so I will let the case of Saint Louis of Gonzaga serve as a type of excess in purification. I think you will agree that this youth carried the elimination of the external and discordant to a point which we cannot unreservedly admire. At the age of ten, his biographer says:—

"The inspiration came to him to consecrate to the Mother of God his own virginity— that being to her the most agreeable of possible presents. Without delay, then, and with all the fervor there was in him, joyous of heart, and burning with love, he made his vow of perpetual chastity. Mary accepted the offering of his innocent heart, and obtained for him from God, as a recompense, the extraordinary grace of never feeling during his entire life the slightest touch of temptation against the virtue of purity. This was an altogether exceptional favor, rarely accorded even to Saints themselves, and all the more marvelous in that Louis dwelt always in courts and among great folks, where danger and opportunity are so unusually frequent. It is true that Louis from his earliest childhood had shown a natural repugnance for whatever might be impure or unvirginal, and even for relations of any sort whatever between persons of opposite sex. But this made it all the more surprising that he should, especially since this vow, feel it necessary to have recourse to such a number of expedients for protecting against even the shadow of danger the virginity which he had thus consecrated. One might suppose that if any one could have contented himself with the ordinary precautions, prescribed for all Christians, it would assuredly have been he. But no! In the use of preservatives and means of defense, in flight from the most insignificant occasions, from every possibility of peril, just as in the mortification of his flesh, he went farther than the majority of saints. He, who by an extraordinary protection of God's grace was never tempted, measured all his steps as if he were threatened on every side by particular dangers. Thence forward he never raised his eyes, either when walking in the streets, or when in society. Not only did he avoid all business with females even more scrupulously than before, but he renounced all conversation and every kind of social recreation with them, although his father tried to make him take part; and he commenced only too early to deliver his innocent body to austerities of every kind." [Meschler's Life of Saint Louis of Gonzaga, French translation by Lebrequier, 1891, p. 40.]

At the age of twelve, we read of this young man that "if by chance his mother sent one of her maids of honor to him with a message, he never allowed her to come in, but listened to her through the barely opened door, and dismissed her immediately. He did not like to be alone with his own mother, whether at table or in conversation; and when the rest of the company withdrew, he sought also a pretext for retiring.... Several great ladies, relatives of his, he avoided learning to know even by sight; and he made a sort of treaty with his father, engaging promptly and readily to accede to all his wishes, if he might only be excused from all visits to ladies."

When he was seventeen years old Louis joined the Jesuit order, against his father's passionate entreaties, for he was heir of a princely house; and when a year later the father died, he took the loss as a 'particular attention' to himself on God's part, and wrote letters of stilted good advice, as from a spiritual superior, to his grieving mother. He soon became so good a monk that if any one asked him the number of his brothers and sisters, he had to reflect and count them over before replying. A Father asked him one day if he were never troubled by the thought of his family, to which, "I never think of them except when praying for them," was his only answer. Never was he seen to hold in his hand a flower or anything perfumed, that he might take pleasure in it. On the contrary, in the hospital, he used to seek for whatever was most disgusting, and eagerly snatch the bandages of ulcers, etc., from the hands of his companions. He avoided worldly talk, and immediately tried to turn every conversation on to pious subjects, or else he remained silent. He systematically refused to notice his surroundings. Being ordered one day to bring a book from the rector's seat in the refectory, he had to ask where the rector sat, for in the three months he had eaten bread there, so carefully did he guard his eyes that he had not noticed the place. One day, during recess, having looked by chance on one of his companions, he reproached himself as for a grave sin against modesty. He cultivated silence, as preserving from sins of the tongue; and his greatest penance was the limit which his superiors set to his bodily penances. He sought after false accusations and unjust reprimands as opportunities of humility; and such was his obedience that, when a room-mate, having no more paper, asked him for a sheet, he did not feel free to give it to him without first obtaining the permission of the superior, who, as such, stood in the place of God, and transmitted his orders.

I can find no other sorts of fruit than these of Louis's saintship. He died in 1591, in his twenty-ninth year, and is known in the Church as the patron of all young people. On his festival, the altar in the chapel devoted to him in a certain church in Rome "is embosomed in flowers, arranged with exquisite taste; and a pile of letters may be seen at its foot, written to the Saint by young men and women, and directed to 'Paradiso.' They are supposed to be burnt unread except by San Luigi, who must find singular petitions in these pretty little missives, tied up now with a green ribbon, expressive of hope, now with a red one, emblematic of love," etc. [Mademoiselle Mori, a novel quoted in Hare's Walks in Rome, 1900, i. 55.]

I cannot resist the temptation to quote from Starbuck's book, p. 388, another case of purification by elimination. It runs as follows:

"The signs of abnormality which sanctified persons show are of frequent occurrence. They get out of tune with other people; often they will have nothing to do with churches, which they regard as worldly; they become hypercritical towards others; they grow careless of their social, political, and financial obligations. As an instance of this type may be mentioned a woman of sixty-eight of whom the writer made a special study. She had been a member of one of the most active and progressive churches in a busy part of a large city. Her pastor described her as having reached the censorious stage. She had grown more and more out of sympathy with the church; her connection with it finally consisted simply in attendance at prayer-meeting, at which her only message was that of reproof and condemnation of the others for living on a low plane. At last she withdrew from fellowship with any church. The writer found her living alone in a little room on the top story of a cheap boarding-house, quite out of touch with all human relations, but apparently happy in the enjoyment of her own spiritual blessings. Her time was occupied in writing booklets on sanctification— page after page of dreamy rhapsody. She proved to be one of a small group of persons who claim that entire salvation involves three steps instead of two; not only must there be conversion and sanctification, but a third, which they call 'crucifixion' or 'perfect redemption,' and which seems to bear the same relation to sanctification that this bears to conversion. She related how the Spirit had said to her, 'Stop going to church. Stop going to holiness meetings. Go to your own room and I will teach you.' She professes to care nothing for colleges, or preachers, or churches, but only cares to listen to what God says to her. Her description of her experience seemed entirely consistent; she is happy and contented, and her life is entirely satisfactory to herself. While listening to her own story, one was tempted to forget that it was from the life of a person who could not live by it in conjunction with her fellows."

Our final judgment of the worth of such a life as this will depend largely on our conception of God, and of the sort of conduct he is best pleased with in his creatures. The Catholicism of the sixteenth century paid little heed to social righteousness; and to leave the world to the devil whilst saving one's own soul was then accounted no discreditable scheme. Today, rightly or wrongly, helpfulness in general human affairs is, in consequence of one of those secular mutations in moral sentiment of which I spoke, deemed an essential element of worth in character; and to be of some public or private use is also reckoned as a species of divine service. Other early Jesuits, especially the missionaries among them, the Xaviers, Brebeufs, Jogues, were objective minds, and fought in their way for the world's welfare; so their lives today inspire us. But when the intellect, as in this Louis, is originally no larger than a pin's head, and cherishes ideas of God of corresponding smallness, the result, notwithstanding the heroism put forth, is on the whole repulsive. Purity, we see in the object-lesson, is not the one thing needful; and it is better that a life should contract many a dirt-mark, than forfeit usefulness in its efforts to remain unspotted.

Proceeding onwards in our search of religious extravagance, we next come upon excesses of Tenderness and Charity. Here saintliness has to face the charge of preserving the unfit, and breeding parasites and beggars. 'Resist not evil,' 'Love your enemies,' these are saintly maxims of which men of this world find it hard to speak without impatience. Are the men of this world right, or are the saints in possession of the deeper range of truth?

No simple answer is possible. Here, if anywhere, one feels the complexity of the moral life, and the mysteriousness of the way in which facts and ideals are interwoven.

Perfect conduct is a relation between three terms: the actor, the objects for which he acts, and the recipients of the action. In order that conduct should be abstractly perfect, all three terms, intention, execution, and reception, should be suited to one another. The best intention will fail if it either work by false means or address itself to the wrong recipient. Thus no critic or estimator of the value of conduct can confine himself to the actor's animus alone, apart from the other elements of the performance. As there is no worse lie than a truth misunderstood by those who hear it, so reasonable arguments, challenges to magnanimity, and appeals to sympathy or justice, are folly when we are dealing with human crocodiles and boa-constrictors. The saint may simply give the universe into the hands of the enemy by his trustfulness. He may by non-resistance cut off his own survival.

Herbert Spencer tells us that the perfect man's conduct will appear perfect only when the environment is perfect: to no inferior environment is it suitably adapted. We may paraphrase this by cordially admitting that saintly conduct would be the most perfect conduct conceivable in an environment where all were saints already; but by adding that in an environment where few are saints, and many the exact reverse of saints, it must be ill adapted. We must frankly confess, then, using our empirical common sense and ordinary practical prejudices, that in the world that actually is, the virtues of sympathy, charity, and non-resistance may be, and often have been, manifested in excess. The powers of darkness have systematically taken advantage of them. The whole modern scientific organization of charity is a consequence of the failure of simply giving alms. The whole history of constitutional government is a commentary on the excellence of resisting evil, and when one cheek is smitten, of smiting back and not turning the other cheek also.

You will agree to this in general, for in spite of the Gospel, in spite of Quakerism, in spite of Tolstoy, you believe in fighting fire with fire, in shooting down usurpers, locking up thieves, and freezing out vagabonds and swindlers.

And yet you are sure, as I am sure, that were the world confined to these hard-headed, hard-hearted, and hard-fisted methods exclusively, were there no one prompt to help a brother first, and find out afterwards whether he were worthy; no one willing to drown his private wrongs in pity for the wronger's person; no one ready to be duped many a time rather than live always on suspicion; no one glad to treat individuals passionately and impulsively rather than by general rules of prudence; the world would be an infinitely worse place than it is now to live in. The tender grace, not of a day that is dead, but of a day yet to be born somehow, with the golden rule grown natural, would be cut out from the perspective of our imaginations.

The saints, existing in this way, may, with their extravagances of human tenderness, be prophetic. Nay, innumerable times they have

proved themselves prophetic. Treating those whom they met, in spite of
the past, in spite of all appearances, as worthy, they have stimulated
them to be worthy, miraculously transformed them by their radiant
example and by the challenge of their expectation.

From this point of view we may admit the human charity which we find
in all saints, and the great excess of it which we find in some saints, to be
a genuinely creative social force, tending to make real a degree of virtue
which it alone is ready to assume as possible. The saints are authors,
auctores, increasers, of goodness. The potentialities of development in
human souls are unfathomable. So many who seemed irretrievably
hardened have in point of fact been softened, converted, regenerated, in
ways that amazed the subjects even more than they surprised the
spectators, that we never can be sure in advance of any man that his
salvation by the way of love is hopeless. We have no right to speak of
human crocodiles and boa-constrictors as of fixedly incurable beings. We
know not the complexities of personality, the smouldering emotional fires,
the other facets of the character-polyhedron, the resources of the
subliminal region. St. Paul long ago made our ancestors familiar with the
idea that every soul is virtually sacred. Since Christ died for us all
without exception, St. Paul said, we must despair of no one. This belief in
the essential sacredness of every one expresses itself today in all sorts of
humane customs and reformatory institutions, and in a growing aversion
to the death penalty and to brutality in punishment. The saints, with
their extravagance of human tenderness, are the great torch-bearers of
this belief, the tip of the wedge, the clearers of the darkness. Like the
single drops which sparkle in the sun as they are flung far ahead of the
advancing edge of a wave-crest or of a flood, they show the way and are
forerunners. The world is not yet with them, so they often seem in the
midst of the world's affairs to be preposterous. Yet they are impregnators
of the world, vivifiers and animaters of potentialities of goodness which
but for them would lie forever dormant. It is not possible to be quite as
mean as we naturally are, when they have passed before us. One fire
kindles another; and without that over-trust in human worth which they
show, the rest of us would lie in spiritual stagnancy.

Momentarily considered, then, the saint may waste his tenderness and
be the dupe and victim of his charitable fever, but the general function of
his charity in social evolution is vital and essential. If things are ever to
move upward, some one must be ready to take the first step, and assume
the risk of it. No one who is not willing to try charity, to try non-resistance
as the saint is always willing, can tell whether these methods will or will
not succeed. When they do succeed, they are far more powerfully
successful than force or worldly prudence. Force destroys enemies; and
the best that can be said of prudence is that it keeps what we already
have in safety. But non-resistance, when successful, turns enemies into
friends; and charity regenerates its objects. These saintly methods are, as
I said, creative energies; and genuine saints find in the elevated
excitement with which their faith endows them an authority and
impressiveness which makes them irresistible in situations where men of

shallower nature cannot get on at all without the use of worldly prudence. This practical proof that worldly wisdom may be safely transcended is the saint's magic gift to mankind. Not only does his vision of a better world console us for the generally prevailing prose and barrenness; but even when on the whole we have to confess him ill adapted, he makes some converts, and the environment gets better for his ministry. He is an effective ferment of goodness, a slow transmuter of the earthly into a more heavenly order.

In this respect the Utopian dreams of social justice in which many contemporary socialists and anarchists indulge are, in spite of their impracticability and non-adaptation to present environmental conditions, analogous to the saint's belief in an existent kingdom of heaven. They help to break the edge of the general reign of hardness, and are slow leavens of a better order.

The best missionary lives abound in the victorious combination of non-resistance with personal authority. John G. Paton, for example, in the New Hebrides, among brutish Melanesian cannibals, preserves a charmed life by dint of it. When it comes to the point, no one ever dares actually to strike him. Native converts, inspired by him, showed analogous virtue. "One of our chiefs, full of the Christ-kindled desire to seek and to save, sent a message to an inland chief, that he and four attendants would come on Sabbath and tell them the gospel of Jehovah God. The reply came back sternly forbidding their visit, and threatening with death any Christian that approached their village. Our chief sent in response a loving message, telling them that Jehovah had taught the Christians to return good for evil, and that they would come unarmed to tell them the story of how the Son of God came into the world and died in order to bless and save his enemies. The heathen chief sent back a stern and prompt reply once more: 'If you come, you will be killed.' On Sabbath morn the Christian chief and his four companions were met outside the village by the heathen chief, who implored and threatened them once more. But the former said:

"'We come to you without weapons of war! We come only to tell you about Jesus. We believe that He will protect us today.'

"As they pressed steadily forward towards the village, spears began to be thrown at them. Some they evaded, being all except one dexterous warriors; and others they literally received with their bare hands, and turned them aside in an incredible manner. The heathen, apparently thunderstruck at these men thus approaching them without weapons of war, and not even flinging back their own spears which they had caught, after having thrown what the old chief called 'a shower of spears,' desisted from mere surprise. Our Christian chief called out, as he and his companions drew up in the midst of them on the village public ground:

"'Jehovah thus protects us. He has given us all your spears! Once we would have thrown them back at you and killed you. But now we come, not to fight but to tell you about Jesus. He has changed our dark hearts. He asks you now to lay down all these your other weapons of war, and to hear what we can tell you about the love of God, our great Father, the only living God.'

"The heathen were perfectly overawed. They manifestly looked on these Christians as protected by some Invisible One. They listened for the first time to the story of the Gospel and of the Cross. We lived to see that chief and all his tribe sitting in the school of Christ. And there is perhaps not an island in these southern seas, amongst all those won for Christ, where similar acts of heroism on the part of converts cannot be recited." [John G. Paton, Missionary to the New Hebrides, An Autobiography, second part, London, 1890, p. 243.]

The next topic in order is Asceticism, which I fancy you are all ready to consider without argument a virtue liable to extravagance and excess. The optimism and refinement of the modern imagination has, as I have already said elsewhere, changed the attitude of the church towards corporeal mortification, and a Suso or a Saint Peter of Alcantara appear to us today rather in the light of tragic mountebanks than of sane men inspiring us with respect. If the inner dispositions are right, we ask, what need of all this torment, this violation of the outer nature? It keeps the outer nature too important. Any one who is genuinely emancipated from the flesh will look on pleasures and pains, abundance and privation, as alike irrelevant and indifferent. He can engage in actions and experience enjoyments without fear of corruption or enslavement. As the Bhagavad-Gita says, only those need renounce worldly actions who are still inwardly attached thereto. If one be really unattached to the fruits of action, one may mix in the world with equanimity. I quoted in a former lecture Saint Augustine's antinomian saying: If you only love God enough, you may safely follow all your inclinations. "He needs no devotional practices," is one of Ramakrishna's maxims, "whose heart is moved to tears at the mere mention of the name of Hari." And the Buddha, in pointing out what he called 'the middle way' to his disciples, told them to abstain from both extremes, excessive mortification being as unreal and unworthy as mere desire and pleasure. The only perfect life, he said, is that of inner wisdom, which makes one thing as indifferent to us as another, and thus leads to rest, to peace, and to Nirvana.

Saint Peter, Saint Teresa tells us in her autobiography (French translation, p. 333), "had passed forty years without ever sleeping more than an hour and a half a day. Of all his mortifications, this was the one that had cost him the most. To compass it, he kept always on his knees or on his feet. The little sleep he allowed nature to take was snatched in a sitting posture, his head leaning against a piece of wood fixed in the wall. Even had he wished to lie down, it would have been impossible, because his cell was only four feet and a half long. In the course of all these years he never raised his hood, no matter what the ardor of the sun or the rain's strength. He never put on a shoe. He wore a garment of coarse sackcloth, with nothing else upon his skin. This garment was as scant as possible, and over it a little cloak of the same stuff. When the cold was great he took off the cloak and opened for a while the door and little window of his cell. Then he closed them and resumed the mantle,— his way, as he told us, of warming himself, and making his body feel a better temperature. It was a frequent thing with him to eat once only in three days; and when I expressed my surprise, he said that it was very easy if one once had acquired the habit. One of his companions has assured me that he has gone sometimes eight days without food.... His poverty was extreme; and his mortification, even in his youth, was such that he told me he had passed three years in a house of his order without knowing any of the monks otherwise than by the sound of their voice, for he never raised his eyes, and only found his way about by following the others. He showed this same modesty on public highways. He spent many years without ever laying eyes upon a woman; but he confessed to me that at the age he had reached it was indifferent to him whether he laid eyes on them or not. He was very old when I first came to know him, and his body so attenuated that it seemed formed of nothing so much as of so many roots of trees. With all this sanctity he was very affable. He never spoke unless he was questioned, but his intellectual right-mindedness and grace gave to all his words an irresistible charm."

We find accordingly that as ascetic saints have grown older, and directors of conscience more experienced, they usually have shown a tendency to lay less stress on special bodily mortifications. Catholic teachers have always professed the rule that, since health is needed for efficiency in God's service, health must not be sacrificed to mortification. The general optimism and healthy-mindedness of liberal Protestant circles today makes mortification for mortification's sake repugnant to us. We can no longer sympathize with cruel deities, and the notion that God can take delight in the spectacle of sufferings self-inflicted in his honor is abhorrent. In consequence of all these motives you probably are disposed, unless some special utility can be shown in some individual's discipline, to treat the general tendency to asceticism as pathological.

Yet I believe that a more careful consideration of the whole matter, distinguishing between the general good intention of asceticism and the uselessness of some of the particular acts of which it may be guilty, ought to rehabilitate it in our esteem. For in its spiritual meaning asceticism stands for nothing less than for the essence of the twice-born philosophy. It symbolizes, lamely enough no doubt, but sincerely, the belief that there is an element of real wrongness in this world, which is neither to be ignored nor evaded, but which must be squarely met and overcome by an appeal to the soul's heroic resources, and neutralized and cleansed away by suffering. As against this view, the ultra-optimistic form of the once-born philosophy thinks we may treat evil by the method of ignoring. Let a man who, by fortunate health and circumstances, escapes the suffering of any great amount of evil in his own person, also close his eyes to it as it exists in the wider universe outside his private experience, and he will be quit of it altogether, and can sail through life happily on a healthy-minded basis. But we saw in our lectures on melancholy how precarious this attempt necessarily is. Moreover it is but for the individual; and leaves the evil outside of him, unredeemed and unprovided for in his philosophy.

No such attempt can be a general solution of the problem; and to minds of sombre tinge, who naturally feel life as a tragic mystery, such optimism is a shallow dodge or mean evasion. It accepts, in lieu of a real deliverance, what is a lucky personal accident merely, a cranny to escape by. It leaves the general world unhelped and still in the clutch of Satan. The real deliverance, the twice-born folk insist, must be of universal application. Pain and wrong and death must be fairly met and overcome in higher excitement, or else their sting remains essentially unbroken. If one has ever taken the fact of the prevalence of tragic death in this world's history fairly into his mind,— freezing, drowning, entombment alive, wild beasts, worse men, and hideous diseases,— he can with difficulty, it seems to me, continue his own career of worldly prosperity without suspecting that he may all the while not be really inside the game, that he may lack the great initiation.

Well, this is exactly what asceticism thinks; and it voluntarily takes the initiation. Life is neither farce nor genteel comedy, it says, but something we must sit at in mourning garments, hoping its bitter taste will purge us of our folly. The wild and the heroic are indeed such rooted parts of it that healthy-mindedness pure and simple, with its sentimental optimism, can hardly be regarded by any thinking man as a serious solution. Phrases of neatness, cosiness, and comfort can never be an answer to the sphinx's riddle.

In these remarks I am leaning only upon mankind's common instinct for reality, which in point of fact has always held the world to be essentially a theatre for heroism. In heroism, we feel, life's supreme mystery is hidden. We tolerate no one who has no capacity whatever for it in any direction. On the other hand, no matter what a man's frailties otherwise may be, if he be willing to risk death, and still more if be suffer it heroically, in the service he has chosen, the fact consecrates him forever. Inferior to ourselves in this or that way, if yet we cling to life, and he is able 'to fling it away like a flower' as caring nothing for it, we account him in the deepest way our born superior. Each of us in his own person feels that a high-hearted indifference to life would expiate all his shortcomings.

The metaphysical mystery, thus recognized by common sense, that he who feeds on death that feeds on men possesses life supereminently and excellently, and meets best the secret demands of the universe, is the truth of which asceticism has been the faithful champion. The folly of the cross, so inexplicable by the intellect, has yet its indestructible vital meaning.

Representatively, then, and symbolically, and apart from the vagaries into which the unenlightened intellect of former times may have let it wander, asceticism must, I believe, be acknowledged to go with the profounder way of handling the gift of existence. Naturalistic optimism is mere syllabub and flattery and sponge-cake in comparison. The practical course of action for us, as religious men, would therefore, it seems to me, not be simply to turn our backs upon the ascetic impulse, as most of us today turn them, but rather to discover some outlet for it of which the fruits in the way of privation and hardship might be objectively useful. The older monastic asceticism occupied itself with pathetic futilities, or terminated in the mere egotism of the individual, increasing his own perfection. But is it not possible for us to discard most of these older forms of mortification, and yet find saner channels for the heroism which inspired them? ["The vanities of all others may die out, but the vanity of a saint as regards his sainthood is hard indeed to wear away." Ramakrishna, his Life and Sayings, 1899, p. 172.]

Does not, for example, the worship of material luxury and wealth, which constitutes so large a portion of the 'spirit' of our age, make somewhat for effeminacy and unmanliness? Is not the exclusively sympathetic and facetious way in which most children are brought up today so different from the education of a hundred years ago, especially in evangelical circles— in danger, in spite of its many advantages, of developing a certain trashiness of fibre? Are there not hereabouts some points of application for a renovated and revised ascetic discipline?

Many of you would recognize such dangers, but would point to athletics, militarism, and individual and national enterprise and adventure as the remedies. These contemporary ideals are quite as remarkable for the energy with which they make for heroic standards of life, as contemporary religion is remarkable for the way in which it neglects them. War and adventure assuredly keep all who engage in them from treating themselves too tenderly. They demand such incredible efforts, depth beyond depth of exertion, both in degree and in duration, that the whole scale of motivation alters. Discomfort and annoyance, hunger and wet, pain and cold, squalor and filth, cease to have any deterrent operation whatever. Death turns into a commonplace matter, and its usual power to check our action vanishes. With the annulling of these customary inhibitions, ranges of new energy are set free, and life seems cast upon a higher plane of power.

"When a church has to be run by oysters, ice-cream, and fun," I read in an American religious paper, "you may be sure that it is running away from Christ." Such, if one may judge by appearances, is the present plight of many of our churches. -

The beauty of war in this respect is that it is so congruous with ordinary human nature. Ancestral evolution has made us all potential warriors; so the most insignificant individual, when thrown into an army in the field, is weaned from whatever excess of tenderness towards his precious person he may bring with him, and may easily develop into a monster of insensibility.

But when we compare the military type of self-severity with that of the ascetic saint, we find a world-wide difference in all their spiritual concomitants.

"'Live and let live,'" writes a clear-headed Austrian officer, "is no device for an army. Contempt for one's own comrades, for the troops of the enemy, and, above all, fierce contempt for one's own person, are what war demands of every one. Far better is it for an army to be too savage, too cruel, too barbarous, than to possess too much sentimentality and human reasonableness. If the soldier is to be good for anything as a soldier, he must be exactly the opposite of a reasoning and thinking man. The measure of goodness in him is his possible use in war. War, and even peace, require of the soldier absolutely peculiar standards of morality. The recruit brings with him common moral notions, of which he must seek immediately to get rid. For him victory, success, must be everything. The most barbaric tendencies in men come to life again in war, and for war's uses they are incommensurably good." [C.V.B.K.: Friedens— und Kriegs-moral der Heere. Quoted by Hamon: Psychologie du Militaire professional, 1895, p. xli.]

These words are of course literally true. The immediate aim of the soldier's life is, as Moltke said, destruction, and nothing but destruction; and whatever constructions wars result in are remote and non-military. Consequently the soldier cannot train himself to be too feelingless to all those usual sympathies and respects, whether for persons or for things, that make for conservation. Yet the fact remains that war is a school of strenuous life and heroism; and, being in the line of aboriginal instinct, is the only school that as yet is universally available. But when we gravely ask ourselves whether this wholesale organization of irrationality and crime be our only bulwark against effeminacy, we stand aghast at the thought, and think more kindly of ascetic religion. One hears of the mechanical equivalent of heat. What we now need to discover in the social realm is the moral equivalent of war: something heroic that will speak to men as universally as war does, and yet will be as compatible with their spiritual selves as war has proved itself to be incompatible. I have often thought that in the old monkish poverty-worship, in spite of the pedantry which infested it, there might be something like that moral equivalent of war which we are seeking. May not voluntarily accepted poverty be 'the strenuous life,' without the need of crushing weaker peoples?

Poverty indeed is the strenuous life,— without brass bands or uniforms or hysteric popular applause or lies or circumlocutions; and when one sees the way in which wealth-getting enters as an ideal into the very bone and marrow of our generation, one wonders whether a revival of the belief that poverty is a worthy religious vocation may not be 'the transformation of military courage,' and the spiritual reform which our time stands most in need of.

Among us English-speaking peoples especially do the praises of poverty need once more to be boldly sung. We have grown literally afraid to be poor. We despise any one who elects to be poor in order to simplify and save his inner life. If he does not join the general scramble and pant with the money-making street, we deem him spiritless and lacking in ambition. We have lost the power even of imagining what the ancient idealization of poverty could have meant; the liberation from material attachments, the unbribed soul, the manlier indifference, the paying our way by what we are or do and not by what we have, the right to fling away our life at any moment irresponsibly,— the more athletic trim, in short, the moral fighting shape. When we of the so-called better classes are scared as men were never scared in history at material ugliness and hardship; when we put off marriage until our house can be artistic, and quake at the thought of having a child without a bank-account and doomed to manual labor, it is time for thinking men to protest against so unmanly and irreligious a state of opinion.

It is true that so far as wealth gives time for ideal ends and exercise to ideal energies, wealth is better than poverty and ought to be chosen. But wealth does this in only a portion of the actual cases. Elsewhere the desire to gain wealth and the fear to lose it are our chief breeders of cowardice and propagators of corruption. There are thousands of conjunctures in which a wealth-bound man must be a slave, whilst a man for whom poverty has no terrors becomes a freeman. Think of the strength which personal indifference to poverty would give us if we were devoted to unpopular causes. We need no longer hold our tongues or fear to vote the revolutionary or reformatory ticket. Our stocks might fall, our hopes of promotion vanish; our salaries stop, our club doors close in our faces; yet, while we lived, we would imperturbably bear witness to the spirit, and our example would help to set free our generation. The cause would need its funds, but we its servants would be potent in proportion as we personally were contented with our poverty.

I recommend this matter to your serious pondering, for it is certain that the prevalent fear of poverty among the educated classes is the worst moral disease from which our civilization suffers.

I have now said all that I can usefully say about the several fruits of religion as they are manifested in saintly lives, so I will make a brief review and pass to my more general conclusions.

Our question, you will remember, is as to whether religion stands approved by its fruits, as these are exhibited in the saintly type of character. Single attributes of saintliness may, it is true, be temperamental endowments, found in non-religious individuals. But the whole group of them forms a combination which, as such, is religious, for it seems to flow from the sense of the divine as from its psychological centre. Whoever possesses strongly this sense comes naturally to think that the smallest details of this world derive infinite significance from their relation to an unseen divine order. The thought of this order yields him a superior denomination of happiness, and a steadfastness of soul with which no other can compare. In social relations his serviceability is exemplary; he abounds in impulses to help. His help is inward as well as outward, for his sympathy reaches souls as well as bodies, and kindles unsuspected faculties therein. Instead of placing happiness where common men place it, in comfort, he places it in a higher kind of inner excitement, which converts discomforts into sources of cheer and annuls unhappiness. So he turns his back upon no duty, however thankless; and when we are in need of assistance, we can count upon the saint lending his hand with more certainty than we can count upon any other person. Finally, his humble-mindedness and his ascetic tendencies save him from the petty personal pretensions which so obstruct our ordinary social intercourse, and his purity gives us in him a clean man for a companion. Felicity, purity, charity, patience, self-severity,— these are splendid excellencies, and the saint of all men shows them in the completest possible measure.

But, as we saw, all these things together do not make saints infallible. When their intellectual outlook is narrow, they fall into all sorts of holy excesses, fanaticism or theopathic absorption, self-torment, prudery, scrupulosity, gullibility, and morbid inability to meet the world. By the very intensity of his fidelity to the paltry ideals with which an inferior intellect may inspire him, a saint can be even more objectionable and damnable than a superficial carnal man would be in the same situation. We must judge him not sentimentally only, and not in isolation, but using our own intellectual standards, placing him in his environment, and estimating his total function.

Now in the matter of intellectual standards, we must bear in mind that it is unfair, where we find narrowness of mind, always to impute it as a vice to the individual, for in religious and theological matters he probably absorbs his narrowness from his generation. Moreover, we must not confound the essentials of saintliness, which are those general passions of which I have spoken, with its accidents, which are the special determinations of these passions at any historical moment. In these determinations the saints will usually be loyal to the temporary idols of their tribe. Taking refuge in monasteries was as much an idol of the tribe in the middle ages, as bearing a hand in the world's work is today. Saint Francis or Saint Bernard, were they living today, would undoubtedly be leading consecrated lives of some sort, but quite as undoubtedly they would not lead them in retirement. Our animosity to special historic, manifestations must not lead us to give away the saintly impulses in their essential nature to the tender mercies of inimical critics.

The most inimical critic of the saintly impulses whom I know is Nietzsche. He contrasts them with the worldly passions as we find these embodied in the predaceous military character, altogether to the advantage of the latter. Your born saint, it must be confessed, has something about him which often makes the gorge of a carnal man rise, so it will be worth while to consider the contrast in question more fully.

Dislike of the saintly nature seems to be a negative result of the biologically useful instinct of welcoming leadership, and glorifying the chief of the tribe. The chief is the potential, if not the actual tyrant, the masterful, overpowering man of prey. We confess our inferiority and grovel before him. We quail under his glance, and are at the same time proud of owning so dangerous a lord. Such instinctive and submissive hero-worship must have been indispensable in primeval tribal life. In the endless wars of those times, leaders were absolutely needed for the tribe's survival. If there were any tribes who owned no leaders, they can have left no issue to narrate their doom. The leaders always had good consciences, for conscience in them coalesced with Will, and those who looked on their face were as much smitten with wonder at their freedom from inner restraint as with awe at the energy of their outward performances.

Compared with these beaked and taloned graspers of the world, saints are herbivorous animals, tame and harmless barn-yard poultry. There are saints whose beard you may, if you ever care to, pull with impunity. Such a man excites no thrills of wonder veiled in terror; his conscience is full of scruples and returns; he stuns us neither by his inward freedom nor his outward power; and unless he found within us an altogether different faculty of admiration to appeal to, we should pass him by with contempt.

In point of fact, he does appeal to a different faculty. Reenacted in human nature is the fable of the wind, the sun, and the traveler. The sexes embody the discrepancy. The woman loves the man the more admiringly the stormier he shows himself, and the world deifies its rulers the more for being willful and unaccountable. But the woman in turn subjugates the man by the mystery of gentleness in beauty, and the saint has always charmed the world by something similar. Mankind is susceptible and suggestible in opposite directions, and the rivalry of influences is unsleeping. The saintly and the worldly ideal pursue their feud in literature as much as in real life.

For Nietzsche the saint represents little but sneakingness and slavishness. He is the sophisticated invalid, the degenerate par excellence, the man of insufficient vitality. His prevalence would put the human type in danger.

"The sick are the greatest danger for the well. The weaker, not the stronger, are the strong's undoing. It is not fear of our fellow-man, which we should wish to see diminished; for fear rouses those who are strong to become terrible in turn themselves, and preserves the hard-earned and successful type of humanity. What is to be dreaded by us more than any other doom is not fear, but rather the great disgust, not fear, but rather the great pity— disgust and pity for our human fellows.... The morbid are our greatest peril— not the 'bad' men, not the predatory beings. Those born wrong, the miscarried, the broken— they it is, the weakest, who are undermining the vitality of the race, poisoning our trust in life, and putting humanity in question. Every look of them is a sigh,— 'Would I were something other! I am sick and tired of what I am.' In this swamp—soil of self-contempt, every poisonous weed flourishes, and all so small, so secret, so dishonest, and so sweetly rotten. Here swarm the worms of sensitiveness and resentment; here the air smells odious with secrecy, with what is not to be acknowledged; here is woven endlessly the net of the meanest of conspiracies, the conspiracy of those who suffer against those who succeed and are victorious; here the very aspect of the victorious is hated— as if health, success, strength, pride, and the sense of power were in themselves things vicious, for which one ought eventually to make bitter expiation. Oh, how these people would themselves like to inflict the expiation, how they thirst to be the hangmen! And all the while their duplicity never confesses their hatred to be hatred." [Zur Genealogie der Moral, Dritte Abhandlung, SS 14. I have abridged, and in one place transposed, a sentence.]

Poor Nietzsche's antipathy is itself sickly enough, but we all know what he means, and he expresses well the clash between the two ideals. The carnivorous-minded 'strong man,' the adult male and cannibal, can see nothing but mouldiness and morbidness in the saint's gentleness and self-severity, and regards him with pure loathing. The whole feud revolves essentially upon two pivots: Shall the seen world or the unseen world be our chief sphere of adaptation? and must our means of adaptation in this seen world be aggressiveness or non-resistance?

The debate is serious. In some sense and to some degree both worlds must be acknowledged and taken account of; and in the seen world both aggressiveness and non-resistance are needful. It is a question of emphasis, of more or less. Is the saint's type or the strong-man's type the more ideal?

It has often been supposed, and even now, I think, it is supposed by most persons, that there can be one intrinsically ideal type of human character. A certain kind of man, it is imagined, must be the best man absolutely and apart from the utility of his function, apart from economical considerations. The saint's type, and the knight's or gentleman's type, have always been rival claimants of this absolute ideality; and in the ideal of military religious orders both types were in a manner blended. According to the empirical philosophy, however, all ideals are matters of relation. It would be absurd, for example, to ask for a definition of 'the ideal horse,' so long as dragging drays and running races, bearing children, and jogging about with tradesmen's packages all remain as indispensable differentiations of equine function. You may take what you call a general all-round animal as a compromise, but he will be inferior to any horse of a more specialized type, in some one particular direction. We must not forget this now when, in discussing saintliness, we ask if it be an ideal type of manhood. We must test it by its economical relations.

I think that the method which Mr. Spencer uses in his Data of Ethics will help to fix our opinion. Ideality in conduct is altogether a matter of adaptation. A society where all were invariably aggressive would destroy itself by inner friction, and in a society where some are aggressive, others must be non-resistant, if there is to be any kind of order. This is the present constitution of society, and to the mixture we owe many of our blessings. But the aggressive members of society are always tending to become bullies, robbers, and swindlers; and no one believes that such a state of things as we now live in is the millennium. It is meanwhile quite possible to conceive an imaginary society in which there should be no aggressiveness, but only sympathy and fairness,— any small community of true friends now realizes such a society. Abstractly considered, such a society on a large scale would be the millennium, for every good thing might be realized there with no expense of friction. To such a millennial society the saint would be entirely adapted. His peaceful modes of appeal would be efficacious over his companions, and there would be no one extant to take advantage of his non-resistance. The saint is therefore abstractly a higher type of man than the 'strong man,' because he is adapted to the highest society conceivable, whether that society ever be concretely possible or not. The strong man would immediately tend by his presence to make that society deteriorate. It would become inferior in everything save in a certain kind of bellicose excitement, dear to men as they now are.

But if we turn from the abstract question to the actual situation, we find that the individual saint may be well or ill adapted, according to particular circumstances. There is, in short, no absoluteness in the excellence of sainthood. It must be confessed that as far as this world goes, any one who makes an out-and-out saint of himself does so at his peril. If he is not a large enough man, he may appear more insignificant and contemptible, for all his saintship, than if he had remained a worldling. Accordingly religion has seldom been so radically taken in our Western world that the devotee could not mix it with some worldly temper. It has always found good men who could follow most of its impulses, but who stopped short when it came to non-resistance. Christ himself was fierce upon occasion. Cromwells, Stonewall Jacksons, Gordons, show that Christians can be strong men also.

We all know daft saints, and they inspire a queer kind of aversion. But in comparing saints with strong men we must choose individuals on the same intellectual level. The under-witted strong man, homologous in his sphere with the under-witted saint, is the bully of the slums, the hooligan or rowdy. Surely on this level also the saint preserves a certain superiority.

How is success to be absolutely measured when there are so many environments and so many ways of looking at the adaptation? It cannot be measured absolutely; the verdict will vary according to the point of view adopted. From the biological point of view Saint Paul was a failure, because he was beheaded. Yet he was magnificently adapted to the larger environment of history; and so far as any saint's example is a leaven of righteousness in the world, and draws it in the direction of more prevalent habits of saintliness, he is a success, no matter what his immediate bad fortune may be. The greatest saints, the spiritual heroes whom every one acknowledges, the Francises, Bernards, Luthers, Loyolas, Wesleys, Channings, Moodys, Gratrys, the Phillips Brookses, the Agnes Joneses, Margaret Hallahans, and Dora Pattisons, are successes from the outset. They show themselves, and there is no question; every one perceives their strength and stature. Their sense of mystery in things, their passion, their goodness, irradiate about them and enlarge their outlines while they soften them. They are like pictures with an atmosphere and background; and, placed alongside of them, the strong men of this world and no other seem as dry as sticks, as hard and crude as blocks of stone or brickbats.

In a general way, then, and 'on the whole,' our abandonment of theological criteria, and our testing of religion by practical common sense and the empirical method, leave it in possession of its towering place in history. Economically, the saintly group of qualities is indispensable to the world's welfare. The great saints are immediate successes; the smaller ones are at least heralds and harbingers, and they may be leavens also, of a better mundane order. Let us be saints, then, if we can, whether or not we succeed visibly and temporally. But in our Father's house are many mansions, and each of us must discover for himself the kind of religion and the amount of saintship which best comports with what he believes to be his powers and feels to be his truest mission and vocation. There are no successes to be guaranteed and no set orders to be given to individuals, so long as we follow the methods of empirical philosophy.

This is my conclusion so far. I know that on some of your minds it leaves a feeling of wonder that such a method should have been applied to such a subject, and this in spite of all those remarks about empiricism which I made at the beginning of Lecture XIII. How, you say, can religion, which believes in two worlds and an invisible order, be estimated by the adaptation of its fruits to this world's order alone? It is its truth, not its utility, you insist, upon which our verdict ought to depend. If religion is true, its fruits are good fruits, even though in this world they should prove uniformly ill adapted and full of naught but pathos. It goes back, then, after all, to the question of the truth of theology. The plot inevitably thickens upon us; we cannot escape theoretical considerations. I propose, then, that to some degree we face the responsibility. Religious persons have often, though not uniformly, professed to see truth in a special manner. That manner is known as mysticism. I will consequently now proceed to treat at some length of mystical phenomena, and after that, though more briefly, I will consider religious philosophy.

LECTURES XVI AND XVII: MYSTICISM

over and over again in these lectures I have raised points and left them open and unfinished until we should have come to the subject of Mysticism. Some of you, I fear, may have smiled as you noted my reiterated postponements. But now the hour has come when mysticism must be faced in good earnest, and those broken threads wound up together. One may say truly, I think, that personal religious experience has its root and centre in mystical states of consciousness; so for us, who in these lectures are treating personal experience as the exclusive subject of our study, such states of consciousness ought to form the vital chapter from which the other chapters get their light. Whether my treatment of mystical states will shed more light or darkness, I do not know, for my own constitution shuts me out from their enjoyment almost entirely, and I can speak of them only at second hand. But though forced to look upon the subject so externally, I will be as objective and receptive as I can; and I think I shall at least succeed in convincing you of the reality of the states in question, and of the paramount importance of their function.

First of all, then, I ask, What does the expression 'mystical states of consciousness' mean? How do we part off mystical states from other states?

The words 'mysticism' and 'mystical' are often used as terms of mere reproach, to throw at any opinion which we regard as vague and vast and sentimental, and without a base in either facts or logic. For some writers a 'mystic' is any person who believes in thought-transference, or spirit-return. Employed in this way the word has little value: there are too many less ambiguous synonyms. So, to keep it useful by restricting it, I will do what I did in the case of the word 'religion,' and simply propose to you four marks which, when an experience has them, may justify us in calling it mystical for the purpose of the present lectures. In this way we shall save verbal disputation, and the recriminations that generally go therewith.

1. Ineffability.— The handiest of the marks by which I classify a state of mind as mystical is negative. The subject of it immediately says that it defies expression, that no adequate report of its contents can be given in words. It follows from this that its quality must be directly experienced; it cannot be imparted or transferred to others. In this peculiarity mystical states are more like states of feeling than like states of intellect. No one can make clear to another who has never had a certain feeling, in what the quality or worth of it consists. One must have musical ears to know the value of a symphony; one must have been in love one's self to understand a lover's state of mind. Lacking the heart or ear, we cannot interpret the musician or the lover justly, and are even likely to consider

him weak-minded or absurd. The mystic finds that most of us accord to his experiences an equally incompetent treatment.

2. Noetic quality.— Although so similar to states of feeling, mystical states seem to those who experience them to be also states of knowledge. They are states of insight into depths of truth unplumbed by the discursive intellect. They are illuminations, revelations, full of significance and importance, all inarticulate though they remain; and as a rule they carry with them a curious sense of authority for after-time.

These two characters will entitle any state to be called mystical, in the sense in which I use the word. Two other qualities are less sharply marked, but are usually found. These are:

3. Transiency.— Mystical states cannot be sustained for long. Except in rare instances, half an hour, or at most an hour or two, seems to be the limit beyond which they fade into the light of common day. Often, when faded, their quality can but imperfectly be reproduced in memory; but when they recur it is recognized; and from one recurrence to another it is susceptible of continuous development in what is felt as inner richness and importance.

4. Passivity.— Although the oncoming of mystical states may be facilitated by preliminary voluntary operations, as by fixing the attention, or going through certain bodily performances, or in other ways which manuals of mysticism prescribe; yet when the characteristic sort of consciousness once has set in, the mystic feels as if his own will were in abeyance, and indeed sometimes as if he were grasped and held by a superior power. This latter peculiarity connects mystical states with certain definite phenomena of secondary or alternative personality, such as prophetic speech, automatic writing, or the mediumistic trance. When these latter conditions are well pronounced, however, there may be no recollection whatever of the phenomenon and it may have no significance for the subject's usual inner life, to which, as it were, it makes a mere interruption. Mystical states, strictly so called, are never merely interruptive. Some memory of their content always remains, and a profound sense of their importance. They modify the inner life of the subject between the times of their recurrence. Sharp divisions in this region are, however, difficult to make, and we find all sorts of gradations and mixtures.

These four characteristics are sufficient to mark out a group of states of consciousness peculiar enough to deserve a special name and to call for careful study. Let it then be called the mystical group.

Our next step should be to gain acquaintance with some typical examples. Professional mystics at the height of their development have often elaborately organized experiences and a philosophy based thereupon. But you remember what I said in my first lecture: phenomena are best understood when placed within their series, studied in their germ and in their over-ripe decay, and compared with their exaggerated and degenerated kindred. The range of mystical experience is very wide, much too wide for us to cover in the time at our disposal. Yet the method of serial study is so essential: for interpretation that if we really wish to reach conclusions we must use it. I will begin, therefore, with phenomena which claim no special religious significance, and end with those of which the religious pretensions are extreme.

The simplest rudiment of mystical experience would seem to be that deepened sense of the significance of a maxim or formula which occasionally sweeps over one. "I've heard that said all my life," we exclaim, "but I never realized its full meaning until now." "When a fellow-monk," said Luther, "one day repeated the words of the Creed: 'I believe in the forgiveness of sins,' I saw the Scripture in an entirely new light; and straightway I felt as if I were born anew. It was as if I had found the door of paradise thrown wide open." This sense of deeper significance is not confined to rational propositions. Single words, and conjunctions of words, effects of light on land and sea, odors and musical sounds, all bring it when the mind is tuned aright. Most of us can remember the strangely moving power of passages in certain poems read when we were young, irrational doorways as they were through which the mystery of fact, the wildness and the pang of life, stole into our hearts and thrilled them. The words have now perhaps become mere polished surfaces for us; but lyric poetry and music are alive and significant only in proportion as they fetch these vague vistas of a life continuous with our own, beckoning and inviting, yet ever eluding our pursuit. We are alive or dead to the eternal inner message of the arts according as we have kept or lost this mystical susceptibility.

'Mesopotamia' is the stock comic instance.— An excellent old German lady, who had done some traveling in her day, used to describe to me her Sehnsucht that she might yet visit 'Philadelphia,' whose wondrous name had always haunted her imagination. Of John Foster it is said that "single words (as chalcedony), or the names of ancient heroes, had a mighty fascination over him. 'At any time the word hermit was enough to transport him.' The words woods and forests would produce the most powerful emotion." [Foster's Life, by Ryland, New York, 1846, p. 3.]

A more pronounced step forward on the mystical ladder is found in an extremely frequent phenomenon, that sudden feeling, namely, which sometimes sweeps over us, of having 'been here before,' as if at some indefinite past time, in just this place, with just these people, we were already saying just these things. As Tennyson writes:

"Moreover, something is or seems,
That touches me with mystic gleams,
Like glimpses of forgotten dreams—
"Of something felt, like something here;
Of something done, I know not where;
Such as no language may declare."

Sir James Crichton-Browne has given the technical name of 'dreamy states' to these sudden invasions of vaguely reminiscent consciousness. They bring a sense of mystery and of the metaphysical duality of things, and the feeling of an enlargement of perception which seems imminent but which never completes itself. In Dr. Crichton-Browne's opinion they connect themselves with the perplexed and scared disturbances of self-consciousness which occasionally precede epileptic attacks. I think that this learned alienist takes a rather absurdly alarmist view of an intrinsically insignificant phenomenon. He follows it along the downward ladder, to insanity; our path pursues the upward ladder chiefly. The divergence shows how important it is to neglect no part of a phenomenon's connections, for we make it appear admirable or dreadful according to the context by which we set it off.

"I have never had any revelations through anaesthetics, but a kind of waking trance— this for lack of a better word— I have frequently had, quite up from boyhood, when I have been all alone. This has come upon me through repeating my own name to myself silently, till all at once, as it were out of the intensity of the consciousness of individuality, individuality itself seemed to dissolve and fade away into boundless being, and this not a confused state but the clearest, the surest of the surest, utterly beyond words— where death was an almost laughable impossibility— the loss of personality (if so it were) seeming no extinction, but the only true life. I am ashamed of my feeble description. Have I not said the state is utterly beyond words?"

Professor Tyndall, in a letter, recalls Tennyson saying of this condition: "By God Almighty! there is no delusion in the matter! It is no nebulous ecstasy, but a state of transcendent wonder, associated with absolute clearness of mind." [Memoirs of Alfred Tennyson, ii. 473.]

Somewhat deeper plunges into mystical consciousness are met with in yet other dreamy states. Such feelings as these which Charles Kingsley describes are surely far from being uncommon, especially in youth:—

"When I walk the fields, I am oppressed now and then with an innate feeling that everything I see has a meaning, if I could but understand it. And this feeling of being surrounded with truths which I cannot grasp amounts to indescribable awe sometimes.... Have you not felt that your real soul was imperceptible to your mental vision, except in a few hallowed moments?" [Charles Kingsley's Life, i. 55, quoted by Inge: Christian Mysticism, London, 1899, p. 341.]

A much more extreme state of mystical consciousness is described by J.A. Symonds; and probably more persons than we suspect could give parallels to it from their own experience.

"Suddenly," writes Symonds, "at church, or in company, or when I was reading, and always, I think, when my muscles were at rest, I felt the approach of the mood. Irresistibly it took possession of my mind and will, lasted what seemed an eternity, and disappeared in a series of rapid sensations which resembled the awakening from anaesthetic influence. One reason why I disliked this kind of trance was that I could not describe it to myself. I cannot even now find words to render it intelligible. It consisted in a gradual but swiftly progressive obliteration of space, time, sensation, and the multitudinous factors of experience which seem to qualify what we are pleased to call our Self. In proportion as these conditions of ordinary consciousness were subtracted, the sense of an underlying or essential consciousness acquired intensity. At last nothing remained but a pure, absolute, abstract Self. The universe became without form and void of content. But Self persisted, formidable in its vivid keenness, feeling the most poignant doubt about reality, ready, as it seemed, to find existence break as breaks a bubble round about it. And what then? The apprehension of a coming dissolution, the grim conviction that this state was the last state of the conscious Self, the sense that I had followed the last thread of being to the verge of the abyss, and had arrived at demonstration of eternal Maya or illusion, stirred or seemed to stir me up again. The return to ordinary conditions of sentient existence began by my first recovering the power of touch, and then by the gradual though rapid influx of familiar impressions and diurnal interests. At last I felt myself once more a human being; and though the riddle of what is meant by life remained unsolved, I was thankful for this return from the abyss—this deliverance from so awful an initiation into the mysteries of skepticism.

"This trance recurred with diminishing frequency until I reached the age of twenty-eight. It served to impress upon my growing nature the phantasmal unreality of all the circumstances which contribute to a merely phenomenal consciousness. Often have I asked myself with anguish, on waking from that formless state of denuded, keenly sentient being, Which is the unreality?— the trance of fiery, vacant, apprehensive, skeptical Self from which I issue, or these surrounding phenomena and habits which veil that inner Self and build a self of flesh-and-blood conventionality? Again, are men the factors of some dream, the dream-like unsubstantiality of which they comprehend at such eventful moments? What would happen if the final stage of the trance were reached?" [H.F. Brown: J.A. Symonds, a Biography, London, 1895, pp. 29-31, abridged.]

In a recital like this there is certainly something suggestive of pathology. The next step into mystical states carries us into a realm that public opinion and ethical philosophy have long since branded as pathological, though private practice and certain lyric strains of poetry seem still to bear witness to its ideality. I refer to the consciousness produced by intoxicants and anaesthetics, especially by alcohol. The sway of alcohol over mankind is unquestionably due to its power to stimulate the mystical faculties of human nature, usually crushed to earth by the cold facts and dry criticisms of the sober hour. Sobriety diminishes, discriminates and says no; drunkenness expands, unites, and says yes. It is in fact the great exciter of the Yes function in man. It brings its votary from the chill periphery of things to the radiant core. It makes him for the moment one with truth. Not through mere perversity do men run after it. To the poor and the unlettered it stands in the place of symphony concerts and of literature; and it is part of the deeper mystery and tragedy of life that whiffs and gleams of something that we immediately recognize as excellent should be vouchsafed to so many of us only in the fleeting earlier phases of what in its totality is so degrading a poisoning. The drunken consciousness is one bit of the mystic consciousness, and our total opinion of it must find its place in our opinion of that larger whole.

Crichton-Browne expressly says that Symonds's "highest nerve centres were in some degree enfeebled or damaged by these dreamy mental states which afflicted him so grievously." Symonds was, however, a perfect monster of many-sided cerebral efficiency, and his critic gives no objective grounds whatever for his strange opinion, save that Symonds complained occasionally, as all susceptible and ambitious men complain, of lassitude and uncertainty as to his life's mission.

Nitrous oxide and ether, especially nitrous oxide, when sufficiently diluted with air, stimulate the mystical consciousness in an extraordinary degree. Depth beyond depth of truth seems revealed to the inhaler. This truth fades out, however, or escapes, at the moment of coming to; and if any words remain over in which it seemed to clothe itself, they prove to be the veriest nonsense. Nevertheless, the sense of a profound meaning having been there persists; and I know more than one person who is persuaded that in the nitrous oxide trance we have a genuine metaphysical revelation.

Some years ago I myself made some observations on this aspect of nitrous oxide intoxication, and reported them in print. One conclusion was forced upon my mind at that time, and my impression of its truth has ever since remained unshaken. It is that our normal waking consciousness, rational consciousness as we call it, is but one special type of consciousness, whilst all about it, parted from it by the filmiest of screens, there lie potential forms of consciousness entirely different. We may go through life without suspecting their existence; but apply the requisite stimulus, and at a touch they are there in all their completeness, definite types of mentality which probably somewhere have their field of application and adaptation. No account of the universe in its totality can be final which leaves these other forms of consciousness quite disregarded. How to regard them is the question,— for they are so discontinuous with ordinary consciousness. Yet they may determine attitudes though they cannot furnish formulas, and open a region though they fail to give a map. At any rate, they forbid a premature closing of our accounts with reality. Looking back on my own experiences, they all converge towards a kind of insight to which I cannot help ascribing some metaphysical significance. The keynote of it is invariably a reconciliation. It is as if the opposites of the world, whose contradictoriness and conflict make all our difficulties and troubles, were melted into unity. Not only do they, as contrasted species, belong to one and the same genus, but one of the species, the nobler and better one, is itself the genus, and so soaks up and absorbs its opposite into itself This is a dark saying, I know, when thus expressed in terms of common logic, but I cannot wholly escape from its authority. I feel as if it must mean something, something like what the hegelian philosophy means, if one could only lay hold of it more clearly. Those who have ears to hear, let them hear; to me the living sense of its reality only comes in the artificial mystic state of mind.

What reader of Hegel can doubt that that sense of a perfected Being with all its otherness soaked up into itself, which dominates his whole philosophy, must have come from the prominence in his consciousness of mystical moods like this, in most persons kept subliminal? The notion is thoroughly characteristic of the mystical level, and the Aufgabe of making it articulate was surely set to Hegel's intellect by mystical feeling.

I just now spoke of friends who believe in the anaesthetic revelation. For them too it is a monistic insight, in which the other in its various forms appears absorbed into the One.

"Into this pervading genius," writes one of them, "we pass, forgetting and forgotten, and thenceforth each is all, in God. There is no higher, no deeper, no other, than the life in which we are founded. 'The One remains, the many change and pass;' and each and every one of us is the One that remains.... This is the ultimatum.... As sure as being— whence is all our care— so sure is content, beyond duplexity, antithesis, or trouble, where I have triumphed in a solitude that God is not above." [Benjamin Paul Blood: The Anaesthetic Revelation and the Gist of Philosophy, Amsterdam, N. Y., 1874, pp. 35, 36.] Mr. Blood has made several attempts to adumbrate the anaesthetic revelation, in pamphlets of rare literary distinction, privately printed and distributed by himself at Amsterdam. Xenos Clark, a philosopher, who died young at Amherst in the '80's, much lamented by those who knew him, was also impressed by the revelation. "In the first place," he once wrote to me, "Mr. Blood and I agree that the revelation. is, if anything, non-emotional. It is utterly flat. It is, as Mr. Blood says, 'the one sole and sufficient insight why, or not why, but how, the present is pushed on by the past, and sucked forward by the vacuity of the future. Its inevitableness defeats all attempts at stopping or accounting for it. It is all precedence and presupposition, and questioning is in regard to it forever too late. It is an initiation of the past.' The real secret would be the formula by which the 'now' keeps exfoliating out of itself, yet never escapes. What is it, indeed, that keeps existence exfoliating? The formal being of anything, the logical definition of it, is static. For mere logic every question contains its own answer— we simply fill the hole with the dirt we dug out. Why are twice two four? Because, in fact, four is twice two. Thus logic finds in life no propulsion, only a momentum. It goes because it is a-going. But the revelation adds: it goes because it is and was a-going. You walk, as it were, round yourself in the revelation. Ordinary philosophy is like a hound hunting his own trail. The more he hunts the farther he has to go, and his nose never catches up with his heels, because it is forever ahead of them. So the present is already a foregone conclusion, and I am ever too late to understand it. But at the moment of recovery from anaesthesis, just then, before starting on life, I catch, so to speak, a glimpse of my heels, a glimpse of the eternal process just in the act of starting. The truth is that we travel on a journey that was accomplished before we set out; and the real end of philosophy is accomplished, not when we arrive at, but when we remain in, our destination (being already there),— which may occur vicariously in this life when we cease our intellectual questioning. That is why there is a smile upon the face of the revelation, as we view it. It tells us that we are forever half a second too late— that's all. 'You could kiss your own lips, and have all the fun to yourself,' it says, if you only knew the trick. It would be perfectly easy if they would just stay there till you got round to them. Why don't you manage it somehow?"

Dialectically minded readers of this farrago will at least recognize the region of thought of which Mr. Clark writes, as familiar. In his latest pamphlet, 'Tennyson's Trances and the Anaesthetic Revelation,' Mr. Blood describes its value for life as follows:

"The Anaesthetic Revelation is the Initiation of Man into the Immemorial Mystery of the Open Secret of Being, revealed as the Inevitable Vortex of Continuity. Inevitable is the word. Its motive is inherent— it is what has to be. It is not for any love or hate, nor for joy nor sorrow, nor good nor ill. End, beginning, or purpose, it knows not of.

"It affords no particular of the multiplicity and variety of things; but it fills appreciation of the historical and the sacred with a secular and intimately personal illumination of the nature and motive of existence, which then seems reminiscent— as if it should have appeared, or shall yet appear, to every participant thereof.

"Although it is at first startling in its solemnity, it becomes directly such a matter of course— so old-fashioned, and so akin to proverbs, that it inspires exultation rather than fear, and a sense of safety, as identified with the aboriginal and the universal. But no words may express the imposing certainty of the patient that he is realizing the primordial, Adamic surprise of Life.

"Repetition of the experience finds it ever the same, and as if it could not possibly be otherwise. The subject resumes his normal consciousness only to partially and fitfully remember its occurrence, and to try to formulate its baffling import,— with only this consolatory afterthought: that he has known the oldest truth, and that he has done with human theories as to the origin, meaning, or destiny of the race. He is beyond instruction in 'spiritual things.'

"The lesson is one of central safety: the Kingdom is within. All days are judgment days: but there can be no climacteric purpose of eternity, nor any scheme of the whole. The astronomer abridges the row of bewildering figures by increasing his unit of measurement: so may we reduce the distracting multiplicity of things to the unity for which each of us stands.

"This has been my moral sustenance since I have known of it. In my first printed mention of it I declared: 'The world is no more the alien terror that was taught me. Spurning the cloud-grimed and still sultry battlements whence so lately Jehovan thunders boomed, my gray gull lifts her wing against the nightfall, and takes the dim leagues with a fearless eye.' And now, after twenty-seven years of this experience, the wing is grayer, but the eye is fearless still, while I renew and doubly emphasize that declaration. I know— as having known— the meaning of Existence: the sane centre of the universe— at once the wonder and the assurance of the soul— for which the speech of reason has as yet no name but the Anaesthetic Revelation."— I have considerably abridged the quotation.

This has the genuine religious mystic ring! I just now quoted J.A. Symonds. He also records a mystical experience with chloroform, as follows:—

"After the choking and stifling had passed away, I seemed at first in a state of utter blankness; then came flashes of intense light, alternating with blackness, and with a keen vision of what was going on in the room around me, but no sensation of touch. I thought that I was near death; when, suddenly, my soul became aware of God, who was manifestly dealing with me, handling me, so to speak, in an intense personal present reality. I felt him streaming in like light upon me.... I cannot describe the ecstasy I felt. Then, as I gradually awoke from the influence of the anesthetics, the old sense of my relation to the world began to return, the new sense of my relation to God began to fade. I suddenly leapt to my feet on the chair where I was sitting, and shrieked out, 'It is too horrible, it is too horrible, it is too horrible,' meaning that I could not bear this disillusionment. Then I flung myself on the ground, and at last awoke covered with blood, calling to the two surgeons (who were frightened), 'Why did you not kill me? Why would you not let me die?' Only think of it. To have felt for that long dateless ecstasy of vision the very God, in all purity and tenderness and truth and absolute love, and then to find that I had after all had no revelation, but that I had been tricked by the abnormal excitement of my brain.

"Yet, this question remains, Is it possible that the inner sense of reality which succeeded, when my flesh was dead to impressions from without, to the ordinary sense of physical relations, was not a delusion but an actual experience? Is it possible that I, in that moment, felt what some of the saints have said they always felt, the undemonstrable but irrefragable certainty of God?" [Op. cit., pp. 78-80, abridged. I subjoin, also abridging it, another interesting anaesthetic revelation communicated to me in manuscript by a friend in England. The subject, a gifted woman, was taking ether for a surgical operation.]

"I wondered if I was in a prison being tortured, and why I remembered having heard it said that people 'learn through suffering,' and in view of what I was seeing, the inadequacy of this saying struck me so much that I said, aloud, 'to suffer is to learn.'

"With that I became unconscious again, and my last dream immediately preceded my real coming to. It only lasted a few seconds, and was most vivid and real to me, though it may not be clear in words.

"A great Being or Power was traveling through the sky, his foot was on a kind of lightning as a wheel is on a rail, it was his pathway. The lightning was made entirely of the spirits of innumerable people close to one another, and I was one of them. He moved in a straight line, and each part of the streak or flash came into its short conscious existence only that he might travel. I seemed to be directly under the foot of God, and I thought he was grinding his own life up out of my pain. Then I saw that what he had been trying with all his might to do was to change his course, to bend the line of lightning to which he was tied, in the direction in which he wanted to go. I felt my flexibility and helplessness, and knew that he would succeed. He bended me, turning his corner by means of my hurt, hurting me more than I had ever been hurt in my life, and at the acutest point of this, as he passed, I saw, I understood for a moment things that

I have now forgotten, things that no one could remember while retaining sanity. The angle was an obtuse angle, and I remember thinking as I woke that had he made it a right or acute angle, I should have both suffered and 'seen' still more, and should probably have died.

"He went on and I came to. In that moment the whole of my life passed before me, including each little meaningless piece of distress, and I understood them. This was what it had all meant, this was the piece of work it had all been contributing to do. I did not see God's purpose, I only saw his intentness and his entire relentlessness towards his means. He thought no more of me than a man thinks of hurting a cork when he is opening wine, or hurting a cartridge when he is firing. And yet, on waking, my first feeling was, and it came with tears, 'Domine non sum digna,' for I had been lifted into a position for which I was too small. I realized that in that half hour under ether I had served God more distinctly and purely than I had ever done in my life before, or than I am capable of desiring to do. I was the means of his achieving and revealing something, I know not what or to whom, and that, to the exact extent of my capacity for suffering.

"While regaining consciousness, I wondered why, since I had gone so deep, I had seen nothing of what the saints call the love of God, nothing but his relentlessness. And then I heard an answer, which I could only just catch, saying, 'Knowledge and Love are One, and the measure is suffering'— I give the words as they came to me. With that I came finally to (into what seemed a dream world compared with the reality of what I was leaving), and I saw that what would be called the 'cause' of my experience was a slight operation under insufficient ether, in a bed pushed up against a window, a common city window in a common city street. If I had to formulate a few of the things I then caught a glimpse of, they would run somewhat as follows:

"The eternal necessity of suffering and its eternal vicariousness. The veiled and incommunicable nature of the worst sufferings; the passivity of genius, how it is essentially instrumental and defenseless, moved, not moving, it must do what it does;— the impossibility of discovery without its price;— finally, the excess of what the suffering 'seer' or genius pays over what his generation gains. (He seems like one who sweats his life out to earn enough to save a district from famine, and just as he staggers back, dying and satisfied, bringing a lac of rupees to buy grain with, God lifts the lac away, dropping one rupee, and says, 'That you may give them. That you have earned for them. The rest is for ME.') I perceived also in a way never to be forgotten, the excess of what we see over what we can demonstrate.

"And so on!— these things may seem to you delusions, or truisms; but for me they are dark truths, and the power to put them into even such words as these has been given me by an ether dream."

With this we make connection with religious mysticism pure and simple. Symonds's question takes us back to those examples which you will remember my quoting in the lecture on the Reality of the Unseen, of sudden realization of the immediate presence of God. The phenomenon in one shape or another is not uncommon.

"I know," writes Mr. Trine, "an officer on our police force who has told me that many times when off duty, and on his way home in the evening, there comes to him such a vivid and vital realization of his oneness with this Infinite Power, and this Spirit of Infinite Peace so takes hold of and so fills him, that it seems as if his feet could hardly keep to the pavement, so buoyant and so exhilarated does he become by reason of this inflowing tide." [In Tune with the Infinite, p. 137.]

Certain aspects of nature seem to have a peculiar power of awakening such mystical moods. Most of the striking cases which I have collected have occurred out of doors. Literature has commemorated this fact in many passages of great beauty— this extract, for example, from Amiel's Journal Intime:—

"Shall I ever again have any of those prodigious reveries which sometimes came to me in former days? One day, in youth, at sunrise, sitting in the ruins of the castle of Faucigny; and again in the mountains, under the noonday sun, above Lavey, lying at the foot of a tree and visited by three butterflies; once more at night upon the shingly shore of the Northern Ocean, my back upon the sand and my vision ranging through the milky way;— such grand and spacious, immortal, cosmogonic reveries, when one reaches to the stars, when one owns the infinite! Moments divine, ecstatic hours; in which our thought flies from world to world, pierces the great enigma, breathes with a respiration broad, tranquil, and deep as the respiration of the ocean, serene and limitless as the blue firmament;... instants of irresistible intuition in which one feels one's self great as the universe, and calm as a god.... What hours, what memories! The vestiges they leave behind are enough to fill us with belief and enthusiasm, as if they were visits of the Holy Ghost."

"I never lost the consciousness of the presence of God until I stood at the foot of the Horseshoe Falls, Niagara. Then I lost him in the immensity of what I saw. I also lost myself, feeling that I was an atom too small for the notice of Almighty God."

I subjoin another similar case from Starbuck's collection:

"In that time the consciousness of God's nearness came to me sometimes. I say God, to describe what is indescribable. A presence, I might say, yet that is too suggestive of personality, and the moments of which I speak did not hold the consciousness of a personality, but something in myself made me feel myself a part of something bigger than I, that was controlling. I felt myself one with the grass, the trees, birds, insects, everything in Nature. I exulted in the mere fact of existence, of being a part of it all— the drizzling rain, the shadows of the clouds, the tree-trunks, and so on. In the years following, such moments continued to come, but I wanted them constantly. I knew so well the satisfaction of losing self in a perception of supreme power and love, that I was unhappy because that perception was not constant." The cases quoted in my third lecture, are still better ones of this type. In her essay, The Loss of Personality, in The Atlantic Monthly (vol. lxxxv. p. 195), Miss Ethel D.

Puffer explains that the vanishing of the sense of self, and the feeling of immediate unity with the object, is due to the disappearance, in these rapturous experiences, of the motor adjustments which habitually intermediate between the constant background of consciousness (which is the Self) and the object in the foreground, whatever it may be. I must refer the reader to the highly instructive article, which seems to me to throw light upon the psychological conditions, though it fails to account for the rapture or the revelation-value of the experience in the Subject's eyes.

Here is a similar record from the memoirs of that interesting German idealist, Malwida von Meysenbug:—

"I was alone upon the seashore as all these thoughts flowed over me, liberating and reconciling; and now again, as once before in distant days in the Alps of Dauphine, I was impelled to kneel down, this time before the illimitable ocean, symbol of the Infinite. I felt that I prayed as I had never prayed before, and knew now what prayer really is: to return from the solitude of individuation into the consciousness of unity with all that is, to kneel down as one that passes away, and to rise up as one imperishable. Earth, heaven, and sea resounded as in one vast world-encircling harmony. It was as if the chorus of all the great who had ever lived were about me. I felt myself one with them, and it appeared as if I heard their greeting: Thou too belongest to the company of those who overcome.'" [Memoiren einer Idealistin, 5te Auflage, 1900, iii. 166. For years she had been unable to pray, owing to materialistic belief.]

The well-known passage from Walt Whitman is a classical expression of this sporadic type of mystical experience.

"I believe in you, my Soul...

Loaf with me on the grass, loose the stop from your throat;...

Only the lull I like, the hum of your valved voice.

I mind how once we lay, such a transparent summer morning.

Swiftly arose and spread around me the peace and knowledge that pass all the argument of the earth,

And I know that the hand of God is the promise of my own,

And I know that the spirit of God is the brother of my own,

And that all the men ever born are also my brothers and the women my sisters and lovers,

And that a kelson of the creation is love."

Whitman in another place expresses in a quieter way what was probably with him a chronic mystical perception: "There is," he writes, "apart from mere intellect, in the make-up of every superior human identity, a wondrous something that realizes without argument, frequently without what is called education (though I think it the goal and apex of all education deserving the name), an intuition of the absolute balance, in time and space, of the whole of this multifariousness, this revel of fools, and incredible make-believe and general unsettledness, we call the world; a soul-sight of that divine clue and unseen thread which holds the whole congeries of things, all history and time, and all events, however trivial, however momentous, like a leashed dog in the hand of the

hunter. [Of] such soul-sight and root-centre for the mind mere optimism
explains only the surface." Whitman charges it against Carlyle that he
lacked this perception. [Specimen Days and Collect, Philadelphia, 1882,
p. 174.]

I could easily give more instances, but one will suffice. I take it from the
Autobiography of J. Trevor. [My Quest for God, London, 1897, pp. 268,
269, abridged.]

"One brilliant Sunday morning, my wife and boys went to the Unitarian
Chapel in Macclesfield. I felt it impossible to accompany them— as though
to leave the sunshine on the hills, and go down there to the chapel, would
be for the time an act of spiritual suicide. And I felt such need for new
inspiration and expansion in my life. So, very reluctantly and sadly, I left
my wife and boys to go down into the town, while I went further up into
the hills with my stick and my dog. In the loveliness of the morning, and
the beauty of the hills and valleys, I soon lost my sense of sadness and
regret. For nearly an hour I walked along the road to the 'Cat and Fiddle,'
and then returned. On the way back, suddenly, without warning, I felt
that I was in Heaven— an inward state of peace and joy and assurance
indescribably intense, accompanied with a sense of being bathed in a
warm glow of light, as though the external condition had brought about
the internal effect— a feeling of having passed beyond the body, though
the scene around me stood out more clearly and as if nearer to me than
before, by reason of the illumination in the midst of which I seemed to be
placed. This deep emotion lasted, though with decreasing strength, until
I reached home, and for some time after, only gradually passing away."

The writer adds that having had further experiences of a similar sort,
he now knows them well.

"The spiritual life," he writes, "justifies itself to those who live it; but
what can we say to those who do not understand? This, at least, we can
say, that it is a life whose experiences are proved real to their possessor,
because they remain with him when brought closest into contact with the
objective realities of life. Dreams cannot stand this test. We wake from
them to find that they are but dreams. Wanderings of an overwrought
brain do not stand this test. These highest experiences that I have had of
God's presence have been rare and brief- flashes of consciousness which
have compelled me to exclaim with surprise— God is here!— or conditions
of exaltation and insight less intense, and only gradually passing away.
I have severely questioned the worth of these moments. To no soul have
I named them, lest I should be building my life and work on mere
phantasies of the brain. But I find that, after every questioning and test,
they stand out today as the most real experiences of my life, and
experiences which have explained and justified and unified all past
experiences and all past growth. Indeed, their reality and their
far-reaching significance are ever becoming more clear and evident. When
they came, I was living the fullest, strongest, sanest, deepest life. I was
not seeking them. What I was seeking, with resolute determination, was
to live more intensely my own life, as against what I knew would be the
adverse judgment of the world. It was in the most real seasons that the

Real Presence came, and I was aware that I was immersed in the infinite ocean of God." [Op. cit., pp. 256, 257, abridged.]

Even the least mystical of you must by this time be convinced of the existence of mystical moments as states of consciousness of an entirely specific quality, and of the deep impression which they make on those who have them. A Canadian psychiatrist, Dr. R.M. Bucke, gives to the more distinctly characterized of these phenomena the name of cosmic consciousness. "Cosmic consciousness in its more striking instances is not," Dr. Bucke says, "simply an expansion or extension of the self-conscious mind with which we are all familiar, but the superaddition of a function as distinct from any possessed by the average man as self-consciousness is distinct from any function possessed by one of the higher animals."

"The prime characteristic of cosmic consciousness is a consciousness of the cosmos, that is, of the life and order of the universe. Along with the consciousness of the cosmos there occurs an intellectual enlightenment which alone would place the individual on a new plane of existence— would make him almost a member of a new species. To this is added a state of moral exaltation, an indescribable feeling of elevation, elation, and joyousness, and a quickening of the moral sense, which is fully as striking, and more important than is the enhanced intellectual power. With these come what may be called a sense of immortality, a consciousness of eternal life, not a conviction that he shall have this, but the consciousness that he has it already." [Cosmic Consciousness: a study in the evolution of the human Mind, Philadelphia, 1901, p. 2.]

It was Dr. Bucke's own experience of a typical onset of cosmic consciousness in his own person which led him to investigate it in others. He has printed his conclusions in a highly interesting volume, from which I take the following account of what occurred to him:—

"I had spent the evening in a great city, with two friends, reading and discussing poetry and philosophy. We parted at midnight. I had a long drive in a hansom to my lodging. My mind, deeply under the influence of the ideas, images, and emotions called up by the reading and talk, was calm and peaceful. I was in a state of quiet, almost passive enjoyment, not actually thinking, but letting ideas, images, and emotions flow of themselves, as it were, through my mind. All at once, without warning of any kind, I found myself wrapped in a flame-colored cloud. For an instant I thought of fire, an immense conflagration somewhere close by in that great city; the next, I knew that the fire was within myself. Directly afterward there came upon me a sense of exultation, of immense joyousness accompanied or immediately followed by an intellectual illumination impossible to describe. Among other things, I did not merely come to believe, but I saw that the universe is not composed of dead matter, but is, on the contrary, a living Presence; I became conscious in myself of eternal life. It was not a conviction that I would have eternal life, but a consciousness that I possessed eternal life then; I saw that all men are immortal; that the cosmic order is such that without any peradventure all things work together for the good of each and all; that the foundation principle of the world, of all the worlds, is what we call love, and that the happiness of each and all is in the long run absolutely certain. The vision lasted a few seconds and was gone; but the memory of it and the sense of the reality of what it taught has remained during the quarter of a century which has since elapsed. I knew that what the vision showed was true. I had attained to a point of view from which I saw that it must be true. That view, that conviction, I may say that consciousness, has never, even during periods of the deepest depression, been lost." [Loc. cit. My quotation follows the privately printed pamphlet which preceded Dr. Bucke's larger work, and differs verbally a little from the text of the latter.]

We have now seen enough of this cosmic or mystic consciousness, as it comes sporadically. We must next pass to its methodical cultivation as an element of the religious life. Hindus, Buddhists, Mohammedans, and Christians all have cultivated it methodically.

In India, training in mystical insight has been known from time immemorial under the name of yoga. Yoga means the experimental union of the individual with the divine. It is based on persevering exercise; and the diet, posture, breathing, intellectual concentration, and moral discipline vary slightly in the different systems which teach it. The yogi, or disciple, who has by these means overcome the obscurations of his lower nature sufficiently, enters into the condition termed samadhi, "and comes face to face with facts which no instinct or reason can ever know." He learns—

"That the mind itself has a higher state of existence, beyond reason, a superconscious state, and that when the mind gets to that higher state, then this knowledge beyond reasoning comes.... All the different steps in yoga are intended to bring us scientifically to the superconscious state or samadhi.... Just as unconscious work is beneath consciousness, so there is another work which is above consciousness, and which, also, is not accompanied with the feeling of egoism.... There is no feeling of I, and yet the mind works, desireless, free from restlessness, objectless, bodiless. Then the Truth shines in its full effulgence, and we know ourselves— for Samadhi lies potential in us all— for what we truly are, free, immortal, omnipotent, loosed from the finite, and its contrasts of good and evil altogether, and identical with the Atman or Universal Soul." [My quotations are from Vivekananda, Raja Yoga, London, 1896. The completest source of information on Yoga is the work translated by Vihari Lala Mitra: Yoga Vasishta Maha Ramayana, 4 vols., Calcutta. 1891-99.]

The Vedantists say that one may stumble into super-consciousness sporadically, without the previous discipline, but it is then impure. Their test of its purity, like our test of religion's value, is empirical: its fruits must be good for life. When a man comes out of Samadhi, they assure us that he remains "enlightened, a sage, a prophet, a saint, his whole character changed, his life changed, illumined."

A European witness, after carefully comparing the results of Yoga with those of the hypnotic or dreamy states artificially producible by us, says: "It makes of its true disciples good, healthy, and happy men.... Through the mastery which the yogi attains over his thoughts and his body, he grows into a 'character.' By the subjection of his impulses and propensities to his will, and the fixing of the latter upon the ideal of goodness, be becomes a 'personality' hard to influence by others, and thus almost the opposite of what we usually imagine a 'medium' so-called, or 'psychic subject' to be." [Karl Kellner: Yoga: Eine Skizze, Munchen, 1896, p. 21.]

The Buddhists use the word 'samadhi' as well as the Hindus; but 'dhyana' is their special word for higher states of contemplation. There seem to be four stages recognized in dhyana. The first stage comes through concentration of the mind upon one point. It excludes desire, but not discernment or judgment: it is still intellectual. In the second stage the intellectual functions drop off, and the satisfied sense of unity remains. In the third stage the satisfaction departs, and indifference begins, along with memory and self-consciousness. In the fourth stage the indifference, memory, and self-consciousness are perfected. [Just what 'memory' and 'self-consciousness' mean in this connection is doubtful. They cannot be the faculties familiar to us in the lower life.] Higher stages still of contemplation are mentioned— a region where there exists nothing, and where the meditator says: "There exists absolutely nothing," and stops. Then he reaches another region where he says: "There are neither ideas nor absence of ideas," and stops again. Then another region where, "having reached the end of both idea and perception, he stops finally." This would seem to be, not yet Nirvana, but as close an approach to it as this life affords. [I follow the account in C.F. Koeppen: Die Religion des Buddha, Berlin, 1857, i. 585 ff.]

In the Mohammedan world the Sufi sect and various dervish bodies are the possessors of the mystical tradition. The Sufis have existed in Persia from the earliest times, and as their pantheism is so at variance with the hot and rigid monotheism of the Arab mind, it has been suggested that Sufism must have been inoculated into Islam by Hindu influences. We Christians know little of Sufism, for its secrets are disclosed only to those initiated. To give its existence a certain liveliness in your minds, I will quote a Moslem document, and pass away from the subject.

Al-Ghazzali, a Persian philosopher and theologian, who flourished in the eleventh century, and ranks as one of the greatest doctors of the Moslem church, has left us one of the few autobiographies to be found outside of Christian literature. Strange that a species of book so abundant among ourselves should be so little represented elsewhere— the absence of strictly personal confessions is the chief difficulty to the purely literary student who would like to become acquainted with the inwardness of religions other than the Christian.

M. Schmolders has translated a part of Al-Ghazzali's autobiography into French: [For a full account of him, see D.B. Macdonald: The Life of Al-Ghazzali, in the Journal of the American Oriental Society, 1899, vol. xx p. 71.]

"The Science of the Sufis," says the Moslem author, "aims at detaching the heart from all that is not God, and at giving to it for sole occupation the meditation of the divine being. Theory being more easy for me than practice, I read [certain books] until I understood all that can be learned by study and hearsay. Then I recognized that what pertains most exclusively to their method is just what no study can grasp, but only transport, ecstasy, and the transformation of the soul. How great, for example, is the difference between knowing the definitions of health, of satiety, with their causes and conditions, and being really healthy or filled. How different to know in what drunkenness consists,— as being a state occasioned by a vapor that rises from the stomach,— and being drunk effectively. Without doubt, the drunken man knows neither the definition of drunkenness nor what makes it interesting for science. Being drunk, he knows nothing; whilst the physician, although not drunk, knows well in what drunkenness consists, and what are its predisposing conditions. Similarly there is a difference between knowing the nature of abstinence, and being abstinent or having one's soul detached from the world.— Thus I had learned what words could teach of Sufism, but what was left could be learned neither by study nor through the ears, but solely by giving one's self up to ecstasy and leading a pious life.

"Reflecting on my situation, I found myself tied down by a multitude of bonds— temptations on every side. Considering my teaching, I found it was impure before God. I saw myself struggling with all my might to achieve glory and to spread my name. [Here follows an account of his six months' hesitation to break away from the conditions of his life at Bagdad, at the end of which he fell ill with a paralysis of the tongue.] Then, feeling my own weakness, and having entirely given up my own will, I repaired to God like a man in distress who has no more resources. He answered, as he answers the wretch who invokes him. My heart no longer felt any difficulty in renouncing glory, wealth, and my children. So I quitted Bagdad, and reserving from my fortune only what was indispensable for my subsistence, I distributed the rest. I went to Syria, where I remained about two years, with no other occupation than living in retreat and solitude, conquering my desires, combating my passions, training myself to purify my soul, to make my character perfect, to prepare my heart for meditating on God— all according to the methods of the Sufis, as I had read of them.

"This retreat only increased my desire to live in solitude, and to complete the purification of my heart and fit it for meditation. But the vicissitudes of the times, the affairs of the family, the need of subsistence, changed in some respects my primitive resolve, and interfered with my plans for a purely solitary life. I had never yet found myself completely in ecstasy, save in a few single hours; nevertheless, I kept the hope of attaining this state. Every time that the accidents led me astray, I sought to return; and in this situation I spent ten years. During this solitary state things were revealed to me which it is impossible either to describe or to point out. I recognized for certain that the Sufis are assuredly walking in the path of God. Both in their acts and in their inaction, whether internal or external, they are illumined by the light which proceeds from the prophetic source. The first condition for a Sufi is to purge his heart entirely of all that is not God. The next key of the contemplative life consists in the humble prayers which escape from the fervent soul, and in the meditations on God in which the heart is swallowed up entirely. But in reality this is only the beginning of the Sufi life, the end of Sufism being total absorption in God. The intuitions and all that precede are, so to speak, only the threshold for those who enter. From the beginning, revelations take place in so flagrant a shape that the Sufis see before them, whilst wide awake, the angels and the souls of the prophets. They hear their voices and obtain their favors. Then the transport rises from the perception of forms and figures to a degree which escapes all expression, and which no man may seek to give an account of without his words involving sin.

"Whoever has had no experience of the transport knows of the true nature of prophetism nothing but the name. He may meanwhile be sure of its existence, both by experience and by what he hears the Sufis say. As there are men endowed only with the sensitive faculty who reject what is offered them in the way of objects of the pure understanding, so there are intellectual men who reject and avoid the things perceived by the prophetic faculty. A blind man can understand nothing of colors save what he has learned by narration and hearsay. Yet God has brought prophetism near to men in giving them all a state analogous to it in its principal characters. This state is sleep. If you were to tell a man who was himself without experience of such a phenomenon that there are people who at times swoon away so as to resemble dead men, and who [in dreams] yet perceive things that are hidden, he would deny it [and give his reasons]. Nevertheless, his arguments would be refuted by actual experience. Wherefore, just as the understanding is a stage of human life in which an eye opens to discern various intellectual objects uncomprehended by sensation; just so in the prophetic the sight is illumined by a light which uncovers hidden things and objects which the intellect fails to reach. The chief properties of prophetism are perceptible only during the transport, by those who embrace the Sufi life. The prophet is endowed with qualities to which you possess nothing analogous, and which consequently you cannot possibly understand. How should you know their true nature, since one knows only what one can comprehend? But the transport which one attains by the method of the Sufis is like an immediate perception, as if one touched the objects with one's hand." [A. Schmolders: Essai sur les ecoles philosophiques chez les Arabes, Paris, 1842, pp. 54-68, abridged.]

This incommunicableness of the transport is the keynote of all mysticism. Mystical truth exists for the individual who has the transport, but for no one else. In this, as I have said, it resembles the knowledge given to us in sensations more than that given by conceptual thought. Thought, with its remoteness and abstractness, has often enough in the history of philosophy been contrasted unfavorably with sensation. It is a commonplace of metaphysics that God's knowledge cannot be discursive but must be intuitive, that is, must be constructed more after the pattern of what in ourselves is called immediate feeling, than after that of proposition and judgment. But our immediate feelings have no content but what the five senses supply; and we have seen and shall see again that mystics may emphatically deny that the senses play any part in the very highest type of knowledge which their transports yield.

In the Christian church there have always been mystics. Although many of them have been viewed with suspicion, some have gained favor in the eyes of the authorities. The experiences of these have been treated as precedents, and a codified system of mystical theology has been based upon them, in which everything legitimate finds its place. The basis of the system is 'orison' or meditation, the methodical elevation of the soul towards God. Through the practice of orison the higher levels of mystical experience may be attained. It is odd that Protestantism, especially evangelical Protestantism, should seemingly have abandoned everything methodical in this line. Apart from what prayer may lead to, Protestant mystical experience appears to have been almost exclusively sporadic. It has been left to our mind-curers to reintroduce methodical meditation into our religious life. [Gorres's Christliche Mystik gives a full account of the facts. So does Ribet's Mystique Divine, 2 vols., Paris, 1890. A still more methodical modern work is the Mystica Theologia of Vallgornera, 2 vols., Turin, 1890.]

The first thing to be aimed at in orison is the mind's detachment from outer sensations, for these interfere with its concentration upon ideal things. Such manuals as Saint Ignatius's Spiritual Exercises recommend the disciple to expel sensation by a graduated series of efforts to imagine holy scenes. The acme of this kind of discipline would be a semi-hallucinatory mono-ideism- an imaginary figure of Christ, for example, coming fully to occupy the mind. Sensorial images of this sort, whether literal or symbolic, play an enormous part in mysticism. But in certain cases imagery may fall away entirely, and in the very highest raptures it tends to do so. The state of consciousness becomes then insusceptible of any verbal description. Mystical teachers are unanimous as to this. Saint John of the Cross, for instance, one of the best of them, thus describes the condition called the 'union of love,' which, he says, is reached by 'dark contemplation.' In this the Deity compenetrates the soul, but in such a hidden way that the soul—

"finds no terms, no means, no comparison whereby to render the sublimity of the wisdom and the delicacy of the spiritual feeling with which she is filled.... We receive this mystical knowledge of God clothed in none of the kinds of images, in none of the sensible representations, which our mind makes use of in other circumstances. Accordingly in this knowledge, since the senses and the imagination are not employed, we get neither form nor impression, nor can we give any account or furnish any likeness, although the mysterious and sweet-tasting wisdom comes home so clearly to the inmost parts of our soul. Fancy a man seeing a certain kind of thing for the first time in his life. He can understand it, use and enjoy it, but he cannot apply a name to it, nor communicate any idea of it, even though all the while it be a mere thing of sense. How much greater will be his powerlessness when it goes beyond the senses! This is the peculiarity of the divine language. The more infused, intimate, spiritual, and supersensible it is, the more does it exceed the senses, both inner and outer, and impose silence upon them.... The soul then feels as if placed in a vast and profound solitude, to which no created thing has access, in an immense and boundless desert, desert the more delicious the more solitary it is. There, in this abyss of wisdom, the soul grows by what it drinks in from the well-springs of the comprehension of love,... and recognizes, however sublime and learned may be the terms we employ, how utterly vile, insignificant, and improper they are, when we seek to discourse of divine things by their means."

I cannot pretend to detail to you the sundry stages of the Christian mystical life. Our time would not suffice, for one thing; and moreover, I confess that the subdivisions and names which we find in the Catholic books seem to me to represent nothing objectively distinct. So many men, so many minds: I imagine that these experiences can be as infinitely varied as are the idiosyncrasies of individuals.

In particular I omit mention of visual and auditory hallucinations, verbal and graphic automatisms, and such marvels as 'levitation,' stigmatization, and the healing of disease. These phenomena, which mystics have often presented (or are believed to have presented), have no essential mystical significance, for they occur with no consciousness of illumination whatever, when they occur, as they often do, in persons of non-mystical mind. Consciousness of illumination is for us the essential mark of 'mystical' states.

The cognitive aspects of them, their value in the way of revelation, is what we are directly concerned with, and it is easy to show by citation how strong an impression they leave of being revelations of new depths of truth. Saint Teresa is the expert of experts in describing such conditions, so I will turn immediately to what she says of one of the highest of them, the 'orison of union.'

"In the orison of union," says Saint Teresa, "the soul is fully awake as regards God, but wholly asleep as regards things of this world and in respect of herself. During the short time the union lasts, she is as it were deprived of every feeling, and even if she would, she could not think of any single thing. Thus she needs to employ no artifice in order to arrest the use of her understanding: it remains so stricken with inactivity that she neither knows what she loves, nor in what manner she loves, nor what she wills. In short, she is utterly dead to the things of the world and lives solely in God.... I do not even know whether in this state she has enough life left to breathe. It seems to me she has not; or at least that if she does breathe, she is unaware of it. Her intellect would fain understand something of what is going on within her, but it has so little force now that it can act in no way whatsoever. So a person who falls into a deep faint appears as if dead....

"Thus does God, when he raises a soul to union with himself, suspend the natural action of all her faculties. She neither sees, hears, nor understands, so long as she is united with God. But this time is always short, and it seems even shorter than it is. God establishes himself in the interior of this soul in such a way, that when she returns to herself, it is wholly impossible for her to doubt that she has been in God, and God in her. This truth remains so strongly impressed on her that, even though many years should pass without the condition returning, she can neither forget the favor she received, nor doubt of its reality. If you, nevertheless, ask how it is possible that the soul can see and understand that she has been in God, since during the union she has neither sight nor understanding, I reply that she does not see it then, but that she sees it clearly later, after she has returned to herself, not by any vision, but by a certitude which abides with her and which God alone can give her. I knew a person who was ignorant of the truth that God's mode of being in everything must be either by presence, by power, or by essence, but who, after having received the grace of which I am speaking, believed this truth in the most unshakable manner. So much so that, having consulted a half-learned man who was as ignorant on this point as she had been before she was enlightened, when he replied that God is in us only by 'grace,' she disbelieved his reply, so sure she was of the true answer; and when she came to ask wiser doctors, they confirmed her in her belief, which much consoled her....

"But how, you will repeat, can one have such certainty in respect to what one does not see? This question, I am powerless to answer. These are secrets of God's omnipotence which it does not appertain to me to penetrate. All that I know is that I tell the truth; and I shall never believe that any soul who does not possess this certainty has ever been really united to God." [The Interior Castle, Fifth Abode, ch. i., in Oeuvres, translated by Bouix, iii. 421-424.]

The kinds of truth communicable in mystical ways, whether these be sensible or supersensible, are various. Some of them relate to this world,— visions of the future, the reading of hearts, the sudden understanding of texts, the knowledge of distant events, for example; but the most important revelations are theological or metaphysical. —

"Saint Ignatius confessed one day to Father Laynez that a single hour of meditation at Manresa had taught him more truths about heavenly things than all the teachings of all the doctors put together could have taught him.... One day in orison, on the steps of the choir of the Dominican church, he saw in a distinct manner the plan of divine wisdom in the creation of the world. On another occasion, during a procession, his spirit was ravished in God, and it was given him to contemplate, in a form and images fitted to the weak understanding of a dweller on the earth, the deep mystery of the holy Trinity. This last vision flooded his heart with such sweetness, that the mere memory of it in after times made him shed abundant tears." [Bartoli-Michel: Vie de Saint Ignace de Loyola, i. 34-36.]

Others have had illuminations about the created world, Jacob Boehme, for instance. At the age of twenty-five he was surrounded by the divine light, and replenished with the heavenly knowledge; insomuch as going abroad into the fields to a green, at Gorlitz, he there sat down, and viewing the herbs and grass of the field, in his inward light he saw into their essences, use, and properties, which was discovered to him by their lineaments, figures, and signatures." Of a later period of experience he writes: "In one quarter of an hour I saw and knew more than if I had been many years together at an university. For I saw and knew the being of all things, the Byss and the Abyss, and the eternal generation of the holy Trinity, the descent and original of the world and of all creatures through the divine wisdom. I knew and saw in myself all the three worlds, the external and visible world being of a procreation or extern birth from both the internal and spiritual worlds; and I saw and knew the whole working essence, in the evil and in the good, and the mutual original and existence; and likewise how the fruitful bearing womb of eternity brought forth. So that I did not only greatly wonder at it, but did also exceedingly rejoice, albeit I could very hardly apprehend the same in my external man and set it down with the pen. For I had a thorough view of the universe as in a chaos, wherein all things are couched and wrapt up, but it was impossible for me to explicate the same." [Jacob Behmen's Theosophic Philosophy, etc., by Edward Taylor, London, 1691, pp. 425, 427, abridged.] So George Fox: "I was come up to the state of Adam in which he was before he fell. The creation was opened to me; and it was showed me, how all things had their names given to them, according to their nature and virtue. I was at a stand in my mind, whether I should practice physic for the good of mankind, seeing the nature and virtues of the creatures were so opened to me by the Lord." Journal, Philadelphia, no date, p. 69. Contemporary 'Clairvoyance' abounds in similar revelations. Andrew Jackson Davis's cosmogonies, for example, or certain experiences related in the delectable ['Reminiscences and Memories of Henry Thomas Butterworth,' Lebanon, Ohio, 1886.]

Similarly with Saint Teresa. "One day, being in orison," she writes, "it was granted me to perceive in one instant how all things are seen and contained in God. I did not perceive them in their proper form, and nevertheless the view I had of them was of a sovereign clearness, and has remained vividly impressed upon my soul. It is one of the most signal of all the graces which the Lord has granted me.... The view was so subtle and delicate that the understanding cannot grasp it."

She goes on to tell how it was as if the Deity were an enormous and sovereignly limpid diamond, in which all our actions were contained in such a way that their full sinfulness appeared evident as never before. On another day, she relates, while she was reciting the Athanasian Creed,—

"Our Lord made me comprehend in what way it is that one God can be in three Persons. He made me see it so clearly that I remained as extremely surprised as I was comforted, and now, when I think of the holy Trinity, or hear It spoken of, I understand how the three adorable Persons form only one God and I experience an unspeakable happiness."

On still another occasion, it was given to Saint Teresa to see and understand in what wise the Mother of God had been assumed into her place in Heaven.

The deliciousness of some of these states seems to be beyond anything known in ordinary consciousness. It evidently involves organic sensibilities, for it is spoken of as something too extreme to be borne, and as verging on bodily pain. But it is too subtle and piercing a delight for ordinary words to denote. God's touches, the wounds of his spear, references to ebriety and to nuptial union have to figure in the phraseology by which it is shadowed forth. Intellect and senses both swoon away in these highest states of ecstasy. "If our understanding comprehends," says Saint Teresa, "it is in a mode which remains unknown to it, and it can understand nothing of what it comprehends. For my own part, I do not believe that it does comprehend, because, as I said, it does not understand itself to do so. I confess that it is all a mystery in which I am lost." In the condition called raptus or ravishment by theologians, breathing and circulation are so depressed that it is a question among the doctors whether the soul be or be not temporarily dissevered from the body. One must read Saint Teresa's descriptions and the very exact distinctions which she makes, to persuade one's self that one is dealing, not with imaginary experiences, but with phenomena which, however rare, follow perfectly definite psychological types.

Saint Teresa discriminates between pain in which the body has a part and pure spiritual pain [Interior Castle, 6th Abode, ch. xi.]. As for the bodily part in these celestial joys, she speaks of it as "penetrating to the marrow of the bones, whilst earthly pleasures affect only the surface of the senses. I think," she adds, "that this is a just description, and I cannot make it better." [Ibid., 5th Abode, ch. i.]

To the medical mind these ecstasies signify nothing but suggested and imitated hypnoid states, on an intellectual basis of superstition, and a corporeal one of degeneration and hysteria. Undoubtedly these pathological conditions have existed in many and possibly in all the cases, but that fact tells us nothing about the value for knowledge of the consciousness which they induce. To pass a spiritual judgment upon these states, we must not content ourselves with superficial medical talk, but inquire into their fruits for life.

Their fruits appear to have been various. Stupefaction, for one thing, seems not to have been altogether absent as a result. You may remember the helplessness in the kitchen and schoolroom of poor Margaret Mary Alacoque. Many other ecstatics would have perished but for the care taken of them by admiring followers. The 'other. worldliness' encouraged by the mystical consciousness makes this over-abstraction from practical life peculiarly liable to befall mystics in whom the character is naturally passive and the intellect feeble; but in natively strong minds and characters we find quite opposite results. The great Spanish mystics, who carried the habit of ecstasy as far as it has often been carried, appear for the most part to have shown indomitable spirit and energy, and all the more so for the trances in which they indulged.

Saint Ignatius was a mystic, but his mysticism made him assuredly one of the most powerfully practical human engines that ever lived. Saint John of the Cross, writing of the intuitions and 'touches' by which God reaches the substance of the soul, tells us that—

"They enrich it marvelously. A single one of them may be sufficient to abolish at a stroke certain imperfections of which the soul during its whole life had vainly tried to rid itself, and to leave it adorned with virtues and loaded with supernatural gifts. A single one of these intoxicating consolations may reward it for all the labors undergone in its life— even were they numberless. Invested with an invincible courage, filled with an impassioned desire to suffer for its God, the soul then is seized with a strange torment— that of not being allowed to suffer enough." [Oeuvres, ii. 320.]

Saint Teresa is as emphatic, and much more detailed. You may perhaps remember a passage I quoted from her in my first lecture. There are many similar pages in her autobiography. Where in literature is a more evidently veracious account of the formation of a new centre of spiritual energy, than is given in her description of the effects of certain ecstasies which in departing leave the soul upon a higher level of emotional excitement?

"Often, infirm and wrought upon with dreadful pains before the ecstasy, the soul emerges from it full of health and admirably disposed for action... as if God had willed that the body itself, already obedient to the soul's desires, should share in the soul's happiness.... The soul after such a favor is animated with a degree of courage so great that if at that moment its body should be torn to pieces for the cause of God, it would feel nothing but the liveliest comfort. Then it is that promises and heroic resolutions spring up in profusion in us, soaring desires, horror of the world, and the clear perception of our proper nothingness.... What empire is comparable to that of a soul who, from this sublime summit to which God has raised her, sees all the things of earth beneath her feet, and is captivated by no one of them? How ashamed she is of her former attachments! How amazed at her blindness! What lively pity she feels for those whom she recognizes still shrouded in the darkness!... She groans at having ever been sensitive to points of honor, at the illusion that made her ever see as honor what the world calls by that name. Now she sees in this name nothing more than an immense lie of which the world remains a victim. She discovers, in the new light from above, that in genuine honor there is nothing spurious, that to be faithful to this honor is to give our respect to what deserves to be respected really, and to consider as nothing, or as less than nothing, whatsoever perishes and is not agreeable to God.... She laughs when she sees grave persons, persons of orison, caring for points of honor for which she now feels profoundest contempt. It is suitable to the dignity of their rank to act thus, they pretend, and it makes them more useful to others. But she knows that in despising the dignity of their rank for the pure love of God they would do more good in a single day than they would effect in ten years by preserving it.... She laughs at herself that there should ever have been a time in her life when she made any case of money, when she ever desired it.... Oh! if human beings might only agree together to regard it as so much useless mud, what harmony would then reign in the world! With what friendship we would all treat each other if our interest in honor and in money could but disappear from earth! For my own part, I feel as if it would be a remedy for all our ills."

Mystical conditions may, therefore, render the soul more energetic in the lines which their inspiration favors. But this could be reckoned an advantage only in case the inspiration were a true one. If the inspiration were erroneous, the energy would be all the more mistaken and misbegotten. So we stand once more before that problem of truth which confronted us at the end of the lectures on saintliness. You will remember that we turned to mysticism precisely to get some light on truth. Do mystical states establish the truth of those theological affections in which the saintly life has its root?

In spite of their repudiation of articulate self-description, mystical states in general assert a pretty distinct theoretic drift. It is possible to give the outcome of the majority of them in terms that point in definite philosophical directions. One of these directions is optimism, and the other is monism. We pass into mystical states from out of ordinary consciousness as from a less into a more, as from a smallness into a vastness, and at the same time as from an unrest to a rest. We feel them as reconciling, unifying states. They appeal to the yes-function more than to the no-function in us. In them the unlimited absorbs the limits and peacefully closes the account. Their very denial of every adjective you may propose as applicable to the ultimate truth,— He, the Self, the Atman, is to be described by 'No! no!' only, say the Upanishads,— though it seems on the surface to be a no-function, is a denial made on behalf of a deeper yes. Whoso calls the Absolute anything in particular, or says that it is this, seems implicitly to shut it off from being that— it is as if he lessened it. So we deny the 'this,' negating the negation which it seems to us to imply, in the interests of the higher affirmative attitude by which we are possessed. The fountain-head of Christian mysticism is Dionysius the Areopagite. He describes the absolute truth by negatives exclusively.

"The cause of all things is neither soul nor intellect; nor has it imagination, opinion, or reason, or intelligence; nor is it reason or intelligence; nor is it spoken or thought. It is neither number, nor order, nor magnitude, nor littleness, nor equality, nor inequality, nor similarity, nor dissimilarity. It neither stands, nor moves, nor rests.... It is neither essence, nor eternity, nor time. Even intellectual contact does not belong to it. It is neither science nor truth. It is not even royalty or wisdom; not one; not unity; not divinity or goodness; nor even spirit as we know it," etc., ad libitum. [T. Davidson's translation, in Journal of Speculative Philosophy, 1893, vol. xxii. p. 399.]

But these qualifications are denied by Dionysius, not because the truth falls short of them, but because it so infinitely excels them. It is above them. It is super-lucent, super-splendent, super-essential, super-sublime, super everything that can be named. Like Hegel in his logic, mystics journey towards the positive pole of truth only by the 'Methode der Absoluten Negativitat.' ["Deus propter excellentiam non immerito Nihil vocatur." Scotus Erigena, quoted by Andrew Seth: Two Lectures on Theism, New York, 1897, p. 55.]

Thus come the paradoxical expressions that so abound in mystical writings. As when Eckhart tells of the still desert of the Godhead, "where never was seen difference, neither Father, Son, nor Holy Ghost, where there is no one at home, yet where the spark of the soul is more at peace than in itself." As when Boehme writes of the Primal Love, that "it may fitly be compared to Nothing, for it is deeper than any Thing, and is as nothing with respect to all things, forasmuch as it is not comprehensible by any of them. And because it is nothing respectively, it is therefore free from all things, and is that only good, which a man cannot express or utter what it is, there being nothing to which it may be compared, to express it by." Or as when Angelus Silesius sings:—

To this dialectical use, by the intellect, of negation as a mode of passage towards a higher kind of affirmation, there is correlated the subtlest of moral counterparts in the sphere of the personal will. Since denial of the finite self and its wants, since asceticism of some sort, is found in religious experience to be the only doorway to the larger and more blessed life, this moral mystery intertwines and combines with the intellectual mystery in all mystical writings.

"Love," continues Behmen, is Nothing, for "when thou art gone forth wholly from the Creature and from that which is visible, and art become Nothing to all that is Nature and Creature, then thou art in that eternal One, which is God himself, and then thou shalt feel within thee the highest virtue of Love.... The treasure of treasures for the soul is where she goeth out of the Somewhat into that Nothing out of which all things may be made. The soul here saith, I have nothing, for I am utterly stripped and naked; I can do nothing, for I have no manner of power, but am as water poured out; I am nothing, for all that I am is no more than an image of Being, and only God is to me I AM; and so, sitting down in my own Nothingness, I give glory to the eternal Being, and will nothing of myself, that so God may will all in me, being unto me my God and all things."

In Paul's language, I live, yet not I, but Christ liveth in me. Only when I become as nothing can God enter in and no difference between his life and mine remain outstanding. [From a French book I take this mystical expression of happiness in God's indwelling presence:]

"Jesus has come to take up his abode in my heart. It is not so much a habitation, an association, as a sort of fusion. Oh, new and blessed life! life which becomes each day more luminous.... The wall before me, dark a few moments since, is splendid at this hour because the sun shines on it. Wherever its rays fall they light up a conflagration of glory; the smallest speck of glass sparkles, each grain of sand emits fire; even so there is a royal song of triumph in my heart because the Lord is there. My days succeed each other; yesterday a blue sky; today a clouded sun; a night filled with strange dreams; but as soon as the eyes open, and I regain consciousness and seem to begin life again, it is always the same figure before me, always the same presence filling my heart.... Formerly the day was dulled by the absence of the Lord. I used to wake invaded by all sorts of sad impressions, and I did not find him on my path. Today he is with me; and the light cloudiness which covers things is not an obstacle to my communion with him. I feel the pressure of his hand, I feel something else which fills me with a serene joy; shall I dare to speak it out? Yes, for it is the true expression of what I experience. The Holy Spirit in not merely making me a visit; it is no mere dazzling apparition which may from one moment to another spread its wings and leave me in my night, it is a permanent habitation. He can depart only if he takes me with him. More than that; he is not other than myself: he is one with me. It is not a juxtaposition, it is a penetration, a profound modification of my nature, a new manner of my being." [Quoted from the MS. 'of an old man' by Wilfred Monod: Il Vit: six meditations sur le mystere chretien, pp. 280-283.]

This overcoming of all the usual barriers between the individual and the Absolute is the great mystic achievement. In mystic states we both become one with the Absolute and we become aware of our oneness. This is the everlasting and triumphant mystical tradition, hardly altered by differences of clime or creed. In Hinduism, in Neoplatonism, in Sufism, in Christian mysticism, in Whitmanism, we find the same recurring note, so that there is about mystical utterances an eternal unanimity which ought to make a critic stop and think, and which brings it about that the mystical classics have, as has been said, neither birthday nor native land. Perpetually telling of the unity of man with God, their speech antedates languages, and they do not grow old. [Compare M. Maeterlinck: L'Ornament des Noces spirituelles de Ruysbroeck, Bruxelles, 1891, Introduction, p. xix.]

'That art Thou!' say the Upanishads, and the Vedantists add: 'Not a part, not a mode of That, but identically That, that absolute Spirit of the World.' "As pure water poured into pure water remains the same, thus, O Gautama, is the Self of a thinker who knows. Water in water, fire in fire, ether in ether, no one can distinguish them; likewise a man whose mind has entered into the Self." "'Every man,' says the Sufi Gulshan-Raz, 'whose heart is no longer shaken by any doubt, knows with certainty that there is no being save only One.... In his divine majesty the me, the we, the thou, are not found, for in the One there can be no distinction. Every being who is annulled and entirely separated from himself, hears resound outside of him this voice and this echo: I am God: he has an eternal way of existing, and is no longer subject to death.'" In the vision of God, says Plotinus, "what sees is not our reason, but something prior and superior to our reason.... He who thus sees does not properly see, does not distinguish or imagine two things. He changes, he ceases to be himself, preserves nothing of himself. Absorbed in God, he makes but one with him, like a centre of a circle coinciding with another centre." "Here," writes Suso, "the spirit dies, and yet is all alive in the marvels of the Godhead... and is lost in the stillness of the glorious dazzling obscurity and of the naked simple unity. It is in this modeless where that the highest bliss is to be found." "Ich bin so gross als Gott," sings Angelus Silesius again, "Er ist als ich so klein; Er kann nicht uber mich, ich unter ihm nicht sein."

In mystical literature such self-contradictory phrases as 'dazzling obscurity,' 'whispering silence,' 'teeming desert,' are continually met with.

They prove that not conceptual speech, but music rather, is the element through which we are best spoken to by mystical truth. Many mystical scriptures are indeed little more than musical compositions.

"He who would hear the voice of Nada, 'the Soundless Sound,' and comprehend it, he has to learn the nature of Dharana.... When to himself his form appears unreal, as do on waking all the forms he sees in dreams; when he has ceased to hear the many, he may discern the ONE— the inner sound which kills the outer.... For then the soul will hear, and will remember. And then to the inner ear will speak THE VOICE OF THE SILENCE.... And now thy Self is lost in SELF, thyself unto THYSELF, merged in that SELF from which thou first didst radiate.... Behold! thou hast become the Light, thou hast become the Sound, thou art thy Master and thy God. Thou art THYSELF the object of thy search: the VOICE unbroken, that resounds throughout eternities, exempt from change, from sin exempt, the seven sounds in one, the VOICE OF THE SILENCE. Om tat Sat." [H.P. Blavatsky: The Voice of the Silence.]

These words, if they do not awaken laughter as you receive them, probably stir chords within you which music and language touch in common. Music gives us ontological messages which non-musical criticism is unable to contradict, though it may laugh at our foolishness in minding them. There is a verge of the mind which these things haunt; and whispers therefrom mingle with the operations of our understanding, even as the waters of the infinite ocean send their waves to break among the pebbles that lie upon our shores.

"Here begins the sea that ends not till the world's end. Where we stand,
Could we know the next high sea-mark set beyond these waves that gleam,
We should know what never man hath known, nor eye of man hath scanned....
Ah, but here man's heart leaps, yearning towards the gloom with venturous glee,
From the shore that hath no shore beyond it, set in all the sea."
[Swinburne: On the Verge, in 'A Midsummer Vacation.']

That doctrine, for example, that eternity is timeless, that our 'immortality,' if we live in the eternal, is not so much future as already now and here, which we find so often expressed today in certain philosophic circles, finds its support in a 'hear, hear!' or an 'amen,' which floats up from that mysteriously deeper level. We recognize the passwords to the mystical region as we hear them, but we cannot use them ourselves; it alone has the keeping of 'the password primeval.' Compare the extracts from Dr. Bucke, quoted earlier in this lecture. [As serious an attempt as I know to mediate between the mystical region and the discursive life is contained in an article on Aristotle's Unmoved Mover, by F.C.S. Schiller, in Mind, vol. ix., 1900.]

I have now sketched with extreme brevity and insufficiency, but as fairly as I am able in the time allowed, the general traits of the mystic range of consciousness. It is on the whole pantheistic and optimistic, or at least the opposite of pessimistic. It is anti-naturalistic, and harmonizes best with twice-bornness and so-called other-worldly states of mind.

My next task is to inquire whether we can invoke it as authoritative. Does it furnish any warrant for the truth of the twice-bornness and supernaturality and pantheism which it favors? I must give my answer to this question as concisely as I can.

In brief my answer is this,— and I will divide it into three parts: (1) Mystical states, when well developed, usually are, and have the right to be, absolutely authoritative over the individuals to whom they come. (2) No authority emanates from them which should make it a duty for those who stand outside of them to accept their revelations uncritically. (3) They break down the authority of the non-mystical or rationalistic consciousness, based upon the understanding and the senses alone. They show it to be only one kind of consciousness. They open out the possibility of other orders of truth, in which, so far as anything in us vitally responds to them, we may freely continue to have faith.

I will take up these points one by one.

1. As a matter of psychological fact, mystical states of a well-pronounced and emphatic sort are usually authoritative over those who have them. They have been 'there,' and know. It is vain for rationalism to grumble about this. If the mystical truth that comes to a man proves to be a force that he can live by, what mandate have we of the majority to order him to live in another way? We can throw him into a prison or a madhouse, but we cannot change his mind— we commonly attach it only the more stubbornly to its beliefs. It mocks our utmost efforts, as a matter of fact, and in point of logic it absolutely escapes our jurisdiction. Our own more 'rational' beliefs are based on evidence exactly similar in nature to that which mystics quote for theirs. Our senses, namely, have assured us of certain states of fact; but mystical experiences are as direct perceptions of fact for those who have them as any sensations ever were for us. The records show that even though the five senses be in abeyance in them, they are absolutely sensational in their epistemological quality, if I may be pardoned the barbarous expression,— that is, they are face to face presentations of what seems immediately to exist.

Example: Mr. John Nelson writes of his imprisonment for preaching Methodism: "My soul was as a watered garden, and I could sing praises to God all day long; for he turned my captivity into joy, and gave me to rest as well on the boards, as if I had been on a bed of down. Now could I say, 'God's service is perfect freedom,' and I was carried out much in prayer that my enemies might drink of the same river of peace which my God gave so largely to me." [Journal, London, no date, p. 172.]

The mystic is, in short, invulnerable, and must be left, whether we relish it or not, in undisturbed enjoyment of his creed. Faith, says Tolstoy, is that by which men live. And faith-state and mystic state are practically convertible terms.

2. But I now proceed to add that mystics have no right to claim that we ought to accept the deliverance of their peculiar experiences, if we are

ourselves outsiders and feel no private call thereto. The utmost they can ever ask of us in this life is to admit that they establish a presumption. They form a consensus and have an unequivocal outcome; and it would be odd, mystics might say, if such a unanimous type of experience should prove to be altogether wrong. At bottom, however, this would only be an appeal to numbers, like the appeal of rationalism the other way; and the appeal to numbers has no logical force. If we acknowledge it, it is for 'suggestive,' not for logical reasons: we follow the majority because to do so suits our life.

But even this presumption from the unanimity of mystics is far from being strong. In characterizing mystic states as pantheistic, optimistic, etc., I am afraid I over-simplified the truth. I did so for expository reasons, and to keep the closer to the classic mystical tradition. The classic religious mysticism, it now must be confessed, is only a 'privileged case.' It is an extract, kept true to type by the selection of the fittest specimens and their preservation in 'schools.' It is carved out from a much larger mass; and if we take the larger mass as seriously as religious mysticism has historically taken itself, we find that the supposed unanimity largely disappears. To begin with, even religious mysticism itself, the kind that accumulates traditions and makes schools, is much less unanimous than I have allowed. It has been both ascetic and antinomianly self-indulgent within the Christian church. It is dualistic in Sankhya, and monistic in Vedanta philosophy, I called it pantheistic; but the great Spanish mystics are anything but pantheists. They are with few exceptions non-metaphysical minds, for whom 'the category of personality' is absolute. The 'union' of man with God is for them much more like an occasional miracle than like an original identity. How different again, apart from the happiness common to all, is the mysticism of Walt Whitman, Edward Carpenter, Richard Jefferies, and other naturalistic pantheists, from the more distinctively Christian sort. The fact is that the mystical feeling of enlargement, union, and emancipation has no specific intellectual content whatever of its own. It is capable of forming matrimonial alliances with material furnished by the most diverse philosophies and theologies, provided only they can find a place in their framework for its peculiar emotional mood. We have no right, therefore, to invoke its prestige as distinctively in favor of any special belief, such as that in absolute idealism, or in the absolute monistic identity, or in the absolute goodness, of the world. It is only relatively in favor of all these things— it passes out of common human consciousness in the direction in which they lie.

So much for religious mysticism proper. But more remains to be told, for religious mysticism is only one half of mysticism. The other half has no accumulated traditions except those which the text-books on insanity, supply. Open any one of these, and you will find abundant cases in which 'mystical ideas' are cited as characteristic symptoms of enfeebled or deluded states of mind. In delusional insanity, paranoia, as they sometimes call it, we may have a diabolical mysticism, a sort of religious mysticism turned upside down. The same sense of ineffable importance in the smallest events, the same texts and words coming with new meanings, the same voices and visions and leadings and missions, the same controlling by extraneous powers; only this time the emotion is pessimistic: instead of consolations we have desolations; the meanings are dreadful; and the powers are enemies to life. It is evident that from the point of view of their psychological mechanism, the classic mysticism and these lower mysticisms spring from the same mental level, from that great subliminal or transmarginal region of which science is beginning to admit the existence, but of which so little is really known. That region contains every kind of matter: 'seraph and snake' abide there side by side. To come from thence is no infallible credential. What comes must be sifted and tested, and run the gauntlet of confrontation with the total context of experience, just like what comes from the outer world of sense. Its value must be ascertained by empirical methods, so long as we are not mystics ourselves.

Once more, then, I repeat that non-mystics are under no obligation to acknowledge in mystical states a superior authority conferred on them by their intrinsic nature.

In chapter i. of book ii. of his work Degeneration, 'Max Nordau' seeks to undermine all mysticism by exposing the weakness of the lower kinds. Mysticism for him means any sudden perception of hidden significance in things. He explains such perception by the abundant uncompleted associations which experiences may arouse in a degenerate brain. These give to him who has the experience a vague and vast sense of its leading further, yet they awaken no definite or useful consequent in his thought. The explanation is a plausible one for certain sorts of feeling of significance; and other alienists [Wernicke, for example, in his Grundriss der Psychiatrie, Theil ii., Leipzig, 1896] have explained 'paranoiac' conditions by a laming of the association-organ. But the higher mystical flights, with their positiveness and abruptness, are surely products of no such merely negative condition. It seems far more reasonable to ascribe them to inroads from the subconscious life, of the cerebral activity correlative to which we as yet know nothing.

3. Yet, I repeat once more, the existence of mystical states absolutely overthrows the pretension of non-mystical states to be the sole and ultimate dictators of what we may believe. As a rule, mystical states merely add a supersensuous meaning to the ordinary outward data of consciousness. They are excitements like the emotions of love or ambition, gifts to our spirit by means of which facts already objectively before us fall into a new expressiveness and make a new connection with our active life. They do not contradict these facts as such or deny anything that our senses have immediately seized. It is the rationalistic critic rather who plays the part of denier in the controversy, and his denials have no strength, for there never can be a state of facts to which new meaning may not truthfully be added, provided the mind ascend to a more enveloping point of view. It must always remain an open question whether mystical states may not possibly be such superior points of view, windows through which the mind looks out upon a more extensive and

inclusive world. The difference of the views seen from the different mystical windows need not prevent us from entertaining this supposition. The wider world would in that case prove to have a mixed constitution like that of this world, that is all. It would have its celestial and its infernal regions, its tempting and its saving moments, its valid experiences and its counterfeit ones, just as our world has them; but it would be a wider world all the same. We should have to use its experiences by selecting and subordinating and substituting just as is our custom in this ordinary naturalistic world; we should be liable to error just as we are now; yet the counting in of that wider world of meanings, and the serious dealing with it, might, in spite of all the perplexity, be indispensable stages in our approach to the final fullness of the truth.

In this shape, I think, we have to leave the subject. Mystical states indeed wield no authority due simply to their being mystical states. But the higher ones among them point in directions to which the religious sentiments even of non-mystical men incline. They tell of the supremacy of the ideal, of vastness, of union, of safety, and of rest. They offer us hypotheses, hypotheses which we may voluntarily ignore, but which as thinkers we cannot possibly upset. The supernaturalism and optimism to which they would persuade us may, interpreted in one way or another, be after all the truest of insights into the meaning of this life.

"Oh, the little more, and how much it is; and the little less, and what worlds away!" It may be that possibility and permission of this sort are all that the religious consciousness requires to live on. In my last lecture I shall have to try to persuade you that this is the case. Meanwhile, however, I am sure that for many of my readers this diet is too slender. If supernaturalism and inner union with the divine are true, you think, then not so much permission, as compulsion to believe, ought to be found. Philosophy has always professed to prove religious truth by coercive argument; and the construction of philosophies of this kind has always been one favorite function of the religious life, if we use this term in the large historic sense. But religious philosophy is an enormous subject, and in my next lecture I can only give that brief glance at it which my limits will allow.

LECTURE XVIII: PHILOSOPHY

The subject of Saintliness left us face to face with the question, Is the sense of divine presence a sense of anything objectively true? We turned first to mysticism for an answer, and found that although mysticism is entirely willing to corroborate religion, it is too private (and also too various) in its utterances to be able to claim a universal authority. But philosophy publishes results which claim to be universally valid if they are valid at all, so we now turn with our question to philosophy. Can philosophy stamp a warrant of veracity upon the religious man's sense of the divine?

I imagine that many of you at this point begin to indulge in guesses at the goal to which I am tending. I have undermined the authority of mysticism, you say, and the next thing I shall probably do is to seek to discredit that of philosophy. Religion, you expect to hear me conclude, is nothing but an affair of faith, based either on vague sentiment, or on that vivid sense of the reality of things unseen of which in my second lecture and in the lecture on Mysticism I gave so many examples. It is essentially private and individualistic; it always exceeds our powers of formulation; and although attempts to pour its contents into a philosophic mould will probably always go on, men being what they are, yet these attempts are always secondary processes which in no way add to the authority, or warrant the veracity, of the sentiments from which they derive their own stimulus and borrow whatever glow of conviction they may themselves possess. In short, you suspect that I am planning to defend feeling at the expense of reason, to rehabilitate the primitive and unreflective, and to dissuade you from the hope of any Theology worthy of the name.

To a certain extent I have to admit that you guess rightly. I do believe that feeling is the deeper source of religion, and that philosophic and theological formulas are secondary products, like translations of a text into another tongue. But all such statements are misleading from their brevity, and it will take the whole hour for me to explain to you exactly what I mean.

When I call theological formulas secondary products, I mean that in a world in which no religious feeling had ever existed, I doubt whether any philosophic theology could ever have been framed. I doubt if dispassionate intellectual contemplation of the universe, apart from inner unhappiness and need of deliverance on the one hand and mystical emotion on the other, would ever have resulted in religious philosophies such as we now possess. Men would have begun with animistic explanations of natural fact, and criticised these away into scientific ones, as they actually have done. In the science they would have left a certain amount of 'psychical research,' even as they now will probably have to re-admit a certain amount. But high-flying speculations like those of either dogmatic or idealistic theology, these they would have had no motive to venture on, feeling no need of commerce with such deities. These speculations must, it seems to me, be classed as over-beliefs, buildings—out performed by the intellect into directions of which feeling originally supplied the hint.

But even if religious philosophy had to have its first hint supplied by feeling, may it not have dealt in a superior way with the matter which feeling suggested? Feeling is private and dumb, and unable to give an account of itself. It allows that its results are mysteries and enigmas, declines to justify them rationally, and on occasion is willing that they should even pass for paradoxical and absurd. Philosophy takes just the opposite attitude. Her aspiration is to reclaim from mystery and paradox whatever territory she touches. To find an escape from obscure and wayward personal persuasion to truth objectively valid for all thinking men has ever been the intellect's most cherished ideal. To redeem religion from unwholesome privacy, and to give public status and universal right of way to its deliverances, has been reason's task.

I believe that philosophy will always have opportunity to labor at this task. We are thinking beings, and we cannot exclude the intellect from participating in any of our functions. Even in soliloquizing with ourselves, we construe our feelings intellectually. Both our personal ideals and our religious and mystical experiences must be interpreted congruously with the kind of scenery which our thinking mind inhabits. The philosophic climate of our time inevitably forces its own clothing on us. Moreover, we must exchange our feelings with one another, and in doing so we have to speak, and to use general and abstract verbal formulas. Conceptions and constructions are thus a necessary part of our religion; and as moderator amid the clash of hypotheses, and mediator among the criticisms of one man's constructions by another, philosophy will always have much to do. It would be strange if I disputed this, when these very lectures which I am giving are (as you will see more clearly from now onwards) a laborious attempt to extract from the privacies of religious experience some general facts which can be defined in formulas upon which everybody may agree.

Religious experience, in other words, spontaneously and inevitably engenders myths, superstitions, dogmas, creeds, and metaphysical theologies, and criticisms of one set of these by the adherents of another. Of late, impartial classifications and comparisons have become possible, alongside of the denunciations and anathemas by which the commerce between creeds used exclusively to be carried on. We have the beginnings of a 'Science of Religions,' so-called; and if these lectures could ever be accounted a crumb-like contribution to such a science, I should be made very happy.

But all these intellectual operations, whether they be constructive or comparative and critical, presuppose immediate experiences as their subject-matter. They are interpretative and inductive operations, operations after the fact, consequent upon religious feeling, not coordinate with it, not independent of what it ascertains.

The intellectualism in religion which I wish to discredit pretends to be something altogether different from this. It assumes to construct religious objects out of the resources of logical reason alone, or of logical reason drawing rigorous inference from non-subjective facts. It calls its conclusions dogmatic theology, or philosophy of the absolute, as the case may be; it does not call them science of religions. It reaches them in an a priori way, and warrants their veracity.

Warranted systems have ever been the idols of aspiring souls. All-inclusive, yet simple; noble, clean, luminous, stable, rigorous, true;— what more ideal refuge could there be than such a system would offer to spirits vexed by the muddiness and accidentality of the world of sensible things? Accordingly, we find inculcated in the theological schools of today, almost as much as in those of the fore-time, a disdain for merely possible or probable truth, and of results that only private assurance can grasp. Scholastics and idealists both express this disdain. Principal John Caird, for example, writes as follows in his Introduction to the Philosophy of Religion:

"Religion must indeed be a thing of the heart; but in order to elevate it from the region of subjective caprice and waywardness, and to distinguish between that which is true and false in religion, we must appeal to an objective standard. That which enters the heart must first be discerned by the intelligence to be true. It must be seen as having in its own nature a right to dominate feeling, and as constituting the principle by which feeling must be judged. In estimating the religious character of individuals, nations, or races, the first question is, not how they feel, but what they think and believe— not whether their religion is one which manifests itself in emotions, more or less vehement and enthusiastic, but what are the conceptions of God and divine things by which these emotions are called forth. Feeling is necessary in religion, but it is by the content or intelligent basis of a religion, and not by feeling, that its character and worth are to be determined."

Cardinal Newman, in his work, The Idea of a University, gives more emphatic expression still to this disdain for sentiment. Theology, he says, is a science in the strictest sense of the word. I will tell you, he says, what it is not— not 'physical evidences' for God, not 'natural religion,' for these are but vague subjective interpretations:

"If," he continues, "the Supreme Being is powerful or skillful, just so far as the telescope shows power, or the microscope shows skill, if his moral law is to be ascertained simply by the physical processes of the animal frame, or his will gathered from the immediate issues of human affairs, if his Essence is just as high and deep and broad as the universe and no more; if this be the fact, then will I confess that there is no specific science about God, that theology is but a name, and a protest in its behalf an hypocrisy. Then, pious as it is to think of Him, while the pageant of experiment or abstract reasoning passes by, still such piety is nothing more than a poetry of thought, or an ornament of language, a certain view taken of Nature which one man has and another has not, which gifted minds strike out, which others see to be admirable and ingenious, and which all would be the better for adopting. It is but the theology of Nature, just as we talk of the philosophy or the romance of history, or the poetry of childhood, or the picturesque or the sentimental or the humorous, or any other abstract quality which the genius or the caprice of the individual, or the fashion of the day, or the consent of the world, recognizes in any set of objects which are subjected to its contemplation. I do not see much difference between avowing that there is no God, and implying that nothing definite can be known for certain about Him."

What I mean by Theology, continues Newman, is none of these things: "I simply mean the Science of God, or the truths we know about God, put into a system, just as we have a science of the stars and call it astronomy, or of the crust of the earth and call it geology."

In both these extracts we have the issue clearly set before us: Feeling valid only for the individual is pitted against reason valid universally. The test is a perfectly plain one of fact. Theology based on pure reason must in point of fact convince men universally. If it did not, wherein would its superiority consist? If it only formed sects and schools, even as sentiment and mysticism form them, how would it fulfill its programme of freeing us from personal caprice and waywardness? This perfectly definite practical test of the pretensions of philosophy to found religion on universal reason simplifies my procedure today. I need not discredit philosophy by laborious criticism of its arguments. It will suffice if I show that as a matter of history it fails to prove its pretension to be 'objectively' convincing. In fact, philosophy does so fail. It does not banish differences; it founds schools and sects just as feeling does. I believe, in fact, that the logical reason of man operates in this field of divinity exactly as it has always operated in love, or in patriotism, or in politics, or in any other of the wider affairs of life, in which our passions or our mystical intuitions fix our beliefs beforehand. It finds arguments for our conviction, for indeed it has to find them. It amplifies and defines our faith, and dignifies it and lends it words and plausibility. It hardly ever engenders it; it cannot now secure it.

As regards the secondary character of intellectual constructions, and the primacy of feeling and instinct in founding religious beliefs, see the striking work of H. Fielding, The Hearts of Men, London, 1902, which came into my hands after my text was written. "Creeds," says the author, "are the grammar of religion, they are to religion what grammar is to speech. Words are the expression of our wants; grammar is the theory formed afterwards. Speech never proceeded from grammar, but the reverse. As speech progresses and changes from unknown causes, grammar must follow" (p. 313). The whole book, which keeps unusually close to concrete facts, is little more than an amplification of this text.

Lend me your attention while I run through some of the points of the older systematic theology. You find them in both Protestant and Catholic manuals, best of all in the innumerable text-books published since Pope Leo's Encyclical recommending the study of Saint Thomas. I glance first at the arguments by which dogmatic theology establishes God's existence, after that at those by which it establishes his nature. [For convenience' sake, I follow the order of A. Stockl's Lehrbuch der Philosophie, 5te Auflage, Mainz, 1881, Band ii. B. Boedder's Natural Theology, London, 1891, is a handy English Catholic Manual; but an almost identical doctrine is given by such Protestant theologians as C. Hodge: Systematic Theology, New York, 1873, or A.H. Strong: Systematic Theology, 5th edition, New York, 1896.]

The arguments for God's existence have stood for hundreds of years with the waves of unbelieving criticism breaking against them, never totally discrediting them in the ears of the faithful, but on the whole slowly and surely washing out the mortar from between their joints. If you have a God already whom you believe in, these arguments confirm you. If you are atheistic, they fail to set you right. The proofs are various. The 'cosmological' one, so-called, reasons from the contingence of the world to a First Cause which must contain whatever perfections the world itself contains. The 'argument from design' reasons, from the fact that Nature's laws are mathematical, and her parts benevolently adapted to each other, that this cause is both intellectual and benevolent. The 'moral argument' is that the moral law presupposes a lawgiver. The 'argument ex consensu gentium' is that the belief in God is so widespread as to be grounded in the rational nature of man, and should therefore carry authority with it.

As I just said, I will not discuss these arguments technically. The bare fact that all idealists since Kant have felt entitled either to scout or to neglect them shows that they are not solid enough to serve as religion's all-sufficient foundation. Absolutely impersonal reasons would be in duty bound to show more general convincingness. Causation is indeed too obscure a principle to bear the weight of the whole structure of theology. As for the argument from design, see how Darwinian ideas have revolutionized it. Conceived as we now conceive them, as so many fortunate escapes from almost limitless processes of destruction, the benevolent adaptations which we find in Nature suggest a deity very different from the one who figured in the earlier versions of the argument. The fact is that these arguments do but follow the combined suggestions of the facts and of our feeling. They prove nothing rigorously. They only corroborate our pre-existent partialities.

It must not be forgotten that any form of disorder in the world might, by the design argument, suggest a God for just that kind of disorder. The truth is that any state of things whatever that can be named is logically susceptible of teleological interpretation. The ruins of the earthquake at Lisbon, for example: the whole of past history had to be planned exactly as it was to bring about in the fullness of time just that particular arrangement of debris of masonry, furniture, and once living bodies. No other train of causes would have been sufficient. And so of any other arrangement, bad or good, which might as a matter of fact be found resulting anywhere from previous conditions. To avoid such pessimistic consequences and save its beneficent designer, the design argument accordingly invokes two other principles, restrictive in their operation. The first is physical: Nature's forces tend of their own accord only to disorder and destruction, to heaps of ruins, not to architecture. This principle, though plausible at first sight, seems, in the light of recent biology, to be more and more improbable. The second principle is one of anthropomorphic interpretation. No arrangement that for us is 'disorderly' can possibly have been an object of design at all. This principle is of course a mere assumption in the interests of anthropomorphic Theism.

When one views the world with no definite theological bias one way or the other, one sees that order and disorder, as we now recognize them, are purely human inventions. We are interested in certain types of arrangement, useful, aesthetic, or moral,— so interested that whenever we find them realized, the fact emphatically rivets our attention. The result is that we work over the contents of the world selectively. It is overflowing with disorderly arrangements from our point of view, but order is the only thing we care for and look at, and by choosing, one can always find some sort of orderly arrangement in the midst of any chaos. If I should throw down a thousand beans at random upon a table, I could doubtless, by eliminating a sufficient number of them, leave the rest in almost any geometrical pattern you might propose to me, and you might then say that that pattern was the thing prefigured beforehand, and that the other beans were mere irrelevance and packing material. Our dealings with Nature are just lines in innumerable directions. We count and name whatever lies upon the special lines we trace, whilst the other things and the untraced lines are neither named nor counted. There are in reality infinitely more things 'unadapted' to each other in this world than there are things 'adapted'; infinitely more things with irregular relations than with regular relations between them. But we look for the regular kind of thing exclusively, and ingeniously discover and preserve it in our memory. It accumulates with other regular kinds, until the collection of them fills our encyclopedias. Yet all the while between and around them lies an infinite anonymous chaos of objects that no one ever thought of together, of relations that never yet attracted our attention.

The facts of order from which the physico-theological argument starts are thus easily susceptible of interpretation as arbitrary human products. So long as this is the case, although of course no argument against God follows, it follows that the argument for him will fail to constitute a knock-down proof of his existence. It will be convincing only to those who on other grounds believe in him already.

If philosophy can do so little to establish God's existence, how stands it with her efforts to define his attributes? It is worth while to look at the attempts of systematic theology in this direction.

Since God is First Cause, this science of sciences says, he differs from all his creatures in possessing existence a se. From this 'a-se-ity' on God's part, theology deduces by mere logic most of his other perfections. For instance, he must be both necessary and absolute, cannot not be, and cannot in any way be determined by anything else. This makes Him absolutely unlimited from without, and unlimited also from within; for limitation is non-being; and God is being itself. This unlimitedness makes

God infinitely perfect. Moreover, God is One, and Only, for the infinitely perfect can admit no peer. He is Spiritual, for were He composed of physical parts, some other power would have to combine them into the total, and his aseity would thus be contradicted. He is therefore both simple and non-physical in nature. He is simple metaphysically also, that is to say, his nature and his existence cannot be distinct, as they are in finite substances which share their formal natures with one another, and are individual only in their material aspect. Since God is one and only, his essentia and his esse must be given at one stroke. This excludes from his being all those distinctions, so familiar in the world of finite things, between potentiality and actuality, substance and accidents, being and activity, existence and attributes. We can talk, it is true, of God's powers, acts, and attributes, but these discriminations are only 'virtual,' and made from the human point of view. In God all these points of view fall into an absolute identity of being.

This absence of all potentiality in God obliges Him to be immutable. He is actuality, through and through. Were there anything potential about Him, He would either lose or gain by its actualization, and either loss or gain would contradict his perfection. He cannot, therefore, change. Furthermore, He is immense, boundless; for could He be outlined in space, He would be composite, and this would contradict his indivisibility. He is therefore omnipresent, indivisibly there, at every point of space. He is similarly wholly present at every point of time,— in other words eternal. For if He began in time, He would need a prior cause, and that would contradict his aseity. If He ended, it would contradict his necessity. If He went through any succession, it would contradict his immutability.

He has intelligence and will and every other creature-perfection, for we have them, and effectus nequit superare causam. In Him, however, they are absolutely and eternally in act, and their object, since God can be bounded by naught that is external, can primarily be nothing else than God himself. He knows himself, then, in one eternal indivisible act, and wills himself with an infinite self-pleasure. Since He must of logical necessity thus love and will himself, He cannot be called 'free' ad intra, with the freedom of contrarieties that characterizes finite creatures. Ad extra, however, or with respect to his creation, God is free. He cannot need to create, being perfect in being and in happiness already. He wills to create, then, by an absolute freedom. For the scholastics the facultas appetendi embraces feeling, desire, and will.

Being thus a substance endowed with intellect and will and freedom, God is a person; and a living person also, for He is both object and subject of his own activity, and to be this distinguishes the living from the lifeless. He is thus absolutely self-sufficient: his self-knowledge and self-love are both of them infinite and adequate, and need no extraneous conditions to perfect them.

He is omniscient, for in knowing himself as Cause He knows all creature things and events by implication. His knowledge is previsive, for He is present to all time. Even our free acts are known beforehand to Him, for otherwise his wisdom would admit of successive moments of enrichment, and this would contradict his immutability. He is omnipotent for everything that does not involve logical contradiction. He can make being— in other words his power includes creation. If what He creates were made of his own substance, it would have to be infinite in essence, as that substance is; but it is finite: so it must be non-divine in substance. If it were made of a substance, an eternally existing matter, for example, which God found there to his hand, and to which He simply gave its form, that would contradict God's definition as First Cause, and make Him a mere mover of something caused already. The things he creates, then, He creates ex nihilo, and gives them absolute being as so many finite substances additional to himself. The forms which he imprints upon them have their prototypes in his ideas. But as in God there is no such thing as multiplicity, and as these ideas for us are manifold, we must distinguish the ideas as they are in God and the way in which our minds externally imitate them. We must attribute them to Him only in a terminative sense, as differing aspects, from the finite point of view, of his unique essence.

God of course is holy, good, and just. He can do no evil, for He is positive being's fullness, and evil is negation. It is true that He has created physical evil in places, but only as a means of wider good, for bonum totius praeeminet bonum partis. Moral evil He cannot will, either as end or means, for that would contradict his holiness. By creating free beings He permits it only, neither his justice nor his goodness obliging Him to prevent the recipients of freedom from misusing the gift.

As regards God's purpose in creating, primarily it can only have been to exercise his absolute freedom by the manifestation to others of his glory. From this it follows that the others must be rational beings, capable in the first place of knowledge, love, and honor, and in the second place of happiness, for the knowledge and love of God is the mainspring of felicity. In so far forth one may say that God's secondary purpose in creating is love.

I will not weary you by pursuing these metaphysical determinations farther, into the mysteries of God's Trinity, for example. What I have given will serve as a specimen of the orthodox philosophical theology of both Catholics and Protestants. Newman, filled with enthusiasm at God's list of perfections, continues the passage which I began to quote to you by a couple of pages of a rhetoric so magnificent that I can hardly refrain from adding them, in spite of the inroad they would make upon our time. He first enumerates God's attributes sonorously, then celebrates his ownership of everything in earth and Heaven, and the dependence of all that happens upon his permissive will. He gives us scholastic philosophy 'touched with emotion,' and every philosophy should be touched with emotion to be rightly understood. Emotionally, then, dogmatic theology is worth something to minds of the type of Newman's. It will aid us to estimate what it is worth intellectually, if at this point I make a short digression.

What God hath joined together, let no man put asunder. The Continental schools of philosophy have too often overlooked the fact that man's thinking is organically connected with his conduct. It seems to me to be the chief glory of English and Scottish thinkers to have kept the organic connection in view. The guiding principle of British philosophy has in fact been that every difference must make a difference, every theoretical difference somewhere issue in a practical difference, and that the best method of discussing points of theory is to begin by ascertaining what practical difference would result from one alternative or the other being true. What is the particular truth in question known as? In what facts does it result? What is its cash-value in terms of particular experience? This is the characteristic English way of taking up a question. In this way, you remember, Locke takes up the question of personal identity. What you mean by it is just your chain of particular memories, says he. That is the only concretely verifiable part of its significance. All further ideas about it, such as the oneness or manyness of the spiritual substance on which it is based, are therefore void of intelligible meaning; and propositions touching such ideas may be indifferently affirmed or denied. So Berkeley with his 'matter.' The cash-value of matter is our physical sensations. That is what it is known as, all that we concretely verify of its conception. That, therefore, is the whole meaning of the term 'matter'— any other pretended meaning is mere wind of words. Hume does the same thing with causation. It is known as habitual antecedence, and as tendency on our part to look for something definite to come. Apart from this practical meaning it has no significance whatever, and books about it may be committed to the flames, says Hume. Dugald Stewart and Thomas Brown, James Mill, John Mill, and Professor Bain, have followed more or less consistently the same method; and Shadworth Hodgson has used the principle with full explicitness. When all is said and done, it was English and Scotch writers, and not Kant, who introduced 'the critical method' into philosophy, the one method fitted to make philosophy a study worthy of serious men. For what seriousness can possibly remain in debating philosophic propositions that will never make an appreciable difference to us in action? And what could it matter, if all propositions were practically indifferent, which of them we should agree to call true or which false?

An American philosopher of eminent originality, Mr. Charles Sanders Peirce, has rendered thought a service by disentangling from the particulars of its application the principle by which these men were instinctively guided, and by singling it out as fundamental and giving to it a Greek name. He calls it the principle of pragmatism, and he defends it somewhat as follows: [In an article, How to make our Ideas Clear, in the Popular Science Monthly for January, 1878, vol. xii. p. 286.]

Thought in movement has for its only conceivable motive the attainment of belief, or thought at rest. Only when our thought about a subject has found its rest in belief can our action on the subject firmly and safely begin. Beliefs, in short, are rules for action; and the whole function of thinking is but one step in the production of active habits. If there were any part of a thought that made no difference in the thought's practical consequences, then that part would be no proper element of the thought's significance. To develop a thought's meaning we need therefore only determine what conduct it is fitted to produce; that conduct is for us its sole significance; and the tangible fact at the root of all our thought-distinctions is that there is no one of them so fine as to consist in anything but a possible difference of practice. To attain perfect clearness in our thoughts of an object, we need then only consider what sensations, immediate or remote, we are conceivably to expect from it, and what conduct we must prepare in case the object should be true. Our conception of these practical consequences is for us the whole of our conception of the object, so far as that conception has positive significance at all.

This is the principle of Peirce, the principle of pragmatism. Such a principle will help us on this occasion to decide, among the various attributes set down in the scholastic inventory of God's perfections, whether some be not far less significant than others.

If, namely, we apply the principle of pragmatism to God's metaphysical attributes, strictly so called, as distinguished from his moral attributes, I think that, even were we forced by a coercive logic to believe them, we still should have to confess them to be destitute of an intelligible significance. Take God's aseity, for example; or his necessariness; his immateriality; his 'simplicity' or superiority to the kind of inner variety and succession which we find in finite beings, his indivisibility, and lack of the inner distinctions of being and activity, substance and accident, potentiality and actuality, and the rest; his repudiation of inclusion in a genus; his actualized infinity; his 'personality,' apart from the moral qualities which it may comport; his relations to evil being permissive and not positive; his self-sufficiency, self-love, and absolute felicity in himself:— candidly speaking, how do such qualities as these make any definite connection with our life? And if they severally call for no distinctive adaptations of our conduct, what vital difference can it possibly make to a man's religion whether they be true or false?

For my own part, although I dislike to say aught that may grate upon tender associations, I must frankly confess that even though these attributes were faultlessly deduced, I cannot conceive of its being of the smallest consequence to us religiously that any one of them should be true. Pray, what specific act can I perform in order to adapt myself the better to God's simplicity? Or how does it assist me to plan my behavior, to know that His happiness is anyhow absolutely complete? In the middle of the century just past, Mayne Reid was the great writer of books of out-of-door adventure. He was forever extolling the hunters and field-observers of living animals' habits, and keeping up a fire of invective against the 'closet-naturalists,' as he called them, the collectors and classifiers, and handlers of skeletons and skins. When I was a boy, I used to think that a closet-naturalist must be the vilest type of wretch under the sun. But surely the systematic theologians are the closet-naturalists of the deity, even in Captain Mayne Reid's sense. What is their deduction of metaphysical attributes but a shuffling and matching of pedantic dictionary-adjectives, aloof from morals, aloof from human needs, something that might be worked out from the mere word 'God' by one of those logical machines of wood and brass which recent ingenuity has contrived as well as by a man of flesh and blood. They have the trail of the serpent over them. One feels that in the theologians' hands, they are only a set of titles obtained by a mechanical manipulation of synonyms; verbality has stepped into the place of vision, professionalism into that of life. Instead of bread we have a stone; instead of a fish, a serpent. Did such a conglomeration of abstract terms give really the gist of our knowledge of the deity, schools of theology might indeed continue to flourish, but religion, vital religion, would have taken its flight from this world. What keeps religion going is something else than abstract definitions and systems of concatenated adjectives, and something different from faculties of theology and their professors. All these things are after-effects, secondary accretions upon those phenomena of vital conversation with the unseen divine, of which I have shown you so many instances, renewing themselves in saecula saeculorum in the lives of humble private men.

So much for the metaphysical attributes of God! From the point of view of practical religion, the metaphysical monster which they offer to our worship is an absolutely worthless invention of the scholarly mind.

What shall we now say of the attributes called moral? Pragmatically, they stand on an entirely different footing. They positively determine fear and hope and expectation, and are foundations for the saintly life. It needs but a glance at them to show how great is their significance.

God's holiness, for example: being holy, God can will nothing but the good. Being omnipotent, he can secure its triumph. Being omniscient, he can see us in the dark. Being just, he can punish us for what he sees. Being loving, he can pardon too. Being unalterable, we can count on him securely. These qualities enter into connection with our life, it is highly important that we should be informed concerning them. That God's purpose in creation should be the manifestation of his glory is also an attribute which has definite relations to our practical life. Among other things it has given a definite character to worship in all Christian countries. If dogmatic theology really does prove beyond dispute that a God with characters like these exists, she may well claim to give a solid basis to religious sentiment. But verily, how stands it with her arguments?

It stands with them as ill as with the arguments for his existence. Not only do post-Kantian idealists reject them root and branch, but it is a plain historic fact that they never have converted any one who has found in the moral complexion of the world, as he experienced it, reasons for doubting that a good God can have framed it. To prove God's goodness by the scholastic argument that there is no non-being in his essence would sound to such a witness simply silly.

No! the book of Job went over this whole matter once for all and definitively. Ratiocination is a relatively superficial and unreal path to the deity: "I will lay mine hand upon my mouth; I have heard of Thee by the hearing of the ear, but now mine eye seeth Thee." An intellect perplexed and baffled, yet a trustful sense of presence— such is the situation of the man who is sincere with himself and with the facts, but who remains religious still.

Pragmatically, the most important attribute of God is his punitive justice. But who, in the present state of theological opinion on that point, will dare maintain that hell fire or its equivalent in some shape is rendered certain by pure logic? Theology herself has largely based this doctrine upon revelation; and, in discussing it, has tended more and more to substitute conventional ideas of criminal law for a priori principles of reason. But the very notion that this glorious universe, with planets and winds, and laughing sky and ocean, should have been conceived and had its beams and rafters laid in technicalities of criminality, is incredible to our modern imagination. It weakens a religion to hear it argued upon such a basis.

We must therefore, I think, bid a definitive good-by to dogmatic theology. In all sincerity our faith must do without that warrant. Modern idealism, I repeat, has said good-by to this theology forever. Can modern idealism give faith a better warrant, or must she still rely on her poor self for witness?

The basis of modern idealism is Kant's doctrine of the Transcendental Ego of Apperception. By this formidable term Kant merely meant the fact that the consciousness 'I think them' must (potentially or actually) accompany all our objects. Former skeptics had said as much, but the 'I' in question had remained for them identified with the personal individual. Kant abstracted and depersonalized it, and made it the most universal of all his categories, although for Kant himself the Transcendental Ego had no theological implications.

It was reserved for his successors to convert Kant's notion of Bewusstsein uberhaupt, or abstract consciousness, into an infinite concrete self-consciousness which is the soul of the world, and in which our sundry personal self-consciousnesses have their being. It would lead me into technicalities to show you even briefly how this transformation was in point of fact effected. Suffice it to say that in the Hegelian school, which today so deeply influences both British and American thinking, two principles have borne the brunt of the operation.

The first of these principles is that the old logic of identity never gives us more than a post-mortem dissection of disjecta membra, and that the fullness of life can be construed to thought only by recognizing that every object which our thought may propose to itself involves the notion of some other object which seems at first to negate the first one.

The second principle is that to be conscious of a negation is already virtually to be beyond it. The mere asking of a question or expression of a dissatisfaction proves that the answer or the satisfaction is already imminent; the finite, realized as such, is already the infinite in posse.

Applying these principles, we seem to get a propulsive force into our logic which the ordinary logic of a bare, stark self-identity in each thing never attains to. The objects of our thought now act within our thought, act as objects act when given in experience. They change and develop. They introduce something other than themselves along with them; and this other, at first only ideal or potential, presently proves itself also to be actual. It supersedes the thing at first supposed, and both verifies and corrects it, in developing the fullness of its meaning.

The program is excellent; the universe is a place where things are followed by other things that both correct and fulfill them; and a logic which gave us something like this movement of fact would express truth far better than the traditional school-logic, which never gets of its own accord from anything to anything else, and registers only predictions and subsumptions, or static resemblances and differences. Nothing could be more unlike the methods of dogmatic theology than those of this new logic. Let me quote in illustration some passages from the Scottish transcendentalist whom I have already named.

"How are we to conceive," Principal Caird writes, "of the reality in which all intelligence rests?" He replies: "Two things may without difficulty be proved, viz., that this reality is an absolute Spirit, and conversely that it is only in communion with this absolute Spirit or Intelligence that the finite Spirit can realize itself. It is absolute; for the faintest movement of human intelligence would be arrested, if it did not presuppose the absolute reality of intelligence, of thought itself. Doubt or denial themselves presuppose and indirectly affirm it. When I pronounce anything to be true, I pronounce it, indeed, to be relative to thought, but not to be relative to my thought, or to the thought of any other individual mind. From the existence of all individual minds as such I can abstract; I can think them away. But that which I cannot think away is thought or self-consciousness itself, in its independence and absoluteness, or, in other words, an Absolute Thought or Self-Consciousness."

Here, you see, Principal Caird makes the transition which Kant did not make: he converts the omnipresence of consciousness in general as a condition of 'truth' being anywhere possible, into an omnipresent universal consciousness, which he identifies with God in his concreteness. He next proceeds to use the principle that to acknowledge your limits is in essence to be beyond them; and makes the transition to the religious experience of individuals in the following words:

"If [Man] were only a creature of transient sensations and impulses, of an ever coming and going succession of intuitions, fancies, feelings, then nothing could ever have for him the character of objective truth or reality. But it is the prerogative of man's spiritual nature that he can yield himself up to a thought and will that are infinitely larger than his own. As a thinking, self-conscious being, indeed, he may be said, by his very nature, to live in the atmosphere of the Universal Life. As a thinking being, it is possible for me to suppress and quell in my consciousness every movement of self-assertion, every notion and opinion that is merely mine, every desire that belongs to me as this particular Self, and to become the pure medium of a thought that is universal— in one word, to live no more my own life, but let my consciousness be possessed and suffused by the Infinite and Eternal life of spirit. And yet it is just in this renunciation of self that I truly gain myself, or realize the highest possibilities of my own nature. For whilst in one sense we give up self to live the universal and absolute life of reason, yet that to which we thus surrender ourselves is in reality our truer self. The life of absolute reason is not a life that is foreign to us."

Nevertheless, Principal Caird goes on to say, so far as we are able outwardly to realize this doctrine, the balm it offers remains incomplete. Whatever we may be in posse, the very best of us in actu falls very short of being absolutely divine. Social morality, love, and self-sacrifice even, merge our Self only in some other finite self or selves. They do not quite identify it with the Infinite. Man's ideal destiny, infinite in abstract logic, might thus seem in practice forever unrealizable.

"Is there, then," our author continues, "no solution of the contradiction between the ideal and the actual? We answer, There is such a solution, but in order to reach it we are carried beyond the sphere of morality into that of religion. It may be said to be the essential characteristic of religion as contrasted with morality, that it changes aspiration into fruition, anticipation into realization; that instead of leaving man in the interminable pursuit of a vanishing ideal, it makes him the actual partaker of a divine or infinite life. Whether we view religion from the human side or the divine— as the surrender of the soul to God, or as the life of God in the soul— in either aspect it is of its very essence that the Infinite has ceased to be a far-off vision, and has become a present reality. The very first pulsation of the spiritual life, when we rightly apprehend its significance, is the indication that the division between the Spirit and its object has vanished, that the ideal has become real, that the finite has reached its goal and become suffused with the presence and life of the Infinite.

"Oneness of mind and will with the divine mind and will is not the future hope and aim of religion, but its very beginning and birth in the soul. To enter on the religious life is to terminate the struggle. In that act which constitutes the beginning of the religious life— call it faith, or trust, or self-surrender, or by whatever name you will— there is involved the identification of the finite with a life which is eternally realized. It is true indeed that the religious life is progressive; but understood in the light of the foregoing idea, religious progress is not progress towards, but within the sphere of the Infinite. It is not the vain attempt by endless finite additions or increments to become possessed of infinite wealth, but it is the endeavor, by the constant exercise of spiritual activity, to appropriate that infinite inheritance of which we are already in possession. The whole future of the religious life is given in its beginning, but it is given implicitly. The position of the man who has entered on the religious life is that evil, error, imperfection, do not really belong to him: they are excrescences which have no organic relation to his true nature: they are already virtually, as they will be actually, suppressed and annulled, and in the very process of being annulled they become the means of spiritual progress. Though he is not exempt from temptation and conflict, [yet] in that inner sphere in which his true life lies, the struggle is over, the victory already achieved. It is not a finite but an infinite life which the spirit lives. Every pulse-beat of its [existence] is the expression and realization of the life of God." [John Caird: An Introduction to the Philosophy of Religion, London and New York, 1880, pp. 243-250, and 291-299, much abridged.]

You will readily admit that no description of the phenomena of the religious consciousness could be better than these words of your lamented preacher and philosopher. They reproduce the very rapture of those crises of conversion of which we have been hearing; they utter what the mystic felt but was unable to communicate; and the saint, in hearing them, recognizes his own experience. It is indeed gratifying to find the content of religion reported so unanimously. But when all is said and done, has Principal Caird— and I only use him as an example of that whole mode of thinking— transcended the sphere of feeling and of the direct experience of the individual, and laid the foundations of religion in impartial reason? Has he made religion universal by coercive reasoning, transformed it from a private faith into a public certainty? Has he rescued its affirmations from obscurity and mystery?

I believe that he has done nothing of the kind, but that he has simply reaffirmed the individual's experiences in a more generalized vocabulary. And again, I can be excused from proving technically that the transcendentalist reasonings fail to make religion universal, for I can point to the plain fact that a majority of scholars, even religiously disposed ones, stubbornly refuse to treat them as convincing. The whole of Germany, one may say, has positively rejected the Hegelian argumentation. As for Scotland, I need only mention Professor Fraser's and Professor Pringle-Pattison's memorable criticisms, with which so many of you are familiar. Once more, I ask, if transcendental idealism were as objectively and absolutely rational as it pretends to be, could it possibly fail so egregiously to be persuasive? [A.C. Fraser: Philosophy of Theism, second edition, Edinburgh and London, 1899, especially part ii. chaps. vii. and viii.; A. Seth [Pringle-Pattison]: Hegelianism and Personality, Ibid., 1890, passim.]

The most persuasive arguments in favor of a concrete individual Soul of the world, with which I am acquainted, are those of my colleague, Josiah Royce, in his Religious Aspect of Philosophy, Boston, 1885; in his Conception of God, New York and London, 1897; and lately in his Aberdeen Gifford Lectures, The World and the Individual, 2 vols., New York and London, 1901-02. I doubtless seem to some of my readers to evade the philosophic duty which my thesis in this lecture imposes on me, by not even attempting to meet Professor Royce's arguments articulately. I admit the momentary evasion. In the present lectures, which are cast throughout in a popular mould, there seemed no room for subtle metaphysical discussion, and for tactical purposes it was sufficient, the contention of philosophy being what it is (namely, that religion can be transformed into a universally convincing science), to point to the fact that no religious philosophy has actually convinced the mass of thinkers. Meanwhile let me say that I hope that the present volume may be followed by another, if I am spared to write it, in which not only Professor Royce's arguments, but others for monistic absolutism shall be considered with all the technical fullness which their great importance calls for. At present I resign myself to lying passive under the reproach of superficiality.

What religion reports, you must remember, always purports to be a fact of experience: the divine is actually present, religion says, and between it and ourselves relations of give and take are actual. If definite perceptions of fact like this cannot stand upon their own feet, surely abstract reasoning cannot give them the support they are in need of. Conceptual processes can class facts, define them, interpret them; but they do not produce them, nor can they reproduce their individuality. There is always a plus, a thisness, which feeling alone can answer for. Philosophy in this sphere is thus a secondary function, unable to warrant faith's veracity, and so I revert to the thesis which I announced at the beginning of this lecture.

In all sad sincerity I think we must conclude that the attempt to demonstrate by purely intellectual processes the truth of the deliverances of direct religious experience is absolutely hopeless.

It would be unfair to philosophy, however, to leave her under this negative sentence. Let me close, then, by briefly enumerating what she can do for religion. If she will abandon metaphysics and deduction for criticism and induction, and frankly transform herself from theology into science of religions, she can make herself enormously useful.

The spontaneous intellect of man always defines the divine which it feels in ways that harmonize with its temporary intellectual prepossessions. Philosophy can by comparison eliminate the local and the accidental from these definitions. Both from dogma and from worship she can remove historic incrustations. By confronting the spontaneous religious constructions with the results of natural science, philosophy can also eliminate doctrines that are now known to be scientifically absurd or incongruous.

Sifting out in this way unworthy formulations, she can leave a residuum of conceptions that at least are possible. With these she can deal as hypotheses, testing them in all the manners, whether negative or positive, by which hypotheses are ever tested. She can reduce their number, as some are found more open to objection. She can perhaps become the champion of one which she picks out as being the most closely verified or verifiable. She can refine upon the definition of this hypothesis, distinguishing between what is innocent over-belief and symbolism in the expression of it, and what is to be literally taken. As a result, she can offer mediation between different believers, and help to bring about consensus of opinion. She can do this the more successfully, the better she discriminates the common and essential from the individual and local elements of the religious beliefs which she compares.

I do not see why a critical Science of Religions of this sort might not eventually command as general a public adhesion as is commanded by a physical science. Even the personally non-religious might accept its conclusions on trust, much as blind persons now accept the facts of optics— it might appear as foolish to refuse them. Yet as the science of optics has to be fed in the first instance, and continually verified later, by facts experienced by seeing persons; so the science of religions would depend for its original material on facts of personal experience, and would have to square itself with personal experience through all its critical reconstructions. It could never get away from concrete life, or work in a conceptual vacuum. It would forever have to confess, as every science confesses, that the subtlety of nature flies beyond it, and that its formulas are but approximations. Philosophy lives in words, but truth and fact well up into our lives in ways that exceed verbal formulation. There is in the living act of perception always something that glimmers and twinkles and will not be caught, and for which reflection comes too late. No one knows this as well as the philosopher. He must fire his volley of new vocables out of his conceptual shotgun, for his profession condemns him to this industry, but he secretly knows the hollowness and irrelevancy. His formulas are like stereoscopic or kinetoscopic photographs seen outside the instrument; they lack the depth, the motion, the vitality. In the religious sphere, in particular, belief that formulas are true can never wholly take the place of personal experience.

In my next lecture I will try to complete my rough description of religious experience; and in the lecture after that, which is the last one, I will try my own hand at formulating conceptually the truth to which it is a witness.

LECTURE XIX: OTHER CHARACTERISTICS

We have wound our way back, after our excursion through mysticism and philosophy, to where we were before: the uses of religion, its uses to the individual who has it, and the uses of the individual himself to the world, are the best arguments that truth is in it. We return to the empirical philosophy: the true is what works well, even though the qualification 'on the whole' may always have to be added. In this lecture we must revert to description again, and finish our picture of the religious consciousness by a word about some of its other characteristic elements. Then, in a final lecture, we shall be free to make a general review and draw our independent conclusions.

The first point I will speak of is the part which the aesthetic life plays in determining one's choice of a religion. Men, I said awhile ago, involuntarily intellectualize their religious experience. They need formulas, just as they need fellowship in worship. I spoke, therefore, too contemptuously of the pragmatic uselessness of the famous scholastic list of attributes of the deity, for they have one use which I neglected to consider. The eloquent passage in which Newman enumerates them puts us on the track of it. Intoning them as he would intone a cathedral service, he shows how high is their aesthetic value. It enriches our bare piety to carry these exalted and mysterious verbal additions just as it enriches a church to have an organ and old brasses, marbles and frescoes and stained windows. Epithets lend an atmosphere and overtones to our devotion. They are like a hymn of praise and service of glory, and may sound the more sublime for being incomprehensible. Minds like Newman's grow as jealous of their credit as heathen priests are of that of the jewelry and ornaments that blaze upon their idols.

Newman's imagination so innately craved an ecclesiastical system that he can write: "From the age of fifteen, dogma has been the fundamental principle of my religion: I know no other religion; I cannot enter into the idea of any other sort of religion." And again, speaking of himself about the age of thirty, he writes "I loved to act as feeling myself in my Bishop's sight, as if it were the sight of God." [Apologia, 1897, pp. 48, 50.]

Among the buildings-out of religion which the mind spontaneously indulges in, the aesthetic motive must never be forgotten. I promised to say nothing of ecclesiastical systems in these lectures. I may be allowed, however, to put in a word at this point on the way in which their satisfaction of certain aesthetic needs contributes to their hold on human nature. Although some persons aim most at intellectual purity and simplification, for others richness is the supreme imaginative requirement. When one's mind is strongly of this type, an individual religion will hardly serve the purpose. The inner need is rather of something institutional and complex, majestic in the hierarchic interrelatedness of its parts, with authority descending from stage to stage, and at every stage objects for adjectives of mystery and splendor, derived in the last resort from the Godhead who is the fountain and culmination of the system. One feels then as if in presence of some vast incrusted work of jewelry or architecture; one hears the multitudinous liturgical appeal; one gets the honorific vibration coming from every quarter. Compared with such a noble complexity, in which ascending and descending movements seem in no way to jar upon stability, in which no single item, however humble, is insignificant, because so many august institutions hold it in its place, how flat does evangelical Protestantism appear, how bare the atmosphere of those isolated religious lives whose boast it is that "man in the bush with God may meet." What a pulverization and leveling of what a gloriously piled-up structure! To an imagination used to the perspectives of dignity and glory, the naked gospel scheme seems to offer an almshouse for a palace.

The intellectual difference is quite on a par in practical importance with the analogous difference in character. We saw, under the head of Saintliness, how some characters resent confusion and must live in purity, consistency, simplicity. For others, on the contrary, superabundance, over-pressure, stimulation, lots of superficial relations, are indispensable. There are men who would suffer a very syncope if you should pay all their debts, bring it about that their engagements had been kept, their letters answered, their perplexities relieved, and their duties fulfilled, down to one which lay on a clean table under their eyes with nothing to interfere with its immediate performance. A day stripped so staringly bare would be for them appalling. So with ease, elegance, tributes of affection, social recognitions— some of us require amounts of these things which to others would appear a mass of lying and sophistication.

In Newman's Lectures on Justification, Lecture VIII. SS 6, there is a splendid passage expressive of this aesthetic way of feeling the Christian scheme. It is unfortunately too long to quote.

It is much like the patriotic sentiment of those brought up in ancient empires. How many emotions must be frustrated of their object, when one gives up the titles of dignity, the crimson lights and blare of brass, the gold embroidery, the plumed troops, the fear and trembling, and puts up with a president in a black coat who shakes hands with you, and comes, it may be, from a 'home' upon a veldt or prairie with one sitting-room and a Bible on its centre-table. It pauperizes the monarchical imagination!

The strength of these aesthetic sentiments makes it rigorously impossible, it seems to me, that Protestantism, however superior in Spiritual profundity it may be to Catholicism, should at the present day succeed in making many converts from the more venerable ecclesiasticism. The latter offers a so much richer pasturage and shade to the fancy, has so many cells with so many different kinds of honey, is so indulgent in its multiform appeals to human nature, that Protestantism will always show to Catholic eyes the almshouse physiognomy. The bitter negativity of it is to the Catholic mind incomprehensible. To intellectual

Catholics many of the antiquated beliefs and practices to which the Church gives countenance are, if taken literally, as childish as they are to Protestants. But they are childish in the pleasing sense of 'childlike,'— innocent and amiable, and worthy to be smiled on in consideration of the undeveloped condition of the dear people's intellects. To the Protestant, on the contrary, they are childish in the sense of being idiotic falsehoods. He must stamp out their delicate and lovable redundancy, leaving the Catholic to shudder at his literalness. He appears to the latter as morose as if he were some hard-eyed, numb, monotonous kind of reptile. The two will never understand each other— their centres of emotional energy are too different. Rigorous truth and human nature's intricacies are always in need of a mutual interpreter. So much for the aesthetic diversities in the religious consciousness.

Compare the informality of Protestantism, where the 'meek lover of the good,' alone with his God, visits the sick, etc., for their own sakes, with the elaborate 'business' that goes on in Catholic devotion, and carries with it the social excitement of all more complex businesses. An essentially worldly-minded Catholic woman can become a visitor of the sick on purely coquettish principles, with her confessor and director, her 'merit' storing up, her patron saints, her privileged relation to the Almighty, drawing his attention as a professional devote, her definite 'exercises,' and her definitely recognized social pose in the organization.

In most books on religion, three things are represented as its most essential elements. These are Sacrifice, Confession, and Prayer. I must say a word in turn of each of these elements, though briefly. First of Sacrifice.

Sacrifices to gods are omnipresent in primeval worship; but, as cults have grown refined, burnt offerings and the blood of he-goats have been superseded by sacrifices more spiritual in their nature. Judaism, Islam, and Buddhism get along without ritual sacrifice; so does Christianity, save in so far as the notion is preserved in transfigured form in the mystery of Christ's atonement. These religions substitute offerings of the heart, renunciations of the inner self, for all those vain oblations. In the ascetic practices which Islam, Buddhism, and the older Christianity encourage we see how indestructible is the idea that sacrifice of some sort is a religious exercise. In lecturing on asceticism I spoke of its significance as symbolic of the sacrifices which life, whenever it is taken strenuously, calls for. But, as I said my say about those, and as these lectures expressly avoid earlier religious usages and questions of derivation, I will pass from the subject of Sacrifice altogether and turn to that of Confession.

In regard to Confession I will also be most brief, saying my word about it psychologically, not historically. Not nearly as widespread as sacrifice, it corresponds to a more inward and moral stage of sentiment. It is part of the general system of purgation and cleansing which one feels one's self in need of, in order to be in right relations to one's deity. For him who confesses, shams are over and realities have begun; he has exteriorized his rottenness If he has not actually got rid of it, he at least no longer smears it over with a hypocritical show of virtue— he lives at least upon a basis of veracity. The complete decay of the practice of confession in Anglo-Saxon communities is a little hard to account for. Reaction against popery is of course the historic explanation, for in popery confession went with penances and absolution, and other inadmissible practices. But on the side of the sinner himself it seems as if the need ought to have been too great to accept so summary a refusal of its satisfaction. One would think that in more men the shell of secrecy would have had to open, the pent—in abbesses to burst and gain relief, even though the ear that heard the confession were unworthy. The Catholic church, for obvious utilitarian reasons, has substituted auricular confession to one priest for the more radical act of public confession. We English-speaking Protestants, in the general self-reliance and unsociability of our nature, seem to find it enough if we take God alone into our confidence. [A fuller discussion of confession is contained in the excellent work by Frank Granger: The Soul of a Christian, London, 1900, ch. xii.]

The next topic on which I must comment is Prayer, and this time it must be less briefly. We have heard much talk of late against prayer, especially against prayers for better weather and for the recovery of sick people. As regards prayers for the sick, if any medical fact can be considered to stand firm, it is that in certain environments prayer may contribute to recovery, and should be encouraged as a therapeutic measure. Being a normal factor of moral health in the person, its omission would be deleterious. The case of the weather is different. Notwithstanding the recency of the opposite belief, every one now knows that droughts and storms follow from physical antecedents, and that moral appeals cannot avert them. But petitional prayer is only one department of prayer; and if we take the word in the wider sense as meaning every kind of inward communion or conversation with the power recognized as divine, we can easily see that scientific criticism leaves it untouched.

Example: "The minister at Sudbury, being at the Thursday lecture in Boston, heard the officiating clergyman praying for rain. As soon as the service was over, he went to the petitioner and said, 'You Boston ministers, as soon as a tulip wilts under your windows, go to church and pray for rain, until all Concord and Sudbury are under water.'" [R.W. Emerson: Lectures and Biographical Sketches, p. 363.]

Prayer in this wide sense is the very soul and essence of religion. "Religion," says a liberal French theologian, "is an intercourse, a conscious and voluntary relation, entered into by a soul in distress with the mysterious power upon which it feels itself to depend, and upon which its fate is contingent. This intercourse with God is realized by prayer. Prayer is religion in act; that is, prayer is real religion. It is prayer that distinguishes the religious phenomenon from such similar or neighboring phenomena as purely moral or aesthetic sentiment. Religion is nothing if it be not the vital act by which the entire mind seeks to save itself by clinging to the principle from which it draws its life. This act is prayer, by which term I understand no vain exercise of words, no mere repetition of certain sacred formula, but the very movement itself of the soul, putting itself in a personal relation of contact with the mysterious power of which it feels the presence,— it may be even before it has a name by which to call it. Wherever this interior prayer is lacking, there is no religion; wherever, on the other hand, this prayer rises and stirs the soul, even in the absence of forms or of doctrines, we have living religion. One sees from this why 'natural religion,' so-called, is not properly a religion. It cuts man off from prayer. It leaves him and God in mutual remoteness, with no intimate commerce, no interior dialogue, no interchange, no action of God in man, no return of man to God. At bottom this pretended religion is only a philosophy. Born at epochs of rationalism, of critical investigations, it never was anything but an abstraction. An artificial and dead creation, it reveals to its examiner hardly one of the characters proper to religion." [Auguste Sabatier: Esquisse d'une Philosophie de la Religion, 2me ed., 1897, pp. 24-26, abridged.]

It seems to me that the entire series of our lectures proves the truth of M. Sabatier's contention. The religious phenomenon, studied as an inner fact, and apart from ecclesiastical or theological complications, has shown itself to consist everywhere, and at all its stages, in the consciousness which individuals have of an intercourse between themselves and higher powers with which they feel themselves to be related. This intercourse is realized at the time as being both active and mutual. If it be not effective; if it be not a give and take relation; if nothing be really transacted while it lasts; if the world is in no whit different for its having taken place; then prayer, taken in this wide meaning of a sense that something is transacting, is of course a feeling of what is illusory, and religion must on the whole be classed, not simply as containing elements of delusion,— these undoubtedly everywhere exist,— but as being rooted in delusion altogether, just as materialists and atheists have always said it was. At most there might remain, when the direct experiences of prayer were ruled out as false witnesses, some inferential belief that the whole order of existence must have a divine cause. But this way of contemplating nature, pleasing as it would doubtless be to persons of a pious taste, would leave to them but the spectators' part at a play, whereas in experimental religion and the prayerful life, we seem ourselves to be actors, and not in a play, but in a very serious reality.

The genuineness of religion is thus indissolubly bound up with the question whether the prayerful consciousness be or be not deceitful. The conviction that something is genuinely transacted in this consciousness is the very core of living religion. As to what is transacted, great differences of opinion have prevailed. The unseen powers have been supposed, and are yet supposed, to do things which no enlightened man can nowadays believe in. It may well prove that the sphere of influence in prayer is subjective exclusively, and that what is immediately changed is only the mind of the praying person. But however our opinion of prayer's effects may come to be limited by criticism, religion, in the vital sense in which these lectures study it, must stand or fall by the persuasion that effects of some sort genuinely do occur. Through prayer, religion insists, things which cannot be realized in any other manner come about: energy which but for prayer would be bound is by prayer set free and operates in some part, be it objective or subjective, of the world of facts.

This postulate is strikingly expressed in a letter written by the late Frederic W.H. Myers to a friend, who allows me to quote from it. It shows how independent the prayer-instinct is of usual doctrinal complications. Mr. Myers writes:—

"I am glad that you have asked me about prayer, because I have rather strong ideas on the subject. First consider what are the facts. There exists around us a spiritual universe, and that universe is in actual relation with the material. From the spiritual universe comes the energy which maintains the material; the energy which makes the life of each individual spirit. Our spirits are supported by a perpetual indrawal of this energy, and the vigor of that indrawal is perpetually changing, much as the vigor of our absorption of material nutriment changes from hour to hour.

"I call these 'facts' because I think that some scheme of this kind is the only one consistent with our actual evidence; too complex to summarize here. How, then, should we act on these facts? Plainly we must endeavor to draw in as much spiritual life as possible, and we must place our minds in any attitude which experience shows to be favorable to such indrawal. Prayer is the general name for that attitude of open and earnest expectancy. If we then ask to whom to pray, the answer (strangely enough) must be that that does not much matter. The prayer is not indeed a purely subjective thing; it means a real increase in intensity of absorption of spiritual power or grace;— but we do not know enough of what takes place in the spiritual world to know how the prayer operates; who is cognizant of it, or through what channel the grace is given. Better let children pray to Christ, who is at any rate the highest individual spirit of whom we have any knowledge. But it would be rash to say that Christ himself hears us; while to say that God hears us is merely to restate the first principle,— that grace flows in from the infinite spiritual world."

Let us reserve the question of the truth or falsehood of the belief that power is absorbed until the next lecture, when our dogmatic conclusions, if we have any, must be reached. Let this lecture still confine itself to the description of phenomena; and as a concrete example of an extreme sort, of the way in which the prayerful life may still be led, let me take a case with which most of you must be acquainted, that of George Muller of Bristol, who died in 1898. Muller's prayers were of the crassest petitional order. Early in life he resolved on taking certain Bible promises in literal sincerity, and on letting himself be fed, not by his own worldly foresight, but by the Lord's hand. He had an extraordinarily active and successful career, among the fruits of which were the distribution of over two million copies of the Scripture text, in different languages; the equipment of several hundred missionaries; the circulation of more than a hundred and eleven million of scriptural books, pamphlets, and tracts; the building of five large orphanages, and the keeping and educating of thousands of orphans; finally, the establishment of schools in which over a hundred and twenty-one thousand youthful and adult pupils were taught. In the course of this work Mr. Muller received and administered nearly a million and a half of pounds sterling, and traveled over two hundred thousand miles of sea and land. During the sixty-eight years of his ministry, be never owned any property except his clothes and furniture, and cash in hand; and he left, at the age of eighty-six, an estate worth only a hundred and sixty pounds. [My authority for these statistics is the little work on Muller, by Frederic G. Warne, New York, 1898.]

His method was to let his general wants be publicly known, but not to acquaint other people with the details of his temporary necessities. For the relief of the latter, he prayed directly to the Lord, believing that sooner or later prayers are always answered if one have trust enough. "When I lose such a thing as a key," he writes, "I ask the Lord to direct me to it, and I look for an answer to my prayer; when a person with whom I have made an appointment does not come, according to the fixed time, and I begin to be inconvenienced by it, I ask the Lord to be pleased to hasten him to me, and I look for an answer; when I do not understand a passage of the word of God, I lift up my heart to the Lord that he would be pleased by his Holy Spirit to instruct me, and I expect to be taught, though I do not fix the time when, and the manner how it should be; when I am going to minister in the Word, I seek help from the Lord, and... am not cast down, but of good cheer because I look for his assistance."

Muller's custom was to never run up bills, not even for a week. "As the Lord deals out to us by the day,... the week's payment might become due and we have no money to meet it; and thus those with whom we deal might be inconvenienced by us, and we be found acting against the commandment of the Lord: 'Owe no man anything.' From this day and henceforward whilst the Lord gives to us our supplies by the day, we purpose to pay at once for every article as it is purchased, and never to buy anything except we can pay for it at once, however much it may seem to be needed, and however much those with whom we deal may wish to be paid only by the week."

The articles needed of which Muller speaks were the food, fuel, etc., of his orphanages. Somehow, near as they often come to going without a meal, they hardly ever seem actually to have done so." Greater and more manifest nearness of the Lord's presence I have never had than when after breakfast there were no means for dinner for more than a hundred persons; or when after dinner there were no means for the tea, and yet the Lord provided the tea; and all this without one single human being having been informed about our need.... Through Grace my mind is so fully assured of the faithfulness of the Lord, that in the midst of the greatest need, I am enabled in peace to go about my other work. Indeed, did not the Lord give me this, which is the result of trusting in him, I should scarcely be able to work at all; for it is now comparatively a rare thing that a day comes when I am not in need for one or another part of the work." [The Life of Trust; Being a Narrative of the Lord's Dealings with George Muller, New American edition, N.Y., Crowell, pp. 228, 194, 219.]

In building his orphanages simply by prayer and faith, Muller affirms that his prime motive was "to have something to point to as a visible proof that our God and Father is the same faithful God that he ever was,— as willing as ever to prove himself the living God, in our day as formerly, to all that put their trust in him." For this reason be refused to borrow money for any of his enterprises. "How does it work when we thus anticipate God by going our own way? We certainly weaken faith instead of increasing it; and each time we work thus a deliverance of our own we find it more and more difficult to trust in God, till at last we give way entirely to our natural fallen reason and unbelief prevails. How different if one is enabled to wait God's own time, and to look alone to him for help and deliverance! When at last help comes, after many seasons of prayer it may be, how sweet it is, and what a present recompense! Dear Christian reader, if you have never walked in this path of obedience before, do so now, and you will then know experimentally the sweetness of the joy which results from it."

When the supplies came in but slowly, Muller always considered that this was for the trial of his faith and patience. When his faith and patience had been sufficiently tried, the Lord would send more means. "And thus it has proved,"— I quote from his diary,— "for today was given me the sum of 2050 pounds, of which 2000 are for the building fund [of a certain house], and 50 for present necessities. It is impossible to describe my joy in God when I received this donation. I was neither excited nor surprised; for I look out for answers to my prayers.— I believe that God hears me. Yet my heart was so full of joy that I could only sit before God, and admire him, like David in 2 Samuel vii. At last I cast myself flat down upon my face and burst forth in thanksgiving to God and in surrendering my heart afresh to him for his blessed service."

George Muller's is a case extreme in every respect, and in no respect more so than in the extraordinary narrowness of the man's intellectual horizon. His God was, as he often said, his business partner. He seems to have been for Muller little more than a sort of supernatural clergyman interested in the congregation of tradesmen and others in Bristol who were his saints, and in the orphanages and other enterprises, but unpossessed of any of those vaster and wilder and more ideal attributes with which the human imagination elsewhere has invested him. Muller, in short, was absolutely unphilosophical. His intensely private and practical conception of his relations with the Deity continued the traditions of the most primitive human thought. When we compare a mind like his with such a mind as, for example, Emerson's or Phillips Brooks's, we see the range which the religious consciousness covers.

I cannot resist the temptation of quoting an expression of an even more primitive style of religious thought, which I find in Arber's English Garland, vol. vii. p. 440. Robert Lyde, an English sailor, along with an English boy, being prisoners on a French ship in 1689, set upon the crew, of seven Frenchmen, killed two, made the other five prisoners, and brought home the ship. Lyde thus describes how in this feat he found his God a very present help in time of trouble:

"With the assistance of God I kept my feet when they three and one more did strive to throw me down. Feeling the Frenchman which hung about my middle hang very heavy, I said to the boy, 'Go round the binnacle, and knock down that man that hangeth on my back.' So the boy did strike him one blow on the head which made him fall.... Then I looked about for a marlin spike or anything else to strike them withal. But seeing nothing, I said, 'LORD! what shall I do?' Then casting up my eye upon my left side, and seeing a marlin spike hanging, I jerked my right arm and took hold, and struck the point four times about a quarter of an inch deep into the skull of that man that had hold of my left arm. [One of the Frenchmen then hauled the marlin spike away from him.] But through GOD's wonderful providence! it either fell out of his hand, or else he threw it down, and at this time the Almighty GOD gave me strength enough to take one man in one hand, and throw at the other's head: and looking about again to see anything to strike them withal, but seeing nothing, I said, 'LORD! what shall I do now?' And then it pleased GOD to put me in mind of my knife in my pocket. And although two of the men had hold of my right arm, yet GOD Almighty strengthened me so that I put my right hand into my right pocket, drew out the knife and sheath,... put it between my legs and drew it out, and then cut the man's throat with it that had his back to my breast: and he immediately dropt down, and scarce ever stirred after."— I have slightly abridged Lyde's narrative.

There is an immense literature relating to answers to petitional prayer. The evangelical journals are filled with such answers, and books are devoted to the subject, but for us Muller's case will suffice. [As, for instance, In Answer to Prayer, by the Bishop of Ripon and others, London, 1898; Touching Incidents and Remarkable Answers to Prayer, Harrisburg, Pa., 1898; H.L. Hastings: The Guiding Hand, or Providential Direction, illustrated by Authentic Instances, Boston, 1898]

A less sturdy beggar-like fashion of leading the prayerful life is followed by innumerable other Christians. Persistence in leaning on the Almighty for support and guidance will, such persons say, bring with it proofs, palpable but much more subtle, of his presence and active influence. The following description of a 'led' life, by a German writer whom I have already quoted, would no doubt appear to countless Christians in every country as if transcribed from their own personal experience. One finds in this guided sort of life, says Dr. Hilty,—

"That books and words (and sometimes people) come to one's cognizance just at the very moment in which one needs them; that one glides over great dangers as if with shut eyes, remaining ignorant of what would have terrified one or led one astray, until the peril is past- this being especially the case with temptations to vanity and sensuality; that paths on which one ought not to wander are, as it were, hedged off with thorns; but that on the other side great obstacles are suddenly removed; that when the time has come for something, one suddenly receives a courage that formerly failed, or perceives the root of a matter that until then was concealed, or discovers thoughts, talents, yea, even pieces of knowledge and insight, in one's self, of which it is impossible to say whence they come; finally, that persons help us or decline to help us, favor us or refuse us, as if they had to do so against their will so that often those indifferent or even unfriendly to us yield us the greatest service and furtherance. (God takes often their worldly goods, from those whom he leads, at just the right moment, when they threaten to impede the effort after higher interests.)

"Besides all this, other noteworthy things come to pass, of which it is not easy to give account. There is no doubt whatever that now one walks continually through 'open doors' and on the easiest roads, with as little care and trouble as it is possible to imagine.

"Furthermore one finds one's self settling one's affairs neither too early nor too late, whereas they were wont to be spoiled by untimeliness, even when the preparations had been well laid. In addition to this, one does them with perfect tranquility of mind, almost as if they were matters of no consequence, like errands done by us for another person, in which case we usually act more calmly than when we act in our own concerns. Again, one finds that one can wait for everything patiently, and that is one of life's great arts. One finds also that each thing comes duly, one thing after the other, so that one gains time to make one's footing sure before advancing farther. And then everything occurs to us at the right moment, just what we ought to do, etc., and often in a very striking way, just as if a third person were keeping watch over those things which we are in easy danger of forgetting.

"Often, too, persons are sent to us at the right time, to offer or ask for what is needed, and what we should never have had the courage or resolution to undertake of our own accord.

"Through all these experiences one finds that one is kindly and tolerant of other people, even of such as are repulsive, negligent, or ill-willed, for they also are instruments of good in God's hand, and often most efficient ones. Without these thoughts it would be hard for even the best of us always to keep our equanimity. But with the consciousness of divine guidance, one sees many a thing in life quite differently from what would otherwise be possible.

"All these are things that every human being knows, who has had experience of them; and of which the most speaking examples could be brought forward. The highest resources of worldly wisdom are unable to attain that which, under divine leading, comes to us of its own accord." [C. Hilty: Gluck, Dritter Theil, 1900, pp. 92 ff.]

Such accounts as this shade away into others where the belief is, not that particular events are tempered more towardly to us by a superintending providence, as a reward for our reliance, but that by cultivating the continuous sense of our connection with the power that made things as they are, we are tempered more towardly for their reception. The outward face of nature need not alter, but the expressions of meaning in it alter. It was dead and is alive again. It is like the difference between looking on a person without love, or upon the same person with love. In the latter case intercourse springs into new vitality. So when one's affections keep in touch with the divinity of the world's authorship, fear and egotism fall away; and in the equanimity that follows, one finds in the hours, as they succeed each other. a series of purely benignant opportunities. It is as if all doors were opened, and all paths freshly smoothed. We meet a new world when we meet the old world in the spirit which this kind of prayer infuses.

Such a spirit was that of Marcus Aurelius and Epictetus. It is that of mind-curers, of the transcendentalists, and of the so-called 'liberal' Christians. As an expression of it, I will quote a page from one of Martineau's sermons:—

"The universe, open to the eye today, looks as it did a thousand years ago: and the morning hymn of Milton does but tell the beauty with which our own familiar sun dressed the earliest fields and gardens of the world. We see what all our fathers saw. And if we cannot find God in your house or in mine, upon the roadside or the margin of the sea; in the bursting seed or opening flower; in the day duty or the night musing; in the general laugh and the secret grief; in the procession of life, ever entering afresh, and solemnly passing by and dropping off; I do not think we should discern him any more on the grass of Eden, or beneath the moonlight of Gethsemane. Depend upon it, it is not the want of greater miracles, but of the soul to perceive such as are allowed us still, that makes us push all the sanctities into the far spaces we cannot reach. The devout feel that wherever God's hand is, there is miracle: and it is simply an indevoutness which imagines that only where miracle is, can there be the real hand of God. The customs of Heaven ought surely to be more sacred in our eyes than its anomalies; the dear old ways, of which the Most High is never tired, than the strange things which he does not love well enough ever to repeat. And he who will but discern beneath the sun, as he rises any morning, the supporting finger of the Almighty, may recover the sweet and reverent surprise with which Adam gazed on the first dawn in Paradise. It is no outward change, no shifting in time or place; but only the loving meditation of the pure in heart, that can reawaken the Eternal from the sleep within our souls: that can render him a reality again, and reassert for him once more his ancient name of 'the Living God.'" [James Martineau: end of the sermon 'Help Thou Mine Unbelief,' in Endeavours after a Christian Life, 2d series. Compare with this page the extract from Voysey, above, and those from Pascal and Madame Guyon.]

"Good Heaven!" says Epictetus, "any one thing in the creation is sufficient to demonstrate a Providence, to a humble and grateful mind. The mere possibility of producing milk from grass, cheese from milk, and wool from skins; who formed and planned it? Ought we not, whether we dig or plough or eat, to sing this hymn to God? Great is God, who has supplied us with these instruments to till the ground; great is God, who has given us hands and instruments of digestion; who has given us to grow insensibly and to breathe in sleep. These things we ought forever to celebrate.... But because the most of you are blind and insensible, there must be some one to fill this station, and lead, in behalf of all men, the hymn to God; for what else can I do, a lame old man, but sing hymns to God? Were I a nightingale, I would act the part of a nightingale; were I a swan, the part of a swan. But since I am a reasonable creature, it is my duty to praise God... and I call on you to join the same song." [Works, book i. ch. xvi., Carter-Higginson translation, abridged.]

When we see all things in God, and refer all things to him, we read in common matters superior expressions of meaning. The deadness with which custom invests the familiar vanishes, and existence as a whole appears transfigured. The state of a mind thus awakened from torpor is well expressed in these words, which I take from a friend's letter: "If we occupy ourselves in summing up all the mercies and bounties we are privileged to have, we are overwhelmed by their number (so great that we can imagine ourselves unable to give ourselves time even to begin to review the things we may imagine we have not). We sum them and realize that we are actually killed with God's kindness; that we are surrounded by bounties upon bounties, without which all would fall. Should we not love it; should we not feel buoyed up by the Eternal Arms?

Sometimes this realization that facts are of divine sending, instead of being habitual, is casual, like a mystical experience. Father Gratry gives this instance from his youthful melancholy period:—

"One day I had a moment of consolation, because I met with something which seemed to me ideally perfect. It was a poor drummer beating the tattoo in the streets of Paris. I walked behind him in returning to the school on the evening of a holiday. His drum gave out the tattoo in such a way that, at that moment at least, however peevish I were, I could find no pretext for fault-finding. It was impossible to conceive more nerve or spirit, better time or measure, more clearness or richness, than were in this drumming. Ideal desire could go no farther in that direction. I was enchanted and consoled; the perfection of this wretched act did me good. Good is at least possible, I said, since the ideal can thus sometimes get embodied." [Souvenirs de ma Jeunesse, 1897, p. 122.]

In Senancour's novel of Obermann a similar transient lifting of the veil is recorded. In Paris streets, on a March day, he comes across a flower in bloom, a jonquil:

"It was the strongest expression of desire it was the first perfume of the year. I felt all the happiness destined for man. This unutterable harmony of souls, the phantom of the ideal world, arose in me complete. I never felt anything so great or so instantaneous. I know not what shape, what analogy, what secret of relation it was that made me see in this flower a limitless beauty.... I shall never inclose in a conception this power, this immensity that nothing will express; this form that nothing will contain; this ideal of a better world which one feels, but which, it seems, nature has not made actual."

We heard in previous lectures of the vivified face of the world as it may appear to converts after their awakening. As a rule, religious persons generally assume that whatever natural facts connect themselves in any way with their destiny are significant of the divine purposes with them. Through prayer the purpose, often far from obvious, comes home to them, and if it be 'trial,' strength to endure the trial is given. Thus at all stages of the prayerful life we find the persuasion that in the process of communion energy from on high flows in to meet demand, and becomes operative within the phenomenal world. So long as this operativeness is admitted to be real, it makes no essential difference whether its immediate effects be subjective or objective. The fundamental religious point is that in prayer, spiritual energy, which otherwise would slumber, does become active, and spiritual work of some kind is effected really.

So much for Prayer, taken in the wide sense of any kind of communion. As the core of religion, we must return to it in the next lecture.

The last aspect of the religious life which remains for me to touch upon is the fact that its manifestations so frequently connect themselves with the subconscious part of our existence. You may remember what I said in my opening lecture about the prevalence of the psychopathic temperament in religious biography. You will in. point of fact hardly find a religious leader of any kind in whose life there is no record of automatisms. I speak not merely of savage priests and prophets, whose followers regard automatic utterance and action as by itself tantamount to inspiration, I speak of leaders of thought and subjects of intellectualized experience. Saint Paul had his visions, his ecstasies, his gift of tongues, small as was the importance he attached to the latter. The whole array of Christian saints and heresiarchs, including the greatest, the Bernards, the Loyolas, the Luthers, the Foxes, the Wesleys, had their visions, voices, rapt conditions, guiding impressions, and 'openings.' They had these things, because they had exalted sensibility, and to such things persons of exalted sensibility are liable. In such liability there lie, however, consequences for theology. Beliefs are strengthened wherever automatisms corroborate them. Incursions from beyond the transmarginal region have a peculiar power to increase conviction. The inchoate sense of presence is infinitely stronger than conception, but strong as it may be, it is seldom equal to the evidence of hallucination. Saints who actually see or bear their Saviour reach the acme of assurance. Motor automatisms, though rarer, are, if possible, even more convincing than sensations. The subjects here actually feel themselves played upon by powers beyond their will. The evidence is dynamic; the God or spirit moves the very organs of their body.

A friend of mine, a first-rate psychologist, who is a subject of graphic automatism, tells me that the appearance of independent actuation in the movements of his arm, when he writes automatically, is so distinct that it obliges him to abandon a psychophysical theory which he had previously believed in, the theory, namely, that we have no feeling of the discharge downwards of our voluntary motor-centres. We must normally have such a feeling, he thinks, or the sense of an absence would not be so striking as it is in these experiences. Graphic automatism of a fully developed kind is rare in religious history, so far as my knowledge goes. Such statements as Antonia Bourignon's, that "I do nothing but lend my hand and spirit to another power than mine," is shown by the context to indicate inspiration rather than directly automatic writing. In some eccentric sects this latter occurs. The most striking instance of it is probably the bulky volume called, 'Oahspe, a new Bible in the Words of Jehovah and his angel ambassadors,' Boston and London, 1891, written and illustrated automatically by Dr. Newbrough of New York, whom I understand to be now, or to have been lately, at the head of the spiritistic community of Shalam in New Mexico. The latest automatically written book which has come under my notice is 'Zertoulem's Wisdom of the Ages,' by George A. Fuller, Boston, 1901.

The great field for this sense of being the instrument of a higher power is of course 'inspiration.' It is easy to discriminate between the religious leaders who have been habitually subject to inspiration and those who have not. In the teachings of the Buddha, of Jesus, of Saint Paul (apart from his gift of tongues), of Saint Augustine, of Huss, of Luther, of Wesley, automatic or semi-automatic composition appears to have been only occasional. In the Hebrew prophets, on the contrary, in Mohammed, in some of the Alexandrians, in many minor Catholic saints, in Fox, in Joseph Smith, something like it appears to have been frequent, sometimes habitual. We have distinct professions of being under the direction of a foreign power, and serving as its mouthpiece. As regards the Hebrew prophets, it is extraordinary, writes an author who has made a careful study of them, to see—

"How, one after another, the same features are reproduced in the prophetic books. The process is always extremely different from what it would be if the prophet arrived at his insight into spiritual things by the tentative efforts of his own genius. There is something sharp and sudden about it. He can lay his finger, so to speak, on the moment when it came. And it always comes in the form of an overpowering force from without, against which he struggles, but in vain. Listen, for instance, [to] the opening of the book of Jeremiah. Read through in like manner the first two chapters of the prophecy of Ezekiel.

"It is not, however, only at the beginning of his career that the prophet passes through a crisis which is clearly not self-caused. Scattered all through the prophetic writings are expressions which speak of some strong and irresistible impulse coming down upon the prophet, determining his attitude to the events of his time, constraining his utterance, making his words the vehicle of a higher meaning than their own. For instance, this of Isaiah's: 'The Lord spake thus to me with a strong hand,'— an emphatic phrase which denotes the overmastering nature of the impulse,— 'and instructed me that I should not walk in the way of this people.'... Or passages like this from Ezekiel: 'The hand of the Lord God fell upon me,' 'The hand of the Lord God was strong upon me.' The one standing characteristic of prophet is that he speaks with the authority of Jehovah himself. Hence it is that the prophets one and all preface their addresses so confidently, 'The Word of the Lord,' or 'Thus saith the Lord.' They have even the audacity to speak in the first person, as if Jehovah himself were speaking. As in Isaiah: 'Hearken unto me, O Jacob, and Israel my called; I am He, I am the First, I also am the last,'— and so on. The personality of the prophet sinks entirely into the background; he feels himself for the time being the mouthpiece of the Almighty." [W. Sanday: The Oracles of God, London, 1892, pp. 49-56, abridged.]

"We need to remember that prophecy was a profession, and that the prophets formed a professional class. There were schools of the prophets, in which the gift was regularly cultivated. A group of young men would gather round some commanding figure— a Samuel or an Elisha— and would not only record or spread the knowledge of his sayings and doings, but seek to catch themselves something of his inspiration. It seems that music played its part in their exercises.... It is perfectly clear that by no means all of these Sons of the prophets ever succeeded in acquiring more than a very small share in the gift which they sought. It was clearly possible to 'counterfeit' prophecy. Sometimes this was done deliberately.... But it by no means follows that in all cases where a false message was given, the giver of it was altogether conscious of what he was doing." [Op. cit., p. 91. This author also cites Moses's and Isaiah's commissions, given in Exodus, chaps. iii. and iv., and Isaiah, chap. vi.]

Here, to take another Jewish case, is the way in which Philo of Alexandria describes his inspiration:—

"Sometimes, when I have come to my work empty, I have suddenly become full; ideas being in an invisible manner showered upon me, and implanted in me from on high; so that through the influence of divine inspiration, I have become greatly excited, and have known neither the place in which I was, nor those who were present, nor myself, nor what I was saying, nor what I was writing; for then I have been conscious of a richness of interpretation, an enjoyment of light, a most penetrating insight, a most manifest energy in all that was to be done; having such effect on my mind as the clearest ocular demonstration would have on the eyes." [Quoted by Augustus Clissold: The Prophetic Spirit in Genius and Madness, 1870, p. 67. Mr. Clissold is a Swedenborgian. Swedenborg's case is of course the palmary one of audita et visa, serving as a basis of religious revelation.]

If we turn to Islam, we find that Mohammed's revelations all came from the subconscious sphere. To the question in what way he got them,—

"Mohammed is said to have answered that sometimes he heard a knell as from a bell, and that this had the strongest effect on him; and when the angel went away, he had received the revelation. Sometimes again he held converse with the angel as with a man, so as easily to understand his words. The later authorities, however,... distinguish still other kinds. In the Itgan (103) the following are enumerated: 1, revelations with sound of bell, 2, by inspiration of the holy spirit in M.'s heart, 3, by Gabriel in human form, 4, by God immediately, either when awake (as in his journey to heaven) or in dream.... In Almawahib alladuniya the kinds are thus given: 1, Dream, 2, Inspiration of Gabriel in the Prophet's heart, 3, Gabriel taking Dahya's form, 4, with the bell-sound, etc., 5, Gabriel in propria persona (only twice), 6, revelation in heaven, 7, God appearing in person, but veiled, 8, God revealing himself immediately without veil. Others add two other stages, namely: 1, Gabriel in the form of still another man, 2, God showing himself personally in dream." [Noldeke, Geschichte des Qorans, 1860, p. 16. Compare the fuller account in Sir William Muir's Life of Mahomet, 3d ed., 1894, ch. iii.]

In none of these cases is the revelation distinctly motor. In the case of Joseph Smith (who had prophetic revelations innumerable in addition to the revealed translation of the gold plates which resulted in the Book of Mormon), although there may have been a motor element, the inspiration seems to have been predominantly sensorial. He began his translation by the aid of the 'peepstones' which he found, or thought or said that he found, with the gold plates,- apparently a case of 'crystal gazing.' For some of the other revelations he used the peep-stones, but seems generally to have asked the Lord for more direct instruction.

The Mormon theocracy has always been governed by direct revelations accorded to the President of the Church and its Apostles. From an obliging letter written to me in 1899 by an eminent Mormon, I quote the following extract:

"It may be very interesting for you to know that the President [Mr. Snow] of the Mormon Church claims to have had a number of revelations very recently from heaven. To explain fully what these revelations are, it is necessary to know that we, as a people, believe that the Church of Jesus Christ has again been established through messengers sent from heaven. This Church has at its head a prophet, seer, and revelator, who gives to man God's holy will. Revelation is the means through which the will of God is declared directly and in fullness to man. These revelations are got through dreams of sleep or in waking visions of the mind, by voices without visional appearance or by actual manifestations of the Holy Presence before the eye. We believe that God has come in person and spoken to our prophet and revelator."

Other revelations are described as 'openings'— Fox's, for example, were evidently of the kind known in spiritistic circles of today as 'impressions.' As all effective initiators of change must needs live to some degree upon this psychopathic level of sudden perception or conviction of new truth, or of impulse to action so obsessive that it must be worked off, I will say nothing more about so very common a phenomenon.

When, in addition to these phenomena of inspiration, we take religious mysticism into the account, when we recall the striking and sudden unifications of a discordant self which we saw in conversion, and when we review the extravagant obsessions of tenderness, purity, and self-severity met with in saintliness, we cannot, I think, avoid the conclusion that in religion we have a department of human nature with unusually close relations to the transmarginal or subliminal region. If the word 'subliminal' is offensive to any of you, as smelling too much of psychical research or other aberrations, call it by any other name you please, to distinguish it from the level of full sunlit consciousness. Call this latter the A-region of personality, if you care to, and call the other the B-region. The B-region, then, is obviously the larger part of each of us, for it is the abode of everything that is latent and the reservoir of everything that passes unrecorded or unobserved. It contains, for example, such things as all our momentarily inactive memories, and it harbors the springs of all our obscurely motived passions, impulses, likes, dislikes, and prejudices. Our intuitions, hypotheses, fancies, superstitions, persuasions, convictions, and in general all our non-rational operations, come from it. It is the source of our dreams, and apparently they may return to it. In it arise whatever mystical experiences we may have, and our automatisms, sensory or motor; our life in hypnotic and 'hypnoid' conditions, if we are subjects to such conditions; our delusions, fixed ideas, and hysterical accidents, if we are hysteric subjects; our supra-normal cognitions, if such there be, and if we are telepathic subjects. It is also the fountain-head of much that feeds our religion. In persons deep in the religious life, as we have now abundantly seen,— and this is my conclusion,— the door into this region seems unusually wide open; at any rate, experiences making their entrance through that door have had emphatic influence in shaping religious history.

With this conclusion I turn back and close the circle which I opened in my first lecture, terminating thus the review which I then announced of inner religious phenomena as we find them in developed and articulate human individuals. I might easily, if the time allowed, multiply both my documents and my discriminations, but a broad treatment is, I believe, in itself better, and the most important characteristics of the subject lie, I think, before us already. In the next lecture, which is also the last one, we must try to draw the critical conclusions which so much material may suggest.

LECTURE XX: CONCLUSIONS

The material of our study of human nature is now spread before us; and in this parting hour, set free from the duty of description, we can draw our theoretical and practical conclusions. In my first lecture, defending the empirical method, I foretold that whatever conclusions we might come to could be reached by spiritual judgments only, appreciations of the significance for life of religion, taken 'on the whole.' Our conclusions cannot be as sharp as dogmatic conclusions would be, but I will formulate them, when the time comes, as sharply as I can.

Summing up in the broadest possible way the characteristics of the religious life, as we have found them, it includes the following beliefs:

1. That the visible world is part of a more spiritual universe from which it draws its chief significance;

2. That union or harmonious relation with that higher universe is our true end;

3. That prayer or inner communion with the spirit thereof— be that spirit 'God' or 'law'— is a process wherein work is really done, and spiritual energy flows in and produces effects, psychological or material, within the phenomenal world.

Religion includes also the following psychological characteristics:

4. A new zest which adds itself like a gift to life, and takes the form either of lyrical enchantment or of appeal to earnestness and heroism.

5. An assurance of safety and a temper of peace, and, in relation to others, a preponderance of loving affections.

In illustrating these characteristics by documents, we have been literally bathed in sentiment. In re-reading my manuscript, I am almost appalled at the amount of emotionality which I find in it. After so much of this, we can afford to be dryer and less sympathetic in the rest of the work that lies before us.

The sentimentality of many of my documents is a consequence of the fact that I sought them among the extravagances of the subject. If any of you are enemies of what our ancestors used to brand as enthusiasm, and are, nevertheless, still listening to me now, you have probably felt my selection to have been sometimes almost perverse, and have wished I might have stuck to soberer examples. I reply that I took these extremer examples as yielding the profounder information. To learn the secrets of any science, we go to expert specialists, even though they may be eccentric persons, and not to commonplace pupils. We combine what they tell us with the rest of our wisdom, and form our final judgment independently. Even so with religion. We who have pursued such radical expressions of it may now be sure that we know its secrets as authentically as any one can know them who learns them from another; and we have next to answer, each of us for himself, the practical question: what are the dangers in this element of life? and in what proportion may it need to be restrained by other elements, to give the proper balance?

But this question suggests another one which I will answer immediately and get it out of the way, for it has more than once already vexed us. Ought it to be assumed that in all men the mixture of religion with other elements should be identical? Ought it, indeed, to be assumed that the lives of all men should show identical religious elements? In other words, is the existence of so many religious types and sects and creeds regrettable?

To these questions I answer 'No' emphatically. And my reason is that I do not see how it is possible that creatures in such different positions and with such different powers as human individuals are, should have exactly the same functions and the same duties. No two of us have identical difficulties, nor should we be expected to work out identical solutions. Each, from his peculiar angle of observation, takes in a certain sphere of fact and trouble, which each must deal with in a unique manner. One of us must soften himself, another must harden himself; one must yield a point, another must stand firm,— in order the better to defend the position assigned him. If an Emerson were forced to be a Wesley, or a Moody forced to be a Whitman, the total human consciousness of the divine would suffer. The divine can mean no single quality, it must mean a group of qualities, by being champions of which in alternation, different men may all find worthy missions. Each attitude being a syllable in human nature's total message, it takes the whole of us to spell the meaning out completely. So a 'god of battles' must be allowed to be the god for one kind of person, a god of peace and heaven and home, the god for another. We must frankly recognize the fact that we live in partial systems, and that parts are not interchangeable in the spiritual life. If we are peevish and jealous, destruction of the self must be an element of our religion; why need it be one if we are good and sympathetic from the outset? If we are sick souls, we require a religion of deliverance; but why think so much of deliverance, if we are healthy-minded? Unquestionably, some men have the completer experience and the higher vocation, here just as in the social world; but for each man to stay in his own experience, whate'er it be, and for others to tolerate him there, is surely best.

From this point of view, the contrasts between the healthy and the morbid mind, and between the once-born and the twice-born types, of which I spoke in earlier lectures cease to be the radical antagonisms which many think them. The twice-born look down upon the rectilinear consciousness of life of the once-born as being 'mere morality,' and not properly religion. "Dr. Channing," an orthodox minister is reported to have said, "is excluded from the highest form of religious life by the extraordinary rectitude of his character." It is indeed true that the outlook upon life of the twice-born— holding as it does more of the element of evil in solution— is the wider and completer. The 'heroic' or 'solemn' way in which life comes to them is a 'higher synthesis' into which healthy-mindedness and morbidness both enter and combine. Evil is not evaded, but sublated in the higher religious cheer of these persons. But the final consciousness which each type reaches of union with the divine has the same practical significance for the individual; and individuals may well be allowed to get to it by the channels which lie most open to their several temperaments. In the cases which were quoted in Lecture IV, of the mind-cure form of healthy-mindedness, we found abundant examples of regenerative process. The severity of the crisis in this process is a matter of degree. How long one shall continue to drink the consciousness of evil, and when one shall begin to short-circuit and get rid of it, are also matters of amount and degree, so that in many instances it is quite arbitrary whether we class the individual a once-born or a twice-born subject.

But, you may now ask, would not this one-sidedness be cured if we should all espouse the science of religions as our own religion? In answering this question I must open again the general relations of the theoretic to the active life.

Knowledge about a thing is not the thing itself. You remember what Al-Ghazzali told us in the Lecture on Mysticism,— that to understand the causes of drunkenness, as a physician understands them, is not to be drunk. A science might come to understand everything about the causes and elements of religion, and might even decide which elements were qualified, by their general harmony with other branches of knowledge, to be considered true; and yet the best man at this science might be the man who found it hardest to be personally devout. Tout savoir c'est tout pardonner. The name of Renan would doubtless occur to many persons as an example of the way in which breadth of knowledge may make one only a dilettante in possibilities, and blunt the acuteness of one's living faith. If religion be a function by which either God's cause or man's cause is to be really advanced, then he who lives the life of it, however narrowly, is a better servant than he who merely knows about it, however much. Knowledge about life is one thing; effective occupation of a place in life, with its dynamic currents passing through your being, is another.

For this reason, the science of religions may not be an equivalent for living religion; and if we turn to the inner difficulties of such a science, we see that a point comes when she must drop the purely theoretic attitude, and either let her knots remain uncut, or have them cut by active faith. To see this, suppose that we have our science of religions constituted as a matter of fact. Suppose that she has assimilated all the necessary historical material and distilled out of it as its essence the same conclusions which I myself a few moments ago pronounced. Suppose that she agrees that religion, wherever it is an active thing, involves a belief in ideal presences, and a belief that in our prayerful communion with them, work is done, and something real comes to pass. She has now to exert her critical activity, and to decide how far, in the light of other sciences and in that of general philosophy, such beliefs can be considered true.

Dogmatically to decide this is an impossible task. Not only are the other sciences and the philosophy still far from being completed, but in their

present state we find them full of conflicts. The sciences of nature know nothing of spiritual presences, and on the whole hold no practical commerce whatever with the idealistic conceptions towards which general philosophy inclines. The scientist, so-called, is, during his scientific hours at least, so materialistic that one may well say that on the whole the influence of science goes against the notion that religion should be recognized at all. And this antipathy to religion finds an echo within the very science of religions itself. The cultivator of this science has to become acquainted with so many groveling and horrible superstitions that a presumption easily arises in his mind that any belief that is religious probably is false. In the 'prayerful communion' of savages with such mumbo-jumbos of deities as they acknowledge, it is hard for us to see what genuine spiritual work— even though it were work relative only to their dark savage obligations— can possibly be done.

The consequence is that the conclusions of the science of religions are as likely to be adverse as they are to be favorable to the claim that the essence of religion is true. There is a notion in the air about us that religion is probably only an anachronism, a case of 'survival,' an atavistic relapse into a mode of thought which humanity in its more enlightened examples has outgrown; and this notion our religious anthropologists at present do little to counteract.

This view is so widespread at the present day that I must consider it with some explicitness before I pass to my own conclusions. Let me call it the 'Survival theory,' for brevity's sake.

The pivot round which the religious life, as we have traced it, revolves, is the interest of the individual in his private personal destiny. Religion, in short, is a monumental chapter in the history of human egotism. The gods believed in— whether by crude savages or by men disciplined intellectually— agree with each other in recognizing personal calls. Religious thought is carried on in terms of personality, this being, in the world of religion, the one fundamental fact. Today, quite as much as at any previous age, the religious individual tells you that the divine meets him on the basis of his personal concerns.

Science, on the other hand, has ended by utterly repudiating the personal point of view. She catalogues her elements and records her laws indifferent as to what purpose may be shown forth by them, and constructs her theories quite careless of their bearing on human anxieties and fates. Though the scientist may individually nourish a religion, and be a theist in his irresponsible hours, the days are over when it could be said that for Science herself the heavens declare the glory of God and the firmament showeth his handiwork. Our solar system, with its harmonies, is seen now as but one passing case of a certain sort of moving equilibrium in the heavens, realized by a local accident in an appalling wilderness of worlds where no life can exist. In a span of time which as a cosmic interval will count but as an hour, it will have ceased to be. The Darwinian notion of chance production, and subsequent destruction, speedy or deferred, applies to the largest as well as to the smallest facts. It is impossible, in the present temper of the scientific imagination, to find

in the driftings of the cosmic atoms, whether they work on the universal or on the particular scale, anything but a kind of aimless weather, doing and undoing, achieving no proper history, and leaving no result. Nature has no one distinguishable ultimate tendency with which it is possible to feel a sympathy. In the vast rhythm of her processes, as the scientific mind now follows them, she appears to cancel herself. The books of natural theology which satisfied the intellects of our grandfathers seem to us quite grotesque, representing, as they did, a God who conformed the largest things of nature to the paltriest of our private wants. The God whom science recognizes must be a God of universal laws exclusively, a God who does a wholesale, not a retail business. He cannot accommodate his processes to the convenience of individuals. The bubbles on the foam which coats a stormy sea are floating episodes, made and unmade by the forces of the wind and water. Our private selves are like those bubbles,— epiphenomena, as Clifford, I believe, ingeniously called them; their destinies weigh nothing and determine nothing in the world's irremediable currents of events.

How was it ever conceivable, we ask, that a man like Christian Wolff, in whose dry-as-dust head all the learning of the early eighteenth century was concentrated, should have preserved such a baby—like faith in the personal and human character of Nature as to expound her operations as he did in his work on the uses of natural things? This, for example, is the account he gives of the sun and its utility:

"We see that God has created the sun to keep the changeable conditions on the earth in such an order that living creatures, men and beasts, may inhabit its surface. Since men are the most reasonable of creatures, and able to infer God's invisible being from the contemplation of the world, the sun in so far forth contributes to the primary purpose of creation: without it the race of man could not be preserved or continued.... The sun makes daylight, not only on our earth, but also on the other planets; and daylight is of the utmost utility to us; for by its means we can commodiously carry on those occupations which in the night-time would either be quite impossible, or at any rate impossible without our going to the expense of artificial light. The beasts of the field can find food by day which they would not be able to find at night. Moreover we owe it to the sunlight that we are able to see everything that is on the earth's surface, not only near by, but also at a distance, and to recognize both near and far things according to their species, which again is of manifold use to us not only in the business necessary to human life, and when we are traveling, but also for the scientific knowledge of Nature, which knowledge for the most part depends on observations made with the help of sight, and, without the sunshine, would have been impossible. If any one would rightly impress on his mind the great advantages which he derives from the sun, let him imagine himself living through only one mouth, and see how it would be with all his undertakings, if it were not day but night. He would then be sufficiently convinced out of his own experience, especially if he had much work to carry on in the street or in the fields.... From the sun we learn to recognize when it is midday, and by knowing this point of time exactly, we can set our clocks right, on which account astronomy owes much to the sun.... By help of the sun one can find the meridian.... But the meridian is the basis of our sun-dials, and generally speaking, we should have no sun-dials if we had no sun." [Vernunftige Gedanken von den Absichten der naturlichen Dinge, 1782, pp. 74-84.]

Or read the account of God's beneficence in the institution of "the great variety throughout the world of men's faces, voices, and handwriting," given in Derham's Physico-theology, a book that had much vogue in the eighteenth century. "Had Man's body," says Dr. Derham, "been made according to any of the Atheistical Schemes, or any other Method than that of the infinite Lord of the World, this wise Variety would never have been: but Men's Faces would have been cast in the same, or not a very different Mould, their Organs of Speech would have sounded the same or not so great a Variety of Notes; and the same Structure of Muscles and Nerves would have given the Hand the same Direction in Writing. And in this Case, what Confusion, what Disturbance, what Mischiefs would the world eternally have lain under! No Security could have been to our persons; no Certainty, no Enjoyment of our Possessions; no Justice between Man and Man; no Distinction between Good and Bad, between Friends and Foes, between Father and Child, Husband and Wife, Male or Female; but all would have been turned topsy-turvy, by being exposed to the Malice of the Envious and ill-Natured, to the Fraud and Violence of Knaves and Robbers, to the Forgeries of the crafty Cheat, to the Lusts of the Effeminate and Debauched, and what not! Our Courts of Justice can abundantly testify the dire Effects of Mistaking Men's Faces, of counterfeiting their Hands, and forging Writings. But now as the infinitely wise Creator and Ruler hath ordered the Matter, every man's Face can distinguish him in the Light, and his Voice in the Dark; his Hand-writing can speak for him though absent, and be his Witness, and secure his Contracts in future Generations. A manifest as well as admirable Indication of the divine Superintendence and Management."

A God so careful as to make provision even for the unmistakable signing of bank checks and deeds was a deity truly after the heart of eighteenth century Anglicanism.

I subjoin, omitting the capitals, Derham's 'Vindication of God by the Institution of Hills and Valleys,' and Wolff's altogether culinary account of the Institution of Water:

"The uses," says Wolff, "which water serves in human life are plain to see and need not be described at length. Water is a universal drink of man and beasts. Even though men have made themselves drinks that are artificial, they could not do this without water. Beer is brewed of water and malt, and it is the water in it which quenches thirst. Wine is prepared from grapes, which could never have grown without the help of water; and the same is true of those drinks which in England and other places they produce from fruit.... Therefore since God so planned the world that men and beasts should live upon it and find there everything required for their necessity and convenience, he also made water as one means whereby to make the earth into so excellent a dwelling. And this is all the more manifest when we consider the advantages which we obtain from this same water for the cleaning of our household utensils, of our clothing, and of other matters.... When one goes into a grinding-mill one sees that the grindstone must always be kept wet and then one will get a still greater idea of the use of water."

Of the hills and valleys, Derham, after praising their beauty, discourses as follows: "Some constitutions are indeed of so happy a strength, and so confirmed an health, as to be indifferent to almost any place or temperature of the air. But then others are so weakly and feeble, as not to be able to bear one, but can live comfortably in another place. With some the more subtle and finer air of the hills doth best agree, who are languishing and dying in the feculent and grosser air of great towns, or even the warmer and vaporous air of the valleys and waters. But contrariwise, others languish on the hills, and grow lusty and strong in the warmer air of the valleys.

"So that this opportunity of shifting our abode from the hills to the vales, is an admirable easement, refreshment, and great benefit to the valetudinarian, feeble part of mankind; affording those an easy and comfortable life, who would otherwise live miserably, languish, and pine away.

"To this salutary conformation of the earth we may add another great convenience of the hills, and that is affording commodious places for habitation, serving (as an eminent author wordeth it) as screens to keep off the cold and nipping blasts of the northern and easterly winds, and reflecting the benign and cherishing sunbeams, and so rendering our habitations both more comfortable and more cheerly in winter.

"Lastly, it is to the hills that the fountains owe their rise and the rivers their conveyance, and consequently those vast masses and lofty piles are not, as they are charged, such rude and useless excrescences of our ill-formed globe; but the admirable tools of nature, contrived and ordered by the infinite Creator, to do one of its most useful works. For, was the surface of the earth even and level, and the middle parts of its islands and continents not mountainous and high as now it is, it is most certain there could be no descent for the rivers, no conveyance for the waters; but, instead of gliding along those gentle declivities which the higher lands now afford them quite down to the sea, they would stagnate and perhaps stink, and also drown large tracts of land.

"[Thus] the hills and vales, though to a peevish and weary traveler they may seem incommodious and troublesome, yet are a noble work of the great Creator, and wisely appointed by him for the good of our sublunary world."

You see how natural it is, from this point of view, to treat religion as a mere survival, for religion does in fact perpetuate the traditions of the most primeval thought. To coerce the spiritual powers, or to square them and get them on our side, was, during enormous tracts of time, the one great object in our dealings with the natural world. For our ancestors, dreams, hallucinations, revelations, and cock-and-bull stories were inextricably mixed with facts. Up to a comparatively recent date such distinctions as those between what has been verified and what is only conjectured, between the impersonal and the personal aspects of existence, were hardly suspected or conceived. Whatever you imagined in a lively manner, whatever you thought fit to be true, you affirmed confidently; and whatever you affirmed, your comrades believed. Truth was what had not yet been contradicted, most things were taken into the mind from the point of view of their human suggestiveness, and the attention confined itself exclusively to the aesthetic and dramatic aspects of events.

Until the seventeenth century this mode of thought prevailed. One need only recall the dramatic treatment even of mechanical questions by Aristotle, as, for example, his explanation of the power of the lever to make a small weight raise a larger one. This is due, according to Aristotle, to the generally miraculous character of the circle and of all circular movement. The circle is both convex and concave; it is made by a fixed point and a moving line, which contradict each other; and whatever moves in a circle moves in opposite directions. Nevertheless, movement in a circle is the most 'natural' movement; and the long arm of the lever, moving, as it does, in the larger circle, has the greater amount of this natural motion, and consequently requires the lesser force. Or recall the explanation by Herodotus of the position of the sun in winter: It moves to the south because of the cold which drives it into the warm parts of the heavens over Libya. Or listen to Saint Augustine's speculations: "Who gave to chaff such power to freeze that it preserves snow buried under it, and such power to warm that it ripens green fruit? Who can explain the strange properties of fire itself, which blackens all that it burns, though itself bright, and which, though of the most beautiful colors, discolors almost all that it touches and feeds upon, and turns blazing fuel into grimy cinders?... Then what wonderful properties do we find in charcoal, which is so brittle that a light tap breaks it, and a alight pressure pulverizes it, and yet is so strong that no moisture rots it, nor any time causes it to decay." [City of God, book xxi. ch. iv.]

Such aspects of things as these, their naturalness and unnaturalness, the sympathies and antipathies of their superficial qualities, their eccentricities, their brightness and strength and destructiveness, were inevitably the ways in which they originally fastened our attention.

If you open early medical books, you will find sympathetic magic invoked on every page. Take, for example, the famous vulnerary ointment attributed to Paracelaus. For this there were a variety of receipts, including usually human fat, the fat of either a bull, a wild boar, or a bear; powdered earthworms, the usnia, or mossy growth on the weathered skull of a hanged criminal, and other materials equally unpleasant— the whole prepared under the planet Venus if possible, but never under Mars or Saturn. Then, if a splinter of wood, dipped in the patient's blood, or the bloodstained weapon that wounded him, be immersed in this ointment, the wound itself being tightly bound up, the latter infallibly gets well,— I quote now Van Helmont's account,— for the blood on the weapon or splinter, containing in it the spirit of the wounded man, is roused to active excitement by the contact of the ointment, whence there results to it a full commission or power to cure its cousin-german, the blood in the patient's body. This it does by sucking out the dolorous and exotic impression from the wounded part. But to do this it has to implore the aid of the bull's fat, and other portions of the unguent. The reason why bull's fat is so powerful is that the bull at the time of slaughter is full of secret reluctancy and vindictive murmurs, and therefore dies with a higher flame of revenge about him than any other animal. And thus we have made it out, says this author, that the admirable efficacy of the ointment ought to be imputed, not to any auxiliary concurrence of Satan, but simply to the energy of the posthumous character of Revenge remaining firmly impressed upon the blood and concreted fat in the unguent. [J.B. Van Helmont: A Ternary of Paradoxes, translated by Walter Charleton, London, 1650.— I much abridge the original in my citations.]

The author goes on to prove by the analogy of many other natural facts that this sympathetic action between things at a distance is the true rationale of the case. "If," he says, "the heart of a horse, slain by a witch, taken out of the yet reeking carcase, be impaled upon an arrow and roasted, immediately the whole witch becomes tormented with the insufferable pains and cruelty of the fire, which could by no means happen unless there preceded a conjunction of the spirit of the witch with the spirit of the horse. In the reeking and yet panting heart, the spirit of the witch is kept captive, and the retreat of it prevented by the arrow transfixed. Similarly hath not many a murdered carcase at the coroner's inquest suffered a fresh hemorrhage or cruentation at the presence of the assassin?— the blood being, as in a furious fit of anger, enraged and agitated by the impress of revenge conceived against the murderer, at the instant of the soul's compulsive exile from the body. So, if you have dropsy, gout, or jaundice, by including some of your warm blood in the shell and white of an egg, which, exposed to a gentle heat, and mixed with a bait of flesh, you shall give to a hungry dog or hog, the disease shall instantly pass from you into the animal, and leave you entirely. And similarly again, if you burn some of the milk either of a cow or of a woman, the gland from which it issued will dry up. A gentleman at Brussels had his nose mowed off in a combat, but the celebrated surgeon Tagliacozzus digged a new nose for him out of the skin of the arm of a porter at Bologna. About thirteen months after his return to his own country, the engrafted nose grew cold, putrefied, and in a few days dropped off, and it was then discovered that the porter had expired, near about the same punctilio of time. There are still at Brussels eye-witnesses of this occurrence," says Van Helmont; and adds, "I pray what is there in this of superstition or of exalted imagination?"

Modern mind-cure literature— the works of Prentice Mulford, for example— of sympathetic magic.

How indeed could it be otherwise? The extraordinary value, for explanation and prevision, of those mathematical and mechanical modes of conception which science uses, was a result that could not possibly have been expected in advance. Weight, movement, velocity, direction, position, what thin, pallid, uninteresting ideas! How could the richer animistic aspects of Nature, the peculiarities and oddities that make phenomena picturesquely striking or expressive, fail to have been first singled out and followed by philosophy as the more promising avenue to the knowledge of Nature's life? Well, it is still in these richer animistic and dramatic aspects that religion delights to dwell, It is the terror and beauty of phenomena, the 'promise' of the dawn and of the rainbow, the 'voice' of the thunder, the 'gentleness' of the summer rain, the 'sublimity' of the stars, and not the physical laws which these things follow, by which the religious mind still continues to be most impressed; and just as of yore, the devout man tells you that in the solitude of his room or of the fields he still feels the divine presence, that inflowings of help come in reply to his prayers, and that sacrifices to this unseen reality fill him with security and peace.

Pure anachronism! says the survival-theory;— anachronism for which deanthropomorphization of the imagination is the remedy required. The less we mix the private with the cosmic, the more we dwell in universal and impersonal terms, the truer heirs of Science we become.

In spite of the appeal which this impersonality of the scientific attitude makes to a certain magnanimity of temper, I believe it to be shallow, and I can now state my reason in comparatively few words. That reason is that, so long as we deal with the cosmic and the general, we deal only with the symbols of reality, but as soon as we deal with private and personal phenomena as such, we deal with realities in the completest sense of the term. I think I can easily make clear what I mean by these words.

The world of our experience consists at all times of two parts, an objective and a subjective part, of which the former may be incalculably more extensive than the latter, and yet the latter can never be omitted or suppressed. The objective part is the sum total of whatsoever at any given time we may be thinking of, the subjective part is the inner 'state' in which the thinking comes to pass. What we think of may be enormous, the cosmic times and spaces, for example,— whereas the inner state may be the most fugitive and paltry activity of mind. Yet the cosmic objects, so far as the experience yields them, are but ideal pictures of something whose existence we do not inwardly possess but only point at outwardly, while the inner state is our very experience itself; its reality and that of our experience are one. A conscious field plus its object as felt or thought of plus an attitude towards the object plus the sense of a self to whom the attitude belongs— such a concrete bit of personal experience may be a small bit, but it is a solid bit as long as it lasts; not hollow, not a mere abstract element of experience, such as the 'object' is when taken all alone. It is a full fact, even though it be an insignificant fact; it is of the kind to which all realities whatsoever must belong; the motor currents of the world run through the like of it; it is on the line connecting real events with real events. That unsharable feeling which each one of us has of the pinch of his individual destiny as he privately feels it rolling out on fortune's wheel may be disparaged for its egotism, may be sneered at as unscientific, but it is the one thing that fills up the measure of our concrete actuality, and any would-be existent that should lack such a feeling, or its analogue, would be a piece of reality only half made up.

Compare Lotze's doctrine that the only meaning we can attach to the notion of a thing as it is 'in itself' is by conceiving it as it is for itself; i. e., as a piece of full experience with a private sense of 'pinch' or inner activity of some sort going with it.

If this be true, it is absurd for science to say that the egotistic elements of experience should be suppressed. The axis of reality runs solely through the egotistic places,— they are strung upon it like so many beads. To describe the world with all the various feelings of the individual pinch of destiny, all the various spiritual attitudes, left out from the description— they being as describable as anything else— would be something like offering a printed bill of fare as the equivalent for a solid meal. Religion makes no such blunder. The individual's religion may be egotistic, and those private realities which it keeps in touch with may be narrow enough; but at any rate it always remains infinitely less hollow and abstract, as far as it goes, than a science which prides itself on taking no account of anything private at all.

A bill of fare with one real raisin on it instead of the word 'raisin,' with one real egg instead of the word 'egg,' might be an inadequate meal, but it would at least be a commencement of reality. The contention of the survival-theory that we ought to stick to non-personal elements exclusively seems like saying that we ought to be satisfied forever with reading the naked bill of fare. I think, therefore, that however particular questions connected with our individual destinies may be answered, it is only by acknowledging them as genuine questions, and living in the sphere of thought which they open up, that we become profound. But to live thus is to be religious; so I unhesitatingly repudiate the survival-theory of religion, as being founded on an egregious mistake. It does not follow, because our ancestors made so many errors of fact and mixed them with their religion, that we should therefore leave off being religious at all. By being religious we establish ourselves in possession of ultimate reality at the only points at which reality is given us to guard. Our responsible concern is with our private destiny, after all.

Even the errors of fact may possibly turn out not to be as wholesale as the scientist assumes. We saw in Lecture IV how the religious conception of the universe seems to many mind-curers 'verified' from day to day by their experience of fact. 'Experience of fact' is a field with so many things in it that the sectarian scientist, methodically declining, as he does, to recognize such 'facts' as mind-curers and others like them experience, otherwise than by such rude heads of classification as 'bosh,' 'rot,' 'folly,' certainly leaves out a mass of raw fact which, save for the industrious interest of the religious in the more personal aspects of reality, would never have succeeded in getting itself recorded at all. We know this to be true already in certain cases; it may, therefore, be true in others as well. Miraculous healings have always been part of the supernaturalist stock in trade, and have always been dismissed by the scientist as figments of the imagination. But the scientist's tardy education in the facts of hypnotism has recently given him an apperceiving mass for phenomena of this order, and he consequently now allows that the healings may exist, provided you expressly call them effects of 'suggestion.' Even the stigmata of the cross on Saint Francis's hands and feet may on these terms not be a fable. Similarly, the time-honored phenomenon of diabolical possession is on the point of being admitted by the scientist as a fact, now that he has the name of 'hystero-demonopathy' by which to apperceive it. No one can foresee just how far this legitimation of occultist phenomena under newly found scientist titles may proceed— even 'prophecy,' even 'levitation,' might creep into the pale.

Thus the divorce between scientist facts and religious facts may not necessarily be as eternal as it at first sight seems, nor the personalism and romanticism of the world, as they appeared to primitive thinking, be matters so irrevocably outgrown. The final human opinion may, in short, in some manner now impossible to foresee, revert to the more personal style, just as any path of progress may follow a spiral rather than a straight line. If this were so, the rigorously impersonal view of science might one day appear as having been a temporarily useful eccentricity rather than the definitively triumphant position which the sectarian scientist at present so confidently announces it to be.

You see now why I have been so individualistic throughout these lectures, and why I have seemed so bent on rehabilitating the element of feeling in religion and subordinating its intellectual part. Individuality is founded in feeling; and the recesses of feeling, the darker, blinder strata of character, are the only places in the world in which we catch real fact in the making, and directly perceive how events happen, and how work is actually done. Compared with this world of living individualized feelings, the world of generalized objects which the intellect contemplates is without solidity or life. As in stereoscopic or kinetoscopic pictures seen outside the instrument, the third dimension, the movement, the vital element, are not there. We get a beautiful picture of an express train supposed to be moving, but where in the picture, as I have heard a friend say, is the energy or the fifty miles an hour?

Hume's criticism has banished causation from the world of physical objects, and 'Science' is absolutely satisfied to define cause in terms of concomitant change— read Mach, Pearson, Ostwald. The 'original' of the notion of causation is in our inner personal experience, and only there can causes in the old-fashioned sense be directly observed and described.

When I read in a religious paper words like these: "Perhaps the best thing we can say of God is that he is the Inevitable Inference," I recognize the tendency to let religion evaporate in intellectual terms. Would martyrs have sung in the flames for a mere inference, however inevitable it might be? Original religious men, like Saint Francis, Luther, Behmen, have usually been enemies of the intellect's pretension to meddle with religious things. Yet the intellect, everywhere invasive, shows everywhere its shallowing effect. See how the ancient spirit of Methodism evaporates under those wonderfully able rationalistic booklets (which every one should read) of a philosopher like Professor Bowne (The Christian Revelation, The Christian Life, The Atonement: Cincinnati and New York, 1898, 1899, 1900). See the positively expulsive purpose of philosophy properly so called:

"Religion," writes M. Vacherot (La Religion, Paris, 1869, pp. 313, 436, et passim), "answers to a transient state or condition, not to a permanent determination of human nature, being merely an expression of that stage of the human mind which is dominated by the imagination.... Christianity has but a single possible final heir to its estate, and that is scientific philosophy."

In a still more radical vein, Professor Ribot (Psychologie des Sentiments, p. 310) describes the evaporation of religion. He sums it up in a single formula— the ever-growing predominance of the rational intellectual element, with the gradual fading out of the emotional element, this latter tending to enter into the group of purely intellectual sentiments. "Of religions sentiment properly so called, nothing survives at last save a vague respect for the unknowable x which is a last relic of the fear, and a certain attraction towards the ideal, which is a relic of the love, that characterized the earlier periods of religious growth. To state this more simply, religion tends to turn into religious philosophy.— These are psychologically entirely different things, the one being a theoretic construction of ratiocination, whereas the other is the living work of a group of persons, or of a great inspired leader, calling into play the entire thinking and feeling organism of man."

I find the same failure to recognize that the stronghold of religion lies in individuality in attempts like those of Professor Baldwin (Mental Development, Social and Ethical Interpretations, ch. x.) and Mr. H. R. Marshall (Instinct and Reason, chaps. viii. to xii.) to make it a purely 'conservative social force.'

Let us agree, then, that Religion, occupying herself with personal destinies and keeping thus in contact with the only absolute realities which we know, must necessarily play an eternal part in human history. The next thing to decide is what she reveals about those destinies, or whether indeed she reveals anything distinct enough to be considered a general message to mankind. We have done as you see, with our preliminaries, and our final summing up can now begin.

I am well aware that after all the palpitating documents which I have quoted, and all the perspectives of emotion-inspiring institution and belief that my previous lectures have opened, the dry analysis to which I now advance may appear to many of you like an anti-climax, a tapering-off and flattening out of the subject, instead of a crescendo of interest and result. I said awhile ago that the religious attitude of Protestants appears poverty-stricken to the Catholic imagination. Still more poverty-stricken, I fear, may my final summing up of the subject appear at first to some of you. On which account I pray you now to bear this point in mind, that in the present part of it I am expressly trying to reduce religion to its lowest admissible terms, to that minimum, free from individualistic excrescences, which all religions contain as their nucleus, and on which it may be hoped that all religious persons may agree. That established, we should have a result which might be small, but would at least be solid; and on it and round it the ruddier additional beliefs on which the different individuals make their venture might be grafted, and flourish as richly as you please. I shall add my own over-belief (which will be, I confess, of a somewhat pallid kind, as befits a critical philosopher), and you will, I hope, also add your over-beliefs, and we shall soon be in the varied world of concrete religious constructions once more. For the moment, let me dryly pursue the analytic part of the task.

Both thought and feeling are determinants of conduct, and the same conduct may be determined either by feeling or by thought. When we survey the whole field of religion, we find a great variety in the thoughts that have prevailed there; but the feelings on the one hand and the conduct on the other are almost always the same, for Stoic, Christian, and Buddhist saints are practically indistinguishable in their lives. The theories which Religion generates, being thus variable, are secondary; and if you wish to grasp her essence, you must look to the feelings and the conduct as being the more constant elements. It is between these two elements that the short circuit exists on which she carries on her principal business, while the ideas and symbols and other institutions form loop-lines which may be perfections and improvements, and may even some day all be united into one harmonious system, but which are not to be regarded as organs with an indispensable function, necessary at all times for religious life to go on. This seems to me the first conclusion which we are entitled to draw from the phenomena we have passed in review.

The next step is to characterize the feelings. To what psychological order do they belong?

The resultant outcome of them is in any case what Kant calls a 'sthenic' affection, an excitement of the cheerful, expansive, 'dynamogenic' order which, like any tonic, freshens our vital powers. In almost every lecture, but especially in the lectures on Conversion and on Saintliness, we have seen how this emotion overcomes temperamental melancholy and imparts endurance to the Subject, or a zest, or a meaning, or an enchantment and glory to the common objects of life. The name of 'faith-state,' by which Professor Leuba designates it, is a good one. It is a biological as well as a psychological condition, and Tolstoy is absolutely accurate in classing faith among the forces by which men live. The total absence of it, anhedonia, means collapse.

The faith-state may hold a very minimum of intellectual content. We saw examples of this in those sudden raptures of the divine presence, or in such mystical seizures as Dr. Bucke described. It may be a mere vague enthusiasm, half spiritual, half vital, a courage, and a feeling that great and wondrous things are in the air.

Example: Henri Perreyve writes to Gratry: "I do not know how to deal with the happiness which you aroused in me this morning. It overwhelms me; I want to do something, yet I can do nothing and am fit for nothing.... I would fain do great things." Again, after an inspiring interview, he writes: "I went homewards, intoxicated with joy, hope, and strength. I wanted to feed upon my happiness in solitude, far from all men. It was late; but, unheeding that, I took a mountain path and went on like a madman, looking at the heavens, regardless of earth. Suddenly an instinct made me draw hastily back— I was on the very edge of a precipice, one step more and I must have fallen. I took fright and gave up my nocturnal promenade." [A. Gratry: Henri Perreyve, London, 1872, pp. 92, 89.]

This primacy, in the faith-state, of vague expansive impulse over direction is well expressed in Walt Whitman's lines [Leaves of Grass, 1872, p. 190]:

"O to confront night, storms, hunger, ridicule, accidents,
rebuffs, as the trees and animals do...
Dear Camerado! I confess I have urged you onward with me, and
still urge you, without the least idea what is our
destination,
Or whether we shall be victorious, or utterly quell'd and
defeated."

This readiness for great things, and this sense that the world by its importance, wonderfulness, etc., is apt for their production, would seem to be the undifferentiated germ of all the higher faiths. Trust in our own dreams of ambition, or in our country's expansive destinies, and faith in the providence of God, all have their source in that onrush of our sanguine impulses, and in that sense of the exceedingness of the possible over the real.

When, however, a positive intellectual content is associated with a faith-state, it gets invincibly stamped in upon belief, and this explains the passionate loyalty of religious persons everywhere to the minutest details of their so widely differing creeds. Taking creeds and faith-state together, as forming 'religions,' and treating these as purely subjective phenomena, without regard to the question of their 'truth,' we are obliged, on account of their extraordinary influence upon action and endurance, to class them amongst the most important biological functions of mankind. Their stimulant and anaesthetic effect is so great that Professor Leuba, in a recent article, goes so far as to say that so long as men can use their God, they care very little who he is, or even whether he is at all. "The truth of the matter can be put," says Leuba, "in this way: God is not known, he is not understood; he is used— sometimes as meat-purveyor, sometimes as moral support, sometimes as friend, sometimes as an object of love. If he proves himself useful, the religious consciousness asks for no more than that. Does God really exist? How does he exist? What is he? are so many irrelevant questions. Not God, but life, more life, a larger, richer, more satisfying life, is, in the last analysis, the end of religion. The love of life, at any and every level of development, is the religious impulse.

[Loc. cit., pp. 571, 572, abridged.] See, also, this writer's extraordinarily true criticism of the notion that religion primarily seeks to solve the intellectual mystery of the world. Compare what W. Bender says (in his Wesen der Religion, Bonn, 1888, pp. 85, 38): "Not the question about God, and not the inquiry into the origin and purpose of the world is religion, but the question about Man. All religious views of life are anthropocentric." "Religion is that activity of the human impulse towards self-preservation by means of which Man seeks to carry his essential vital purposes through against the adverse pressure of the world by raising himself freely towards the world's ordering and governing powers when the limits of his own strength are reached." The whole book is little more than a development of these words.

At this purely subjective rating, therefore, Religion must be considered vindicated in a certain way from the attacks of her critics. It would seem that she cannot be a mere anachronism and survival, but must exert a permanent function, whether she be with or without intellectual content, and whether, if she have any, it be true or false.

We must next pass beyond the point of view of merely subjective utility, and make inquiry into the intellectual content itself.

First, is there, under all the discrepancies of the creeds, a common nucleus to which they bear their testimony unanimously?

And second, ought we to consider the testimony true?

I will take up the first question first, and answer it immediately in the affirmative. The warring gods and formulas of the various religions do indeed cancel each other, but there is a certain uniform deliverance in which religions all appear to meet. It consists of two parts:

1. An uneasiness; and
2. Its solution.

1. The uneasiness, reduced to its simplest terms, is a sense that there is something wrong about us as we naturally stand.

2. The solution is a sense that we are saved from the wrongness by making proper connection with the higher powers.

In those more developed minds which alone we are studying, the wrongness takes a moral character, and the salvation takes a mystical tinge. I think we shall keep well within the limits of what is common to all such minds if we formulate the essence of their religious experience in terms like these:

The individual, so far as he suffers from his wrongness and criticises it, is to that extent consciously beyond it, and in at least possible touch with something higher, if anything higher exist. Along with the wrong part there is thus a better part of him, even though it may be but a most helpless germ. With which part he should identify his real being is by no means obvious at this stage; but when stage 2 (the stage of solution or salvation) arrives, the man identifies his real being with the germinal higher part of himself; and does so in the following way. He becomes conscious that this higher part is conterminous and continuous with a MORE of the same quality, which is operative in the universe outside of him, and which he can keep in working touch with, and in a fashion get on board of and save himself when all his lower being has gone to pieces in the wreck.

Remember that for some men it arrives suddenly, for others gradually, whilst others again practically enjoy it all their life.

It seems to me that all the phenomena are accurately describable in these very simple general terms. They allow for the divided self and the struggle; they involve the change of personal centre and the surrender of the lower self; they express the appearance of exteriority of the helping power and yet account for our sense of union with it; and they fully justify our feelings of security and joy. There is probably no autobiographic document, among all those which I have quoted, to which the description will not well apply. One need only add such specific details as will adapt it to various theologies and various personal temperaments, and one will then have the various experiences reconstructed in their individual forms.

So far, however, as this analysis goes, the experiences are only psychological phenomena. They possess, it is true, enormous biological worth. Spiritual strength really increases in the subject when he has them, a new life opens for him, and they seem to him a place of conflux where the forces of two universes meet; and yet this may be nothing but his subjective way of feeling things, a mood of his own fancy, in spite of the effects produced. I now turn to my second question: What is the objective 'truth' of their content?

The word 'truth' is here taken to mean something additional to bare value for life, although the natural propensity of man is to believe that whatever has great value for life is thereby certified as true.

The part of the content concerning which the question of truth most pertinently arises is that 'MORE of the same quality' with which our own higher self appears in the experience to come into harmonious working relation. Is such a 'more' merely our own notion, or does it really exist? If so, in what shape does it exist? Does it act, as well as exist? And in what form should we conceive of that 'union' with it of which religious geniuses are so convinced?

It is in answering these questions that the various theologies perform their theoretic work, and that their divergencies most come to light. They all agree that the 'more' really exists; though some of them hold it to exist in the shape of a personal god or gods, while others are satisfied to conceive it as a stream of ideal tendency embedded in the eternal structure of the world. They all agree, moreover, that it acts as well as exists, and that something really is effected for the better when you throw your life into its hands. It is when they treat of the experience of 'union' with it that their speculative differences appear most clearly. Over this point pantheism and theism, nature and second birth, works and grace and karma, immortality and reincarnation, rationalism and mysticism, carry on inveterate disputes.

At the end of my lecture on Philosophy I held out the notion that an impartial science of religions might sift out from the midst of their discrepancies a common body of doctrine which she might also formulate in terms to which physical science need not object. This, I said, she might adopt as her own reconciling hypothesis, and recommend it for general belief. I also said that in my last lecture I should have to try my own hand at framing such an hypothesis. [Above, Lecture XVIII.]

The time has now come for this attempt. Who says 'hypothesis' renounces the ambition to be coercive in his arguments. The most I can do is, accordingly, to offer something that may fit the facts so easily that your scientific logic will find no plausible pretext for vetoing your impulse to welcome it as true.

The 'more,' as we called it, and the meaning of our 'union' with it, form the nucleus of our inquiry. Into what definite description can these words be translated, and for what definite facts do they stand? It would never do for us to place ourselves offhand at the position of a particular theology, the Christian theology, for example, and proceed immediately to define the 'more' as Jehovah, and the 'union' as his imputation to us of the righteousness of Christ. That would be unfair to other religions, and, from our present standpoint at least, would be an over-belief.

We must begin by using less particularized terms; and, since one of the duties of the science of religions is to keep religion in connection with the rest of science, we shall do well to seek first of all a way of describing the 'more,' which psychologists may also recognize as real. The subconscious self is nowadays a well-accredited psychological entity; and I believe that in it we have exactly the mediating term required. Apart from all religious considerations, there is actually and literally more life in our total soul than we are at any time aware of. The exploration of the transmarginal field has hardly yet been seriously undertaken, but what Mr. Myers said in 1892 in his essay on the Subliminal Consciousness is as true as when it was first written: "Each of us is in reality an abiding psychical entity far more extensive than he knows— an individuality which can never express itself completely through any corporeal manifestation. The Self manifests through the organism; but there is always some part of the Self unmanifested; and always, as it seems, some power of organic expression in abeyance or reserve." Much of the content of this larger background against which our conscious being stands out in relief is insignificant. Imperfect memories, silly jingles, inhibitive timidities, 'dissolutive' phenomena of various sorts, as Myers calls them, enter into it for a large part. But in it many of the performances of genius seem also to have their origin; and in our study of conversion, of mystical experiences, and of prayer, we have seen how striking a part invasions from this region play in the religious life.

Proceedings of the Society for Psychical Research, vol. vii. p. 305. For a full statement of Mr. Myers's views, I may refer to his posthumous work, 'Human Personality in the Light of Recent Research,' which is already announced by Messrs. Longmans, Green & Co. as being in press. Mr. Myers for the first time proposed as a general psychological problem the exploration of the subliminal region of consciousness throughout its whole extent, and made the first methodical steps in its topography by treating as a natural series a mass of subliminal facts hitherto considered only as curious isolated facts, and subjecting them to a systematized nomenclature. How important this exploration will prove, future work upon the path which Myers has opened can alone show. Compare my paper: 'Frederic Myers's Services to Psychology,' in the said Proceedings, part xlii., May, 1901.

Let me then propose, as an hypothesis, that whatever it may be on its farther side, the 'more' with which in religious experience we feel ourselves connected is on its hither side the subconscious continuation of our conscious life. Starting thus with a recognized psychological fact as our basis, we seem to preserve a contact with 'science' which the ordinary theologian lacks. At the same time the theologian's contention that the religious man is moved by an external power is vindicated, for it is one of the peculiarities of invasions from the subconscious region to take on objective appearances, and to suggest to the Subject an external control. In the religious life the control is felt as 'higher'; but since on our hypothesis it is primarily the higher faculties of our own hidden mind which are controlling, the sense of union with the power beyond us is a sense of something, not merely apparently, but literally true.

This doorway into the subject seems to me the best one for a science of religions, for it mediates between a number of different points of view. Yet it is only a doorway, and difficulties present themselves as soon as we step through it, and ask how far our transmarginal consciousness carries us if we follow it on its remoter side. Here the over-beliefs begin: here mysticism and the conversion-rapture and Vedantism and transcendental idealism bring in their monistic interpretations and tell us that the finite self rejoins the absolute self, for it was always one with God and identical with the soul of the world. Here the prophets of all the different religions come with their visions, voices, raptures, and other openings, supposed by each to authenticate his own peculiar faith.

"If this room is full of darkness for thousands of years, and you come in and begin to weep and wail, 'Oh, the darkness,' will the darkness vanish? Bring the light in, strike a match, and light comes in a moment. So what good will it do you to think all your lives, 'Oh, I have done evil, I have made many mistakes'? It requires no ghost to tell us that. Bring in the light, and the evil goes in a moment. Strengthen the real nature, build up yourselves, the effulgent, the resplendent, the ever pure, call that up in every one whom you see. I wish that every one of us had come to such a state that even when we see the vilest of human beings we can see the God within, and instead of condemning, say, 'Rise, thou effulgent One, rise thou who art always pure, rise thou birthless and deathless, rise almighty, and manifest your nature.'... This is the highest prayer that the Advaita teaches. This is the one prayer: remembering our nature."... "Why does man go out to look for a God?... It is your own heart beating, and you did not know, you were mistaking it for something external. He, nearest of the near, my own self, the reality of my own life, my body and my soul.— I am Thee and Thou art Me. That is your own nature. Assert it, manifest it. Not to become pure, you are pure already. You are not to be perfect, you are that already. Every good thought which you think or act upon is simply tearing the veil, as it were, and the purity, the Infinity, the God behind, manifests itself— the eternal Subject of everything, the eternal Witness in this universe, your own Self. Knowledge is, as it were, a lower step, a degradation. We are It already; how to know It?" [Swami Vivekananda: Addresses, No. XII., Practical Vedanta, part iv. pp. 172, 174, London, 1897; and Lectures, The Real and the Apparent Man, p. 24, abridged.]

Those of us who are not personally favored with such specific revelations must stand outside of them altogether and, for the present at least, decide that, since they corroborate incompatible theological doctrines, they neutralize one another and leave no fixed result. If we follow any one of them, or if we follow philosophical theory and embrace monistic pantheism on non-mystical grounds, we do so in the exercise of our individual freedom, and build out our religion in the way most congruous with our personal susceptibilities. Among these susceptibilities intellectual ones play a decisive part. Although the religious question is primarily a question of life, of living or not living in the higher union which opens itself to us as a gift, yet the spiritual excitement in which the gift appears a real one will often fail to be aroused in an individual until certain particular intellectual beliefs or ideas which, as we say, come home to him, are touched. These ideas will thus be essential to that individual's religion;— which is as much as to say that over-beliefs in various directions are absolutely indispensable, and that we should treat them with tenderness and tolerance so long as they are not intolerant themselves. As I have elsewhere written, the most interesting and valuable things about a man are usually his overbeliefs.

For instance, here is a case where a person exposed from her birth to Christian ideas had to wait till they came to her clad in spiritistic formulas before the saving experience set in:—

"For myself I can say that spiritualism has saved me. It was revealed to me at a critical moment of my life, and without it I don't know what I should have done. It has taught me to detach myself from worldly things and to place my hope in things to come. Through it I have learned to see in all men, even in those most criminal, even in those from whom I have most suffered, undeveloped brothers to whom I owed assistance, love, and forgiveness. I have learned that I must lose my temper over nothing, despise no one, and pray for all. Most of all I have learned to pray! And although I have still much to learn in this domain, prayer ever brings me more strength, consolation, and comfort. I feel more than ever that I have only made a few steps on the long road of progress; but I look at its length without dismay, for I have confidence that the day will come when all my efforts shall be rewarded. So Spiritualism has a great place in my life, indeed it holds the first place there." Flournoy Collection.

Disregarding the over-beliefs, and confining ourselves to what is common and generic, we have in the fact that the conscious person is continuous with a wider self through which saving experiences come, a positive content of religious experience which, it seems to me, is literally and objectively true as far as it goes. If I now proceed to state my own hypothesis about the farther limits of this extension of our personality, I shall be offering my own over-belief— though I know it will appear a sorry under-belief to some of you— for which I can only bespeak the same indulgence which in a converse case I should accord to yours.

The further limits of our being plunge, it seems to me, into an altogether other dimension of existence from the sensible and merely 'understandable' world. Name it the mystical region, or the supernatural region, whichever you choose. So far as our ideal impulses originate in this region (and most of them do originate in it, for we find them possessing us in a way for which we cannot articulately account), we belong to it in a more intimate sense than that in which we belong to the visible world, for we belong in the most intimate sense wherever our ideals belong. Yet the unseen region in question is not merely ideal, for it produces effects in this world. When we commune with it, work is actually done upon our finite personality, for we are turned into new men, and consequences in the way of conduct follow in the natural world upon our regenerative change. But that which produces effects within another reality must be termed a reality itself, so I feel as if we had no philosophic excuse for calling the unseen or mystical world unreal.

That the transaction of opening ourselves, otherwise called prayer, is a perfectly definite one for certain persons, appears abundantly in the preceding lectures. I append another concrete example to reinforce the impression on the reader's mind:

"Man can learn to transcend these limitations [of finite thought] and draw power and wisdom at will.... The divine presence is known through experience. The turning to a higher plane is a distinct act of consciousness. It is not a vague, twilight or semi-conscious experience. It is not an ecstasy; it is not a trance. It is not super-consciousness in the Vedantic sense. It is not due to self-hypnotization. It is a perfectly calm, sane, sound, rational, common-sense shifting of consciousness from the phenomena of sense-perception to the phenomena of seership, from the thought of self to a distinctively higher realm.... For example, if the lower self be nervous, anxious, tense, one can in a few moments compel it to be calm. This is not done by a word simply. Again I say, it is not hypnotism. It is by the exercise of power. One feels the spirit of peace as definitely as heat is perceived on a hot summer day. The power can be as surely used as the sun's rays can be focused and made to do work, to set fire to wood." [The Higher Law, vol. iv. pp. 4, 6, Boston, August, 1901.]

God is the natural appellation, for us Christians at least, for the supreme reality, so I will call this higher part of the universe by the name of God. We and God have business with each other; and in opening ourselves to his influence our deepest destiny is fulfilled. The universe, at those parts of it which our personal being constitutes, takes a turn genuinely for the worse or for the better in proportion as each one of us fulfills or evades God's demands. As far as this goes I probably have you with me, for I only translate into schematic language what I may call the instinctive belief of mankind: God is real since he produces real effects.

Transcendentalists are fond of the term 'Over-soul,' but as a rule they use it in an intellectualist sense, as meaning only a medium of communion. 'God' is a causal agent as well as a medium is communion, and that is the aspect which I wish to emphasize.

The real effects in question, so far as I have as yet admitted them, are exerted on the personal centres of energy of the various subjects, but the spontaneous faith of most of the subjects is that they embrace a wider sphere than this. Most religious men believe (or 'know,' if they be mystical) that not only they themselves, but the whole universe of beings to whom the God is present, are secure in his parental hands. There is a sense, a dimension, they are sure, in which we are all saved, in spite of the gates of hell and all adverse terrestrial appearances. God's existence is the guarantee of an ideal order that shall be permanently preserved. This world may indeed, as science assures us, some day burn up or freeze; but if it is part of his order, the old ideals are sure to be brought elsewhere to fruition, so that where God is, tragedy is only provisional and partial, and shipwreck and dissolution are not the absolutely final things. Only when this farther step of faith concerning God is taken, and remote objective consequences are predicted, does religion, as it seems to me, get wholly free from the first immediate subjective experience, and bring a real hypothesis into play. A good hypothesis in science must have other properties than those of the phenomenon it is immediately invoked to explain, otherwise it is not prolific enough. God, meaning only what enters into the religious man's experience of union, falls short of being an hypothesis of this more useful order. He needs to enter into wider cosmic relations in order to justify the subject's absolute confidence and peace.

That the God with whom, starting from the hither side of our own extra-marginal self, we come at its remoter margin into commerce should be the absolute world-ruler, is of course a very considerable over-belief. Over-belief as it is, though, it is an article of almost every one's religion. Most of us pretend in some way to prop it upon our philosophy, but the philosophy itself is really propped upon this faith. What is this but to say that Religion, in her fullest exercise of function, is not a mere illumination of facts already elsewhere given, not a mere passion, like love, which views things in a rosier light. It is indeed that, as we have seen abundantly. But it is something more, namely, a postulator of new facts as well. The world interpreted religiously is not the materialistic world over again, with an altered expression; it must have, over and above the altered expression, a natural constitution different at some point from that which a materialistic world would have. It must be such that different events can be expected in it, different conduct must be required.

This thoroughly 'pragmatic' view of religion has usually been taken as a matter of course by common men. They have interpolated divine miracles into the field of nature, they have built a heaven out beyond the grave. It is only transcendentalist metaphysicians who think that, without adding any concrete details to Nature, or subtracting any, but by simply calling it the expression of absolute spirit, you make it more divine just as it stands. I believe the pragmatic way of taking religion to be the deeper way. It gives it body as well as soul, it makes it claim, as everything real must claim, some characteristic realm of fact as its very own. What the more characteristically divine facts are, apart from the actual inflow of energy in the faith-state and the prayer-state, I know not. But the over-belief on which I am ready to make my personal venture is that they exist. The whole drift of my education goes to persuade me that the world of our present consciousness is only one out of many worlds of consciousness that exist, and that those other worlds must contain experiences which have a meaning for our life also; and that although in the main their experiences and those of this world keep discrete, yet the two become continuous at certain points, and higher energies filter in. By being faithful in my poor measure to this over-belief, I seem to myself to keep more sane and true. I can, of course, put myself into the sectarian scientist's attitude, and imagine vividly that the world of sensations and of scientific laws and objects may be all. But whenever I do this, I hear that inward monitor of which W. K. Clifford once wrote, whispering the word 'bosh!' Humbug is humbug, even though it bear the scientific name, and the total expression of human experience, as I view it objectively, invincibly urges me beyond the narrow scientific bounds. Assuredly, the real world is of a different temperament,— more intricately built than physical science allows. So my objective and my subjective conscience both hold me to the over-belief which I express. Who knows whether the faithfulness of individuals here below to their own poor over-beliefs may not actually help God in turn to be more effectively faithful to his own greater tasks?

POSTSCRIPT

In writing my concluding lecture I had to aim so much at simplification that I fear that my general philosophic position received so scant a statement as hardly to be intelligible to some of my readers. I therefore add this epilogue, which must also be so brief as possibly to remedy but little the defect. In a later work I may be enabled to state my position more amply and consequently more clearly.

Originality cannot be expected in a field like this, where all the attitudes and tempers that are possible have been exhibited in literature long ago, and where any new writer can immediately be classed under a familiar head. If one should make a division of all thinkers into naturalists and supernaturalists, I should undoubtedly have to go, along with most philosophers, into the supernaturalist branch. But there is a crasser and a more refined supernaturalism, and it is to the refined division that most philosophers at the present day belong. If not regular transcendental idealists, they at least obey the Kantian direction enough to bar out ideal entities from interfering casually in the course of phenomenal events. Refined supernaturalism is universalistic supernaturalism; for the 'crasser' variety 'piecemeal' supernaturalism would perhaps be the better name. It went with that older theology which today is supposed to reign only among uneducated people, or to be found among the few belated professors of the dualisms which Kant is thought to have displaced. It admits miracles and providential leadings, and finds no intellectual difficulty in mixing the ideal and the real worlds together by interpolating influences from the ideal region among the forces that causally determine the real world's details. In this the refined supernaturalists think that it muddles disparate dimensions of existence. For them the world of the ideal has no efficient causality, and never bursts into the world of phenomena at particular points. The ideal world, for them, is not a world of facts, but only of the meaning of facts; it is a point of view for judging facts. It appertains to a different '-ology,' and inhabits a different dimension of being altogether from that in which existential propositions obtain. It cannot get down upon the flat level of experience and interpolate itself piecemeal between distinct portions of nature, as those who believe, for example, in divine aid coming in response to prayer, are bound to think it must.

Notwithstanding my own inability to accept either popular Christianity or scholastic theism, I suppose that my belief that in communion with the Ideal new force comes into the world, and new departures are made here below, subjects me to being classed among the supernaturalists of the piecemeal or crasser type. Universalistic supernaturalism surrenders, it seems to me, too easily to naturalism. It takes the facts of physical science at their face-value, and leaves the laws of life just as naturalism finds them, with no hope of remedy, in case their fruits are bad. It confines itself to sentiments about life as a whole, sentiments which may be admiring and adoring, but which need not be so, as the existence of systematic pessimism proves. In this universalistic way of taking the ideal world, the essence of practical religion seems to me to evaporate. Both instinctively and for logical reasons, I find it hard to believe that principler, can exist which make no difference in facts. But all facts are particular facts, and the whole interest of the question of God's existence seems to me to lie in the consequences for particulars which that existence may be expected to entail. That no concrete particular of experience should alter its complexion in consequence of a God being there seems to me an incredible proposition, and yet it is the thesis to which (implicitly at any rate) refined supernaturalism seems to cling. It is only with experience en bloc, it says, that the Absolute maintains relations. It condescends to no transactions of detail.

Transcendental idealism, of course, insists that its ideal world makes this difference, that facts exist. We owe it to the Absolute that we have a world of fact at all. 'A world' of fact!— that exactly is the trouble. An entire world is the smallest unit with which the Absolute can work, whereas to our finite minds work for the better ought to be done within this world, setting in at single points. Our difficulties and our ideals are all piecemeal affairs, but the Absolute can do no piecework for us; so that all the interests which our poor souls compass raise their heads too late. We should have spoken earlier, prayed for another world absolutely, before this world was born. It is strange, I have heard a friend say, to see this blind corner into which Christian thought has worked itself at last, with its God who can raise no particular weight whatever, who can help us with no private burden, and who is on the side of our enemies as much as he is on our own. Odd evolution from the God of David's psalms!

I am ignorant of Buddhism and speak under correction, and merely in order the better to describe my general point of view; but as I apprehend the Buddhistic doctrine of Karma, I agree in principle with that. All supernaturalists admit that facts are under the judgment of higher law; but for Buddhism as I interpret it, and for religion generally so far as it remains unweakened by transcendentalistic metaphysics, the word 'judgment' here means no such bare academic verdict or platonic appreciation as it means in Vedantic or modern absolutist systems; it carries, on the contrary, execution with it, is in rebus as well as post rem, and operates 'causally' as partial factor in the total fact. The universe becomes a gnosticism pure and simple on any other terms. But this view that judgment and execution go together is that of the crasser supernaturalist way of thinking, so the present volume must on the whole be classed with the other expressions of that creed. [See my Will to Believe and other Essays in Popular Philosophy, 1897.]

I state the matter thus bluntly, because the current of thought in academic circles runs against me, and I feel like a man who must set his back against an open door quickly if he does not wish to see it closed and locked. In spite of its being so shocking to the reigning intellectual tastes, I believe that a candid consideration of piecemeal supernaturalism and a complete discussion of all its metaphysical bearings will show it to be the hypothesis by which the largest number of legitimate requirements are met. That of course would be a program for other books than this; what I now say sufficiently indicates to the philosophic reader the place where I belong.

If asked just where the differences in fact which are due to God's existence come in, I should have to say that in general I have no hypothesis to offer beyond what the phenomenon of 'prayerful communion,' especially when certain kinds of incursion from the subconscious region take part in it, immediately suggests. The appearance is that in this phenomenon something ideal, which in one sense is part of ourselves and in another sense is not ourselves, actually exerts an influence, raises our centre of personal energy, and produces regenerative effects unattainable in other ways. If, then, there be a wider world of being than that of our every-day consciousness, if in it there be forces whose effects on us are intermittent, if one facilitating condition of the effects be the openness of the 'subliminal' door, we have the elements of a theory to which the phenomena of religious life lend plausibility. I am so impressed by the importance of these phenomena that I adopt the hypothesis which they so naturally suggest. At these places at least, I say, it would seem as though transmundane energies, God, if you will, produced immediate effects within the natural world to which the rest of our experience belongs.

The difference in natural 'fact' which most of us would assign as the first difference which the existence of a God ought to make would, I imagine, be personal immortality. Religion, in fact, for the great majority of our own race means immortality, and nothing else. God is the producer of immortality; and whoever has doubts of immortality is written down as an atheist without farther trial. I have said nothing in my lectures about immortality or the belief therein, for to me it seems a secondary point. If our ideals are only cared for in 'eternity,' I do not see why we might not be willing to resign their care to other hands than ours. Yet I sympathize with the urgent impulse to be present ourselves, and in the conflict of impulses, both of them so vague yet both of them noble, I know not how to decide. It seems to me that it is eminently a case for facts to testify. Facts, I think, are yet lacking to prove 'spirit-return,' though I have the highest respect for the patient labors of Messrs. Myers, Hodgson, and Hyslop, and am somewhat impressed by their favorable conclusions. I consequently leave the matter open, with this brief word to save the reader from a possible perplexity as to why immortality got no mention in the body of this book.

The ideal power with which we feel ourselves in connection, the 'God' of ordinary men, is, both by ordinary men and by philosophers, endowed with certain of those metaphysical attributes which in the lecture on philosophy I treated with such disrespect. He is assumed as a matter of course to be 'one and only' and to be 'infinite'; and the notion of many finite gods is one which hardly any one thinks it worth while to consider, and still less to uphold. Nevertheless, in the interests of intellectual clearness, I feel bound to say that religious experience, as we have studied it, cannot be cited as unequivocally supporting the infinitist belief. The only thing that it unequivocally testifies to is that we can experience union with something larger than ourselves and in that union find our greatest peace. Philosophy, with its passion for unity, and mysticism with its monoideistic bent, both 'pass to the limit' and identify the something with a unique God who is the all-inclusive soul of the world. Popular opinion, respectful to their authority, follows the example which they set.

Meanwhile the practical needs and experiences of religion seem to me sufficiently met by the belief that beyond each man and in a fashion continuous with him there exists a larger power which is friendly to him and to his ideals. All that the facts require is that the power should be both other and larger than our conscious selves. Anything larger will do, if only it be large enough to trust for the next step. It need not be infinite, it need not be solitary. It might conceivably even be only a larger and more godlike self, of which the present self would then be but the mutilated expression, and the universe might conceivably be a collection of such selves, of different degrees of inclusiveness, with no absolute unity realized in it at all. Thus would a sort of polytheism return upon us— a polytheism which I do not on this occasion defend, for my only aim at present is to keep the testimony of religious experience clearly within its proper bounds. [Compare Lectures VI and VII above.]

Upholders of the monistic view will say to such a polytheism (which, by the way, has always been the real religion of common people, and is so still today) that unless there be one all-inclusive God, our guarantee of security is left imperfect. In the Absolute, and in the Absolute only, all is saved. If there be different gods, each caring for his part, some portion of some of us might not be covered with divine protection, and our religious consolation would thus fail to be complete. It goes back to what was said in Lectures VI and VII, about the possibility of there being portions of the universe that may irretrievably be lost. Common sense is less sweeping in its demands than philosophy or mysticism have been wont to be, and can suffer the notion of this world being partly saved and partly lost. The ordinary moralistic state of mind makes the salvation of the world conditional upon the success with which each unit does its part. Partial and conditional salvation is in fact a most familiar notion when taken in the abstract, the only difficulty being to determine the details. Some men are even disinterested enough to be willing to be in the unsaved remnant as far as their persons go, if only they can be persuaded that their cause will prevail— all of us are willing, whenever our activity-excitement rises sufficiently high. I think, in fact, that a final philosophy of religion will have to consider the pluralistic hypothesis more seriously than it has hitherto been willing to consider it. For practical life at any rate, the chance of salvation is enough. No fact in human nature is more characteristic than its willingness to live on a chance. The existence of the chance makes the difference, as Edmund Gurney says, between a life of which the keynote is resignation and a life of which the keynote is hope.

www.ingramcontent.com/pod-product-compliance
Lightning Source LLC
Chambersburg PA
CBHW020600270326
41927CB00005B/103